THE ULTIMATE EU TEST BOOK
Administrators 2018

Also from John Harper Publishing

The Ultimate EU Test Book is available in separate editions for
– ADMINISTRATORS,
– ASSISTANTS,
– ASSESSMENT CENTRE.

Also in the series is THE ULTIMATE EU CAREER DEVELOPMENT BOOK

Full details may be found at **www.johnharperpublishing.co.uk**

To keep up to date with developments on EPSO exams and any updates on The Ultimate EU Test Book, visit www.eu-testbook.com, from which you can also link to the Ultimate EU Test Book Facebook page to gather information from and make contact with others taking the exams.

THE ULTIMATE EU TEST BOOK
ADMINISTRATORS 2018

András Baneth

JOHN HARPER
PUBLISHING

The Ultimate EU Test Book Administrators 2018
ISBN 978-1-9999595-2-4

Published by John Harper Publishing
27 Palace Gates Road
London N22 7BW, United Kingdom.
www.johnharperpublishing.co.uk

Sales and distribution: Turpin Distribution Services Ltd.

The Ultimate EU Test Book – edition history
First edition, November 2005
Second edition, May 2007
Third edition, March 2008
Fourth edition, April 2009
Fifth edition, March 2010
Assistant edition 2011, November 2010
Administrator edition 2011, February 2011
Assistant edition 2012, October 2011
Administrator edition 2012, October 2011
Assistant edition 2013, January 2013
Administrator edition 2013, January 2013
Administrator edition 2015, December 2014
Assistant edition 2015, December 2014
Assessment Centre edition, May 2015
Administrator edition 2016, February 2016
Assistant edition 2016, February 2016
Assessment Centre 2018, February 2018
Administrators 2018, March 2018
Assistants 2018, March 2018

© John Harper Publishing 2018

Typeset mainly in 9 & 10/11pt Palatino

Printed and Bound in Malta at the Gutenberg Press.

TABLE OF CONTENTS

Introduction vii

About the Authors ix

1. The EU Personnel Selection and Recruitment Process. 1

2. Verbal, Numerical and Abstract Reasoning Tests in EPSO Administrator Exams. 25

3. Succeeding in Verbal Reasoning Tests 31

4. Verbal Reasoning Test
    *   Questions 45
    *   Answers 109

5. Succeeding in Numerical Reasoning Tests 141

6. Numerical Reasoning Test
    *   Questions 157
    *   Answers. 188

7. Succeeding in Abstract Reasoning Tests 265

8. Abstract Reasoning Test
    *   Questions 275
    *   Answers 329

9. Succeeding in Situational Judgement Tests 351

10. Situational Judgement Test
    *   Questions 357
    *   Answers 369

INTRODUCTION

Purpose of the Book

The purpose of *The Ultimate EU Test Book* is to help candidates prepare and practise for the European Personnel Selection Office (EPSO) competitions, so as to be eligible for jobs in the EU institutions.

EPSO competitions (often called by their French name, *concours*) are divided into two main types: those for Administrator (AD) level positions and those for Assistants (AST), with a sub-category being Secretaries (AST-SC). The AD level includes Linguists and many Specialist roles.

While the structure of competitions shows some variability (in essence, the more specialised and specific the role, the greater the weight put on applied specialised and specific job-related knowledge), the core elements of competitions are the reasoning tests (psychometric tests) and as the final stage the assessment of a candidate's "competencies" at the Assessment Centre.

The resoning tests, which for the vast majority of candidates constitute the first phase of the exams, make up the "pre-selection" round. This comprises a range of psychometric tests, administered on a computer, which measure candidates' skills in numerical, verbal and abstract reasoning and (possibly) situational judgement tests. Nowadays almost everybody must take all of these tests.

For most candidates, it is the pre-selection round that proves the stumbling block, and in the big "generalist" competitions a large majority fall at this hurdle. For this reason, the focus of the *The Ultimate EU Test Book Administrators 2018* is on the pre-selection tests. Successive chapters explain what the various types of test involve, the skills needed to tackle them, and the errors to avoid – and in each case this methodology is followed by extensive practice questions with detailed explanations of the answers. All the questions have been specifically designed to mirror Administrator-level competitions.

Only a minority of candidates make it as far as the Assessment Centre phase, and they are in reach of becoming "laureates", eligible to take up permanent posts in the EU institutions. A more specialised book, with guidance and practice exercises specifically for those who reach the Assessment Centre, is now available: *The Ultimate EU Test Book Assessment Centre 2018*.

Overview of the chapters

Chapter 1 provides a detailed step-by-step guide with timeline describing each stage of the whole EPSO selection process. Including dozens of useful tips and hints, it gives signposts to all the areas covered in greater detail later in the book.

Few candidates instinctively feel comfortable with the full range of pre-selection psychometric tests: everyone has their strengths and weaknesses, and there are also many hazards in tests which people think they are good at. **Chapter 2** offers a brief overview of what these tests are and why EPSO uses them, with a much fuller look at each test type in the following chapters. Candidates who do not reach the required level in these tests will not be offered the chance to proceed further in the competition. It is therefore vital to study carefully the methodology to learn the principles and shortcuts involved and then make sure to practise to increase your speed, accuracy and ratio of correct answers.

With **verbal reasoning tests**, a common problem is that candidates consider them relatively "easy", without being aware of the traps they contain. In an EPSO competition you are presented with a short text and have to say which one of a series of statements is correct, based on the information in the passage. The nub of the problem for many proves to be the requirement "based on information in the passage", because the statements always include superficially attractive answer options which "seem" right, but in fact cannot be properly based on what the passage actually says. Sometimes, too, the correct answer is a statement which seems rather bland or even immaterial but is in fact soundly based. **Chapter 3** explains the common errors candidates make, and then **Chapter 4** provides a full test exercise with questions designed to probe your ability to spot the hazards.

In the case of **numerical reasoning tests**, the questions are not designed to assess your high-level mathematical skills: nothing is required beyond the maths you will have learned at school. What is tested, however, is your ability to grasp the essence of a problem quickly – to work out what data in the jumble of information in the tables or charts is actually needed to solve the problem, and to calculate in the fastest and most direct way possible. Sometimes, indeed, no or scarcely any real calculations are needed at all, if you know how to see this. For this reason, **Chapter 5** focuses on the fundamental types of calculation needed and how to speed up your application of these. **Chapter 6** not only tests your ability to apply these calculations but provides numerous tips on "shortcuts" and "pitfalls" which can make the difference between making basic errors or simply running out of time, on the one hand, and working quickly and accurately on the other.

You are not alone if your first reaction to **abstract reasoning tests** is one of anxiety or even dismay, as you try to work out which in a series of shapes is "next in the series". However, as **Chapter 7** shows, such tests involve in a systematic way the application of often quite simple rules – and the key thing is to learn to spot what those rules are. Chapter 7 explains the patterns and operations test designers use, and then in **Chapter 8** you can test yourself in applying those rules in practice. In each case, the answers explain the rules so if you get the answer wrong, you can work backwards from the rules to see where you made your mistake.

Chapter 9 explains the principles and methodology of **situational judgement tests** (SJTs), which are based on real-life workplace scenarios, where a complex interplay of factors is often involved. SJTs have not been used in all recent competitions, but are covered fully in this book. Here you are being measured against the "competencies" EPSO uses more intensively at a later stage at the Assessment Centre. Unlike with the verbal, numerical and abstract reasoning tests, there is not a simple "right" or "wrong" answer with SJTs – rather there is a progression from a "most" to a "least" appropriate or effective response to a given situation. **Chapter 10** gives you the opportunity to see how your responses match those set as standards in a test exercise. While, unlike with the other psychometric tests, you cannot simply improve your SJT scores by learning and practising techniques, how you do in the test should help guide you as to what interpersonal or other skills you need to think about and work on.

The Assessment Centre exercises are very different from the reasoning tests and are covered in *The Ultimate EU Test Book Assessment Centre 2018*.

Keep up to date!

As is emphasised at many points in this book, you must always check carefully the exact rules for your competition (as announced in the Notice of Competition), because the shape of competitions, including such important matters as the weighting of marks between different tests, can vary. Make sure also that you keep up-to-date with the EPSO website and, for more informal but often useful news and tips, www.eu-testbook.com and *The Ultimate EU Test Book* Facebook page.

András Baneth
Brussels, January 2018.

ABOUT THE AUTHORS

András Baneth wishes to express his appreciation to all those who have over the years contributed ideas and content to *The Ultimate EU Test Book*, including Barnabas Bóta, Zoltán Csipke, Delphine Galon, Christine J. Ruzicka, Thomas A. Williams and many others – not the least of them being the "Golden Tailor".

ANDRÁS BANETH, an SHL-certified assessor, is a trainer, consultant and partner at Arboreus Online EU Training. He is also managing director of the Public Affairs Council's European office. His bestselling *Ultimate EU Test Book* has helped thousands of candidates prepare for EPSO competitions since 2005. András has a wide knowledge of EU policies, institutions and communication, his career having included seven years' experience at the European Commission and the European Court of Justice, where his roles included coordinating briefings for Commission President Barroso and serving as member of the *cabinet* of Commissioner Kovács. He holds an M.A. in law and political sciences and the degree of Master of European Public Administration from the College of Europe, Bruges, Belgium. He is always open to invitations to speak about EU careers, strategic communication or public affairs. His personal website is available at www.baneth.eu and his direct e- mail is andras@baneth.eu

MÁRTON MAGYAR is a graduate in English and philosophy with a keen interest in technology and design. He has designed, fine-tuned, and updated thousands of practice test questions for EPSO competitions, and moderated dozens of methodology and preparation webinars and training sessions. A specialist in psychometric testing, abstract reasoning is his particular field.

GÁBOR MIKES is the former managing director of Arboreus Online EU Training and an expert on successful methodologies, including both the theory and practice of passing pre-selection tests. With an M.A. in English Language and Literature and former Kellner Scholar at Trinity College in Hartford, Connecticut (USA), Gábor has worked at an NGO specialising in EU affairs communication and at Ericsson, the Swedish telecom giant. Gábor has held dozens of training courses for hundreds of people around Europe on verbal, abstract and numerical reasoning, many of whom are now working for various EU institutions.

BENJAMIN WILLIAMS is an HPC Registered Occupational Psychologist and a Chartered Associate Fellow of the British Psychological Society (BPS). Ben has led the design and implementation of Assessment Centres for over 300 public and private sector clients across Europe and the Middle East. He has developed practice materials for the EPSO assessments for over a decade. Ben began his career reading Experimental Psychology at Oxford University followed by a Masters in Organisational and Occupational Psychology. After his studies, Ben worked for three large consultancy firms before launching Sten10, a firm that specialises in designing bespoke people assessments.

1. The EU Personnel Selection and Recruitment Process

Introduction

There are thousands of applicants, including trainees and those already working for the EU with a fixed term contract, who attempt to pass the open (or the rarer internal) competitions knowing that this is the only way to become a permanent official of the European Union institutions and bodies. EPSO, being aware of the high interest from candidates and also from its "clients", the EU institutions and bodies, realised the need for strategic and transparent planning by introducing annual (therefore regular) cycles in 2010.

In this chapter, I provide a detailed overview of the system now in force, the candidates, the eligibility criteria, the exam steps and other relevant information with numerous practical tips that I hope may improve your chances of success.

The Selection and Recruitment Procedure

Applications in General

Owing to the exclusive nature of open competitions, EPSO cannot consider any ad hoc applications or CVs that are submitted outside the framework of an official competition, not least because EPSO itself is never recruiting new staff: it "only" selects applicants who can later be hired by EU institutions and bodies (see more details about this later). On the other hand, vacancies for non-permanent posts or a limited number of senior positions (Director level and above) that do not require the selection procedure described below are regularly posted on the EPSO website with links to the given Agency or body where applications should be submitted directly. (You can find more information about non-permanent jobs below and a list, updated daily, on *http://www.eutraining.eu/eu_jobs*.)

Planning and Transparency

One of the key aims of EPSO is to make selection and, ultimately, recruitment as transparent as possible by giving more information to candidates about the stages and methodology of the system, along with detailed and timely feedback about the applicants' very own performance in the tests.

It is in this framework that strategic human resource planning is now used in all institutions, meaning that each Directorate General, Service or high-level administrative unit must signal a forecast of its staffing needs for the upcoming three or so years. This is to help EPSO to plan competitions and to try to avoid situations, such as used to occur, when a successful laureate received no job offer for months or even years. Planning is further reinforced by analysing employee fluctuations, political developments (e.g. the creation of the European External Action Service) or other factors affecting staff turnover or intake.

Increasing transparency is an ongoing effort that includes disclosing the names of Selection Board members, the aim to communicate test results and Assessment Centre reports to candidates and help candidates plan their preparation efforts by knowing a relatively precise timeline of exam schedules. This trend is certainly highly appreciated by all applicants.

Skills vs. Knowledge

The most significant element in the current selection system is the shift from the old pre-2010 knowledge-based testing to an emphasis on **reasoning skills (psychometric tests) and competencies ("soft skills")**. This means that multiple choice tests and essays focused on memorising "EU knowledge" facts and figures – such as the infamous "How many women Commissioners are there in the European Commission?" type of question – are completely a thing of the past. Broadly speaking, reasoning skills are tested in the first pre-selection phase of competitions and the competencies at the final Assessment Centre stage.

EPSO has instead created a competency framework against which candidates are evaluated. This way EU-specific and domain-specific knowledge is only of secondary importance and these aspects are only tested to evaluate a candidate's final suitability for the job, provided they possess all the required skills.

While not contradicting the above, EPSO nonetheless wishes to select candidates who are "operational from day one"– therefore the Assessment Centre case study and oral presentation exercises (or in the case of Assistants and generalist Administrators, e-tray exercise or the practical linguistic tests for Linguists), which are the items most closely related to the specific knowledge required for the job are just as important, being the main elements of testing on-the-job suitability. This is often reflected by the weighting system used in most specialist competitions (different from the generalist ones): the domain specific knowledge or skills can be attributed a 55% weight in the final scoring, as opposed to 45% for the "general" competencies. (Note that the percentages may vary from one competition to another, so it is always advised to read the Notice of Competition carefully.)

Core Competencies

According to EPSO, the following are considered as core competencies (which are required for all profiles independent of the competition):

- **Analysis and Problem Solving** – Identifies the critical facts in complex issues and develops creative and practical solutions

- **Communicating** – Communicates clearly and precisely both orally and in writing

- **Delivering Quality and Results** – Takes personal responsibility and initiative for delivering work to a high standard of quality within set procedures

- **Learning and Development** – Develops and improves personal skills and knowledge of the organisation and its environment

- **Prioritising and Organising** – Prioritises the most important tasks, works flexibly and organises own workload efficiently

- **Resilience** – Remains effective under a heavy workload, handles organisational frustrations positively and adapts to a changing work environment

- **Working with Others** – Works co-operatively with others in teams and across organisational boundaries and respects differences between people

- **Leadership** – Manages, develops and motivates people to achieve results (only for Administrator grades)

For senior or management-level posts (usually AD9 and above), one or two further competencies may be identified for specific job profiles or competitions, depending on the analysis of the given position. The above general competencies are always tested by two different exercises to ensure their validity and reliability as organisational psychologists and human resource experts have created a specific method to ensure the above quality criteria. (For more details on what each competency means and how it is measured, see *The Ultimate EU Test Book Assessment Centre 2018*.)

Duration

EPSO has tried to streamline and professionalise the selection procedure as much as possible. This in practice means that instead of ad hoc competitions, **exams are in principle announced each year on a regular, cyclical basis** (although other factors sometimes prevent this), complemented by exams for Specialists based on a need basis. The annual cycles usually start with the announcement of **Administrator** exams in March, followed by the publication of exams for **Linguists** around July, and closing with the call for application of **Assistants** in November or December. It is essential to check the EPSO website for the latest information on the schedule as changes in policy or priorities may always happen.

Each cycle is intended to be completed within a year from announcement until the publication of the reserve list, though in practice the timescale can be longer and of course actual recruitment takes longer still. However, it is possible to plan ahead your preparation as it is fairly clear what type of competition is to be announced and when.

On a related note, it is advisable to focus your efforts on only preparing for the given upcoming exam phase (pre-selection, intermediate or Assessment Centre) and not the entire procedure as such from the very beginning. This book accordingly concentrates on the pre-selection phase while the very different tests used at the Assessment Centre are covered in *The Ultimate EU Test Book Assessment Centre 2018*.

Soon-to-be Graduates Welcome

The "cut-off date", meaning the date by which a candidate must meet all eligibility criteria, especially that of possessing a degree or other qualification, is often moved to a later specified date instead of the application deadline for a given competition. This is true for most of the Administrator and Linguist exams, though not necessarily for Assistant profiles. However, always check this requirement in the Notice of Competition to ensure that you are eligible for the exam.

Take a practical example. EPSO announces a competition in March 2018. The way the system works means that if you are a graduating student and you expect to receive your degree in June 2018 but the EPSO exam, where a university degree is a pre-requisite, has its application deadline in April, you can still apply, as long as the degree is obtained by the time of the date specified. The rationale behind this is to offer soon-to-be graduates the opportunity to apply in their last year of studies, thus broadening the scope of the candidate pool.

Candidates with Special Needs

European Union institutions have always been keen to respect the principles of equal access and non-discrimination given this policy's pivotal place in the EU Member States' legislation and obviously inside the institutions themselves. Therefore in the EU selection procedure candidates with special needs, such as seriously limited eyesight, physical disability or other issues that require adaptation in the test centres, should notify EPSO well in advance to make sure that both their access to the testing and the scoring of their exams are adapted to their condition. Supervised one-on-one tests or other measures may exceptionally also be made available to encourage such candidates to apply.

Chances of Succeeding

The total number of applications per year is very high – it can be above 30,000 for the generalist Administrator exams, for instance. (Numbers tend to be lower for Assistant competitions.) This should, however, not discourage anyone from applying as this figure is less intimidating once put into perspective. Consider that about 10% of these applicants never actually show up at the test centre (they change their minds, were not really serious about sitting the exam, could not make it due to personal reasons etc.) and thus your chances are already higher.

Further, the pre-selection phase is very challenging for those who see verbal, numerical and abstract reasoning questions for the first time at the exam centre. Those having done their "homework" to prepare well are therefore immediately at an advantage. This is the stage at which most will drop out.

On average, at the Assessment Centre stage of the exams 1200 Administrators, 600 Linguists and 300 Specialists are tested in a year along with 900 Assistant candidates. (These figures fluctuate due to the changing needs of the EU institutions and the exams announced in any given year. Staff numbers have been subject to a 5% cut in recent years, which has had an impact on the intake of new staff. Nonetheless, due to staff turnover, retiring and other reasons, EU institutions have still been hiring about 1000 or more new staff each year.)

The above figures also mean that there is intense competition at the pre-selection phase (varying considerably among the profiles, which is discussed further below). It also means that it is not enough to just pass – you should aim for the highest possible score to do better than others who also reach the pass mark. This is primarily true for the pre-selection phase as those candidates who win through to the Assessment Centre are measured against the pre-established competencies and only afterwards are they measured against each other. Note, however, that for Specialist profiles, you usually only need to reach a 50% score on the abstract, verbal and numerical tests, though this often depends on the number of applicants for the given competition.

Competition and Sifting-in

In the EPSO system, the concept of "**sifting-in**" is used for most **Specialist competitions** (though for general Administrators and for most Assistant profiles the eligibility is slightly more flexible): this means that Specialists are required to fill out a so-called "**talent-screener**", a questionnaire about their professional experience and qualifications that are relevant to the field of the competition. EPSO selection board members then check these answers and award points for each answer, usually on a scale of 0-3.

Pre-selection tests with proper ranking of the top candidates are then organised only if there are more than X times more eligible candidates remaining even after setting a pass mark (or cut-off score) on the basis of the points awarded in the talent screener, which by definition eliminates many candidates. If, however, there are only a handful of suitable candidates, the abstract, verbal and numerical reasoning tests that they will be required to pass will be part of the Assessment Centre and not used as a pre-selection test. Moreover, candidates will only need to pass with a minimum of 50% score – and they are not ranked on the basis of their performance in these tests as long as they reached the pass-mark (the final ranking being based on other exercises in the Assessment Centre, i.e. their domain-specific and general competencies).

As a general rule when pre-selection tests are used, the Selection Board of the given competition will be looking at the overall results and the number of candidates, and then determine the threshold score above which all candidates are considered for the next phase. This does not mean that all those having scored above this limit will be admitted to the Assessment Centre; however the Selection Board will examine their formal qualifications and eligibility to make sure they are fully eligible for an EU job.

This also means that **you must consider carefully which exam profile to apply for**. For example, if you have a qualification in human resource management and relevant professional experience, you can sit an Assistant exam and maybe also an Administrator exam (if your qualification is a university degree), and may also be eligible for a Specialist exam if that fits your profile. Similarly, if you are an economist who considers that, based on the earmarked figures disclosed in the Notice of Competition (published on EPSO's website and in the Official Journal), you have more chances in the Economist sub-profile than in the Public Administration one, you are free to choose either one as long as your degree and other formal criteria make you eligible for both.

Let's consider an imaginary but practical example. Depending on your profile, you may look at the Notice of Competition and discover that EPSO plans to create a reserve list of 200 Public Administration profiles and 80 lawyer profiles in the framework of an Administrator (AD5) competition. If you have a legal background, you are thus eligible to compete in either of the two categories.

While at first glance it might seem logical to apply for the one where more people are taken and thus your chances seem higher, practice shows that far more candidates apply in the "generalist" Public Administration profile – which changes the equation. If we assume that 12,000 people apply in the Public Administration profile and 3000 people apply for the lawyer one, your chances are 200:12,000 compared to 80:3000 for the lawyers, therefore the latter is the smarter choice. The only problem in this logic is the lack of actual statistics: nobody knows exactly how many applicants will apply until the deadline is up; therefore this is a unique mix of logical reasoning and chance.

Another aspect to consider is the long-term repercussions of your choice: not only will your exam profile determine the required professional knowledge but it will also affect your recruitment prospects once placed on the reserve list. It is for obvious reasons that EPSO creates sub-profiles and specialist profiles in the selection process: if an expert on environment law is sought, those on a lawyers' reserve list may have better chances of being offered a job than those on a Public Administration list (though this is not a formal rule and depends a lot on other external and individual factors as well). Important to note, however, is that de facto *anyone* can be recruited from ANY reserve list as long as their personal profile and the function group (Secretary, Assistant or Administrator) matches the specific vacancy's requirements, though EU institutions try to respect an internal policy of not "poaching" candidates from other reserve lists than the one from which they are meant to recruit.

Deciding on which exam profile to sit is therefore a tough decision for many, given its repercussions on the chances to succeed. Nevertheless, **you can apply for an unlimited number of competitions** (provided the Notice of competition does not specifically exclude this). As long as you are aware of these aspects, you can evaluate the position better for yourself – this will, in fact, be your first numerical reasoning practice exercise!

Feedback and Complaints

When discussing feedback and complaints, it must be borne in mind that given the significant number of candidates, both are handled in an automated way in the first place until human intervention is required.

Feedback (on test results) is only given in an automated format for the pre-selection phase while those who take part in an Assessment Centre are given more comprehensive feedback in the form of a written report called a "**competency passport**", which is provided for everyone regardless of whether they passed or failed. EPSO also often requests feedback online or immediately after the computer-based test on screen, so as to improve its procedures.

Only well founded and serious complaints can be taken into account by the Selection Board, for the above reasons. This also means that individual cases are always examined by the Selection Board or exceptionally by EPSO as a body. Moreover, complaints can only concern the lack of respect for the exam rules or other administrative procedures and they can hardly ever relate to "revision" of the scores or exam results. As an example, if you missed the pass mark by one point, you cannot argue in favour of leniency or flexibility unless there was an error in one of the exam questions and it must be "neutralised" for all candidates (more on this below). Another scenario when your complaint may be substantiated is when an exam rule was not respected, e.g. your relevant qualification was not accepted by the Selection Board even though the issuing university is accredited and recognised by your Member State.

As mentioned above, the first place to lodge a complaint with is the Selection Board where strict deadlines apply (usually within 10 days from the communication of the results), but both the Ombudsman and ultimately, the Civil Service Tribunal may deal with the case. While the Ombudsman can only deal with "maladministration" (this term refers to a situation when an EU institution or body fails to respect the exam rules or procedures – as opposed to individual exam results or evaluations of the Selection Board), the EU Civil Service Tribunal does examine individual cases on their merits but acts only as a second level judicial review body after the Selection Board has refused your formal complaint. It must nevertheless be borne in mind that these are long and cumbersome procedures that are only worth the effort if you are truly and reasonably convinced that you have been discriminated against or that your application's treatment can be challenged on legal grounds.

Another important aspect is that regardless of any failed efforts to pass the exams you can, as mentioned above, apply for new competitions without any limitations. If you do not pass an exam, EPSO does not retain your scores or keep a file on your results, therefore **you can start with a "clean slate" if you decide to have another go at passing the exams**, and you may even apply in parallel for multiple competitions (provided you meet the eligibility criteria and there is no clause in the Notice of Competition forbidding this).

The Selection Boards

Selection Boards have traditionally been composed of EU officials who volunteer to take part in such tasks. Their background, motivation and interests vary greatly which ensures objective and fair treatment based on strict guidelines that each of them must follow. Selection Boards, including most assessors, are still chosen from among volunteering active and even retired personnel, though some expertise, especially in developing multiple choice tests and administering the exams in various locations around the world, is now provided by external contractors. EPSO has been trying to professionalise the Selection Boards by extending the scope of their members' assignments for several months or even years instead of using them on an ad hoc basis, thus ensuring the accumulation of more insight and knowledge on their part, and also by providing proper training before their assignment commences.

Members of the Selection Boards generally perform the entire administration of an exam while being independent from EPSO and, legally speaking, they are the ones who are solely responsible for the administration of a competition and not EPSO. Each competition has its own Selection Board, which takes on tasks such as preparing the tests, admitting candidates on the basis of their files or marking the exercises. In a case brought before the European Court of Justice, a candidate in the 2010 Administrator exam challenged the Selection Board's ability to control and supervise the computer-based tests created and run by an external company. He won the case, requiring a re-run of the 2010 Administrator exams in 2013. This case demonstrates the importance of the Selection Board and their duty to supervise all elements of the competition.

You, of course, **may never approach a Selection Board member** for any additional information other than that formally communicated to you, even though the board members' names are always made public on EPSO's website for reasons of transparency. Some candidates think that a quick online search to find the professional background of board members could help identify their favourite topics (e.g. if a member works in DG Competition of the European Commission, it may have some bearing on the questions they ask), though this is rarely the case especially since the Assessment Centres have a very different approach in testing candidates.

Venues and Costs

The **pre-selection exams take place all over Europe** and in several other locations around the world. Where citizens of all Member States are eligible for a competition (which is the normal situation), there will be exam centres in each country's capital, and in case of bigger countries, also in other large cities.

As almost all exams under the EPSO system are administered on computers, exams are generally held over a certain period of time at the designated centres.

Candidates are required to pick and book a date and venue online that suits them most within this period, though you must be very careful in your first choice as revisions or changes are almost never allowed after the booking period is over (the very few exceptions may include issues such as childbirth or medical events).

After you validate your application (i.e. submit it formally online), booking will be made available shortly thereafter. The minute the booking is opened, be sure to sign up as soon as possible given that places tend to fill up fast, and to avoid any last minute internet blackout or server crash that may prevent you from securing your place in time.

No contribution is made towards any travelling or subsistence expenses associated with the pre-selection phase of the exam. As these exams take place in your own country or at multiple venues elsewhere in the world, travelling from your home to these centres is always on your own budget.

For the assessment phase, you will be given a specific date some time in advance with limited or no option to amend it unless compelling events prevent you from attending and you can duly justify the reason.

Assessment Centres are located centrally in Brussels though exceptionally and only for lawyer-linguists, there is an Assessment Centre in Luxembourg too. Candidates who need to travel there are reimbursed for their travel costs and also given a daily subsistence allowance for hotel and food costs. The specific rules are always communicated in advance either as early as in the Notice of Competition or later to those who actually make it through to the assessment phase. The underlying principle is that nobody should suffer any disadvantage in attending the competitions due to budgetary issues. The same rule of equal opportunities applies for those flying in or travelling to a specific job interview unless a telephone or videoconference is a feasible alternative.

Motivation

Before applying, it is useful to reflect on what factors motivate you in wanting to work for an EU institution. Usually it is a mixture of various considerations – such as the desire to work on international affairs, the opportunity to travel, getting an attractive salary and benefits, having an interesting and varied job, speaking and learning foreign languages, job security etc.

Being aware of which factors are the most important for you personally can help in identifying which profile to apply for – and it should also help in the structured interview, if you get to the Assessment Centre, when assessors try to find out more about your personality. "Being part of something larger than yourself" is a vital aspect that you may also emphasise in your application's motivation section. Also on this topic, at the start of 2018 EPSO was considering the introduction of an "EU Motivation Interview" at the Assessment Centre, to assess candidates' commitment to the "European idea".

The Candidates

It is very hard, if not impossible, to outline a "typical" candidate profile given the large number and diverse backgrounds of applicants. However, I have formed the impression that most of the serious applicants have five things in common. They:

- Are interested in EU affairs, committed to European integration and wish to work for a "good cause"

- Have a solid knowledge of at least two foreign languages

- Are flexible and willing to work abroad in a multi-cultural environment

- Have a strong motivation to study for and pass the exams to get into the EU institutions

- Understand and accept that EU institutions are different from the private sector inasmuch as they are a hybrid of a diplomatic corps, an international organisation and a government administration that is based on a hierarchic model

The above qualities will also be looked at by assessors if only on an indirect or informal level. EU institutions deal with such a wide variety of issues that you can certainly find the job that best suits your interests and personality if your motivation is right.

Age

There is no limitation on an applicant's age (minimum age is determined by the requirement of a degree/diploma or work experience, therefore it is never formally spelled out). Obviously the EU is keen on ensuring a level playing field in terms of candidates' backgrounds, ensuring equal opportunities for all based on merit, regardless of whether they belong to any particular religious, sexual, ethnic or other minority, social segment or age group.

Whatever your age, you will be required to pass a medical check that will serve as a benchmark for your social security and health insurance file before taking up an EU job. This also serves to ensure that you are physically capable of doing the job you are to be required to perform.

Quotas

It is frequently asked whether the EU institutions apply a quota system for allocating posts to a certain number of officials from each Member State.

In fact, the Staff Regulations provide that officials are to be "recruited on the broadest possible geographical basis from among nationals of Member States of the Union". This reference to "the broadest possible geographical basis" explains the special competitions in recent years e.g. to select candidates exclusively from Croatia based on their recent accession to the EU, but such targeted competitions are the exception, not the rule.

Apart from such special circumstances, where new Member States are starting from a base of zero, the "broadest possible geographical basis" provision in practice means there is an ongoing effort to maintain an allocation of posts that more-or-less reflects the proportion of each Member State's population in the EU as a whole. This is true for all grades, including senior management. Yet, despite this principle, there are no hard-coded quotas for Irish or Cypriot or any other citizens given the merit-based competition system. Natural imbalances therefore always exist and they could only be challenged by the introduction of specific staff allocations, which would then likely infringe upon the principle of non-discrimination based on nationality. This is certainly not an easy issue to handle politically as it touches on the very essence of the principles guiding European integration.

Language Rules

One of the most common misunderstandings regarding EU competitions is the language regime: what is the exact meaning of the so-called first and second language? In fact the **first language** refers to your **mother tongue, as long as it is an official EU language**. The reason why this latter point needs to be specified is because a Lithuanian candidate, for example, may have Russian as their mother tongue but that cannot be considered as their first language since it is not an official EU language.

In some cases, especially for enlargement-related or Linguist exams, the candidate's citizenship or the given exam's specific language profile automatically determines the required first language. Examples would be competitions for Croatian Administrators and Assistants requiring the first language to be Croatian; or having French as the compulsory first language for translator exams in the French language. In other instances you are free to choose your first language as long as the above rules on citizenship and the official EU language requirements are respected. Thus, for instance, if you have Luxembourgish citizenship, your "first language" may well be French or German as Luxembourgish is not an official EU language.

It is important to note that "mother tongue" can also mean that if you have a perfect command of a language that you "learned" – and if you are confident that your speaking and writing is close to perfect in that language, you can indicate it as your first language. For example, if your citizenship is Slovak but you speak Greek perfectly, and you wish to apply for an exam where one of the first language choices is Greek, feel free to do so. But bear in mind that your second language must also be at a high level.

The second language is in fact your first foreign language and traditionally you have only been allowed to choose between English, French or German. However following a ruling by the European Court of Justice (which actually led to the cancellation of the AD5 generalist competition in 2016) EPSO is now offering as language 2 the five languages most frequently declared by candidates at B2 level or higher in the first part of their application form for the competition in question (meaning it can vary from one competition to another).

The first time this new procedure was applied, for the 2017 AD5 generalist competition (EPSO/AD/338/17) the following 5 languages were declared by the most people: English, French, Spanish, Italian and German (in that order, from highest to lowest number), which was as might have been expected. How this rule will be applied in future is uncertain because for the most recent Secretaries/Clerks competition more candidates actually declared Greek than German as one of their languages. However, it is worth pointing out that the Notice of Competition in this case (as in others) states that while EPSO intends to offer as language 2 "the 5 languages most frequently declared by candidates" this would be only *"while also taking into account the needs of the service"*.

Therefore there is discretion in deciding which languages will be treated as language 2 – and it seems unlikely, for instance, that this will be interpreted as meaning that the Assessment Centre should be offered in Greek.

For Linguist exams (and sometimes for certain Assistant exams) the second language is usually the one for which candidates are sought. For example, if EPSO announces a Linguist exam for Bulgarian translators, the first language is required to be Bulgarian, the second language may be any other EU official language, and there may be a third language (in fact, second foreign language) requirement as well. Note that I did not mention any Bulgarian citizenship requirement here as the goal is the perfect command of a language regardless of which EU citizenship you may have. This is a fundamental rule in the system: the citizenship requirement is almost always decoupled from the language requirements.

EPSO now provides for abstract reasoning, verbal reasoning and numerical reasoning tests to be done in your first language. This shows that the aim of such tests is not to test your linguistic knowledge but to assess your psychometric reasoning skills, which can be done best in your "EU mother tongue". Situational judgement tests and other tests (e.g. domain specific tests for Specialists, Assessment Centre exams and others), however, are in language 2.

Once recruited, AD level officials will also need to demonstrate their ability to work in a **second foreign language** (their "**third language**") before their first promotion, though many candidates have already shown this ability at the exam if such an option was available. In any case, always be very mindful which language(s) you select when signing up for the exam, as you would certainly not like to decode French abbreviations in your test if you had intended to take the exam in English!

Another crucial piece of advice to bear in mind is that once you know which language you will be assessed in (i.e. the choice for "second language"; in case of linguists/interpreters, your first language will also be tested), read all preparation materials only in that/those language(s). Needless to say, French, German and all other names of EU institutions, abbreviations, programmes and concepts may differ significantly from each other, and you certainly do not wish to mix up the European Council with the Council of Europe because of a language issue.

Formal Criteria

As a candidate applying for EU exams, you must meet certain formal (objective) criteria. These, as a general rule, say you must:

- Be a citizen of a Member State of the European Union (though exceptions might occur as in the case of enlargement-related competitions)

- Be entitled to full rights as such a citizen (e.g. no legal limitations as a result of criminal acts or other issues) and meet the character requirements for the duties involved

- Have fulfilled any obligations imposed by the laws on military service (only relevant for those Member States where such service is compulsory, and even there you may prove that you were exempted from the service)

- Have a thorough knowledge of one of the official languages of the European Union and a satisfactory knowledge of a second (this is the minimum requirement but further linguistic prerequisites may be set out in the given Notice of Competition as also mentioned above)

- Have the sufficient minimum education and/or work experience as set out in the Notice of Competition

These formal criteria are required for all profiles, regardless of the specific provisions of

	Administrators (AD)	Linguists (AD)	Assistants (AST) Secretaries (AST-SC)	Specialists (AD or AST)
Minimum Qualification	Degree (min. BA level or 3 years of studies, EPSO may require it to be related to the chosen sub-profile, e.g. Audit)	Degree (min. BA level or 3 years of studies)	Relevant high school diploma or post-secondary qualification (a minimum of 3 years study-related work might also be required)	Same as for ASTs and ADs
Work Experience	None (AD5); 6 years (AD7); 12 years (AD9) (exception: see Specialists' column)	None (AD5); 6 years (AD7); 12 years (AD9)	None to 3 or 6 years, depending on the qualification (AST3 and above and SC1 and SC2 unless relevant diploma available)	Same as for ASTs and ADs (with possible exceptions, e.g. AD7 lawyer-linguists may need only 3 years of work experience instead of 6)
Type of Qualification (in many cases, though not always, qualifications are eliminatory, so make sure to read EPSO's Notice of Competition carefully)	Arts, Law, Economics, Political Science, Statistics etc.	Language Studies, Interpreting	Clerical Studies, Arts, Finances, IT, Technical skills etc.	Lawyers, Linguists, Engineers, Scientists, Doctors, Veterinaries

Important note: the terminology relating to qualifications varies greatly from country to country – what is called a "degree" in one country is a "diploma" in another, and so forth. For a country-by-country list of what EPSO regards as examples of qualifications corresponding to those required by the Notices of Competition, see http://europa.eu/epso/doc/diplomes-fortheweb_en.pdf

Please note that the above table is for information purposes only and the actual requirements may differ; please always consult EPSO's official communications for up-to-date information

an exam announcement; meeting these does not lead to passing any stage but their lack certainly leads to non-eligibility or if discovered later, disqualification from the exam.

The Profiles

The EPSO system comprises five main job categories generally referred to as **profiles** – Administrators (AD), Linguists (AD), Assistants (AST), Secretaries (AST-SC), and Specialists (AD or AST). These are summarised in the table above. Note, however, that many staff are also recruited these days on a more flexible contract basis, for so-called Contract Agents for Specific Tasks (CAST) positions, not included in the table. CAST competitions are different from the "regular" EPSO open competitions because only a limited number of pre-selected candidates are asked to sit the types of selection tests described in this book. However, verbal, numerical and abstract reasoning tests, as well as a specific competency test in the field being recruited for, are likely to be used for candidates who get past the initial screening.

Choosing a profile is determined by both objective and subjective factors: depending on your qualifications and work experience (which are "objective" facts you cannot change overnight), you may be limited to only one "choice"; it may nevertheless happen that you are formally eligible for multiple profiles and it remains your individual choice which one to sit for. For example, a lawyer with three years' experience and fluent knowledge of three languages might be eligible for all the profiles, including Specialists (lawyer-linguists).

Multiple Applications

A general approach taken by many candidates is to apply for all competitions they are eligible for, this way increasing their chances. This is in fact a highly recommended strategy though you should be very careful not to apply for two exams in parallel that are mutually exclusive **nor should you create two accounts (profiles)** on EPSO's website, because this will lead to disqualification from the competition.

Such rules are usually indicated in the Notice of Competition and are limited to the sub-profiles of a given exam. Thus an Administrator (AD5) or Assistant (AST) competition in the annual cycle may have multiple domains such as Public Administration, Law, Economics, Audit, Finance and Statistics, where candidates are required to pick only one of these options. Apart from the risk of being disqualified from both, it is also technically impossible to choose two domains at the same time given the features of the online application form. If in doubt whether you may run parallel applications for different competitions (for example an AD or AST exam and a Specialist exam), better to ask EPSO than lose out on both counts.

The Exam Procedure Step-by-Step

Having overviewed the above general principles and hints, we can now move on to the phases and possible pitfalls of the EPSO system.

As seen in the table opposite, the system comprises up to five main phases:

1. Notice of Competition, Self-Assessment, Registration

2. Pre-selection Phase (first round of exams)

3. Intermediate exam (e-tray test for AD generalists)

4. Assessment Centre (second full round of exams)

5. Reserve List, Recruitment

Below we have tried to provide an introduction to each of the stages and tests, along with some practical advice. Later chapters in this book provide very detailed coverage and practice materials for the critical pre-selection phase.

Phase 1: Notice of Competition, Self-Assessment, Registration

The Notice of Competition

As mentioned earlier, the Notice of Competition (NoC) is a special administrative notice addressed to all EU citizens and it is therefore published in the Official Journal of the EU both in print and online. It is important to underline that the NoC is the only official source of information, therefore if you see any contradicting or different interpretation in the press or on a website, make sure to check the original authentic source which is always referenced on EPSO's website.

The NoC is a rather extensive document that sets out all the formal eligibility criteria, language requirements, deadlines and other practical arrangements linked to the exam. Just as important, the NoC contains a wealth of information that you can use to your benefit by reading it attentively, such as the size of the reserve list (so you can estimate

Month(s)	Administrators	Assistants and Secretaries	Linguists	Specialists
0	Notice of competition + self-assessment	Notice of competition + self-assessment	Notice of competition + self-assessment	Notice of competition + self-assessment
1	Online registration	Online registration	Online registration	Online registration
2-4	Pre-selection: verbal + numerical + abstract reasoning tests + situational judgement tests (possibly)	Pre-selection: AST: numerical + abstract + verbal reasoning tests + situational judgement tests (possibly) + accuracy tests + prioritising and organising tests SC: verbal reasoning tests + accuracy tests + prioritising and organising tests + language comprehension tests	Pre-selection: verbal (in 2 or 3 languages) + numerical + abstract reasoning tests	"Talent Screener" (if the No. of candidates exceeds a specified threshold, abstract + verbal + numerical reasoning tests are also used in this phase)
	Intermediate test (e-tray)			
5-7	Admission + Assessment Centre: case study + group exercise + oral presentation + structured interview	Admission + Assessment Centre: AST: professional skills test + in-tray + case study + group exercise + structured interview SC: document processing + drafting skills + in-tray + structured interview + IT literacy	Admission + Assessment Centre: practical linguistic tests (translation or interpreting from the source language/s) + structured interview + oral presentation + group exercise	Admission + detailed case study and/or domain specific interview + structured interview + group exercise (+verbal + numerical + abstract reasoning tests, if not used at pre-selection, no minimum pass mark)
8-9	Reserve lists/recruitment	Reserve lists/recruitment	Reserve lists/recruitment	Reserve lists/recruitment

The details in this table are only indicative – timelines and specific tests vary from one competition to another

your chances and thus decide which sub-profile or domain to apply for after analysing the earmarked number of applicants to be accepted for the assessment phase and how many people are to be placed on the reserve list).

The basic "job description", also detailed in the NoC, is particularly interesting as it is not only an indication of what sort of tasks you would need to carry out once employed but you can also deduce lots of hints about the topics to cover when preparing for the domain-specific parts of the assessment phase, especially the case study.

On the next page, by way of illustration, are extracts from a **Notice of Competition for a general Administrator competition**, where the main aspects of the role are described.

It is crucial to understand and analyse every detail provided in the NoC to make sure you can gain valuable insights. This also helps you avoid seemingly evident pitfalls that might lead to disqualification (such as a requirement to submit a certain certificate or sign a submitted document) – you would be surprised to know how many people get rejected on formal grounds by accidentally overlooking a date, a provision or a prerequisite

AD 5 is the grade at which graduates begin their careers as administrators in the European institutions. Administrators recruited at this grade can undertake, under supervision, three main types of work in the institutions: policy formulation, operational delivery, and resource management. We are particularly looking for candidates with a potential for career development.

The general role of administrators is to support decision-makers in fulfilling the mission of their institution or body.

Their main duties, which may vary from one institution to another, include:

- devising, implementing, monitoring and control of programmes and action plans,
- managing resources including staff, finances, and equipment,
- assisting decision-makers by means of written or oral contributions,
- drafting policy analysis briefings,
- external communication as well as internal reporting and communication,
- relations with external stakeholders and with the Member States,
- inter-service and inter-institutional coordination and consultation regarding policy,
- coordinating working groups set up by the Member States, the institutions and other external stakeholders,
- drafting contracts, preparing calls for proposals and invitations to tender, and participating in evaluation committees for monitoring selection procedures and the allocation of proposals.

Self-Assessment

Self-assessment as a tool is widely used in international organisations and multinational private sector companies and EPSO makes use of it as well. The objective is to ensure candidates realise what EU jobs are really about and dispel misconceptions or misperceptions at the earliest stage. This is hoped to result in a reduction in non-eligible applications and candidate frustration and so to decreasing overhead expenses related to the organisation of exams caused by registered applicants not showing up or refusing job offers because they had a very different idea of what working for the EU means.

Self-assessment, which is not to be confused with the talent screener used for Specialists, is non-eliminatory, meaning that you cannot pass or fail based on your answers.

Registration

Registration is done exclusively online on the EPSO (EU Careers) website at the start of the procedure, which also means that you will not need to hand in any proof, paper or document at this stage – you only need to make an honest declaration. The first step is to create an **EPSO account or profile**, which is an online personal profile where your correspondence with EPSO's contractual supplier will take place. If you change your postal or e-mail address during the procedure or any other contact information becomes obsolete, make sure to update your online account immediately.

If, after registration, the confirmation e-mail does not arrive in your inbox within a few hours, check your spam or bulk mail folder as it may have been misfiled by your e-mail application; should you still not receive anything, ask EPSO for technical assistance. Make sure, however, that you do not register twice as it may lead to potential disqualification if other signs show you had second thoughts when doing so.

As in all other steps of the competition, make sure to re-read all input you provide, as a wrong click with your mouse can lead to sitting the exam in a different language than intended, or an error in choosing your citizenship from a drop-down menu may even result in you being refused for the pre-selection. Finally, never leave anything to the last moment as many candidates may rush to complete their account in the last few days of application and it may cause service interruptions or outages and prevent you from securing your place – which is every candidate's worst nightmare!

Phase 2: Pre-Selection

Having taken the above steps and provided that you meet all formal eligibility criteria, you should receive an official invitation to the pre-selection phase, communicated to you in your online EPSO profile. Once this eagerly awaited message arrives, you should start planning seriously your preparation as the booking period may open straightaway and the exam be imminent.

Once the booking is open, you can choose a venue and a time from the available exam centres and time slots. If you live outside Europe, you can choose an exam centre outside the Member States; EPSO has extended the reach of exam centres to other continents via international test centres in China, the USA and elsewhere, which is a welcome development (though it does not necessarily apply for all exams, e.g. for the Croatian exams, test centres were only available in Europe).

When choosing an exam centre, make sure you are fully aware of the logistical issues: print the map of its location, find out which public transport goes there on the exam day, make sure that no strike or service interruption is foreseen for that day, and have a fallback plan in case you are running late, such as the phone number of a reliable taxi company.

My general advice for test-takers is to start practising as early as you can; preferably straight after deciding to sit for an EPSO exam. Even though you will not need any EU knowledge in the pre-selection phase, competition is still fierce and you must achieve the highest possible score in demanding psychometric tests. (Note, however, that for certain Specialist competitions, the "pre-selection" phase is the talent screener, and the psychometric tests are part of the Assessment Centre.) This book teaches the basic skills you need for these tests, with plenty of practice questions. In addition, various websites provide online preparation tests and courses, and a number of companies offer training in Brussels and elsewhere in Europe.

I strongly advise creating a concrete study plan where you allocate sufficient time for the upcoming weeks and months for practice, revision, simulation and preparation. Simply saying "I'll find the time whenever I have nothing else to do" will not lead to tangible results, as watching the next episode of *Game of Thrones* will always seems more fun than dealing with rhombuses in abstract reasoning quizzes.

Scoring

As opposed to the system commonly used in French competitions and exams, there is only one correct answer for any given test question except for situational judgement tests (see below).

A small but very important piece of advice is to read the question extremely carefully to avoid overlooking words such as "not" in a question that reads "Which of the following is not an EU policy?" I have been told more than a dozen times that a certain question in the previous editions of this book was wrong when it turned out that the readers had misread the question. This of course relates to verbal and numerical reasoning tests as much as other multiple choice questions.

Another important aspect to note is that **EPSO does not simply add up all your scores across the board to produce an aggregate mark**. You may have to achieve a minimum score, for instance 50%, in every one or some of the tests, if you are to go further, regardless of how well you do in aggregate; alternatively, it could be that while the results of two tests are combined another is considered on its own. Thus, to give an example, you may find that if you do brilliantly at abstract and verbal reasoning but don't make the pass mark on numerical reasoning, you could be failed for that reason alone. Similarly, the situational judgement test has been both eliminatory and a stand-alone, with the pass mark for situational judgement tests usually 24 points out of 40, which is 60%.

The exact rules for scoring, how scores are weighted and aggregated, and which tests are eliminatory in their own right can and do vary between competitions, so you must be sure what rules apply to your competition – always check the Notice of Competition. Equally, it means you cannot afford to rely on doing well in just some tests – you need to get to the highest possible standard across the board.

Computer Screens

As all tests in the pre-selection phase are administered on computers located in accredited exam centres, you should be prepared for the difficulties this entails. Reading a text is always slower on a computer screen than on paper, speed being also influenced by the font size and screen resolution. Highlighting, underlining or adding comments on screen is technically not available, therefore you need to take notes on the scrap paper or erasable slate that the exam centres provide. (This is even more relevant when it comes to the case study, which is formally part of the Assessment Centre, even if it is usually organised separately for logistical reasons.) Even though an on-screen calculator is usually available, handling it is less easy than using a physical one, especially if you could not practise such operations beforehand.

Computer-based exams do have a few advantages however. The display of the available time (which is not meant to put pressure on you but rather to help time management); the automatic registration of answered and unanswered questions (which should help you keep track of the questions); the flexibility of choosing a convenient exam day for all candidates (as opposed to having a single exam day for all candidates); and the faster (and more reliable) correction of your answers given the electronic evaluation, are among the advantages of computer based exams.

Verbal and Numerical Reasoning Tests

The verbal and numerical reasoning tests, along with abstract reasoning, are commonly known as **psychometric tests**. These are one of the most popular methods to evaluate cognitive skills and the intelligence of prospective employees. They are widely used by multinational companies and civil service recruiters around the world given their flexible application, cost-effectiveness and proven relevance to gauge candidates' skills. The relevant chapters of this book provide a full methodology and hundreds of practice exercises: what follows here is more of a description of how these tests are administered along with some general advice on how to tackle them.

Verbal reasoning tests are essentially reading comprehension tests where you are required to answer a question based on a text. A fundamental rule is to only consider information contained in the text.

Numerical reasoning, on the other hand, is a calculation exercise using statistical charts, tables and graphs, based on which you are required to find a certain percentage, figure, or decide on relative values (e.g. "Based on the table, which country had the highest birth rate in 2008?"). Questions can be tricky as in many cases no or minimal exact calculation is required given that you can simplify the riddle by applying calculation methods and shortcuts. A comprehensive toolkit is offered in the relevant chapter of this book.

EPSO has been using verbal and numerical reasoning tests for some years in its competitions and they have proven to be one of the most challenging parts of the exam procedure. The likely reason is that while EU knowledge could be memorised by dedicating sufficient time to this end, succeeding in verbal and numerical reasoning requires a completely different approach. Learning the methodology, and then plenty of practice in using it, is therefore crucial to succeed.

As mentioned in the section on languages above, since 2011 all verbal and numerical reasoning tests are in your first language (along with abstract reasoning, but there the choice of language has no relevance). Linguists can expect to have two or three different verbal reasoning tests: one in their main language (which depends on which linguistic profile they had applied for, e.g. Bulgarian translator or German interpreter); while the other two depend on the source languages available for that given exam (English, French and German have privileged status and almost always appear among the languages).

Work as hard as you can to improve your overall vocabulary in the exam's language by reading quality news websites, boost your spelling skills for complex words, your understanding of measurement units (billions vs. millions, how many litres in one cubic metre, etc.) and revise basic mathematical operations. In addition to the extensive resources in this book, you will find tests in 14 different languages on the Online EU Training website.

Abstract Reasoning Tests

Abstract reasoning is another test type that various international employers commonly use; it is a common feature of popular IQ tests as well. Abstract reasoning is different from the other two tests as it requires no linguistic skills: there is only one main question for all tasks, such as "Which figure is the next in the series?"

Using these questions for personnel selection is practical for EPSO given that there is no need to translate the exercise into any language and also because abstract reasoning tests have been scientifically proven to be culture-neutral while effectively testing candidates' so-called "fluid intelligence". This latter term refers to the capability to solve new problems and understand the relationship between various concepts, independent of any acquired knowledge.

The main skill you need to efficiently resolve abstract reasoning tests is "imagination" – that is, the ability to mentally rotate, flip or turn certain figures according to a certain logic or rule. This rule is one of the main challenges of this question type as you should be able to "dissect" a figure and identify its component elements. Those capable of performing such tasks are likely to be able to cope with unknown or new situations in the workplace: this skill therefore does have more practical value for predicting actual job performance than may seem at first glance. You can find a large number of abstract reasoning test questions in the relevant chapter of this book, along with an in-depth methodology that is highly practical and applicable.

Situational Judgement Tests

Situational judgement tests (or SJTs for short) have been employed for decades by different organisations, such as the Canadian Civil Service, and companies that have wished to measure potential candidates in real-life work scenarios. The objective of SJTs is to create **realistic work-related scenarios** in which you must determine the proper course of action given the parameters and situation. In other words, the test basically asks what you would do in a particular circumstance.

An important element of SJTs is that there are no absolutely "right" or "wrong" answers when testing your judgement. Rather, judgement is about your ability to assess a given situation and make clearly defined decisions on how to proceed from there, based on your own unique set of experiences in life and understanding of the EU institutions' culture and ethical rules, while applying a certain common sense to workplace situations.

For example, given a sample question about witnessing malpractice in your unit committed by a colleague, your reaction or response may be to confront that person first while another person may feel it is most appropriate to let your Head of Unit know about what has happened. This is therefore closely linked to the competencies that EPSO is seeking to find in future EU officials.

Since there are no right or wrong answers as such, the decision whether one answer is better than another lies in the hands of the test administrators; however, the benchmark for deciding the value of each answer is the competency list that EPSO has established and against which it evaluates candidates.

It is important to point out that while real world situations can certainly be summarised into brief sentences or paragraphs, rarely do we come across situations in life that resemble these questions precisely. As in the above example, you could be confronted with a colleague who may be stealing but who may also be a friend, or someone with whom you are in direct competition for a promotion. Such factors would certainly influence your judgement and response.

For further background details on SJTs, how they are created, including a full sample that covers the competencies that EPSO tests with specific exercises (rather than only by observation of behaviour in assessment exercises), refer to the relevant chapters below.

Professional Skills Tests

These types of tests are widely used by assessors and recruiters around the world to gauge candidates' ability to concentrate, attention to detail and computer literacy skills. Such tests used by EPSO for **AST and Secretary (AST-SC)** exams are prioritising and organising (planning skills involving allocation of limited resources) and accuracy tests with icons (spotting typos, misquotes or spelling errors in a large set of data, table or chart); e-tray simulations (a series of emails coming in to a simulated interface where you need to process and understand them); and for SC posts, IT literacy tests (knowledge of Microsoft Office and other computer and information technology tools).

Testing of AST professional skills is carried out in both the pre-selection phase and in the Assessment Centre. However, in the pre-selection phase the focus is on general "prioritising and organising" and "accuracy" tests which are relevant to every AST sub-profile, while at the Assessment Centre the emphasis is on specific knowledge in the chosen field of the exam.

Notification of Results

After the pre-selection phase, or in the case of Specialist profiles, after the successful sifting-in of your CV, candidates are notified both of their positive or negative results. The scores and the answers you had given are communicated to you in all cases though for practical reasons EPSO cannot disclose the multiple choice questions themselves, only the answers you had marked.

Since the number of applicants in the pre-selection phase runs into the tens of thousands, EPSO decided to require the submission of supporting documents only for those who have passed the pre-selection or were Specialists short-listed on the basis of their

CV. This means that even those who have already cleared the first hurdle may not take their eligibility for the assessment phase for granted: EPSO will first of all require you to send in a completed and signed application form along with annexes listing your educational qualifications and if necessary, documents attesting your professional experience or other required information.

As soon as the above documents are validated and accepted, you receive an official notification in your EPSO profile that you have been admitted to the assessment phase. Shortly afterwards you will be required to confirm your presence at a given venue and date to undergo the assessment exams.

Phase 3: Intermediate Test

The intermediate test is a relatively new addition to the EPSO selection process. It consists of an e-tray exercise for generalist AD (Administrator) candidates who have passed the pre-selection tests and made the "top cut", that is, they were among the best X number of candidates. The number asked to take the intermediate test will likely be around ten times the number intended to be placed on the final reserve list. As this exam is another filter to get to the Assessment Centre, it has enabled more than three times more candidates to pass the pre-selection and be evaluated in this phase rather than being "selected out" earlier, in the pre-selection phase. The e-tray is covered in detail in the *The Ultimate EU Test Book Assessment Centre 2018*.

Phase 4: Assessment

Generic Assessment Centre Exercises

An Assessment Centre is used as the **second full round of exams** for Administrators (including Linguists) and Assistants and Secretaries (but in most cases, the first round for Specialists). At the Assessment Centre several trained observers called "assessors" evaluate your performance throughout half a day or a full day of exercises that have been developed specifically for this purpose. EPSO uses multiple types of exercises based on their competency framework: the idea is that each competency (listed above, such as "Delivering quality and results") will be tested by two types of exercises to make sure that the observations are valid.

The reason why different competencies are tested by using various exercises for various profiles is that EPSO has linked certain competencies to each profile and therefore only wishes to test you on those that are relevant for your field. Thus, for example, Assistants will not be required to give an oral presentation as their job roles will not include giving presentations.

The core generic exercises currently used at the Assessment Centre are:

1. The Case Study (not for AST-SC)

2. The Group Exercise (not for AST-SC)

3. The Structured Interview (the general competency based interview)

4. The Oral Presentation (AD only)

5. The e-Tray (or in-tray) exercise (AST and SC only)

The above exercises are generic in the sense that they test personal behaviours and qualities in ways which are relevant to the wide range of roles that candidates may be called on to undertake in the course of their career.

In addition to these "core" elements of assessment, for more specialised roles the competition will involve other tests focusing on specialised knowledge.

Professional Skills Tests

Linguists' Skills Tests (Translators, Interpreters, Lawyer-Linguists)

For the Linguist profiles, the pre-selection tests include two extra verbal reasoning tests that concern their two "source" languages. The main verbal reasoning test is in their "target" language (which is the language of the chosen exam profile, e.g. for Spanish interpreters it is Spanish). More information on the languages is given in the section above on this topic.

As for the professional skills tests, they are similar to a classic language exam, comprising the translation of two 500 to 1500-word-long texts from each of the source languages into the target language (for translators) and a "live" interpretation with the above language combinations (for interpreters).

Translators and interpreters have various exercises in the assessment phase such as the structured interview, group exercise, oral presentation and the above- mentioned professional skills test. These exercises do not necessarily cover EU affairs, though they will certainly cover a wide range of topics such as economics, history or politics, given that these issues feature prominently in the day-to-day work of an EU translator or interpreter.

For lawyer-linguists the translation of a legal (though not necessarily EU) text is faced in the Assessment Centre phase, along with verbal, numerical and abstract reasoning tests and other competency tests (structured interview, group exercise). Traditionally, lawyer-linguists have not been allowed to use a dictionary for their translations, which made this testing more challenging than that of translators. Interestingly and importantly, lawyer-linguists have an extra test in the Assessment Centre which covers their general knowledge of and linguistic skills related to national (!) law. The reason for this test is not so much the knowledge of national paragraphs and regulations but the requirement to be familiar with the judicial and legal terminology that is a pre-requisite to performing a lawyer-linguist's job well.

Specialists' Tests

It is important to note that for Specialists, the pre-selection exams described above may be moved into the Assessment Centre stage, depending on the number of applicants.

As a general rule, EPSO says that if the number of Specialist applicants (e.g. nuclear scientist, cohesion policy expert, competition lawyer etc.) exceeds X times the number of places available on the reserve list, it will organise a pre-selection round for them as well. If not, then these exam items will be included in the assessment phase.

Moreover, Specialists need to go through an online pre-screening questionnaire, called a talent screener. The purpose of this is to identify their work experience in the given field, whether they have had publications in academic journals, done research in the field and many other declarations that can help the Selection Board evaluate Specialist candidates' suitability and eligibility for the post. (Even though these are declared on "word of honour", they may be checked by requesting supporting documents any time in the selection process or at recruitment.)

Should a large number of such candidates remain even after the pre-screening, a pre-selection round may be organised to filter candidates further. For Administrator and Assistant competitions, a pre-selection phase is the default rule without any in-depth online screening other than basic formal eligibility criteria.

Specialist knowledge is tested in the assessment phase mainly in the form of a practical exercise, a special domain-focused and targeted interview, and/or in the framework of the case study. This latter is closely related to the exam profile and the sub-profile or domain that the candidate chose at the time of application.

Specialist knowledge is tested for all profiles, as no capable candidate who otherwise lacks the proper knowledge of the chosen field can be recruited, given EPSO's wish that all new officials should be operational from "day one". Moreover, even Specialists need a solid understanding of EU institutions, procedures and stakeholders, which can add valuable points to your performance in the assessment phase of the exam. For instance, if you are familiar with the overall context of the EU's environmental policy, know which institutions and agencies are involved, which are the formal rules to enact policy in this field, which European associations and NGOs are taking an active part in influencing decision-makers and what the strategic thinking is on this policy's future, you are immediately in a position to make more out of the group exercise, the case study or the oral presentation than many other candidates who lack such knowledge would be able to do.

Assessment of Heads of Unit

The assessment for Head of Unit and Director posts has traditionally been carried out via an Assessment Centre. Potential Heads of Unit should prepare along the same lines as Administrators, even though the competency model against which they are evaluated is somewhat different, having a strong focus on management-related issues. This means that questions testing the candidate's skills in variously managing people, time, teams, finance, operations and conflict feature prominently in the structured interview and possibly impact other exam items such as the group exercise and the case study as well. Moreover, candidates for these exams are advised to be familiar with the EU Financial Regulations and general principles of handling budgets and funds.

Assessment Report

After both the Assessment Centre and other forms of assessment, a report with a competency passport will be drawn up by the assessors to evaluate you against the pre-established competencies. This also means that first and foremost you will not be judged against other candidates but rather against the objective behavioural criteria EPSO seeks in candidates. The ranking of suitable candidates will come afterwards and will be influenced by your performance in professional knowledge metrics.

Based on a streamlined and structured methodology, assessors draw up a report that summarises your performance, along with your strengths and weaknesses. EPSO provides this report to all candidates regardless of whether or not they were successful in the assessment phase. This report can add a lot to your self-development as it provides a comprehensive analysis of your personality traits as observed during the assessment. It can also be very helpful in deciding which of your skills or competencies may need to be developed.

Phase 5: Reserve List, Recruitment

For those candidates who successfully passed both exam stages and survived other potential pitfalls in the procedure, a notification including the words "we are happy to inform you" arrives in their virtual EPSO account's mailbox. This also means that your name will be published in the reserve lists that appear in the EU's Official Journal and on EPSO's website (unless you opt out) and your competency passport, based on the above assessment, will be added to your profile once you take up employment. Those who did not succeed this time should not despair as they can re-apply for any later exam with the advantage of being familiar with the working methods of the system.

Validity of the Reserve List

Once a reserve list is published, it is always clearly indicated when it expires, meaning until which date you can be recruited from it. However, EPSO has in practice regularly extended the validity period of a reserve list to make sure that all available candidates are recruited from it.

The idea is to have the Administrator and Assistant competitions' reserve lists valid until the next annual cycle results in a new list; for Linguists it is the same approach but instead of the next annual cycle, it will be the next competition in the same language that replaces the previous list; for Specialists, the lists are valid for at least three years as long as they still contain recruitable (available) laureates.

Flagging

Once on the reserve list, candidates (or as they are called at this stage, "**laureates**") are "flagged" by the institutions. This means that your profile listed in the "E-laureates" database can be assigned different statuses (marked in colours) as follows:

- **Green**: Any institution may recruit the candidate – a candidate may receive multiple offers in parallel and can choose accordingly

- **Red**: The laureate has already been recruited or their recruitment is happening right now

- **Grey**: The laureate is temporarily not available (e.g. the person is interested in taking up a job but currently cannot due to family or work reasons)

Job Interview

Once on the reserve list, you can try to lobby for yourself by indicating your exam's reference number and presenting your CV to targeted Heads of Unit; this, however, is of mixed effectiveness: while it works for some, it may yield no result at all for others. EPSO much rather recommends that you wait to be contacted by interested institutions or if you wish to get in touch with them yourself, they provide a candidate contact service list on their website where you may also ask for the list of internal vacancies that they might be willing to send you. Those candidates who are already working in one of the EU institutions (e.g. as a temporary agent) can have direct access to the internal vacancy list. Application to these posts is sometimes limited to "internal" candidates; however, sometimes "external" candidates are also considered if they meet the specific requirements of the post.

Finally, if you have a chance to make personal contacts, it can go a long way as you can make a good impression on a Head of Unit or demonstrate your abilities instead of depending on an impersonal message. Friday afternoons may be your best bet to manage to talk to or meet with a person in charge, but you may need to travel to Brussels at your own expense in the hope of effective networking.

Any time between a few weeks and several months, you may receive a phone call or e-mail asking whether you would be interested in an interview for a position at x or y EU institution. Always make sure your contact data is up-to-date and that you regularly check your EPSO profile as well in order not to miss such important events.

Once offered the chance to attend a job interview, it is highly recommended to participate even if the job itself may not be the most appealing. You can always decide to decline and wait for a better or different offer, but it is better to have such options than decline flatly in the first place and take a gamble. You can also gain useful interview experience and find out more about the position; you might even realise that the job is in fact meant for you.

The job interview itself is different from other parts of the selection competition as it is focused on your suitability for the specific position and it may only include some basic general EU questions. If you apply for a consumer health expert position, for example, you can expect a number of technical questions on this specific topic but nothing on e.g. the Treaty of Lisbon or the EU's immigration policy (unless the job in question is in the Commission's DG Home).

Your interviewers will most likely speak in English, French or German, unless you are applying for a translator or interpreter post where the rule is rather your second language (if different from the above three). Be aware, however, that questions may be put to you in any other language specified in your CV. Should you feel that you need to further clarify matters, take care not to patronise the interviewer and that your body language is also entirely respectful.

Medical Check

A medical check is required for all new recruits; it may take place even before you know the result of your job interview. Should you not be chosen, the medical check results are valid for a few months so you will not need to re-take it if you attend another interview and you are accepted for another post. In any case, avoid the temptation of having that delicious-looking ham-and-eggs for breakfast or you risk further check-ups due to an excessive cholesterol level.

Travelling

You will most likely need to travel to Brussels or Luxembourg for the interview unless a video- or phone-conference call can be arranged at the EU representation or delegation office of your country of residence. Should you need to travel, all costs will be reimbursed and you will be given a modest daily subsistence allowance as well (based on strict formal conditions), but be prepared to receive the reimbursement only several weeks later.

Recruitment

If your interview was successful, you will be offered a job first by phone or e-mail, then formally by letter. Should this not arrive in time, make sure you ask your future EU institution's HR department or the unit in which you will work to send it to you. Generally you can agree on the starting date of employment with your future boss, so you can look for accommodation (if in Belgium, try *www.immoweb.be* or the European Commission's Intranet also has a fine small ads section with real estate ads) and arrange paperwork in due course.

Moving costs are paid for unless you have lived in the country where you were recruited to for more than a certain period of time (e.g. if you had done an EU traineeship at the Commission in Brussels right before you got recruited, this may prevent you from having your moving costs paid or being granted a so-called "expatriation allowance", though the rule is generally six months of residence and for traineeships, the duration is five months). The detailed rules can be found in the EU officials' Staff Regulations.

Preparation Methods

Preparing for EPSO tests is far from being an easy exercise and most candidates have had feelings of apprehension. The way of preparing for the tests is really an individual choice. You may find that simply looking at the tests' objectives and preparing on your own makes you feel confident; conversely, you may want to read text books, take web-based training courses, or actually go through instructor-led preparatory classes offered by a training centre.

Whatever method you choose, know that timing and motivation are the linchpins. As you prepare for your test, make sure to start soon enough and take it very seriously all the way. Knowing when to begin your preparation process is critical to having enough time without feeling rushed. EPSO normally publishes the timelines of competitions with plenty of advance notice, and it is strongly advised to start preparation at least two months before the exam day.

The key thing to remember is that tests are not written with the intention of catching you out. In fact they are only meant to probe your skills and competencies in various "reasoning" exercises and assess whether you have a concise understanding of the chosen field while ensuring that you possess the right competencies at the same time.

What to Study

Regarding your EU knowledge, make sure to have a good basic understanding of the "Treaties", meaning the Treaty on European Union and the Treaty on the Functioning of the European Union. This is something that can add greatly to your performance if you get through to the Assessment Centre and save you from using the wrong EU terminology, which, even if not evaluated, may give a bad impression, especially since the assessors are EU officials themselves who are very familiar with the topics.

A good knowledge of how EU institutions and decision-making procedures work and what the key priorities of the European Commission and Parliament are; an idea about some milestones in EU history; and some basic familiarity with the latest European Council Presidency Conclusions, key judgements of the European Courts, basic Eurostat data, and strategic policy papers such as the EU2020 programme – these are all useful for learning the specific character and vocabulary of the EU. Lastly, reading EU news on a daily or weekly basis can help you understand how a seemingly abstract or complex piece of legislation works in real life.

Preparation Resources

For the pre-selection phase, I recommend reading through this book's concise methodology chapters and practising the exercises multiple times. Additional tests are available online from EU Training. For the assessment phase, make sure to use *The Ultimate EU Test Book Assessment Centre 2018.* Various YouTube videos can help you see real life examples and tips for each exercise.

Browsing the Commission Directorates Generals' websites for "hot" issues and checking the relevant Commissioner's website and speeches on your topic will help you understand where to focus your attention for the Assessment Centre (especially for the case study); having a look at the various European Parliament committees' meeting reports can also serve as time-saving and efficient tools.

Linguists can find excellent resources on the Commission DG Translation's website regarding terminology; finding and comparing the terminology of various EU documents in different linguistic versions is also a powerful preparation method.

Having reviewed the above rules and general advice, let's get started with the preparation!

2. Verbal, Numerical and Abstract Reasoning Tests in EPSO Administrator Exams

Introduction

EPSO has, since its inception, used verbal reasoning and numerical reasoning tests in the so-called pre-selection or admission phase of open competitions (while for some Specialist profiles these are required in the assessment phase). Although it is often said that taking such tests does not require specific knowledge and they are therefore "easy" to pass, they have been dreaded by many candidates – and for good reasons. From 2010 onwards, the so-called abstract reasoning test also became part of the pre-selection stage of the competitions.

When it comes to abstract, verbal and numerical reasoning tests (commonly referred to as "psychometric tests"), it is important to answer the following questions:

- What exactly are these tests like?
- What do they measure?
- What is the concept behind their design?
- What is the rationale for their use?
- What are the factors determining success?
- How are these tests scored?
- And finally: how to prepare and practice for them?

An Overview of the Three Test Types

Each test type will be described in detail in the relevant upcoming chapters, but it is important to first get a sense of what these tests are like in general terms.

Format

All three test types, verbal, numerical and abstract reasoning, are in multiple-choice format. Based on EPSO's practice, all three "reasoning" tests have either four or five answer options for each question or text passage. In both cases, there is always only one correct answer and no penalty for wrong answers.

Verbal Reasoning

Verbal reasoning tests are designed to measure a candidate's ability to comprehend complex texts on various topics. These may vary from the description of an EU policy through current news, culture, history, or even natural sciences – in other words, the topic can be almost anything.

The length of the text is typically around 150 words and you are normally asked to decide which of four answer options is correct, based on the information in the text.

The answer options will then measure whether you:

- understood key concepts
- have the necessary vocabulary to comprehend a wide range of topics (believe it or not, this may be an issue in your native language as well)
- are able to deduce arguments from the text
- can accurately interpret key indicators (such as chronology, causality, quantities) in the text

For more information and practice tests, turn to chapters 3 and 4.

Numerical Reasoning

Numerical reasoning tests are designed to measure a candidate's ability to interpret data and numbers, with a special emphasis on the relationship between various data sets and on performing quick calculations based on intuitive insight. This means in practice that the focus is not on complex mathematics but on identifying how one can arrive at the correct answer in the most efficient way.

The data on which the test question is based is usually a table with several rows and columns. The rows usually indicate various groups (countries, age groups, regions, industries, and so on), while the columns often contain various metrics (GDP, average income, amount transported, percentages, and so on). Alternatively, the data can also be presented in the form of a chart or several charts (pie chart, bar chart, etc.), or any combination of the above-mentioned items.

The test question usually seeks either a figure ("200", "0.3", "45%", "1/5", etc.) or one of the groups in the data set ("France", "People aged between 15-64", "Europe", "Agriculture", etc.) as the answer.

By arriving at the answer in a timely manner, you can demonstrate your ability to:

- identify relevant data
- understand the relationship between various metrics
- determine the level of accuracy needed to answer the question
- perform quick mental calculations, and
- make fast but relatively accurate estimates

For more information and practice tests, turn to chapters 5 and 6.

Abstract Reasoning

Abstract reasoning tests always involve geometric shapes. Although there are test types where the shapes are three-dimensional, EPSO has so far decided against using such tests and therefore candidates will only be given questions with two-dimensional objects.

The figures in the questions can be geometrical ones, such as circles, rectangles, triangles, lines, and combinations of these, but they can also be the simplified representations of real-life objects, for example bodies, faces, vehicles, animals, and so on. Another important aspect is to avoid any gender, nationality or other bias regarding candidates' abilities to solve them; EPSO (or, more precisely, the company that has created the tests) also makes sure that those with visual challenges are not being discriminated against either.

The tests are designed so that there is a linear relationship among the items in the set of illustrations included with the question. The figures in the test item form a series going from left to right and the test-taker is expected to select which of the five answer options would come next in the series.

Abstract reasoning tests measure your ability to:

- interpret abstract concepts that do not carry actual real-life meaning
- draw conclusions in new and unfamiliar scenarios
- discover relationships between seemingly unrelated concepts, and
- use your so-called "fluid intelligence" and apply it to any intellectual problem

For more information and practice tests, turn to chapters 7 and 8.

Why these Tests are Used

When someone first looks at verbal or numerical reasoning test questions, and especially in the case of abstract reasoning, a thought that often comes to mind is *"How is this related to my potential performance as an Administrator in the European Commission?"* It is a fair question and one which deserves a good answer.

According to one approach, these tests are generic indicators of intelligence. Their results are standardized and are simply good predictors of performance in any work situation where intelligence, creativity and independent thinking is required. While this is certainly true, it is also easy to identify much more concrete work scenarios where the "skills" measured by these tests can actually be put to good use.

As mentioned above, **verbal reasoning** tests measure a general ability to interpret texts, regardless of the topic. One can easily imagine the wide array of topics, formats and styles an Administrator at the European Commission or the Committee of the Regions will be expected to read about and make sense of in the course of their career. One day you might be reading about some new internal procedures to follow, the next day you might be asked by your superior to skim through a report on the effects of the increasing price of fertilizers on the Latvian farmers' standard of living. Regardless of the topic, one thing is certain: you will need to be able to make sense of the text in a timely manner, draw the right conclusions, avoid common misunderstandings and eventually summarize your findings. Sounds familiar? Hopefully it does as this is exactly what you will be expected to do in the verbal reasoning test as well.

The same goes for the **numerical reasoning** tests. You might also be given a statistical report one day at work. It may contain a mind-numbingly large number of tables and charts, and although you are looking for one single figure or piece of data, it's just not in there. There may be a wealth of other (irrelevant) data, but not the bit you are looking for though you are expected to come up with an answer based on that report and nothing else. What you will need to do is sort through all the data, disregard everything you do not need and find a way to "extract" the useful information. This is exactly what you will do when taking the numerical reasoning tests.

When it comes to **abstract reasoning**, the above analogy will of course not work. Not even in an institution with as widespread responsibilities as the EU will you face a situation where you need to select a shape with four circles and one rectangle (as opposed to two rectangles) in order to get through the day! You do, however, stand a good chance of going to your office one Monday morning and facing a situation or being given a task that will be completely unfamiliar; it might be about something you have never even heard about. Situations like this are the ones where the above-mentioned "fluid intelligence", the ability to manage the "unfamiliar" and apply logic, patterns and common sense becomes useful and that is exactly what abstract reasoning tests measure, as proven by various psychological experiments.

The Factors Determining Success

Just as is the case with any other test, success and good performance in EPSO's pre-selection exam is determined by several factors. We will now briefly discuss the four most important ones:

- Motivation
- Habits and hobbies
- Educational background
- Preparation and practice (most important)

Motivation

EPSO's pre-selection exam is certainly an event that one must prepare for and set aside significant amounts of time for this purpose: expect to experience a lot of stress both in the process of preparing and in the exam itself. In short, it takes time and effort, and it is easy to be distracted or discouraged on the way. This is exactly why having a clear and strong motivation is so important.

One essential component of self-motivation is knowing why you are expected to carry out a given task and how you can benefit from the effort that must be dedicated to it. Even if performing well at these tests is just a means to an end, it is still much easier to put in the required effort if you have a clear sense of why you are expected to do them and understand their objective benefits, such as getting an EU job or performing much better in job tasks requiring psychometric skills.

The above section on how these test types can be related to actual work situations may be thought of as one component of the motivation needed to succeed – knowing why you are expected to do these tests at the exam rather than something else.

Motivation is also about setting clear and attainable goals. There is an acronym that nicely sums up this challenge: being SMART.

A SMART strategy is one that includes goals that are:

Specific –   "I will practice X hours a day for X days a week in order to get the job I have always wanted. Each week I will do X number of tests and revise X previous tests. I will also start reading about EU affairs to familiarise myself with the institutions."

Measureable –   "I will improve this or that much every week, and will be able to get X per cent at these tests by the time of the exam. I will do a benchmark test against which I can measure my progress."

Achievable –   "I have never been particularly good with numbers so I will not try to score 100% at numerical reasoning, but I will make sure to score as much as possible above the 50% threshold and to make it up in the other test types."

Relevant –   "I will do all of the above because my goal is to work in the Directorate General for Development of the European Commission. I would also like to get this job so I will have the financial means to pursue my long-time dream of visiting a friend in Australia. Even if I find these tests challenging or tedious at times, I understand that they are required for the exam and in any case I can improve my skills too."

Time-bound –   "I will set aside this amount of time for the next X months to achieve this or that goal. I will have a clear timetable for the next two months where I indicate the days and hours I plan to spend on practicing. I will be able to stick to my schedule because I see the end of the tunnel."

Educational Background

Educational background is another important factor in success. In addition to the obvious fact that the quality of education one received can make a huge difference, there are various fields of study that provide a more relevant background for performing well at these tests than others. Mathematics or other disciplines that make use of logic and deduction may help in solving the test questions better under time pressure.

Obviously, your educational background is not something you can change at the time you decide to participate in an EPSO Administrator competition. If you have a more relevant background, so much the better – though if you do not, there is certainly no reason for despair either: there are numerous important factors in success, all of which you can improve significantly (see relevant tips below and in each consequent chapter).

Habits and Hobbies

Before turning to the "controllable" factors mentioned above, we must also mention that there are certain hobbies and activities that, if you are a fan of them, may provide some temporary advantage. When it comes to verbal, numerical and abstract reasoning, people who have done crossword puzzles, Sudoku and other mind games might be at some advantage.

Preparation and Practice

The factor, however, that is the single most important one is what this book is all about: *the quality and quantity of preparation and practice you complete in the run-up to the exam.*

In the following chapters, we will introduce in detail:

• the three test types and how they are designed

• the typical problems and challenges they pose

• the methods and skills that can greatly improve your performance

• the best ways to approach and interpret the test questions, and

• the optimal way to prepare and practice for these tests

With a clear grasp of the methods that can be used to efficiently take these tests and with the right amount of focused practice, powered by the correct motivation, even those candidates who feel that such tests are not their strong suit can improve significantly and pass this stage of the exam.

How these Tests are Scored

When you are preparing for the exam, you might often wonder exactly how well you are expected to perform in order to succeed. To answer this question, let us overview the marking system for these tests. The score candidates receive will have to satisfy two conditions:

Pass Mark – this is a simple "objective" barrier, usually 50% (but in some profiles, this is lowered to 40% for certain test types) that must be reached in each test separately, to be considered for the shortlist. It often happens, however, that for Administrator exams EPSO will set a pass mark for two or more tests combined (e.g. they will consider your numerical and abstract reasoning test scores as one and establish a 50% pass mark for the aggregate score of these two tests) – this is a somewhat easier situation because you can compensate for poorer performance in one test by excelling in the other one(s).

The Best X – this is a "relative" barrier, meaning that in addition to scoring higher than the objective pass mark, you must also be among a given number of best-performing candidates in all the tests combined. Some of the test results may be excluded from this relative barrier, meaning that numerical reasoning, for example, sometimes doesn't count toward your total score: all you need to do is achieve the pass mark.

Mixed Version –   EPSO may also use the "pass mark" approach to create a larger pool of potential candidates and then "sift in" a certain number whose qualifications or professional experience (in the case of "specialist" Administrator exams) match various objective, pre-determined criteria, though the "best X" may also be factored in the decision.

In Practice

- Although you can hope to compensate for your weakness in one test type by performing better in another and thus still reaching a relatively high overall score, this option is limited by the requirement to reach the pass mark in each test separately (except for the cases outlined above when two test types have a combined pass mark)

- A "good" score in the context of one group of candidates (e.g. those who sit exams for the human resources sub-profile) might be an insufficient score in another group (e.g. those who have chosen the financial management sub-profile) – so examples of "successful scores" from the past are not really relevant

The figure below shows what is known as a "bell curve". Although it is just an illustration and it is not based on statistics, it quite accurately shows the typical distribution of scores candidates get at such tests. As we can see, there are few candidates with very low scores and very high scores. Most of the candidates will get scores in a very narrow range, for example between 60% and 70%, or 70% and 80%.

If "successful" candidates are selected by the best X number of participants in the exam, you must certainly score higher than others. *Looking at the bell curve, it is easy to see that only a few percentage points of improvement can mean that you have beaten a large number of additional candidates!*

Why is this important? The way we must approach this information is that the goals you set when you start preparing and practicing for these tests do not have to be unrealistic or unattainable. Also, you can take comfort in the fact that every small improvement will make a huge difference at the exam and will improve your chances exponentially – all thanks to the bell curve.

In the following chapters, we will see what the best methods and skills to achieve success are, accompanied by a large number of quality practice tests.

After all, the best way of learning things is by doing them a lot.

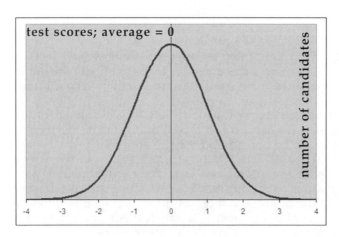

3.   Succeeding in Verbal Reasoning Tests

In the world of standardized testing, the term "verbal reasoning" is commonly used to designate various test types relating to the interpretation and comprehension of texts. Although EPSO uses currently only one of these verbal reasoning test types, some of the models below measure skills that underlie the verbal reasoning tests EPSO uses to test candidates. It is therefore worth taking a quick look at each of them:

- **Spelling tests** are designed to test a person's ability to spell words correctly and also to differentiate between words with similar spellings yet completely or partially different meanings (for example, "steal" and "steel" or the correct spelling of "miscellaneous")
- **Word meaning tests** measure a person's vocabulary and their ability to select the best definition for words that have complex meanings (for example, to correctly identify the meaning of "exasperation" or "innuendo")
- **Word relationship tests** are designed to test a person's ability to determine the relationship between two concepts based on the analogy of another pair of concepts (for example, "what law is to anarchy, medicine is to ...")
- **Comprehension tests** measure a person's ability to comprehend complex texts and determine whether statements about a text are correct, incorrect, or impossible to tell (this is the "classical" type used by EPSO)
- **Verbal deduction tests** are the most advanced form of verbal reasoning exercises – they measure the reader's ability to make correct and logical conclusions based on the information provided (for example, a text describing the mating habits of penguins followed by various questions such as "What are the right conditions for penguins to start mating?", "How do male penguins draw attention to themselves?" etc; this is a somewhat different approach from the "Which of the following statements is false?" question)

EPSO's verbal reasoning tests are closest in design to the comprehension test type. It is, however, easy to see how good performance in a comprehension test is based on the candidate's ability to identify correct spelling, the meaning of complex expressions and the relationship between various concepts. In this respect, this type of test is at the top in a hierarchy where success in comprehension depends on skills stemming from good performance on each of the lower levels.

In the following, we will overview several issues to look out for in a text, as well as a number of methods and skills that, once mastered, can greatly improve your performance. These include:

- How verbal reasoning tests are designed
- The role of familiar and unfamiliar topics
- Sources of information
- Assumptions
- Correct versus incorrect statements
- Near-equivalent versus identical statements
- Omission of information
- General versus particular
- Determiners and quantities

- Frequency
- Verbs: time and mode
- Causality versus chronology

We must mention here that a few of the methods and tips discussed in this chapter are discussed in the context of English-language test questions – this does not mean, however, that they cannot be applied in taking tests in other languages as well. In addition, the overwhelming majority of test-taking strategies discussed here are language-independent and are extremely useful in taking these tests in any language.

We will also discuss the best way to deal with each test question, the suggested order of reading the various components of the test (the text, the question and the answer options) and the recommended methods to practice for the test.

The sample test below is representative of the type of test questions EPSO currently uses as well as the expected level of difficulty at an EPSO competition. It consists of:

- A passage of text of between 100 and 200 words
- A standard question asking which of the supplied statements is correct or true
- Four statements as answer options, one being the right answer, i.e. the only correct statement

A Sample Test

Bacteria growing in near darkness use a previously unknown process for harvesting energy and producing oxygen from sunlight, a research team discovered. The discovery lays the foundation for further research aimed at improving plant growth and harvesting energy from the Sun.

"We have shown that some cyanobacteria, also called blue-green algae, can grow in far-red wavelengths of light, a range not seen well by most humans," said a researcher. "Most cyanobacteria can't 'see' this light either. But we have found a new subgroup that can absorb and use it, and we have discovered some of the surprising ways they manipulate their genes in order to grow using only these wavelengths," he said.

The experiments revealed that these cyanobacteria replace seventeen proteins in three major light-using complexes while also making new chlorophyll pigments that can capture the far-red light. The scientists also discovered that the organisms accomplish this feat by quickly turning on a large number of genes to modify cellular metabolism and simultaneously turning off a large number of other genes.
(*Science Daily*, 26 August 2014)

Which of the following statements is correct?

A. The mechanism by which some cyanobacteria capture far-red light may in the future be used to harness solar power.
B. Blue-green algae utilise far-red light by substituting three light-using proteins for chlorophyll pigments.
C. Some cyanobacteria cannot activate the genes necessary to absorb far-red light because they lack the necessary proteins.
D. The light-absorbing process described requires replacing 17 proteins but does not necessitate major genetic changes.

We will now consider the factors and methods listed above one by one. Before we do that, however, it is essential to gain some insight into how verbal reasoning tests are designed by their authors – if you understand the concepts and strategies behind the creation of verbal reasoning tests, taking those tests will become incomparably easier.

How are verbal reasoning tests designed?

When psychologists whose specialty is the creation of psychometric tests design verbal reasoning items, they essentially follow two design steps:

1. Selecting an appropriate piece of text.
2. Authoring appropriate answer options.

Let us see what considerations go into each of these two steps.

1. Selecting an appropriate piece of text

When selecting excerpts for a verbal reasoning text, several factors are considered, such as:

- Does the text include a good variety of verbs, nouns, adjectives, and so on?
- Is the difficulty of vocabulary appropriate for the purposes of the test (e.g. for assessing Assistant or Administrator candidates for an EU job?)
- Is the text free of jargon?
- Are abbreviations explained at least once in the text?
- Is the text free of topics that might be objectionable from a political, moral or ethical point of view?

The difficulty of the text and its vocabulary is a complex issue: suffice it to say that such things are considered as the length of the sentences (in number of words) or the length and complexity of the words themselves.

2. Authoring appropriate answer options

The creation of the answer options is the most difficult and most important task in the design of verbal reasoning tests. Let us overview what kind of answer options exist – being aware of the types of answer options that you might face will be highly useful in the EPSO pre-selection as well.

"Correct" or "True" statements: Such statements are clearly and demonstrably correct based on the information in the text. No outside knowledge is required to prove their correctness; it is possible to determine that on the basis of the excerpt and by drawing well-founded conclusions. Obviously, each verbal reasoning test item features only one such statement, and that statement will be the right answer. It is worth noting that the difficulty of the test item can be greatly influenced by how this statement is formulated:

- Does the right answer use similar expressions to those found in the text? The more similar the wording, the easier it is to spot that it is the correct statement.
- Is the right answer simply a reworded version of a statement in the passage, or is it a conclusion that can be drawn by utilizing several pieces of information from various parts of the excerpt?

"Incorrect" or "False" statements: Such statements are clearly and demonstrably incorrect based on the information in the text passage. It is important to point out that these statements are not simply unfounded (that is, no evidence exists as to whether they are correct or incorrect) but can be clearly disproved by utilizing information in the text. The difficulty of spotting such statements is, again, dependent on several factors:

- Is part of the statement correct? If so, it may be more difficult to realize that it is an incorrect statement, because only part of the information contained in it makes it so.
- Is the topic of the text expected to be familiar to test-takers? If so, it is much easier to decide a statement is incorrect, because most candidates will know it to be false and it will immediately "stand out".

You may now think that the above two statement types are all there is to verbal reasoning tests, but we will see very soon that there is one more statement type which makes the whole thing much more complicated. Nevertheless, we can already see that the degree of difficulty of test items that utilize only these two statement types can also vary greatly based on the factors listed above.

"Insufficient information" or "Cannot say" statements: This is the type of statement which usually causes the greatest confusion and represents the most dangerous trap when taking a verbal reasoning test. "Insufficient information" statements can belong to one of two categories:

- Statements that are *incorrect* if assessed using outside knowledge: such statements are easier to handle, because they will "feel" incorrect – you might know the statement to be incorrect based on your knowledge of facts, but it is impossible to classify the statement as incorrect based solely on information in the test passage. Fortunately, you are not expected to do that – just remember that **any statement which cannot be clearly proven by information in the excerpt is "incorrect"** in the context of a verbal reasoning test
- Statements that are *correct* if assessed using outside knowledge: such statements are the hardest to spot because they will "feel" correct upon first reading. The reason they are dangerous is exactly because you instinctively want to agree with the statement you know to be true. The important thing to remember here is that the **only correct statement in a verbal reasoning test is one that is fully supported and proven by information in the text passage**.

We can now easily realize that verbal reasoning tests can be designed using any mixture of the above statement types.

Here are a few:

- 1 true statement, 3 false statements: this is probably the easiest type, as true and false statements are easier to spot
- 1 true statement, 2 false statements, 1 "insufficient information" or "cannot say" statement: this test would be a bit harder, because in addition to the correct answer, one additional answer option might at first "feel" correct – remember the tips above and you will be able to easily avoid this trap
- 1 true statement, 3 "insufficient information" statements: this is the "crown jewel" of verbal reasoning tests – the most difficult type. This is because due to the nature of the statement types used, you might feel that *all four statements* are correct upon first reading, but, again, you can discard those with insufficient information by remembering the principles described above

Based on experience and consulting with occupational psychologists, the great majority of verbal reasoning test questions that you will encounter at an EPSO Administrator competition will feature at least one "insufficient information" statement and it is quite likely that you will face at least a few questions where three of the four answer options will be of this type. You should, however, be aware of the existence of the other combinations listed above as well – better safe than sorry, as the saying goes.

Let us now consider a concrete example and return to the sample test item above. Let us analyze the answer options based on the criteria we established.

A. The mechanism by which some cyanobacteria capture far-red light may in the future be used to harness solar power.

This is a true statement:

- the passage describes the way certain bacteria can absorb and use far-red light
- the passage states that this discovery lays the foundation for further research
- one of the future research areas mentioned is harvesting the energy of the sun
- we can draw the well-supported conclusion that the mechanism may in the future be used to harness the power of the sun

B. Blue-green algae utilise far-red light by substituting three light-using proteins for chlorophyll pigments.

This statement is false. Although all of the components of the statement have a basis in the text passage, things are completely mixed up. The number of proteins is 17, three is the number of light-using complexes. Also, chlorophyll pigments are not substituted, rather, new ones are grown. The only correct part of the statement is the one that states that it is blue-green algae that can utilise far-red light.

C. Some cyanobacteria cannot activate the genes necessary to absorb far-red light because they lack the necessary proteins.

This is a typical insufficient information type statement which is made even more difficult by the fact that the claim it makes feels logical and true.

- it is true that some cyanobacteria cannot use far-red light
- it seems logical that this may be caused by the necessary genes not being activated
- it also seems logical that this might be because the necessary proteins are missing

What we have to realise here is that we used several unfounded assumptions to arrive at this conclusion. In reality, we have no idea what causes some cyanobacteria not to be able to absorb far-red light, and we are not given enough information to make claims about what proteins are necessary to activate which genes.

D. The light-absorbing process described requires replacing 17 proteins but does not necessitate major genetic changes.

This statement is false. While it starts out making a correct claim (the process does require replacing 17 proteins), the last paragraph of the passage is in clear contradiction to the second part of the statement: it describes major genetic changes taking place in these bacteria and a large number of genes are activated and turned off to achieve this ability.

Now that we have analyzed the above four statements, we can see that our sample test item contains one true statement (the right answer), one "insufficient information" or "cannot say" statement, and two false statements. From a design perspective, the above test item is of medium difficulty, and the EPSO verbal reasoning test for Administrators will include items of comparable or greater difficulty.

Let us now turn our attention to the factors listed a few pages earlier – familiarity with such techniques as verb time and mode or generalizations will help you quickly determine which category each statement in a test belongs to, allowing you to find the correct answer in record time.

The Role of Familiar and Unfamiliar Topics

The topics of the texts in the verbal reasoning test can be varied. They may be closely EU-related (descriptions of policies, EU news) or they may be completely unrelated, dealing with history, art, nature, science and technology, music, and so on. Based on their interests or hobbies, most candidates have one or several preferred topics; however, the topic of the text should be completely irrelevant from the point of view of performing well in the test. While it is troubling to be faced with a topic that is completely alien to you, a familiar topic has its own dangers, because you must only use the information in the text, not your own knowledge.

Let us consider the pros and cons of familiar and unfamiliar topics.

As we can see, there is no significant argument either for or against wishing for familiar topics. Each has its distinct pitfalls and advantages.

As an example, if a candidate is very interested in space exploration and reads a text on a topic they know a lot about, for instance the New Horizons spacecraft currently heading to Pluto, it may seem a comfortable situation but may also backfire. Having a deep knowledge of a topic may make it hard to separate the information in the text from the information we already have about the subject – and, as we will see, it is one of the main mistakes test takers commit. In the above example, the candidate may, for instance, be aware that New Horizons is moving faster than any other space probe launched previously. This could lead the candidate to choose a statement about the spacecraft's speed as being correct when it is actually a "cannot say" statement because the speed is not mentioned in the text or any reference is ambiguous.

On the other hand, many candidates panic when faced with a text about a subject they have never been interested in. There may even be words and expressions that they have never even heard of. Yet it often happens that it is exactly the distance from the topic and "objectivity" that allows us to consider only the information in the text and select the right answer quickly and systematically.

Familiar Topic (space exploration)		Unfamiliar Topic (e.g. molecular biology)	
Pros	*Cons*	*Pros*	*Cons*
Mainstream vocabulary	*Bias*	*No bias*	*May be colloquial*
Familiarity	*Technical vocabulary*	*May be everyday topic*	*May include exotic vocabulary*
No colloquialisms	*Assumptions*	*No assumptions*	*Not familiar*

Sources of Information

When we discussed the familiarity of the subject, we touched upon the fact that it is crucial to always keep in mind what information we use when assessing whether statements in the answer options are correct.

Let us consider the following sentence from an imaginary verbal reasoning text passage: *"nearly one in five European adult males still smoke cigarettes on a daily basis"*.

Now let's look at a theoretical answer option where pre-existing knowledge could cause a problem: *"Almost 40 million European adult males still regularly smoke cigarettes."*

If the candidate happens to know that there are approximately 200 million adult males in Europe and uses that knowledge when taking the test, they might end up selecting the above answer option as correct – and lose a point, because the statement cannot be correct if the text does not contain information about the adult male population of Europe.

It is thus crucial to remember that statements in the answer options must be assessed based solely on the information in the text.

It can be particularly dangerous when a statement includes information of the sort that it may seem "everybody" knows, not just that is familiar to you because of your own specialist knowledge. Examples of this would be: "The German economy is bigger than that of Greece"; "the Olympic Games are held every four years"; "more of the Earth's surface is ocean than land". Be very alert to this risk. The test questions in the next chapter have many such examples.

Assumptions

In the previous example, we saw a situation where an assumption (regardless of whether true or false) was made about a statement based on "outside" knowledge. Let us consider another example.

"Performing specific physical exercises daily decreases the chances of developing certain movement-related difficulties in old age."

A possible answer option: *"Cycling for 30 minutes every day decreases the chances of developing rheumatism later."*

One might be tempted to select the above answer option as correct. If we do so, we make two assumptions:

1. Cycling is one of those specific physical exercises that are useful for such purposes.

2. Rheumatism is one of those movement-related difficulties that can be prevented in such a way.

Whether the above answer option is indeed the correct one depends entirely on what other information regarding the specific physical exercises and the types of movement-related difficulties is included in the text. For example, if there is no mention of cycling in the text, considering it as one of those exercises will be a false assumption which will cause us to lose a valuable point in the test. Also, it is merely our interpretation (assumption) that rheumatism is a movement-related difficulty that can be prevented this way – unless the text itself gives that information.

Correct versus Incorrect Statements

Although the verbal reasoning test in EPSO competitions almost exclusively includes items where the question is of the *"Which of the following statements is correct?"* type, it is important to mention another possibility – when the question is *"Which of the following statements is incorrect?"*.

The same principles that we discussed apply in this situation as well, but we will need to look for the false statement – that will be the right answer. It is also important to point out that if the question is seeking the incorrect statement, we can still encounter "insufficient information" statements – in this case, however, such statements will often be designed to "feel" incorrect – thereby leading you to think that they indeed are. Just remember: if you are expected to pick the incorrect answer option, look for a statement that can be clearly and unambiguously disproved based on the information in the text passage.

As a final point, it is worth mentioning something that may seem obvious, but must be noted. It is crucial to always carefully read the question (the one immediately after the text) and keep in mind whether you are supposed to look for the correct or incorrect statement. As simple as this may sound, many candidates have lost points in verbal reasoning tests by not taking the extra two seconds to read the question, especially under the stress and time pressure of the exam.

Near Equivalent versus Identical Statements

Consider the following example.

"Not many inventions last for more than a hundred years without major modifications. One of them is the barometer."

A possible answer option: *"Since it was invented, the barometer has not been modified."*

The statement in the answer option is very similar to the information in the excerpt. It uses many of the same words, and it essentially conveys a fairly similar meaning. Yet in the context of a verbal reasoning test, we cannot infer that "without major modifications" is equivalent to "has not been modified". The former implies *little* has been changed, the latter that *nothing* has been changed in the design of the barometer.

It is always dangerous to look for similar words and expressions in the answer option. Similarity can hide small but important differences in meaning and can prevent you from reading on and seriously considering other answer options among which the correct one can be found.

Another piece of advice is to always look for prefixes or adjectives that change the meaning or the scope of a statement, such as "some", "hardly", "almost", "not always", "any", "completely", "at all", "partially", "to some extent", "mostly", "generally", "exclusively", "sometimes", "largely", "arguably", "seemingly" and others (see more examples below).

Although since 2011 this problem has eased as you are now able to take the verbal reasoning test in your native (official EU) language, it is still worth taking some time to think about words and expressions in your own language that slightly modify the meaning of the sentence in which they are included. This is especially true because we use our native language much less consciously than a second language and slight shifts in meaning are often overlooked in everyday speech.

Omission of Information

Here is an excerpt from another text:

"Shakepeare's plays are still well-liked by audiences. In 2010, almost 100 countries had theatres where a Shakespeare play was in the programme and tickets to these productions were sold to nearly 15 million people."

A possible answer option: *"There are still theatres that stage Shakespeare productions."*

Note that this answer option has a completely different approach than the excerpt from the text. Having read the text, readers might be inclined to look for answer options that emphasize how well-liked Shakespeare's plays still are. Our example answer option does not do that, it simply states that Shakespeare productions are still being staged in an unspecified number of theatres.

At first reading, the statement in the answer option seems to be in conflict with the excerpt by not conveying the popularity of these plays. Yet it is a perfectly valid and correct statement.

We must, then, remember that the fact that a statement fails to convey all the information that was included in the text about something does not mean that it is an incorrect statement. In short and all other factors being equal, omission of information is not necessarily disagreement or contradiction.

General versus Particular

Another typical mistake many candidates make has to do with the difference between general categories and particular instances. This mistake can take one of two forms:

- Generalisation
- Over-specification

Let us consider an example.

"The oceanic climate is one of the wettest ones in the world. Average precipitation is significantly higher than in continental habitats. Some areas of the Atlantic Ocean do not go a full week without rain for decades."

A possible answer option: *"Oceanic areas do not have completely dry weeks for decades."*

The above statement is an example of a generalisation where a statement made about certain instances of a category (in this case, Atlantic areas) is assumed to be correct about the entire category (that is, all oceanic climate areas).

Let us consider another example.

"Some oceanic areas have wetter winters and springs while others experience more rainfall in the summer and autumn."

A possible answer option: *"The amount of rainfall in oceanic areas differs by season, depending on the geographical location."*

The above answer option is correct in stating that the amount of rainfall differs by season, but it is overly specific in stating that this depends on the geographical location – this is unfounded information not included in the text.

Determiners and Quantities

We now come to more language-specific problems. While most of the points raised so far are valid in all languages the test is administered in, there are always language-specific issues to consider. If the test is administered in English these tips will be directly useful to your preparation.

If you take your test in another language, the following few sections can serve as a guideline along which you can consider the peculiarities of your own language and come up with a list of things to look out for. A good way of doing this is to read newspaper articles with higher than usual attention – professional journalists are always careful about how they formulate their statements and use many of the linguistic devices demonstrated here to make their statements more accurate.

Determiners and words expressing certain or uncertain quantities can be hard to notice; many candidates tend not to attribute much meaning to them in everyday situations even though they may greatly alter the meaning of a statement in the context of a verbal reasoning test.

Be mindful of the exact meaning of some of the most common determiners:

- "the" usually signifies one concrete object or person, or one concrete group: "the apple","the fruit", "the pencils [on the table]", and so on.
- "a/an" and nouns without any determiner usually refer to one unspecified object or person, or an unspecified group of objects or persons: "an apple", "a fruit", "people in the United Kingdom", and so on.

When the answer option lacks the determiner found in the text or features a different one, we must always be suspicious and consider whether this distinction changes the meaning of the statement.

A similar pattern can be observed when it comes to quantities: "some", "many", "several", "a number of" refer to an unspecified number of objects of persons. "All", "the entire", "every", and "each" signifies that the statement is about every single member of a group, or an object in its entirety, without exception.

It is important to bear in mind that these determiners of quantity are not interchangeable and if the text mentions "many countries", an answer option that extends that claim to "all countries" will not be correct.

Frequency

A very similar situation can be created by the use of adverbs signifying the frequency at which an action takes place. Always pay special attention to the use of the adverbs "sometimes", "often", "usually", "frequently", "never", "hardly ever", "occasionally", "always" and so on.

Although the only two concrete indicators are "never" and "always", and it is very hard to define the difference between "sometimes" and "occasionally", we must be mindful of the fact that they do carry meaning and can significantly change the meaning of a statement.

The same also can be said about adjectives and adverbs expressing chronology:

- "before", "previously", "earlier", "prior to that" are hints that one event took place sooner than another one
- "meanwhile", "concurrently", "simultaneously", and others indicate that two events occured at the same time

- "after", "subsequently", "followed by", "later", and similar words help us establish that one event followed another event in time

Think of the following statements: "I occasionally go to work after eating breakfast" and "I sometimes eat breakfast after going to work". The implied sequence of actions and their frequencies are very different. Another example is "Birds have colourful feathers" versus "Some birds have colourful feathers": the scope and extent are very different.

Verbs: Time and Mode

Closely related to the previous point, the tense of verbs also plays a crucial role in re-creating a series of events. Take an example:

"Until his brother successfully launching his internet startup, Gerorge was the richest member of the family thanks to his burgeoning career as a successful attorney."

A possible answer option: *"George is the richest member of the family."*

The above option is incorrect because according to the text, he had been the richest member of the family only until his brother successfully launched his internet startup. This fact is indicated by the use of the expression "until" and also the past tense.

Verb mode also plays an important part in determining whether a statement is correct:

- Probability – "would happen" does not necessarily mean that something "will happen"; "would have happened" commonly means that the event did not in fact happen at all
- "Could happen" indicates that a certain event is only one of several possible outcomes
- "Should do something" indicates that a certain course of action is recommended or likely, but not necessarily unavoidable or mandatory
- "About to happen" shows that an event was going to take place but may or may not have actually happened
- "Was about to" (e.g. "he was about to go home when") refers to an intention or plan that was likely to take place when a certain event interrupted it or took place

Causality versus Chronology

As a last point, we must mention two phenomena that are frequently confused. Let us look at an example.

"The San Francisco Zoo has been visited by record numbers of visitors ever since 2005. In 2012, it received a gold medal from the World Zoological Society."

A possible answer option: *"Record numbers of visitors go to see the San Francisco Zoo every year, which resulted in it receiving the Gold Medal from the World Zoological Society."*

The statement in the above answer option incorrectly makes the assumption that there is a cause-and-effect relationship between the record number of visitors to the zoo in recent years and the receipt of the gold medal. As far as the statement goes, the relationship between the two things is merely chronological. There is no evidence that the gold medal was awarded because of the high number of visitors: it could just as well wave been given as a commendation for good animal keeping conditions or other factors, we simply do not know.

It is easy to mistake a merely chronological relationship for a cause-and-effect one, but one thing that will help decide is the verbal clues mentioned above. Since test-makers tend not to include ambiguous information in tests, we can always count on indicators of a cause-and-effect relationship ("led to", "consequently", "resulted in") or a mere chronological relationship to appear in the text.

Methods for Approaching the Test Questions

Let us return to our sample text:

> Bacteria growing in near darkness use a previously unknown process for harvesting energy and producing oxygen from sunlight, a research team discovered. The discovery lays the foundation for further research aimed at improving plant growth and harvesting energy from the Sun.
>
> "We have shown that some cyanobacteria, also called blue-green algae, can grow in far-red wavelengths of light, a range not seen well by most humans," said a researcher. "Most cyanobacteria can't 'see' this light either. But we have found a new subgroup that can absorb and use it, and we have discovered some of the surprising ways they manipulate their genes in order to grow using only these wavelengths," he said.
>
> The experiments revealed that these cyanobacteria replace seventeen proteins in three major light-using complexes while also making new chlorophyll pigments that can capture the far-red light. The scientists also discovered that the organisms accomplish this feat by quickly turning on a large number of genes to modify cellular metabolism and simultaneously turning off a large number of other genes.
> (*Science Daily*, 26 August 2014)
>
> *Which of the following statements is correct?*
>
> A. The mechanism by which some cyanobacteria capture far-red light may in the future be used to harness solar power.
> B. Blue-green algae utilise far-red light by substituting three light-using proteins for chlorophyll pigments.
> C. Some cyanobacteria cannot activate the genes necessary to absorb far-red light because they lack the necessary proteins.
> D. The light-absorbing process described requires replacing 17 proteins but does not necessitate major genetic changes.

When somebody first looks at a verbal reasoning test like the one above, the natural instinct is to start reading the text, then read the question, and finally read the four answer options. If we wish to consider all the factors we discussed in this chapter and make mental "notes" of them by underlining the key expressions in the text using the above method, it would look like this:

> Bacteria growing in <u>near</u> darkness use a <u>previously</u> unknown process for harvesting energy and producing oxygen from sunlight, a research team discovered. The discovery lays the foundation for <u>further</u> research aimed at improving plant growth and harvesting energy from the Sun.
>
> "We have shown that <u>some</u> cyanobacteria, also called blue-green algae, <u>can</u> grow in far-red wavelengths of light, a range not seen <u>well</u> by most humans," said a researcher. "Most cyanobacteria can't 'see' this light either. But we have found a <u>new</u> subgroup that <u>can</u> absorb and use it, and we have discovered <u>some</u> of the surprising ways they manipulate their genes in order to grow using <u>only</u> these wavelengths," he said.
>
> The experiments revealed that these cyanobacteria replace <u>seventeen</u> proteins in <u>three major</u> light-using complexes <u>while</u> also making new chlorophyll pigments that can capture the far-red light. The scientists also discovered that the organisms accomplish this feat by <u>quickly</u> turning on a <u>large number</u> of genes to modify cellular metabolism and simultaneously turning off a <u>large number</u> of other genes.

Which of the following statements is correct?

A. The mechanism by which some cyanobacteria capture far-red light <u>may in the future</u> be used to harness solar power.
B. Blue-green algae utilise far-red light by substituting <u>three</u> light-using proteins for chlorophyll pigments.
C. <u>Some</u> cyanobacteria cannot activate the genes necessary to absorb far-red light <u>because</u> they lack the necessary proteins.
D. The light-absorbing process described requires replacing 17 proteins but does <u>not</u> necessitate <u>major</u> genetic changes.

The underlined expressions are "suspect phrases" because of the various factors we discussed.

But what if most of the factors that we concentrated on when reading the text for the first time later turn out to be completely irrelevant because the answer options do not relate to those bits of the text? In order to avoid wasting time on irrelevant information, it is a good idea to read the question and the answer options first, looking for keywords and key concepts, and then read the text, already focusing on and searching for those bits that we know we need to answer the question.

Our mental notes using this recommended method would therefore look like this:

Bacteria growing in near darkness use a previously unknown process for harvesting energy and producing oxygen from sunlight, a research team discovered. The discovery lays the foundation for further research aimed at improving plant growth and harvesting energy from the Sun.

"We have shown that some cyanobacteria, also called blue-green algae, can grow in far-red wavelengths of light, a range not seen well by most humans," said a researcher. "Most cyanobacteria can't 'see' this light either. But we have found a new subgroup that can absorb and use it, and we have discovered some of the surprising ways they manipulate their genes in order to grow using only these wavelengths," he said.

The experiments revealed that these cyanobacteria replace seventeen proteins in three major light-using complexes while also making new chlorophyll pigments that can capture the far-red light. The scientists also discovered that the organisms accomplish this feat by quickly turning on a large number of genes to modify cellular metabolism and simultaneously turning off a large number of other genes.

Using this method, we can immediately discard option B when we read that chlorophyll pigments are not substituted, but capture far-red light. Option D can be discarded when we read that significant genetic changes take place to allow for the absorption of far-red light. Option C is a bit trickier, but when we realise that the text passage does not actually explain why certain cyanobacteria can not absorb far-red light, the entire explanation given in the statement becomes an unfounded assumption and we can discard that quickly as well.

Let us summarize the above method in a few points:

1. Read the question first – are we looking for the correct or incorrect statement?
2. Read the answer options and make a mental note of the important keywords and themes included in those statements.
3. Read the text by focusing on the themes and keywords you made a mental note of when reading the answer options.
4. If you encounter a statement in the text that is clearly in agreement with an answer option (or in clear disagreement, if you are looking for the incorrect statement), and you are sure about your assessment, you can even stop reading and move on, thereby saving precious time.
5. If you are not sure about your assessment, you can continue reading and then eliminate the answer options one by one. This is where your knowledge of the possible statement types (true, false, insufficient information) will prove extremely useful – if you apply this knowledge right, and factor in the methods we discussed in this chapter, no amount of "witchcraft" on the part of the test item's author will confuse you.

Practice Methods

As a last point, it might be useful to make a few suggestions as to what the best methods are for preparing for the verbal reasoning test.

• Start practicing by taking your time, reading all kinds of high level English texts, making mental notes of the "suspect phrases" we covered in this chapter
• Continue by doing the same, this time with the actual test questions in this book (for

the sake of practicing, you may wish to underline or outline these concepts and also write down in your own words why a certain answer option is wrong)
- Once you have established the necessary routine in identifying the key phrases and concepts, you can start timing yourself – begin by simply measuring how much time it takes for you to answer one test question
- Check how much time you will have at the exam, and how many questions you will need to answer (**as a general rule, you will have 35 minutes for 20 questions**).
- Start decreasing the amount of time you let yourself use for answering one question – ideally, by the time of the exam, you should be able to answer more questions in the given time than required in the exam (this is necessary because you cannot re-create the stress of the exam, which can decrease performance, not to mention the slower pace when reading texts on a computer screen for the pre-selection exams)
- Try to re-create as much of the atmosphere and infrastructure of the exam as you can – do not interrupt the test, go to a quiet place, use an alarm clock, and so on
- If you have access to such a service, practice tests online, e.g. the *www.eutraining.eu* site – since the EPSO exam will also be computer-based, and it is a good idea to get used to the "interface" before going to the exam. Most such websites also offer the opportunity to revise the practice tests you took and look at detailed statistics, comparing your performance to others and measuring your improvement in a test type over time – experience shows that such statistics can have an extremely positive psychological effect as well as help to reveal the weaknesses and strengths of your skills in various tests.
- Try to read as much as possible on screen and measure the time it takes to read texts of comparable length (e.g. one page copied into Word) so you can measure and improve your performance.

For advice and tips on tackling verbal reasoning questions – see the previous chapter.

For the answers to this test – see at end of questions.

4. Verbal Reasoning Test

180 QUESTIONS – ANSWERS follow questions

In each question below, you have to decide which of four statements, A, B, C or D is correct, based on the preceding passage of text.

There is only one correct answer to each question, *which is "True" in terms of the information given in the text: the other statements will either be "False" or "Cannot say" from the information given in the text. Each question must be considered without reference to any other knowledge you may have of the subject matter –* **only information included in the passage itself may be used** *in deciding your answer.*

For practice purposes, you should try to complete 20 questions in 35 minutes.

1. English has been the unofficial language of pilots for many years, but a tragic accident in the Canary Islands in 1977 emphasized the need for a universal aviation language. In this case, two 747 jets—one Pan Am, one KLM—collided on the runway at Tenerife airport. At one point, the KLM pilot told the tower in a heavy Dutch accent either "We're now at take-off" or "We're uh...taking off." The tower didn't understand the message and told KLM to standby, but a simultaneous communication from Pan Am garbled the instruction. Reviews by the National Transportation Safety Board (NTSB) of the cockpit recorder transcriptions determined that the KLM pilot's use of non-standard phraseology during the critical moments leading up to the accident contributed to the disaster. (*mentalfloss.com*)

A. English was chosen as the universal aviation language because it is so widely spoken.

B. It took a tragedy before people officially adopted English for use in aviation.

C. The tragedy in the Canary Islands demonstrated the importance of standardised language.

D. The Dutch pilot's inability to speak English resulted in the tragedy on the Canary Islands.

2. **Most of us consider our personality to be an integral and unchanging part of who we are – perhaps the essence of that thing we call the self. In 1887, psychologist William James went so far as to argue that it becomes "set like plaster" by the age of 30. His idea stuck. Psychologists have long debated how to measure personality, settling eventually on the "big five" traits. But at least they were able to agree on a definition: personality refers to an individual's thought patterns and behaviours, which tend to persist over time. Now mounting evidence is undermining that notion. Personality is far more mutable than we thought. That may be a little unsettling. But it's also good news for the almost 90 percent of us who wish our personalities were at least a little different.** (*newscientist.com*)

A.   By the time people reach the age of 30 their personalities are mostly set in stone.

B.   William James was the psychologist who defined the "big five" psychological traits.

C.   Nearly everyone wishes that their personality was strikingly different.

D.   Personalities are now believed to be much more malleable before and after the age of 30.

3. **One theory regarding Edgar Allen Poe's death is that he may have been a victim of a violent crime. Because the tavern where Poe was found prior to his death was being used as a polling place (it was common practice in the 19th century for voting to take place in drinking establishments), it has been proposed that he may have been caught up in an unusual form of electoral fraud known as "cooping." In a cooping scheme, gangs working for corrupt politicians would grab unwilling bystanders off the street and force them to vote repeatedly for a certain candidate. Victims were often beaten or forced to drink alcohol to make them comply. Disguises were used to allow the victims to vote multiple times. This could explain the bizarre outfit that Poe was wearing when he was discovered.** (*Britannica.com*)

A.   Voting usually took place in drinking establishments in the 19th century.

B.   Poe's mysterious death may be explained as the product of electoral fraud.

C.   In the 19th century, people were allowed to vote on multiple occasions in elections.

D.   When Poe was found it was discovered that he had voted on multiple occasions.

4. **Chromatic aberration, also known as "colour fringing" or "purple fringing", is a common optical problem that occurs when a lens is either unable to bring all wavelengths of colour to the same focal plane, and/or when wavelengths of colour are focused at different positions in the focal plane. Chromatic aberration is caused by lens dispersion, with different colours of light travelling at different speeds while passing through a lens. As a result, the image can look blurred or noticeable coloured edges (red, green, blue, yellow, purple, magenta) can appear around objects, especially in high-contrast situations.** (*photographylife.com*)

A.   Chromatic aberration is caused by lens dispersion in lenses that are inexpensive.

B.   Chromatic aberration is also called purple fringing because that is the most common colour.

C.   Lenses unable to bring all colour wavelengths to the same focal plane produce colour fringing.

D.   The effect of chromatic aberration will not be seen in situations featuring low contrast.

5. **Education does not stop. Professors must update and develop their technical skills throughout their careers. But as they progress, few take the time – or are offered the opportunity – to become educated in how to be an effective leader. As a consequence, academic teams waste time dealing with unproductive interpersonal issues, lack of motivation and unnecessary conflict. When things do not run smoothly, the costs in terms of money, productivity and retention of talent are high. Leaders should inspire others to achieve goals. Professors lead research teams and manage teaching staff. They also have to lead intellectually, making advances in engineering and science that benefit society. The importance of leadership skills grows as scientists gain seniority. Even well-meaning professors can create chaos by bossing people and failing to take into account the emotions of others.**

Equally, those who take a back seat can create teams that are much less effective. (*nature.com*)

A. Academic teams fail due to the conflict caused by poor leadership that does not tackle inter-personal issues and low motivation.

B. It is important that senior academics build strong leadership and technical skills in order to be effective in their roles.

C. An abundance of opportunities for promotion explains why academics do not focus on developing their leadership skills.

D. Seniority is not relevant when considering the leadership skills necessary for scientists whereas the ability to read emotions is.

6. At the *ludi meridiani*, or midday games, criminals, barbarians, prisoners of war and other unfortunates, called *damnati*, or "condemned," were executed. (Despite numerous accounts of saints' lives written in the Renaissance and later, there is no reliable evidence that Christians were killed in the Colosseum for their faith.) Some damnati were released in the arena to be slaughtered by fierce animals such as lions, and some were forced to fight one another with swords. Others were dispatched in what a modern scholar has called "fatal charades," executions staged to resemble scenes from mythology. The Roman poet Martial, who attended the inaugural games, describes a criminal dressed as Orpheus playing a lyre amid wild animals; a bear ripped him apart. Another suffered the fate of Hercules, who burned to death before becoming a god. (*smithsoniamag.com*)

A. Historical evidence proves that no Christians were killed at the Colosseum, along with war prisoners and barbarians.

B. All *damnati* were forced to participate in staged executions involving characters and scenes from mythology.

C. During the morning games, spectators could witness wild beast hunts involving fierce animals such as lions and bears.

D. As part of their execution, a criminal could find themselves facing a wild beast or sword fighting another person.

7. Dr Caroline Lyon, Professor Chrystopher Nehaniv and Dr Joe Saunders have carried out experiments as part of the iTalk project with the childlike iCub humanoid robot to show how language learning emerges. Initially the robot can only babble and perceives speech as a string of sounds, not divided up into words. After engaging in a few minutes of "conversation" with humans, in which the participants were instructed to speak to the robot as if it were a small child, the robot adapted its output to the most frequently heard syllables to produce some word forms such as the names of simple shapes and colours. Dr Caroline Lyon said: "It is known that infants are sensitive to the frequency of sounds in speech, and these experiments show how this sensitivity can be modelled and contribute to the learning of word forms by a robot." (*Science Daily*)

A. According to Dr Caroline Lyon, our current knowledge of how infants perceive language can help robots learn word forms.

B. When robots are starting to learn language skills, they readily recognize individual speech units including words.

C. Experiments that are part of the iTalk project have shown that robots develop language skills more quickly than humans.

D. After a few minutes of "conversation" with humans, a robot will adapt its output to the most frequently heard inflections.

8. Leonardo da Vinci's *Vetruvian Man* is the attempt to illustrate the idea, set down by Vitruvius in the *Ten Books*, that the human body can be made to fit inside a circle and a square. This was more than a geometrical statement. Ancient thinkers had long invested the circle and the square with symbolic powers. The circle represented the cosmic and the divine; the square, the earthly and the secular. Anyone proposing that a man could be made to fit inside both shapes was making a metaphysical proposition: The human body wasn't just designed according to the principles that governed the world; it *was* the world, in miniature. This was the theory of the microcosm, and Leonardo hitched himself to it early in his career. "By the ancients," he wrote around 1492, "man was termed

a lesser world, and certainly the use of this name is well bestowed, because … his body is an analogue for the world." (*smithsonianmag.com*)

A. Viewing the body as a miniature representation of the world was the key to Leonardo da Vinci's success as an artist.

B. According to ancient thinkers, the circle symbolizes the non-spiritual while the square symbolizes the spiritual.

C. *Vetruvian Man,* as an attempt to fit the human body inside a circle and a square, reflects Leonardo's belief in God.

D. *Vetruvian Man* is a statement of the metaphysical idea that the human body is a microcosm of the world.

9. **Quantum cryptography is, in principle, a foolproof way to prevent hacking. It ensures that any attempt by an eavesdropper to read encoded communication data will lead to disturbances that can be detected by the legitimate users. Therefore, quantum cryptography allows the transmission of an unconditionally secure encryption key between two users, "Alice" and "Bob", in the presence of a potential hacker, "Eve". The encryption key is communicated using light signals and is received using photon detectors. The challenge is that Eve can intercept and manipulate these signals. When quantum hacking occurs, light signals subvert the photon detectors, causing them to only see the photons that Eve wants Bob to see. (*Science Daily*)**

A. In quantum cryptography, the encryption key is transmitted with photon detectors and received with light signals.

B. Quantum cryptography uses light signals that can be captured and manipulated by a would-be hacker.

C. Quantum hacking, in which light signals subvert photon detectors, is the least common form of hacking.

D. If a hacker attempts to access data encoded with quantum cryptography, legal users have no way of knowing.

10. **The European economy is largely linear by design. This design results in avoidable environmental and human** health impacts, inefficient use of natural resources and over-dependency on resources from outside Europe. Moving to a circular economy would alleviate these pressures and concerns, and deliver several economic, social and environmental benefits and affect current trade practices. In the past the creation of waste in connection with production and consumption was accepted as a necessary evil. Today, that apparent common sense is increasingly being challenged: circular economy, zero waste, closed-cycle, resource efficiency, waste avoidance, re-use, recycling – all these terms can be attributed to the ideal of achieving a world largely without waste, with a responsible attitude to resources, materials, products and the environment. (*European Parliamentary Research Service*)

A. There is universal agreement that the manufacture of goods in the European economy will always create waste.

B. European member states have agreed to pursue a closed-cycle economy based on the ideal of a world largely without waste.

C. Progressing towards the model of a circular economy could help Europe use raw materials more efficiently.

D. Moving towards a circular economy would cause a fall in trade between Europe and the rest of the world.

11. **The Higgs boson is one of the final puzzle pieces required for a complete understanding of the standard model of physics – the so-far successful theory that explains how fundamental particles interact with the elementary forces of nature. The so-called God particle was proposed in the 1960s by Peter Higgs to explain why some particles, such as quarks – building blocks of protons, among other things – and electrons have mass, while others, such as the light-carrying photon particle, do not. Higgs's idea was that the universe is bathed in an invisible field similar to a magnetic field. Every particle feels this field – now known as the Higgs field – but to varying degrees. If a particle can move through this field with little or no interaction, there will be no drag, and that particle will have little or no mass. Alternatively,**

if a particle interacts significantly with the Higgs field, it will have a higher mass. The idea of the Higgs field requires the acceptance of a related particle: the Higgs boson. (*National Geographic*)

A. The Higgs boson helps explain why, in the standard model of physics, some particles have mass and others do not.

B. According to the Higgs theory, a particle with high mass could travel through the Higgs field with few interactions.

C. Without the existence of the Higgs field, atoms, electrons, and chemical bonds would have difficulty forming.

D. Higgs boson particles attach themselves to fundamental particles like quarks, electrons, and atoms, causing drag.

12. When [Arthur Conan] Doyle graduated from Stonyhurst College in 1876, his parents expected that he would follow in his family's footsteps and study art, so they were surprised when he decided to pursue a medical degree at the University of Edinburgh instead. At medical school, Doyle met his mentor, Professor Dr. Joseph Bell, whose keen powers of observation would later inspire Doyle to create his famed fictional detective character, Sherlock Holmes. Doyle became increasingly invested in Spiritualism or "Psychic religion," a belief system that he would later attempt to spread through a series of his written works. By the time he received his Bachelor of Medicine degree in 1881, Doyle had denounced his Roman Catholic faith. Doyle's first paying job as a doctor took the form of a medical officer's position aboard the steamship Mayumba, travelling from Liverpool to Africa. (*biography.com*)

A. Arthur Conan Doyle's renunciation of his Roman Catholic faith was largely due to the influence of his father.

B. Following family tradition, Arthur Conan Doyle studied art before he decided to pursue a medical degree.

C. The powerful observational skills of Sherlock Holmes were modeled on a doctor he met while aboard the Mayumba.

D. After receiving his medical degree, Doyle served as a medical officer on a steamship for his first paying position as a doctor.

13. Warm-blooded birds need about 20 times more oxygen than cold-blooded reptiles, and they have evolved a unique lung structure that allows for a high rate of gas exchange and high activity level. Their unusual thigh complex helps support the lung and prevent its collapse. But the scientists said that every other animal – including humans, elephants, dogs, lizards and, in the ancient past, dinosaurs – that has walked on land has had a moveable thigh bone that was involved in the animal's motion. The implication of these facts, the researchers said, is that birds almost certainly did not descend from theropod dinosaurs such as the tyrannosaurus or allosaurus. The scientists' findings add to a growing body of evidence in the past two decades that challenge some of the most widely held beliefs about animal evolution. (*Science Daily*)

A. Scientists have concluded that dinosaurs such as tyrannosaurus are probably not the ancient ancestors of birds.

B. Cold-blooded reptiles have a special structure in their lungs allowing them to exchange gases at a rapid rate.

C. Dinosaurs had a flexible thigh bone that allowed them to walk on land with more efficiency than elephants.

D. Birds were able to survive what likely killed the dinosaurs because their thigh complex prevented lung collapse.

14. Van Gogh's art helped him stay emotionally balanced. In 1885, he began work on what is considered to be his first masterpiece, *Potato Eaters*. His brother Theo, by this time living in Paris, believed the painting would not be well-received in the French capital, where impressionism had become the trend. Nevertheless, Van Gogh decided to move to Paris, and showed up at Theo's house uninvited. In Paris, Van Gogh first saw impressionist art, and he was inspired by the color and light. He began studying with Toulouse-Lautrec, Pissarro and others. Van Gogh was passionate, and he argued with other painters about their works, alienating those who became tired of his bickering. In February 1888, Van Gogh boarded a train to the south of France. He moved into the "little yellow

house" and spent his money on paint rather than food. He lived off of coffee, bread and absinthe, and found himself feeling sick and strange, even sipping turpentine and eating paint. (*biography. com*)

A.   Despite Van Gogh's love of passionate argument, he maintained friendships with Pissarro and other painters.

B.   Van Gogh was emotionally volatile and had turbulent relationships with other painters throughout his life.

C.   When Van Gogh first moved to Paris, he was introduced to impressionism and was inspired by the colour and light.

D.   Despite his brother's initial scepticism, Van Gogh's first masterpiece, *Potato Eaters,* was well received in Paris.

15.   **Until recently, black holes were thought to come in only two sizes: small stellar varieties that are several times heavier than our sun, and supermassive black holes that pack the gravitational punch of many millions of suns – large enough to swallow our entire solar system. Notorious for ripping apart and swallowing stars, extra-large black holes live exclusively in the hearts of most galaxies, including our own Milky Way. The new middleweight black hole is between these two types – equal to the matter of about 90,000 suns. Supermassive black holes might form when a single intermediately sized black hole gobbles enough matter to grow into a supermassive black hole with at least a million solar masses. Or perhaps a number of intermediate black holes merged in the early universe to form the supermassive black holes we see today. Either way, without further surveys, it's impossible to tell how common middleweight black holes are across the universe. (*National Geographic*)**

A.   A supermassive black hole may have formed when a group of intermediate black holes merged in the early universe.

B.   Intermediate black holes, equal to the matter of about 90,000 suns, are instrumental in the formation of solar systems.

C.   Supermassive black holes live at the centre and outskirts of most galaxies, dismantling and consuming stars.

D.   Based on existing research data, it is possible to forecast the number of intermediate black holes that exist in the universe.

16.   **The challenge to "transform Europe into a low-carbon economy and increase its energy security" is one of the Grand Challenges facing European policymakers. The EU has set itself a legally binding goal to cut greenhouse gas emissions from all primary energy sources by at least 20% by 2020, compared to 1990 levels. It will also push for an international agreement to succeed the Kyoto Protocol aimed at achieving a 30% cut by all developed nations by 2020. In October 2009, EU leaders endorsed a long-term target of cutting up to 50% of carbon emissions from primary energy sources by 2050, compared to 1990 levels. In parallel, the European Commission has put forward a Strategic Energy Technology Plan "to accelerate the development and deployment of cost-effective low carbon technologies". Both actions, which originated from the Climate Action and Energy Commissioners, respectively, coincide in the need for appropriate research, such as that done by the European Research Council. (*European Research Council*)**

A.   The European Research Council has been asked by the European Commission to fund appropriate research into cost-effective low-carbon technologies.

B.   In 2009 the EU agreed to adopt a legally binding target of reducing its greenhouse gas emissions by 50% by 2050, compared to 1990 levels.

C.   The Strategic Energy Technology Plan being put forward by the European Commission was originated from the Commissioner for Energy.

D.   The EU is negotiating with all developed nations with the aim of achieving a cut of 30% of their greenhouse gas emissions by 2020.

17.   **Videogame technology is proving to be a valuable tool for helping people of all ages improve lifestyle and health habits and manage disease. New research is showing that so-called "exergames" significantly benefit older adults by providing them with cognitive stimulation and a source of social interaction, exercise, and fun. Thus, the games help lead them to fuller, more**

independent lives for a longer time. "The elderly often forsake their lifelong activities in exchange for the safety, security, and care of institutional living," says Editor-in-Chief Bill Ferguson, PhD. "This trade-off need not require the sacrifice of physical activity and fitness. Furthermore, videogames offer an escape from routine. All of these benefits can improve the well-being of elderly adults." Digital games offer a home-based method of supporting behavior modification, motivating patients to take better care of themselves and to self-manage chronic conditions. (*Science Daily*)

A. According to Bill Ferguson the elderly must give up physical activity and fitness for safety and security.

B. Elderly adults living in assisted care facilities reap greater benefits from exergames than do their peers living in their own homes.

C. Elderly adults who regularly use exergames are more mentally healthy and more fulfilled socially than those who do not.

D. Videogame technology can benefit the elderly by helping to motivate them and manage some of their chronic conditions.

18. René Lacoste's mechanical mind never really lagged behind his athletic pursuits. A tenacious perfectionist, he had once been criticized by a coach for overtraining. His tendency to wear out practice partners proved so frustrating that Lacoste created the world's first tennis ball machine, a hand-cranked device he called "lance-balle." His inventive mind worked in areas outside of tennis, too. Between the mid-1960s and late 1980s Lacoste filed 20 new patents. But a clothing line that bore his name proved to be Lacoste's greatest post-game success. As a player, Lacoste went against traditional on-court fashion, opting to compete in short-sleeved knit shirts rather than dress shirts. Sensing a market for this look, Lacoste formed a small company to manufacture the apparel soon after leaving the game. By 1950, Lacoste's shirt, with its signature crocodile emblem on the left breast, entered the U.S. market. (*biography.com*)

A. Gifted in tennis, mechanical engineering, and fashion design, Lacoste's main passion was always invention.

B. After his tennis career, Lacoste's greatest success was his invention of the world's first tennis ball machine.

C. Lacoste was a perfectionist, quickly went through practice partners, and wore short-sleeved knit shirts on court.

D. The Lacoste name and crocodile symbol conquered the US market and became status symbols in the world of fashion.

19. Cleopatra's father had thrown in his lot with Pompey the Great. Good fortune seemed eternally to shine on Pompey, that brilliant Roman general, at least until Julius Caesar dealt him a crushing defeat in central Greece. Pompey fled to Egypt, where, in 48 BC, he was stabbed and decapitated. Twenty-one-year-old Cleopatra was at the time a fugitive in the Sinai – on the losing side of a civil war against her brother and at the mercy of her brother's troops and advisers. Quickly, she managed to ingratiate herself with the new master of the Roman world, Julius Caesar. Caesar arrived in Alexandria just days after Pompey's murder. He barricaded himself in the Ptolemies' palace, the home from which Cleopatra had been exiled. From the desert, Cleopatra engineered a clandestine return, skirting enemy lines and Roman barricades, arriving after dark inside a sturdy sack. Over the succeeding months she stood at Caesar's side – pregnant with his child – while he battled her brother's troops. With their defeat, Caesar restored her to the throne. (*smithsonianmag.com*)

A. After Caesar returned Cleopatra to the throne, she went on to rule the Mediterranean region for many years.

B. In 48 BC, the Roman general Pompey the Great escaped to Egypt, where he was stabbed and beheaded.

C. In 48 BC, the young Cleopatra was living in the Sinai following a civil war victory against her brother.

D. The young Cleopatra was able to quickly win the favour of Julius Caesar, a new leader in the Roman world.

20. George Frideric Handel's *Messiah* was originally an Easter offering. It burst onto the stage of *Musick Hall* in Dublin

on April 13, 1742. Handel's superstar status was not the only draw; many also came to glimpse the contralto, Susannah Cibber, then embroiled in a scandalous divorce. [Handel] was born in Halle, Germany, into a religious, affluent household. His father, Georg Händel, a celebrated surgeon in northern Germany, wanted his son to study the law. But an acquaintance, the Duke of Weissenfels, heard the prodigy, then barely 11, playing the organ. The nobleman's recognition of the boy's genius likely influenced the doctor's decision to allow his son to become a musician. By 18, Handel had composed his first opera, *Almira*. During the next five years, he was employed as a musician, composer and conductor at courts and churches in Rome, Florence, Naples and Venice, as well as in Germany, where the Elector of Hanover, the future King George I of England, was briefly his patron. (*smithsonianmag.com*)

A.   Handel was born into a religious family, the son of a successful surgeon who wanted him to study law.

B.   Handel mostly preferred to work for one or two main benefactors, rather than seeking patronage more widely.

C.   On its opening night of April 13, 1742, the *Messiah* drew crowds solely because of Handel's dazzling reputation.

D.   Contralto Susannah Cibber drew crowds not because of her voice but because of the scandalous divorce she was going through.

21.   Suzanne de la Monte, M.D., has found a link between brain insulin resistance (diabetes) and two other key mediators of neuronal injury that help Alzheimer's disease (AD) to propagate. The research found that once AD is established, therapeutic efforts must also work to reduce toxin production in the brain. Alzheimer's disease is one of the most common degenerative dementias, and more than 115 million new cases are projected worldwide in the next 40 years. There is clinical and experimental evidence that treatment with insulin or insulin sensitizer agents can enhance cognitive function and in some circumstances help slow the rate of cognitive decline in AD. Alzheimer's and other neurodegenerative diseases

destroy the brain until the patients finally succumb. In order to effectively halt the process of neurodegeneration, the forces that advance and perpetuate the disease, particularly with regard to the progressive worsening of brain insulin/IGF resistance, must be understood. (*Science Daily*)

A.   The underlying causes of brain insulin resistance (diabetes) and Alzheimer's disease are almost identical.

B.   If Alzheimer's disease is diagnosed early, the rate of neurodegeneration can likely be decreased effectively.

C.   Clinical and experimental evidence suggests that insulin treatment can improve cognitive function in Alzheimer's patients.

D.   Alzheimer's disease is the most common degenerative dementia and more than 115 million new cases are projected worldwide in the next 40 years.

22.   A painter, sculptor, printmaker, ceramist and writer, Gauguin stands today as one of the giants of Post-Impressionism and a pioneer of Modernism. He was also a great storyteller, creating narratives in every medium he touched. Some of his tales were true, others near-fabrications. For instance, the lush Tahitian masterpieces for which he is best known reflect an exotic paradise more imaginary than real. The fables Gauguin spun were meant to promote himself and his art, an intention that was more successful with the man than his work; he was well known during his lifetime, but his paintings sold poorly. Certainly the artist would have been pleased by the renewed attention; his goal, after all, was to be famous. He dressed bizarrely, wrote self-serving critiques of his work, courted the press and even handed out photographs of himself to his fans. He was often drunk, belligerent and promiscuous – and possibly suicidal. (*smithsonianmag.com*)

A.   Gauguin's Tahitian masterpieces provide a remarkably accurate and detailed record of the lush tropical environment.

B.   Gauguin used his gift for telling stories to please his friends and fans and to advance the cause of art in general.

C. Along with painting, Gauguin spent time drinking, promoting himself, telling stories, and engaging in sexual relations.

D. Gauguin never made much money selling his paintings because of his strange and provoking behaviour with the press and the public.

23. When cats are on what they perceive to be safe ground they can and do behave affectionately towards their owners. They show this in a whole variety of ways including: raising their tails upright when they see us, rubbing their heads or flanks on our legs, licking us when they're sitting next to us, and purring when we stroke them. How do we know that these are signs of affection? Well, it has to be said that we will never know precisely what's going on inside a cat's head (or a dog's for that matter), but we do know that these are the ways in which cats indicate their affection for other cats. The fact that cats get along with other cats at all is something of an achievement for a species that was exclusively solitary just 10,000 years ago. Our domestic cat's wild relatives, the Arabian wildcat Felis lybica, spend most of their lives alone. During the breeding season, males consort with females for just a few days of the year, but otherwise avoid other cats as much as possible, unlike male lions and cheetahs, both of which are able to form "brotherhoods", competing with other groups for the attention of females. (*theguardian.com*)

A. Male lions and cheetahs are similar to domestic cats in that they have evolved over the years to have specific behavioural tendencies towards one another.

B. 10,000 years ago the Arabian wildcat Felis lybica spent most of its time alone until the breeding season meant it sought out a mate with which to breed.

C. It is not possible to know precisely what goes on in the mind of a cat but we can make assumptions by observing their behaviour.

D. Unlike lions and cheetahs the Felis lybica form groups, which allow them to compete effectively with big cats for the attention of females.

24. Fake news flourished in the 19th century. One such fake correspondent was Theodor Fontane, a German pharmacist-turned-journalist who would go on to write some of the most important German Realist novels. In 1860, Fontane joined the staff of the Kreuzzeitung, an ultra-conservative Berlin newspaper. The paper assigned him to cover England, and for a decade, he published story after story "from" London, spellbinding his readers with "personal" accounts of dramatic events, like the devastating Tooley Street Fire of 1861. But during the entire decade, he never actually crossed the English Channel. Fontane sifted through existing accounts to get a sense for what readers already knew about the catastrophe. He cut up the old articles, picked out the most relevant texts, and glued them together for his own account. Then, to elevate the drama, he wrote some new passages with details and characters that were completely fabricated. (*theconversation. com*)

A. In 1860 the German writer Theodor Fontane created the journalistic practice that we now call fake news.

B. During the decade that he wrote about English affairs for the Kreuzzeitung newspaper, Theodor Fontane never left his home country.

C. All of the details in the story written by Theodor Fontane about the Tooley Street fire were invented.

D. The journalistic practice that we now call fake news was widely practised in a previous century.

25. Morse gave up painting entirely; relinquishing the whole career he had set his heart on since college days. No one could dissuade him. He had to attend to one thing at a time, as his father had long ago advised him. The "one thing" henceforth would be his telegraph, the crude apparatus that was housed in his New York University studio apartment. Later it would be surmised that, had Morse not stopped painting when he did, no successful electromagnetic telegraph would have been developed when it was, or at least not a Morse electromagnetic telegraph. Essential to Morse's idea, as he had set forth earlier in notes written in 1832, was that signals would be sent by the opening and closing of an electrical circuit, that the receiving apparatus would, by electromagnet, record signals

as dots and dashes on paper, and that there would be a code whereby the dots and dashes would be translated into numbers and letters. (*smithsonianmag. com*)

A.   Morse made many attempts to develop a code for his telegraph before finding one that worked.

B.   Morse planned for telegraph signals to be sent by the opening and closing of an electrical circuit and recorded by electromagnet.

C.   Morse pursued the design of his electromagnetic telegraph even as he was working as a commissioned painter.

D.   Although his telegraph was not immediately successful, Morse continued to refine his invention, undeterred.

26.   Peat wetlands in northwest Europe are well-known for their bog bodies. The wetlands provide cold, acidic, oxygen-free conditions, which prevent decay and mummify human flesh. The two new Irish bog men were named after the places where they were found: Croghan Hill and Clonycavan. Oldcroghan man was preserved so perfectly that his discovery sparked a police murder investigation before archaeologists were called in. Radiocarbon dating showed that he lived between 362 BC and 175 BC, while Clonycavan man dates from 392 BC to 201 BC. A team led by researchers at the National Museum of Ireland studied the two bodies. The scientists say the fingerprint whorls of Oldcroghan man are as clear as any living person's. While both bog men appeared to be aristocratic dandies of their day, they still met horrible deaths. Oldcroghan man shows signs of cruel torture before he was beheaded. Meanwhile, Clonycavan man suffered three axe blows to the head, plus one to his chest. (*National Geographic*)

A.   The two new Irish bog bodies show signs of torture, indicating that they were killed as part of a ritual to pagan gods.

B.   The two bodies were found preserved in the cold, acidic conditions of the bogs Croghan Hill and Clonycavan.

C.   The two bog bodies were apparently men of low social rank, which may explain why they were buried in the bog.

D.   Oldcroghan man and Clonycavan man offer evidence of Iron Age burial modes occurring across Western Europe and beyond.

27.   Scientists have long known that the body rids itself of excess copper and various other minerals by collecting them in the liver and excreting them through the liver's bile. However, a new study suggests that when this route is impaired, there's another exit route just for copper: a molecule sequesters only the copper and routes it from the body through urine. The researchers found this additional copper escape hatch by studying an animal model of Wilson's disease, a rare disorder most often diagnosed in children. People with this disease accumulate abnormally large amounts of copper in the liver, eventually leading to liver damage and failure. Micronutrients such as copper, zinc and iron are indispensible for human development. Copper is required for embryonic development, respiration, and cardiovascular function, among other processes; too little copper can be fatal whereas too much can cause neurological impairment and organ failure. (*Science Daily*)

A.   Individuals with Wilson's disease were either over or under exposed to the micronutrient copper before birth.

B.   In individuals with Wilson's disease, liver cells die off at increasingly rapid rates without regenerating.

C.   Too much of the micronutrient copper leads to death, but too little leads to neurological damage rather than death.

D.   Collection in the liver and excretion through the liver's bile is just one way that excess copper exits the body.

28.   In 2001, the Human Genome Project and Celera Genomics announced that after 10 years of work at a cost of some $400 million, they had completed a draft sequence of the human genome. Today, sequencing a human genome is something that a single researcher can do in a couple of weeks for less than $10,000. Since 2002, the rate at which genomes can be sequenced has been doubling every four months or so, whereas computing power doubles only every 18 months.

Without the advent of new analytic tools, biologists' ability to generate genomic data will soon outstrip their ability to do anything useful with it. Researchers talk about a new algorithm that drastically reduces the time it takes to find a particular gene sequence in a database of genomes. And in fact, the more genomes the algorithm searches, the greater the speedup it affords, so its advantages will only compound as more data is generated. (*Science Daily*)

A.   A lone scientist is able to sequence a human genome over the course of a few weeks for less than $10,000.

B.   Celera Genomics finished a draft sequence of the human genome after 10 years of work for less than $10,000.

C.   The new algorithm reduces the time it takes to locate a gene sequence by utilizing related species' genomes.

D.   Since 2002 the rate at which scientists can sequence genomes has doubled.

29.   Since they became widely known in the late 1920s, the mysterious desert drawings known as the Nasca lines have puzzled archaeologists, anthropologists, and anyone fascinated by ancient cultures in the Americas. For just as long, waves of scientists – and amateurs – have inflicted various interpretations on the lines, as if they were the world's largest set of Rorschach inkblots. At one time or another, they have either been explained as Inca roads, irrigation plans, images to be appreciated from primitive hot-air balloons, or, most laughably, landing strips for alien spacecraft. Almost all of these iconic animal figures, such as the spider and the hummingbird, were single-line drawings; a person could step into them at one point and exit at another without ever crossing a line, suggesting to archaeologists that at some point in early Nasca times the lines evolved from mere images to pathways for ceremonial processions. (*National Geographic*)

A.   Since the 1920s due to the influence of popular culture, amateurs proposed that the Nasca lines were alien spacecraft landing strips.

B.   Recently scientists have proved that the Nasca lines were initially images that evolved into ceremonial pathways.

C.   Inca roads, irrigation plans, and landing strips are three interpretations of the single-line Nasca drawings.

D.   The Nasca lines, including the spider and hummingbird, always served the dual purpose of irrigation and ceremony.

30.   Italy managed to borrow in the financial markets at slightly lower rates Friday, despite a downgrade of its sovereign debt by a credit rating agency that threatened to deal a new blow to its efforts to escape the debt crisis. The Italian Treasury sold out its offering of €5.25 billion, or $6.4 billion, with three-year government bonds at 4.65 per cent, the lowest rate since May but still at a high price by historical standards. Moody's Investors Service lowered Italy's government bond rating Friday by two steps to Baa2 from A3, citing concerns that Italy faces higher financing costs and an increased risk of being locked out of lending markets as it battles contagion emanating from Greece and Spain. Nicholas Spiro, managing director of Spiro Sovereign Strategy, a London-based consultancy specialising in sovereign credit risk, described the Italian auction as a "mixed bag" but called the outcome more positive than negative. (*New York Times*)

A.   Moody's Investors Service downgraded Italy's government bond rating because of the country's unsuccessful efforts to escape the debt crisis.

B.   Despite the auction, the stakes for Italy remain high because the country is too big for the euro zone to bail out.

C.   The Italian Treasury sold three-year government bonds at 4.65 per cent, a price that is high by historical standards.

D.   Italy may become caught in a downward cycle, with recessionary trends adding an unsustainable debt burden.

31.   Nothing about elephants is small, and their pregnancies are no exception. Before giving birth to a 110-kilogramme calf, mothers carry the foetus for 22 months, the longest gestation period of any mammal. And whereas most mammals have only one corpus luteum – a temporary gland that controls hormone levels during pregnancy – elephants have as many as 11. Now, by giving 17

elephants blood tests and ultrasound scans throughout their pregnancies, researchers have discovered a key to this remarkable form of motherhood. The researchers found that the animals formed, on average, five corpora lutea during each menstrual cycle. And surprisingly, whereas one corpus luteum was derived from an egg-generating follicle, as happens in mammals such as humans, the rest of the structures formed from separate follicles at a different point in the reproductive cycle. The observation could lead to methods for controlling elephant ovulation or timing artificial insemination. (*sciencemag.org*)

A. Young female elephants that have not yet reached sexual maturity are not able to develop multiple corpora lutea.

B. Multiple corpora lutea form from separate follicles in female elephants in order to maintain steady hormone levels.

C. Female elephants form about five corpora lutea during each menstrual cycle, all from one egg-generating follicle.

D. Elephant mothers carry the foetus for 22 months, which is the longest gestation period among mammals.

32. Physicists are often interested in mathematically describing how a system behaves: for instance, a formula tracks the motions of the planets and their moons in their complicated dance around the sun. Researchers work out these equations by measuring the objects at various points in time and then developing a formula that links all of those points together, such as filling in a video from a set of snapshots. With each new variable, however, it becomes tougher to find the right equation. Computers can speed things up by sifting through potential solutions at breakneck speed, but even the world's top supercomputers meet their match with a certain class of problems, known as "hard" problems. These problems take exponentially more time to solve with every additional variable that is thrown into the mix – an extra planet's motion, for instance. (*sciencemag.org*)

A. With each variable that is added, so-called "hard" problems take exponentially more time to solve, even for computers.

B. As researchers work to describe a system mathematically, each variable makes it easier to find the correct equation.

C. Problems considered "hard" can still be solved at breakneck speed by the best supercomputers of the world.

D. Any algorithm that turns data into a formula describing a system over time can't be simplified to run on a computer.

33. This new, irrational art movement would be named Dada. It got its name, according to Richard Huelsenbeck, a German artist living in Zurich, when he and Ball came upon the word in a French-German dictionary. To Ball, it fit. "Dada is 'yes, yes' in Rumanian, 'rocking horse' and 'hobby horse' in French," he noted in his diary. "For Germans it is a sign of foolish naiveté, joy in procreation, and preoccupation with the baby carriage." Romanian artist Tristan Tzara, who later claimed that he had coined the term, quickly used it on posters, put out the first Dada journal and wrote one of the first of many Dada manifestoes, few of which made much sense. But the absurdist outlook spread like a pandemic – Tzara called Dada "a virgin microbe" – and there were outbreaks from Berlin to Paris, New York and even Tokyo. And for all its zaniness, the movement would prove to be one of the most influential in modern art, foreshadowing abstract and conceptual art, performance art, op, pop and installation art. (*smithsonianmag.com*)

A. The irrational art movement of Dada appealed particularly to those who could not make sense of the events of the early 20th century.

B. The first of many Dada manifestoes, issued by Romanian artist Tristan Tzara, were all highly logical and meaningful.

C. The term "dada" means "hobby horse" in French and for Germans it has associations with joy in procreation.

D. The element of Dada that paved the way for abstract and conceptual art was its absurdity and irrationality.

34. The international Cassini mission has concluded its remarkable exploration of the Saturnian system in spectacular style, by plunging into the gas planet's atmosphere. Confirmation of the

end of mission arrived at NASA's Jet Propulsion Laboratory at 13:55 CEST (Central European Summer Time) with the loss of the spacecraft's signal having occurred 83 minutes earlier at Saturn, some 1.4 billion km from Earth. With the rocket propellant for manoeuvring the spacecraft fully expended as planned touring Saturn and its moons for the last 13 years, the mission concluded with the intentional plunge into the gas planet. This ensures that Saturn's icy moons, in particular, ocean-bearing Enceladus, do not risk being contaminated by microbes that might have remained on board the spacecraft from Earth, and are left pristine for future exploration. (*European Space Agency*)

A. The Cassini spacecraft plunged onto Enceladus after its signal was lost.

B. The Cassini spacecraft travelled more than 1.4 billion km during its mission to explore Saturn.

C. The Cassini spacecraft discovered an ocean-bearing icy moon.

D. Scientists want to avoid future exploration of Saturn's moons, to avoid contaminating them with microbes from Earth.

35. In 1565, ambitious for the English throne, Mary Queen of Scots married her cousin, Henry Stewart, Lord Darnley, a grandson of Margaret Tudor, but became disgusted by his debauchery, and was soon alienated from him. The birth of a son, the future James VI, failed to bring a reconciliation. While ill with smallpox, Darnley was mysteriously killed in an explosion at Kirk o' Field (1567); the chief suspect was the Earl of Bothwell, who underwent a mock trial and was acquitted. Mary's involvement is unclear, but she consented to marry James Hepburn of Bothwell, a divorcé with whom she had become infatuated. The Protestant nobles under Morton rose against her; she surrendered at Carberry Hill, was imprisoned at Loch Leven, and compelled to abdicate in favour of her son James VI. After escaping, she raised an army, but was defeated again by the confederate lords at Langside (1568). Placing herself under the protection of Queen Elizabeth, she found herself instead a prisoner for life. (*biography.com*)

A. Mary Queen of Scots married James Hepburn of Bothwell with whom she had a son, the future James VI.

B. In 1567 Mary's husband, Lord Darnley, was in strange circumstances killed in an explosion while sick with smallpox.

C. Queen Elizabeth I had Mary arrested and imprisoned because she saw her as a serious threat to the throne.

D. After gathering an army, Mary Queen of Scots successfully defeated the confederate lords at Landside in 1568.

36. Neurosurgeons and researchers are adapting an ultraviolet camera to possibly bring planet-exploring technology into the operating room. If the system works when focused on brain tissue, it could give surgeons a real-time view of changes invisible to the naked eye and unapparent even with the magnification of current medical imaging technologies. The pilot study seeks to determine if the camera provides visual detail that might help surgeons distinguish areas of healthy brain from deadly tumors called gliomas, which have irregular borders as they spread into normal tissue. Because tumor cells are more active and require more energy than normal cells, a specific chemical (nicotinamide adenine dinucleotide hydrogenase or NADH) accumulates in tumor cells but not in healthy cells. NADH emits ultraviolet light that may be captured by the camera and displayed in a high-resolution image. The camera employs the ultraviolet technology used in space to study planets and distant galaxies. (*Science Daily*)

A. Neurosurgeons do not use images taken by the ultraviolet camera in making decisions or to aid surgical technique.

B. Healthy cells require more energy than tumor cells and typically display irregular borders as they grow.

C. The ultraviolet camera will revolutionise how brain tumors and other neurological disorders are treated.

D. Ultraviolet technology used to study galaxies and planets could be adapted for the benefit of neurosurgery.

37. It was hailed in 2010 as the most "alien" life-form yet: bacteria that reportedly,

and unprecedentedly, had rewritten the recipe for DNA. And the secret ingredient was arsenic. Researchers led by then NASA astrobiologist Felisa Wolfe-Simon had found the organism, dubbed GFAJ-1, in arsenic-rich sediments of California's Mono Lake. They later reported that the bacterium thrived in arsenic-rich, phosphorus-poor lab conditions. The team concluded that GFAJ-1 must be incorporating arsenic into its DNA in place of phosphorous, which is essential for the DNA of all other known organisms. The find was exciting to astrobiologists, who had previously speculated that extraterrestrial life might survive in unexpected places if only such a swap were possible – arsenic and phosphorous being chemically similar. But when the amount of phosphorous was reduced even further than in Wolfe-Simon's experiments, GFAJ-1 stalled. The new conclusion: the arsenic-loving life-form does in fact need phosphorous to grow, but shockingly tiny amounts of it. (*National Geographic*)

A. Wolfe-Simon and her team concluded that GFAJ-1 was able to incorporate hosphorous into its DNA in place of arsenic.

B. Wolfe-Simon and her team found the GFAJ-1 organism in sediments of Mono Lake.

C. GFAJ-1's ability to exchange phosphorous and arsenic would confirm the existence of extraterrestrial life.

D. The fact that GFAJ-1 requires miniscule amounts of phosphorous for growth confirms the extraterrestrial life hypothesis.

38. By the time Paul Morphy was felled by a stroke on July 10, 1884, he had become an odd but familiar presence on Canal Street in New Orleans: a trim little man in sack suit and monocle, muttering to himself, smiling at his own conceits, swinging his cane at most who dared approach. Sometimes he would take a fancy to a passing woman, following her for hours at a distance. He lived in fear of being poisoned, eating only food prepared by his mother or sister, and he believed that neighbourhood barbers were conspiring to slit his throat. His family tried to have him committed to an asylum, but he argued his sanity so convincingly that the authorities declined to admit him. It had

been a quarter-century since he became a world-renowned chess champion, and for the last decade of his life he was loath to discuss the game at all. (*smithsonianmag.com*)

A. Morphy's obsessions and paranoia, which bordered on madness, were probably the necessary counterpart to his genius.

B. Morphy wore a monocle, believed that barbers would cut his throat, and ate only food that his family prepared.

C. In his later years, Morphy came to believe that time spent playing chess was nothing more than wasted time.

D. Morphy's behaviour eventually became so disturbing that his family had him committed to a mental asylum.

39. Research shows a twenty-fold enhancement in harvesting light by combining graphene with metallic nanostructures, and this new discovery could pave the way for advances in high-speed internet and other communications. By putting two closely spaced metallic wires on top of graphene and shining light on this structure, researchers generated electric power. This simple device is actually an elementary solar cell. Such graphene devices can transfer data tens and potentially hundreds of times faster than communication rates in the fastest internet cables; this is due to the uniquely high mobility and velocity of electrons in graphene. But the major stumbling block towards practical applications of these otherwise promising devices has been their low efficiency. The problem is that graphene – the thinnest material in the world – absorbs little light, approximately only 3 per cent of the total light shined on it, while the rest penetrates the graphene without contributing to the generation of electrical power. (*Science Daily*)

A. Graphene devices can transfer data so fast that they will replace existing internet cables.

B. A graphene solar cell can be made only by placing graphene on top of a metallic wire and then shining light on it.

C. Graphene devices owe their incredible speed to the high mobility and velocity of graphene's electrons.

D. Graphene devices are promising to communications because of their high efficiency and lightning speed.

40. **Shrapnel from mortars, grenades and, above all, artillery projectile bombs, or shells, would account for an estimated 60 per cent of the 9.7 million military fatalities of World War I. And it was soon observed that many soldiers arriving at the casualty clearing stations who had been exposed to exploding shells, although clearly damaged, bore no visible wounds. Rather, they appeared to be suffering from a remarkable state of shock caused by blast force. This new type of injury, a British medical report concluded, appeared to be "the result of the actual explosion itself, and not merely of the missiles set in motion by it." In other words, it appeared that some dark, invisible force had in fact passed through the air and was inflicting novel and peculiar damage to men's brains. "Shell shock," the term that would come to define the phenomenon, first appeared in the British medical journal *The Lancet* in February 1915, only six months after the commencement of the war. (*smithsonianmag.com*)**

A. Shell shock causes no visible wounding but those who suffer from the condition display symptoms similar to a concussion.

B. From early in World War I, soldiers appeared at casualty clearing stations suffering from an unusual state of shock.

C. The term "shell shock" was coined by military doctors in the barracks before appearing in the February 1915 edition of *The Lancet*.

D. About 60 per cent of the 9.7 million World War I military deaths were due to what would become known as shell shock.

41. **Overexploitation, pollution, habitat loss or emerging diseases have led a large number of species to extinction. This has made zoos and wildlife enclosures expand their goals beyond entertainment and fun; their participation in conservation and research programs is important for the recovery of multiple species. To ensure success, staff need to know the specific requirements of each species. In the case of the Iberian ibex, different mange outbreaks caused dramatic declines of some ibex** populations, which led managers and researchers to explore strategies aimed at preventing and controlling this disease and to reduce its impact on ibex populations. The objective of the Iberian ibex stock reservoir El Toril, as a key part of a general management plan, is to keep in captivity a sex and age structured representation of the free-ranging population, with most of its genetic variability, destined for conservation programs. (*Journal for Nature Conservation*)

A. Iberian ibex are being kept in captivity at El Toril in order to preserve the species from threatened extinction.

B. The ibex being kept at El Toril are planned to have a similar mix of hereditary characteristics to those which still roam free.

C. Mange outbreaks have increased in the Iberian ibex population due to overexploitation, pollution and habitat loss.

D. Ibex bred at El Toril have been successfully released into the wild.

42. **From the Middle Ages to the Baroque period, tapestry enjoyed a prestige far beyond that of painting. Royalty and the church commissioned whole series of designs – called cartoons – from the most sought-after artists of their times: Raphael, Rubens, Le Brun. Later artists from Goya to Picasso and Miró and beyond have carried on the tradition. Still, by 20th-century lights, tapestries fit more naturally into the pigeonhole of crafts than of fine arts. In their Golden Age, however, tapestries were seen to offer many advantages. They are portable, for one thing, as frescoes and wall paintings on a similar scale are not. For another, tapestries helped take the edge off the cold in large, drafty spaces. They had snob appeal, since only the richest of the rich could afford them. To hang tapestries was to show that you not only could appreciate the very best but that cost was no object. The materials alone could be worth a fortune, not to mention the massive costs of scarce, highly skilled labour. (*smithsonianmag.com*)**

A. During their Golden Age, tapestry cartoons could be licensed and woven in multiples by different artists.

B. After the 18th century, there was a great decline in the creation of tapestries as oil painting became in vogue.

C. Tapestry was associated with the peasant classes during the Middle Ages through the Baroque period.

D. Tapestries were favoured at one time for their convenience, ability to block cold air, and role as status symbols.

43. An interesting pattern over the last four decades is that inequality has grown much faster for households with children than it has for households over all – an indication that changes in family structure (as opposed to wages and employment alone) have increased inequality. Bruce Western and Tracey Shollenberger of the Harvard sociology department compared households at the 90th percentile and the 10th percentile. In 1970, the top households had 8.9 times the income of the bottom. By 2011 they had nearly 11.7 times as much – inequality between them grew 31 per cent. But among households with children it grew 121 per cent – the ratio went from 4.8 in 1970 to 10.6 last year. Most of that growth, it should be noted, occurred by 1994, while births to unwed mothers have continued to rise. And though no one has suggested that it is the sole or even main driving force behind the increases in inequality, rates of single parenthood are important but sometimes overlooked. (*New York Times*)

A. Children raised in single-parent households have more difficulty moving up the income ladder than their peers.

B. Single parenthood could be an important factor in inequality, and it's one that can also be ignored or missed.

C. A pattern emerging over the last forty years suggests that inequality has increased due only to wages and unemployment.

D. Between 1970 and 2011, income inequality between the top and bottom households grew by 121 per cent overall.

44. In 1956, Mandela and 150 others were arrested and charged with treason for their political advocacy, though they were eventually acquitted. Meanwhile, the African National Congress (ANC) was being challenged by the Africanists, a new breed of Black activists who believed that the pacifist method of the ANC was ineffective. In 1961, Mandela, who was formerly committed to non-violent protest, began to believe that armed struggle was the only way to achieve change. He co-founded Umkhonto we Sizwe, also known as MK, an armed offshoot of the ANC dedicated to sabotage and guerilla war tactics to end apartheid. He orchestrated a three-day national workers strike in 1961 for which he was arrested in 1962. He was sentenced to five years in prison for the strike, and then he was brought to trial again in 1963. This time, he and 10 other ANC leaders were sentenced to life imprisonment for political offences, including sabotage. (*biography.com*)

A. Mandela first began to consider guerilla war tactics shortly after he was arrested and charged with treason in 1956.

B. Umkhonto we Sizwe changed its pacifist tactics after Mandela was put on trial.

C. Mandela was arrested in 1962 and later sentenced to life imprisonment for sabotage and other political crimes.

D. The Africanist Black activists accepted the leadership role of the African National Congress and its pacifist method.

45. For centuries, scientists have tried to solve the mystery of how the colossal stone statues of Easter Island moved. The multi-ton behemoths travelled up to 18 kilometres from the quarry where most of them were carved, without the benefit of wheels, cranes, or even large animals. Scientists have tested many ideas in the past, figuring that the islanders must have used a combination of log rollers, ropes, and wooden sledges. Now a pair of archaeologists have come up with a new theory: Perhaps the statues, known as moai, were "engineered to move" upright in a rocking motion, using only manpower and rope. Last year, Hunt and Lipo showed that as few as 18 people could, with three strong ropes and a bit of practice, easily and relatively quickly manoeuvre a three-meter, five-ton moai replica a few hundred meters. No logs were required. (*National Geographic*)

A. Islanders designed the moai specifically so the statues could be moved using rope and a rocking motion.

B. Islanders used wheels, cranes, and strong animals to move the stone statues from the quarry.

C. All of the stones were carved at a rock quarry and then moved 18 kilometers to their resting places.

D. As few as 18 islanders could have moved the stone statues with three ropes using a rocking motion.

46. The Thames has been synonymous with rowing for almost three centuries. In August 1715, half a dozen "watermen" – oarsmen who ferried passengers on the river – convened beneath London Bridge for Britain's first rowing race. Nearly 200 years later, at the London Summer Olympic Games in 1908, spectators thronged the banks of Henley-on-Thames, site of the annual Royal Regatta, as British scullers competed against crews from seven countries, including Canada, Hungary and the Netherlands. Eton College, the nearly 600-year-old prep school whose graduates include novelist Ian Fleming, Prime Minister David Cameron and Prince William, is famed for its fanatic devotion to rowing. Dozens of Etonians have gone on to row in the Olympics, including four-time gold medalist Sir Matthew Pinsent, now 42. Before the 1990s, Eton's crews practiced and competed on the Thames, but today recreational boat traffic makes rowing there too dangerous. (*smithsonianmag. com*)

A. Britain's first rowing race took place in 1715 with six watermen gathering on the Thames beneath London Bridge.

B. Etonians have rowed in the Olympics, and students of the College continue to row on the Thames even today.

C. Olympic boating events are no longer held on the Thames due to varying currents that would cause unfair conditions.

D. At the London Summer Olympics in 1908, the British crew was more successful than those of Canada and the Netherlands.

47. With his work "Reason's Oxymorons" that premiered at the Lyon Biennial art festival in 2015, Kader Attia created an expansive video installation. It contained interviews with philosophers, ethnologists, historians, psychiatrists, psychoanalysts, musicologists, patients, healers, and fetishists. Its volumes are edited following different themes like "Genocide," "Totem and Fetish," "Reason and Politics," or "Trance." Each individually and also as a whole they make up an essay on the psychiatric pathology as it is perceived in traditional Non-Western cultures, on the one hand, and in modern Western societies, on the other. In its mix of rational explanations and irrational representations of what the West calls psychiatry, the work is particularly concerned with the question of the unrepairable, inherent in the idea of "repair" and it calls into question the ambivalence of the psyche of modern Western societies towards traditional Non-Western societies. (*europenowjournal.org*)

A. Kader Attia's work "Reason's Oxymorons" functions as a video library and explores the causes and effects of psychiatric illness.

B. "Reason's Oxymorons" explores the theme of "Genocide" and the way that it was perpetrated historically by Western societies on non-Western societies.

C. Kader Attia has explored the theme of psychiatric pathology using the experience of experts and individuals who have undergone treatment.

D. "Reason's Oxymorons" relies on absurd images of psychiatrists to question the idea that some mental illnesses are fundamentally unrepairable.

48. Researchers used data from the UK's census to examine how health varied across the country, finding that people were more likely to have good health the closer they live to the sea. The analysis also showed that the link between living near the coast and good health was strongest in the most economically deprived communities. The results show that on average, populations living by the sea report rates of good health more than similar populations living inland. The authors were keen to point out that although this effect is relatively small, when applied to the whole population the impacts on public health could be substantial. Along with other studies the

results of this work suggest that access to 'good' environments may have a role in reducing inequality in health between the wealthiest and poorest members of society. (*Science Daily*)

A.   In the UK, living further inland affords higher health benefits than living by the coast.

B.   Researchers believe that some of the features and benefits of living by the sea can be transferred to other locations.

C.   Living near the coast confers good health because it offers stress reduction and cleaner air compared to inland locations.

D.   In the UK, the connection between living near the sea and good health was found to be strongest for the poorest people.

49.   **Painter, provocateur, risk taker and revolutionary, Gustave Courbet might well have said, "I offend; therefore I am." Arguably modern art's original enfant terrible, he had a lust for controversy that makes the careers of more recent shockmeisters like Jeff Koons, Damien Hirst and Robert Mapplethorpe seem almost conventional. As a rebellious teenager from a small town in eastern France, Courbet disregarded his parents' desire for him to study law and vowed, he wrote, "to lead the life of a savage" and free himself from governments. He did not mellow with age, disdaining royal honours, turning out confrontational, even making salacious canvases and attacking established social values when others of his generation were settling into lives cushioned with awards and pensions. As the standard-bearer of a new "realism," which he defined as the representation of familiar things as they are, he would become one of the most innovative and influential painters of mid-19th-century France. (*smithsonianmag.com*)**

A.   Although Courbet originally stated his intent to live the life of a savage, he softened considerably in his later years.

B.   Courbet's rebellious spirit and corresponding vision were precisely what made him such a brilliant modern artist.

C.   Courbet's sometimes salacious paintings were intended to change the public's taste and way of seeing.

D.   Courbet rejected his parents' wish that he study law, instead becoming a key figure of new realism in modern art.

50.   **John Gotti, born in the Bronx on October 27, 1940, was the Boss of the New York City Gambino crime family. He was known for his outspoken personality and flamboyant style, resulting in the nickname, "The Dapper Don." Between 1957 and 1961, Gotti pursued a life of crime on a full-time basis. His arrest record included street fighting, public intoxication, and car theft. By his 21st birthday, Gotti had been arrested five times, but served little gaol time. On March 6, 1962, Gotti married 17-year-old Victoria DiGiorgio. At the time of their marriage, DiGiorgio had already given birth to their first child, Angela, and was pregnant with their second. Gotti briefly tried his hand at legitimate jobs for the sake of his family: first, as a presser in a coat factory, and then as an assistant to a truck driver. In 1992, Gotti was convicted of 13 murders and various other charges and was sentenced to life in prison without parole. He died there 10 years later. (*biography.com*)**

A.   Although Gotti was arrested five times by the time he was 21, he left crime entirely when he married Victoria DiGiorgio.

B.   Born in the Bronx, Gotti was known as "The Dapper Don" and at one time worked in a coat factory.

C.   Although Gotti was arrested many times, no court ever punished him for a crime.

D.   By the time he was 21, Gotti had served five years in prison for public intoxication, street fighting, and car theft.

51.   **A battle-scarred, eighth-century town unearthed in northern Germany may be the earliest Viking settlement in the historical record, archaeologists announced recently. Ongoing excavations at Füsing, near the Danish border, link the site to the "lost" Viking town of Sliasthorp, which was first recorded in AD 804 by royal scribes of the powerful Frankish ruler Charlemagne. Some 30 buildings have been uncovered since excavations began in 2010. Chief among them is a Viking longhouse measuring more than a hundred feet (30 metres)**

long and 30 feet (9 metres) wide. The longhouse's burnt-out remains seemingly bear witness to a violent attack: Arrowheads found embedded in its charred wall posts suggest the communal building was at some point set on fire and shot at, Dobat said. A caltrop – a type of small, spiked iron weapon that was scattered on the ground for the enemy to step on – was also found at the entrance. Other finds include precious jewellery, glass beads, and silver coins. (*National Geographic*)

A. The "lost" Viking town of Sliasthorp, located in Germany near the Danish border, was once visited by Charlemagne.

B. Scribes of the Frankish ruler Charlemagne first recorded the Viking settlement of Sliasthorp in AD 804.

C. The caltrop is a type of large arrowhead weapon that sticks into the walls of wooden buildings like Viking longhouses.

D. Arrowheads found in scorched wall posts of a Viking longhouse indicate that Danish warriors attacked the building.

52. Just days after a poacher's snare had killed one of their own, two young mountain gorillas worked together Tuesday to find and destroy traps in their Rwandan forest home, according to conservationists on the scene. Bush-meat hunters set thousands of rope-and-branch snares in Rwanda's Volcanoes National Park, where the mountain gorillas live. The traps are intended for antelope and other species but sometimes capture the apes. Adults are generally strong enough to free themselves. Youngsters aren't always so lucky. Just last week an ensnared infant named Ngwino, found too late by workers from Karisoke, died of snare-related wounds. Her shoulder had been dislocated during escape attempts, and gangrene had set in after the ropes cut deep into her leg. The hunters seem to have no interest in the gorillas. Even small apes, which would be relatively easy to carry away for sale, are left to die. (*National Geographic*)

A. It is almost always the young male gorillas who dismantle the snares because it is their role to protect the clan.

B. Volcanoes National Park employees look for and dismantle snares, and young gorillas often help them with the task.

C. Poachers in Rwanda set snares to capture young mountain gorillas because they can sell them for large profits.

D. While adult gorillas are often strong enough to free themselves from the snares, young ones often cannot.

53. Rhinovirus infection is linked to about 70 per cent of all asthma exacerbations with more than 50 per cent of these patients requiring hospitalisation. Furthermore, over 35 per cent of patients with acute chronic obstructive pulmonary disease (COPD) are hospitalised each year due to respiratory viruses including rhinovirus. A new antiviral drug to treat rhinovirus infections is being developed by Melbourne company Biota Holdings Ltd, targeted for those with these existing conditions where the common cold is a serious threat to their health and could prove fatal. A team of researchers is now using information on how the new drug works to create a 3D simulation of the complete rhinovirus using Australia's fastest supercomputer. (*Science Daily*)

A. Every year, nearly one in four patients with COPD are hospitalised due to respiratory viruses such as rhinovirus.

B. The antiviral drug being developed by Biota Holdings Ltd disables rhinovirus by binding to the shell that surrounds it.

C. Using Australia's supercomputer technology allows researchers to monitor how a drug will work at a molecular level.

D. For individuals with asthma and COPD, respiratory viruses such as rhinovirus can be extremely serious and even fatal.

54. Climate change has had a significant impact on the timing of river floods across Europe over the past 50 years, according to a new study. In some regions, such as southern England, floods are now occurring 15 days earlier than they did half a century ago; however, around the North Sea, in the Netherlands, Denmark and Scotland, the trend is towards later floods. The scientists believe this is due to changes in the North Atlantic Oscillation (NAO), the weather phenomenon that

pushes storms across the ocean into Europe. The study has been published in the journal Science. Floods caused by rivers impact more people than any other natural hazard, and the estimated global damages run to roughly a 100 billion dollars a year. (*BBC News online*)

A.   Scientists have found that climate change is usually resulting in later flooding in Europe.

B.   Floods caused by rivers result in estimated damage of nearly 100 billion dollars to European economies every year.

C.   Changes in the North Atlantic Oscillation may be causing later river floods in northern European countries.

D.   In southern England river floods are now occurring at a much earlier time than river floods in Scotland.

55.   The third plague pandemic lasted roughly from 1855 to 1959 and marked the first time that bubonic plague reached all inhabited continents, leaving more than 12 million dead. Plague made its first major appearance in the Crown Colony of Hong Kong in 1894. It then spread first to India (1896) and then, rapidly, on a global scale; between 1898 and 1900 alone it struck Hawaii, California, Manchuria, Australia, Madagascar, Paraguay, Portugal, Scotland, Egypt, and Japan. During its course the third plague pandemic functioned as a catalyst for major public health and urban planning reforms, colonial policies, geopolitical struggles, and medical theories and techniques. This was not simply on account of the mortality and morbidity crisis in different parts of the world induced by plague. It was also because incidents of this pandemic were systematically photographed and documented from beginning to end, with images from local outbreaks making newspaper headlines across the globe. (*Royal Historical Society website*)

A.   The third plague pandemic spread quickly around the globe due to colonialism and global conflict.

B.   The third plague pandemic started in Hong Kong in roughly 1894 and then spread to India in 1896.

C.   The third plague pandemic was widely documented during the course of 1855 to 1959.

D.   The third plague pandemic reached Europe in 1898 when outbreaks occurred in Portugal and Scotland.

56.   A recently published study examined how decision-making would be affected by a human-like aid. The study focused on adults' trust, dependence, and performance while using a computerised decision-making aid for persons with diabetes. The study is one of the first to examine how the design of decision-support aids on consumer devices can influence the level of trust that users place in that system and how much they use it. Many people interact with computerised decision aids or automation on a daily basis, whether they're using smart phones, digital cameras or global positioning systems. When automation is only reliable sometimes, a person's level of trust becomes an important factor that determines how often the aid will be used. The research findings have revealed that the inclusion of an image of a person can significantly alter perceptions of a computerised aid when there is no difference in the aid's reliability or presentation of information. (*Science Daily*)

A.   An individual's level of trust in computerised decision aids has influence on how they use a device.

B.   An individual's level of trust in computerised decision aids is highly influenced by the design used.

C.   Research shows that computerised decision-making aids that include an image of a person change how such an aid is perceived.

D.   Research shows that human-like computerised decision aids may reduce decision-making reaction time for adults.

57.   In all, Francis of Assisi, noted ascetic, holy man and future saint, found that he bore five marks: two on his palms and two on his feet, where the nails that fixed Christ to the cross were traditionally believed to have been hammered home, and the fifth on his side, where the Bible says Jesus had received a spear thrust from a Roman centurion. This was the first case of stigmata – the appearance of marks or actual wounds paralleling those Christ

received during Crucifixion – described. Later stigmatics (and there have been several hundred of them) have exhibited similar marks, though some bear only one or two wounds, while others also display scratches on their foreheads, where Christ would have been injured by his crown of thorns. Through the centuries, stigmata has become one of the best-documented, and most controversial, of mystical phenomena. The extensive record makes it possible to compare cases that occurred centuries apart. At least ten more were recorded in the 13th century. (*smithsonianmag.com*)

A.   Stigmatics bear the five marks that mimic those wounds that Christ received during the Crucifixion.

B.   Among the stigmata marks borne by ascetic and holy man Francis of Assisi were scratches on his forehead.

C.   Stigmata is a controversial mystical occurrence that has been reportedly experienced by several hundred individuals.

D.   Francis of Assisi, who has been recognized as a saint, was the first person to bear the wounds of Christ.

58.   Modern cats diverged in skull shape from their sabre-toothed ancestors early in their evolutionary history and then followed separate evolutionary trajectories, according to new research. The study also found that the separation between modern domestic cats and big cats such as lions and tigers is also deeply rooted. Scientists studied the skull shape of extinct sabre-toothed cats, modern (conical-toothed) cats and prehistoric 'basal' cats (ancestors of modern cats). This is the first time these three different types of cats have been analysed together in a single dataset. The researchers quantified skull shape by taking various measurements, adjusting these measurements for size differences, then investigating the distribution of cat skulls in shape-space. They found an early and conspicuous divergence between the conical-toothed cats and sabre-toothed cats, with all sabre-toothed cats being more closely related to each other than they were to modern conical-toothed cats. (*Science Daily*)

A.   Their parallel evolutionary trajectories underlie the close connection between modern big cats such as lions and tigers and modern domestic cats.

B.   Despite the divergence between the skull shapes of extinct sabre-toothed cats and modern domestic cats, these two different types of cats are closely related to each other.

C.   Skull shape indicates that all types of sabre-toothed cats were more closely related to one another than to modern conical-toothed cats.

D.   The skull shapes of sabre-toothed and conical-toothed cats indicate that they followed different evolutionary trajectories.

59.   Future high-energy accelerators will need stronger magnetic fields and the magnets of the future will most probably be manufactured from high-temperature superconductors (HTS). These materials are thus named because they exhibit superconducting behaviour at higher temperatures than niobium-titanium and niobium-tin, which are both known as low-temperature superconductors (LTS) and must operate at extremely low temperatures to reach and retain their superconductive state. In the Large Hadron Collider, which is the world's largest and most powerful particle accelerator, for example, the niobium-tin magnets are cooled to just 1.9 Kelvin (–271.3 °C) using liquid helium as a coolant. Above a critical temperature and above a critical magnetic field, the superconductors fail to maintain their superconductive state, and stop operating correctly (they are said to undergo a "quench"), which is very undesirable behaviour for a magnet, because it results in the appearance of voltage and a rapid temperature increase. (*European Organization for Nuclear Research*)

A.   Niobium-tin magnets are likely to undergo a quench when operating at a temperature of 1.9 Kelvin (–271.3 °C).

B.   Niobium-titanium and niobium-tin are both low-temperature superconductors used in the magnets of the Large Hadron Collider.

C.   Liquid helium is used as a coolant in the Large Hadron Collider because alternative coolants cannot achieve a temperature of 1.9 Kelvin (–271.3 °C).

D.   Low-temperature superconductors only work properly within a critical range of temperature and magnetic field.

60. The massive population decline of Lord Howe Island stick insects began with a shipwreck in 1918, on their namesake Lord Howe Island, a small, lush landmass jutting out of the ocean off the east coast of Australia. The ship contained a horde of rats that quickly invaded. With no larger mammals to predate on the rats, their population exploded. The stick insect was eventually classified as extinct in 1983. In 1960, a group of rock climbers visited another small volcanic rock island nearby, named Ball's Pyramid. It was there that they found what appeared to be the dead remains of the "extinct" stick creatures. It wasn't until 2001 that researchers returned to Ball's Pyramid. Atop a tea tree, 213 feet above sea level, sat a few living examples of what appeared to be Lord Howe Island stick insects. However, the identity of the insects has been the subject of debate. Visually, the captive-bred stick insects looked different. It wasn't until genome sequencing was conducted on both museum specimens and the captive-bred stick insects that scientists realised they had a less than one percent genetic variance—enough to officially classify them as the same species. (*nationalgeographic.com*)

A. In 1960 stick insects were found on Ball's Pyramid, a rocky outcrop on Lord Howe Island.

B. The rock climbers retrieved samples of what appeared to be the extinct stick insects.

C. Until the rats came along, the Lord Howe Island stick insects had no large predators.

D. The scientists compared the extinct samples to the living stick insects to find they are of the same species.

61. The biggest known crocodile has been found – and the 8.3-metre-long predator likely swallowed early humans whole, a new study says. *Crocodylus thorbjarnarsoni* lurked in deep lakes near present-day Lake Turkana in Kenya between about two and four million years ago. According to research, the ancient animal would have resembled a heavyset Nile crocodile, some of which can reach up to 6 metres long. Other species in the wider category of crocodyliforms – part of a group that includes modern-day alligators, caimans, and more – are bigger,

such as the 12-metre-long SuperCroc. The prehistoric reptile likely got so big from eating plentiful large prey – including our ancestors, who at the time stood about 1.2 metres tall as adults. When *C. thorbjarnarsoni* gobbled an early human, "the whole thing [probably went] down the gullet, so nothing gets fossilized," said Hastings, who discovered a prehistoric crocodile species in 2011. (*National Geographic*)

A. The giant *Crocodylus thorbjarnarsoni* likely ambushed our 1.2-metre tall ancestors when they went to collect water.

B. *Crocodylus thorbjarnarsoni* is the biggest species in the category of crocodyliforms, which also includes caimans.

C. *Crocodylus thorbjarnarsoni*, the largest crocodile known, is a distant ancestor of the Nile crocodile.

D. The 8.3-metre-long *C. thorbjarnarsoni* lived about two to four million years ago in lake waters of present-day Kenya.

62. In 1848, the British East India Company sent Robert Fortune on a trip to China's interior, an area forbidden to foreigners. Fortune's mission was to steal the secrets of tea horticulture and manufacturing. The Scotsman donned a disguise and headed into the Wu Si Shan hills in a bold act of corporate espionage. Although the concept of tea is simple – dry leaf infused in hot water – the manufacture of it is not intuitive at all. Tea is a highly processed product. At the time of Fortune's visit the recipe for tea had remained unchanged for two thousand years, and Europe had been addicted to it for at least two hundred of them. But few in Britain's dominions had any firsthand or even secondhand information about the production of tea before it went into the pot. Fortune's horticultural contemporaries in London and the directors of the East India Company all believed that tea would yield its secrets if it were held up to the clear light and scrutiny of Western science. (*smithsonianmag.com*)

A. Robert Fortune's "corporate espionage" trip to China was the first attempt by the British East India Company to steal the secrets of tea horticulture and manufacturing.

B. Tea is nothing more than an infusion of dry leaf in hot water, and the process of manufacturing tea is just as simple.

C. In 1848 when Robert Fortune visited the Wu Si Shan hills of China, the recipe for tea had not changed for two thousand years.

D. In 1848 within the British East India Company, only a few people had firsthand or secondhand knowledge of tea production.

63. Text messaging may offer tweens a quick way to send notes to friends and family, but it could lead to declining language and grammar skills, according to researchers. Tweens who frequently use language adaptations – "techspeak" – when they text performed poorly on a grammar test, said Drew Cingel, a former undergraduate student in communications, Penn State, and currently a doctoral candidate in media, technology and society, Northwestern University. When tweens write in techspeak, they often use shortcuts, such as homophones and omissions of non-essential letters and initials, to quickly and efficiently compose a text message. "Overall, there is evidence of a decline in grammar scores based on the number of adaptations in sent text messages, controlling for age and grade," Cingel said. Not only did frequent texting negatively predict the test results, but both sending and receiving text adaptations were associated with how poorly they performed on the test, according to Sundar. (*Science Daily*)

A. Research shows that tweens who text daily with friends and family are better adapted socially but perform less efficiently on grammar than their peers.

B. Studies show that how tweens perform on a grammar test is unrelated to how many text adaptations they send and receive.

C. Research shows that tweens who use techspeak when texting could experience a decline in grammar and language skills.

D. According to research, the use of techspeak is the primary reason for the decline in grammar scores among tweens.

64. Embedding family doctors in casualty departments to free up emergency staff slashes waiting times and hospital admissions for children, but increases antibiotic prescriptions, a study has shown. The measure follows an ongoing increase in casualty department admissions as they struggle to cope with the numbers. Two researchers had this to say: "The results presented in this study highlight both advantages and challenges", said Professor Taylor. "During this period patients seen by the family doctor were significantly less likely to be admitted, exceed the four-hour waiting target or leave before being seen. However, they were more likely to receive antibiotics."

"The most common medical presentations in emergency departments are breathing difficulty, febrile illness, diarrhoea and vomiting, abdominal pain, seizures and rash, all of which could be potentially serious", said Professor Carroll. "Long wait times and overcrowding in emergency departments are associated with delays in delivering urgent treatments such as antibiotics for sepsis." (*www.telegraph.co.uk*)

A. It is likely that casualty departments will reduce the use of family doctors after this report.

B. Professor Taylor and Professor Carroll disagree on the value of the increased use of antibiotics in casualty departments.

C. Family doctors working in casualty departments have had some positive effects, according to research.

D. Embedding family doctors in casualty departments has led to a major increase in the use of antibiotics in hospitals.

65. The job of a renaissance court portraitist was to produce likenesses of his sovereigns to display at the palace and give to foreign dignitaries or prospective brides. It went without saying the portraits should be flattering. Yet, in 1590, Giuseppe Arcimboldo painted his royal patron, the Holy Roman Emperor Rudolf II, as a heap of fruits and vegetables. With pea pod eyelids and a gourd for a forehead, he looks less like a king than a crudité platter. Lucky for Arcimboldo, Rudolf had a sense of humour. Arcimboldo served the Hapsburg family for more than 25 years, creating oddball "composite heads" made of sea creatures, flowers, dinner roasts and other materials. Part scientist, part

sycophant, part visionary, Arcimboldo was born in 1526 in Milan. Giuseppe's father was also an artist, and Giuseppe's early career suggests the young man designed cathedral windows and tapestries rife with angels, saints and evangelists. Though apples and lemons appear in some of the divine scenes, the produce is, comparatively, less remarkable than that of the fruit portraits. (*smithsonianmag.com*)

A.   Giuseppe was not only a visionary painter and a scientist, but evidence suggests that he also designed tapestries.

B.   Giuseppe most likely learned from his father how to paint sea creatures, flowers, dinner roasts, pea pods, gourds, and more.

C.   In 1590, Arcimboldo painted Holy Roman Emperor Rudolf II at the emperor's request.

D.   From the beginning of his career as an artist, Arcimboldo used only fruits and vegetables as the elements of his works.

66.   What does a robot feel when it touches something? Researchers published a study showing that a specially designed robot can outperform humans in identifying a wide range of natural materials according to their textures, paving the way for advancements in prostheses, personal assistive robots and consumer product testing. The robot was equipped with a new type of tactile sensor built to mimic the human fingertip. So, is touch another task that humans will outsource to robots? Fishel and Loeb point out that while their robot is very good at identifying which textures are similar to each other, it has no way to tell what textures people will prefer. Instead, they say this robot touch technology could be used in human prostheses or to assist companies who employ experts to assess the feel of consumer products and even human skin. (*Science Daily*)

A.   A robot with a special tactile sensor that simulates the fingertip of a human can outperform humans in identifying materials.

B.   Robots with a special tactile sensor could be used to advance some types of health products or assist with testing consumer products.

C.   Robots with a special tactile sensor are able to identify many materials including plastic, wood, wool, silk, and polyester.

D.   Robots with a special tactile sensor can outperform humans at jobs that deal with texture comparison and people's texture preferences.

67.   A new study concludes that among older adults – especially those who are frail – low levels of vitamin D can mean a much greater risk of death. The randomised, nationally representative study found that older adults with low vitamin D levels had a 30 per cent greater risk of death than people who had higher levels. Overall, people who were frail had more than double the risk of death than those who were not frail. Frail adults with low levels of vitamin D tripled their risk of death over people who were not frail and who had higher levels of vitamin D. Because of the cross-sectional nature of the survey, researchers could not determine if low vitamin D contributed to frailty, or whether frail people became vitamin D deficient because of health problems. However, Smit said the longitudinal analysis on death showed it may not matter which came first. (*Science Daily*)

A.   Individuals who are frail develop vitamin D deficiency primarily because of their health problems.

B.   Frail older adults with low vitamin D levels are three times as likely to die as those who are not frail and have higher levels.

C.   According to the new study, older adults with low vitamin D levels faced a lower risk of dying than those with higher levels.

D.   According to most studies, researchers have concluded that low vitamin D levels contribute to frailty in older adults.

68.   Mariza, the internationally known Portuguese singer, is captivating yet another audience with the haunting sounds of fado – the music called the soul of Portugal and often compared to American blues. As her voice fills the hall – alternately whispering and shouting, rejoicing and lamenting – the wildly receptive audience confirms her rising reputation as the new queen of fado, and the genre's increasing world appeal. The roots of fado, Portuguese for fate or destiny, are a mystery. But musicologists see it as an amalgam of cultures, especially African and Brazilian,

stemming from Portugal's maritime and colonial past, combined with its oral poetry tradition and, possibly, some Berber-Arab influence from the long Moorish presence that spanned the 8th through the 13th centuries. In the 19th century, fado became popular among the urban poor of Lisbon. It was sung in bars, back streets and brothels. (*smithsonainmag.com*)

A. The urban poor of 19th-century Lisbon were drawn to fado because they could sing it any time or place.

B. According to musicologists, fado comes from just Portuguese, Moorish, and Berber-Arab cultures and oral poetry traditions.

C. Fado music is currently more popular around the world than it was among the urban poor of 19th-century Lisbon.

D. Fado, which means "fate" or "destiny" in Portuguese, is called the soul of Portugal and is compared to American blues.

69. Autism spectrum disorders, including Asperger syndrome, have generally been associated with uneven intellectual profiles and impairment, but according to a new study of Asperger individuals, this may not be the case – as long as intelligence is evaluated by the right test. Both autistic and Asperger individuals display uneven profiles of performance in commonly used intelligence test batteries such as Wechsler scales, and their strongest performances are often considered evidence for deficits. However, this study reports that Asperger individuals' scores are much higher when they are evaluated by a test called Raven's Progressive Matrices, which encompasses reasoning, novel problem-solving abilities, and high-level abstraction. By comparison, scores for non-Asperger individuals are much more consistent across different tests. (*Science Daily*)

A. A recent study of Asperger individuals suggests that the measure of intelligence is exactly quantifiable.

B. Asperger individuals score higher than non-Asperger individuals on the Raven's Progressive Matrices test.

C. In general Asperger individuals score more unevenly on different types of intelligence tests than their non-Asperger peers.

D. High-level abstraction and the ability to solve novel problems are considered higher forms of intelligence.

70. Few insects capture the imagination like bees do. Honeybees (*Apis mellifera*) in particular, with their social hierarchy and sweet product, have long been part of our literary and agricultural heritage. Honeybees are the workhorses of modern farms, which rely on them to pollinate crops. That dependence has made reports of declining bee populations and colony collapse all the more alarming. Although bees are known to be affected by environmental shifts, including habitat loss and climate change, public attention has been focused on a class of pesticide called neonicotinoids, or neonics. But the link between these pesticides and colony collapse remains obscure. Daunting as the prospect is of losing our main pollinators, the furore has masked wider issues. Not only honeybees are at risk – solitary bees face greater threats. Like humans, bees have microbes in their guts that provide a host of benefits, and studying the honeybee provides insights into how biological and synthetic systems interact. (*nature.com*)

A. The interaction of biological and synthetic systems within the gut of a bee can prove as harmful to a bee as it is for a human.

B. The decline in the honeybee population means they may be wiped out altogether in some areas.

C. Solitary bees face the same threat as honeybees as environmental changes lead to the loss of their natural habitat.

D. Neonicotinoids have been linked with the decline in the number of bees, however this link has not been categorically confirmed.

71. Superconductivity is one of the most fascinating phenomena known to humankind. When a superconductor is cooled below its 'critical temperature', the fluid of electrons, which is responsible for the conduction of electricity through the material, undergoes a radical re-organisation. The electrons form 'Cooper pairs' and these Cooper pairs condense into a single, collective quantum state, which means they all behave as a single entity. This allows the manifestation of quantum-mechanical effects, which

are normally confined to the world of sub-microscopic particles, on a scale that is visible to the naked eye. While in conventional superconductors (and also in some high-temperature superconductors) the electrons in a Cooper pair have their intrinsic 'spins' pointing in opposite directions, so that the total spin of the Cooper pair is zero, in other, more exotic 'triplet' superconductors the electronic spins line up, so the Cooper pair has some intrinsic spin of its own. (*Science Daily*)

A.   Electrons that form Cooper pairs act as one entity, rendering quantum-mechanical effects visible to the naked eye.

B.   In conventional superconductors, the electrons form Cooper pairs so that the electronic spins form a cloud.

C.   In triplet superconductors, Cooper pairs allow for quantum-mechanical effects, but they are not visible to the naked eye.

D.   Conventional, high-temperature, and triplet superconductors all cannot operate above the same critical temperature.

72.   Once a required stop on caravan routes that brought Asian goods west to eager Romans, Palmyra has "always been conceived as an oasis in the middle of the desert, but it's never been quite clear what it was living from," said Michal Gawlikowski, the retired head of the University of Warsaw's Polish Mission at Palmyra. And what an oasis: Among the ruins are grand avenues lined with columns, triumphal arches, and the remains of an ancient market where traders once haggled over silk, silver, spices, and dyes from India and China. The landscape around the city, it now appears, was intensively farmed and most likely included olive, fig, and pistachio groves-crops known in the region from Roman accounts and still common in Syria. Barley too was grown, according to a pollen analysis Meyer's team conducted on a mud brick from the survey area. (*National Geographic*)

A.   Palmyra served not only as a caravan stop but it was most likely an agricultural centre of the region thanks to the intensive cultivation.

B.   Ancient residents of Palmyra likely grew a number of different crops in the surrounding area including figs and barley.

C.   Ancient residents of Palmyra likely captured the small amount of annual rainfall to water their crops and pistachio groves.

D.   Palmyra once served as a caravan stop where traders bargained over silks, spices, and other goods from all over the world.

73.   Several centuries ago, many practising Christians, and those of other religions, had a strong belief that the Devil could give certain people known as witches the power to harm others in return for their loyalty. A "witchcraft craze" rippled through Europe from the 1300s to the end of the 1600s. Tens of thousands of supposed witches – mostly women – were executed. Though the Salem trials came on just as the European craze was winding down, local circumstances explain their onset. The Salem witch trials occurred in colonial Massachusetts between 1692 and 1693. More than 200 people were accused of practising witchcraft – the Devil's magic – and 20 were executed. Eventually, the colony admitted the trials were a mistake and compensated the families of those convicted. Since then, the story of the trials has become synonymous with paranoia and injustice, and it continues to beguile the popular imagination more than 300 years later. (*smithsonianmag. com*)

A.   The "witchcraft craze" in Europe between the 13th and 16th centuries was the gravest period in the history of witch-hunts.

B.   More than 200 accused witches were executed in the Salem trials in colonial Massachusetts between 1692 and 1693.

C.   Colonial Massachusetts ultimately acknowledged that the witch trials were an error and recompensed families of the convicted.

D.   Practising Christians in Europe were largely responsible for stirring up paranoia about witches.

74.   For the first four decades of competition, the Olympics awarded official medals for painting, sculpture, architecture, literature and music, alongside those for the athletic competitions. From 1912 to 1952, juries awarded a total of 151 medals to original works in the fine arts inspired by athletic endeavours. The story goes all the way back to the

Baron Pierre de Coubertin, the founder of the IOC and the modern Games, who saw art competitions as integral to his vision of the Olympics. "He was raised and educated classically, and he was particularly impressed with the idea of what it meant to be a true Olympian – someone who was not only athletic, but skilled in music and literature," Stanton says. "He felt that in order to recreate the events in modern times, it would be incomplete to not include some aspect of the arts." (*smithsonianmag.com*)

A. For the first four decades of the Olympics, juries awarded medals for works of fine art depicting any subject matter.

B. Between 1912 and 1952, Olympic juries awarded 151 medals to gifted artists who were also highly skilled athletes.

C. Baron Pierre de Coubertin felt that the modern Olympics would not be complete without some inclusion of the arts.

D. For the first four decades of the Olympics, the majority of art medals were awarded for paintings of the games themselves.

75. Nicolaus Copernicus was the first to demonstrate that the earth orbited the sun, upsetting the prevailing notion that the earth was the centre of the cosmos. A 30-year project, *On the Revolutions of the Heavenly Spheres* was Copernicus' response to the unwieldy mathematics used since the days of the ancient Greeks to explain the motion of the sun, moon and five known planets (Mercury, Venus, Mars, Jupiter and Saturn). Astronomers had worked from the assumption that the earth was the centre of the universe, forcing them to draw convoluted orbits for the planets, which even had to reverse directions for the theory to be consistent with their observed trajectories. Once Copernicus put the sun at the centre of the picture and adjusted the mathematics, the planetary orbits became regular, smooth and elegant. His inspiration came early, but the cautious scholar took half a lifetime to check his figures before publishing them in 1543, the year he died at age 70. (*smithsonianmag.com*)

A. Nicolaus Copernicus used convoluted mathematics and planetary orbits to demonstrate that the earth orbited the sun.

B. Copernicus delayed publishing his conclusions until he was 70 because he was cautious about his calculations and feared he would be persecuted as a heretic for his work.

C. Prior to Copernicus, astronomers used mathematics and complex planetary orbits to deduce that the earth was the centre of the universe.

D. Prior to Copernicus, astronomers had most likely explained the motions of heavenly bodies using mathematics dating to the ancient Greeks.

76. Pavegen tiles are designed to collect the kinetic energy created by the estimated 40 million pedestrians who will use that walkway in a year, generating several hundred kilowatt-hours of electricity from their footsteps. Once a Pavegen tile converts energy to electricity, 5 per cent of it is used to light the round LED-lighted logo in the centre of each tile. The other 95 per cent is either directly fed to the application or stored in a battery for later use. Pavegen is also working on a new system that will feed the power directly into a grid. The tiles are completely waterproof, so they can endure rain, snow, and ice. Pavegen's tiles are designed to have a minimal carbon footprint. All of the rubber comes from recycled truck tires, and about 80 per cent of the polymers used for the other components can be recycled. On average, one footstep generates 7 watts of electricity, though the amount varies depending on a person's weight. (*National Geographic*)

A. The amount of electricity generated by a person's single footstep depends solely on that person's weight.

B. Pavegen tiles are made with rubber from recycled tires and have a carbon footprint that is less than that of any other energy source.

C. The more recyclable components an energy source contains, the less carbon footprint it has.

D. Pavegen tiles are waterproof, have a minimal carbon footprint, and collect an average of 7 watts of electricity per footstep.

77. UC Irvine scientists have discovered intriguing differences in the brains and mental processes of an extraordinary group of people who can effortlessly recall every moment of their lives since about age 10. All had variations in nine structures of their brains compared

to those of control subjects, including more robust white matter linking the middle and front parts. Surprisingly, the people with stellar autobiographical memory did not score higher on routine laboratory memory tests or when asked to use rote memory aids. Yet when it came to public or private events that occurred after age 10½, they were remarkably better at recalling the details of their lives. The study also found statistically significant evidence of obsessive-compulsive tendencies among the group, but the authors do not yet know if or how this aids recollection. Many of the individuals have large, minutely catalogued collections of some sort, such as magazines, videos, shoes, stamps or postcards. (*Science Daily*)

A. People with remarkable autobiographical memories are more likely to have obsessive-compulsive tendencies than control subjects.

B. Obsessive-compulsive behaviours share the same neural pathways as those used to store and recall autobiographical memories.

C. The brains of people with extraordinary autobiographical memories may have larger prefrontal lobes than those of control subjects.

D. People who could remember every moment of their lives from around age 10 also scored higher when using rote memory aids.

78. Music was a key ingredient in ancient Egyptian religion. Teeter explains that it was believed to soothe the gods and encourage them to provide for their worshippers. Nehemes-Bastet was one of many priestess-musicians who performed inside the sanctuaries and in the courts of the temples. The musical instruments typically used were the menat, a multi-strand beaded necklace they would shake, and the sistrum, a handheld rattle whose sound was said to evoke wind rustling through papyrus reeds. Other musicians would have played drums, harps, and lutes during religious processions. "For years people have debated what kind of music it was," says Teeter. "But there's no musical notation left, and we're not sure how they tuned the instruments or whether they sang or chanted." The emphasis was definitely on percussion. Images often show people stamping their feet and clapping. Examples of

song lyrics are recorded on temple walls. (*archaeology.org*)

A. In ancient Egypt, priestesses and musicians both sang and chanted during religious ceremonies.

B. Evidence recorded on temple walls suggests that ancient Egyptian music was like an early form of modern percussion music.

C. Music in ancient Egypt accompanied religious processions and was made using the menat and the sistrum and probably drums, lutes, and harps.

D. Musical instruments of ancient Egypt include the menat, a necklace that might have also had a decorative function.

79. The European Union has signed a fisheries agreement with Mauritania in west Africa. The total cost to the EU budget for fishing rights off the coast of the former French colony will be €70 million per year, according to the European Commission. The agreement allows EU ships to fish for demersal – a group of fish that lives or feeds near the bottom of the sea. Though the annual payment to the Mauritanian government will remain the same, access to fish has been reduced. Fish can now only be caught more than 20 miles from the shore, up from 13 miles in the previous agreement. There is also a new requirement that 2% of the catch must be given to the Mauritanian government. "The EU will pay the same amount of money but for much less fish," said Gerard van Balsfoort of the Pelagic Freezer-Trawler Association. "50–60% of the fleet was catching between 13 and 20 miles from the shore." Balsfoort said the restrictions will make the fishing rights worthless to EU fishermen. (*European Voice*)

A. Under a new fisheries agreement with Mauritania, the EU will no longer have to give 2% of its catch to Mauritania.

B. The new fisheries agreement does not allow the EU to catch fish between 13 miles and 20 miles from the shore because it is Mauritania's richest fishing area.

C. The EU will pay €70 million per year for fishing rights off the coast of Mauritania, including rights to fish for demersal.

D.	Although Gerard van Balsfoort has been critical of the fishing agreement, a sizeable portion of fishermen may support it.

80.	**Many of the predictions we make in everyday life are vague, and many of them are wrong – like when we predict the weather – because we have incomplete information. But in quantum mechanics, the outcomes of certain experiments generally can't be predicted perfectly beforehand, even if all of the information is available. This inability to accurately predict the results of experiments in quantum physics has been the subject of a long debate, going back to Einstein and his co-workers, about whether quantum mechanics is the best way to predict outcomes. Randomness in quantum theory is one of its key features and is widely recognized, even outside the scientific community, says Tittel. "Its appeal is its fundamental nature and broad range of implications: knowing the precise configuration of the universe at the big bang would not be sufficient to predict its entire evolution, for example, in contrast to classical theory." (*Science Daily*)**

A.	Randomness is a central feature of quantum theory with practical applications for fields as diverse as chemistry and politics.

B.	The question of whether quantum mechanics offers the best way to predict outcomes dates to Einstein and his colleagues.

C.	Per quantum theory, if the universe's exact arrangement at the time of the big bang was known, its evolution could be partly predicted.

D.	According to quantum mechanics, if you know all the available information at the outset, you will be able to accurately predict an outcome.

81.	**Consider Jan Lievens, born in Leiden in western Holland on October 24, 1607, just 15 months after the birth of Rembrandt van Rijn, another Leiden native. While the two were alive, admirers spoke of them in the same breath, and the comparisons were not always in Rembrandt's favour. After their deaths, Lievens dropped out of sight – for centuries. Though the artists took quite different paths, their biographies show many parallels. Both**
served apprenticeships in Amsterdam with the same master, returned to that city later in life and died there in their 60s. The work the two produced in their early 20s in Leiden was not always easy to tell apart, and as time went on, many a superior Lievens was misattributed to Rembrandt. Quality aside, it mattered that Rembrandt spent virtually his entire career in one place, cultivating a single, highly personal style, whereas Lievens moved around, absorbing many different influences. Equally important, Rembrandt lent himself to the role of the lonely genius, a figure dear to the Romantics, whose preferences would shape the tastes of generations to come. (*smithsonianmag.com*)**

A.	Had Lievens developed a single personal style as a painter, he would have stolen the cloak of fame from Rembrandt.

B.	Although Lievens and Rembrandt produced work that is remarkably similar, critics of their time universally favoured Rembrandt.

C.	Rembrandt and Lievens were both born in Leiden, apprenticed with the same master, and created some works of great similarity.

D.	Lievens' life centred on continuous change, which put him out of favour with the Romantics who idolised the lonely genius.

82.	**Human diversity in Africa is greater than in any other place on Earth. Differing food sources, geographies, diseases and climates offered many opportunities for natural selection to force Africans to change and adapt to their local environments. The individuals who adapted best were the most likely to reproduce and pass on their genomes to the generations who followed. A recent study identifies several million previously unknown genetic mutations in humans. It finds evidence that the direct ancestors of modern humans may have interbred with members of an unknown ancestral group of hominids. It suggests that different groups evolved distinctly in order to reap nutrition from local foods and defend against infectious disease. "A message we're seeing is that even though all the individuals we sampled are hunter-gatherers, natural selection has acted differently in these different groups." (*Science Daily*)**

A. Evidence indicates that ancestors of modern humans who did not interbreed with different hominid groups failed to evolve.

B. A recent study suggests that in human evolution, natural selection functioned the same in different hunter-gatherer groups.

C. A recent study suggests that humans evolved differently in order to maximise sources of nutrition and defend against diseases.

D. Early hunter-gatherers who had access to the most diverse food sources and lived in the most temperate climates were most likely to reproduce, according to one study.

83. Each new woolly mammoth carcass to emerge from the Siberian permafrost triggers a flurry of speculation about resurrecting this Ice Age giant. The two fundamental steps involved in cloning a mammoth, or any other extinct animal, are to recover its complete DNA sequence – in the case of mammoths, estimated to be more than 4.5 billion base pairs long – and to express this data in flesh and blood. The publication of the partial mammoth genome is a good start on the first problem, though the remaining 30 per cent of the genome would have to be recovered and the entire genome resequenced several more times to weed out errors. Scientists would also have to package the DNA into chromosomes – and at present they don't even know how many chromosomes the mammoth had. Yet none of these tasks appears insurmountable, especially in light of recent technical advances, such as a new generation of high-speed sequencers and a simple, inexpensive technique for recovering high-quality DNA from mammoth hair. (*National Geographic*)

A. Despite recent promising advances in technology, resurrecting a woolly mammoth in flesh and blood is not likely to happen.

B. Scientists have already sequenced part of the woolly mammoth's DNA but still have to work out how many chromosomes it had.

C. Scientists will be able to recover the 30 per cent of the mammoth genome that remains unknown from mammoth skin cells or mammoth hair.

D. Cloning a mammoth involves recovering its full DNA sequence and then recreating both male and female sex cells of the animal.

84. Harriet Menloy established the modern British field of inequality and poverty studies. She has worked on inequality and poverty for over five decades. Harriet's work is predominantly focused on income distributions and the economics of public policy for third world countries, from which an inequality measure was named after her: the Menloy index. In her recent book *"Inequality: options and strategies for reform"*, she argues that high levels of inequality are not inevitable and that policies can be designed to make our societies both more equitable and more efficient. Harriet's protégé Kingly Fisher's work is predominantly focused on macro and development economics. Much of his work concerns understanding the determinants of cross-country income differences, in particular arguing that financial underdevelopment is an important determinant of poverty and examining the effects of policies in the presence of such financial underdevelopment. His work analyses the causes and consequences of inequality within developed countries. (*eib.org*)

A. Harriet's strategies for reform have had a positive impact on society where implemented, making it both more equitable and efficient.

B. The Menloy index was named after her by Harriet Menloy's protégé Kingly Fisher.

C. Kingly's work only concerns the causes and effects of inequality in developing countries.

D. Kingly's position on the causes of poverty revolves around the consequences of financial underdevelopment.

85. The Rev. Charles Lutwidge Dodgson was a teacher of mathematics at Oxford and a deacon of the Anglican Church. Some colleagues knew him as a somewhat reclusive stammerer, but he was generally seen as a devout scholar; one dean said he was "pure in heart." To readers all over the world, he became renowned as Lewis Carroll, the author of *Alice's Adventures in Wonderland*. *Alice* was popular almost from the moment it was published, in 1865, and it has remained in print ever since, influencing such disparate artists as Walt Disney and Salvador Dali. Charles Dodgson was born in 1832 in Daresbury, a village in northwest

England. After enrolling at Oxford in 1850, at age 18, Dodgson became a "senior student" at the university's College of Christ Church. According to college rules, senior students had to be ordained as priests and take a vow of celibacy; Dodgson evaded the ordination rule and lived at the college unmarried, until his death in 1898, less than two weeks before his 66th birthday. (*smithsonianmag.com*)

A.   Charles Lutwidge Dodgson, who used the pseudonym Lewis Carroll, was viewed as a serious scholar, a solitary man with a good heart and a stammerer.

B.   Many of the characters in *Alice's Adventures in Wonderland* may have been inspired by the priests and academics that Charles Lutwidge Dodgson knew.

C.   Charles Lutwidge Dodgson devoted much of his life to the craft of writing, though he did not publish much of his work.

D.   Lewis Carroll's *Alice's Adventures in Wonderland* influenced Walt Disney, Salvador Dali and American filmmaker Tim Burton, among others.

86.   Researchers have developed a way for security systems to combine different biometric measurements – such as eye colour, face shape or fingerprints – and create a learning system that simulates the brain in making decisions. The algorithm can learn new biometric patterns and associate data from different data sets, allowing the system to combine information, such as fingerprint, voice, gait or facial features, instead of relying on a single set of measurements. The key is in the ability to combine features from multiple sources of information, prioritise them by identifying more important/prevalent features to learn and adapt the decision-making to changing conditions. Biometric information is becoming more common in our daily lives, being incorporated in drivers' licences, passports and other forms of identification. The work is not only pioneering the intelligent decision-making methodology for human recognition but is also important for maintaining security in virtual worlds and avatar recognition. (*Science Daily*)

A.   Security systems that can learn new biometric patterns and associate data from different data sets could contribute to solving crimes.

B.   Security systems that can learn new biometric patterns and associate data from different data sets can make decisions better than a human.

C.   While biometric information is being incorporated into passports and drivers' licences, it has no other practical applications.

D.   Security systems are now capable of combining information from multiple sources and altering decision-making to shifting conditions.

87.   The most popular entertainments offered by the circuses of Rome were the gladiators and chariot racing, the latter often as deadly as the former. As many as 12 four-horse teams raced one another seven times around the confines of the greatest arenas and rules were few, collisions all but inevitable, and hideous injuries to the charioteers commonplace. Ancient inscriptions record the deaths of famous racers in their early 20s, crushed against the stone *spina* that ran down the centre of the race track or dragged behind their horses after their chariots were smashed. Charioteers, who generally started out as slaves, took these risks because they could win fortunes. Successful, surviving racers could grow enormously wealthy. Spectators wagered and also won substantial sums – enough for the races to be plagued by all manner of dirty tricks; there is evidence that the fans sometimes hurled nail-studded curse tablets onto the track in an attempt to disable their rivals. (*smithsonianmag. com*)

A.   Chariot racing and the gladiators were the most popular attractions at Rome's circuses, but the gladiators were always the most deadly.

B.   Ancient inscriptions suggest that the majority of the charioteers in any race were killed by being dragged behind their horses.

C.   Spectators could win so much money betting on chariot races that many of them lost their lives due to underhanded schemes.

D.   Charioteers at Rome's circuses would have faced opposing racers, stone *spina*, and possibly curse tablets full of nails.

88. One hundred years ago, in 1912, astronomer Vesto Slipher found that the Andromeda galaxy was heading straight for us at a speed of 400,000 kilometres per hour. Scientists were unsure what this would mean for our galaxy in the long-term. Would we collide directly with Andromeda, a galaxy roughly the same size as our Milky Way? Or would we slide past it, like two ships passing in the night? Now, we know the Milky Way's ultimate fate: a galactic collision. The Milky Way and Andromeda galaxies will be slowly drawn together due to their mutual gravitational pull, colliding roughly 4 billion years from now. Subsequently, the two galaxies will orbit around each other before merging in one big galactic pile-up. The resulting supergalaxy will be different from either of the current ones: Instead of the elegant, flat, spiral-shaped disc we know and love, the new galaxy will be a three-dimensional ball of stars. Astoundingly, this massive crash won't have an enormous impact on earth or the solar system as a whole. (*smithsonianmag.com*)

A. While the Milky Way and Andromeda galaxies will collide, other galaxies in the same situation simply slide past each other.

B. The collision of the Milky Way with Andromeda will not significantly impact the earth because the process will take millions of years to complete.

C. When the Milky Way and Andromeda galaxies collide with each other, they will immediately form one big supergalaxy.

D. Scientists now predict that the Andromeda galaxy and the Milky Way galaxy will merge in several billion years to form a new galaxy.

89. Physicists at The University of Texas at Austin, in collaboration with colleagues in Taiwan and China, have developed the world's smallest semiconductor laser, a breakthrough for emerging photonic technology with applications from computing to medicine. Miniaturisation of semiconductor lasers is key for the development of faster, smaller and lower energy photon-based technologies, such as ultrafast computer chips; highly sensitive biosensors for detecting, treating and studying disease; and next-generation communication technologies.

The device is constructed of a gallium nitride nanorod that is partially filled with indium gallium nitride. Both alloys are semiconductors used commonly in LEDs. The nanorod is placed on top of a thin insulating layer of silicon that in turn covers a layer of silver film that is smooth at the atomic level. (*Science Daily*)

A. The smooth arrangement of atoms in a layer of silver film inside the world's smallest semiconductor laser differentiates it from similar devices.

B. One component of the world's smallest semiconductor laser is a nanorod that is partly filled with indium gallium nitride.

C. The world's smallest semiconductor laser is composed of a thin layer of silicon that covers a gallium nitride nanorod.

D. The world's smallest semiconductor laser will soon be on the market in the form of computer chips, among other things.

90. Germany's industrial sector suffers as the eurozone slides back towards recession. The manufacturing sector in the eurozone suffered a steep decline in activity in July, according to figures recently released. It is the eurozone's worst PMI reading for three years and looks likely to contribute to the eurozone sliding back into recession. One of the sharpest falls in industrial orders came in Germany, showing that the main driver of the eurozone economy is now feeling the effects of the economic crisis. Its reading was also at a three-year low, at 43. Greece and Spain were the only two countries where the manufacturing sector contracted more rapidly. Only one country, Ireland, saw its manufacturing sector expand, with a score of 53.9. Chris Williamson said that July had been characterised by "faster rates of decline in output and new orders, leading manufacturers to cut back on head counts and inventory holdings and suggesting a fear among companies towards ongoing weakness". (*European Voice*)

A. Spain's manufacturing sector in July suffered a more severe setback than Greece, Germany, or Ireland.

B. In July, the manufacturing sectors of Germany, Greece, and Spain declined while the same sector in Ireland expanded.

C.   According to Chris Williamson, July's manufacturing sector slowdown reflects a temporary and seasonally-related lapse.

D.   Although Ireland's manufacturing sector expanded in July, its score of 53.9 is still the lowest it has seen in three years.

91. **In the spring of 1963, Martin Luther King Jr. organised a demonstration in downtown Birmingham, Alabama. City police turned dogs and fire hoses on demonstrators. Martin Luther King was gaoled along with large numbers of his supporters, but the event drew nationwide attention. From the gaol in Birmingham, King eloquently spelled out his theory of non-violence: "Nonviolent direct action seeks to create such a crisis and foster such a tension that a community, which has constantly refused to negotiate, is forced to confront the issue." By the end of the Birmingham campaign, Martin Luther King Jr. and his supporters were making plans for a massive demonstration on the nation's capital asking for peaceful change. On August 28, 1963, the historic March on Washington drew more than 200,000 people into the shadow of the Lincoln Memorial. It was here that King made his famous "I Have a Dream" speech, emphasising his belief that someday all men could be brothers.** (*biography.com*)

A.   King delivered his "I Have a Dream" speech at the March on Washington just months after being gaoled in Birmingham, Alabama.

B.   Without the publicity generated by the Birmingham demonstration, the March on Washington would not have drawn 200,000 people.

C.   King believed that non-violence was a way to voice concerns and work toward solutions while avoiding crisis and confrontation.

D.   The "I Have a Dream" speech was written to motivate and educate all Americans about the civil rights movement.

92. **On May 6, 1937 the Hindenburg airship was about to complete its 35th trip across the Atlantic, having departed from Frankfurt, Germany and nearly arrived in New Jersey, U.S.A. Then, suddenly, after thousands of kilometres of uneventful travel, the great zeppelin caught fire while less than 90 metres from the ground. Within a minute of the first signs of trouble, the entire ship was incinerated, and the burning wreckage crashed to the ground. Immediately after the accident, observers disagreed about what exactly sparked the explosion and what caused the airship to burn so quickly. In the years since, scientists, engineers and others have weighed in on the debate and attempted to solve the mystery of the Hindenburg. Possible causes of the explosion include a buildup of static electricity, a bolt of lightning or a backfiring engine, but at this point it's impossible to determine what exactly caused the spark.** (*smithsonianmag.com*)

A.   The Hindenburg airship never reached New Jersey, as the zeppelin caught fire and crashed to the ground just metres from where it was scheduled to land.

B.   In 1937, after travelling from Germany to the United States, the Hindenburg caught fire and crashed to the ground.

C.   Since the Hindenburg disaster, scientists and engineers have concluded that the explosion was not caused by human error.

D.   A bolt of lightning most likely caused the Hindenburg to burst into flames while less than 90 metres from the ground.

93. **Despite claims in the 1890s that Mars was filled with canals teeming with water, research over the past several decades has suggested that in fact, Mars has only a tiny amount of water, mostly near its surface. During the 1970s, as part of NASA's Mariner space orbiter programme, dry river beds and canyons on Mars were discovered – the first indications that surface water may have once existed there. The Viking programme subsequently found enormous river valleys on the planet, and in 2003 it was announced that the Mars Odyssey spacecraft had actually detected minute quantities of liquid water on and just below the surface, which was later confirmed by the Phoenix lander. Now there is evidence that Mars is home to vast reservoirs of water in its interior as well. The research also provides us with an answer for how underground water may have made its way to the Martian surface: volcanic activity.** (*smithsonianmag.com*)

A. The Viking programme discovered small amounts of liquid water on and just beneath the surface of Mars.

B. NASA's Mariner space orbiter programme discovered canyons and other formations on Mars during the 1970s.

C. Evidence that water exists on or near Mars' surface and in its interior suggests that the planet once possibly supported life.

D. Scientists claim that Mars has only a tiny amount of water, mostly near its surface.

94. The founding of the People's Liberation Army on 1 August 1927 is a date known to all in China. It is commemorated annually with speeches and promotions and every five years by major cultural celebrations. The events this year include operas, choral performances, photography shows and the "National Exhibition of Artistic Works in Celebration of the 85th Anniversary of the Chinese People's Liberation Army." Since the earliest days, the Communist Party and the People's Liberation Army, or P.L.A., have maximised the value of the arts as tools of propaganda. As Mao Zedong said in 1942, "To defeat the enemy we must rely primarily on the army with guns. But this army alone is not enough; we must also have a cultural army, which is absolutely indispensable for uniting our own ranks and defeating the enemy." The P.L.A. is one of the most important arts organizations in China. In Beijing, it has an arts university, opera house, opera, symphony orchestra, drama troupe and numerous bands. (*New York Times*)

A. Every year in China, the founding of the People's Liberation Army is remembered with major cultural celebrations.

B. Without the so-called cultural army, China would not be as united as it is today, nor as able to defeat its enemies.

C. In China, art is leveraged as a means of propa-ganda which, according to Mao Zedong, is essential for defeating the enemy.

D. China's Communist Party and P.L.A. have proven that art flourishes best when it is wedded to politics and national defence.

95. Before the Euro Cup, the International Football Association Board (IFAB) gave the green light to try goal line sensors from two of 10 competing companies: GoalRef and Hawkeye. In early July, IFAB approved both technologies, although they will remain optional. The distinction between these two technologies is that one is camera-based and one is not. And that difference could be the deciding factor. Unlike tennis, where there is almost never any thing or person obstructing the line of sight between the cameras and the ball, football presents unique challenges – especially during free kicks and corner kicks. In such situations, 10 players might be close to the goal, making it harder for cameras to unambiguously record when the ball passes the line. Not everyone is keen on goal line technology. Michel Platini, head of the UEFA, worried that introduction of this technology would begin a slippery slope toward more intrusions to the game, and he stood staunchly opposed to the technology. (*smithsoanianmag.com*)

A. The fact that the game of football presents chal-lenges that are different from tennis is of no consequence to goal line sensor technology.

B. While the IFAB approved the optional use of two types of goal line sensors, the move was not unanimously embraced.

C. Although the IFAB has approved the use of goal line sensors, the head of UEFA is opposed and may "veto" their use.

D. Tennis most likely favours the use of GoalRef's technology because the line of sight between the ball and the cameras is rarely blocked.

96. A government investigation into insider trading in Tokyo has extended onto the trading floors of some of Wall Street's largest companies, including Goldman Sachs, UBS and Deutsche Bank. Regulators are scrutinising suspicious trading activity ahead of at least 12 public offering announcements over the last three years. The committee has been working with regulators to stiffen insider trading laws in Japan. Among the trades being investigated are those made by Goldman clients who bet against All Nippon Airways just days before the airline's stock offering last month. A company's share price typically drops when a new share issuance is announced. The commission is expected to issue an order and call for fundamental changes in

the way the company, which is based in Tokyo, handles information. The scandal has further undermined faith in Japanese stock markets, experts say, which remain some of the world's most depressed after the global financial crisis. (*New York Times*)

A. In Tokyo, a government committee investigation into insider trading involves Goldman Sachs and Deutsche Bank.

B. Of all the cases, just one company, Deutsche Bank, has clients suspected of misconduct in betting against an airway company.

C. A government investigation in Tokyo into insider trading will most likely result in more severe trading laws in Japan.

D. Suspicions of insider trading violations have caused Japanese stock markets to plunge in recent weeks.

97. Drawing on research from psychology and linguistics, the researchers seek to better understand how using different languages to discuss and express emotions in a multilingual family might play an important role in children's emotional development. They propose that the particular language parents choose to use when discussing and expressing emotion can have significant impacts on children's emotional understanding, experience, and regulation. Research from linguistics suggests that when bilingual individuals switch languages, the way they experience emotions changes as well. Bilingual parents may use a specific language to express an emotional concept because they feel that the language provides a better cultural context for expressing the emotion. Overall, the authors argue that research from psychological science and linguistics suggests that a child's emotional competence is fundamentally shaped by a multilingual environment. (*Science Daily*)

A. Research indicates that due to cultural differences native Spanish speakers experience emotions more intensely than native Finnish speakers.

B. Research suggests that growing up in a multilingual home has minor impact on a child's emotional development.

C. Children who grow up with bilingual parents are better able to express their emotions compared to their peers.

D. The perception of some bilingual parents it is that one language may provide a better means for expressing a given emotion.

98. The story about the first Penguin paperbacks may be apocryphal, but it is a good one. In 1935, Allen Lane, chairman of the eminent British publishing house Bodley Head, had a "Eureka!" moment: What if quality books were available at places like train stations and sold for reasonable prices – the price of a pack of cigarettes, say? Bodley Head did not want to finance his endeavour, so Lane used his own capital. He called his new house Penguin, apparently upon the suggestion of a secretary, and sent a young colleague to the zoo to sketch the bird. He then acquired the rights to ten reprints of serious literary titles and went knocking on non-bookstore doors. When Woolworth's placed an order for 63,500 copies, Lane first realised he had a viable financial model. Lane's paperbacks were cheap. They cost two and a half pence, the same as ten cigarettes, the publisher touted. Volume was key to profitability; Penguin had to sell 17,000 copies of each book to break even. (*smithsoanianmag.com*)

A. The key to Penguin's success was its advertising campaign comparing the price of a book to a pack of cigarettes.

B. Immediately after his "Eureka!" moment about reasonably priced books, Lane saw that his financial model would succeed.

C. If Woolworth's had not placed an early order for 63,500 books, Penguin would never have succeeded as it did.

D. After he had a "Eureka!" moment, Lane financed Penguin books and initially acquired the rights to ten reprints.

99. Born Agnes Bojaxhiu in 1910, Mother Teresa attended a convent-run primary school and then a state-run secondary school. The congregation made an annual pilgrimage to the chapel of the Madonna of Letnice atop Black Mountain in Skopje, and it was on one such trip at the age of twelve that Mother Teresa first felt

a calling to a religious life. In 1928, an 18-year-old Agnes Bojaxhiu decided to become a nun and set off for Ireland to join the Loreto Sisters of Dublin. It was there that she took the name Sister Mary Teresa after Saint Thérèse of Lisieux. A year later, she travelled on to Darjeeling, India for the novitiate period; afterward she was sent to Calcutta, where she was assigned to teach at Saint Mary's High School for Girls, a school dedicated to teaching girls from the city's poorest Bengali families. Mother Teresa had to learn to speak both Bengali and Hindi fluently as she taught geography and history and dedicated herself to alleviating the girls' poverty through education. (*biography.com*)

A.   Had Agnes Bojaxhiu not joined her congregation on a pilgrimage to Skopje, she might never have felt a religious calling.

B.   Agnes Bojaxhiu first took the name of Sister Mary Teresa on a trip to Darjeeling, India with the Loreto Sisters.

C.   Mother Teresa taught history and geography in Bengali and Hindi at Saint Mary's High School for Girls in Calcutta.

D.   After Agnes Bojaxhiu felt a religious calling, she became a nun and eventually travelled to Darjeeling and Calcutta and never left India again.

100.   Prior to the 17th century, Ottoman succession had been governed by the "law of fratricide" drawn up by Mehmed II in the middle of the 15th century. Under the terms of this remarkable piece of legislation, whichever member of the ruling dynasty succeeded in seizing the throne on the death of the old sultan was not merely permitted, but enjoined, to murder all his brothers (together with any inconvenient uncles and cousins) in order to reduce the risk of subsequent rebellion and civil war. Although it was not invariably applied, Mehmed's law resulted in the deaths of at least 80 members of the House of Osman over a period of 150 years. These victims included all 19 siblings of Sultan Mehmed III – some of whom were still infants at the breast, but all of whom were strangled with silk handkerchiefs immediately after their brother's accession in 1595. (*smithsonianmag.com*)

A.   Without the "law of fratricide", chaos and coups would have reigned in the Ottoman empire between the 15th and 17th centuries.

B.   During the 15th century, the Ottoman Mehmed II instituted legislation that commanded a new ruler to commit fratricide.

C.   The murder of the 19 siblings of Sultan Mehmed III was the most appalling incident of fratricide in the Ottoman succession between the 15th and 17th centuries.

D.   Between the 15th and 17th centuries all family members of the new ruler were murdered in order to reduce the risk of subsequent rebellion and civil war.

101.   Twins offer a precious opportunity to untangle the influence of genes and the environment – of nature and nurture. Because identical twins come from a single fertilised egg that splits in two, they share virtually the same genetic code. Any differences between them – one twin having younger looking skin, for example – must be due to environmental factors such as less time spent in the sun. Alternatively, by comparing the experiences of identical twins with those of fraternal twins, who come from separate eggs and share on average half their DNA, researchers can quantify the extent to which our genes affect our lives. If identical twins are more similar to each other with respect to an ailment than fraternal twins are, then vulnerability to the disease must be rooted at least in part in heredity. Lately, however, twin studies have helped lead scientists to a radical, almost heretical new conclusion: that nature and nurture are not the only elemental forces at work. (*National Geographic*)

A.   Fraternal twins are more suitable than identical twins for studying how our environment impacts our lives.

B.   Studies of identical and fraternal twins indicate that we are equally influenced by our genetics and our environment.

C.   If one fraternal twin suffers from a disease while the other twin does not, the cause of the disease is hereditary.

D.   Identical twins share nearly 100 per cent of their DNA while, on average, fraternal twins share 50 per cent of their DNA.

102. Economic growth and urbanisation go hand in hand and are critical to poverty reduction. Ultimately, cities provide both the living and working environment for most people in high-income countries, and an increasing number of middle income ones. Cities have the potential to reap major economies of scale. The United Kingdom has launched a three year programme of research funded by the World Bank and undertaken jointly by London School of Economics and Oxford University. It will look at the development of city systems – the urban hierarchy within and across countries – and at urban form – the internal organisation of particular cities, focusing on Africa. The programme of research will aim to build a credible database documenting the speed, magnitude and form of urban development in selected countries. Once completed this data will establish the facts about urbanisation. It will also predict the determinants of and consequences of differing patterns of urban growth. (*economics.ox.ac.uk*)

A. The research programme will help to antici-pate the causes and effects of different types of urban growth.

B. Collaboration between academics and govern-ment officials in Africa will be required in order to collect the data on urban form.

C. Urban growth is the primary driver of poverty reduction and this study aims to document the speed, size and form of urban development.

D. Most people live outside the city in high income countries, a pattern replicated across an increasing number of middle income countries.

103. A new Internet-enabled power outlet will soon allow users to control household appliances via their smartphones and reduce their energy costs significantly. Soon there will be no need for special timers to switch lighting on and off or operate household appliances when the homeowner is absent. In the future, all of these things will be doable by means of a smartphone or PC thanks to Internet-enabled wireless power outlets that support the IPv6 Internet protocol. The wireless power outlets are a component of the HexaBus home automation system. "The HexaBus components make the smart home of the future a reality. They

enable household appliances to be controlled intelligently, thus optimizing or reducing electricity consumption. For example, the householder can start the washing machine during cheap-rate off-peak hours, or run the dishwasher when the photovoltaic panels on the roof are generating sufficient power," says industrial engineer Mathias Dalheimer. (*Science Daily*)

A. Homes equipped with Internet-enabled power outlets will automatically optimise or reduce the household's use of electricity without any human control.

B. The HexaBus home automation system will soon be installed in the majority of smart homes that support the IPv6 Internet protocol.

C. Soon homeowners can start a load of laundry remotely with a smartphone or PC and Internet-enabled wireless power outlets.

D. When homeowners can control appliances and lighting from their smartphone or PC, energy consumption will drop.

104. Not only are healthy organs in short supply but donor and patient also have to be closely matched, or the patient's immune system may reject the transplant. A new kind of solution is incubating in medical labs: "bioartificial" organs grown from the patient's own cells. Thirty people have received lab-grown bladders already, and other engineered organs are in the pipeline. Researchers take healthy cells from a patient's diseased bladder, cause them to multiply profusely in petri dishes, then apply them to a balloon-shaped scaffold made partly of collagen, the protein found in cartilage. Muscle cells go on the outside, urothelial cells (which line the urinary tract) on the inside. "It's like baking a layer cake," says Atala. "You're layering the cells one layer at a time, spreading these toppings." The bladder-to-be is then incubated at body temperature until the cells form functioning tissue. The whole process takes six to eight weeks. (*National Geographic*)

A. A lab-grown bioartificial bladder is made by layering urothelial cells around muscle cells.

B. To grow a bladder in a lab, researchers must take some of the patient's healthy collagen cells.

C. A lab-grown bioartificial bladder involves petri dishes, a scaffold, cell layering, and incubation.

D. After bladder cells are transferred to the scaffold, they remain there for a period of three weeks.

105. Recent studies indicate that the brain's insular cortex may help a sprinter drive his body forward just a little more efficiently than his competitors. This region may prepare a boxer to better fend off a punch his opponent is beginning to throw as well as assist a diver as she calculates her spinning body's position so she hits the water with barely a splash. The insula does all this by anticipating an athlete's future feelings, according to a new theory. Researchers suggest that an athlete possesses a hyper-attuned insula that can generate strikingly accurate predictions of how the body will feel in the next moment. That model of the body's future condition instructs other brain areas to initiate actions that are more tailored to coming demands than those of also-rans and couch potatoes. Emerging evidence now also suggests that this brain area can be trained using a meditation technique called mindfulness – good news for Olympians and weekend warriors alike. (*smithsonianmag.com*)

A. Research shows that the brain's insular cortex can be tuned only by physically practising a given sport or skill.

B. The insular cortex may contribute to athletic excellence by anticipating how the physical body will soon feel.

C. Sprinters, boxers and divers are those athletes who benefit most from a hyper-attuned insular cortex.

D. Research indicates that, compared to boxers, athletes have larger insular cortexes.

106. The British mathematician Alan Turing probed one of computing's biggest theoretical questions: Could machines possess a mind? If so, how would we know? In 1950, he proposed an experiment: If judges in typed conversations with a person and a computer programme couldn't tell them apart, we'd come to consider the machine as "thinking." He predicted

that programmes would be capable of fooling judges 30 per cent of the time by the year 2000. They came closest at the 2008 Loebner Prize competition when the top chatbot (as a human-mimicking programme is called) fooled 3 of 12 judges, or 25 per cent. Chatbots betray themselves in many ways, some subtle. They're unlikely to gracefully interrupt or be interrupted. Their responses, often cobbled together out of fragments of stored conversations, make sense at a local level but lack long-term coherence. (*smithsonianmag.com*)

A. A chatbot tricked a quarter of the judges into thinking it was human at the 2008 Loebner Prize competition.

B. The absence of sustained logical consistency most frequently alerts Turing test judges that they are talking to a chatbot.

C. Turing's prediction that computers would trick people 30 per cent of the time by the year 2000 was proven correct.

D. Within the next several years, chatbots will be able to adequately imitate how humans interrupt and are interrupted.

107. The predominant theory of sleep is that the brain demands it. But the trick is to confirm this assumption with real data. How does sleeping help the brain? The answer may depend on what kind of sleep you are talking about. Recently, researchers at Harvard tested undergraduates on various aptitude tests, allowed them to nap, then tested them again. They found that those who had engaged in REM sleep subsequently performed better in pattern recognition tasks, such as grammar, while those who slept deeply were better at memorisation. Other researchers have found that the sleeping brain appears to repeat a pattern of neuron firing that occurred while the subject was recently awake, as if in sleep the brain were trying to commit to long-term memory what it had learned that day. Yet another study showed that the sleeping brain seems to weed out redundant or unnecessary synapses or connections. So the purpose of sleep may be to help us remember what's important by letting us forget what's not. (*National Geographic*)

A. According to the study referenced, REM sleep is the most valuable in assisting memorisation.

B. The patterned neuron firing that occurs during REM sleep facilitates long-term memory.

C. Removing unneeded synapses while asleep allows us to recognise patterns while awake.

D. Some research shows that sleep may facilitate better pattern recognition and memory.

108. **Bingo Friendzy, developed by the British online gambling company Gamesys, was introduced on Facebook this morning. It allows players to stake cash in 90 bingo and slot machine games. The app is marketed with cartoon graphics featuring characters that have been compared to those on Moshi Monsters, the popular children's social network. It has prompted anger from Christian groups, who called on the Advertising Standards Authority to act. Facebook has allowed the first real gambling app as it comes under unprecedented pressure to increase its revenues. Since its flotation in May the firm has reported a $157m loss and its shares have almost halved in value amid concerns about Facebook's effectiveness as an advertising medium. Facebook will take 30 per cent of revenues from Bingo Friendzy and a host of other gambling apps expected to be introduced in the coming months. (*Daily Telegraph*)**

A. Christian groups angered by Bingo Friendzy believe that children should not be exposed to the sin of gambling.

B. Facebook will not benefit financially from Bingo Friendzy or any other gambling app to appear on the site.

C. Facebook shares lost half their value primarily because investors do not have faith in the company's advertising.

D. Bingo Friendzy appeared on Facebook at a time when the company was suffering from economic loss.

109. **At least 10 million of the world's poorest people are set to go hungry this year because of failing crops caused by one of the strongest El Niño climatic events on record, Oxfam, the charity, has warned. The charity said several countries were already facing a "major emergency", such as Ethiopia, where 4.5 million are in need of food aid because of a prolonged**
scarcity of rain this year. Floods, followed by drought, have slashed Malawi's maize production by more than a quarter, farmers in central America have suffered from two years of drought and El Niño conditions have already reduced the Asian monsoon over India, potentially triggering a wider drought across the east of the continent. El Niño is a periodic climatic phenomenon where waters of the eastern tropical Pacific warm, triggering a range of potential consequences for global weather. While parts of South America are typically doused in heavy rainfall, warmer, drought-like conditions are experienced in Australia, south-east Asia and southern Africa. (*theguardian. com*)

A. El Niño is an annual event where waters of the eastern tropical Pacific warm up, causing a range of consequences in the weather.

B. The results of El Niño include floods and droughts and the effects can be observed in Malawi, India and South America, among others.

C. 4.5 million people in Ethiopia are in need of food aid because of initial floods and then a prolonged scarcity of rain, worsened by El Niño.

D. All countries effected by El Niño first experience heavy floods and then a drought.

110. **Thomas, or Doubting Thomas as he is commonly known, was one of the "Twelve Apostles", disciples sent out after Christ's Crucifixion to spread the newborn faith. He was joined by Peter, Andrew, James the Greater, James the Lesser, John, Philip, Bartholomew, Matthew, Thaddaeus, Simon – and Matthias, who replaced the former disciple and alleged traitor, Judas Iscariot. In time the terms "apostle" and "apostolic" (derived from the Greek *apostolos*, or messenger) were applied to others who spread the word. In the case of Paul, he claimed the title of apostle for himself, believing he had seen the Lord and received a spiritual commission from him. Mary Magdalene is known as the apostle to the Apostles for her role of announcing the resurrection to them. Although only two of the four Evangelists – Matthew and John – were amongst the original Apostles, Mark and Luke are considered apostolic because of**

the importance of their work in writing the New Testament Gospels. (*National Geographic*)

A.   For at least a century following the crucifixion, the word "apostle" was only used in reference to Christ's twelve disciples.

B.   Simon, Philip and Mary Magdalene are all considered apostles, a term that traces to the Greek word meaning messenger.

C.   Despite their contributions to the New Testament, some conservative Christians still do not consider Mark and Luke to be apostles.

D.   The twelve apostles are Thomas, Peter, Andrew, James the Greater, James the Lesser, John, Philip, Bartholomew, Matthew, Thaddaeus, Simon, and Judas Iscariot.

111.   The 17th century Dutch painter Frans Hals made two great contributions. One was to combine an intense sense of realism with flamboyant brushwork – which gives his work a highly personal quality. Hals' other contribution is to fill his paintings with evident psychological intensity, the quality known as "psychological insight." His figures feel as if we could speak to them. It's surely no accident that Hals's life (1580–1666) overlapped with that of Shakespeare (1564–1616), and the way he evoked a sense of character provides interesting parallels to the characters in Shakespeare's plays who are generally two or more people in one body, engaged in internal dialogue. In that sense, Hals's portraits document the emergence of the modern self: they display a new awareness that the "self" is not a single, uniform thing, but the product of conflicting forces and disparate impulses, ruled by a consciousness filled with self-doubt. (*smithsonianmag.com*)

A.   Frans Hals' use of subtle brushwork in his paintings conveyed his impression of the people he painted.

B.   Frans Hals's paintings have been described as conveying a sense of realism along with psychological insight.

C.   In his portraits, Frans Hals intentionally tried to impart a sense of the modern self, riddled with complexity and doubt.

D.   Hals frequently attended performances of Shakespeare's plays, and the bard's influence on his painting is obvious.

112.   A new genetic analysis has reconstructed the history of North Africa's Jews, showing that these populations date to biblical-era Israel and are not largely the descendants of natives who converted to Judaism. The study also shows that these Jews form two distinct groups, one of which is more closely related than the other to their European counterparts, reflecting historical migrations. The findings are the latest in a series of genetic studies, which began in the 1990s, indicating that the world's Jews share biological roots, not just cultural and religious ties. In many cases the analyses have confirmed what scholars had gleaned from archaeological finds and historical accounts. The scientists found that the Jewish populations of North Africa became genetically distinct over time, with those of each country carrying their own DNA signatures. This suggests they mostly married within their own religious and cultural group. (*Science Daily*)

A.   Genetic analysis shows that the ancestors of North African Jews share biological roots with at least two other groups.

B.   Forced segregation prevented the Jews of North Africa from marrying outside their culture and religion.

C.   Country-specific Jewish populations in North Africa each have their own unique genetic markers.

D.   Studies consistently show that while Jews are culturally and religiously similar, they are biologically dissimilar.

113.   Paris has a deeper and stranger connection to its underground than almost any city, and that underground is one of the richest. The arteries and intestines of Paris, the hundreds of miles of tunnels that make up some of the oldest and densest subway and sewer networks in the world, are just the start of it. Under Paris there are spaces of all kinds: canals and reservoirs, crypts and bank vaults, wine cellars transformed into nightclubs and galleries. Most surprising of all are the *carrières* – the old limestone quarries that fan out in a deep and intricate web under many neighbourhoods, mostly in the southern part of the metropolis. Into the 19th

century those caverns and tunnels were mined for building stone. After that farmers raised mushrooms in them, at one point producing hundreds of tons a year. During World War II, French Resistance fighters – the underground – hid in some quarries; the Germans built bunkers in others. (*National Geographic*)

A.   Underground limestone mining was primarily carried out under the northern part of Paris into the 19th century.

B.   Today, anyone is welcome to visit the many galleries, nightclubs, and other establishments underneath Paris.

C.   Underneath Paris, one can find *carrières,* bank vaults, galleries, sewers, nightclubs, tunnels, crypts, and caverns.

D.   At one point in Paris' history, the tons of mush-rooms produced beneath ground were most likely more than the amount produced above ground.

114.   More than 200,000 individual animal species, by varying strategies, help flowers make more flowers. Flies and beetles are the original pollinators, going back to when flowering plants first appeared 130 million years ago. As for bees, scientists have identified some 20,000 distinct species so far, and about one-fifth of those pollinate flowers in the United States. Hummingbirds, butterflies, moths, wasps, and ants are also up to the task. Snails and slugs smear pollen as they slide over flower clusters. Mosquitoes carry pollen for batches of orchids, and bats, with diverse muzzles and tongues adapted to tap differently shaped blossoms, move pollen for 360 plants in the Americas alone. Flowering plants – there are more than 240,000 species of them – have evolved in step with their pollinators, using sweet scents and bright colours to lure with the promise of a meal. Flower receptacles are wonderfully varied, from tubes and gullets to flaps, brushes, and spurs. (*National Geographic*)

A.   At the time plants began flowering on the planet 130 million years ago, among others flies, beetles, bees and bats spread their pollen.

B.   More than 240,000 species of flowering plants are pollinated by more than 200,000 animal species, including ants and bats.

C.   Hundreds of plants have evolved to match the tongue shape of some bat species that pollinate them.

D.   While beetles, snails, and bees all serve to polli-nate plants, only the mosquito can carry pollen for orchids.

115.   Microplastics used in sewage plants could be contributing to the problem of plastic pollution in oceans, according to a new report. Dozens of UK wastewater treatment plants use tiny plastic pellets, known as Bio-Beads, to filter chemical and organic contaminants from sewage. Once the Bio-Beads are in the ocean they are hard to spot and almost impossible to remove – yet can cause significant harm to marine wildlife. Industrial pellets and small bits of plastic such as Bio-Beads are mistaken for food by birds, fish, and other marine animals. These particles can kill animals, not only by causing digestive blockages, but also as a result of the high concentrations of pollutants. Plastic pollution can also enter the food chain, which is a concern to many people. Last August, the results of a study by Plymouth University reported plastic was found in a third of UK-caught fish, including cod, haddock, mackerel and shellfish. "We are learning more all the time about the environmental impact of consumer microplastics in wastewater such as laundry fibres, cosmetic microbeads and tyre dust," said the author of the report, Claire Wallerstein. "However, it now seems that microplastics used in the wastewater plants' own processes could also be contributing to the problem." (*theguardian.com*)

A.   Humans have themselves consumed Bio-Beads through eating fish such as cod, haddock and mackerel.

B.   The Bio-Beads, which come from sewage plants, can poison or cause suffocation in marine wildlife.

C.   Sewage plants, whether accidentally or on purpose, leak the microplastics called Bio-Beads into the ocean.

D.   Most people are aware of the environmental impact of other microplastics such as laundry fibres.

116. The oldest extant play and the only
      surviving Greek tragedy about
      a contemporaneous (rather than
      mythological) topic, *The Persians* was
      written by Aeschylus in 472 BC. The play
      chronicles the 480 BC Battle of Salamis,
      one of the most significant battles in
      world history: As the turning point
      in the Persian Empire's downfall, it
      allowed the Greeks – and therefore the
      West's first experiment with democracy
      – to survive. Aeschylus, a veteran of the
      Persian Wars, also made the unusual
      choice of recounting the battle from
      the Persian perspective, creating what's
      generally seen as an empathetic, rather
      than triumphalist, narrative of their loss.
      Today, the play is unexpectedly trendy.
      It has been produced about 30 times
      over the last five years. Why? Consider
      the plot: a superpower's inexperienced,
      hubristic leader – who hopes to
      conquer a minor enemy his father tried
      unsuccessfully to fell a decade earlier –
      charges into a doomed military invasion.
      (*smithsonianmag.com*)

A.   *The Persians* has enjoyed a renaissance in recent
      years because of its insight into the history of
      the Persian Empire.

B.   In *The Persians,* Greek playwright Aeschylus
      tells of the Battle of Salamis from the Greek
      point of view.

C.   *The Persians* is popular with contemporary
      audiences because it proves that history repeats
      itself.

D.   Aeschylus, who fought in the Persian Wars,
      provides an empathetic account of how the
      Persians lost the Battle of Salamis in 480 BC.

117. We now know that Stonehenge was in
      the making for at least 400 years. The
      first phase, built around 3000 BC, was
      a simple circular earthwork enclosure
      similar to many "henges" (sacred
      enclosures typically comprising a circular
      bank and a ditch) found throughout the
      British Isles. Around 2800 BC, timber
      posts were erected within the enclosure.
      Archaeologists have long believed that
      Stonehenge began to take on its modern
      form two centuries later, when large
      stones were brought to the site in the
      third and final stage of its construction.
      The first to be put in place were the 80
      or so bluestones, which were arranged

in a double circle with an entrance
facing northeast. The importance of
the bluestones is underscored by the
immense effort involved in moving
them a long distance – some were as
long as three metres and weighed
four tons. Geological studies in the
1920s determined that they came from
the Preseli Mountains in southwest
Wales, 140 miles from Stonehenge.
(*smithsonianmag.com*)

A.   Stonehenge was constructed in two main
      stages: first it was a circle-shaped enclosure and
      then the large stones were added.

B.   Research suggests that the bluestones of
      Stonehenge were moved from their source 140
      miles away using only manpower.

C.   According to archaeologists, the bluestones of
      Stonehenge were added to the structure around
      2800 BC.

D.   Around 2600 BC, bluestones from southwest
      Wales were added to the Stonehenge site in a
      double circle.

118. Children who think their parents
      are poor monitors or nag a lot tend
      to play videogames more than other
      kids, according to a study funded by
      the National Science Foundation. The
      study is one of the first to link parental
      behaviour to kids' videogame playing.
      The researchers surveyed more than 500
      students from 20 middle schools and
      found that the more children perceived
      their parents' behaviour as negative (e.g.,
      "nags a lot") and the less monitoring
      parents did, the more the children played
      videogames. The next step, said lead
      researcher Linda Jackson, is to find out
      what's fueling children's videogame
      behaviour – a topic Jackson and her team
      plan to examine. Jackson said an equally
      interesting question is the relationship
      between videogame playing and actual
      rather than perceived behaviour of parents.
      Perceptions don't always mirror reality, she
      said, and this may be the case in the child-
      parent relationship. (*Science Daily*)

A.   According to a study, children play more vide-
      ogames if they perceive that they have parents
      who closely supervise them.

B.   Videogame playing causes children to inter-
      pret their parents' behaviour toward them as
      negative.

C. According to a study, children who think their parents pester them a lot play more videogames.

D. Research shows that children who play a lot of videogames are less likely to have parents who behave positively.

119. Walking upright on two legs is the trait that defines the hominid lineage: Bipedalism separated the first hominids from the rest of the four-legged apes. It took a while for anthropologists to realise this. At the turn of the 20th century, scientists thought that big brains made hominids unique. This was a reasonable conclusion since the only known hominid fossils were of brainy species – Neanderthals and *Homo erectus*. In more recent decades, anthropologists have determined that bipedalism has very ancient roots. The earliest hominid with the most extensive evidence for bipedalism is the 4.4-million-year-old *Ardipithecus ramidus*. Although the earliest hominids were capable of upright walking, they retained primitive features – such as long, curved fingers and toes as well as longer arms and shorter legs – that indicate they spent time in trees. It's not until the emergence of *H. erectus* 1.89 million years ago that hominids grew tall, evolved long legs and became completely terrestrial creatures. (*smithsonianmag. com*)

A. Fossils indicate that *Ardipithecus ramidus* became the first fully bipedal and terrestrial species 4.4 million years ago.

B. Fossils of Neanderthals suggest that the hominid species walked upright but was better at climbing trees.

C. Hominid species with shorter legs, longer arms, and fingers and toes that curl likely spent at least some time in trees.

D. Hominid species developed bigger brains just after they walked upright – around 4.4 million years ago.

120. In the warfare that raged in Cambodia from 1970 until 1998, all sides used land mines. There are more than 30 different types. Villagers have prosaic names for them based on their appearance: the frog, the drum, the corncob. Most were manufactured in China, Russia, or Vietnam, a few in the United States.

Khmer Rouge commander Pol Pot, whose regime was responsible for the deaths of some 1.7 million Cambodians between 1975 and 1979, purportedly called land mines his "perfect soldiers." They never sleep. Although weapons of war, land mines are unlike bullets and bombs in two distinct ways. First, they are designed to maim rather than kill, because an injured soldier requires the help of two or three others, reducing the enemy's forces. Second, and most sinister, when a war ends, land mines remain in the ground, primed to explode. Only 25 per cent of land mine victims around the world are soldiers. The rest are civilians – boys gathering firewood, mothers sowing rice, girls herding goats. (*National Geographic*)

A. Land mines are different from some other weapons of war in that their intent is not to kill but to disable.

B. In Cambodia between 1975 and 1979, 75 per cent of land mine victims were civilians.

C. "Perfect soldiers" is one of many names that only Cambodian villagers use to describe land mines.

D. As weapons of war, land mines are more successful at reducing soldier forces than bullets or bombs.

121. Our working memory capacity is decidedly finite – it reflects our ability to focus and control attention and strongly influences our ability to solve problems. Converging evidence from many psychological science studies suggests that high working memory capacity is associated with better performance at mathematical problem-solving. In fact, decreased working memory capacity may be one reason why math anxiety leads to poor math performance. Overall, working memory capacity seems to help analytical problem-solvers focus their attention and resist distraction. However, these very features of working memory capacity seem to impair creative problem-solving. With creative problems, reaching a solution may require an original approach or a novel combination of diverse pieces of information. As a result, too much focus may actually impair creative problem solving. (*Science Daily*)

A. Scientific studies suggest that people who tend to be anxious are better able to solve problems creatively.

B. Scientific evidence indicates that a razor-sharp focus likely helps people to creatively solve problems.

C. A high working memory capacity is associated with the ability to focus and solve mathematical problems.

D. While our working memory capacity is limited, our ability to find creative solutions to problems is unlimited.

122. **The explosion of personal devices with built in web connectivity, office applications and email can improve working practices but also comes with risks not limited to time wasting. The portability, connectivity, and storage capacity of mobile devices means they bring with them the threat of data leakage, data theft, and the introduction of viruses or other malware into workplace computing systems. Portable storage devices of every ilk whether mp3 player, tablet or mobile phone now have several ways of connecting to other devices and networks including Wi-Fi, Bluetooth, and USB. Many of these devices also now have several gigabytes of storage capacity and are often expandable and so have the ability to capture vast quantities of data, whether for legitimate work purposes or for illicit use. Many businesses and organisations are rightly concerned about the loss or disclosure of intellectual property or sensitive information about customers and employees. (*Science Daily*)**

A. Businesses that issue mobile devices to employees face just two risks: data theft and potential loss of productivity.

B. Before the appearance of the mobile devices with vast storage capacity the threat of data leakage and data theft was minimal.

C. Personal technology devices like mobile phones and tablets can compromise privacy and spread viruses and malware.

D. Portable storage devices with the most storage capacity put businesses and organisations most at risk of malware attacks.

123. **In northern Europe, public opinion is increasingly exasperated by what many**

view as an attempt by the south to rob it of its savings. A recent letter signed by 160 German economists claiming that the European Union's plan for a banking union was little more than an attempt to make Germany pay for Spanish mistakes is revealing in this respect. In turn, southern Europe is getting angry. One man saw this coming. American economist Martin Feldstein wrote in 1997 that monetary union would create conflict within Europe. Unfortunately, his insight was correct: European countries today are at loggerheads not despite the common currency but precisely because of it. History suggests that international disputes over debt and transfers are a serious danger. In the 1920s and the 1930s, representatives of European states devoted countless meetings to resolving them (at the time, mainly German reparations). Despite US goodwill, they were unable to overcome their differences. (*New York Times*)

A. Sharing a common currency is the main and only factor contributing to quarrels between northern and southern Europe.

B. Some economists in northern Europe believe their countries are being forced to pay for mistakes made by southern Europe.

C. In the 1920s and 1930s, European state representatives resolved international debt disagreements.

D. The common currency in Europe is a source of trouble because of inherent inequalities between north and south.

124. **The Roman Catholic Sagrada Família has always been revered and reviled. The surrealists claimed architect Antoni Gaudí as one of their own, while George Orwell called the church "one of the most hideous buildings in the world." As idiosyncratic as Gaudí himself, it is a vision inspired by the architect's religious faith and love of nature. He understood that the natural world is rife with curved forms, not straight lines. And he noticed that natural construction tends to favour sinewy materials such as wood, muscle, and tendon. With these organic models in mind, Gaudí based his buildings on a simple premise: If nature is the work of God, and if architectural forms are derived from nature, then the best way to**

honour God is to design buildings based on his work. Gaudí's faith was his own. But his belief in the beautiful efficiency of natural engineering clearly anticipated the modern science of biomimetics. (*National Geographic*)

A. The design of Antoni Gaudí's Sagrada Família is intended to bring nature into the church.

B. Antoni Gaudí's Sagrada Família directly influenced the modern field of biomimetics.

C. Antoni Gaudí's Sagrada Família incorporates wood, rounded lines, and sinewy effects.

D. Antoni Gaudí drew inspiration from his religious faith and the forms he saw in nature.

125. A bronze statue's orphaned arm. A corroded disc adorned with a bull. Preserved wooden planks. These are among the latest treasures that date back to the dawn of the Roman Empire, discovered amid the ruins of the Antikythera shipwreck, a sunken bounty off the coast of a tiny island in Greece. Marine archaeologists working on a project called Return to Antikythera announced these findings on Wednesday from this most recent excavation of the roughly 2,000-year-old wreck, which was first discovered 115 years ago. They said the haul hints at the existence of at least seven more bronze sculptures still buried beneath the seafloor. Bronze sculptures from that era are rare because they were often melted down to make swords, shields and other items. Only about 50 intact examples have survived, so if the team can salvage the submerged statues, it would be a remarkable recovery of ancient artifacts. For more than a century the wreck has yielded a trove of antiquities, from bronze and marble statues of Olympian gods and heroes to the mysterious Antikythera mechanism, a hand-held device for tracking planetary movements and predicting eclipses that is often called the "first computer." (*nytimes.com*)

A. It is highly unusual to discover bronze sculptures as humans have historically used bronze for swords and shields.

B. It is not yet known if all the bronze sculptures can be retrieved from the shipwreck.

C. This project is the first time archaeologists

have been able to excavate the Antikythera shipwreck.

D. The Antikythera mechanism was among the first treasures excavated from the shipwreck.

126. The antibacterial substance triclosan, which was first developed in the 1960s to prevent bacterial infections in hospitals, has since been incorporated into everything from hand soaps to toothpastes to mouthwashes and toys. Manufacturers see it as a marketing bonus, increasing consumer confidence that a particular product kills harmful bacteria. In recent years, though, research has shed light on a number of problems with employing triclosan so widely. Studies have shown that the chemical can disrupt the endocrine systems of several different animals, binding to receptor sites in the body, which prevents the thyroid hormone from functioning normally. Additionally, triclosan penetrates the skin and enters the bloodstream more easily than previously thought, and has turned up everywhere from aquatic environments to human breast milk in troubling quantities. To this list of concerns, add one more: A new paper indicates that triclosan impairs muscle function in both animals and humans. (*smithsonianmag.com*)

A. Consumers are more confident in a product's antibacterial qualities when triclosan is listed as an ingredient.

B. People who use products that contain triclosan face a high risk of developing conditions of the endocrine system.

C. Triclosan interferes with the proper functioning of muscles and the thyroid and has been found in human breast milk.

D. The intended purpose of developing the antibacterial triclosan in the '60s was to treat infections in hospitals.

127. A pioneering technology to detect fingermarks at crime scenes is a step closer to being incorporated into traditional forensic investigations. The technology uses Matrix Assisted Laser Desorption Ionisation Mass Spectrometry Imaging (MALDI-MSI) to provide crime scene investigators with key extra details about suspects. These details, such as any

substances they might have touched, can provide crucial background information in a criminal investigation. A fingermark is made up of material from the surface of the skin and from gland secretions. Conventionally, fingermarks found at the scene of a crime are lifted, often using a powder, and are compared with prints on a police database to identify a suspect. The new technology uses MALDI-MSI for the first time to produce multiple images of fingermarks that can provide extra information on a suspect. These details can be important background information in a criminal investigation, especially if the suspect's fingermark is not on the police database. (*Science Daily*)

A. Conventional fingermark processing and MALDI-MSI both require that a suspect's prints are on the police database.

B. MALDI-MSI technology does not yield the information conventional fingermark processing does.

C. MALDI-MSI technology, which produces several images of a fingermark, may sooner or later be part of criminal investigations.

D. MALDI-MSI technology can provide the necessary details and background information to convict a criminal suspect.

128. Travel apps are increasingly popular as more people travel abroad. Over the past five years, international travel has grown 4-5% annually, exceeding 1.1 billion overnight visitors in 2014, according to the World Tourism Organisation. With competition heating up, developers are targeting niches. For PokDok – a Finnish start-up launched in early 2015 – it's "Pocket Doctor," an app that offers easy access to healthcare. PokDok offers a way around language barriers with a directory, location service and map view to help users navigate to an appropriate point of care. "People don't necessarily bring a computer with them on vacation – but everybody takes their smart phone. If something unexpected should happen, you just get your phone and immediately see where to go next," said PokDok co-founder Jussi Lipponen, who has lived in six different countries and knows first-hand the difficulty of finding good medical care in a foreign country. (*politico.eu*)

A. International travel has grown rapidly in the past 5 years, with nearly 1.1 billion overnight visitors in that period, according to the World Tourism Organisation.

B. PokDok has already helped large numbers of people to find good medical care in a foreign country since its launch in early 2015.

C. PokDok is a free app that offers easy access to healthcare and was launched in 2015.

D. The app, PokDok, helps people find appropriate medical care in a way that avoids the disadvantages of not knowing the country's language, with a directory and help with locating suitable care.

129. Burials both rich and gruesome have recently been discovered in the Pyramid of the Moon of Teotihuacan. Tunnelling deep into the 140-foot-tall stone structure, archaeologists located five burial sites. Evidence indicates that all the victims were ritually killed to consecrate successive stages of the pyramid's construction. The earliest sacrifice, from about AD 200, marked a substantial enlargement of the building. A wounded foreigner, most likely a prisoner of war, was apparently buried alive with his hands tied behind him. Animals representing mythical powers and military might surrounded him, some buried alive in cages. Finely crafted offerings included weapons of obsidian and a figurine of solid greenstone, perhaps a war goddess to whom the burial was dedicated. Each subsequent burial was different, but all had the same aim: "Human sacrifice was important to control the people," says Sugiyama, "to convince them to do what their rulers wanted." (*National Geographic*)

A. Teotihuacan's Pyramid of the Moon and the burials made there were intended to appease an honored war goddess.

B. Five burial sites, animals in cages, a greenstone figurine, and obsidian weapons were all discovered in the Pyramid of the Moon.

C. Humans were ritually sacrificed in Teotihuacan for the sole purpose of sanctifying the building of the Pyramid of the Moon.

D. Victims were buried alive in the Pyramid of the Moon so rulers could keep control of the masses.

130. Freshwater eels, of the genus *Anguilla*, are ancient fishes. They began evolving more than 50 million years ago, branching into 16 species and three subspecies. Most migratory fish, such as salmon and shad, are anadromous, spawning in fresh water and living as adults in salt water. The freshwater eel is one of the few fishes that do the opposite, spawning in the ocean and spending their adulthood in lakes, rivers, and estuaries – a life history known as catadromy. In general, female eels are found upstream in river systems, while males stay in the estuaries. Eels may spend decades in rivers before returning to the ocean to spawn, after which they die. No one has ever been able to witness freshwater eels spawning, and for eel biologists, solving this eel-reproduction mystery remains a kind of Holy Grail. Eel larvae were thought to be a separate species of fish until 1896, when two Italian biologists watched one in a tank metamorphose into an eel. (*National Geographic*)

A. Eels are catadromous, living as adults in salt water and travelling to fresh water for spawning.

B. Although biologists in 1896 saw an eel larva transform into an eel, they have not yet watched the fish spawning.

C. After spawning, eels return to lakes, rivers, and estuaries where they may remain for decades before dying.

D. That male eels mainly occupy estuaries while females occupy upstream waters is fundamental to how the fish spawn.

131. In the 19th century, coffee was a huge business in Europe with cafes flourishing across the continent. But coffee brewing was a slow process and, as is still the case today, customers often had to wait for their brew. Seeing an opportunity, inventors across Europe began to explore ways of using steam machines to reduce brewing time – this was, after all, the age of steam. Though there were surely innumerable patents and prototypes, the invention of the machine and the method that would lead to espresso is usually attributed to Angelo Moriondo of Turin, Italy, who was granted a patent in 1884 for "new steam machinery for the economic and instantaneous confection of coffee beverage." The machine consisted of a large boiler, heated to 1.5 bars of pressure, that pushed water through a large bed of coffee grounds on demand, with a second boiler producing steam that would flash the bed of coffee and complete the brew. With the exception of his patent, Moriondo has been largely lost to history. (*smithsonianmag.com*)

A. The precursor to the espresso machine invented by Angelo Moriondo used steam alone to brew coffee.

B. In the 19th century, Angelo Moriondo produced hundreds of machines that used steam to brew coffee.

C. In Europe during the 19th century, inventors sought ways to reduce the amount of time required to brew coffee.

D. Angelo Moriondo of Turin, Italy was the first to invent a machine that used steam to brew coffee.

132. Do you smile when you're frustrated? Most people think they don't, but they actually do, a new study from MIT has found. When asked to feign frustration, 90 per cent of research subjects did not smile. But when presented with a task that caused genuine frustration – filling out a detailed online form, only to then find the information deleted after pressing the "submit" button – 90 per cent of them smiled. Still images showed little difference between these frustrated smiles and the delighted smiles elicited by a video of a cute baby, but video analysis showed that the progression of the two kinds of smiles was quite different: Often, the happy smiles built up gradually, while frustrated smiles appeared quickly but faded fast. The research could pave the way for computers that better assess the emotional states of their users and respond accordingly. It could also help train those who have difficulty interpreting expressions to more accurately gauge the expressions they see. (*Science Daily*)

A. Video and still images both recorded a marked difference between frustrated and delighted smiles.

B. Computers may soon be able to provide individualised help based on the feelings of the people using them.

C. The majority of study participants who performed a frustrating task developed a smile that both appeared and disappeared quickly.

D. People who cannot easily figure out facial expressions fail to pick up on how an expression develops.

133. **Double-baked biscuits with a long shelf-life were the food of choice for European voyagers starting in the 1500s. A few hundred years later, airtight and reusable biscuit tins were invented. They allowed their valuable cookie contents to travel easily, stay oven-fresh and not crumble. Credit for introducing biscuit tins goes to Huntley and Palmers, a Quaker firm in Reading, England, which, by 1900, was the largest biscuit manufacturer in the world. Huntley & Palmers' tins came in all sizes and shapes. They were elaborately decorated, from miniature replicas of vehicles to reusable tins engraved with intricate still life tableaux to street-scene designs inspired by impressionist art. Biscuits weren't a luxury item in the 1800s, but the tins served a Victorian middle class eager to show good taste. The tins became independent *objets d'art* in and of themselves. For manufacturers, branding gradually took a different tone. The tins came to represent their country, an origin, a pride, an artist's whim. (*smithsonianmag.com*)**

A. While airtight tins originally kept biscuits fresh and travel-ready, they eventually became *objets d'art*.

B. Huntley & Palmers' tins came in a variety of decorations, sizes, and shapes but they all bore the same branding.

C. Beginning in the 1500s, tins provided a way to keep biscuits fresh; only later did they become *objets d'art*.

D. In the nineteenth century, the Huntley & Palmers' tins inspired by impressionist art were the most favoured by the Victorian middle class.

134. **Our galaxy is far larger, brighter, and more massive than most other galaxies. From end to end, the Milky Way's starry disk, observable with the naked eye and through optical telescopes, spans 120,000 light-years. Encircling it is another disk, composed mostly of hydrogen gas, detectable by radio telescopes. And engulfing all that our telescopes can see is an enormous halo of dark matter that they can't. While it emits no light, this dark matter far outweighs the Milky Way's hundreds of billions of stars, giving the galaxy a total mass one to two trillion times that of the sun. Indeed, our galaxy is so huge that dozens of lesser galaxies scamper about it, like moons orbiting a giant planet. Because we reside within the Milky Way, we actually know less about its overall appearance than we do about distant galaxies – just as, absent a mirror, you know more about your friends' faces than your own. (*National Geographic*)**

A. Scientists have learned a great deal about the Milky Way by observing galaxies that orbit it.

B. Milky Way stars weigh much less than the dark matter, which telescopes can't detect.

C. A ring of hydrogen gas surrounding a ring of stars constitutes the Milky Way galaxy.

D. Scientists know the mass of our galaxy's dark matter by calculating the mass of its stars.

135. **Christopher Williams is somewhat of a revolutionary as well as a whiskey distiller. This month, led by Mr Williams, nine New York State craft distilleries — including his Coppersea Distilling — will each introduce a whiskey labelled Empire Rye.**
      Empire Rye — an appellation that requires, among other things, that distillers use New York State grain and age their whiskey for at least two years — represents a novel turn in American distilling. At a time when bourbon is made by small distillers in 48 of 50 states, Mr. Williams and his co-conspirators are betting that consumers will buy into the idea of a spirit distinguished by its regional pedigree, in the same way, that millions of drinkers worldwide identify Jack Daniel's as Tennessee whiskey or Château Latour as Bordeaux wine. Empire Rye is a potential answer to a problem born of craft distilling's phenomenal success: Ten years ago there were about 100 companies making spirits in the United States; today there are nearly 1,400, according to the American

Distilling Institute. "You have all these distilleries, all going the same way, so there's no touchstone," Mr Williams said. (*nytimes.com*)

A.   This new whiskey can only be called Empire Rye if it meets more than two requirements.

B.   This new whiskey can be called Empire Rye provided it uses grain from New York State and it is aged for at least two years.

C.   Empire Rye will be made using a different method than bourbon and Tennessee whiskey.

D.   Nine New York State distilleries will be introducing Empire Rye and others will follow them.

136.   Bacteria are organisms that are equipped to reproduce themselves; antibiotics attack that machinery. But a virus is a parasite: It invades a host cell and co-opts the cell's own machinery to make copies of itself – thousands of copies at once, which means thousands of chances to mutate and develop drug resistance. A drug that disables a part of the human cell that helps the virus reproduce, though, could stop it with little risk of resistance. The key is finding the right target – a gene, and the protein it encodes, that the human cell doesn't need but the virus does. Human DNA contains more than 20,000 genes, but in any given cell at any given time, many are dormant; some, for instance, are only switched on during embryonic development. With the human genome now fully decoded, investigators can search for targets systematically by disabling individual genes in many cells and seeing what happens. (*National Geographic*)

A.   Viruses resist drugs by changing which proteins in the host cell they use to reproduce themselves.

B.   To combat viruses, researchers are looking to target a gene that is important to both the virus and the host cell.

C.   Antibiotics work by scrambling the reproductive mechanism of the bacteria, causing fatal mutations.

D.   Of the 20,000 genes that make up human DNA, some may be inactive and others may be used by viruses.

137.   Data privacy rules are tightening in the European Union, creating a niche for start-ups that shield personal details. Even as innovators increasingly use massive sets of data from digital devices to develop products and services, security problems are increasing. The number of business data breaches worldwide rose 49 percent in 2014 from the year earlier, according to the latest annual figures from the Breach Level Index, a database run by Gemalto, a Dutch digital security firm. To protect individual privacy, companies will soon be required to protect personal details "by design or by default," under the EU's General Data Protection Regulation, adopted in 2012 and set to take effect this year. Penalties can range up to 2 percent of global turnover, capped at €100 million. The tough new law "has raised awareness about data privacy," said Jason du Preez, co-founder and CEO of London-based Privitar, a start-up that sells a "de-identification tool" that it claims can obscure personal information within large data sets while permitting a company's work on analysis. (*politico.eu*)

A.   The number of business data infringements rose by almost half between 2013 and 2014.

B.   Privitar's de-identification tool can help companies avoid fines of up to 2 percent of their global turnover.

C.   The EU's General Data Protection Regulation has made data privacy more confusing for companies and for the general public.

D.   Problems with privacy are decreasing as innovators increasingly use enormous sets of data for development purposes.

138.   A 40-year retrospective study on the impact of technology in classrooms suggests that technology delivers content and supports student achievement. The research brought together data from 60,000 elementary school, high school, and post-secondary students. It compared achievement in classrooms that used computer technology versus those that used little or none. In those classrooms where computers were used to support teaching, the technology was found to have a small to moderate positive impact on both learning and attitude. "We deduce that the impact would be

even greater if observed over a student's entire educational experience," says co-author Richard Schmid. The research team found technology works best when students are encouraged to think critically and communicate effectively. "A standard PowerPoint presentation will most likely not enhance the learning experience beyond providing content or enhancing teacher-directed lectures or class discussions," says Schmid. (*Science Daily*)

A.   Critical thinking skills were more developed in students whose classrooms used computer technology than in those whose classrooms did not.

B.   Research shows that a student's learning is enhanced by creating and giving a PowerPoint presentation on their own.

C.   Research shows that a student's attitude and ability to learn and achieve are all positively influenced by the use of computers in the classroom.

D.   The extent to which technology in the classroom positively influences students' social lives correlates to the length of their exposure to it.

139.   Linguistics has undergone two great revolutions in the past 60 years, on seemingly opposite ends of the discipline. In the late 1950s Noam Chomsky theorised that all languages were built on an underlying universal grammar embedded in human genes. A second shift in linguistics – an explosion of interest in small and threatened languages – has focused on the variety of linguistic experience. Field linguists are more interested in the idiosyncrasies that make each language unique and the ways that culture can influence a language's form. Some 85 per cent of languages have yet to be documented. Understanding them can only enrich our comprehension of what is universal to all languages. Different languages highlight the varieties of human experience, revealing as mutable aspects of life that we tend to think of as settled and universal, such as our experience of time, number, or colour. In Tuva, for example, the past is always spoken of as ahead of one, and the future is behind one's back. (*National Geographic*)

A.   How we perceive and experience concepts like time and colour is universal and therefore not influenced by language.

B.   By studying how languages relate to culture, linguists will discover a set of characteristics that all languages share.

C.   While some linguists have theorised about the common foundations of language, others have chosen to investigate their differences.

D.   In Tuva, it is possible to say, "I'm looking forward to getting together with you tomorrow."

140.   Until recently, gene therapy has been reserved for severe diseases with few treatment options. But the recent report of its successful use to treat hemophilia B, which would offer patients a therapeutic alternative that could replace the need for regular, lifelong protein replacement infusions, has brought gene therapy to the forefront as a technology capable of competing with and disrupting traditional forms of treatment. Although gene therapy for hemophilia B is still in early-stage clinical testing, a similar approach is in development to treat hemophilia A, and together these life-threatening diseases represent a $6.5 billion market for current protein replacement therapies. The technical feasibility of gene therapy "has been established in multiple diseases and with different technology platforms," says Dr. Wilson. He predicts that "2012 will usher in an era of commercial development of gene therapy that, although likely to begin slowly, will quickly gather momentum." (*Science Daily*)

A.   Gene therapy has been shown to be a technically feasible option for treating numerous diseases.

B.   Dr. Wilson's prediction that gene therapy would be developed commercially in 2012 has been proven correct.

C.   Gene therapy for hemophilia A and B would cost less than what is required for protein replacement therapy.

D.   The technical viability of gene therapy for hemophilia B has been established through late-stage clinical trials.

141.   Just six days after the Bank downgraded its inflation outlook, paving the way for more quantitative easing (QE), official

figures showed that the consumer prices index (CPI) rose from 2.4pc in June to 2.6pc in July. According to Alliance Trust, the investment company, pensioners aged 75 and over were hardest hit by the price rises as food and energy costs account for a larger proportion of their outgoings. Alliance calculated their effective inflation rate was 3pc, above June's reading of 2.9pc. "It is the over 75 year old households which continue to face the highest rate of inflation, as has now been the case since the end of last year," Alliance said. People aged between 30 and 64 had the lowest inflation rate, of 2.5pc – due largely to slower petrol inflation. The Office for National Statistics (ONS) put the surprise jump in inflation down to lower discounting by clothing and footwear retailers and an unusual spike in air fares. (*The Telegraph*)

A. Economists agree that the recent increase in inflation was driven by a sudden rise in energy and food prices.

B. People between the ages of 30 and 64 faced the lowest rate of inflation for the most part due to petrol costs.

C. Fewer discounts on clothing and footwear meant that inflation in July particularly hit poorer families.

D. Inflation has most severely affected pensioners aged 75 and over because a greater proportion of their income derives from stocks and bonds.

142. Tsunamis strike somewhere in the world almost every year, and giant ones have arguably changed history. Some archaeologists have argued, for instance, that a Mediterranean tsunami struck the north shore of Crete a bit over 3,500 years ago; the disaster, they say, sent Minoan civilisation, one of the most sophisticated of the age, into a tailspin, leading it to succumb to Mycenaean Greeks. In 1755, when an earthquake and tsunami killed tens of thousands in Lisbon, the tragedy had a lasting impact on Western thought: It helped demolish the complacent optimism of the day. In the fifth century BC the Greek historian Thucydides was the first person to document the connection between earthquakes and tsunamis. He noticed that the first sign of a tsunami is often the abrupt draining of a harbour, as the sea pulls away from the coast. "Without an earthquake I do not see how such things could happen," he wrote. (*National Geographic*)

A. Greek historian Thucydides was incorrect in his belief that earthquakes were the only cause of a tsunami.

B. Greek historian Thucydides observed that a harbour will suddenly empty out just before a tsunami strikes.

C. Had a tsunami not hit Crete 3,500 years ago, the Mycenaean culture would not have prevailed over the Minoan.

D. In the city of Lisbon in 1755, many thousands of people were tragically killed by an earthquake only.

143. Bats and toothed whales had many opportunities to evolve echolocation techniques that differ from each other, since their nearest common ancestor was incapable of echolocation. Nevertheless – as scientists have known for years – bats and toothed whales rely on the same range of ultrasonic frequencies, between 15 to 200 kilohertz, to hunt their prey. This overlap in frequencies is surprising because sound travels about five times faster in water than in air, giving toothed whales an order of magnitude more time than bats to make a choice about whether to intercept a potential meal. Bats increase the number of calls per second (what researchers call a "buzz rate") while in pursuit of prey. Whales were thought to maintain a steady rate of calls or clicks no matter how far they were from a target. But new research shows that wild whales also increase their rate of calls or clicks during a kill – and that whales' buzz rates are nearly identical to that of bats, at about 500 calls or clicks per second. (*Science Daily*)

A. Before developing the ability to increase their buzz rate while pursuing prey, toothed whales emitted a steady rate of calls.

B. Five hundred is the maximum number of calls that both bats and toothed whales can process per second.

C. Bats typically use an ultrasonic frequency range of 150 to 200 kilohertz to hunt while toothed whales use a range of 15 to 200.

D. Bats and toothed whales developed similar echolocation techniques despite their different environments.

144. The nocebo effect is the phenomenon in which inert substances or mere suggestions of substances actually bring about *negative* effects in a patient or research participant. For some, being informed of a pill or procedure's potential side effects is enough to bring on real-life symptoms. Researchers from the Technical University of Munich in Germany have published one of the most thorough reviews to date on the nocebo effect. Breaking down 31 empirical studies that involved the phenomenon, they examined the underlying biological mechanisms and the problems it causes for doctors and researchers in clinical practice. Their conclusion: although perplexing, the nocebo effect is surprisingly common and ought to be taken into consideration by medical professionals on an everyday basis. The researchers suggest that doctors reconsider conventional beliefs about pain management to avoid magnifying painful side effects. (*smithsonianmag. com*)

A. Patients always feel pain when taking a pill or undergoing a procedure if it is first mentioned as a possible side effect by a doctor.

B. After reviewing studies on the nocebo effect, researchers have concluded that the phenomenon is of little consequence.

C. A review of empirical studies of the nocebo effect indicates that the phenomenon has several identifiable biological causes.

D. If a person swallows 2 sugar pills, but is told they have swallowed pills that may cause dizziness, they could experience that side effect.

145. A painful British economic recession and rising unemployment may have driven more than 1,000 people in England to commit suicide, according to a scientific study published today. The study, a so-called time-trend analysis which compared the actual number of suicides with those expected if pre-recession trends had continued, reflects findings elsewhere in Europe where suicides are also on the rise. "This is a grim reminder after the euphoria of the Olympics of the challenges we face and those that lie ahead," said David Stuckler, a sociologist at Cambridge University who co-led the study, published in the British Medical Journal (BMJ). The analysis found that between 2008 and 2010 there were 846 more suicides among men in England than would have been expected if previous trends continued, and 155 more among women. Between 2000 and 2010 each annual 10pc increase in the number of unemployed people was associated with a 1.4pc increase in the number of male suicides, the study found. (*The Telegraph*)

A. Had it not been for the Olympic games more suicides would have occurred in England during the summer.

B. Tough economic times and high unemployment may have contributed to higher suicide rates in England between 2008 and 2010.

C. According to a time-trend analysis, the ratio of male to female suicides remained constant between 2000 and 2010.

D. Rising unemployment rates and economic decline are a direct cause of suicides in England and Europe.

146. A fall alarm. Automatic nightlight. Oven reminder. Refrigerator alarm. These are just a few of the new welfare technology solutions that may become a normal part of the lives of the elderly in the future. New technology and ways of organising activities are needed if we are to meet the challenges facing the welfare state and the enormous needs for health and care services. But technology must not replace personal care and human warmth. The aim is to enhance the quality of life of elderly people who want to live at home as long as possible. By 2050 a third of Europe's population will be over 60 years of age, and by 2035 the number of people over 80 will have doubled. The World Health Organisation estimates that the need for capacity in the health sector under the current system may increase by 130,000 person-years up until 2050 – a dramatic growth rate of 120 per cent. (*Science Daily*)

A. A third of Europe's population will be using welfare technology by 2050.

B. Welfare technology's goal is to help elderly people live on their own longer.

C. Welfare technology is an effective alternative for human care services.

D. Oven reminders and fall alarms will enhance the quality of life for all elderly people.

147. Canines were the earliest domesticated animal, a process that started somewhere between 20,000 and 15,000 years ago, most likely when grey wolves began scavenging around human settlements. Eventually the relationship became a mutual one, as we began employing dogs for hunting, guarding, and companionship. Sheltered from the survival-of-the-fittest wilderness, those semi-domesticated dogs thrived even though they harboured deleterious genetic mutations – stumpy legs, for instance – that would have been weeded out in smaller wild populations. Thousands of years later, breeders would seize on that diverse raw material when they began creating modern breeds. They tended to grab traits they desired from across multiple breeds – or tried to rapidly replicate mutations in the same one – in order to get the dog they wanted. They also favoured novelty, since the more distinct a line of dogs appeared, the more likely it was to garner official recognition as a new breed. (*National Geographic*)

A. Some early partly domesticated dogs had characteristics that would likely have threatened their survival in the wild.

B. Domesticated dogs are the evolutionary consequence of early humans' need for companionship.

C. Dog breeders usually selected for those traits that would make for the most loyal companions.

D. Semi-domesticated dogs continued to evolve according to the theory of "survival of the fittest."

148. Throughout history, periods of religious and political repression have provoked an exodus of creative and entrepreneurial talent from various countries – from 17th century Huguenots fleeing France (after the king revoked religious freedoms), to 20th century Russian writers evading the Kremlin, to Jewish intellectuals escaping Nazi Germany. Likewise, many prominent Chinese artists and intellectuals who came of age during the Cultural Revolution later left China to garner fame and fortune abroad. For sixty years, upheavals in Chinese politics have not only remade the country's economy – they have remade Chinese art. During the Mao era, Soviet-inspired "socialist realism" was the only acceptable style in the strictly controlled authoritarian society. However, in 1979 Deng Xiaoping's monumental economic reforms also paved the way for the emergence of contemporary Chinese art. Over the next decade, Chinese artists had much greater access to international news and scholarship. (*smithsonianmag.com*)

A. Under the leadership of Mao, the diversity of artistic expression in China was fostered and encouraged.

B. The Huguenots, Russian writers, Jewish intellectuals, and Chinese artists all share a common experience.

C. Deng Xiaoping's influential reforms of 1979 prevented many talented artists from leaving China.

D. History shows that artistic talents flourish best in the face of political persecution.

149. Despite their modern reputation, the original Luddites were neither opposed to technology nor inept at using it. Many were highly skilled machine operators in the textile industry. The Luddite disturbances started in circumstances at least superficially similar to our own. British working families at the start of the 19th century were enduring economic upheaval and widespread unemployment. Food was scarce and rapidly becoming more costly. On March 11, 1811, in Nottingham, a textile manufacturing centre, British troops broke up a crowd of protesters demanding more work and better wages. That night, angry workers smashed textile machinery in a nearby village. Similar attacks occurred nightly at first, then sporadically, and then in waves. Fearing a national movement, the government soon positioned thousands of soldiers to defend factories. Parliament passed a measure to make machine-breaking a capital offence. But the Luddites were neither as organised nor as dangerous as authorities believed. (*smithsonianmag.com*)

A. Although the working classes faced economic turmoil in early 19th century England, the upper classes did not.

B.   The Luddite uprising of the 19th century occurred amid high levels of unemployment and high food costs.

C.   Luddite protests probably ceased for the most part after the British parliament made breaking machines a capital offence.

D.   Luddites in 19th century England destroyed textile machinery only to demand better wages.

150. Gian Lorenzo Bernini was said to have been only 8 when he carved a stone head that "was the marvel of everyone" who saw it, according to a contemporary biographer. He was not much older when he dazzled Pope Paul V, who reportedly declared "We hope that this youth will become the Michelangelo of his century." Prophetic words: over a long lifetime, Bernini undertook commissions for eight popes, transforming the look of 17th-century Rome as Michelangelo had helped shape Florence and Rome a century before. Much of the Baroque grandeur of the Eternal City – its churches, fountains, piazzas and monuments – can be credited to Bernini and his followers. Indeed, Bernini was a highly original thinker, not merely a consummate craftsman. In the many different arts he pursued – sculpture, architecture, painting, even playwriting – his works expressed ideas. Behind every Bernini masterpiece there lies a *concetto*, its governing concept or conceit. (*smithsonianmag.com*)

A.   Without the recognition and commissions of eight popes, Bernini might have lived and died an unknown artist.

B.   Bernini thoroughly explored a *concetto* through painting before translating it to a sculpture or building.

C.   Bernini's paintings, sculptures, and building designs irrevocably changed the face of 17th century Florence.

D.   Bernini's talent was apparent from a young age, and it is still apparent today, immortalised in the Eternal City.

151. The European Central Bank (ECB) and the Bank of England (BOE) said they are concerned about the "shrinking" market for asset backed securities, or bundles of mortgage, small business and other loans that are packaged and sold to investors. Securitization became a bad word during the financial crisis, when it was largely blamed for reckless lending decisions by banks, which were then sold to hapless investors. But the ECB has argued lately that regulation should take into account that European securitization instruments have performed far better than their U.S. counterparts. "Despite its long-term value, securitization today suffers from stigma, reflecting both its adverse reputation amongst investors and conservatism among regulators," the central banks said. ECB President Mario Draghi said at the central bank's last news conference that the ECB and BOE would present their paper at the meetings of the International Monetary Fund, currently taking place in Washington, D.C. (*online.wsj.com*)

A.   The BOE and ECB maintain that securitization is worthwhile although it is not in favour at present.

B.   European securitization products have not fluctuated in price as much as U.S. products.

C.   The central banks believe that securitization was the major cause of the financial crisis.

D.   The BOE and ECB are not worried about the size of the bundled loan market in Europe.

152. Kimbal Musk, 45, got rich working in technology alongside his older brother, Elon. Now he wants to do for food what his brother has done for electric cars and space travel. Although Mr Musk has food ventures active in Colorado, where he lives, as well as in big cities like Chicago and Los Angeles, he has become enamoured of places like Tennessee, Indiana and Ohio — parts of the country he believes are the ripest for a revolution in eating and agriculture. Mr Musk is promoting a philosophy he calls "real food," which nourishes the body, the farmer and the planet. It doesn't sound much different than what writers like Michael Pollan and everyone who has ever helped start a farmers' market or community garden have preached for years. But Mr Musk has big ideas about what the Silicon Valley crowd likes to call the food space, which is as exciting to him as the internet was in 1995. In short, he wants to create a network of business, educational and agricultural ventures big

enough to swing the nation's food system back to one based on healthy, local food grown on chemical-free farms. (*nytimes. com*).

A. A businessman living in Colorado has ambitions to change the nation's food system in the direction of "real food".

B. The Silicon Valley crowd believe Tennessee, Indiana and Ohio are ripe for a revolution in in what they call the "food space".

C. Kimbal Musk's vision for the food space will most likely be as revolutionary as the internet was in 1995.

D. Kimbal Musk's aim is to have only farms that are chemical-free in the United States

153. Mars' atmosphere was probably never thick enough to keep temperatures on the planet's surface above freezing for the long term, suggests research published today in *Nature Geoscience*. Although the planet's topography indicates that liquid water has flooded Mars in the distant past, evidence increasingly suggests that those episodes reflect occasional warm spells, not a consistently hospitable phase of the planet's history. Signs of flowing water on Mars include layered sediments presumed to have been laid down in ancient lakes, as well as rugged canyons and lowlands apparently sculpted by massive floods. These had once prompted researchers to suggest that the red planet, now frigid and dry, was warm and wet throughout its early history. But that would have required an atmosphere much thicker than today's, a prospect that now seems unlikely, says Edwin Kite, a planetary scientist at Princeton University in New Jersey. (*www.nature.com*)

A. In contrast to its cold past, Mars is currently in a relatively temperate period, researchers think.

B. The research indicates that floods on Mars occurred only intermittently rather than during a long continuous period.

C. Floods were partly responsible for the canyons and lowlands existing on Mars.

D. Mars' atmosphere has very rarely been such as to keep water above its freezing temperature.

154. Ever since the first metal workers of antiquity dug copper from a Cyprus hillside and fashioned it into tools, copper has been in high demand. So high, in fact, that researchers in February raised the prospect that international copper production could peak within a few decades. (The original Cypriot copper mine lives on in the chemical symbol Cu, drawn from the Latin name for the island's metal.) A recent discovery describes improvements to copper as a catalyst that could streamline ethanol production. A catalyst helps chemical reactions occur more efficiently. In theory, better copper catalysts could offer an efficient method to convert carbon dioxide to liquid, carbon-based fuels. The traditional copper-catalysed conversion of carbon dioxide to liquid fuel proceeds through an intermediate of carbon monoxide. Many catalysts can perform the first step, but only copper can mix the carbon monoxide with water to produce fuel. (*www.nature.com*)

A. The copper market was small before labourers began extracting the metal from Cypriot mines.

B. Copper is the sole agent that can change carbon dioxide into carbon monoxide.

C. Copper extraction will likely reach its maximum point within 25 years.

D. Improvements in the production of ethanol could result from a discovery in the use of copper as a catalyst.

155. A below-ground experiment at the South Pole discovered three of the highest-energy neutrinos ever found. These neutrinos have energies at the absurdly high scale of petaelectronvolts — roughly the energy equivalent of one million times a proton's mass. Famous physicist Albert Einstein showed in his $E = mc2$ equation that energy and mass are equivalent, and such a large amount of mass converts to an extreme level of energy. The experiment, called IceCube, reported the discovery of the first two, nicknamed Ernie and Bert last year, and announced the third, Big Bird, Monday at the American Physical Society meeting. These neutrinos are valuable because they are extremely standoffish, rarely ever interacting with other particles, and uncharged, their direction never swayed by magnetic fields. Astronomers think the neutrinos could emanate from

a variety of intense events such as large black holes accreting matter, explosions called gamma-ray bursts or galaxies forming stars at furious rates. (*www.nature.com*)

A.   Ernie and Bert were identified last year by IceCube in a sub-surface test at the South Pole.

B.   Ernie, Bert, and Big Bird are most probably among the highest-energy neutrinos in the universe.

C.   Its aloof tendency bars a neutrino from being affected by other particles within the universe.

D.   An intense process of star creation could be the source of the vigorous particles found by IceCube.

156.   When planning vacation itineraries, graveyard visits may not be top of mind. But Loren Rhoads, author of the new book *199 Cemeteries to See Before You Die*, makes the case for going out of your way to see burial grounds. While it's fun to see where famous leaders and celebrities are buried, it's also instructive to see how ordinary people came to rest, too. Visiting your local cemetery can reveal the families who lent their names to the streets and neighbourhoods in your town, and looking at their groupings and ages can bring history to life. "Up until fairly recently when there were written records, the things we know about the past, for the most part, we know about because of people who've been buried — how they were buried, what they were buried with. Even the Greeks and Romans, we've learned a lot because of their tombs. And now with the move toward cremation and scattering and all that, we don't have that, and there hasn't been a replacement. So we can guess what a normal person ate in the Middle Ages, we can guess what they wore in pre-history, but we won't know that about us," Rhoads says. "Once we're gone and our ashes are scattered, there won't be any record." (*time.com*)

A.   Cemeteries are one of the least popular places for tourists to visit when they are holidaying in foreign countries.

B.   Our understanding of Ancient Greek culture has been significantly influenced by recent research into their places of burial.

C.   Loren Rhoads believes that because of cremation a type of historical record is being lost.

D.   Most streets and neighbourhoods are named after families who lived there previously.

157.   The collision of a pair of neutron stars, marked by ripples through the fabric of space-time and a flash brighter than a billion suns, has been witnessed for the first time in the most intensely observed astronomical event to date. The extraordinary sequence, in which the two ultra-dense stars spiralled inwards, violently collided and, in all likelihood, immediately collapsed into a black hole, was first picked up by the Laser Interferometer Gravitational-Wave Observatory (Ligo). Albert Einstein, the German-born theoretical physicist first predicted the existence of gravitational waves a century ago, but the first experimental proof that space itself can be stretched and squeezed took until 2015 when Ligo scientists detected a collision of black holes. This time, as the stars collided, they emitted an intense beam of gamma rays and the sky was showered with heavy elements, resolving a decades-old debate about where gold and platinum come from. Neutron stars are the smallest, densest stars known to exist: about 12 miles wide, with a teaspoon of neutron star material having a mass of about a billion tons. The core is a soup of pure neutrons, while the crust is smooth, solid and 10 billion times stronger than steel. (*theguardian.com*)

A.   The collision of a pair of neutron stars has attracted exceptional interest.

B.   The phenomenon of stars immediately collapsing into a black hole was observed by the Laser Interferometer Gravitational-Wave Observatory.

C.   Einstein predicted 100 years ago that this event would happen, but we did not know for sure until 2015 if it could happen.

D.   Due to this event, we are now even closer to resolving where gold and platinum comes from.

158.   Most eggshells have a barrier to repel germs but microbes that penetrate encounter an antimicrobial enzyme called lysozyme in the whites of bird eggs. Brush turkey eggs have roughly the same amount of lysozyme as chicken eggs, but their shells are 1.5 times thinner

than those of chickens. This should make them more susceptible to microbes, not less, but infections occur in only about 9% of Australian brush turkey eggs, for example. The eggs incubate in moist piles of rotting vegetation to keep them warm from the heat generated as microbes in the soil and compost decompose organic matter. Those same microbes can get through eggshells and kill the embryos, but researchers found that the shells are covered in a layer of nanometre-sized spheres of calcium phosphate, making them more water-repellent than chicken eggs and helping them to fend off bacterial attachment and penetration. The findings could one day lead to new antimicrobial coatings for plastics and other surfaces. (*www.nature.com*)

A. Diseases affect Australian brush turkey eggs less than the eggs of other related bird species.

B. Bird eggs contain chemicals within their yolks that render bacteria and other pathogens inactive.

C. Chicken eggs resist water less than those of brush turkeys but contain about equal levels of lysozyme.

D. The temperature emanating from decay in the ground negatively affects brush turkey eggs.

159. The site of the world's next generation ground-based gamma-ray detector, the Cherenkov Telescope Array (CTA), is still undecided but a panel of funders has narrowed the field slightly, following a meeting in Munich, Germany. Scientists had originally hoped to select two sites, a large one in the Southern Hemisphere and a smaller one in the North, by the end of 2013, but the selection process for the €200 million project has taken longer than originally foreseen. Representatives from 12 government ministries narrowed the potential southern sites from five to two: Aar, a site in Southern Namibia, and Armazones in Chile's Atacama desert while picking a reserve site in Argentina. The committee, a panel of representatives from Argentina, Austria, Brazil, France, Germany, Italy, Namibia, Poland, Spain, South Africa, Switzerland and the United Kingdom, decided that all four possible northern sites in Mexico, Spain and the United States needed further analysis. (*blogs.nature.com*)

A. All the potential southern hemisphere locations for the detector are in one of the 12 countries making the selection.

B. The nations financing the venture met in Germany because its economy is the largest among them.

C. The number of southern hemisphere countries with potential sites for the detector does not exceed the number of countries in the northern hemisphere with potential sites.

D. Building the southern hemisphere CTA will most likely cost more than its northern counterpart due to its greater scale.

160. The top two cement makers hope their merger isn't going to run into antitrust worries. Lafarge, based in France and Holcim, in Switzerland, plan to put $8 billion of assets around the world up for sale in a bid to secure antitrust clearance for their merger, which would create the world's largest construction-materials company with a combined market value of about $50 billion. The companies disclosed Friday that they were in advanced talks but said a deal wasn't certain. The swift progress toward completing a merger suggests the companies are confident they can overcome what are likely to be lofty antitrust hurdles. The boards of both companies approved the merger plan and Holcim executives are expected in Paris, France to announce the merger. It's not clear what production facilities or other assets the two companies will propose to part with as part of their agreement, or whether that will be enough to mollify regulators' likely concerns with the potential tie-up. (*online.wsj.com*)

A. If the organisations sell some of their assets, they will be able to combine their operations.

B. The management of one company is traveling to the national base of the other to announce their merger.

C. The companies have disclosed which resources will be disposed of in order to secure their union.

D. Government regulators are interested in the implications of the companies' combination.

161. Governments have wasted billions of dollars stockpiling antiviral drugs for use in seasonal and pandemic flu, a

non-profit group of medical experts said this week, after analysing the results of previously unpublished clinical trials. The Cochrane Collaboration, another international organisation headquartered in Oxford, UK, has been arguing its case against the efficacy of the antiviral Tamiflu, also known as oseltamivir, for more than four years, initially on the basis of a previous analysis of the limited published data available. Today, it published an analysis of more than 500 pages after a campaign with the British Medical Journal (BMJ) to access the full, unpublished, clinical-trial data on Tamiflu. But other scientists say that although scrutiny is welcome, the review has uncovered little new information and in itself does not make a strong case to stop stockpiling. (*www.nature.com*)

A.   The Cochrane Collaboration launched its campaign based on access to undisclosed information while the non-profit group had to rely on widely known data.

B.   The Cochrane Collaboration's evaluation produced insufficient evidence to alter antiviral policy.

C.   Governments have spent more than a billion dollars on stockpiling Tamiflu.

D.   The Cochrane Collaboration has argued a case based on limited published data.

162.   In 1963, an inventor called Walter Munk led a team of scientists studying how swells generated by Antarctic storms travel more than 16,000km across the Pacific Ocean. The team set up stations to measure the waves as they travelled in a great circle from New Zealand to Alaska. Munk and his family spent more than a month in American Samoa for the experiment, monitoring pressure sensors mounted on the ocean floor and recording data on paper tape punched with holes. The experiment yielded a surprising discovery. The waves showed very little decay in energy on their journey across the Pacific. The biggest change was a shift in the observed period of the wave – that is, the time between passing crests. Munk's team found that the period increased as the waves moved northwards. This happens because ocean waves are dispersive, meaning that the speed of

the wave depends on the period. Long-period waves move more rapidly, so they run to the front of the pack, while shorter-period waves lag behind. The phenomenon is well known to surfers, who experience this dispersive ordering as a gradual shortening of the time between sets of waves. (*time.com*)

A.   The energy of the waves that Munk observed did not deplete significantly as they travelled across the Pacific Ocean.

B.   The study in 1963 confirmed what a few ocean scientists had hypothesised for years, that ocean waves are dispersive.

C.   We know from the passage that ocean waves speed up as they move northwards.

D.   Waves travel directly in a continuous straight line northward from New Zealand to Alaska and increase in lengths of periods.

163.   Chancellor Angela Merkel's government approved legislation revamping Germany's sweeping plan to generate more than 40 percent of its energy needs through renewable resources by 2025 by slowing the rapid expansion of solar and wind parks in an effort to hold down spiraling prices. Already, 25 percent of German energy comes from renewable resources, but that advance has come at a cost to consumers, who have borne the brunt of the surcharges that funded the expansion. Keeping power prices in check is a key element of the government's revised policy, even as it upholds exemptions for crucial industries that require high amounts of energy. "Restart means no longer following the illusion that the energy transformation can be achieved by expanding renewable energy as quickly as possible, but to make sure that the expansion will be safe and predictable," Sigmar Gabriel, the energy and economics minister, said in announcing the changes to the legislation, the Renewable Energy Sources Act. (*www.nytimes.com*)

A.   Solar and wind power installations make up twenty-five percent of Germany's energy production.

B.   Angela Merkel has stated that Germany's sweeping plan to generate more than 40 percent of its energy needs through renewable resources by 2025 was too fast.

C. Some business users pay lower charges for energy than consumers, who mostly finance Germany's shift to renewables.

D. Sigmar Gabriel thinks Germany can develop renewable energy as fast as possible without too much risk.

164. Belovezhskaya National Park houses a huge forest of old-growth evergreen, beech, oak, alder, and spruce trees. Despite its size the park protects only about 10 percent of the Białowieża Primeval Forest, which dates back some 10,000 years and stands as the sole large remnant of the ancient forests that once covered much of Europe. The park has more than a thousand trees that are 300 to 600 years old and many more in old-growth stands of 250 to 200 years old. The park is home to a number of notable ancient oak trees; some are more than 500 years old. The Białowieża Forest creates an inviting ecosystem for many other plant species, including hundreds of lichens and mosses and thousands of different fungi. Belovezhskaya borders Poland and an adjacent national park across the border, Białowieski National Park, is Poland's oldest and one of the first in Europe at its founding in 1932. (*travel.nationalgeographic.com*)

A. Belovezhskaya National Park, founded in the 1930s, contains Europe's oldest trees.

B. The country of Poland has Europe's oldest park, which is adjacent to the Belovezhskaya National Park.

C. Belovezhskaya National Park shelters a fraction of the forest having the same name as a park in Poland.

D. Woodlands in a park in a country neighbouring Poland include some trees that have existed for at least three centuries.

165. Overfishing is still the most important threat to Mediterranean underwater ecosystems, "more than pollution, invasive species, or climate change", says Enric Sala, one of the authors of the most comprehensive study made of the sea, published this week in the science journal PLoS ONE. The assessment, presented in a paper entitled Large-Scale Assessment of Mediterranean Marine Protected Areas Effects on Fish Assemblages, drew on the work of a dozen researchers. A marine ecologist and a National Geographic Explorer-in-Residence, Sala is actively engaged in exploration, research and communications to advance ocean policy and conservation. Sala believes that without radical changes to fishing practices, we're just going to reduce the Mediterranean Sea to a soup of microbes and jellyfish. (*newswatch. nationalgeographic.com*)

A. If the current rate of fishing in the Mediterranean continues, then the sea's microbe levels will increase.

B. Sala had collaborators in his research focusing on protected regions within the Mediterranean Sea.

C. Twelve researchers think that excessive fishing will do more harm to marine life than pollution.

D. Enric Sala announced the results of the research in National Geographic just this week.

166. Many avalanches are small slides of dry powdery snow that move as a formless mass and account for a tiny fraction of the death and destruction wrought by bigger, more organized avalanches. Disastrous avalanches occur when massive slabs of snow break loose from a mountainside and shatter like broken glass as they race downhill. These moving masses can reach speeds of 80 miles (130 kilometers) per hour within about five seconds and victims caught in these events seldom escape. Avalanches are most common during, and in the 24 hours right after, a storm that dumps 12 inches (30 centimeters) or more of fresh snow. The quick pileup overloads the underlying snowpack, which causes a weak layer beneath the slab to fracture. The layers are an archive of winter weather: big dumps, drought, rain, a hard freeze, more snow, and how the layers bond often determines how easily one will weaken and cause a slide. (*environment. nationalgeographic.com*)

A. Avalanches occur when strata of frozen precipitation from previous winters splinter and cause rapid movement of snow.

B. Avalanches can occur while winter storms are still happening and advance at up to eighty miles per hour.

C. Larger avalanches are less frequent than small ones but account for more damage than the latter.

D. Avalanches that do not break up as they move downhill are the most severe.

167 A ruin facing ruin, Pompeii looks to one of its doomed sister cities in its latest rescue effort. Italian officials this month unveiled details of the Great Pompeii Project, a 105-million-euro ($145 million U.S. dollar) project to restore the famed Roman town, pillaged by treasure hunters, overrun by tourists, and wracked by the elements in the four centuries since its rediscovery. A highly innovative, "maintenance-based" approach to restoration will guide the project, said Massimo Osanna, the newly appointed superintendent of the site, in a statement. Instead of piecemeal patches to individual buildings or attractions, the effort will take its cues from the conservation of the nearby buried Roman town of Herculaneum, which was a 20-million-euro ($27.7 million U.S. dollar) effort. The hope is that by putting comprehensive maintenance concerns first, more of the site can be opened to visitors. (*news.nationalgeographic.com*)

A. The previous superintendent of the Pompeii site employed a traditional piecemeal approach.

B. Both Roman towns have been ruined by weather and overwhelmed by visitors since being unearthed.

C. The new strategy for Pompeii will primarily involve piecemeal restoration of specific important structures.

D. Herculaneum's restoration cost over 20 million dollars while Pompeii's will cost under 145 million euros.

168. Lafarge and Holcim are leading players in construction materials like cement, gravel and asphalt, which are used to pave roads. Because the cement market is largely local—cement is cheap to make but expensive to transport—both companies have expanded in many of the same markets around the world. The companies' combined market share of cement-making capacity is around 60% in France, Canada and Morocco and 30% in the U.S. The two companies have combined annual sales of nearly $43 billion, dwarfing rivals such as Germany's HeidelbergCement, with $18 billion in sales, and Mexico's Cemex, with $15 billion. The European Commission has been investigating Holcim, Lafarge and six other companies for operating a suspected cartel in cement and cement-based products since December 2010. (*online.wsj.com*)

A. HeidelbergCement is being probed like Holcim and Lafarge for engaging in collusive behavior.

B. Cement producers operate only in their home countries because cement is costly to ship.

C. The profits realized by Lafarge and Holcim from non-U.S. sources are greater than those from the U.S.

D. Lafarge and Holcim make over $40 billion in annual sales combined without having half of the U.S. cement market.

169. Greece's highest mountain, Olympus, is also the legendary abode of the gods. The favor of the deities gave the mountain an honored place in Classical Greek culture and that mythical status has been passed down through the centuries across Western civilization. The mountain's highest peak, Mytikas, tops out at 9,573 feet (2,918 meters) and was called "Pantheon" by the ancients, who believed it was the meeting place of the deities. The 12 gods were believed to have lived in the alpine ravines, which Homer described as the mountain's "mysterious folds." The village of Dion, on the mountain's flanks, was a Macedonian holy city where King Archelaus (r. 414-399 B.C.) held nine days of games to honor the god Zeus and today, the Olympus Festival held in the summer there includes performances at the ancient theater. Modern-day Dion also houses a remarkable archaeological site, where work is ongoing, and an archaeological museum in which much of the region's rich Classical history is on display. (*travel.nationalgeographic.com*)

A. Greek divinities were said to have assembled on the highest mountain of the Classical world.

B. A location with antique artifacts and a theatre from antiquity still exist on the sides of Olympus.

C. Dion served as the location of a week-long event involving sports to celebrate a Macedonian royal.

D. Homer believed that Greek divinities inhabited the fissures within Greece's highest mountain.

170. **The park, Snowdonia, is a Welsh landscape of mountains, valleys, forests, and lakes established in 1951 and covering 2,132 square kilometers. Snowdonia is punctuated by the park's namesake mountain peak, Snowdon - Yr Wyddfa in the local Welsh tongue - standing at 1,085 meters and the highest point in Wales and England. The Welsh name for Snowdonia is Eryri (the Highland), and nine mountain ranges cover fully half of Snowdonia with a breathtaking array of jagged peaks, gorges, and windswept uplands. King Arthur is the region's most legendary inhabitant and it is said that it was on the top of Snowdon itself that he fought an epic battle with the king-killing giant Rhita Gawr. Rhita Gawr's resting place, under summit rocks, presumably lent the mountain its ancient Welsh names Yr Wyddfa Fawr (the Great Tomb) and Carnedd y Cawr (the Cairn of the Giant).** (*travel.nationalgeographic.com*)

A. A famous monarch who lived in the area of the modern-day park slayed a giant known for having killed a king.

B. The park's mountain peak has the same Welsh name as the park it is located in.

C. A series of mountain ranges spans over two thousand square kilometers within Snowdonia as well as outside its borders.

D. The mountain's ancient names, in the local language, refer to the reputed burial place of a giant who fought a legendary king.

171. **Recent photos taken by NASA's Mars rover might appear to show a gleaming alien bonfire burning in the distance—at least according to some on the internet—but that's not exactly what's happening. Fact is, there still isn't any evidence for life on Mars. None. The provocative, shiny smears of light appear in two images snapped by rover Curiosity's navigation camera, one on April 2 and the other on April 3, provoking excitement among some in the UFO-spotting crowd. The photos come courtesy of the camera's right eye and show nearly vertical bright smudges emerging from a spot near the horizon. Photos of the same spot shot by the camera's left eye, meanwhile, show no such things. Rather than emanating from an underground Martian disco, the bright spots are probably caused by cosmic rays colliding with the rover's camera or by glinting rocks reflecting the Martian sunlight, according to NASA's Jet Propulsion Laboratory's Justin Maki, lead imaging scientist for the Curiosity team.** (*news.nationalgeographic.com*)

A. The rover's camera was interfered with by radiation and by rubble redirecting light into its lens.

B. The right eye of Curiosity's camera failed to detect illumination found by the camera's left eye.

C. More than one snapshot has caused internet users to consider there might be extraterrestrial activity on Mars.

D. NASA says that data confirming activity by extraterrestrials on the planet Mars is lacking.

172. **Most mornings at nine, the emergency responders assigned to the Seine pull on their wet suits and swim around the Île de la Cité, a teardrop-shaped island in the middle of the river in the middle of Paris. The firemen-divers scour the bottom and retrieve bikes, cutlery (which they clean and use in the nearby houseboat where they live), cell phones, old coins, crucifixes, guns, keys tossed in the water by couples hoping to affirm the eternal nature of their love, and once, a museum-grade Roman clasp. Historically, the left bank of the Seine was bohemian while its right bank was aristocratic, and as the central artery of Paris, the Seine naturally accrues the detritus of human civilization and relationships. However, through the centuries the river has also served as highway, moat, water tap, sewer, and washtub. The river's scimitar arc still slices the city, dividing it into left and right banks, but the distinctions of living on either have blurred over time.** (*ngm. nationalgeographic.com*)

A. Roman money and eating utensils have been found by divers at the bottom of the river.

B. Most of the keys thrown into the river are symbols of eternal love and can't actually open anything.

C.   A residence on a teardrop-shaped island in the middle of the Seine is where the firemen-divers patrolling the river live.

D.   The different character of the two sides of the river is less marked than was once the case.

173.   Agriculture is among the greatest contributors to global warming, emitting more greenhouse gases than all our cars, trucks, trains, and airplanes combined—largely from the methane gas released by cattle and rice farms, nitrous oxide from fertilized fields, and carbon dioxide from the cutting of rain forests to grow crops or raise livestock. Farming is the thirstiest user of our precious water supplies and a major polluter, as runoff from fertilizers and manure disrupts fragile lakes, rivers, and coastal ecosystems across the globe. Agriculture also accelerates the loss of biodiversity when areas of grassland and forest are cleared for farms, resulting in the loss of crucial habitat and making agriculture a major driver of wildlife extinction. (*www.nationalgeographic. com*)

A.   Substances used to enrich the land contaminate bodies of water and partly cause the world to heat up.

B.   Animal species are dying due to the increasing amounts of carbon dioxide released by deforestation.

C.   Cultivating land and taking care of cattle are the principle causes of the world's temperature rising.

D.   Land and air transport vehicles produce more greenhouse gases than does farming.

174.   Garajonay Park is on the island of La Gomera in Spain's Canary Islands, off the northwest coast of Africa, and covered more than two-thirds by a thick laurel forest. Laurel forests are now rare in North Africa and southern Europe, where they thrived during the Tertiary, a geologic period from 66 million to 2.588 million years ago. The landscape is fed by springs, streams, and nurtured by volcanic soils, but La Gomera is the only one of the Canary Islands that has not had a volcanic eruption in the modern era.

No people live inside the park but La Gomera has an unusual cultural heritage. The island's Guanche people, possibly

North African Berbers, developed a language, dubbed the silbo gomero, ideal for communicating across forested hillsides and valleys. Spain colonized the Canaries in the 15th century and the islands long served as an important stopover on sea routes from Europe to the Americas, and were Christopher Columbus's last port of call before making landfall in the Americas. (*travel. nationalgeographic.com*)

A.   A Spanish explorer made a brief stop on La Gomera during his travels before continuing to America.

B.   The origin of La Gomera's inhabitants may be from a region lying to the south and east of the island.

C.   A type of woodland frequently found in southern Europe populates the largest proportion of the park.

D.   All of the islands have experienced a volcanic event in their existence except the one with the park.

175.   Montenegro houses the enormous Durmitor Massif and three breathtaking canyons, including that of the wild Tara River, which is home to Europe's deepest gorge at 1,300 meters. A massif is a demarcated portion of a planet's crust, a famous example being the massif resembling a face on Mars. Rivers also flow under Montenegro's massif with waters from Black Lake travelling below it to the upper canyon valley of the River Komarnica. A park sharing the same name as the massif was established in 1952 and spans 339 square kilometers. It is dotted with more than a dozen sparkling lakes and thickly forested with both deciduous and pine forests—including one of Europe's last virgin stands of black pine near Crna Poda. These trees are more than 400 years old and tower some 50 meters high. In the summer, many of the park's high pastures are home to grazing sheep and cattle owned by the 1,500-some people living within the park and by others in the nearby village of Zabljak. (*travel. nationalgeographic.com*)

A.   A depression 1300 meters deep and 100km long has been carved out by a river in Montenegro.

B.   Inhabitants of a Montenegrin community outside of Durmitor's boundaries possess foraging animals.

C.   Waters from a lake travel under Durmitor's surface along with the Tara River, which makes Europe's deepest gorge.

D.   An area having centuries old forest life and human inhabitants contains over twelve bodies of water.

176.   **The environmental challenges posed by agriculture are enormous, and they will only become more pressing as we try to meet the growing need for food worldwide. We'll likely have two billion more mouths to feed by mid-century— more than nine billion people, but sheer population growth is not the only reason we will need more food. The spread of prosperity across the world, especially in China and India, is driving an increased demand for meat, eggs, and dairy, boosting pressure to grow more corn and soybeans to feed more cattle, pigs, and chickens. If these trends continue, the double whammy of population growth and richer diets will require us to roughly double the amount of crops we grow by 2050. (***www.nationalgeographic.com***)**

A.   Rising demand for animal derived products is a lesser cause of overall rising food demand than other factors.

B.   The food demand forecast for the century's midpoint necessitates an increase in the number of farms.

C.   Growing soybean consumption by Asian people has resulted from greater wealth and living standards.

D.   The trend in soybean and corn consumption by livestock results from rising global incomes.

177.   **It turns out that both cosmic rays and glinting rocks are pretty common on Mars and have been spotted in images sent by several of NASA's Mars rovers to Earth. NASA is the U.S. space exploration agency and cosmic rays are particles originating outside of the solar system with very high energy. A NASA scientist explained that maybe one percent of the hundreds of weekly images include cosmic ray-induced bright spots but the junked-up pixels normally don't cause much of a stir. The scientist pointed out**

that NASA might not see cosmic rays for two or three days in the images but certainly does at least once a week, the reason being that Mars's atmosphere is thinner and doesn't block as much cosmic radiation as Earth's does. (*news. nationalgeographic.com***)**

A.   Martian conditions are causing the weekly rate of luminous marks found in NASA's photographs.

B.   Photographs of light-reflecting rubble are frequently beamed back by various countries' exploratory vehicles on Mars.

C.   Earth's surrounding layer prevents cameras on Earth from being interfered with by energetic matter.

D.   The pictures are free from irregularities for the most part and lack abnormalities in some weeks.

178.   **Some 80 percent of all the planet's earthquakes occur along the rim of the Pacific Ocean, called the "Ring of Fire" because of the preponderance of volcanic activity there as well. Most earthquakes occur at fault zones, where tectonic plates—giant rock slabs that make up the Earth's upper layer—collide or slide against each other. These impacts are usually gradual and unnoticeable on the surface; however, immense stress can build up between plates. When this stress is released quickly, it sends massive vibrations, called seismic waves, often hundreds of miles through the rock and up to the surface. Other quakes can occur far from fault zones when plates are stretched or squeezed. Scientists assign a magnitude rating to earthquakes based on the strength and duration of their seismic waves. A quake measuring 3 to 5 is considered minor or light; 5 to 7 is moderate to strong; 7 to 8 is major; and 8 or more is great. (***environment. nationalgeographic.com***)**

A.   Tremors can result far from fault zones when sections of the Earth's upper layer contract and expand but occur mostly where they meet.

B.   The Atlantic, Indian, and Arctic Oceans are where twenty percent of oceanic earthquakes happen.

C.   The perimeter of an ocean gets its name from the frequency of earthquakes that occur along it.

D.   Grading an earthquake from magnitude three to five means that its effects are usually gradual and unnoticeable at the surface.

179. **Blanketed with ash by the A.D. 79 eruption of Italy's Mount Vesuvius then rediscovered, Pompeii has seen almost three-quarters of its homes, temples, and streets exposed to the elements due to the removal of the deadly, preserving ash that once roughly buried the town. Once home to perhaps 12,000 people, Pompeii is now one of the world's great tourist sites, seeing more than two million visitors a year. Tourists, thieves, and time have made the 163-acre (66-hectare) ruin more of a ruin, with three walls suffering collapses and vandals stealing a fresco in March. Herculaneum was a nearby town buried even deeper by Vesuvius, under about 82 feet (25 meters) of ash, and is a smaller tourist site but underwent a restoration in which roofing and drains made much of the difference. (*news. nationalgeographic.com*)**

A.   The same eruption from the Italian volcano that covered Pompeii in ash also enveloped Herculaneum.

B.   Overhead cover and better drainage could play a major role in Pompeii's restoration as they did in another city.

C.   Some walls have given way but under three-quarters of Pompeii's houses, churches, and roads are vulnerable to weather damage.

D.   Herculaneum's number of visitors is unknown while just under two million per year visit Pompeii.

180. **In contrast to the huge surpluses that have been typical in recent years, Germany bought almost as much from its neighbors in February as it sold to them. German exports to the euro zone totaled 34.9 billion euros, or $48.2 billion, in February, a 3.7 percent increase from a year earlier. That compares with the 8.4 percent jump in imports, which were valued at €34.6 billion, according to the German Federal Statistical Office. German exports worldwide rose 4.6 percent during February to €92.4 billion. The increase in imports from the rest of Europe is mostly good news, economists say, especially for countries like Greece and Italy that suffer from very high unemployment and desperately need customers for their exports. But some analysts warn that Germany, which has Europe's largest economy, could be squandering hard-fought gains in competitiveness. (*www.nytimes.com*)**

A.   A rise in Germany's imports has produced more jobs in Greece and Italy.

B.   Thanks to an 8.4% percent year-on-year increase, Germany's imports from the euro zone in February were less than half a billion euro lower than its exports to the euro zone.

C.   Germany's worldwide exports increased under 4 percent while those just to the euro zone increased over 4 percent.

D.   Greece and Italy shipped more products to Germany in February than Germany shipped to them.

ANSWERS

1.   C

A.   Cannot say. While this may seem a likely answer, the passage does not actually tell us why, or even if, English was chosen as the universal aviation language.

B.   Cannot say. The passage does not say that English was officially adopted after the tragedy, only that it emphasized the need for a universal aviation language.

C.   True. This is clearly stated in the first sentence.

D.   False. It was not the pilot's inability to speak English, but a combination of a heavy accent, non-standard language and radio interference that contributed to the accident.

2.   D

A.   False. While it was once believed that personality patterns and behaviours persist over time, "mounting evidence is undermining that notion".

B.   Cannot say. We are not told who defined the "big five" traits.

C.   False. According to the passage, most people would like to change their personalities "a little", but not to have "strikingly different" personalities.

D.   True. While William James believed that personalities are set by the age of 30, and "his idea stuck", new evidence strongly suggests otherwise.

3.   B

A.   Cannot say. It was "common practice" to use drinking establishments but we are not told if voting "usually" took place in them.

B.   True. As the passage states, Edgar Allen Poe may have been caught up in a form of electoral fraud known as "cooping".

C.   False. Victims of the electoral fraud method known as "cooping" were disguised so that they could vote in multiple locations because it would have otherwise been prevented.

D.   False. While there is reason to believe Poe may have been made to vote on multiple occasions, there is no evidence that he actually did. Therefore, to say that it was discovered that he had done so, is an inaccurate statement.

4.   C

A.   Cannot say. The topic of lens price is not mentioned.

B.   Cannot say. Although one might assume purple fringing is the most common colour, given that it is one of the other names for chromatic aberration, the passage does not actually state that this is the most common colour.

C.   True. All that information is given in the text.

D.   Cannot say. The passage states that chromatic aberration can be especially visible in high-contrast situations, but it does not say anything in regard to low-contrast situations.

5.   B

A.   Cannot say. This cannot be inferred from the passage as it only indicates that teams waste time on these issues, not that they fail due to conflict.

B.   True. The passage tells us that both technical and leadership skills are important elements of their role.

C.   Cannot say. We are told that "few take the time" to develop leadership skills but not whether this is because there are plenty of opportunities for promotion.

D.   False. On the contrary, the passage indicates that the importance of leadership skills grows with seniority.

6.   D

A.   False. The passage merely states that "there is *no reliable evidence* that Christians were killed in the Colosseum for their faith".

B.   False. The passage says that just some of the *damnati* were forced to participate in such executions.

C.   Cannot say. The text addresses the midday games; what occurred at the morning games, or even if morning games were held, is not said.

D.   True. Each of these facts is given in the text.

7.   A

A.   True. All these facts are stated in the final sentence.

B.   False: "initially the robot can only babble and perceives speech as a string of sounds, not divided up into words".

C.   Cannot say from the information contained in the passage, which does not address the comparative rates at which robots and humans acquire language skills.

D.   Cannot say. While the passage states that, after a few minutes of "conversation" with humans, a robot will adapt its output to the most frequently heard syllables, it does not address inflections.

8.   D

A.   Cannot say. While the passage does state that Leonardo "hitched himself" to the theory of the microcosm, there is no information that this was "the key" to his success as an artist.

B.   False. The passage clearly states that the opposite is true.

C.   Cannot say. While the passage states that the idea that the human body can fit inside both a circle and a square is a metaphysical proposition to which Leonardo subscribed, based on this information alone we cannot deduce or disprove his belief in God.

D.   True based on information in the text.

9.   B

A.   False. The passage states: "The encryption key is communicated using light signals and is received using photon detectors."

B.   True. The passage states that "the encryption key is communicated using light signals" and a potential hacker can intercept and manipulate such signals.

C.   Cannot say. While the passage states that quantum hacking involves light signals subverting photon detectors, whether this form of hacking is the least (or most) common is not given.

D.   False. The passage states that quantum cryptography "ensures that any attempt by an eavesdropper...will lead to disturbances that can be detected by the legitimate users".

10.   C

A.   False. The text states: "In the past, the creation of waste in connection with production...

was accepted as a necessary evil", but that this view is "increasingly being challenged". There cannot therefore be universal agreement on the matter.

B.   Cannot say. There is nothing in the text to say whether member states have or have not reached such an agreement.

C.   True. The passage states that: "Moving to a circular economy would alleviate... pressures", and that one of those pressures is "the inefficient use of natural resources".

D.   Cannot say. While the text states that a linear economy has resulted in "over-dependency on resources from outside Europe" it does not clearly state, nor does it necessarily follow, that the move to a circular economy will decrease trade.

11.   A

A.   True. The passage clearly states that the Higgs boson is part of the standard model of physics and that it explains "why some particles... have mass, while others...do not".

B.   False. The passage states that "if a particle interacts significantly with the Higgs field, it will have a higher mass"

C.   Cannot say. The passage does not provide relevant information to determine what would happen in the absence of the Higgs field.

D.   Cannot say. There is no evidence in the text as to whether the particles attach themselves in this way and so cause drag.

12.   D

A.   Cannot say. While the passage states that Doyle denounced his Roman Catholic faith, nothing is said about whether this was due to his father.

B.   False. The passage clearly states that Doyle surprised his family by choosing to study art rather than medicine.

C.   False: Sherlock Holmes' keen powers of observation were inspired by Doyle's medical school mentor, Professor Dr. Joseph Bell.

D.   True. "Doyle's first paying job as a doctor took the form of a medical officer's position aboard the steamship Mayumba, travelling from Liverpool to Africa".

13. A

A.   True: "birds almost certainly did not descend from theropod dinosaurs, such as tyrannosaurus".

B.   Cannot say. While the passage refers to warm-blooded birds having "a unique lung structure that allows for a high rate of gas exchange," it does not indicate whether cold-blooded reptiles also have this.

C.   Cannot say. The text makes no comparison of their relative efficiency in walking.

D.   Cannot say. While the passage states that birds have a unique thigh complex that "helps support the lung and prevent its collapse", there is no indication as to whether or not this feature allowed them to survive what killed the dinosaurs.

14. C

A.   Cannot say. The passage refers to him arguing with other painters, and "alienating those who became tired of his bickering", but does not say whether or not he had friendships with any of them.

B.   Cannot say. We are told that he "was passionate, and he argued with other painters" while in Paris, but not whether he had such turbulent relationships throughout his life.

C.   True: "in Paris, Van Gogh first saw impressionist art, and he was inspired by the color and light".

D.   Cannot say. While the passage states that Theo "believed the painting would not be well-received" there is no information as to whether this belief proved correct.

15. A

A.   True. The passage clearly states that a supermassive black hole could have formed when "a number of intermediate black holes merged in the early universe to form the supermassive black holes we see today".

B.   Cannot say. While the passage states that intermediate black holes are equal to the matter of about 90,000 suns, there is no information as to whether they are instrumental in the formation of solar systems.

C.   False. The passage clearly states that supermassive black holes live *exclusively* at the heart of galaxies.

D.   False: "without further surveys, it's impossible to tell how common middleweight black holes are across the universe".

16. C

A.   Cannot say. There is no reference to what the European Commission has asked the European Research Council to do.

B.   Cannot say. Although the passage refers to a "legally binding goal" having been agreed for 2020 emissions, and EU leaders have "endorsed" a target for 2050, there is no indication as to whether the 2050 target is "legally binding".

C.   True. The text describes two European Commission actions. The first is "a long-term target of cutting up to 50% of carbon emissions... by 2050". The second is "a Strategic Energy Technology Plan". The text states that the actions "originated from the Climate Action and Energy Commissioners, respectively". This means that the first action originated from the Climate Action Commissioner, and the second from the Energy Commissioner.

D.   Cannot say. The text states that the EU will be "pushing for an international agreement to succeed the Kyoto Protocol aimed at achieving a 30% cut by all developed nations by 2020", but does not clearly state whether negotiations have started.

17. D

A.   False. He says the opposite.

B.   Cannot say. No such distinction is made in the text between those in their own homes and those in assisted care facilities.

C.   Cannot say. While the passage states that "so-called 'exergames' have significant benefits for older adults by providing cognitive stimulation and a source of social interaction, exercise, and fun", whether or not elderly adults who regularly use exergames are *more mentally healthy* and *more fulfilled socially* is not said.

D.   True. All these facts are stated in the text.

18. C

A.   Cannot say. While the passage describes his inventiveness, whether his main passion was always invention is not stated.

B.   False: "it was a clothing line that bore his name that proved to be Lacoste's greatest post-game success".

C.   True. All of these aspects of Lacoste are clearly stated in the passage.

D.   Cannot say. While the passage says Lacoste's clothing line "entered" the US market, it provides no information as to whether it "conquered" that market or the name and crocodile symbol became status symbols.

19. D

A.   Cannot say. The text says that Caesar returned Cleopatra to the throne, but not whether she went on to rule the Mediterranean region for many years.

B.   Cannot say. The passage only tells us that Pompey was *stabbed and decapitated* in 48 BC and it leaves room for us to speculate about how long Pompey was in Egypt before this occurred.

C.   False. The passage states that the "twenty-one-year-old Cleopatra was at the time [48 BC] a fugitive in the Sinai on the losing side of a civil war against her brother".

D.   True. "Quickly, she managed to ingratiate herself with the new master of the Roman world, Julius Caesar."

20. A

A.   True. All these facts are stated in the text.

B.   Cannot say. There is no information as to his preferences in this regard.

C.   False. "Handel's superstar status was not the only draw; many also came to glimpse the contralto, Susannah Cibber".

D.   Cannot say. While the passage states that "many also came to glimpse the contralto, Susannah Cibber, then embroiled in a scandalous divorce", whether Cibber drew crowds because of her singing or her divorce is not stated.

21. C

A.   Cannot say. While research shows "a link between brain insulin resistance (diabetes) and two other key mediators of neuronal injury that help Alzheimer's disease (AD) to propagate", whether the *underlying causes* of diabetes and Alzheimer's disease are almost identical is not discussed.

B.   Cannot say. The passage does not address this issue.

C.   True. "There is clinical and experimental evidence that treatment with insulin... can enhance cognitive function... in AD."

D.   False. The passage states that Alzheimer's disease is *one of the most* common degenerative dementias.

22. C

A.   False: "the lush Tahitian masterpieces for which he is best known reflect an exotic paradise more imaginary than real".

B.   Cannot say. While "the fables Gauguin spun were meant to promote himself and his art", whether Gauguin meant to promote the cause of art in general cannot be derived from the text.

C.   True. The passage states that Gauguin engaged in all of the pursuits listed.

D.   Cannot say. While the passage states that Gauguin's paintings sold poorly in his lifetime, whether this was because of his behaviour is not stated.

23. C

A.   Cannot say. The passage makes no reference to the evolution of behaviour.

B.   Cannot say. The passage does not tell us whether Felis lybica existed 10,000 years ago.

C.   True. The passage tells us that we can infer cats are showing affection towards humans when they behave in ways which are known to be how they show affection to other cats.

D.   False. It is lions and cheetahs which form brotherhoods, not the Felis lybica, which is a solitary animal.

24. D

A.   Cannot say. The text says that Fontane was "one such fake correspondent" but does not state that he was the first.

B.   Cannot say. We are told he never crossed the English Channel during the decade in question, but he may have travelled elsewhere

C.   Cannot say. Fontane wrote about the Tooley Street fire, but there is no information about how much of his story was invented.

D.   True. "Fake news flourished in the 19th century."

25. B

A.   Cannot say from the information contained in the passage, which does not say how many attempts were needed.

B.   True. The passage clearly states that "signals would be sent by the opening and closing of an electrical circuit, that the receiving apparatus would, by electromagnet, record signals as dots and dashes".

C.   False. The passage clearly states that Morse quit painting before he began work on his telegraph.

D.   Cannot say. The passage does not address how Morse's telegraph was received.

26. B

A.   Cannot say. While the bodies showed signs of torture, there is no reference as to whether they may have been killed as part of such a ritual.

B.   True. All these facts are given in the text.

C.   False. The passage states that "both bog men appeared to be aristocratic dandies of their day."

D.   Cannot say from the information contained in the passage, which does not address the topic of evidence of Iron Age burial modes.

27. D

A.   Cannot say. There is no mention of the issue of exposure to copper before birth.

B.   Cannot say. While those with Wilson's disease suffer liver damage and failure, whether liver cells die off at increasing rates without regenerating is not discussed.

C.   False. It is the other way round: "too little copper can be fatal whereas too much can cause neurological impairment".

D.   True. The passage states: "the body rids itself of excess copper and various other minerals by collecting them in the liver and excreting them through the liver's bile. However...when this route is impaired, there's another exit route just for copper...through urine."

28. A

A.   True. This information is clearly given in the passage.

B.   False. It cost $400 million.

C.   Cannot say. While the new algorithm reduces the time it takes, whether it does this by utilizing the genomes of related species is not stated.

D.   False. The passage states that "since 2002, the rate at which genomes can be sequenced has been *doubling every four months or so*".

29. C

A.   Cannot say. While "landing strips for alien spacecraft" has been suggested as an explanation, there is no information provided in the text about the influence of popular culture.

B.   False. There is only evidence "suggesting" this – so it is at this point a theory, not a proven fact.

C.   True. All these interpretations are stated in the text.

D.   Cannot say. While interpretations include that the lines were used for "ceremonial processions" and that they were "irrigation plans", their exact purpose and whether they had a dual purpose is not known according to the passage.

30. C

A.   False. "Moody's Investors Service lowered Italy's government bond rating ...citing concerns that Italy *faces higher financing costs and an increased risk of being locked out of lending markets.*" No "unsuccessful efforts to escape the debt crisis" are mentioned.

B.   Cannot say. The passage makes no reference to the question of Italy being too big for the euro zone to bail out.

C.   True. All these facts are stated in the text.

D.   Cannot say. There is no reference to whether Italy may become caught in this way.

31. D

A.   Cannot say. This topic is not discussed.

B.   Cannot say. While we are told that the corpus luteum "controls hormone levels during pregnancy" we are not told whether the formation of multiple corpora lutea is to maintain *steady* hormone levels.

C.   False. The passage states: "one corpus luteum was derived from an egg-generating follicle, as happens in mammals such as humans, the rest of the structures formed from separate follicles…"

D.   True. These facts are stated in the text.

32. A

A.   True. The passage states that hard problems "take exponentially more time to solve with every additional variable that is thrown into the mix".

B.   False. "With each new variable, however, it becomes tougher to find the right equation."

C.   False. "Even the world's top supercomputers meet their match with a certain class of problems, known as 'hard' problems. These problems take exponentially more time to solve with every additional variable that is thrown into the mix."

D.   Cannot say. The topic is not discussed.

33. C

A.   Cannot say. While the passage states that Dada was an "irrational art movement", it does not indicate whether it appealed particularly to those who could not make sense of the events of the *early 20th century.*

B.   False. While the passage states that Romanian artist Tristan Tzara put out the first of many Dada manifestoes, it also states that few of them "made much sense".

C.   True. This information is given in the text.

D.   Cannot say. While the passage states that Dada influenced abstract and conceptual art, whether the element of Dada that paved the way for abstract and conceptual art was its absurdity and irrationality is not discussed.

34. B

A.   False. It plunged into Saturn's atmosphere to avoid contaminating Saturn's icy moons, in particular Enceladus.

B.   True. The text states that Saturn is "some 1.4 billion km from Earth", so Cassini must have travelled more than that distance during the course of its mission, which involved reaching Saturn and touring its system for 13 years.

C.   Cannot say. The text refers to "ocean-bearing Enceladus" as one of Saturn's icy moons but says nothing about whether the Cassini spacecraft discovered it.

D.   False. The passage states that Saturn's icy moons are to be "left pristine for future exploration", so scientists must be open to the idea.

35. B

A.   False. Mary did marry James Hepburn of Bothwell, but it was Lord Darnley with whom she had her son, the future James VI.

B.   True. The passage clearly states: "While ill with smallpox, Darnley was mysteriously killed in an explosion at Kirk o' Field (1567)."

C.   Cannot say from the information. While "placing herself under the protection of Queen Elizabeth, she found herself instead a prisoner for life", whether Queen Elizabeth I had Mary arrested and imprisoned because she saw her as *a serious threat to the throne* is not discussed.

D.   False. The passage states that Mary "raised an army, but was defeated again by the confederate lords at Langside (1568)".

36. D

A.   Cannot say. Whether or not neurosurgeons use images taken by the ultraviolet camera in making decisions or to aid surgical technique is not stated

B.   False. The passage clearly states that tumor cells have irregular borders as they grow and require more energy than healthy cells.

C.   Cannot say. The passage states that the use of the camera is in the pilot study stage, but not whether it will revolutionise how brain tumors and other neurological disorders are treated.

D.   True. "Neurosurgeons and researchers are adapting an ultraviolet camera to possibly bring planet-exploring technology into the operating room" and "The camera employs the ultraviolet technology used in space to study planets and distant galaxies."

37. B

A.   False. It was the other way round. "The team concluded that GFAJ-1 must be incorporating *arsenic* into its DNA in place of *phosphorous*".

B.   True. "NASA astrobiologist Felisa Wolfe-Simon had found the organism, dubbed GFAJ-1, in arsenic-rich sediments of California's Mono Lake."

C.   Cannot say. While the passage states that the discovery was "exciting" to astrobiologists who had "previously speculated that extraterrestrial life might survive in unexpected places if only such a swap were possible" it is not stated that the existence of extraterrestrial life had been confirmed.

D. Cannot say. We are told that all *known* living organisms require some phosphorous, and so does GFAJ-1, but nothing in the text either precludes or confirms that *as yet unknown* organisms might not require phosphorous.

38. B

A. Cannot say. There is no reference in the text to any relationship between his behaviour and genius.

B. True. The passage clearly states all of these facts about Morphy.

C. Cannot say. While the passage states that "for the last decade of his life he was loath to discuss the game at all", it does not say whether or not he believed that time spent playing chess was nothing more than wasted time.

D. False. "His family tried to have him committed to an asylum, but he argued his sanity so convincingly that the authorities declined to admit him."

39. C

A. Cannot say. While the passage discusses the speed of data transfer by graphene devices, there is no reference to whether they will replace existing internet cables.

B. False. A cell is made by "putting *two* closely-spaced metallic wires *on top of graphene*".

C. True. This information is all given in the text.

D. False: "the major stumbling block towards practical applications of these otherwise promising devices has been their low efficiency".

40. B

A. Cannot say. The passage states that shell shock inflicted "novel and peculiar damage to men's brains", but not whether the symptoms were similar to a concussion.

B. True. The passage says that "many soldiers arriving at the casualty clearing stations… appeared to be suffering from a remarkable state of shock" and that the term "shell shock" first appeared in *The Lancet* "only six months after the commencement of the war".

C. Cannot say. We are told only that the term "shell shock" first appeared in *The Lancet* in February 1915, but not whether it may already have been coined by military doctors in the barracks.

D. False. It was not shell shock but "Shrapnel from mortars, grenades and, above all, artillery projectile bombs, or shells" which accounted for about 60 per cent of the military fatalities.

41. B

A. Cannot say. We are told that there have been "dramatic declines of some ibex populations", but not whether the Iberian ibex is under threat of extinction.

B. True. The passage says that the "objective of the Iberian ibex stock reservoir El Toril" is to have "most of the genetic variability" of the free-ranging population of ibex.

C. Cannot say. "Overexploitation, pollution, habitat loss" have led species to extinction, but there is nothing to say whether they are responsible for the mange outbreaks among some ibex populations.

D. Cannot say. There is no reference to this topic in the text.

42. D

A. Cannot say. There is no reference in the passage to the licensing of designs.

B. Cannot say. While it may seem a plausible inference that the creation of tapestries declined after their "Golden Age", this is not explicitly stated and nor is any information given as to the relationship between the creation of tapestries and that of oil paintings.

C. False. The passage states that tapestries "had snob appeal, since only the richest of the rich could afford them."

D. True. Each of these reasons is referred to in the text.

43. B

A. Cannot say. While the passage refers to the increase in single-parent households as a factor in increasing inequality between households, whether or not children raised in such households subsequently have more difficulty moving up the income ladder is not discussed.

B.   True: "though no one has suggested that it is the sole or even main driving force behind the increases in inequality, rates of single parenthood are important but sometimes overlooked."

C.   False. The passage clearly states to the contrary: "changes in family structure (as opposed to wages and employment alone) have increased inequality."

D.   False. The passage states that between 1970 and 2011, income inequality between the top and bottom households grew by *31 per cent* overall.

44. C

A.   False. The passage tells us that it was *in 1961* that "Mandela, who was formerly committed to non-violent protest, began to believe that armed struggle was the only way to achieve change".

B.   False. It was *founded* as an armed offshoot of the ANC.

C.   True. The passage states: "he was arrested in 1962. He was sentenced to five years in prison for the strike, and then brought to trial again in 1963. This time, he and 10 other ANC leaders were sentenced to life imprisonment for political offences, including sabotage."

D.   False. The passage states: "The African National Congress (ANC) was being challenged by the Africanists, a new breed of Black activists who believed that the pacifist method of the ANC was ineffective."

45. D

A.   Cannot say. At the moment this is merely a "new theory".

B.   False. The passage states that they "travelled… without the benefit of wheels, cranes, or even large animals."

C.   False. The passage tells us that "*most* of them", not "*all* of them", were carved in the quarry.

D.   True. This was precisely what Hunt and Lipo demonstrated.

46. A

A.   True. All this information is given in the second sentence.

B.   False. While the passage informs us that many Etonians have rowed in the Olympics, it also states: "For generations, Eton's crews practiced and competed on the Thames, but by the 1990s,

recreational boat traffic made rowing there dangerous."

C.   Cannot say. There is no reference to whether Olympic events are now held on the Thames.

D.   Cannot say. We are told that British, Canadian and Dutch crews competed, but not which of them had the most success.

47. C

A.   Cannot say. The text tells us that the work contains video interviews, but we don't know whether or not it is a kind of video library.

B.   Cannot say. Although "Genocide" is one of the themes of the video installation, there is no reference in the text to the topic of this being perpetrated by Western societies on non-Western societies.

C.   True. We are told that Kader Attia created the work and that it is an "essay on… psychiatric pathology" and "contained interviews with philosophers, ethnologists, historians, psychiatrists, psychoanalysts, musicologists, patients, healers, and fetishists".

D.   Cannot say. The text states that the work uses "irrational representations" but does not say that psychiatrists are represented in an absurd way.

48. D

A.   False. Researchers found the opposite; people were more likely to have good health the closer they lived to the sea.

B.   Cannot say. There is no reference to this topic.

C.   Cannot say. While the research shows a link between the likelihood of having good health and living close to the sea, the passage does not indicate what the reasons for that might be.

D.   True. "The link between living near the coast and good health was strongest in the most economically deprived communities."

49. D

A.   False. The passage tells us that Courbet vowed "to lead the life of a savage" and that "he did not mellow with age".

B.   Cannot say. While the passage states that Courbet "would become one of the most innovative and influential painters of mid-19th-century France", it does not say that his rebellious spirit and corresponding vision were what made him such.

C.   Cannot say. While the text states that Courbet produced "salacious canvases", it does not tell us if these *were intended to change the public's taste and way of seeing.*

D.   True. The passage clearly states these facts about Courbet.

50.   B

A.   False. He became "the Boss of the New York City Gambino crime family" and in 1992 was convicted of 13 murders, among other crimes.

B.   True. All this information is given in the text.

C.   False. The passage states that Gotti "was sentenced to life in prison without parole."

D.   False. His arrest record by age 21 included all those offences but he had "served little gaol time".

51.   B

A.   Cannot say. While the town's existence was known to his royal scribes, whether it was once visited by Charlemagne himself is not mentioned.

B.   True. The passage clearly states these facts.

C.   False. The passage tells us that caltrops were small, spiked iron weapons that were scattered on the ground.

D.   Cannot say. While the passage states that "Arrowheads found embedded in [the long-house's] charred wall posts suggest the communal building was at some point set on fire and shot at", there is no information given as to who the attackers were.

52.   D

A.   Cannot say. The passage does not tell us whether this was an isolated case or a pattern of behaviour or, if the latter, whether it almost always involved young male gorillas and whether it was their role to protect the clan.

B.   Cannot say. While it may seem quite likely that park employees look for and dismantle snares, and even more unlikely that young gorillas often help them with the task, the text provides no information either way on either count.

C.   False. The passage clearly states that the poachers set snares for antelope and other species but that they have no interest in the gorillas.

D.   True. "Adults are generally strong enough to free themselves. Youngsters aren't always so lucky."

53.   D

A.   False. The relevant figure is "over 35 per cent".

B.   Cannot say. The passage does not tell us how the drug works.

C.   Cannot say. The passage makes no reference to whether the supercomputer is used to "monitor how a drug will work at a molecular level".

D.   True. The passage clearly states that for individuals with asthma and COPD, "the common cold is a serious threat to their health and could prove fatal."

54.   C

A.   Cannot say. In some areas the flooding is earlier and in some later, but we are not told which of these is the more usual.

B.   Cannot say. While flood damage globally runs to "roughly a 100 billion dollars a year" and it would seem highly probable that Europe's share of this would be much less than "nearly 100 billion dollars", the text does not provide definite information on this topic.

C.   True. We are told that "around the North Sea... the trend is towards later floods. The scientists believe this is due to changes in the North Atlantic Oscillation".

D.   Cannot say. The text states that: "In... southern England, floods are now occurring 15 days earlier than they did half a century ago" and that "in... Scotland, the trend is towards later floods". But the text gives no dates as to when floods are happening, so we cannot be certain that floods in southern England take place much earlier than those in Scotland.

55.   C

A.   Cannot say. The text states that "the third plague pandemic functioned as a catalyst for... colonial policies [and] geopolitical struggles", but does not say that these helped spread the plague.

B.   False. The third plague pandemic "lasted roughly from 1855 to 1959".

C.   True. The text tells us that the pandemic "lasted roughly from 1855 to 1959" and that "incidents of this pandemic were systematically photographed and documented from beginning to end, with images from local outbreaks making newspaper headlines across the globe."

D.   Cannot say. The passage tells us that "between 1898 and 1900... it struck... Portugal [and] Scotland", so we cannot be certain that the outbreaks occurred in 1898. It could have been 1898, 1899, or 1900.

56. C

A.   Cannot say. The passage says that "When automation is only reliable sometimes, a person's level of trust becomes an important factor that determines *how often the aid will be used*." We are not told if it influences *how they use* the device.

B.   Cannot say. While the "inclusion of an image" of a person can "significantly alter perceptions of a computerised aid", whether the overall "design" of the device will highly influence an individual's level of trust is not discussed.

C.   True: "research findings have revealed that the inclusion of an image of a person can significantly alter perceptions of a computerised aid".

D.   Cannot say. The passage does not discuss "reaction time".

57. C

A.   False. The passage states that Francis of Assisi bore five marks but that "later stigmatics...bear only one or two wounds".

B.   False. Francis of Assisi "bore five marks: two on his palms and two on his feet...and the fifth on his side".

C.   True. The passage clearly states these facts about stigmata.

D.   Cannot say. "This was the *first case* of stigmata...*described*". There may have been earlier cases that were *not* described.

58. C

A.   False. The passage states that "the separation between modern domestic cats and big cats such as lions and tigers is also deeply rooted".

B.   False. "Modern cats diverged in skull shape from their sabre-toothed ancestors early in their evolutionary history *and then followed separate evolutionary trajectories*."

C.   True. Researchers "quantified skull shape... They found an early and conspicuous divergence between the conical-toothed cats and sabre-toothed cats, with all sabre-toothed cats being more closely related to each other than they were to modern conical-toothed cats."

D.   Cannot say. While the skull shapes of sabre-toothed and modern (conical-toothed) cats diverged early and they "*then*" followed separate evolutionary trajectories" there is no information as to whether *the skull shapes alone* indicate that they followed different evolutionary trajectories.

59. D

A.   False. The text states that "niobium-tin magnets are cooled to just 1.9 Kelvin (–271.3 °C)" in order "to reach and retain their superconductive state". A "quench" is when "superconductors fail to maintain their superconductive state".

B.   Cannot say. The passage tells us that *niobium-tin* magnets are used in the Large Hadron Collider but does not state whether or not *niobium-titanium* magnets are also used.

C.   Cannot say. We are told that liquid helium is used as a coolant in the Large Hadron Collider, but not whether there are any alternatives.

D.   True. The text states that "above a critical temperature and above a critical magnetic field, the superconductors fail to maintain their superconductive state".

60. D

A.   False. Ball's Pyramid is "another small volcanic rock island nearby".

B.   Cannot say. We are told that the rock climbers found what looked like to be the extinct stick insects, but we do not know if they took samples with them.

C.   Cannot say. There is no information on what kind of predators the stick insects had; we only know that the rats did not have large mammals to predate them.

D.   True. The scientists used genome sequencing to compare museum specimens and the captive-bred stick insects and to officially classify them as the same species.

61. D

A. Cannot say. While the passage clearly states that *Crocodylus thorbjarnarsoni* ate our 1.2-metre tall ancestors, whether the beast likely ambushed the early humans when they went to collect water is not mentioned.

B. False. The passage states: "Other species in the wider category of crocodyliforms ...are bigger".

C. Cannot say. While the passage states that *Crocodylus thorbjarnarsoni* "would have resembled a heavyset Nile crocodile", whether it is its distant ancestor is not stated.

D. True. The passage clearly states these facts.

62. C

A. Cannot say. While the passage tells us that Robert Fortune engaged in a "corporate espionage" trip to China for this purpose, whether this was the first such attempt by the British East India Company to steal the secrets is not stated.

B. False. While the passage states that "the concept of tea is simple – dry leaf infused in hot water" it also states that "the manufacture of it is not intuitive at all. Tea is a highly processed product".

C. True. The passage clearly states each of these facts.

D. Cannot say. While the passage tells us that *"few in Britain's dominions* had any firsthand or even secondhand information about the production of tea before it went into the pot", there is no reference as to whether *anyone* within the British East India Company had that information.

63. C

A. Cannot say. While the research showed that the frequent use of "language adaptations" by tween texters was reflected in lower scores in a grammar test, no information is provided as to which group of tweens are "better adapted socially".

B. False. The passage states: "there is evidence of a decline in grammar scores based on the number of adaptations in sent text messages, controlling for age and grade".

C. True. This is the main point of the passage.

D. Cannot say. While techspeak is given as *a* reason for a decline in grammar skills among tweens, there is no information that it is the *primary* reason.

64. C

A. Cannot say. The benefits and drawbacks of employing family doctors in casualty departments are discussed, but not whether this is likely to be reduced.

B. Cannot say. There is no information as to whether they disagree with each other.

C. True. Professor Taylor describes the positive effects: "patients seen by the family doctor were significantly less likely to be admitted, exceed the four-hour waiting target or leave before being seen."

D. Cannot say. We are told it "increases antibiotic prescriptions" but this is not quantified and we cannot be sure it is a "major increase".

65. A

A. True. The passage states all these facts about Giuseppe Arcimboldo.

B. Cannot say. While the passage states that Giuseppe painted sea creatures, flowers, dinner roasts, pea pods, gourds, and more, there is no information about where he learned to paint them.

C. Cannot say. Whether Arcimboldo painted Rudolf II *at the emperor's request* is not stated.

D. False. The passage refers to other elements, such as sea creatures and dinner roasts.

66. B

A. Cannot say. While the passage tells us that such a robot "can outperform humans in identifying a *wide range of natural materials* according to their textures", whether it can do this for *all* materials is not stated.

B. True. The passage clearly states these facts.

C. Cannot say. The passage refers to a robot being able to identify "natural materials", but whether it is also able to identify materials such as plastic and synthetics is not discussed.

D. False. The passage clearly states that the robot with a special tactile sensor "has no way to tell what textures people will prefer".

67. B

A. Cannot say. The passage states that "researchers could not determine if low vitamin D contributed to frailty, or whether frail people became vitamin D deficient because of health problems".

B.   True. "Frail adults with low levels of vitamin D tripled their risk of death over people who were not frail and who had higher levels of vitamin D."

C.   False. The passage states that older and frail adults with low vitamin D have a 30 per cent *higher* risk of dying than those with higher levels.

D.   Cannot say. The passage only discusses the "new study" in which the researchers did not conclude whether frailty caused vitamin D deficiency or vice versa, while it does not discuss what the majority of studies say about the link between these two conditions.

68. D

A.   Cannot say. While it was sung in "bars, back streets and brothels" there is no information as to whether they could sing it at any time or place or that this was its attraction.

B.   False. The passage tells us that musicologists see fado "as an amalgam of cultures, especially African and Brazilian, stemming from Portugal's maritime and colonial past, combined with its oral poetry tradition and, possibly, some Berber-Arab influence".

C.   Cannot say. While it is enjoying "increasing world appeal," there is no comparison of its current world popularity with that among the urban poor of 19th-century Lisbon.

D.   True. The passage clearly states these facts.

69. C

A.   Cannot say. While the passage explains that according to the study, intellectual profiles of Asperger individuals depend on which type of test is used, whether *the measure of intelligence is exactly quantifiable* is not given.

B.   Cannot say. The passage tells us that Asperger individuals score much higher in Raven's Progressive Matrices than they do in other types of test, but there is no indication as to how their scores compare with those of non-Asperger individuals who take that test.

C.   True. The passage explains that Asperger individuals score unevenly on Wechsler tests but higher on the Raven's Progressive Matrices test while "scores for non-Asperger individuals are much more consistent across different tests".

D.   Cannot say. While the passage states that "this study reports that Asperger individuals' scores are much higher when they are evaluated by a test called Raven's Progressive Matrices, which encompasses reasoning, novel problem-solving abilities, and high-level abstraction", whether high-level abstraction and the ability to solve novel problems are considered *higher forms of intelligence* cannot be deduced from the information provided.

70. D

A.   Cannot say. No such comparison is made in the text.

B.   Cannot say. The passage refers to "declining bee populations and colony collapse" in reference to the honeybee but does not tell us whether they could be wiped out altogether in some areas.

C.   False. The passage states that solitary bees face a *greater* threat than honeybees.

D.   True. The passage states the link remains "obscure", therefore it cannot have been categorically confirmed.

71. A

A.   True. All these facts are stated in the text.

B.   Cannot say. The formation of a "cloud" is not referred to.

C.   False. The passage refers to "quantum-mechanical effects… on a scale that is visible to the naked eye."

D.   Cannot say. The topic of operating above the same critical temperature is not discussed.

72. B

A.   Cannot say. While "the landscape around the city, it now appears, was intensively farmed", whether it was *most likely an agricultural centre of the region* thanks to the intensive cultivation is not given.

B.   True. These facts are given in the text.

C.   Cannot say. There is no reference to the capture of the small amount of rainfall.

D.   Cannot say. The passage tells us goods were brought from India and China, but there is no information as to whether they came from "all over the world".

73. C

A.   Cannot say. The passage tells us of the "witch-craft craze" during that period, but not whether it was "the gravest period" in the history of witch-hunts.

B.   False. "More than 200 people were accused... and 20 were executed."

C.   True. "Eventually, the colony admitted the trials were a mistake and compensated the families of those convicted."

D.   Cannot say. While the passage states that *"many practising Christians, and those of other religions,* had a strong belief that the Devil could give certain people known as witches the power to harm others", it does not say whether practising Christians in Europe were largely responsible for stirring up paranoia about witches.

74. C

A.   False. The medals were awarded for "original works in the fine arts *inspired by athletic endeavours."*

B.   Cannot say. While we are told the juries awarded 151 such medals, there is no information as to whether the artists were also highly skilled athletes.

C.   True. The passage states that Baron Pierre de Coubertin "felt that in order to recreate the events in modern times, it would be incomplete to not include some aspect of the arts".

D.   Cannot say. While the medals were awarded for works "inspired by athletic endeavours", whether the majority were awarded for *paintings of the games themselves* is not discussed.

75. D

A.   False. "Once Copernicus put the sun at the centre of the picture...the planetary orbits became regular, smooth and elegant."

B.   Cannot say. While Copernicus "took half a lifetime to check his figures before publishing them... at age 70", whether he also feared persecution is not stated.

C.   False: prior to Copernicus, "astronomers *had worked from the assumption* that the earth was the centre of the universe, forcing them to draw convoluted orbits for the planets".

D.   True. The passage states that Copernicus' work was a "response to the unwieldy mathematics used since the days of the ancient Greeks to explain the motion of the sun, moon and five known planets".

76. D

A.   Cannot say. We are told that "on average, one footstep generates 7 watts of electricity, though the amount varies depending on a person's weight", but not whether the amount depends *solely* on a person's weight.

B.   Cannot say. The tiles are made from recycled tires and have a "minimal carbon footprint" but we are not told that this is "less than that of any other energy source".

C.   Cannot say. There is no information about the relationship between the proportion of recyclable components an energy source contains and the size of its carbon footprint.

D.   True. The passage clearly states each of these facts.

77. A

A.   True. The study "found statistically significant evidence of obsessive-compulsive tendencies" among people with remarkable autobiographical memories.

B.   Cannot say. While researchers "found statistically significant evidence of obsessive-compulsive tendencies" among those with extraordinary autobiographical memories, it also states that the researchers "do not yet know if or how this aids recollection".

C.   Cannot say. The size of prefrontal lobes is not discussed.

D.   False. The passage states the opposite: "the people with stellar autobiographical memory *did not* score higher...when asked to use rote memory aids".

78. C

A.   Cannot say: "we're not sure...whether they sang or chanted".

B.   Cannot say. While "the emphasis was definitely on percussion" whether it was *like an early form of modern percussion music* is not stated.

C.   True. The passage clearly states these facts.

D.   Cannot say. While the passage states that instruments included "the menat, a multi-strand beaded necklace they would shake," whether it might have also had a decorative function is not said.

79. C

A.   False. The requirement to give 2% of the catch is a provision of the *new* agreement.

B.   Cannot say. While the passage states that "fish can now only be caught more than 20 miles from the shore, up from 13 miles in the previous agreement," whether this is because between 13 and 20 miles from the shore is Mauritania's richest fishing area is not said.

C.   True. The passage states: "The total cost to the EU budget for fishing rights off the coast of the former French colony will be €70 million per year...The agreement allows EU ships to fish for demersal."

D.   Cannot say. Nothing in the text refers to the level of support for the agreement among fishermen.

80. B

A.   Cannot say. While the passage states that "randomness in quantum theory is one of its key features" whether it has *practical applications* for fields as diverse as chemistry and politics is not discussed.

B.   True. "This inability to accurately predict the results of experiments in quantum physics has been the subject of a long debate, going back to Einstein and his co-workers, about whether quantum mechanics is the best way to predict outcomes."

C.   Cannot say. While the passage states that randomness in quantum theory means that "knowing the precise configuration of the universe at the big bang would not be sufficient to predict its *entire* evolution", there is no information to indicate whether its evolution could be *partly* predicted.

D.   False. The passage clearly states that "in quantum mechanics, the outcomes of certain experiments generally can't be predicted perfectly beforehand, even if all of the information is available".

81. C

A.   Cannot say. The passage provides no information to make this assessment.

B.   False. The passage states: "While the two were alive, admirers spoke of them in the same breath, and the comparisons were not always in Rembrandt's favour."

C.   True. The passage clearly states these facts about Rembrandt and Lievens.

D.   Cannot say. While "the role of the lonely genius" was "a figure dear to the Romantics" and "Lievens moved around, absorbing many different influences," whether his *life centred on continuous change* and this put him out of favour with the Romantics, is not discussed.

82. C

A.   Cannot say. While "the direct ancestors of modern humans may have interbred with members of an unknown ancestral group of hominids," there is no information as to whether those who did not do so failed to evolve.

B.   False: "even though all the individuals we sampled are hunter-gatherers, natural selection has acted differently in these different groups."

C.   True. The study "suggests that different groups evolved distinctly in order to reap nutrition from local foods and defend against infectious disease".

D.   Cannot say. While "Differing food sources, geographies, diseases and climates offered many targets for natural selection to exert powerful forces...The individuals who adapted best were the most likely to reproduce," there is no information as to the effect of having "the most diverse food sources" or living "in the most temperate climates".

83. B

A.   Cannot say. While the passage states that none of the tasks involved in resurrecting a woolly mammoth "appears insurmountable" whether or not it is likely to happen is not given.

B.   True. The passage clearly states that part of the mammoth genome has been published and that scientists at present "don't even know how many chromosomes the mammoth had".

C.   Cannot say. While the passage states that "30 per cent of the genome would have to be recovered" and references "a simple, inexpensive technique for recovering high-quality DNA from mammoth hair," whether scientists will be able to recover the 30 per cent of the mammoth genome that remains unknown is not stated.

D.   Cannot say. The text makes no reference to the issue of recreating male and female sex cells.

84. D

A.   Cannot say. In her book she argues that policies can be designed to have this effect but the passage does not say whether they have been implemented anywhere.

B.   Cannot say. We are told that the Menloy index was named after her but not who gave it its name.

C.   False. His work includes "the causes and consequences of inequality within developed countries".

D.   True. The passage states that he argues that financial underdevelopment is an important determinant of poverty.

85. A

A.   True. The passage states each of these facts about Charles Lutwidge Dodgson.

B.   Cannot say. There is no reference to the sources of inspiration for the characters in *Alice's Adventures in Wonderland*.

C.   Cannot say. While the passage tells us he wrote *Alice's Adventures in Wonderland* it does not say what else he published or whether he devoted *much of his life* to the craft of writing.

D.   Cannot say. While the passage states that *Alice's Adventures in Wonderland* influenced Walt Disney and Salvador Dali, there is no mention of Tim Burton.

86. D

A.   Cannot say. The use of such security systems in solving crimes is not mentioned.

B.   Cannot say. While the passage refers to researchers creating a "learning system that simulates the brain in making decisions", whether such a system can make decisions better than a human is not discussed.

C.   False. The passage states that additional practical applications for biometric information include "intelligent decision-making methodology for human recognition…maintaining security in virtual worlds and avatar recognition".

D.   True. "The key is the ability to combine features from multiple sources of information, prioritise them… and adapt the decision-making to changing conditions".

87. D

A.   False. "The most popular entertainments offered by the circuses of Rome were the gladiators and chariot racing, *the latter often as deadly as the former.*"

B.   Cannot say. While the passage says that "ancient inscriptions frequently record the deaths of famous racers… crushed against the stone *spina*… or dragged behind their horses," there is no reference to whether the *majority in any race* were killed in the latter way.

C.   Cannot say. While the passage states that "spectators wagered and also won substantial sums – enough for the races to be plagued by all manner of dirty tricks", whether many of them lost their lives as a result is not mentioned.

D.   True. The passage clearly states all these facts.

88. D

A.   Cannot say. While the passage states that the two galaxies will collide and that scientists were initially uncertain about whether they might just pass one another "like two ships passing in the night," whether other galaxies in the same situation do in fact simply slide past each other is not given.

B.   Cannot say. While the passage states that the collision between the two galaxies "won't have an enormous impact on earth or the solar system as a whole," whether this is because the process will take millions of years to complete is not stated.

C.   False. When the two galaxies collide, they will first "orbit around each other before merging in one big galactic pile-up".

D.   True. The passage clearly states these facts.

89. B

A.   Cannot say. While the passage states that the laser includes "a layer of silver film that is smooth at the atomic level", it does not say whether this is what differentiates this laser from similar devices.

B.   True. "The device is constructed of a gallium nitride nanorod that is partially filled with indium gallium nitride."

C.   False. The passage clearly states that the nanorod is placed on top of the thin layer of silicon, not vice versa.

D.   Cannot say. While the passage tells us that the laser "is key for the development of faster, smaller and lower energy photon-based technologies, such as ultrafast computer chips," there is no information whether the laser will *soon be on the market in the form of computer chips*.

90. B

A.   Cannot say. While the passage states that in July "Greece and Spain were the only two countries where the manufacturing sector contracted more rapidly", whether Spain's contraction was greater than Greece's is not given.

B.   True. The passage clearly states these facts.

C.   False. Chris Williamson said that the July slowdown suggested "a fear among companies towards ongoing weakness".

D.   Cannot say. While Ireland "saw its manufacturing sector expand, with a score of 53.9", there is no information as to the meaning of this score or whether this is the lowest it has seen in three years.

91. A

A.   True. The passage clearly states these facts.

B.   Cannot say. While the passage states that the Birmingham demonstration "drew nationwide attention," whether the March on Washington would not otherwise have drawn 200,000 people is not discussed.

C.   False. The passage tells us that King believed "'nonviolent direct action seeks to create such a crisis and foster such a tension that a community, which has constantly refused to negotiate, is forced to confront the issue".

D.   Cannot say. While the speech emphasised King's belief that "someday all men could be brothers," there is no reference to whether its message was written to motivate and educate all Americans about the civil rights movement.

92. B

A.   Cannot say. While the passage states that "the great zeppelin caught fire while less than 90 metres from the ground," whether it crashed to the ground *just metres from where it was scheduled to land* cannot be determined from the information provided.

B.   True. The passage clearly states each of these facts.

C.   Cannot say. While the possible causes listed in the text do not include human error, the reason for the explosion remains a "mystery... at this point it's impossible to determine what exactly caused the spark."

D.   Cannot say. While the passage states that a bolt of lightning is one realistic explanation for what caused the Hindenburg to burst into flames, it also states that "at this point it's impossible to determine what exactly caused the spark".

93. B

A.   False. It was the Mars Odyssey spacecraft that detected minute quantities of liquid water on and just below the surface of Mars.

B.   True. The passage clearly states these facts.

C.   Cannot say. While the passage details evidence indicating that water exists on or near Mars' surface and in its interior, whether such evidence suggests that the planet once possibly supported life is not stated.

D.   False. "Now there is evidence that Mars is home to vast reservoirs of water in its interior as well."

94. C

A.   False. The passage states that the P.L.A. "is commemorated *annually* with speeches and promotions and *every five years* by major cultural celebrations".

B.   Cannot say. While Mao Zedong said that "we must also have a cultural army, which is absolutely indispensable for uniting our own ranks and defeating the enemy", there is no reference in the text to whether, without this cultural army, China would in fact not be as united as it is today, nor as able to defeat its enemies.

C.   True. The passage states: "the Communist Party and the People's Liberation Army....have maximised the value of the arts as tools of propaganda. As Mao Zedong said.... a cultural army...is absolutely indispensable for... defeating the enemy."

D.   Cannot say. There is no discussion of this question in the text.

95. B

A.   False. The passage states: "The distinction between these two technologies is that one is camera-based and one is not. And that difference could be the deciding factor. Unlike tennis, where there is almost never any thing or person obstructing the line of sight between the cameras and the ball, soccer presents unique challenges".

B. True. "IFAB gave the green light to try goal line sensors from… GoalRef and Hawkeye. In early July, IFAB approved both technologies…Michel Platini, head of the UEFA…stood staunchly opposed to the technology."

C. Cannot say. While the passage states that IFAB has approved the use of goal line sensors and that Platini, the head of the UEFA, is opposed, whether he has either the power or the intention to veto it is not discussed.

D. Cannot say. The text does not say which of the two technologies is favoured by tennis or whether it is GoalRef or Hawkeye where the line of sight is not an issue.

96. A

A. True. "A government investigation into insider trading in Tokyo has extended onto the trading floors of some of Wall Street's largest companies, including Goldman Sachs, UBS and Deutsche Bank."

B. False. The passage states that some of Goldman Sachs' clients are being investigated for trading misconduct involving All Nippon Airways, so it is impossible that Deutsche Bank is the only company with clients in such a situation.

C. Cannot say. While a government committee in Tokyo "has been working with regulators to stiffen insider trading laws in Japan," whether this will *most likely result* in more severe laws is not stated.

D. Cannot say. While the passage states that the insider trading scandal has "undermined faith in Japanese stock markets," there is no information that markets have plunged in recent weeks.

97. D

A. Cannot say. The differences between native Spanish and Finnish speakers are not discussed.

B. False: "research from psychological science and linguistics suggests that a child's emotional competence is fundamentally shaped by a multilingual environment".

C. Cannot say. No information is given on this topic.

D. True. "Bilingual parents may use a specific language to express an emotional concept because they feel that language provides a better cultural context for expressing the emotion."

98. D

A. Cannot say. There is no information that an advertising campaign making this comparison was "the key to Penguin's success".

B. False. "When Woolworth's placed an order for 63,500 copies, Lane first realised he had a viable financial model."

C. Cannot say. While the passage states that when Woolworth's placed an order for 63,500 books Lane realised he had a viable financial model, there is no statement that Penguin would never have succeeded without it.

D. True. The passage states each of these facts about the founding of Penguin.

99. C

A. Cannot say. While the passage tells us that "it was on one such trip…that Mother Teresa first felt a calling to a religious life," there is no information to allow us to conclude whether or not she might have felt such a calling on another occasion.

B. False. The passage states that she took the name of Sister Mary Teresa while in Ireland, a year before she travelled to Darjeeling.

C. True. The passage clearly states these facts about Mother Teresa's life.

D. Cannot say. While the passage states that Agnes Bojaxhiu felt a religious calling and then travelled to Darjeeling and Calcutta, there is no mention of whether she ever left India again.

100. B

A. Cannot say. While the passage tells us that the law of fratricide was applied "in order to reduce the risk of subsequent rebellion and civil war," there is no information as to whether *chaos and coups would have reigned* without the law.

B. True. All these facts are given in the text.

C. Cannot say. We are told that "Mehmed's law resulted in the deaths of at least 80 members of the House of Osman over a period of 150 years." While it may seem quite likely that the murder of all 19 siblings of Sultan Mehmed III, nearly one-quarter of the 150-year total, was therefore the most appalling incident, no information in the text confirms or negates that conclusion.

D. False. The passage states that the new ruler was "enjoined to murder all his *brothers*, together with any inconvenient *uncles and cousins*", i.e. not *all* family members.

101. D

A. False. The passage clearly states that it is the other way round: "identical twins…share virtually the same genetic code. Any differences between them…must be due to environmental factors".

B. Cannot say. While the passage states that "twins offer a precious opportunity to untangle the influence of genes and the environment – of nature and nurture," no information is given as to whether or not "we are *equally influenced* by our genetics and our environment".

C. Cannot say. While the passage states that "if identical twins are more similar to each other with respect to an ailment than fraternal twins are, then vulnerability to the disease must be rooted at least in part in heredity", whether the cause of a disease is necessarily hereditary if one fraternal twin suffers from it while the other twin does not is not discussed.

D. True. The passage states that "identical twins come from a single fertilised egg that splits in two, they share *virtually* the same genetic code" while fraternal twins "come from separate eggs and share *on average* half their DNA".

102. A

A. True. The passage tells us exactly that.

B. Cannot say. The passage refers to work within Africa but makes no mention of how this will be achieved.

C. Cannot say. The passage tells us that "economic growth and urbanisation go hand in hand and are critical to poverty reduction" but not whether urban growth itself is the primary driver.

D. False. Cities provide the work and living environment for most people in high income countries.

103. C

A. False. The passage clearly states that Internet-enabled power outlets do not *automatically* optimise and reduce the use of electricity, but "will soon allow users to control household appliances via their smartphones".

B. Cannot say. No information is given as to the likely take-up of the HexaBus home automation system.

C. True. All this information is in the text.

D. Cannot say. While the passage tells us that the technology will enable homeowners to reduce their energy costs, whether energy consumption will *in fact* drop is not discussed.

104. C

A. False. It is the other way round: "muscle cells go on the outside, urothelial cells (which line the urinary tract) on the inside".

B. Cannot say. Collagen cells are used, but there is no information as to where they come from.

C. True. The passage clearly states that the process involves all these elements.

D. Cannot say. We are told that the entire process of making a bioartificial bladder takes six to eight weeks, but not the length of time that the bladder cells are on the scaffold.

105. B

A. False. "Emerging evidence now also suggests that this brain area can be trained using a meditation technique called mindfulness."

B. True. The passage states: "an athlete possesses a hyper-attuned insula that can generate strikingly accurate predictions of how the body will feel in the next moment."

C. Cannot say. While sprinters, boxers and divers are mentioned in the text, it is not stated whether they will gain more benefit than other athletes.

D. Cannot say. The question of the relative size of boxers' and athletes' cortexes is not discussed.

106. A

A. True. The passage states that at the 2008 Loebner Prize competition the top chatbot fooled 3 of the 12 judges.

B. Cannot say. While the passage states that a lack of long-term coherence is one way that chatbots "betray themselves," there is no information as to whether this is the most frequent way.

C. False. The closest so far was at the 2008 Loebner Prize competition when the top chatbot fooled 3 of 12 judges.

D. Cannot say from the information contained in the passage. While they do not yet have this ability, there is no information as to whether they will in the future.

107. D

A.   False. The passage states that researchers found that "those who had engaged in REM sleep subsequently performed better in pattern recognition tasks, such as grammar, while *those who slept deeply* were better at memorisation".

B.   Cannot say. While the passage states that "researchers have found that the sleeping brain appears to repeat a pattern of neuron firing that occurred while the subject was recently awake, as if in sleep the brain were trying to commit to long-term memory what it had learned that day," it does not say whether such neuron firing occurs *during REM sleep.*

C.   Cannot say. While the weeding out of redundant or unnecessary synapses is referred to, there is no reference to a connection with recognition of patterns.

D.   True. The passage states that researchers "found that those who had engaged in REM sleep subsequently performed better in pattern recognition tasks, such as grammar, while those who slept deeply were better at memorisation".

108. D

A.   Cannot say. While the passage states that Bingo Friendzy "has prompted anger from Christian groups", there is no reference to whether the groups believe that children should not be exposed to the sin of gambling.

B.   False. "Facebook will take 30 per cent of revenues from Bingo Friendzy".

C.   Cannot say. While the passage states that the shares "have almost halved in value amid concerns about Facebook's effectiveness as an advertising medium", whether they lost half their value *primarily* because investors do not have faith in the company as an advertising medium is not given.

D.   True. All these facts are given in the text.

109. B

A.   Cannot say. We are told El Niño is periodic, but not how often it happens.

B.   True. All this information is given in the text.

C.   Cannot say. We are told only that 4.5 million are in need of food aid in Ethiopia because of a scarcity of rain, not whether this followed floods as occurred in Malawi.

D.   False. There are different consequences for different countries: South America experiences heavy rainfall, whereas drought-like conditions are experienced in Australia, south-east Asia and southern Africa.

110. B

A.   Cannot say. While the passage states that "in time" the word "apostle" was applied to others besides the original 12, the exact timescale is not given.

B.   True. The passage clearly states these facts.

C.   Cannot say. The views of conservative Christians on this matter are not mentioned in the text.

D.   False. The passage clearly states that Matthias was one of the twelve apostles, replacing the former disciple and alleged traitor, Judas Iscariot.

111. B

A.   False. The passage clearly states that Hals used flamboyant brushwork and that his paintings conveyed "a sense of intense realism" rather than his impressions.

B.   True. The passage states: "Hals made two great contributions. One was to combine an intense sense of realism with flamboyant brushwork... Hals' other contribution is to fill his paintings with evident psychological intensity, the quality known as 'psychological insight'."

C.   Cannot say. While "Hals's portraits document the emergence of the modern self", there is no reference to whether this was intentional.

D.   Cannot say. There is no information as to whether Hals attended performances of Shakespeare's plays or was influenced by them.

112. C

A.   Cannot say. While the passage states that genetic analysis shows that North Africa's Jews "form two distinct groups, one of which is more closely related than the other to their European counterparts", and "the findings are the latest in a series of genetic studies... indicating that the world's Jews share biological roots", whether the ancestors of North African Jews share biological roots with at least *two other* groups is not given.

B.   Cannot say. While the Jewish populations of North Africa "mostly married within their own religious and cultural group", whether this was a result of forced segregation is not mentioned.

C.   True. The passage states that "the Jewish populations of North Africa became genetically distinct over time, with those of each country carrying their own DNA signatures".

D.   False. "The findings are the latest in a series of genetic studies, which began in the 1990s, indicating that the world's Jews share biological roots, not just cultural and religious ties."

113. C

A.   False. The quarries were "mostly in the *southern* part".

B.   Cannot say. While the passage tells us that "crypts and bank vaults, wine cellars transformed into nightclubs and galleries" are located underneath Paris, whether *anyone is welcome to visit* them is not stated.

C.   True. All these features are mentioned in the text.

D.   Cannot say. While the passage states that farmers raised mushrooms beneath Paris, "at one point producing hundreds of tons a year", no comparison is made with the quantity produced above ground.

114. B

A.   False. "*Flies and beetles* are the original pollinators, going back to when flowering plants first appeared 130 million years ago."

B.   True. These facts are all stated in the text.

C.   Cannot say. While the passage tells us that "bats, with diverse muzzles and tongues adapted to tap differently shaped blossoms" it also states that "flowering plants...have evolved in step with their pollinators," and whether the plants have evolved to match the bats or vice versa is not indicated.

D.   Cannot say. While the passage states that mosquitos carry pollen for orchids, there is no information as to whether *only* the mosquito can do this.

115. C

A.   Cannot say. The passage tells us that plastic pollution can enter the food chain, but not whether humans have consumed the Bio-Beads.

B.   Cannot say. While we are told that Bio-Beads can cause digestive blockages and poison marine animals, we do not know if they suffocate as a result.

C.   True. We are told that it is sewage plants that are leaking Bio-Beads into the ocean but not whether this has been deliberate or accidental, so it could be either.

D.   Cannot say. There is no information in the text as to whether this is true or not.

116. D

A.   Cannot say. There is no reference to the topic of providing insight into the history of the Persian Empire.

B.   False. The passage clearly states that *The Persians* is told from the *Persian* perspective.

C.   Cannot say. While the passage may seem to *imply* such an interpretation ("Consider the plot: a superpower's inexperienced, hubristic leader – who hopes to conquer a minor enemy his father tried unsuccessfully to fell a decade earlier – charges into a doomed military invasion"), whether the play is popular with contemporary audiences specifically *because it proves that history repeats itself* is not said.

D.   True. All this information is given in the text.

117. D

A.   False. The passage clearly mentions *three* phases in the construction of Stonehenge.

B.   Cannot say. While the passage states that "immense effort" was involved in moving the bluestones, there is no information as to whether only manpower was used in this task.

C.   False. The passage clearly states that archaeologists believe the bluestones were added two centuries after about 2800 BC.

D.   True. These facts are all given in the text.

118. C

A.   False. The study found the opposite: "the less monitoring parents did, the more the children played videogames."

B.   Cannot say. While the study "found that the more children perceived their parents' behaviour as negative...the more the children played videogames", it is not stated which of these is *cause* and which is *effect*.

C. True. The passage clearly states that the more children perceived their parents as nagging them, the more the children played videogames.

D. Cannot say. The study shows that children who play a lot of videogames are more likely to *perceive* their parents as behaving negatively, but whether the parents are *actually* behaving negatively is not discussed.

119. C

A. False. The passage states: "It's not until the emergence of *H. erectus* 1.89 million years ago that hominids grew tall, evolved long legs and became completely terrestrial creatures."

B. Cannot say. While the passage states that "although the earliest hominids were capable of upright walking, they retained primitive features...that indicate they spent time in trees", there is no information as to whether the hominid species was *better at climbing trees* or *fossils of Neanderthals* suggest this to be the case.

C. True. The passage states: "Although the earliest hominids were capable of upright walking, they retained primitive features – such as long, curved fingers and toes as well as longer arms and shorter legs – that indicate they spent time in trees."

D. Cannot say. While the passage states that "the earliest hominid with the most extensive evidence for bipedalism is the 4.4-million-year-old *Ardipithecus ramidus*", there is no information whether hominid species developed bigger brains just after this.

120. A

A. True. The passage states: "land mines are unlike bullets and bombs in two distinct ways. First, they are designed to maim rather than kill."

B. Cannot say. While the passage tells us that "only 25 per cent of land mine victims around the world are soldiers. The rest are civilians", whether the same proportion holds true for Cambodia between 1975 and 1979 is not given.

C. False. The passage states that Pol Pot called land mines his "perfect soldiers".

D. Cannot say. There is no information given on the relative success of the different types of weapons.

121. C

A. Cannot say. While we are told that "math anxiety leads to poor math performance", there is no information on the relationship between anxiety levels and ability to solve problems creatively.

B. False: studies indicate "too much focus may actually impair creative problem solving".

C. True. The passage states that "working memory capacity seems to help analytical problem-solvers focus their attention and resist distraction."

D. Cannot say. While the passage states that "our working memory capacity is decidedly finite", there is no statement as to whether our ability to find creative solutions is unlimited.

122. C

A. False. The passage clearly states that data leakage and the introduction of viruses or other malware into workplace computing systems are among other risks faced.

B. Cannot say. While the passage tells us that "The portability, connectivity, and storage capacity of mobile devices means they bring with them the threat of data leakage, data theft...", there is no information as to whether the threat of data leakage and data theft was *minimal* before the appearance of such devices.

C. True. The passage clearly states that mobile devices "bring with them the threat of data leakage, data theft, and the introduction of viruses or other malware".

D. Cannot say. While the availability of mobile devices with large storage capacity is linked to "the ability to capture vast quantities of data, whether for legitimate work purposes or for illicit use", no link is mentioned between storage capacity and the risk of malware attacks.

123. B

A. Cannot say. While the passage states: "European countries today are at loggerheads not despite the common currency but precisely because of it", whether sharing a common currency is the *main and only factor* contributing to their quarrels cannot be concluded.

B. True. The passage states: "A recent letter signed by 160 German economists claiming that the European Union's plan for a banking union was little more than an attempt to make Germany pay for Spanish mistakes."

C.   False. The representatives were "unable to over-come their differences."

D.   Cannot say. While the passage highlights the economic conflict between northern and southern Europe and mentions Martin Feldstein's prediction that "monetary union would create conflict within Europe", whether the common currency in Europe is a source of trouble because of *inherent inequalities between north and south* is not said.

124. D

A.   Cannot say. While the passage tells us that "Gaudí based his buildings on a simple premise: If nature is the work of God, and if architectural forms are derived from nature, then the best way to honour God is to *design buildings based on his work*", whether or not the design of the Sagrada Família is intended to *bring nature into the church* is not given.

B.   Cannot say. While Gaudí's "belief in the beautiful efficiency of natural engineering clearly anticipated the modern science of biomimetics", whether his Sagrada Família directly influenced the field is not said.

C.   Cannot say. While the passage states that Gaudí "understood that the natural world is rife with curved forms, not straight lines. And he noticed that natural construction tends to favour sinewy materials such as wood, muscle, and tendon", whether the Sagrada Família itself incorporates wood, rounded lines, and sinewy effects is not stated.

D.   True. The passage states that Gaudí's Sagrada Família was inspired by his religious faith and mentions his "belief in the beautiful efficiency of natural engineering".

125. B

A.   Cannot say. We are told that bronze sculptures from *one particular era* are rare because they were often melted down to make swords, shields and other items, but we do not know if bronze sculptures from *other eras* are highly unusual.

B.   True. The passage says that "if the team can salvage the submerged statues, it would be a remarkable recovery", meaning that it isn't known if all bronze sculptures can be retrieved from the shipwreck.

C.   False. The phrase "from this most recent excava-tion" tells us there have been other excavations.

D.   Cannot say. We are not told when it was excavated.

126. C

A.   Cannot say. While the passage states that "manufacturers see [triclosan] as a marketing bonus, increasing consumer confidence that a particular product kills harmful bacteria", whether consumers are more confident in a product's antibacterial qualities when triclosan is *listed as an ingredient* is not stated.

B.   Cannot say. The text mentions studies showing that "the chemical can disrupt the endocrine systems of several different animals", but there is no mention of such an effect in people.

C.   True. The passage clearly states each of these facts.

D.   False. The passage tells us that the reason triclosan was developed in the 1960s was to help *prevent* bacterial infections in hospitals.

127. C

A.   False. The passage states that MALDI-MSI tech-nology is especially useful "if the suspect's fingermark is not on the police database".

B.   Cannot say. While the passage tells us that MALDI-MSI can provide "key extra details about suspects", whether it *does not yield the information conventional fingermark processing does* is not stated.

C.   True. The passage tells us that MALDI-MSI technology "is a step closer to being incorpo-rated into traditional forensic investigations", therefore it *may* sooner or later be part of crim-inal investigations.

D.   Cannot say. While the technology "can provide extra information on a suspect" and "important background information in a criminal inves-tigation", whether it can provide the *necessary details and background information to convict a criminal suspect* is not stated in the text.

128. D

A.   False. International travel exceeded 1.1 billion overnight visitors *in 2014 alone* according to the World Tourism Organisation.

B.   Cannot say. There is nothing in the passage about how many people have made use of the app.

C. Cannot say. We are not told whether or not it is free.

D. True. All this information is in the text.

129. B

A. Cannot say. While archaeologists found "a figurine of solid greenstone, perhaps a war goddess to whom the burial was dedicated", whether the pyramid and/or the burials were in fact intended to appease a war goddess is not given.

B. True. The passage clearly states these facts about the Pyramid of the Moon.

C. False. An additional purpose was "to control the people...to convince them to do what their rulers wanted".

D. Cannot say. While a case of burial alive is mentioned and human sacrifice was used to "control the people", it is not stated whether all the victims were buried alive for that purpose.

130. B

A. False. While the passage states that eels are catadromous – or "have a life history known as catadromy" – it also explains that this means they spawn in the ocean and spend their adulthood in fresh water.

B. True. The passage clearly states these facts about eels.

C. False. "Eels may spend decades in rivers before returning to the ocean to spawn, after which they die."

D. Cannot say. While "female eels are found upstream in river systems, while males stay in the estuaries", whether this is *fundamental* to how the fish spawn is not stated.

131. C

A. False. The passage clearly states that the machine used both water and steam.

B. Cannot say. No information is provided about how many machines he produced.

C. True. The passage clearly states these facts.

D. Cannot say. While the passage tells us that Moriondo was granted a patent for a machine that used steam to brew coffee, it also says that "there were surely innumerable patents and prototypes" for such a machine, and whether his was the first is not stated.

132. C

A. False. "Still images showed little difference... but video analysis showed that the progression of the two kinds of smiles was quite different."

B. Cannot say. The passage refers to the possibility of computers "that better assess the emotional states of their users and respond accordingly" but there is no reference to the topic of computers being able to provide *individualised help*.

C. True. The passage states that "when presented with a task that caused genuine frustration...90 per cent... did smile" and that "frustrated smiles appeared quickly but faded fast".

D. Cannot say. There is no reference to this topic in the text.

133. A

A. True. All these aspects are mentioned in the text.

B. Cannot say. While we are told that Huntley & Palmers' tins came in all sizes and shapes and with a variety of decorations, there is no reference to whether their tins all bore the same branding.

C. False. The passage states that biscuit tins were not invented until a few hundred years after biscuits became "the food of choice for European voyagers starting in the 1500s".

D. Cannot say. While the elaborately decorated tins "served a Victorian middle class eager to show good taste", there is no information as to whether it was the tins inspired by impressionist art that were the *most* favoured.

134. B

A. Cannot say from the information. While the passage states that the Milky Way "is so huge that dozens of lesser galaxies scamper about it, like moons orbiting a giant planet", there is no information as to whether observation of these galaxies has helped scientists learn about the Milky Way.

B. True. The passage clearly states that the Milky Way's dark matter "far outweighs the Milky Way's hundreds of billions of stars" and that it cannot be detected by telescopes.

C. False: surrounding both stars and hydrogen is "an enormous halo of dark matter".

D.   Cannot say. While the passage states that the dark matter of our galaxy "far outweighs the Milky Way's hundreds of billions of stars, giving the galaxy a total mass one to two trillion times that of the sun", whether scientists know the mass of our galaxy's dark matter by calculating the mass of its stars is not said.

135. A

A.   True. The following are given as requirements for whiskey to be named Empire Rye: (1) it uses grain from New York State (2) it is aged for at least two years and (3) "other things", which means that there are in total at least 4 requirements.

B.   False. The passage tells us that "other things" are also required.

C.   Cannot say. We are not told whether the method of making whiskey differs between Empire Rye, bourbon and Tennessee whiskey, only that they are distinguished by their "regional pedigree".

D.   Cannot say. We do not know the intentions of distilleries other than the nine referred to in the text.

136. D

A.   Cannot say. While the passage states that a virus "invades a host cell and co-opts the cell's own machinery to make copies of itself – thousands of copies at once, which means thousands of chances to mutate and develop drug resistance" and that disabling this process requires "finding the right target – a gene, and the protein it encodes", we are not told whether viruses resist drugs by *switching which proteins in the host cell they use to reproduce themselves*.

B.   False. Regarding the search for a drug that disables part of the human cell to destroy a virus, the passage states that "the key is finding the right target – *a gene*, and the protein it encodes, *that the human cell doesn't need but the virus does*".

C.   Cannot say. While the passage states that "bacteria are organisms that are equipped to reproduce themselves; antibiotics attack that machinery", whether antibiotics work specifically by causing fatal mutations by scrambling the reproductive mechanism of the bacteria is not stated.

D.   True. "Human DNA contains more than 20,000 genes, but in any given cell at any given time, many are dormant" and a virus "co-opts the cell's own machinery."

137. A

A.   True. This is as stated in the text.

B.   Cannot say. While we are told Privitar has developed a "de-identification tool" to obscure personal data within large data sets, we have no information as to whether this is effective in preventing data breaches that could result in fines.

C.   Cannot say. According to Jason du Preez, the EU's General Data Protection Regulation had "raised awareness", but the passage does not indicate whether it has made the topic easier or more difficult to understand.

D.   False. The passage states the opposite.

138. C

A.   Cannot say. While "in those classrooms where computers were used to support teaching, the technology was found to have a small to moderate positive impact on both learning and attitude", no impact on "critical thinking skills" is mentioned.

B.   Cannot say. Although research suggests "a standard PowerPoint presentation will most likely not enhance the learning experience beyond providing content or enhancing teacher-directed lectures or class discussions", whether a student's learning is enhanced by *creating and giving* a PowerPoint presentation *on their own* is not discussed.

C.   True: "in those classrooms where computers were used to support teaching, the technology was found to have a small to moderate positive impact on both learning and attitude".

D.   Cannot say. There is no reference in the text to the influence on students' social lives.

139. C

A.   False. "Different languages highlight the varieties of human experience, revealing as mutable aspects of life that we tend to think of as settled and universal, such as our experience of time, number, or colour."

B.   Cannot say. No information is provided either way on this topic.

C.   True. The passage states that "Noam Chomsky theorised that all languages were built on an underlying universal grammar embedded in human genes," whereas "field linguists are more interested in the idiosyncrasies that make each language unique."

D.   False. The passage explains that in this language "the past is always spoken of as ahead of one, and the future is behind one's back".

140. A

A.   True. "The technical feasibility of gene therapy 'has been established in multiple diseases and with different technology platforms,' says Dr. Wilson."

B.   Cannot say. We are given Dr. Wilson's prediction to this effect, but no information as to whether he has been proved correct.

C.   Cannot say. While we are told these diseases represent a $6.5 billion market for current protein replacement therapies, whether gene therapy would cost more or less is not stated.

D.   False. The passage states that "gene therapy for hemophilia B is still in early-stage clinical testing".

141. B

A.   False. The passage states that "the Office for National Statistics (ONS) put the surprise jump in inflation down to lower discounting by clothing and footwear retailers and an unusual spike in air fares".

B.   True. The passage states: "People aged between 30 and 64 had the lowest inflation rate, of 2.5pc – due largely to slower petrol inflation."

C.   Cannot say. While we are told that "lower discounting by clothing and footwear retailers" was a factor in the increase in inflation, we are not given any information on the comparative effect of this on poorer families.

D.   Cannot say. There is reference to the "outgoings" of pensioners aged 75 and over but not to their sources of income.

142. B

A.   Cannot say. While the passage tells us that Thucydides "was the first person to document the connection between earthquakes and tsunamis", there is no information as to whether earthquakes are or are not the *only* cause of tsunamis.

B.   True. The passage states that Thucydides "noticed that the first sign of a tsunami is often the abrupt draining of a harbour".

C.   Cannot say. While a tsunami "sent Minoan civilization…into a tailspin, leading it to succumb to Mycenaean Greeks", whether or not this might have happened anyway cannot be concluded from the text.

D.   False. The passage clearly states that in 1755 an earthquake *and tsunami* killed many thousands of people in Lisbon.

143. D

A.   Cannot say. There is no information on what toothed whales did before developing this ability.

B.   Cannot say. The passage states that "whales' buzz rates are nearly identical to that of bats, at about 500 calls or clicks per second", but also that both whales and bats have variable click rates, which increase while hunting – so whether 500 is the *maximum* number they can process cannot be concluded.

C.   False. The passage states that bats and toothed whales both rely on the same range of ultrasonic frequencies, between 15 to 200 kilohertz, to hunt.

D.   True. These facts are clearly stated in the passage.

144. D

A.   False. "*For some*, being informed of a pill or procedure's potential side effects is enough to bring on real-life symptoms."

B.   False: researchers concluded it "ought to be taken into consideration by medical professionals on an everyday basis."

C.   Cannot say. The review "examined the underlying biological mechanisms" but whether it indicates that the phenomenon has *several identifiable biological causes* is not stated.

D.   True. The passage explains: "The nocebo effect is the phenomenon in which inert substances or mere suggestions of substances actually bring about *negative* effects in a patient or research participant."

145. B

A.   Cannot say. While the passage refers to the study being "a grim reminder after the euphoria of the Olympics of the challenges we face and those that lie ahead", no connection is discussed between the staging of the Olympics and the number of suicides.

B.   True. "A painful British economic recession and rising unemployment may have driven more than 1,000 people in England to commit suicide…between 2008 and 2010 there were 846 more suicides among men in England than would have been expected if previous trends continued, and 155 more among women."

C.   Cannot say. There is no information on the ratio of male to female suicides.

D.   Cannot say. While the passage states that "a painful British economic recession and rising unemployment *may* have driven more than 1,000 people in England to commit suicide" and that the trend "reflects findings elsewhere in Europe where suicides are also on the rise", there is no information to conclude whether rising unemployment rates and economic decline are a *direct* cause of suicides.

146. B

A.   Cannot say. While the passage states that "by 2050 a third of Europe's population will be over 60 years of age", there is no statement of what proportion of Europe's population will be using welfare technology.

B.   True. "The aim [of welfare technology] is to enhance the quality of life of elderly people who want to live at home as long as possible."

C.   False. The passage clearly states that "technology must not replace personal care and human warmth".

D.   Cannot say. While oven reminders and fall alarms are cited as examples of technology "to enhance the quality of life of elderly people who want to live at home as long as possible", whether they will enhance the quality of life for *all* elderly people is not discussed.

147. A

A.   True. This information is clearly given in the text.

B.   Cannot say. While "companionship" is mentioned as one of the reasons why humans began to employ dogs, there is no information as to whether domesticated dogs are the *evolutionary consequence* of a human need for companionship.

C.   False: breeders "favoured novelty, since the more distinct a line of dogs appeared, the more likely it was to garner official recognition as a new breed".

D.   False. "Sheltered from the survival-of-the-fittest

wilderness, those semi-domesticated dogs thrived…"

148. B

A.   False. "During the Mao era, Soviet-inspired 'socialist realism' was the only acceptable style in the strictly controlled authoritarian society."

B.   True. All these groups are referred to in the text as examples of how "periods of religious and political repression have provoked an exodus of creative and entrepreneurial talent".

C.   Cannot say. There is reference to the impact of Deng Xiaoping's economic reforms on Chinese art and access of Chinese artists to international news and scholarship, but no information as to whether his reforms prevented many talented artists from leaving China.

D.   Cannot say. The topic is not discussed in the text.

149. B

A.   Cannot say. We are told that "British working families at the start of the 19th century were enduring economic upheaval," but there is no reference to the circumstances of the upper classes.

B.   True. All this information is given in the text.

C.   Cannot say. While the passage states that "Parliament passed a measure to make machine-breaking a capital offence", there is no information as to whether the protests *ceased for the most part*.

D.   False. "British troops broke up a crowd of protesters demanding *more work and better wages*. That night, angry workers smashed textile machinery in a nearby village."

150. D

A.   Cannot say. While Bernini "undertook commissions for eight popes", there is nothing in the text to suggest whether he might or might not have otherwise died an unknown artist.

B.   Cannot say. While the passage tells us that "Behind every Bernini masterpiece there lies a *concetto*, its governing concept or conceit", nothing is said about whether Bernini thoroughly explored a *concetto* through *painting* before translating it to a sculpture or building.

C. False. The passage clearly states that Bernini's work transformed the look of 17th century Rome, not Florence.

D. True. "Bernini was said to have been only 8 when he carved a stone head that 'was the marvel of everyone' who saw it" and "much of the Baroque grandeur of the Eternal City – its churches, fountains, piazzas and monuments – can be credited to Bernini and his followers".

151. A

A. True. "'Despite its *long-term value*, securitization today *suffers from stigma*, reflecting both its adverse reputation amongst investors and conservatism among regulators,' the central banks said."

B. Cannot say. The passage only says that the ECB has argued that regulation should take into account European securitization instruments performing better than their U.S. counterparts. We cannot say what "performing better" means or if this has anything to do with fluctuations in price.

C. Cannot say. The passage states that securitization became a "bad word" during the financial crisis, when it was largely blamed for reckless lending decisions by banks. We cannot say for certain, however, that securitization was the *major cause* of the financial crisis given the information in the passage, nor that this is the belief of the central banks.

D. False. On the contrary, the text tells us that "The European Central Bank (ECB) and the Bank of England (BOE) said they are concerned about the 'shrinking' market for asset backed securities, which are bundles of loans that are packaged and sold to investors."

152. A

A. True. This information is all in the text.

B. Cannot say. We know that Kimbal Musk believes this but there is no indication of what the Silicon Valley crowd believe.

C. Cannot say. The text says that the food space is as "exciting" to Kimbal Musk as the internet was in 1995, but we don't know if it will "most likely be as revolutionary".

D. Cannot say. We are told that he would like the US to be a country based on healthy, local food grown on chemical-free farms, but not that his aim is having only farms that are chemical-free.

153. B

A. False. The passage says the opposite: Mars is now "frigid and dry" but in the past had been "warm and wet".

B. True. The passage states that floods have occurred on Mars because of "occasional warm spells" and not because of a "consistently hospitable phase".

C. Cannot say. The text says that signs of flowing water on Mars include rugged canyons and lowlands "apparently" sculpted by massive floods but this is not given as a certain fact.

D. Cannot say. The passage tells us only that "Mars' atmosphere was *probably* never thick enough to keep temperatures on the planet's surface above freezing for the long term", but that is not given as a certainty, and we are not told how frequent any above-freezing periods may have been.

154. D

A. Cannot say. The passage tells us that *ever since* the first metal workers dug copper from a Cyprus hillside and fashioned it into tools, copper has been in high demand. It does not refer to whether there was a copper market *before* that point and what its scale was: it is possible there was a market for copper for purposes other than making tools – we are not told.

B. False. It is true according to the passage that copper is the only catalyst that can mix carbon monoxide with water to produce fuel. However, the passage also states that the traditional copper-catalysed conversion of carbon dioxide to liquid fuel proceeds through an intermediate of carbon monoxide and that many catalysts can perform this first step, the opposite of the statement.

C. Cannot say. Researchers raised the prospect that international copper production could "peak within a few decades" but the timescale for that is indefinite and could be more or less than 25 years.

D. True. "A recent discovery describes improvements to copper as a catalyst that could streamline ethanol production."

155. D

A. Cannot say. The passage states that IceCube *reported* the discovery of Ernie and Bert last year but not when they were actually discovered.

B.   Cannot say. The passage only tells us that Ernie, Bert, and Big Bird are "three of the highest-energy neutrinos ever found", but makes no reference to their likely ranking in the universe as a whole.

C.   False. The passage states that neutrinos "rarely ever" – as opposed to *never* – interact with other particles because they are "extremely standoffish".

D.   True. The passage asserts that neutrinos could emanate from "galaxies forming stars at furious rates" and the particles found by IceCube were neutrinos.

156. C

A.   Cannot say. We are told only that cemeteries may not be "top of mind" for tourists, not that they are "one of the least popular places for tourists to visit".

B.   Cannot say. Loren Rhoads has said that "we've learned a lot" about the Greeks from their tombs, but we do not know whether our understanding has been "significantly influenced by recent research".

C.   True. Loren Rhoads says exactly that.

D.   Cannot say. The passage says that visiting your local cemetery can reveal the families who lent their names to the streets and neighbourhoods in your town, but we are not told if *most* streets and neighbourhoods are named this way.

157. A

A.   True. It has been "the most intensely observed astronomical event to date".

B.   Cannot say. The collision of the neutron stars was observed by the Laser Interferometer Gravitational-Wave Observatory; the stars "in all likelihood" collapsed into a black hole, so we cannot be certain this was observeD.

C.   Cannot say. Einstein first predicted the existence of gravitational waves a century ago, but we do not know if he predicted the event of the collision of a pair of neutron stars.

D.   False. The passage says that this event has resolved a decades-old debate about where gold and platinum come from, meaning not that we are "now even closer" to finding out, but that we definitely know.

158. C

A.   Cannot say. The passage tells us that infections occur in about 9% of Australian brush turkey eggs, but it does not say whether this percentage is more or less than for other related bird species.

B.   Cannot say. We are told that egg whites have an enzyme called lysozyme that is antimicrobial but there is no reference to chemicals in the yolks.

C.   True. All this information is in the text.

D.   False. The passage states that the heat generated as microbes in the soil decompose organic matter is actually helpful for the eggs, keeping them warm for incubation.

159. C

A.   False. One of the potential southern hemisphere locations is in Chile, which is not included on the 12-member selection committee.

B.   Cannot say. The passage does not refer to the size of the economies of the countries on the panel nor does it say why the members met in Germany.

C.   True. There are two potential southern hemisphere sites, in Namibia and Chile, with a reserve in Argentina, making three countries, whereas there are four potential northern hemisphere sites, in Mexico, Spain and the United States, i.e. also three countries.

D.   Cannot say. The text tells us that the site for the southern hemisphere detector will be larger than the northern one but it does not say how the project's money will be allocated between the two sites. Other factors than the size of the sites could affect the costs.

160. B

A.   Cannot say. The passage tells us that Lafarge and Holcim "plan to put $8 billion of assets around the world up for sale in a bid to secure antitrust clearance for their merger", but we cannot say for sure whether their plan will work. Their merger may not be cleared even if they sell $8 billion of assets.

B.   True. Holcim is based in Switzerland and Holcim executives are expected in Paris, France to announce the merger. Lafarge, the company Holcim is merging with, is based in France.

C.   False. The text tells us that "it's not clear what production facilities or other assets the two companies will propose to part with as part of their agreement".

D.   Cannot say. The actions the companies are taking are in response to the "likely" regulatory hurdles facing their merger. However, the passage does not explicitly say that any regulators are actually interested in the merger.

161. D

A.   False. "The Cochrane Collaboration ... has been arguing its case... *initially* on the basis of a previous analysis of the *limited published data available*", whereas the non-profit group reported "after analysing the results of *previously unpublished clinical trials*" – the exact opposite of the statement.

B.   Cannot say. It is only the opinion of some other scientists that the review by the Cochrane Collaboration did not make a strong case to stop stockpiling. We cannot say for certain that the group's evaluation produced insufficient evidence to alter antiviral policy.

C.   Cannot say. We are told that governments have spent billions of dollars stockpiling antiviral drugs, but not how much of that was spent on Tamiflu.

D.   True. It is stated that the Cochrane Collaboration "has been arguing its case against the efficacy of the antiviral Tamiflu ... for more than four years, initially on the basis of a previous analysis of the limited published data available."

162. A

A.   True. The passage clearly states that the waves showed very little decay in energy on their journey across the Pacific

B.   Cannot say. The text states that the experiment yielded a "surprising discovery", but we do not know whether it had been hypothesised previously.

C.   False. The opposite is true: long-period waves move quickly, short-period waves move slowly. As the passage tells us that the period increases as waves move northwards, it can be inferred that ocean waves slow down as they move northwards.

D.   False. Waves travel in a great circle from New Zealand to Alaska, not in a continuous straight line.

163. C

A.   Cannot say. We are told that 25 percent of German energy is derived from renewable sources but not whether there are other renewable sources than solar and wind power.

B.   Cannot say. The passage makes no mention of a statement by Angela Merkel on this subject.

C.   True. The passage gives all this information.

D.   False. Sigmar Gabriel says that it is an "illusion" that "energy transformation can be achieved by expanding renewable energy as quickly as possible"; instead, he says that Germany should make sure that the expansion is "safe and predictable".

164. D

A.   Cannot say. Although the text tells us that Belovezhskaya National Park contains ancient trees, including some that are 600 years old, it does not say whether they are the oldest trees in Europe. Furthermore, it is *Białowieski* National Park which was founded in 1932, while the date of founding of *Belovezhskay*a National Park is not given.

B.   Cannot say. The passage tells us that Białowieski National Park is Poland's oldest and *"one of the first* in Europe" but not whether it was *the* first.

C.   False. It is true that Belovezhskaya National Park protects only about 10 percent of the Białowieża Primeval Forest, but that forest's name is not the same as Poland's park, Białowieski National Park.

D.   True. All this information is given in the text.

165. B

A.   Cannot say. While Enric Sala "believes" that the Mediterranean Sea will be reduced to "a soup of microbes and jellyfish" without radical changes to fishing practices, we cannot say for certain that this will be the outcome given the information in the passage.

B.   True. The passage states that Sala was only one of the authors of the study, which was itself called "Large-Scale Assessment of *Mediterranean Marine Protected Areas* Effects on Fish Assemblages".

C.   Cannot say. The study drew on the work of a dozen researchers but we cannot say for certain whether they all share Sala's opinion that overfishing is the most important threat to

Mediterranean marine ecosystems, more than pollution, invasive species, or climate change.

D.   False. Sala published the results of his study this week but in the science journal PLoS ONE.

166. B

A.   Cannot say. The passage tells us that avalanches occur when a weak layer in the snowpack fractures under pressure from pileups of snow but not when these layers were formed. They could have originated in the current or previous winters.

B.   True. The passage tells us that avalanches are most common "*during*, and in the 24 hours right after, a storm" and "can reach speeds of 80 miles (130 kilometers) per hour within about five seconds".

C.   Cannot say. While the passage tells us that bigger avalanches cause more death and destruction than small ones, it does not discuss their comparative frequency.

D.   False. The text says that disastrous avalanches occur when massive slabs of snow break loose from a mountainside and shatter like broken glass as they race downhill.

167. D

A.   Cannot say. The passage does not discuss the approach adopted by the previous superintendent of the site, or indeed whether there was a superintendent before Massimo Osanna.

B.   Cannot say. While we are told that Pompeii has been "overrun by tourists, and wracked by the elements in the four centuries since its rediscovery", we are not given such information about Herculaneum.

C.   False. There will be "comprehensive maintenance" rather than "piecemeal patches to individual buildings or attractions".

D.   True. The passage gives the dollar and euro values for each restoration. Herculaneum was a 20-million-euro ($27.7 million U.S. dollar) effort while the Great Pompeii Project will be a 105-million-euro ($145 million U.S. dollar) project.

168. D

A.   Cannot say. Holcim and Lafarge along with six other companies are being investigated by the European Commission but we do not know

who the other six are. The passage does not mention HeidelbergCement as being among the group being investigated.

B.   False. The passage says that the cement market is "largely" local and that cement is expensive to transport but it also says that Holcim and Lafarge "have expanded in many of the same markets around the world", not just in their home countries.

C.   Cannot say. The passage only refers to their *market shares* in the U.S. and in some other countries. There is no reference to the relative contribution to profits.

D.   True. This information is clearly stated in the passage.

169. B

A.   Cannot say. While we are told that Olympus was believed to the "meeting place of the deities" and that it is Greece's highest mountain, there is no reference to whether the territory of the "Classical world" corresponds to modern Greece or what other mountains there may have been in that territory.

B.   True. The passage includes all this information.

C.   False. In Dion King Archelaus held nine days, not seven days (a week) of games and these were "to honor the god Zeus", not a Macedonian royal.

D.   Cannot say. The passage only tells us that "12 gods were believed to have lived in the alpine ravines", which Homer described as the mountain's "mysterious folds." It does not explicitly state that Homer himself believed the gods resided there.

170. D

A.   Cannot say. It is only given as conjecture ("it is said") and not fact that King Arthur fought an epic battle with the king-killing giant Rhita Gawr. Further, the passage never says that Arthur slayed the giant; it only says that he battled with him.

B.   False. Snowdonia's highest peak, Snowdon, is known as Yr Wyddfa in Welsh, whereas the park, Snowdonia, is known as Eryri.

C.   Cannot say. The passage only says that Snowdonia covers 2,132 square kilometers with nine mountain ranges covering half of the park. These ranges may be fully contained within the park or spread outside its borders, and in total cover over or under 2000 square kilometers.

D. True. We are told that Welsh is the local tongue and that the mountain has two ancient Welsh names, Yr Wyddfa Fawr (the Great Tomb) and Carnedd y Cawr (the Cairn of the Giant), derived from Rhita Gawr's resting place. Rhita Gawr was a "king-killing giant" that fought an epic battle with King Arthur, who is Snowdonia's most legendary inhabitant.

171. C

A. Cannot say. NASA scientist Justin Maki says that "the bright spots are *probably* caused by cosmic rays colliding with the rover's camera or by glinting rocks reflecting the Martian sunlight" – so this is a hypothesis not a definite fact.

B. False. The statement is the opposite of what happened. The camera on Curiosity showed nearly vertical bright smudges emerging from a spot near the horizon in its *right* eye but these did not show up in the camera's left eye.

C. True. All this information is given in the text.

D. Cannot say. Although the passage says that no evidence exists for life on Mars, it does not explicitly state what NASA's stance is on this subject. The text only refers to a NASA scientist's analysis of Curiosity's photos.

172. D

A. Cannot say. The passage only says that divers once found a museum-grade Roman clasp. Although they have found old coins and cutlery, the text does not tell us whether these were Roman in origin.

B. Cannot say. Although there are "keys tossed in the water by couples hoping to affirm the eternal nature of their love", there is no information as to whether most of these keys can open anything.

C. False. The text states that they live on a houseboat.

D. True. This is clearly stated in the passage.

173. A

A. True. All this information is given in the text.

B. Cannot say. The text tells us that agriculture is "a major driver of wildlife extinction" but this is in the context of loss of habitat when land is cleared for farming; it also says that agriculture,

through deforestation, is leading to increased levels of carbon dioxide, but it does *not* refer to whether those increased levels are resulting in the death of animal species.

C. Cannot say. The passage only says that agriculture is "among" the greatest contributors, not that it is the greatest contributor, to global warming.

D. False. The statement is the opposite of what is in the text. The passage says that agriculture emits "more greenhouse gases than all our cars, trucks, trains, and airplanes combined".

174. B

A. Cannot say. The passage does not refer to a "Spanish explorer".

B. True. The passage says that La Gomera's Guanche people were possibly North African Berbers. It also tells us that the island of La Gomera is off the northwest coast of Africa; therefore it follows that North Africa lies to the south and east of the island.

C. False. The type of thick laurel forest covering over two-thirds of the park is "now rare in … southern Europe".

D. False. We know from the passage that La Gomera is the only one of the Canary Islands that has not had a volcanic eruption *in the modern era*. However, we can also deduce from the passage that it has experienced volcanic activity at some point in its history as we are told that the landscape is "nurtured by volcanic soils".

175. D

A. Cannot say. The canyon of the Tara River in Montenegro is "home to Europe's deepest gorge at 1,300 meters", but its length is not given.

B. Cannot say. The passage says that people in the nearby village of Zabljak own grazing sheep and cattle that roam the park in the summer, but it does not say if the village is Montenegrin.

C. Cannot say. Although the passage states that waters from the Black Lake travel below the Durmitor massif, and that the Tara River is home to Europe's deepest gorge, it only says that *rivers* flow under the massif, and not whether this includes the Tara.

D. True. All this information can be found in the passage.

176. D

A. Cannot say. Although the passage states that the spread of prosperity across the world is increasing demand for animal derived products, it does not measure the extent of this demand (as less or more) in comparison to other factors responsible for the overall rising food demand, such as population increase.

B. Cannot say. The passage only gives a hypothesis that if trends continue we will have to roughly double the amount of crops we grow, not necessarily double the number of farms, by 2050.

C. Cannot say. The text says only that there is pressure to grow more soybeans to feed cattle, pigs, and chickens – not necessarily humans.

D. True. "The spread of prosperity across the world … is driving an increased demand for meat … boosting pressure to grow more corn and soybeans to feed more cattle… ".

177. A

A. True. The passage says that NASA sees cosmic rays in the images at least once a week because Mars's atmosphere is thinner and doesn't block as much cosmic radiation as Earth's does. The cosmic rays are responsible for creating bright spots in the images.

B. Cannot say. Although "glinting rocks are pretty common on Mars and have been spotted in images sent by several of NASA's Mars rovers to Earth", we are not told if this phenomenon has been observed by other countries' rovers or even if other countries have rovers on Mars.

C. Cannot say. We only know that Mars's atmosphere is thinner and doesn't block as much cosmic radiation as Earth's does. We are not told if Earth's atmosphere blocks cosmic radiation to the extent that it thereby prevents interference with terrestrial cameras.

D. False. Although the scientist says that maybe one percent of the hundreds of weekly images include cosmic ray-induced bright spots, he follows that by saying that they are certainly found once a week.

178. A

A. True. "Most earthquakes occur at fault zones, where tectonic plates—giant rock slabs that make up the Earth's upper layer—collide or slide against each other … Other quakes can occur far from fault zones when plates are stretched or squeezed."

B. Cannot say. The passage says that 80 percent of all the planet's earthquakes occur along the rim of the Pacific Ocean, but there is no reference to where 20 percent of oceanic earthquakes occur.

C. False. The Pacific Ocean's rim gets its name, "Ring of Fire," from all of the volcanic activity that occurs along it, not the frequency of earthquakes.

D. Cannot say. A magnitude rating of 3 to 5 "is considered minor or light", but the passage doesn't explain what "minor" or "light" equates to for this type of event. It says that most earthquakes occur at fault zones and their impacts are "usually gradual and unnoticeable on the surface" – but we are not told whether such earthquakes are less or more than magnitude 3.

179. C

A. Cannot say. The passage never explicitly states that the events in Pompeii and Herculaneum occurred at the same date, only that both towns were buried by Vesuvius in ash.

B. Cannot say. Although "roofing and drains made much of the difference" in Herculaneum's restoration, we cannot conclude that they would do the same in a restoration of Pompeii. Pompeii may have its own unique circumstances and some are given in the passage.

C. True. According to the text three walls have collapsed at Pompeii and *almost* three-quarters of its homes, temples, and streets are exposed to the elements.

D. False. The number of visitors to Herculaneum is not given but the passage explicitly states that Pompeii sees *more than*, not under, two million visitors a year.

180. B

A. Cannot say. While we are told that the increase in imports by Germany "is mostly good news, economists say, especially for countries like Greece and Italy that suffer from very high unemployment", there is no information in the text as to whether the increase has actually produced more jobs in those two countries.

B. True. All these facts are given in the passage.

C. False. The statement is the reverse of the truth. German exports worldwide rose 4.6 percent while German exports to the euro zone increased 3.7 percent.

D. Cannot say. We are not given any figures for Germany's trade with Greece and Italy.

5.   Succeeding in Numerical Reasoning Tests

Introduction

It is often said that the difficulty in taking numerical reasoning tests lies not in finding the actual answer to the question but doing it within the limited time available. This observation is correct inasmuch as these tests do not require complex mathematical calculations but rather the ability to:

• identify data relevant to answering the question from a larger set of information

• identify the quickest way to extract the answer from the relevant data

• discover one or several possible shortcuts that will allow us to arrive at the answer quickly

• determine the level of accuracy required to select the correct answer, and

• make quick mental calculations

In order to be prepared for the above, there are certain aspects of numerical reasoning tests that we must be aware of.

First of all, the "alternative reality" of a numerical reasoning test is different from what we are used to in everyday life – relevant data is not provided in a clean format but is rather hidden among other pieces of information that we may call "noise". Our first task is to always identify what we will need to work with from the information provided and avoid getting bogged down in wondering why other data might also be present.

Secondly, such tests have a surprising tendency to reach back to basic mathematical skills that may in fact come naturally to a secondary school student but are often lost during later academic stages and at the workplace. It is essential to refresh our basic calculus (see for instance www.calculus.org or www.sosmath.com and the "math refresher" Webinar on Online EU Training).

Also, many candidates dread the numerical reasoning test simply because it is based on mathematics and they have always considered this discipline their weakness. What we must realize here is that the "mathematical" aspect of numerical reasoning tests is rather basic – addition, subtraction, multiplication, division, fractions and percentages will always be sufficient to perform the necessary calculations. As we will see, in some cases even such calculations are unnecessary and arriving at the correct answer is rather based on an intuitive insight or the realization of a relationship between figures that is in fact right in front of our eyes – we just need to learn to see it.

It is also useful to note here that, just like in the case of verbal reasoning, the broad term "numerical reasoning" may be used to designate various test types related to the handling of numbers, calculations and data, such as:

- **Computation tests** are basic tests that measure the speed at which the test-taker is able to make basic mental calculations such as addition, subtraction, multiplication and division (e.g. "how much is (15+65) / 2 ?").
- **Estimation tests** resemble computation tests in that the calculations to be made are very similar, but the numbers with which you have to work may be greater. The point of the test is not to measure ability to perform the actual calculation but rather the speed and accuracy at which candidates can approximate the result of the calculation. The aim is to select an answer option that will be close to what the result would be if the actual calculation was performed (e.g. 3.98 times 997 is approximately 4000).
- **Numerical reasoning tests** represent a higher level where the focus is not on the actual ability to make calculations but rather the insight required to find out which calculations need to be performed to arrive at the answer. In other words, *applied reasoning* is tested. These tests are usually text-based in which a certain scenario involving numbers is described – it is this situation that the test-taker is expected to interpret in mathematical terms. To take an example of such a scenario: "There are 60 children at a camp site. Each child either wants to play hide and seek or go to the movies. Twice as many children want to play hide and seek. How many children want to go to the movies?"
- **Data interpretation tests** are similar to the above but instead of using a text, a "scenario" or story as the input, the basis of the exercise is a data set presented in the form of a table, a chart, or any combination of these (e.g. "Based on the data in the chart, by what percentage did the proportion of English-speaking people in cities change in France between 2000 and 2010?").

EPSO's numerical reasoning tests are most closely modelled on the latter two test types. Yet it is easy to see how each subsequent test type in this "hierarchy" builds on skills and routine that is measured in a lower-level test type. Quick estimations can only be made if we can make quick calculations as well. When you are faced with text-based numerical reasoning tests and you need to find a way to arrive at the answer, once you have done that, you must actually perform the required calculations or estimations to end up with the correct figure. When it comes to data interpretation based on tables and charts, the task is very similar to those in a text-based numerical reasoning test, with the added twist of having the data presented in a tabular or graphical format.

Let's now turn our attention to a real numerical reasoning test item and see how the above skills come into play.

High-Definition Television Sets in Various Countries (thousands)			
	2000	**2005**	**2010**
Belgium	345	612	880
Slovakia	230	462	510
Netherlands	702	950	1002
Spain	810	1230	1600

Q. Approximately what percentage of total high-definition television sets across the four countries shown were in Belgium in 2010?

A.   10%   B.   15%   C.   22%   D.   30%   E.   35%

Using this sample test item, we can demonstrate how the above-described skills (data interpretation, numerical reasoning, estimation and computation) can be used to quickly and efficiently solve EPSO's numerical reasoning tests.

The first step is to interpret the data that we need to work with.

In the present case, the first step is to determine which figures from the table we actually need. The question concerns the number of high-definition television sets in 2010, so we can concentrate on the 2010 column in the table knowing that all the other figures are irrelevant to the task.

Next, we need to figure out what calculations we actually need to perform – in other words, we apply our numerical reasoning skills to the task at hand. Since the question is about Belgium's share of the total number of television sets in the four countries shown in the table, we need to calculate the total (by adding up the individual figures for the four countries), and then calculate Belgium's share in it (by dividing Belgium's number by the total). Finally, we need to convert the result of this division into a percentage figure (multiplying it by 100).

The next question we have to decide is whether we actually need to perform the exact above calculations at all. We can decide this by considering if there is any possibility of estimating certain results. Let's look at the four numbers we need to add up from this perspective:

880

510

1002

1600

Whenever making a decision about the use of estimation, we must take into account the answer options first. In our case, these are percentages which are quite far apart from one another: 10%, 15%, 22%, 30% and 35% – this will tell us that the level of accuracy required to answer the question is not too high and you can feel free to "guesstimate".

Looking at the numbers, we can see that they lend themselves quite nicely to rounding up and down. By doing this, we can arrive at some more "convenient" numbers:

900 (rounded up)

500 (rounded down)

1000 (rounded down)

1600 (stays the same)

Now that the numbers are easy to work with, we can perform some actual computation. Since all numbers end in 00, we can disregard those two digits and work with one and two-digit numbers as their relative proportions (percentages) will remain the same. Add up these four numbers to get to the total number of subscriptions:

9+5+10+16 = 40

Remember that we are looking for a percentage. This means that we do not need to add back the two zeroes – that would only be needed if we had to arrive at an actual value. Instead, we can just compare our total (40) with Belgium's number: 9.

9 / 40 = 0.225

To convert this to a percentage, simply multiply the number by 100:

0.225 x 100 = 22.5%

Remember at this point that we rounded all the numbers up and down a bit – this explains why our result is not exactly the same as any of the answer options provided. It is, however, overwhelmingly clear that it is closest to Answer C (22%), which will be the correct answer.

Let's take stock of what we did in solving this test problem:

1. We interpreted the data in the table.

2. We applied our reasoning to determine what calculations we needed to perform.

3. We made estimations to simplify our calculations.

4. Finally, we performed the actual calculations.

Hopefully, this example demonstrates how the various skills required for succeeding in numerical reasoning depend on one another. If you keep these simple principles in mind and follow the steps laid out above, you will gain a systematic approach to solving all numerical reasoning tests successfully. There are, of course, things to look out for in test items, traps to avoid and tactics to use and become accustomed to.

Based on the required skills and the aspects introduced above, we will now provide an overview of the following:

- Mental calculus
- Order of magnitude
- Percentages and percentage points
- Estimation
- Equations
- Tables and charts

After reviewing these various methods and aspects, we will discuss how to approach numerical reasoning tests, what to focus on in each exercise and how to practice for the exam.

Mental Calculus

If you read through the information made available to candidates before the exam it will, based on recent data, be stated that an on-screen calculator may be used during the numerical reasoning test. EPSO may also make a physical calculator available for you to use at the exam centre. In light of this, you might be doubtful as to why it is so important to be able to perform quick mental calculations. There are several important reasons for this:

- The calculator provided may be quite slow to use and its layout may be unfamiliar to you, which might make its use counter-productive
- There are certain calculations that are always faster to perform in your head
- Overreliance on a calculator may make you less intuitive and prevent you from realizing whether certain calculations are really required to answer the question

It is therefore strongly advised to first practice as if no calculators were provided and start to use such devices only later when you have learned all the necessary ways of carrying out calculations.

Fractions

As mentioned above, certain types of calculations can quite simply be performed more efficiently without any "technical assistance". One such example is the handling of fractions (as in the illustration below).

Consider the following scenario. We are looking for the proportion of households living in one-bedroom apartments with access to a garden from all households in the United Kingdom. Based on the data provided, let's say that you realize that approximately one in six households in the United Kingdom live in a one-bedroom apartment

Numerator

$$\frac{1}{6} \times \frac{2}{3}$$

Denominator

and among those, two out of three have access to a garden. One way of approaching this calculation would be to use the calculator to do the following:

$1 \div 6 = 0.1667$ (proportion of UK households living in one-bedroom apartments)

$2 \div 3 = 0.6667$ (proportion of these that have access to a garden)

$0.6667 * 0.16667 = 0.1111$ (proportion of UK households living in one-bedroom apartments with access to a garden)

If we also have the total number of households, say 19,540,000, we then perform one additional calculation:

$0.1111 * 19,540,000 = 2,170,894$

Now, let's see how this calculation would go without the use of a calculator, by using fractions:

$$\frac{1}{6} \times \frac{2}{3} = \frac{2}{18} \quad \frac{\text{Numerator}}{\text{Denominator}}$$

How did we do this calculation? Fractions are multiplied by multiplying the first numerator by the second numerator and the first denominator by the second denominator.

We can then simplify the fraction by finding a number that both the numerator and the denominator can be divided by – in our case, this is the number 2:

$$\frac{2}{18} = \frac{1}{9}$$

It is easy to see that the above two calculations can be performed very quickly by mental arithmetic. Also, the final figure we arrive at is extremely convenient – now we know that one in nine UK households are one-bedroom apartments with garden access. If we consider that there are 19,540,000 households, the remaining calculation will also be very simple:

$19,540,000 / 9 = 2,171,111$

You can see that the number we get this way is slightly different from the number we get using the first method. We can be sure that the latter is more accurate because we did not have to do any rounding in the interim calculation stages.

There are two observations to make here:

• We arrived at the required figure by making extremely simple calculations with easy, round numbers
• Using fractions is actually more accurate than the calculator, because during the first method, we "truncated" many of the figures.

Calculations with Fractions

Multiplication: **Division:**   **Addition and subtraction:**

Lowest Common Multiple

$$\frac{3}{5} \times \frac{4}{6} = \frac{12}{30} \qquad \frac{4}{7} \div \frac{2}{3} = \frac{4}{7} \times \frac{3}{2} = \frac{12}{14} \qquad \frac{2}{3} + \frac{3}{7} = \frac{14}{21} + \frac{9}{21} = \frac{23}{21}$$

Multiplication

Method

If we need to multiply two fractions, we first multiply the two numerators (the numbers at the top) and then the two denominators (the numbers at the bottom).

Example of Application

Imagine that you are given a table showing IBM's 2013 revenues in billions. You are also given the following two pieces of information in the question text itself:

- 30% of revenue was made from selling datacenter components
- Of the datacenter revenue, 40% was generated in China

Your task could be to calculate either how much or what percentage of revenue was generated from datacenter components in China. A quick answer to this question can be found using fractions.

30% can be transcribed as a fraction, 3/10 and 40% as 4/10. Based on this, the calculation would go as follows:

$$\frac{3}{10} \times \frac{4}{10} = \frac{12}{100}$$

If the question was "what percentage", we are extremely lucky because the fraction we arrived at after the multiplication is already "per hundred", so the answer is 12%. If the question was "how much", we simply calculate the 12% of the total revenue by multiplying it by 0.12.

Division

Method

If we need to divide a fraction by another fraction, our first task is to turn the operation into multiplication. We do this by "inverting" the numerator and the denominator in one of the fractions. This way, $\frac{2}{3}$ would become $\frac{3}{2}$, and so on.

Next, we multiply the two numerators and then the two denominators in the same way as we do when multiplying fractions.

Example of Application

Q. 20% of France's annual wine production is equal to half of England's annual consumption. If all of the wine consumed in England were French, what percentage of France's production would be imported into England?

We can transcribe the above information with fractions as follows.

$$20\% = \frac{1}{5} \qquad\qquad half = \frac{1}{2}$$

We are looking for England's total consumption in terms of France's total production. We have the following information:

$$\frac{1}{5} \times Production_{France} = \frac{1}{2} Consumption_{England}$$

We want only England's total consumption on one side of the equation, so we need to divide both sides of the equation by one half:

$$\frac{1}{5} \div \frac{1}{2} \times Production_{France} = Consumption_{England}$$

We can now invert the numerator and the denominator (say, in the second fraction) and then perform the multiplication as described above:

$$\frac{1}{5} \times \frac{2}{1} \times Production_{France} = Consumption_{England}$$

$$\frac{1}{5} \times 2 \times Production_{France} = Consumption_{England}$$

$$\frac{2}{5} \times Production_{France} = Consumption_{England}$$

With a little practice, we can readily see that two-fifths is equal to four-tenths, or, in more familiar terms, 40%.

In the above very simple example, we could have calculated this even more easily by simply saying that if 50% of England's consumption is equal to 20% of France's production, then the full consumption (which is twice as much), will represent twice as much of France's production, or 40%. In other situations, however, things are not as self-evident and fractions can serve a very useful purpose.

Addition and Subtraction

Method

When adding or subtracting fractions, we need to make sure first that the denominators are the same in both fractions. We can do this by finding the smallest number that can be divided by both denominators. If our two denominators are 3 and 7, as in the illustration at the start of this section on Calculation with fractions, that number will be 21. Once we have done that, we need to multiply the numerators by the same number as the one with which we had to multiply the denominator in the same fraction. In the illustration, the numerator in the left fraction needs to be multiplied by 7 and the numerator in the right fraction needs to be multiplied by 3.

The last step is to simply add up the two numerators.

Example of Application

Imagine that you have the following three pieces of information:

- 30% of Italians believe that the minimum wage must be increased
- three in five Italians believe that the minimum wage must remain unchanged
- the rest believe it should be eliminated to increase competitiveness

Based on the wording of the above, we can be sure that there is no overlap between the groups – one group believes in an increase, the other in maintaining the current level, the third in eliminating it.

We have to answer the following question:

Q. What percentage of Italians believe that the minimum wage must remain unchanged or increase?

To answer the above question with fractions, we need to express "30%" and "three in five" in the form of fractions and then add up the two.

"30%" = 3 / 10

"three in five" = 3 / 5

The proportion we are looking for, then, is as follows:

3/10 + 3/5

You will notice that in this particular case, only the second fraction will need to be "converted". If we multiply both the numerator and the denominator of that fraction by 2, the two denominators will be identical and we can perform the addition.

3/10 + 6/10 = 9/10

By using fractions, we can answer the question by saying that 90% of Italians believe the minimum wage needs to be retained or increased, and 10% believe it should be eliminated. When solving numerical reasoning tests, it is always worth considering for a second whether we can take advantage of fractions – they are an extremely powerful tool in reducing seemingly complex relationships into the simplest of calculations.

Order of Magnitude

	Apple Production in Various European Countries			
		Apple Production (thousands of tonnes)		
	Population in 2000 (thousands)	1990	2000	2010
Slovakia	4 895	31	25	35
Croatia	4 290	103	98	112
Bulgaria	8 930	120	90	134
Austria	10 354	546	490	560

Note: 1 tonne=1000kg

Q. What was the production of apples per person in Croatia in 2000?

A.   0.23 kg

B.   2.29 kg

C.   22.84 kg

D.   228.4 kg

E.   2.28 tonnes

An order of magnitude is a scale of amounts where each amount is in a fixed ratio to the amount preceding it. The most common ratio is 1:10, which means that the next amount in a scale can be calculated by multiplying the previous figure by 10.

For example: 1, 10, 100, 1000, 10000 …and so on…

If we look at the above answer options, we can see that that is exactly the situation we have here:

0.23, 2.29, 22.84, 228.4, 2.28 tonnes, (which is 2280 kg) – with some small variations from exact multiples of ten which slightly disguise the relationship.

When we are faced with a set of numbers like the ones above, it gives us an important hint that the actual calculation of the figure may not really be necessary – all we need to figure out is the order of magnitude of the correct answer.

Let us consider the above sample test from the perspective of whether we can take advantage of this observation.

We have the following information:

• The amount of apples produced in Croatia in 2000 in thousands of tonnes – 98
• The population of Croatia in thousands – 4290

Since the answer options only differ in their order of magnitude, we can be quite flexible in rounding our numbers up or down to simplify our calculations.

Let us round 98 up to 100 and 4290 down to 4000. You can disregard the exact number of digits for a second. What is the relationship between the numbers 100 and 4000? If you think about that for a second, you will realize that 100 and 4000 are in a relationship to each other that is similar to that between 1 and 4 – that is, to one quarter. Expressed in decimal terms, this is 0.25. Our answer options are close to this (this is especially apparent in option A – the difference of 0.23 versus 0.25 is caused by having rounded down the numbers). Remember – we do not need to be particularly accurate in this case, all that we are looking for is the number of digits in the correct answer. Now turn your attention to those zeroes we disregarded so far.

Apple Production: 98 thousand tonnes – we will add 6 zeroes here to make it kilogrammes: 98 000 000 kg

Population: 4 290 thousand – we will need to add three zeroes here: 4 290 000

If we turn back to our simplified figures, our calculation would look like this:

100 million divided by 4 million

We could use a calculator to obtain the result here, but let us recall what we said earlier – this is very close to one quarter of 100, which is 25.

25 is closest to Option C and that is the correct answer.

Percentages and Percentage points

The information in this section may seem trivial, yet mixing up two concepts (*percentage change* and *percentage point change*) can prove fatal when taking a numerical reasoning test.

Let us consider the following example (some lines are blocked out):

In many numerical reasoning tests, you will be faced with data where calculation of the

Bus Companies in the United States, 2013				
Company	Profit (in million USD)	Number of Passengers (in millions)	Number of vehicles	Average vehicle utilization (%)
Greyhound	46	289	4560	73

correct answer will require working with percentages. A straightforward case is where one figure (for example the number of cars in Italy) is an amount, and the other figure (for example the proportion of foreign-made cars) is a percentage. In such cases, the calculation is obvious:

No. of cars in Italy * % of foreign-made cars = No. of foreign made cars in Italy

Let us, however, consider another example. There are cases when *both* figures are proportions or percentages. What happens when the first piece of data (in the table, the average utilization of Greyhond buses) and the second piece of data (the % change in average utilization, for example) are both percentages?

Suppose that the question based on the above table is the following:

Q. What was the average vehicle utilization of Greyhound in 2012 if its vehicle utilization was 22% worse than in 2013?

In this example, where average utilization in 2013 is 73%, and it was 22% worse in 2012, our natural instinct might well be to perform the following calculation:

73% - 22% = 51%, therefore the average utilization in 2012 was 51%.

Not surprisingly, this would not be the correct answer. For comparison, keep in mind how we would calculate a 22% decrease of a regular amount, for example 1200:

1200 * (100% − 22%) = 1200 * 78% = 1200 * 0.78 = 936

Now apply the above logic to capacity utilization:

73% * (100% − 22%) = 73% * 78% = 73% * 0.78 = 56.94%

We can see that the correct calculation yields a significantly different result from what our initial instinct suggested.

When it comes to percentage changes in values that are themselves percentages, what many people think of as a 22 per cent change (for example 62% to 40%) is in fact a 22 percentage point change.

Through an intuitive example, we will be able to appreciate the fundamental difference between the two concepts.

Suppose that a bank in Switzerland pays 10% interest on deposits (we wish!). Now let's take a look at possible changes to this interest rate:

- If the interest rate drops by 5 percentage points, the new interest rate will be 5%
- If the interest rate drops by 5 percent, the new interest rate will be 9.5%
- A 10% interest rate can decrease by a maximum of 10 percentage points, but it can decrease by as much as 100 per cent – both resulting in a 0% interest rate

Estimation

In a previous section, when calculating the per-capita apple production of Croatia, we applied a sort of estimation to get to the correct answer. In that case, the estimation took the form of concentrating only on the number of digits in the correct answer. There are cases, however, where we need to be a little more precise than that

Let's go back to our table and ask a different question:

Bus Companies in the United States, 2013				
Company	Profit (in million USD)	Number of Passengers (in millions)	Number of vehicles	Average vehicle utilization (%)
Greyhound	46	289	4560	73

Q. How many passengers would Greyhound carry in 2014 if its average vehicle utilization improves by 10% and its number of vehicles doesn't change?

a) 317.9 million

b) 356.6 million

c) 232.07 million

d) 260.1 million

Again, let us first consider the less innovative (and therefore more time-consuming) way of calculating the correct answer.

The data we will work with are:

- Number of passengers in millions in 2013: 289
- Average vehicle utilization in 2013: 73%
- The fact that average vehicle utilization in 2014 is forecast to increase by 10%

The first thing we would do is calculate the new utilization. An important point to remember here is the difference between percentage change and percentage point change, as discussed above.

New capacity utilization = 73% * (100% + 10%) = 73% * 110% = 73% * 1.1 = 80.3%

One mistake we could make here is equating the 2014 figure for passengers carried with the following:

289 million * 80.3% = 289 million * 0.803 = 232.07 million (note that this is one of the answer options)

Why is the above calculation incorrect? We must bear in mind that the number 289 million is actually equal to 73% of the total vehicle capacity of Greyhound, since its average utilization according to the table was 73%.

We also know the new capacity utilization figure (80.3%), but we must also calculate total capacity (X). We know the following:

X * 0.73 = 289 million (73% of the total capacity is 289 million passengers)

Let's solve the equation for X:

X = 289 million / 0.73 = 395.9 million

We can now calculate the number of passengers transported at 80.3% capacity utilization:

395.9 * 0.803 = 317.9 million

Answer A is in fact the correct answer.

While the above series of calculations were all correct, we must always be suspicious when so many raw calculations are required to get to the correct answer. Do not forget that numerical reasoning in EPSO exams is not primarily a mathematical exercise, so this might be a hint that an easier solution may exist.

We need to make two observations here:

- Some of the data is irrelevant
- The "distance" between the values in the answer options allows for estimation

Let's go back to the problem. As the question referred to average vehicle utilization, we immediately started to work with that number. However, we should reconsider the meaning of this term. If average vehicle utilization increases by 10%, and the number of vehicles does not change, is this not just another way of saying that Greyhound carried 10% more passengers? This immediately simplifies our calculation:

289 million + 10% = 289 million * 110% = 289 million * 1.1

Now let us look at the answer options again:

a)   317.9 million

b)   356.6 million

c)   232.07 million

d)   260.1 million

Answers C and D can be immediately ruled out because those numbers are smaller than the 289 million in the table, which is impossible when the utilization increases.

Answer B has a greater number than in the table, but if we estimate 10% of 289 million (about 30 million, or exactly 28.9 million) we will immediately see that Answer B's 356.6 million is simply too large an amount, which leaves only Answer A as a feasible option.

The correctness of Answer A can also be verified very quickly, with a simple subtraction:

317.9 million – 28.9 million = 317.9 million – (17.9 million + 11 million) = 300 million – 11 million = 289 million

The above calculation also shows an example of how to make subtractions easier. In this example, we reformulated 28.9 million as 17.9 million + 11 million so it became much easier to first subtract 17.9 million from 317.9 million (leaving the round number of 300 million), and then deal with the rest.

Equations

Equations might sound too mathematical, yet they are a brilliantly inventive way of dealing with problems where multiple calculations must be made. Consider this:

Q. There are 13 600 customers in a café in a month. Out of them, 45% order coffee; of these, 30% opt for coffee with milk, of whom 200 ask for soy milk. Of the other customers, 25% ask for espresso macchiato, for which 60 millilitres of regular milk is used per customer. How much regular milk is used in a month for espresso macchiatos?

A.   245.4 litres

B.   245.4 millilitres

C.   24.54 litres

D.   29.54 litres

One way of approaching the problem would be to perform a series of individual calculations. First, we would calculate 45% of 13 600 customers to get 6120, then 30% of 6120 to get 1836, then we would subtract 200 from that to get 1636, then we would calculate 25% of this to get 409. Finally, we would multiply 409 by the amount of milk (60 ml, or 0.06 litres) and get the correct result, which is answer C. This is all perfectly reasonable.

However, by denoting the amount of milk used for macchiatos (which is the answer we are looking for) by X, we can create an equation which will make the calculation faster:

X = (13 600 * 0.45 * 0.3 – 200) * 0.25 * 60 (where 0.45 equals 45%, 0.3 equals 30%, and 0.25 equals 25%)

We can further simplify the equation:

X = (13 600 * 0.135 – 200) / 4 * 60

X = (1836 – 200) / 4 * 60

X = 1636 / 4 * 60

X = 409 * 60

X = 24 540

The final thing we need to remember is that this is in millilitres. Since this doesn't match any of the available answer options, let's convert it into litres:

24 540 / 1 000 = 24.54 litres

This matches Answer C. By denoting the figure we are looking for as X and then using the data to find X, we can work systematically with all levels of difficulty in the figures and reduce the risk of "getting lost" in a jumble of numbers.

Tables and Charts

Bus Companies in the United States, 2013				
Company	Profit (in million USD)	Number of Passengers (in millions)	Number of vehicles	Average vehicle utilization (%)
Trailways	12	123	2140	71
National	14	150	2400	69
Roger's	7	65	1300	75
Greyhound	46	289	4560	73

Q. How many passengers would Greyhound carry in 2014 if its average vehicle utilization improves by 10% and its number of vehicles doesn't change?

A.   317.9 million

B.   356.6 million

C.   232.07 million

D.   260.1 million

The above table may seem familiar. This is because we previously used a version of this table with some rows "blacked out" for demonstrating certain methods. In real numerical tests, however, the table always contains lots of superfluous data that you will not need for your calculations – this is what we referred to as "noise" in the introduction. When starting to solve a numerical reasoning question, it is always important to first decide exactly what data is necessary for the calculation because the superfluous information will just confuse you and can take valuable time if you become distracted.

For this reason, it is good advice to mentally "black out" that data from the table which you will not need. In this instance, the first thing we will realize is that we don't need any of the data about the other three bus companies (Trailways, National, Roger's). So let's black out the data for the other companies.

Bus Companies in the United States, 2013				
Company	Profit (in million USD)	Number of Passengers (in millions)	Number of vehicles	Average vehicle utilization (%)
Greyhound	46	289	4560	73

Since the question refers to the number of passengers carried, we will certainly not need profit data to answer the question, so let's black out that data:

Bus Companies in the United States, 2013				
Company	Profit (in million USD)	Number of Passengers (in millions)	Number of vehicles	Average vehicle utilization (%)
Greyhound		289	4560	73

Based on our reasoning in the section on Estimation, we will also realize that the number of vehicles is a superfluous figure, as is average vehicle utilization, so let's black those out too:

Bus Companies in the United States, 2013				
Company	Profit (in million USD)	Number of Passengers (in millions)	Number of vehicles	Average vehicle utilization (%)
Greyhound		289		

If we systematically exclude all superfluous data, the task will seem significantly less complicated. As it turns out, in our example, the table's only purpose is to tell us that Greyhound carried 289 million passengers in 2013!

How to Approach Numerical Reasoning Tests

This chapter demonstrated the number of factors we must consider in order to efficiently solve the problems posed in numerical reasoning tests. Consider aspects such as the required level of accuracy, the relevance of data or the possibility of estimation, then decide the approach to take – whether to perform raw calculations, apply estimates, draw up an equation, or simply read a relationship or a trend off a chart.

As is true in the case of verbal and abstract reasoning tests, a systematic approach will make your test-taking experience much more efficient. Below, you will find a a summary of the recommended approach:

1. Read the question and the answer options first as carefully as possible.
2. The question will help you identify which data sets will be relevant and necessary for answering the question and know what to ignore.
3. Looking at the answer options will help you decide the level of accuracy required. If, for example, the values in the answer options are very far apart, you may consider estimation.
4. Based on the question, determine the relevant information and mentally "black out" the unnecessary data.
5. Having looked at the answer options and the data in the table, you can now make a final decision about whether to go for an exact figure or make an estimate, whether to use an equation, and so on.
6. Make sure you exclude all unrealistic answer options (for example numbers representing an increase when the question refers to a decrease).
7. Once you have performed your calculations, you can match the result against the remaining answer options. If you estimated, look for the answer option closest to your estimated result. If the result is significantly closer to one answer option than to all others, you were probably on the right track.

Practice Methods

Finally, a few suggestions for how to practice for the numerical reasoning test:

- Start your practice by identifying your weaknesses. Percentages? Subtraction? Estimation? Equations? Calculus in general?
- Once you have identified your weaknesses, you should particularly practice these operations, all of which are tested in the next chapter
- Make sure you check how many questions you will face in the actual exam and how much time you will have to answer them
- In the next chapter, start without timing yourself but tackle the same number of test questions as at the exam (in most cases 20). Measure the average time you require.
- Start decreasing the time needed to answer the questions so it gets closer to the time available at the exam
- Ideally, by the time of the exam, you should be able to answer more questions in the time available than required at the exam, because you cannot account for stress and other outside factors are impossible to recreate at home
- The EPSO test will be administered on a computer, which will make it much more challenging (and stranger) to take than a paper-based test where you can scribble on the paper and make quick calculations, write down equations, underline key concepts and so on – so if you have access to such services, try to practice online

6. Numerical Reasoning Test

55 Sets – Total 165 Questions

ANSWERS follow Set 55

You should aim to eventually be able to answer these questions at a rate of 10 in 20 minutes, which is a typical EPSO scenario. However you will most likely struggle to achieve these speeds at first. Read the answer explanations carefully and focus on the range of strategies they give for speeding up your calculations until they become second nature to you.

Remember, too, to check the exact rules of your competition for the number of questions, time allowed and pass mark and use those for your practice.

Note: the symbols × and * are both used for multiplication.

Set 1

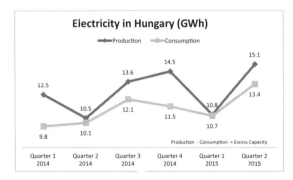

Q1. If 5% of production in Quarter 1 2014 came from 50 wind farms and the same percentage of Quarter 2 2014 production was also contributed by wind farms, how many wind farms produced electricity in that quarter? You should assume that all operational wind farms produce identical amounts of electricity as each other and in each quarter.

A. 42
B. 48
C. 52

D. 55
E. Cannot say

Q2. In 2014, Hungary exported 79% of its excess capacity. How many GWh of excess electricity does Hungary still need to generate in the rest of 2015 to achieve the same export volume in 2015 if in the first half of 2015 it exported 50% of its excess capacity?

A. 4.2 GWh
B. 5.1 GWh
C. 5.8 GWh
D. 6.7 GWh
E. It cannot achieve the same export volume

Q3. The Paks nuclear power plant in Hungary produces 14.8 GWh annually and its rate of production is constant. In how many of the quarters shown was Paks's production more than 30% of total production?

A. In none of them
B. 1
C. 2
D. 4
E. In all of them

Set 2

Wine Consumption in Europe		
Country	Population (thousands)	Annual Wine Consumption (million litres)
Austria	8412	59.6
Belgium	7992	53.7
Netherlands	16884	106.3
Norway	4840	29.4
Portugal	11041	71.6

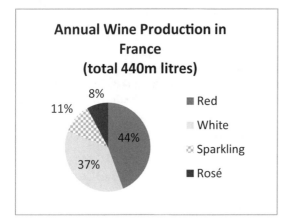

Annual Wine Production in France (total 440m litres)

- 44% Red
- 37% White
- 11% Sparkling
- 8% Rosé

Q1. On average how much more wine is consumed per person in Austria than in Norway in a year?

A. 0.1 litres
B. 1.02 litres
C. 2.44 litres
D. 3.42 litres
E. 7.29 litres

Q2. In Belgium, 43% of all wine consumed is red, of which 41% is French. What percentage of French red wine production is exported to Belgium?

A. 1.3%
B. 2.8%
C. 4.9%
D. 5.8%
E. 8.4%

Q3. In the Netherlands they drink twice as much white wine as red, twice as much red wine as rosé and twice as much rosé as sparkling. How much white wine does each person drink on average in the Netherlands in a year?

A. 3.36 litres
B. 3.92 litres
C. 4.88 litres
D. 6.44 litres
E. 7.02 litres

Set 3

Unemployment in Europe					
Country	Population ('000)	Workforce (% of Population)		Unemployed (% of workforce)	
	2005	2005	2010	2005	2010
Austria	8232	47.2	47.7	7.7	7.9
France	61013	48.9	48.6	7.8	8.4
Ireland	4187	43.7	44.4	9.4	8.9
Poland	38198	48.2	48.7	12.6	11.3
Sweden	9066	47.3	48.1	6.9	6.8

Q1. In Ireland the population grew by a total of 4% between 2005 and 2010. How many more or fewer people were unemployed in 2010 than in 2005?

A. 7,800 more
B. 78 more
C. No change
D. 78 fewer
E. 7,800 fewer

Q2. What percentage of the population of Sweden was unemployed in 2010 if the population grew by 0.8% each year between 2005 and 2010?

A. 1.34%
B. 2.81%
C. 3.27%
D. 5.85%
E. 8.42%

Q3. If the population of Austria grew by 3% between 2005 and 2010, what was the percentage increase in the number of people unemployed in Austria over that time?

A. 2.8%

B. 3.8%

C. 4.8%

D. 5.8%

E. 6.8%

Set 4

Country	Export (2014,% of production)	Export Volume (2014, million t)	Change from 2013 (volume)
China	34%	279.5	+ 3%
USA	27%	23.8	+ 5%
Japan	19%	21	– 2 %
EU	34%	55.9	–
Rest of World	62%	285.4	+ 9%

Domestic consumption = Production – Export + Import

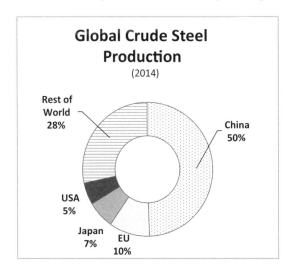

Global Crude Steel Production
(2014)

Rest of World 28%
China 50%
USA 5%
Japan 7%
EU 10%

Q1. If China exported 30% of its steel production to the United States in 2014, how much steel did the US use in that year?

A. 143.85 million tonnes

B. 166.05 million tonnes

C. 310.97 million tonnes

D. 328.82 million tonnes

E. Cannot say

Q2. How much more steel did the EU export in 2013 than Japan?

A. 66.2% more

B. 71.6% more

C. 161% more

D. 166.2% more

E. 171.6% more

Q3. Approximately what percentage of global steel production did 2013 exports make up if production in every region was the same in 2013 as in 2014?

A. Around 6%

B. Around 14%

C. Around 38%

D. Around 50%

E. Around 70%

Set 5

Acme Company Accounts					
Income (£ '000)			Expenditure (£ '000)		
	2009	2010		2009	2010
Sales	26192	28344	Materials	13442	13894
Interest	46	43	Labour	6899	7114
Rental	487	494	Utilities	1884	1907
Other	106	103	Misc	3099	2986

Q1. If profit is the total income less the total expenditure, by how much did the profit increase between 2009 and 2010?

    A. £1576

    B. £3083

    C. £220,000

    D. £893,000

    E. £1.58m

Q2. By what percentage did the 'non-misc' expenditure rise between 2009 and 2010?

    A. 2.7%

    B. 3.1%

    C. 3.6%

    D. 4.4%

    E. 5.7%

Q3. In 2009, 14% of the miscellaneous expenditure was spent on advertising. This increased by 12.2% in 2010. What percentage of the miscellaneous expenditure was spent on advertising in 2010?

    A. 15.7%

    B. 16.3%

    C. 19.1%

    D. 21.2%

    E. 26.2%

Set 6

Car Efficiency		
Model	Urban (miles per gallon)	Extra Urban (miles per gallon)
Alpha	38.9	47.6
Beta	44.8	50.2
Gamma	76.3	88.9
Delta	28.7	32.1
Epsilon	40.6	47.4

Q1. You are driving the Epsilon on a journey which consists of 28% urban driving and 72% extra urban. You use 3.3 gallons of fuel. Approximately how many miles is the journey?

    A. 45

    B. 74

    C. 104

    D. 150

    E. 205

Q2. You drive 50 urban miles in an Alpha and then 30 urban miles in a Beta. Your overall average fuel consumption in miles per gallon is closest to which of the figures below?

    A. 39.6

    B. 40.1

    C. 40.9

    D. 41.2

    E. 41.8

Q3. On an urban journey, how much more fuel efficient is the Gamma than the Delta?

    A. 62.4%

    B. 81.6%

    C. 103.9%

    D. 147.2%

    E. 165.9%

Set 7

100m Men's Final	
Runner	*Time (s)*
Adams	9.95
Best	9.98
Carter	10.03
Davies	10.07

Q1. Davies ran the last 10m at a speed 8% faster than his overall average speed. By what distance, to the nearest centimetre, did he miss out on the bronze medal (3rd place)?

    A. 43

    B. 37

    C. 32

    D. 26

    E. 18

Q2. How much faster did Adams run than Best on average?

    A. 0.1%

    B. 0.3%

    C. 0.7%

    D. 1.0%

    E. 1.2%

Q3. Carter ran the final 1.3% faster than he ran in the semi-final which was 1.8% faster than his performance in the heat (the race before the semi-final). He won his heat by 3 hundredths of a second. What was the finishing time of the runner who came second in Carter's heat?

    A. 10.09

    B. 10.18

    C. 10.29

    D. 10.34

    E. 10.37

Set 8

Birth Rates in Europe			
Country	*Population ('000)*	*Birth Rate (per 100,000 of Population)*	
	2005	*2005*	*2010*
Denmark	5417	1644	1612
Finland	5244	1680	1616
Ireland	4187	1844	1750
Lithuania	3416	1576	1582
Netherlands	16316	1702	1661

Q1. How many more births were there in Finland than in Ireland in 2005?

    A. 11

    B. 109

    C. 1089

    D. 10891

    E. 108909

Q2. If the table were ordered by percentage change in birth rate between 2005 and 2010, which country would be in the middle?

    A. Denmark

    B. Finland

    C. Ireland

    D. Lithuania

    E. Netherlands

Q3. If the population of Lithuania increased by 1.6% between 2005 and 2010, how many more births were there in 2010 than in 2005 in Lithuania?

    A. 886

    B. 1070

    C. 1290

    D. 1334

    E. 1427

Set 9

Population Density		
Country	Area ('000 km²)	Density in 2000 (people per km²)
France	544	110.49
Latvia	64.6	34.68
Ireland	70.3	59.56
Spain	495	86.55

Q1. If the population of Ireland grew by 6% between 2000 and 2010, what was its population density in 2010?

A. 55.99

B. 59.56

C. 61.34

D. 63.13

E. 64.28

Q2. In Spain, 74% of the population live in urban areas which occupy just 17% of the total land. What was the average population density of rural Spain in 2000?

A. 27.11

B. 49.67

C. 77.17

D. 132.37

E. 376.75

Q3. By how much would the population of Latvia need to increase for its average density of population to be precisely one-third that of France (assuming France remains constant)?

A. 2150

B. 15,800

C. 139,000

D. 721,000

E. 2.38 million

Set 10

Spending on Education (€/person)			
Country	Population in 2005 (× 1000)	2005	2010
Belgium	10415	1575	1630
France	61013	1615	1685
Netherlands	16316	1645	1715
Spain	43060	1490	1535
UK	60261	1580	1625

Q1. Which country had the largest percentage increase in per capita spending on education between 2005 and 2010?

A. Belgium

B. France

C. Netherlands

D. Spain

E. UK

Q2. If the population of Belgium increased by 454 thousand between 2005 and 2010, what was the percentage increase in total spending on education in Belgium over that period?

A. 4%

B. 5%

C. 6%

D. 7%

E. 8%

Q3. How much more was spent on education in the UK in 2005 than in the Netherlands and Spain combined?

A. €4.213m

B. €42.13m

C. €421.3m

D. €4213m

E. €42,130m

Set 11

European Rail Travel – normal journey times		
Brussels to …	*Distance (km)*	*Time (hours:mins)*
Amsterdam	210	1:24
Berlin	770	5:20
Luxembourg	220	1:35
Paris	320	2:40
Strasbourg	435	3:45

Q1. You travel from Brussels to Strasbourg, departing and arriving on time. The cruising speed of your train is 15% faster than its overall average speed. What is its cruising speed to the nearest kilometre per hour?

A. 100

B. 116

C. 125

D. 133

E. 150

Q2. You are travelling from Brussels to Luxembourg but due to adverse conditions the train travels 10% slower than normal. How late do you arrive in Luxembourg?

A. 5m 35s

B. 9m 30s

C. 10m 31s

D. 12m 45s

E. 15m 10s

Q3. Trains leave Brussels for Berlin every 2 hours starting at 0600 and similarly from Berlin starting at 0500. If you depart Brussels at 0800, how many Brussels-bound trains do you pass on your journey to Berlin?

A. 4

B. 5

C. 6

D. 7

E. 8

Set 12

Percentage of people who…		
	Men	*Women*
Can identify the Pole star	37	29
Know the capital of Country X	18	16
Own a car	83	79
Can make a Hollandaise sauce	28	38
Can swim 1km	32	42

Q1. In a representative group of 50 men and 50 women, 25 people who owned a car could also swim 1km. How many neither owned a car nor could swim 1km?

A. 7

B. 12

C. 19

D. 31

E. 37

Q2. In another, also representative group (which means that the above percentages are valid in this group as well), 80 people could make a Hollandaise sauce. There were 82 men in the group. How many women were in the group?

A. 80

B. 82

C. 100

D. 133

E. 150

Q3. In a representative group of 200 men, what is the minimum number who can identify the Pole Star but do not know the capital of Country X?

A. 0

B. 24

C. 38

D. 50

E. 76

Set 13

Octogenarians (% of population)				
Country	*Pop 2005 ('000)*	*1985*	*1995*	*2005*
Croatia	4443	3.75	3.81	3.84
Greece	11064	4.11	4.31	4.34
Netherlands	16316	5.29	5.38	5.64
Spain	43060	4.77	4.82	4.88
Sweden	9066	5.44	5.48	5.57

Q1. In the Netherlands, 4.3% of all people who were over 80 years old in 2005 were also over 90 and 3.2% of those are also over 100. How many centenarians were there in the Netherlands in 2005?

    A. 1

    B. 13

    C. 126

    D. 1266

    E. 12662

Q2. If the population of Sweden has increased 6% every ten years between 1985 and 2005, what is the percentage increase in the number of Octogenarians in Sweden between 1985 and 2005?

    A. 2.4%

    B. 8.5%

    C. 14.7%

    D. 15%

    E. 17.5%

Q3. If the population of Greece rose by 0.5% each year between 1985 and 1995, what was the % rise in the number of Greeks who were octogenarians per head of total population over that time?

    A. 2.9%

    B. 3.9%

    C. 4.9%

    D. 5.9%

    E. 6.9%

Set 14

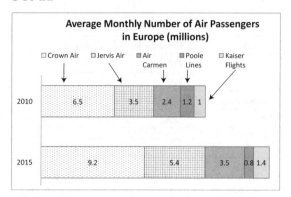

Q1. Between 2010 and 2015, by how many passengers did the increase in average monthly Crown Air traffic exceed the increase in Jervis Air traffic?

    A. 80 000

    B. 800 000

    C. 1 100 000

    D. 1 900 000

    E. 8 000 000

Q2. By how many passengers did the monthly average number of European air passengers increase between 2010 and 2015 in Europe if the 5 airlines shown represented 50% of the total in both years?

    A. 5.7 million

    B. 11.4 million

    C. 14.6 million

    D. 20.3 million

    E. 29.2 million

Q3. How many passengers did Crown Air carry in 2010?

    A. 6.5 million

    B. 9.2 million

    C. 42 million

    D. 78 million

    E. 110.4 million

Set 15

Factory annual production and wood supplier figures, tonnes				
		Utilisation of forestry production volume for:		
Forestry (number of employees)	Production Volume	Roofing	Outdoor Furn-iture	Indoor Furn-iture
Craybourne Woodlands (50)	8 000	2 000	4 000	850
Stirling Forest (80)	14 000	3 800	5 900	2450
Woodcombe Hills Woods (30)	3 000	1 600	1 200	0
Hampton Forest (30)	3 000	1 600	1 300	55
Frasier Green (40)	8 000	4 000	2 800	1 045

Q1. Which forestry has the most productive employees?

   A. Craybourne Woodlands

   B. Stirling Forest

   C. Woodcombe Hills Woods

   D. Hampton Forest

   E. Frasier Green

Q2. If 50 tonnes of wood are needed for each outdoor furniture shipment, how many shipments could have been manufactured in total relying on all forestries if 10% of the wood used for roofing had been shifted to outdoor furniture?

   A. 26

   B. 88

   C. 114

   D. 304

   E. 330

Q3. Based on the average of all five forestries, how much roofing wood is supplied by each forestry employee?

   A. 56.52 tonnes

   B. 66.09 tonnes

   C. 156.52 tonnes

   D. 565.2 tonnes

   E. 156.2 tonnes

Set 16

Marathon Results 2010 (42.2 km)	
Runner	Time (h:mm:ss)
Anderson	2:12:14
Benoit	2:12:38
Canard	2:13:31
Dennis	2:14:12
Ekimov	2:14:20

Q1. Canard passed the halfway marker at 1:07:50. What was his average speed for the second half of the race?

   A. 15.20 km/h

   B. 17.38 km/h

   C. 18.63 km/h

   D. 19.27 km/h

   E. 20.31 km/h

Q2. Dennis and Ekimov passed the "1km to go" marker at exactly the same time, 2:11:00. How much faster than Ekimov did Dennis run in the last kilometre?

   A. 1%

   B. 4.2%

   C. 6.6%

   D. 8%

   E. 12.5%

Q3. Benoit ran the last 150m at a speed 5% faster than his overall average for the race. How far was Benoit from the finishing line when Anderson finished?

   A. 84m

   B. 92m

   C. 100m

   D. 133m

   E. 149m

Set 17

Acme Closing Share Prices (€)		
	Buy	Sell
Monday	2.37	2.32
Tuesday	2.41	2.37
Wednesday	2.39	2.34
Thursday	2.28	2.25
Friday	2.34	2.29

Q1. You buy 2000 shares on Tuesday at 1.4% below the previous day's closing price. There is a €15.95 dealing charge. How much does it cost you?

    A. €4673.64

    B. €4689.59

    C. €4734.37

    D. €4761.47

    E. €4768.47

Q2. You sell 2000 shares on Friday which incurs a €15.95 dealing charge. Your total proceeds amount to €4664.05. By what percentage had the price risen since yesterday's close?

    A. 2%

    B. 3%

    C. 4%

    D. 5%

    E. 6%

Q3. The difference between the buying price and the selling price on a given day is known as 'the spread'. If the percentage spread is calculated as a percentage of the higher value, which day has the largest percentage spread?

    A. Monday

    B. Tuesday

    C. Wednesday

    D. Thursday

    E. Friday

Set 18

The Planets		
Planet	Distance from Sun (million km)	Orbital Period (Earth Days)
Mercury	58	88
Venus	101	224.7
Earth	150	365.25
Mars	228	687

Q1. As a planet travels around the Sun (orbital period), the distance it covers is 6.3 times its distance from the Sun. At what speed does the Earth travel around the Sun in km/sec?

    A. 0.03

    B. 0.3

    C. 3

    D. 30

    E. 300

Q2. How much faster than Venus is Mercury travelling? The distance travelled by a planet around the Sun is the distance of the planet from the Sun multiplied by 6.3.

    A. 24%

    B. 47%

    C. 67%

    D. 85%

    E. 125%

Q3. A future astronaut on Mars has to wait at least 8m 40s to get a response from Earth to his messages. This minimum delay occurs when the distance of Mars from Earth is the distance of Mars from the Sun minus Earth's distance from the Sun. At what speed do his messages travel (in km/sec)?

    A. 120,000

    B. 150,000

    C. 210,000

    D. 270,000

    E. 300,000

Set 19

Belgium (Population 10.84m)	
	Percentage of Population
Under-18	31.2
Have a driver's licence	64.7
Employed	42.7
Never been outside Belgium	2.9
Watch more than 10h of TV per week	59.8

Q1. If 98.3% of the people who have never been outside Belgium are under 18 years old, how many people over 18 have never been outside Belgium?

A. 10

B. 186

C. 798

D. 5344

E. 9827

Q2. Employed people are 25% less likely to watch 10h or more of TV in a week. What percentage of the non-employed people watch more than 10h per week of TV?

A. 38.1

B. 59.8

C. 68.8

D. 74.2

E. 84.8

Q3. At least what percentage of non-employed people have a driver's licence based on the data in the table?

A. 22%

B. 29.7%

C. 35.1%

D. 38.4%

E. 44.7%

Set 20

Bakery Sales (€'000)		
	2009	*2010*
Bread	86.3	87.2
Pastries	27.9	30.1
Pies/Pasties	18.6	18.8
Drinks	43.7	44.9

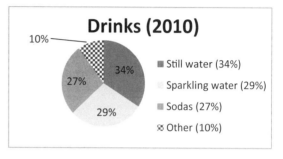

Drinks (2010)

10%

34%

27%

29%

- Still water (34%)
- Sparkling water (29%)
- Sodas (27%)
- Other (10%)

Q1. In 2008 bread sales were 7% less than in 2010. By how much did they rise in 2009?

A. 3.9%

B. 4.7%

C. 5.9%

D. 6.4%

E. 6.8%

Q2. In 2010 sparkling water sales rose 10% from 2009. What was the value of sparkling water sales in 2009?

A. €11,837

B. €11,881

C. €16,228

D. €18,493

E. €21,276

Q3. What was the difference between sales of water (sparkling + still) and pastries in 2010?

A. €782

B. €992

C. €1230

D. €1684

E. €1813

Set 21

Customer Survey 2010		
	Responses	Average (values are rounded to the nearest 1 decimal place)
Greeting	99	8.1
Ambiance	93	8.3
Cleanliness	90	7.7
Quality	102	6.9
Value for money	88	6.8
Overall satisfaction	110	7.2

Note: Averages that are closer to a lower value are rounded down and all other values are rounded up.

Q1. There were 110 surveys returned but not all questions were answered on every card. What was the average number of responses per question?

    A. 99

    B. 97

    C. 50

    D. 6.1

    E. 5.3

Q2. Questions 1 and 6 both got the same number of total marks when all their scores were added up. How many was this (rounded to the nearest whole number)?

    A. 792

    B. 795

    C. 797

    D. 800

    E. 802

Q3. The average mark for overall satisfaction dropped 10% from its 2009 value. What was the overall satisfaction score in 2009?

    A. 6.5

    B. 7.2

    C. 7.7

    D. 7.9

    E. 8.0

Set 22

Off Licence Sales		
	Percentage of sales by value	
	2009	2010
Beer	29.1	30.4
Wine	28.8	29.2
Spirits	12.1	10.6
Tobacco	11.8	10.3
Miscellaneous	18.2	19.5

Q1. In 2010, sales went up by 5% on 2009. What was the increase in sales of beer between 2009 and 2010?

    A. 1.5%

    B. 5.2%

    C. 6.7%

    D. 8.1%

    E. 9.7%

Q2. Sales of tobacco were €122 thousand in 2009 and increased by 0.3% in 2010. What was the total value of all sales in 2010?

    A. €1.073 million

    B. €1.188 million

    C. €1.201 million

    D. €1.224 million

    E. €1.278 million

Q3. In 2010, by how much would the sales of wine need to increase to equal those of beer in the same year?

    A. 1.2%

    B. 1.9%

    C. 3.9%

    D. 4.1%

    E. 4.4%

Set 23

Vaccinations in Europe				
		Percentage of Population Vaccinated		
Country	Population in 2010 ('000)	MMR	DPT	Polio
Estonia	1339	87.3	83.2	49.6
Italy	60098	94.8	93.7	51.9
Netherlands	16653	96.2	97.3	54.6
UK	61899	91.6	92.2	46.2

Q1. How many more people were vaccinated against MMR in Italy than in the UK?

A. 274

B. 2740

C. 27,400

D. 274,000

E. 2,740,000

Q2. In 2005, the population of the Netherlands was 5% lower than in 2010 but the percentage of the population vaccinated against Polio was 2 percentage points higher. How many more or fewer people were vaccinated against Polio in 2005 than in 2010?

A. 333,000 fewer

B. 139,000 fewer

C. No change

D. 139,000 more

E. 333,000 more

Q3. What is the minimum possible number of people who have been vaccinated against both MMR and DPT in Estonia in 2010?

A. 1.3m

B. 1.17m

C. 1.11m

D. 944K

E. 55K

Set 24

Shoe Shops in Europe (per 100,000 population)				
	Population in 2010 ('000)	2000	2005	2010
France	62139	8.3	8.4	8.6
Italy	60098	9.3	9.6	9.5
Netherlands	16653	8.2	8.4	8.4
Spain	45317	7.3	7.6	7.2

Q1. How much higher than the lowest per capita rate is the highest per capita rate of shoe shops in the countries shown across all three years?

A. 2.4%

B. 12.5%

C. 25%

D. 33.3%

E. 50%

Q2. If the population of France increased by 5% each five years, how many more shoe shops were there in France in 2010 than in 2000?

A. 381

B. 598

C. 666

D. 742

E. 848

Q3. If the population of Spain increased by 7% between 2000 and 2005, what was the percentage increase in the number of shops over that time?

A. 4.1%

B. 7.0%

C. 11.1%

D. 11.4%

E. 12.3%

Set 25

Supermarket Sales (€m)		
	2009	*2010*
Food	6.62	6.84
Clothing	1.98	2.04
Electrical	1.87	1.99
Other	2.11	2.23

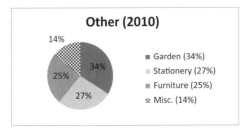

Other (2010)

- Garden (34%)
- Stationery (27%)
- Furniture (25%)
- Misc. (14%)

Q1. What was the percentage rise in revenue in the electrical department between 2009 and 2010?

A.   3.9%

B.   4.7%

C.   5.9%

D.   6.4%

E.   6.8%

Q2. In 2010, sales in the garden department rose by 4% from 2009. What was the garden department's value of sales in 2009?

A.   €344,000

B.   €542,000

C.   €633,000

D.   €729,000

E.   €802,000

Q3. Stationery sales fell by 3.2% between 2009 and 2010. What percentage of total sales did stationery account for in 2009?

A.   1.98%

B.   4.94%

C.   12.91%

D.   21.66%

E.   27.62%

Set 26

Chocolate Consumption in Europe ('000 tonnes)			
	Population 2005 ('000)	*2005*	*2010*
Belgium	10415	175	183
Estonia	1346	16.6	17.5
Hungary	9973	131	138
Italy	58645	932	989
Switzerland	7441	129	133

Q1. Which country has the highest per capita consumption of chocolate in 2005?

A.   Belgium

B.   Estonia

C.   Hungary

D.   Italy

E.   Switzerland

Q2. The population of Hungary increases by 8.3% between 2005 and 2010. What is the percentage change in per capita consumption of chocolate over that time?

A.   +5.31%

B.   +1.97%

C.   No change

D.   -2.73%

E.   -5.31%

Q3. In Switzerland, 78% of consumption is of homemade chocolate, which accounts for 12% of total home production, the remainder being exported. How much chocolate did Switzerland export in 2005?

A.   20,000 tonnes

B.   198,00 tonnes

C.   738,000 tonnes

D.   839,000 tonnes

E.   928,00 tonnes

Set 27

Forests in Europe			
	Area of Country (×1000km²)	*1990 (×1000ha)*	*2010 (×1000ha)*
Denmark	43.1	63.9	67.2
France	544	602.4	649.5
Georgia	69.7	110.2	112.9
Poland	312.7	715.9	706.8
UK	242.9	189.1	193.2
1km²=100ha (hectares)			

Q1. Which country experienced the largest percentage growth in forested area between 1990 and 2010?

  A. Denmark

  B. France

  C. Georgia

  D. Poland

  E. UK

Q2. How many more hectares of forest would Denmark have needed in 2010 to have had the same percentage coverage as Georgia?

  A. 2.622

  B. 69.8

  C. 897

  D. 2622

  E. 69810

Q3. What is the average percentage coverage of forested area in 2010 across the five countries shown?

  A. 1.39%

  B. 1.43%

  C. 1.49%

  D. 1.52%

  E. 1.56%

Set 28

Results for Swimming Championships (m:ss.ss)				
In medley races, the swimmers swim equal distances in four different styles: butterfly, backstroke, breaststroke, freestyle.				
	100m Freestyle	*200m Backstroke*	*400m Medley*	*100m Breast-stroke*
Gold	50.91	1:58.31	3:48.7	1:03.41
Silver	50.99	1:59.72	3:49.6	1:04.06
Bronze	51.31	1:59.88	3:53.2	1:04.92

Q1. In the medley, the winner spent 26.2% of the time on the butterfly section of the race. What was his average speed during that leg of the race?

  A. 1.67 m/s

  B. 1.75 m/s

  C. 1.8 m/s

  D. 2.0 m/s

  E. 2.25 m/s

Q2. How much faster was the gold medal winner than the bronze medal winner in the 200m backstroke event?

  A. 0.1%

  B. 1.0%

  C. 1.3%

  D. 1.5%

  E. 2.0%

Q3. From the moment that the gold medallist finished until he himself finished, the freestyle silver medal winner swam 10% faster than his overall average. To the nearest centimetre, by what distance did the gold medallist beat the silver medallist?

  A. 14

  B. 17

  C. 25

  D. 36

  E. 51

Set 29

European Rail Passengers			
	Population ('000)	Number of Passengers (m)	
	2005	2005	2010
France	61013	308.9	312.4
Germany	82409	526.3	531.9
Italy	58645	292.3	287.6
Spain	43060	183.9	189.4
UK	60261	514.2	534.6

*passenger-kilometres is total passengers multiplied by average journey length

Q1. In France in 2005, the average length of a rail journey is 170km, yet the total number of passenger-kilometres is exactly the same as in the UK. What is the average length of journey in the UK in 2005?

A. 98.8km

B. 100km

C. 102.1km

D. 110.9km

E. 126km

Q2. If the population of Germany increased by 3.7% between 2005 and 2010, what is the change in average number of journeys per person over that time?

A. +2.5%

B. +1.1%

C. No change

D. -1.1%

E. -2.5%

Q3. How many more rail journeys did the average Italian make in 2005 than the average Spaniard?

A. 0

B. 0.71

C. 1.22

D. 1.65

E. 1.91

Set 30

Music DVD Sales in the UK (million discs)		
	2009	2010
Pop	43.6	39.2
Jazz	1.4	1.8
Classical	2.9	3.4
R&B	1.6	1.5
Other	4.4	4.6

Q1. What is the overall percentage change in DVD discs sold between 2009 and 2010?

A. -3.4%

B. -4.7%

C. -5.9%

D. -6.3%

E. -6.7%

Q2. What was the percentage increase in market share of Jazz DVDs between 2009 and 2010?

A. 0.96%

B. 5%

C. 10%

D. 25%

E. 37%

Q3. The population of the UK in 2010 was 61.092m. If 94.3% of pop DVDs are bought by teenagers who comprise 12.1% of the population, how many pop DVDs did the average teenager buy in 2010?

A. 2

B. 3

C. 4

D. 5

E. 6

Set 31

Restaurant Wine List		
	Glass (€)	Bottle (€)
Chablis	8.95	31.95
Chardonnay	7.50	28.50
Margaux	7.15	27.00
Sancerre	9.20	34.80
Tavel	7.95	29.50

Q1. Assuming a glass is a fifth of a bottle, which wine provides the most extra profit in euro terms when sold by the glass?

A. Chablis

B. Chardonnay

C. Margaux

D. Sancerre

E. Tavel

Q2. The restaurant makes 220% profit on all bottles of wine. In one evening they make €287.10 profit on Sancerre alone. How many bottles of Sancerre did they sell?

A. 6

B. 10

C. 12

D. 15

E. 18

Q3. If a glass is 187.5ml and a bottle is 750ml, what is the percentage increase in revenue on a bottle of Tavel when sold by the glass?

A. 5.9%

B. 7.8%

C. 8.3%

D. 9.4%

E. 11.1%

Set 32

Dutch Holiday Destinations (x1000 people)		
	2005	2010
France	301	312
Germany	225	234
Greece	170	164
Spain	192	188
UK	195	202

Q1. What percentage increase on the 2010 level of Dutch visitors does Greece need to recover to its 2005 level?

A. 2.91%

B. 3.53%

C. 3.66%

D. 3.91%

E. 4.22%

Q2. If both Germany and France increase their number of Dutch visitors by the same percentage as they did between 2005 and 2010, how many more Dutch people will visit France than Germany in 2015?

A. 80K

B. 123K

C. 135K

D. 189K

E. 201K

Q3. In 2005, 1.805m Dutch people went abroad for their holidays. What percentage of them went to the countries listed in the table, assuming each person visited only one country?

A. 25%

B. 33%

C. 50%

D. 60%

E. 75%

Set 33

French Car Sales (thousands)			
	2008	*2009*	*2010*
Renault	1584	1710	1723
Citroen	1087	1094	1107
Peugeot	1306	1396	1422

Q1. In 2008 a franchise dealer in France with 44 showrooms sold on average 90 Renault cars each month in each branch. What percentage of national Renault sales did they sell?

A. 0.3%

B. 0.67%

C. 1%

D. 1.67%

E. 3%

Q2. How many more Peugeot cars would need to have been sold in 2009 for them to have had precisely one-third of the sales shown, assuming that all other sales volumes remain unchanged?

A. 4

B. 6

C. 400

D. 4000

E. 6000

Q3. In 2010, Citroen accounted for 13.7% of all car sales in France. What percentage did the three manufacturers shown account for combined?

A. 34.8%

B. 52.6%

C. 59.1%

D. 64.8%

E. 69.2%

Set 34

Marriages in Europe			
	Population ('000)	Number of Marriages (hundreds)	
	2005	*2000*	*2010*
Bosnia	3781	714	702
Finland	5244	1008	998
Ireland	4187	904	923
Slovakia	5386	908	899
Switzerland	7441	1120	1131

Q1. If the population of Ireland increased by 5% between 2005 and 2010, what percentage of the population got married in 2010?

A. 2.1%

B. 3.0%

C. 4.2%

D. 42%

E. 54%

Q2. How many marriages per 100,000 people were there in Finland in 2010 if the population decreased by 1.5% between 2005 and 2010?

A. 1.93

B. 19.3

C. 193

D. 1932

E. 19321

Q3. Which of the counties shown had the lowest per capita marriage rate in 2000 if the populations did not change from 2000 to 2005?

A. Bosnia

B. Finland

C. Ireland

D. Slovakia

E. Switzerland

Set 35

Electricity Generation in the Netherlands (%)		
	2005	*2010*
Fossil Fuel	81.1	76.4
Wind	6.8	8.1
Solar	3.4	5.2
Nuclear	3.9	3.8
Other	4.8	6.5

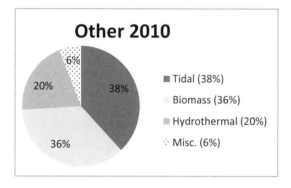

Other 2010

- ■ Tidal (38%)
- Biomass (36%)
- ■ Hydrothermal (20%)
- ∴ Misc. (6%)

Q1. Generation of electricity rose by 10% between 2005 and 2010. Tidal power generation doubled over that period. What percentage of the electricity was generated by tidal power in 2005?

A. 1.12%

B. 1.36%

C. 1.59%

D. 1.73%

E. 1.94%

Q2. In 2010, 2.4 million kWh of electricity was generated from biomass. How much was generated from solar power (in millions of kWh)?

A. 5.3

B. 5.9

C. 6.2

D. 6.8

E. 7.3

Q3. If total electricity generation rose by 10% between 2005 and 2010, what was the percentage change in fossil fuel generated electricity over that time?

A. +3.6%

B. +1.8%

C. No change

D. -1.8%

E. -3.6%

Set 36

Prison Populations			
	Population ('000)	Number of Prisoners (hundreds)	
	2005	2005	2010
Austria	8232	115.9	119.6
Estonia	1347	22.4	22.8
Poland	38198	702.2	707.9
Sweden	9066	106.8	105.3
Ukraine	46936	912.2	916.8

Q1. If the population of Poland increased by 700,000 between 2005 and 2010, what was the percentage change in the number of prisoners per capita over that time?

A. -1%

B. -0.1%

C. Less than 0.01% change

D. +0.1%

E. +1%

Q2. Estonia's per capita rate of prisoners was unchanged between 2005 and 2010. What was the population of Estonia in 2010 (in thousands)?

A. 1323

B. 1339

C. 1347

D. 1355

E. 1371

Q3. How much worse than Sweden's per capita rate of prisoners was Austria's in 2005? (The higher the rate, the worse it is.)

A. 0.23%

B. 3.9%

C. 8.3%

D. 19.52%

E. 31.1%

Set 37

Bullion Exchange				
	€	£	US$	CHF
€	–	0.784	1.225	1.202
£	1.275	–	1.563	1.533
US$	0.816	0.640	–	0.981
CHF	0.832	0.652	1.020	–

Q1. You have £1000 which you want to change into Swiss francs (CHF). There is a £3 transaction charge and the customer rate (the rate you get) is 1.5% below the bullion rate. How many Swiss francs do you get?

A. 1504.87

B. 1505.47

C. 1505.81

D. 1510.01

E. 1528.40

Q2. You have €5000 which you change into US$ at 1% below bullion rate. The bank only deals in multiples of US$5. There is no transaction fee. How much change do you get back in euros?

A. €1.71

B. €2.33

C. €2.87

D. €3.09

E. €3.38

Q3. You pay for your CHF49.36 meal in a Zurich restaurant with your credit card. The rate drops by 2% from the one shown in the table by the time the payment is processed and your card issuer charges a 2.5% fee. How much does the meal cost you in euro?

A. 38.77

B. 40.34

C. 41.25

D. 42.32

E. 43.79

Set 38

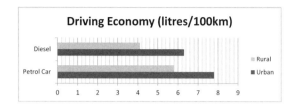

Driving Economy (litres/100km)

Q1. You drive the petrol car on a journey that is 38% urban and use 12.2 litres of fuel during the whole journey. How long is the journey?

- A. 122km
- B. 145km
- C. 156km
- D. 171km
- E. 186km

Q2. Diesel costs €1.48/litre and you drive 120km, 80% of which is rural. How much does it cost?

- A. €6.76
- B. €8.06
- C. €10.24
- D. €11.01
- E. €12.14

Q3. How many more kilometres per litre does the diesel car do on rural journeys than the petrol car on urban journeys?

- A. 3.7
- B. 7.1
- C. 11.6
- D. 13.2
- E. 14.2

Set 39

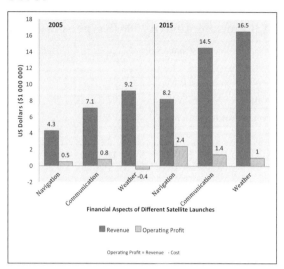

Q1. How much more operating profit was generated from satellite launches in 2015 than in 2005?

- A. About 182% more
- B. About 282 % more
- C. About 433% more
- D. About 533% more
- E. Impossible to tell

Q2. Approximately how much more revenue was generated on average per satellite type in 2015 than in 2005?

- A. 1.3 million US dollars
- B. 6.2 million US dollars
- C. 18.6 million US dollars
- D. 21.6 million US dollars
- E. 28.6 million US dollars

Q3. If there were 25 satellite launches in 2015, what was the average cost of a launch?

- A. 192 thousand US dollars
- B. 788 thousand US dollars
- C. 824 thousand US dollars
- D. 1.376 million US dollars
- E. 1.568 million US dollars

Set 40

Fat Consumption in 2005 (Kg/person/year)			
	Population ('000)	Saturated Fat	Unsaturated Fat
Greece	11064	1.93	2.82
Italy	58645	2.02	2.88
Netherlands	16316	1.77	3.02
Sweden	9066	1.82	3.11
UK	60120	2.44	2.19

Q1. What is the total amount of fat consumed per day in the UK?

A. 76.26kg

B. 762.6 kg

C. 7.626 tonnes

D. 76.26 tonnes

E. 762.6 tonnes

Q2. Between 2005 and 2010, a health drive in Italy reduced the saturated fat consumption by 15% and increased the unsaturated fat consumption by 12.5%. What was the net change in fat consumption in Italy if the population remained unchanged?

A. +2.5%

B. +1.2%

C. No change

D. −1.2%

E. −2.5%

Q3. What is the average amount of fat consumed per person per year in the Netherlands and Sweden combined?

A. 4.79kg

B. 4.82kg

C. 4.84kg

D. 4.86kg

E. 4.93kg

Set 41

Sales Figures for Single Lens Reflex Cameras					
Camera Model	Retail Price	Profit*	Extended Warranty Surcharge**	Cameras Sold	Extended Warranties Sold
300F	€ 450	23%	8%	5500	100
200D	€ 360	18%	10%	?	150

* The percentage of the retail price that is the seller's profit
** The percentage of the retail price that the seller charges additionally for the extended warranty
The entire revenue generated from selling extended warranties is considered profit.

Q1. Due to a clerical error, the number of 200D cameras sold was lost. If the total profit on both camera models is € 1 096 650, how many 200D models were sold?

A. 3 268

B. 8 000

C. 8 139

D. Impossible to tell

Q2. By what percentage would the total profit made on 300F cameras have been higher if ten times as many extended warranties had been sold (rounded to two decimal places)?

A. 4.67%

B. 5.66%

C. 6.32%

D. 8.46%

Q3. How much more or less profit would be generated by increasing the profit rate on 300F camera sales by 1 percentage point than by increasing the number of extended warranties sold for the model tenfold, achieved by dropping the surcharge to 5%?

A. € 11 250 less

B. € 9 450 less

C. € 2 250 more

D. € 5 850 more

Set 42

Manufacturing Statistics – Furniture World					
Furniture	Costs per piece of furniture			Retail Price	Output*
	Assembly	Materials	Packaging		
Dining table	€10.50	€57	€15	€97	150
Armchair	€8	€30	€10.50	€55	200
Book shelf	€12.50	€60	€15.50	€99	350
Sofa bed	€25	€149	€24.50	€225.50	55

* Output is the number of units manufactured and sold per month
Profit = Retail price – costs

Q1. A new machine will allow Furniture World to reduce assembly costs for sofa beds by €4.50 and increase output to 100 units. Given constant retail prices and no change in other costs, by what percentage will the company's total monthly profit from sofa beds increase thanks to these changes?

- A. 16.67%
- B. 18.75%
- C. 52.85%
- D. 112.12%
- E. 156%

Q2. For which type of furniture does the cost of assembly represent the smallest proportion of the costs?

- A. Dining table
- B. Arm chair
- C. Book shelf
- D. Sofa bed
- E. Dining table and sofa bed combined

Q3. How much would Furniture World spend on materials in a month if it decreased its output of every type of furniture by 12%?

- A. 4 374.50 euros
- B. 5 249.40 euros
- C. 38 495.60 euros
- D. 39 370.50 euros
- E. 43 745.00 euros

Set 43

Amenities in ABC Apartment Buildings, 2014						
	% with air conditioning		% with dishwasher		Number of units	
	Studio	1-bed	Studio	1-bed	Studio	1-bed
Austria	20	50	50	70	100	200
France	20	30	40	65	130	300
Germany	14	23	76	91	300	100
Spain	65	85	50	80	200	250

All ABC Apartment Buildings comprise only studio and 1-bedroom apartments.

Q1. ABC Apartments built 20 studio apartments in Spain in 2014 and now has the number of units shown in the table. How many studio apartments with air conditioning did it have in 2013 if the proportion of studios with various amenities was the same?

- A. 90
- B. 117
- C. 130
- D. 143
- E. 176

Q2. ABC Apartments will increase the overall number of its apartments by 120 in 2015, adding equal numbers of new units in all countries and both categories. How many studio apartments with dishwasher will it have in France in 2015 if the proportion of such units remains the same as in 2014?

- A. 32
- B. 52
- C. 58
- D. 64
- E. 215

Q3. What percentage of ABC Apartments' total number of units are studio apartments without air conditioning in Germany?

- A. 2.66%
- B. 4.43%
- C. 4.56%
- D. 14.62%
- E. 16.33%

Set 44

Inkjet Printer Models – PrintWare Factory				
	FR-7	*FR-10*	*TG-4*	*RZ-10*
Production time	10 mins	11 mins	24 mins	15 mins
% of produced units sold	96%	92%	84%	89%
Retail price	$90	$110	$115	$130
Revenue = Retail price * Units sold Factory operation: 12 hours per day, from Monday through Saturday				

Q1. The PrintWare factory manufactures 4 printer models. Which of the four models generates the smallest revenue per week?

    A. FR-7

    B. FR-10

    C. TG-4

    D. RZ-10

    E. FR-7 and FR-10

Q2. Approximately how many days would it take to manufacture $27 000 worth of FR-7 printers if production time increased by 20% due to a technical failure?

    A. 2

    B. 2.5

    C. 4

    D. 5

    E. 50

Q3. Approximately how many additional printers (all models combined) could be manufactured if the factory remained in operation on Sunday for the usual operating hours?

    A. 12

    B. 48

    C. 215

    D. 336

    E. 430

Set 45

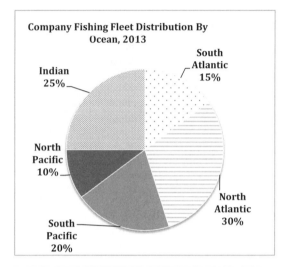

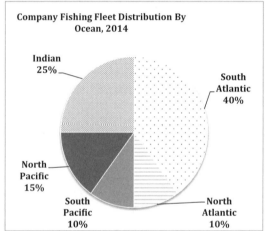

* *The Indian Ocean is not considered part of the Pacific Ocean.*

Q1. The company is realigning its fishing fleet distribution according to changing catch expectations. If, in 2013, the company had 42 fishing boats in the South Atlantic and the company increases its total fleet size by 15% in 2014, how many fishing boats will it have overall in the Atlantic Ocean in 2014, rounded to the nearest whole boat?

    A.   105

    B.   112

    C.   129

    D.   140

    E.   161

Q2. By approximately what percentage does the number of the company's fishing boats in the Pacific Ocean change between 2013 and 2014 if the overall fleet grows by 15% between the two years?

A. -16.67%

B. -5.00%

C. -4.17%

D. -1.25%

E. +27.78%

Q3. If the Pacific Ocean is 2.3 times as large as the Indian Ocean, by what percentage is the company's number of boats per square kilometer in the Indian Ocean greater than in the Pacific Ocean in 2014?

A. 30%

B. 92%

C. 130%

D. 230%

E. Impossible to tell

Set 46

Costs of Introducing New Accounting Software				
	Accounts Pro 10	BSheet 12	BSheet Lite	BookKeeper Standard
Licence fee (€)	4500 / year	3500 / year	8000 / year	9000 one-time fee
Installation fee (€)	130	150	200	550
Staff needed to operate*	4	4	3	5
Working hours needed to operate / person (monthly)	20	20	25	15

* The hourly wage of staff operating the accounting software is 20 (€)

Q1. Which of the accounting software shown in the table is projected to cost the least to acquire and operate over a two-year period?

A. Accounts Pro 10

B. BSheet 12

C. BSheet Lite

D. BookKeeper Standard

E. BSheet 12 and BookKeeper Standard

Q2. If the company manages to negotiate a 15% discount on the licence fees and the installation is done free of charge, how much would it cost to introduce and operate the BSheet 12 software for 5 years?

A. 16 475 €

B. 19 100 €

C. 110 875 €

D. 113 500 €

E. 111 025 €

Q3. How much money will the company save or lose over 3 years if it introduces BookKeeper Standard instead of Accounts Pro 10?

A. 2 605 € in savings

B. 6 840 € in savings

C. 7 680 € in savings

D. 10 320 € in losses

E. 13 820 € in losses

Set 47

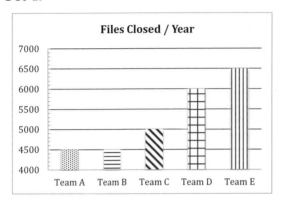

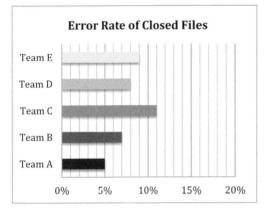

Q1. Five teams work on closing financial audit files and each team sometimes makes errors. Which team closes the lowest number of files per year without errors?

A. Team A

B. Team B

C. Team C

D. Team D

E. Team E

Q2. If Team C's error rate deteriorated to 17% and Team B's improved to 2%, how many fewer files would Team C be able to close without errors than Team B?

A. 35

B. 250

C. 260

D. 350

E. 500

Q3. If teams progress through files at a constant rate from month to month, how many files will the five teams close by the end of September?

A. 16525

B. 17667

C. 18258

D. 19875

E. 22083

Set 48

Tax Systems

SYSTEM 1	SYSTEM 2	SYSTEM 3
Tax free allowance: 10000	Tax free allowance: Nil	Tax free allowance: 15000
10001–30000: 15%	0–30000: 15%	15001–30000: 17%
30001–50000: 25%	30001+: 21%	30001–60000: 22%
50001+: 31%	Insurance tax: 50 per month	60001+: 28%
Insurance tax: 100 per month		Insurance tax: 200 per month

All amounts are in euro and are annual except where otherwise indicated. Tax rates are marginal (the percentage indicated is levied only on that part of the income falling in the given range).
Effective tax rate (%) = tax / income × 100

Q1. A country is considering the adoption of a new tax system. Under which system does a person earning 55 000 € / year owe the least in taxes?

A. System 1

B. System 2

C. System 3

D. Systems 1 and 2 are the same

E. All Systems are the same

Q2. What is the effective tax rate of a person earning 62 000 € annually under System 3?

A. 15.66%

B. 15.98%

C. 19.53%

D. 19.77%

E. 23.65%

Q3. A person earns 75 000 € a year. By what percentage is their after-tax income greater or smaller under System1 than under System 3?

A. Approximately 1% smaller

B. Approximately 2% smaller

C. Approximately 2% greater

D. Approximately 3.9% smaller

E. Approximately 3.9% greater

Set 49

Power Station	Country	Annual Electricity Production (TWh)
Itaipu Dam	Brazil	98.30
Three Gorges Dam	China	98.50
Krasnoyarsk	Russia	20.40
Grand Coulee	USA	20.00
Guri	Venezuela	53.41

Country Annual Electricity Consumption Statistics (MWh)	
Brazil	455 700 000
China	5 322 300 000
Russia	1 016 500 000
USA	3 886 400 000
Venezuela	85 850 000
1 TWh = 1 000 000 MWh	

Q1. If they are ranked by the percentage that a power station generates of the total electricity consumption of the given country, which station would be in the middle?

A. Three Gorges Dam

B. Itaipu Dam

C. Guri

D. Grand Coulee

E. Krasnoyarsk

Q2. Venezuela plans to build another power station of the same production capacity as that of Guri. If existing power stations produce 78% of the electricity consumed in Venezuela, how much electricity will Venezuela have available for export after completion of the new power station?

A. 20.97 TWh

B. 34.523 MWh

C. 34 523 MWh

D. 20 970 000 MWh

E. 34 523 000 MWh

Q3. If the electricity produced by the Three Gorges Dam would be enough to cover 3.24% of the electricity consumed in the EU, and the EU produces 30% of the electricity it consumes from nuclear power, how much electricity in the EU is produced from nuclear power?

A.   912.04 MWh

B.   91.20 TWh

C.   912.00 TWh

D.   912.04 TWh

E.   3040.12 TWh

Set 50

Energy Ratings of Selected Household Appliances, 2014					
Appliance	A+ / A	B	C	D	Total units
Air conditioners	10%	45%	20%	25%	3 400
Washing machines	45%	35%	10%	10%	5 500
Dryers	25%	10%	50%	15%	2 000
Refrigerators	40%	25%	25%	10%	9 000

Appliances with A+, A and B energy ratings are considered energy-efficient.

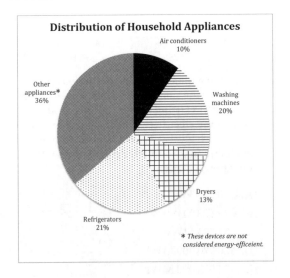

Distribution of Household Appliances

Air conditioners 10%

Other appliances* 36%

Washing machines 20%

Dryers 13%

Refrigerators 21%

* These devices are not considered energy-effiecient.

Q1. What percentage of all household appliances are energy-efficient washing machines?

A.   9%

B.   13%

C.   16%

D.   20%

E.   80%

Q2. If the share of energy-efficient units among refrigerators and air conditioners rose by 20%, how many energy-efficient refrigerators and air conditioners would there be?

A.   4 728

B.   6 024

C.   6 420

D.   9 264

E.   10 200

Q3. If D-rated household appliances are ranked by the number of such units in a highest-to-lowest list, which one would be at the top of the list?

A.   Air conditioners

B.   Washing machines

C.   Dryers

D.   Refrigerators

E.   Impossible to tell

Set 51

Crop Production in France (thousands of tonnes)			
	2005	2010	2015
Corn	12 107	12 211	12 409
Rapeseed	4 541	5 472	5 801
Sugar	2 814	2 920	2 702
Sunflowers	18 442	19 194	21 199
Wheat	7 422	7 719	7 792

Q1. If the table were ordered by percentage increase in production between 2010 and 2015, which crop would be in the middle of the table?

    A. Corn

    B. Rapeseed

    C. Sugar

    D. Sunflowers

    E. Wheat

Q2. How many more tonnes of sugar would France have needed to produce in 2010 for its percentage increase from 2005 (to the nearest whole percentage point) to be the same as the corresponding increase for wheat?

    A. 245.6

    B. 6560

    C. 191

    D. 224.7

    E. 2926.6

Q3. The yield (tonnes produced per hectare) of rapeseed is 3.1 tonnes per hectare in 2005. This improves by 6% by 2015. What is the percentage increase in land usage for rapeseed production between 2005 and 2015?

    A. 27.7%

    B. 13.7%

    C. 35.4%

    D. 26.2%

    E. 20.5%

Set 52

Percentage of Total Power Generated in the UK				
Source	2000	2005	2010	2015
Fossil Fuel	85.2	78.8	66.4	53.0
Wind	1.7	3.7	9.8	15.4
Solar	0.3	0.9	7.8	12.3
Tide/Wave	0.1	1.3	1.8	3.3
Nuclear	10.9	12.4	10.4	9.8
Other	1.8	2.9	3.8	6.2

Q1. The total power generated in the UK increased by 7.25% between 2000 and 2005. What was the percentage increase in nuclear power generation over the same period?

    A. 14.8%

    B. 22%

    C. 19.3%

    D. 13.8%

    E. 96%

Q2. Which form of power generation shows the greatest percentage increase in the percentage of total power generated between 2010 and 2015?

    A. Fossil fuel

    B. Wind

    C. Solar

    D. Tide/Wave

    E. Nuclear

    F. Other

Q3. In 2005, 20% of the 'Other' power was generated by biomass. By 2010 this amount had increased by 50%. If the total power generated in the UK had increased by 10% over the same period, what percentage of 'Other' power was generated by biomass in 2010?

    A. 30%

    B. 63.6%

    C. 22.9%

    D. 48.6%

    E. 20.8%

Set 53

Populations	
	2005 ('000)
Croatia	4 443
Denmark	5 417
Portugal	10 547
Sweden	9 293

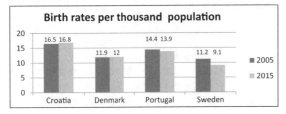

Set 54

Netherlands Population	
Year	Pop ('000)
2005	16 316
2010	16 492
2015	16 714

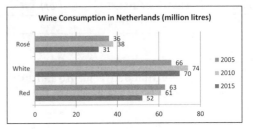

Q1. The population of Croatia increased by 7.5% between 2005 and 2015. How many more births were there in Croatia in 2015 than in 2005 (*rounded to the nearest whole number*)?

A. 6931

B. 1433

C. 1333

D. 73310

E. 80241

Q2. What is the average number of births across all four countries shown in 2005 (*rounded to the nearest whole number*)?

A. 92704

B. 102314

C. 98433

D. 96154

E. 100238

Q3. In Portugal there were 4 more births in 2015 than there were in 2005. What was the percentage change in population of Portugal over this time?

A. 5%

B. −5%

C. 0.1%

D. −0.1%

E. 3.6%

F. −3.6%

Q1. If the average cost of a 75cl bottle of red wine in the Netherlands was €6.63 in 2015, what was the per capita spending on red wine in 2015?

A. €18.15

B. €27.87

C. €20.62

D. €27.50

E. €37.02

Q2. If the change in consumption of white wine between 2010 and 2015 had been the same as the change for rosé wine over the same period, what would the consumption figure for white wine have been in 2015?

A. 56

B. 60

C. 67

D. 14

E. 66

Q3. What was the percentage change in per capita consumption of red wine between 2005 and 2010?

A. −4.2%

B. −4.4%

C. −5.1%

D. −3.2%

E. −3.9%

Set 55

	Pop 2015 ('000)	Workforce (% of Pop)	
		2010	2015
Croatia	4887	41.9	42.1
Hungary	11086	46.1	46.7
Ireland	4606	48.7	48.5
Portugal	11602	41.8	42.1
Ukraine	51629	46.1	47.6

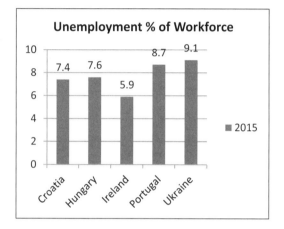

Q3. The percentage of the workforce unemployed in Croatia rose by 5% between 2010 and 2015 and the population rose by 3.3% over the same period. What was the rise in the number of unemployed in Croatia between 2010 and 2015?

A. 5715

B. 18912

C. 7939

D. 104680

E. 12542

Q1. In 2015 the number of unemployed in Ireland was 10000 more than in 2010 and the percentage of the workforce unemployed was 0.1 percentage points less in 2010 than 2015. What was the percentage change in population in Ireland between 2010 and 2015?

A. −0.5%

B. 0%

C. 5.7%

D. 6.8%

E. −3.8%

Q2. What percentage of the number of unemployed people in Portugal is the number of unemployed in Hungary in 2015?

A. 87.4%

B. 92.6%

C. 96.9%

D. 96.6%

E. 103%

ANSWERS

SET 1, Q1. Correct Answer: A

Reasoning

First, we must calculate 5% of the total electricity production in Q1 2014, and then work out the production per wind farm. We then calculate the total wind farm production in Q2 2014 and from that, the number of operational wind farms in that quarter.

Calculation

5% of the total Q1 2014 production gives us the production from wind farms:

12.5 x 0.05 = 0.625 GWh

There were 50 wind farms operating in this quarter, so the production of one wind farm is:

0.625 / 50 = 0.0125 GWh

Now let's calculate the total wind farm production in Q2 2014:

10.5 x 0.05 = 0.525 GWh

We now know the total wind energy production in this quarter and the production value for 1 wind farm, so we can calculate the number of wind farms that were operating in this quarter:

0.525 / 0.0125 = 42

Potential Shortcuts / Pitfalls

First, it is important to make sure to use the production figures from the chart, not the consumption figures.

Secondly, a moment's reflection will show that *no real calculations are required at all* in this case. We are told in the question text that that all operational wind farms produce identical amounts of electricity as each other and in each quarter. This means we can immediately rule out Answer E, as we have all the data we need to answer the question. We also know from the chart that production *fell* between the two quarters, which means therefore that the total number of operational wind farms must also have fallen – which rules out Answers C and D. The scale of the drop, from 12.5 to 10.5 GWh, is also clearly bigger than that from 50 to 48 (answer B), leaving

answer A as the only possible option.

SET 1, Q2. Correct Answer: B

Reasoning

The definition of excess capacity as production minus consumption is given in the chart. Using this, we must first calculate the excess capacity for 2014, and from that calculate the amount exported.

We then calculate the excess capacity in the first half of 2015 and from that the amount exported.

Finally, we calculate the difference between the two export amounts to see how much more electricity Hungary needs to export in the second half of 2015 to match the 2014 export amount.

Calculation

The total excess capacity for 2014 is the sum of the excess capacities for the 4 quarters:

12.5 – 9.8 + 10.5 – 10.1 + 13.6 – 12.1 + 14.5 – 11.5 = 7.6 GWh

The exported amount is 79% of this:

7.6 x 0.79 = 6.004 GWh

The excess capacity in the first half of 2015 was:

10.8 – 10.7 + 15.1 – 13.4 = 1.8 GWh

50% of this was exported:

1.8 x 0.5 = 0.9 GWh

In order for the country to export as much as it did in 2014, it needs to export a total of 6.004 GWh. To achieve this, it still needs to generate the following excess capacity:

6.004 – 0.9 = 5.104 GWh

Which is Answer B (rounded).

Potential Shortcuts / Pitfalls

This question is basically straightforward but it involves a sequence of calculations which you have to do systematically to avoid getting lost: excess capacity first, then the export amount, then the difference between the two years, and so on. The incorrect answer options are deliberately designed so that if you forget any of these steps, your incorrect result might match one of the incorrect answer options.

SET 1, Q3. Correct Answer: C

Reasoning

First we must calculate the quarterly production figure for Paks. Then we calculate 30% of each quarterly production value and count the number of quarters in which the Pak production figure was higher.

Calculation

The quarterly production figure for Paks is:

14.8 / 4 = 3.7 GWh

We now calculate 30% of the total quarterly production figures:

Q1 2014: 12.5 x 0.3 = 3.75 GWh
Q2 2014: 10.5 x 0.3 = 3.15 GWh
Q3 2014: 13.6 x 0.3 = 4.08 GWh
Q4 2014: 14.5 x 0.3 = 4.35 GWh
Q1 2015: 10.8 x 0.3 = 3.24 GWh
Q2 2015: 15.1 x 0.3 = 4.53 GWh

We can see that the Paks production figure of 3.7 GWh is greater than 30% in the case of two of the quarterly production figures.

Potential Shortcuts / Pitfalls

There is no real need to calculate 30% of each quarterly production figure. We know that Paks always produces 3.7 GWh per quarter. Therefore it will produce more than 30% of the total in any quarter in which total production is less than 3.7 / (100 / 30) = 12.33 GWh. A glance at the chart shows that this is the case in two quarters. We have replaced six calculations with one.

SET 2, Q1. Correct Answer: B

Reasoning

Per capita consumption is the average amount consumed by an entire population. We need to calculate this for both Austria and Norway and take the difference.

Calculation

In Austria 59.6m litres are consumed by 8412 (thousand) people. It is helpful to convert the population from thousands into millions by dividing by 1000 and then everything is now in millions:

8412 / 1000 = 8.412

The per capita consumption is now simply the total consumed divided by the population:

59.6 / 8.412 = 7.09 litres/person

Similarly, for Norway:

4840 / 1000 = 4.84
29.4 / 4.84 = 6.07

Finally, we need to take the difference between these, which is:

7.09 – 6.07 = 1.02 litres/person

SET 2, Q2. Correct Answer: C

Reasoning

We need to calculate how much French red wine is consumed in Belgium and the amount of red wine produced in France. We can then calculate the proportion of French red wine that is exported to Belgium.

Calculation

This question requires data from both the table and the pie chart. From the table we can see that Belgium consumes 53.7m litres of wine. The question tells us that 43% of this wine is red. The 43% can be expressed as 0.43 and so the amount of red wine consumed is:

53.7 * 0.43 = 23.1m litres

Also in the question we are told that 41% of this is from France. The 41% can be expressed as 0.41 and so the amount of French red wine consumed is:

23.1 * 0.41 = 9.47m litres

Now we need to calculate how much red wine France produces. From the title of the pie chart we can see that France produces 440m litres of wine in total and 44% of this is red wine:

440 * 0.44 = 193.6m litres of red wine

So, 9.47m litres out of a total of 193.6m litres produced is sent to Belgium. To calculate this as a percentage, we simply divide the amount consumed by the total produced and multiply it by 100 to make it into a percentage:

$(9.47 / 193.6) \times 100 = 4.9\%$

SET 2, Q3. Correct Answer: A

Reasoning

We need to calculate the proportion of white wine consumed and then how much each person consumes on average. We only have indirect knowledge of how much white wine is consumed.

What do we know exactly? We know the total amount consumed, and that this is made up of four types of wines: sparkling, rosé, red and white. The key thing is to notice that the *only real unknown* is the amount of sparkling wine.

When we have such an unknown amount, it should always suggest to us that using 'X' for the unknown amount and an equation format is the right way to approach the exercise.

An unknown amount (X) of sparkling wine
Twice as much (2x) rosé wine
Twice as much red wine as rosé wine
$(2 \times 2X = 4x)$
Twice as much white wine as red wine
$(2 \times 4X = 8x)$

Now that we have managed to express the consumption of all wine types using only one unknown, we can come up with our equation.

Calculation

Using the above definitions, we can express the total amount of wine consumed in the Netherlands as follows:

$X + 2X + 4X + 8X = 15X$ litres

However, we know from the table that the total consumed is 106.3m litres of wine:

$106.3m = 15X$

Looking at our equation again, we can see that we have 15X on one side, so we need to divide that by 15 to get to 1X. Remember, we need to do this to both sides of the equation:

$106.3m / 15 = 15X / 15$
$7.087 = X$

Remember that × is the amount of sparkling wine consumed, and 8 times as much white wine is consumed as sparkling wine:

$7.087 \times 8 = 56.7m$ litres

This is the total consumed in the Netherlands, but the question referred to *per capita consumption*. This is the total consumed divided by the total population. The population is given in thousands which is best converted to millions to keep thing equal:

$16884 / 1000 = 16.884$

The per capita consumption is then:

$56.7m / 16.884m = 3.36$ litres/person

SET 3, Q1. Correct Answer: B

Reasoning

The number of people unemployed is the percentage unemployed multiplied by the size of the workforce. The size of the workforce is the percentage of the population employed multiplied by the size of the population. We need to calculate this figure for both 2005 and 2010 and then take the difference.

Calculation

The population in 2010 has increased by 4%. Because it is an increase on an existing value, we add 1 (representing the original value) to the 0.04 (representing the 4% increase) and so we multiply the 2005 population by 1.04:

$4187 \times 1.04 = 4354.48$

The workforce is 44.4% of this new population and so we multiply by 0.444 to get:

$4354.48 \times 0.444 = 1933.389$

The unemployed is 8.9% of the workforce which is:

$1933.389 \times 0.089 = 172.072$

Remember that the population is given in the table in thousands and so this answer is also in thousands. Now we do the same for 2005 although we don't have to increase the population first. The number of unemployed in 2005 was:

$4187 \times 0.437 \times 0.094 = 171.994$

Take the difference of these two and multiply by 1000 to get the real figure (not in thousands):

172.072 – 171.994 = 0.078
0.078 × 1000 = 78

SET 3, Q2. Correct Answer: C

Reasoning

The proportion of the population unemployed is simply the number of unemployed divided by the population. This is then multiplied by 100 to make it a percentage. Since we already know the *proportion* of the workforce unemployed in 2010 and we also know the *proportion* of the population that is in the workforce in 2010, we can use these two values and *disregard the actual population figure* to get to the correct answer.

Calculation

We know that 48.1% of the population is in the workforce in Sweden. Let's convert 48.1% to 0.481. We also know that 6.8% of the workforce is unemployed. Let's also convert this to 0.068.

Now let's make the following statement: 6.8% of the workforce is unemployed.

Using the data above, we can also state this as follows: 6.8% of (48.1% of the population) is unemployed.

How can we express this in mathematical terms?

0.068 × 0.481 × 100 = percentage of the population unemployed, that is 3.27%, which is the correct answer.

Potential Shortcuts / Pitfalls
The main problem here is the risk of getting bogged down calculating unnecessary values because they seem to be relevant. This is especially tempting when the superfluous information is embedded in the question itself: in this case, the population growth of Sweden between 2005 and 2010.

The easiest way to avoid such time-consuming distractions is to always take a moment to think about what *exactly* the question is. In this example, the question was about the *percentage* of the population that is unemployed. This should be a hint that calculating the actual value (for which the population growth would indeed be needed) is unnecessary.

SET 3, Q3. Correct Answer: E

Reasoning

The percentage increase in the unemployed is the size of the increase divided by the original number of the unemployed. To calculate the number of unemployed people, we need to calculate the size of the workforce for both 2005 and 2010, and then use the unemployment rate to calculate the actual numbers. We also need to calculate the 2010 population.

Calculation

The number of unemployed is the percentage of the workforce unemployed multiplied by the size of the workforce. The size of the workforce is the percentage of the population multiplied by the size of the population. The population in 2010 must first be adjusted because it has increased by 3% from the 2005 figure given:

8232 × 1.03 = 8478.96

The size of the workforce is then:

8478.96 × 0.477 = 4044.46

And the number of unemployed is:

4044.46 × 0.079 = 319.51

Bear in mind also that this figure is in thousands due to the population being given in thousands. For 2005 this can be done similarly as:

8232 × 0.472 × 0.077 = 299.18

The percentage increase is then the difference between these divided by the starting value (2005 figure) and then multiplied by 100 to make it a percentage:

319.51 – 299.18 = 20.33 (the increase in the number of unemployed people)
(20.33 / 299.18) × 100 = 6.8% (the increase expressed as a percentage, which is also the correct answer)

SET 4, Q1. Correct Answer: E

Reasoning

Domestic consumption is defined in the note to the table as production minus exports plus imports so we need to establish how much of its own production the US used itself and how much was added to this by imports.

From the table we know what 27% of US production amounts to, so we can calculate the quantity that the US does *not* export, which will be 100% - 27% = 73% of its production:

23.8 / 27 x 73 = 64.35 million tonnes

We can also establish the amount of imports to the USA from China. The Chinese export quantity, 279.5 million tonnes, is known, and we also know that this represents 34% of Chinese production. Further, we are told in the question text that 30% of Chinese production is exported to the US:

279.5 / 34 x 30 = 246.62 million tonnes

We now have a total of 64.35 + 246.62

= 310.97 million tonnes

At this point, however, we hit a problem because we do not have any data on the proportion of exports from any of the other regions that went to the USA. Without this information we cannot complete the calculation and so must choose Answer option E, "Cannot say".

Calculation

Following the reasoning above, we cannot do this calculation.

Potential Shortcuts / Pitfalls
The risk with this question is that you assume it must be possible to determine the quantity and waste valuable time in trying to make the data do this.

A particular danger is that you successfully calculate the amount of US production used domestically and the quantity of imports from China, as above, but forget about the lack of data for imports from other regions. If you do this you will choose Answer C, which is 310.97 million tonnes.

SET 4, Q2. Correct Answer: C

Reasoning

We must calculate the 2013 export volume for both Japan and EU by using the % change between 2013 and 2014 shown in the table.

Calculation

The 2013 export volume for the EU is identical to the 2014 export volume: 55.9 million tonnes.

To calculate the 2013 export volume for Japan, we need to consider the % change from 2013 to 2014. If we think of the 2013 export volume as X, we can write the following equation:

2013 export volume (X) – 2% = 2014 export volume = 21 million tonnes

In more usable terms:

98% of 2013 export volume = 21 million tonnes

From this, it is easy to calculate the 2013 export volume by dividing by 98 and multiplying by 100:

21 / 98 x 100 = 21.43 million tonnes (rounded)

We can now calculate the difference between the EU and Japanese export volumes:

55.9 – 21.43 = 34.47

And from this, the percentage difference:

34.47 / 21.43 = 1.6085 x 100 = 160.85%

Rounded, this is 161%.

Potential Shortcuts / Pitfalls
Be careful with data expressed as a percentage change between two years. Imagine we know a value for 2014 is 50 and that it is 20% higher than the figure for 2013. The temptation is to simply deduct 20% from the 2014 value to get the 2013 value. If we do that we get a 2013 value of 40, which is incorrect. Think of the problem in terms of having an unknown number (X = the 2013 value) that increases by 20% to result in the known value (50). Thus we calculate X + 20% = 50, which becomes 50/120 x 100, giving us 41.66 (rounded). If you approach the problem this way, you can ensure that you will perform the correct calculation.

SET 4, Q3. Correct Answer: C

Reasoning

Using data from both the chart and the table, and the statement in the question that production in every region was the same in 2013 as in 2014, we need to calculate the 2013 share of exports from the production of the various regions in 2013 and then what percentage total exports make up of total global production.

Calculation

To calculate the 2013 share of exports in the various regions, we need to take into account the percentage changes. To do this, the easiest thing to do is to think of the 2013 export percentages as unknown values (X) and see how they compare to the 2014 percentages. In the case of China, this would be:

X + 3% of X = 34%
1.03X = 34%

The 2013 export share in China is then:

X = 34 / 1.03 = 33%

For the other regions:

USA: X = 27/1.05 = 25.7% (rounded)
Japan: X = 19 / 0.98 = 19.4% (rounded)
EU: X = 34% (as there was no change between 2013 and 2014)
Rest of World: X = 62 / 1.09 = 56.9% (rounded)

Next, we can calculate what share of global production each of the above export shares makes up by multiplying the share of each region's production from the global total by the export share. For example, for China, this is:

50% x 33% = 50% x 0.33 = 16.5%

For the other regions the figures are:

USA: 5% x 0.257 = 1.285%
Japan: 7% x 0.194 =1.358%
EU: 10% x 0.34 = 3.4%
Rest of World: 28% x 0.569 = 15.9% (rounded)

To get the total export share, we simply add up the above percentages:

16.5 + 1.285 + 1.358 + 3.4 + 15.9 = 38.443%

This is roughly 38%, so the correct answer is C.

Potential Shortcuts / Pitfalls

The calculations described above would be very time-consuming to perform, which you should take as a hint that they might not actually be necessary.

The key words in this question are "approximately" in the question text and "around" in the answer options. This should tell you that you can estimate the correct answer without calculating it to a high degree of accuracy. The level of accuracy you need to

achieve depends on how much the answer options differ from each other so you need to make an initial judgement on this.

Let's look at the shortcuts.

1. We can see from the 4th column of the table that the export share of production while rising a bit didn't change radically from 2013 to 2014 overall. So we can try using the 2014 figures to aim for an approximate result, saving a lot of calculations. Very importantly, the answer options – 6%, 14%, 38%, 50%, 70% – are far apart, which suggests we can be fairly generous with our approximating.

2. The 3rd column of the table tells us that China and Rest of the World were overwhelmingly the dominant factors in exports so we can put aside the other regions unless we can't get a clear result from the China and Rest of the World data.

3. The 2nd column of the table tells us that in 2014 China exported 34% of its production and the Rest of the World 62%. Although the 2013 shares for each were lower, they are still in the same ballpark relative to the spread in the answer options. We can immediately tell therefore that answers A (6%) and B (14%) are far too low and E (70%) is far too high. That leaves us with just C (38%) and D (50%) to decide between.

4. At this point we can't avoid doing some calculations, but we can do some serious rounding:

Export % of Rest of World = ca. 60%
Global production share of Rest of World = ca. 30%
Share of exports from global production = ca. 60 x 0.3 = 20%
Export % of China = ca. 30%
Global production share of China = 50%
Share of exports from global production = ca. 30 x 0.5 = 15%
Total: 20% + 15% = 35%

The net result of all of this is very approximate, but it's close enough for our purposes to choose answer option C, 38%. We can get closer by calculating more of the variables but in this case it's unnecessary as the only alternative answer we were left with, 50%, is too far away.

SET 5, Q1. Correct Answer: E

Reasoning

We need to sum each of the data columns to get the totals. We can then calculate the profit for each of the two years and take the difference.

Calculation

First we sum each of the columns of data:

26192 + 46 + 487 + 106 = 26831 (2009 income)
28344 + 43 + 494 + 103 = 28984 (2010 income)
13442 + 6899 + 1884 + 3099 = 25324 (2009 expenditure)
13894 + 7114 + 1907 + 2986 = 25901 (2010 expenditure)

The profit in 2010 is then calculated by taking the total income (28984) and subtracting the total expenditure (25901):

28984 − 25901 = 3083

And similarly for 2009:

26831 − 25324 = 1507

The increase in profit is then the difference between these two years:

3083 − 1507 = 1576

Now check the column headings and note that the values are quoted in thousands and so this answer is also in thousands and the final answer is £1.576m, which is rounded to £1.58m.

Potential Shortcuts / Pitfalls

You may notice that the 2010 profit value (3083) is also among the answer options. This is another example of how test designer try to anticipate the errors you might make and confuse you by including them among the incorrect answer options.

SET 5, Q2. Correct Answer: B

Reasoning

The expenditure is the sum of the specified items for each of the years. The percentage increase is then the difference divided by the 2009 value and then finally multiplied by 100 to make it a percentage.

Calculation

The expenditure relevant to this question is just the sum of the three data items for each of the years. For 2009 it is:

13442 + 6899 + 1884 = 22225

And for 2010 it is:

13894 + 7114 + 1907 = 22915

This gives an increase or difference of:

22915 − 22225 = 690

And so the percentage increase is:

(690 / 22225) × 100 = 3.1%

Potential Shortcuts / Pitfalls

Note that because we are dealing here with percentages (which means we have to divide by one of the values), the *order of magnitude* (the fact that the values are actually in thousands) *does not affect the answer*. If we had applied the magnitude factor to each of the values, then the extra thousands would simply have cancelled each other out and we would have ended up with the same answer – but we would have been typing many more numbers into our calculators, thereby increasing the chance of making a mistake.

SET 5, Q3. Correct Answer: B

Reasoning

We need to calculate the amount spent on advertising in 2009, increase this value by 12.2% and then calculate what percentage this new value is of the 2010 'Misc' expenditure.

Calculation

First we must calculate the amount spent on advertising in 2009. This is 14% of 3099:

3099 × 0.14 = 433.86

This is increased by 12.2% in 2010:

433.86 × 1.122 = 486.79

This is how much was spent on advertising in 2010. To calculate the percentage of the 2010 'Misc' spending we need to divide it by the total (2986) and multiply it by 100 to make it a percentage:

(486.79 / 2986) × 100 = 16.3%

Potential Shortcuts / Pitfalls

One serious mistake we might make is misunderstanding the information given.

We know that 14% of the 2009 'misc' spending was on advertising, and we are also told that this spending increased by 12.2% in the 2010. It might be tempting to interpret this as meaning that in 2010, advertisement spending increased to:

14% + 12.2% = 26.2% of 'misc' spending

This would be the wrong answer. If, however, the question had said that spending on advertising increased by 12.2 *percentage points* of 'misc' spending from 2009 to 2010, then that would indeed be the correct answer.

SET 6, Q1. Correct Answer: D

Reasoning

We need to calculate the amount of fuel used for each part of the journey. It is important to quickly identify the unknown in the test, which is the total distance of the journey.

Let us assume that the total journey length is × miles. From the question we know that we drove 28% of this as urban driving:

28% × X = 0.28X

Similarly for extra urban:

72% × X = 0.72X

How do we express the amount of fuel used in terms of the distance X? Clearly, we need to use the fuel efficiency figure, but exactly how? Looking at the units is always useful in answering such questions.

Distance = miles
Efficiency = miles / gallon

We now need to come up with a way to express the amount of fuel used:

$$\frac{\text{Distance}}{\text{Efficiency}} = \frac{\text{Miles}}{\frac{\text{Miles}}{\text{Gallon}}}$$

Let's notice that *miles* appears in both the numerator and the denominator. In fractions, this means that they cancel each other out or, in other words, we can simply delete them, leaving us with *gallons*, that is, the amount of fuel used during the journey.

Calculation

As we said above, the amount of fuel used for a journey is the distance divided by the efficiency of that part of the journey. Since we have already established that the units cancel each other out, we don't need to write them out from now on.

For the first part of the journey, the calculation is:

(0.28X / 40.6) = 0.0069X

And for the second part:

(0.72X / 47.4) = 0.0152X

Now we can simply add these together to give us the total amount of fuel used:

0.0069X + 0.0152X = 0.0221X

We now know the total amount of fuel used in terms of X. However, we also know from the question that the total fuel used during the journey is 3.3 gallons, so we can say that:

0.0221X = 3.3

Remember that we can perform any operation on equations as long as we perform it on both sides. Also recall that in order to get meaningful information out of equations, we need to create a situation where 1X and *only* 1X is on one side, and everything else is on the other side. Here we do this by dividing both sides of the equation by 0.0221:

X = 3.3/0.0221 = 149.3

Which is approximately 150 miles.

SET 6, Q2. Correct Answer: C

Reasoning

We need to calculate the amount of fuel used by each car to find the total amount used and then calculate the overall efficiency. To determine the amount of fuel used by each car, we divide the distance travelled by the fuel efficiency.

Calculation

The amount of fuel used is the distance travelled divided by the efficiency. In the Alpha this is:

50 / 38.9 = 1.2853

And for the Beta it is:

30 / 44.8 = 0.66696

And so the total amount of fuel used is:

1.2853 + 0.6696 = 1.9549

We have travelled a total of 80 miles using 1.9549 gallons of fuel which gives an overall fuel efficiency of:

80 / 1.9549 = 40.92 or 40.9

Potential Shortcuts / Pitfalls

There may be a temptation to say that for 50/80 of the total distance, our full efficiency was 38.9 mpg and in 30/80 of the total distance it was 44.8. This would then lead you to say that the average fuel efficiency would be calculated as follows:

50 × 38.9 + 30 × 44.8 / 80

This would produce the incorrect answer of 41.1 mpg. Make sure you read the question and do what is asked! The average fuel consumption is the *total journey length divided by the total amount of fuel used* and this is indeed the easiest way to calculate the answer.

SET 6, Q3. Correct Answer: E

Reasoning

First, look at the answer options. This will tell you that we need to express how much more efficient the Gamma is than the Delta as *a percentage*. The percentage difference is the difference in values divided by the lower value and multiplied by 100.

Calculation

The difference in fuel efficiencies is simply:

76.3 – 28.7 = 47.6

The percentage difference is then:

100 × (47.6 / 28.7) = 165.9%

Potential Shortcuts / Pitfalls

There are two things to look out for in the question.

The first important thing is to realise that when it comes to fuel efficiency expressed in miles per gallon, *the greater the number, the better*. This is especially important for candidates from those many European countries where fuel efficiency is usually defined differently (in litres / 100 kilometres, where the *lower* the number, the better).

Also, there is an *alternative method of calculating a percentage increase* which might constitute a shortcut for some. Using this method, we divide the increased value by the base value first:

76.3 / 28.7 = 2.659

But be careful here: many people make the mistake of simply multiplying this by 100 and then saying that the increase is 265.9%. This is incorrect. The above calculation tells us how much less fuel the Gamma consumes. In other words, the calculation yields a ratio.

Think of it this way. Two apples is *100% more* than one apple (this is the calculation you need for the percentage increase). Similarly, if a pair of shoes costs 25 euros and the price is then increased by 25 euros, the new price will be *100% more* than the original.

But 2 apples is also *twice as much (200% as much)* as 1 apple. Using the example of the shoes again, we have the base value (25 euros) and we double it, so the new price is 50 euros. Let's convert it into percentages. The base value is always 1 (or 100% if we multiply it by 100 to make it a percentage) and 50 euros is 2, twice as much (or 200% after the conversion) as the base value.

What can we do then if we follow the above calculation method? We can simply subtract 1 (representing the base value) before multiplying by 100:

2.659 – 1 = 1.659

SET 7, Q1. Correct Answer: A

Reasoning

We need to calculate the speed of the runner and then the distance he would cover at that speed over the time difference between the two runners. We also need to remember when calculating the speed that Davies ran the last 10 metres (when the fate of the bronze medal was decided) 8% faster than his overall average.

Calculation

First, we calculate Davies' overall average speed, which is the distance covered divided by the time taken:

100 m / 10.07 s = 9.93m/s

In the closing 10 metres, he was actually running 8% faster than this, which is:

9.93 × 1.08 = 10.72m/s

He finished 4th, just 0.04s behind the 3rd placed runner. In those 0.04 seconds he ran the following distance:

10.72 * 0.04 = 0.43m

which is 43cm.

Potential Shortcuts / Pitfalls
A risk in this question is that of confusing speeds and times because they are very similar in value. A runner covering 100m in 10s is travelling at 10m/s. As the times chosen are very close to 10 then so are the speeds, so care must be taken to ensure you keep track of each step.

Another thing to be careful about is the fact that we need to work with the 8% increased speed to calculate the distance covered in the last 0.04 seconds as this was the speed Davies ran at in the final 10 metres.

SET 7, Q2. Correct Answer: B

Reasoning

We need to calculate the speed of each runner and then the percentage difference between these speeds.

Calculation

The speed of the runner is calculated by dividing the distance run by the time taken. For Adams this is:

100 / 9.95 = 10.05 m/s

And for Best it is:

100 / 9.98 = 10.02 m/s

The percentage difference is the difference divided by the slower speed and then multiplied by 100 to make it a percentage:

100 × (10.05 − 10.02) / 10.02 = 0.3%

Potential Shortcuts / Pitfalls
If you try and do this in one step then you would get:

$$\frac{100 / 9.95}{100 / 9.98}$$

When we divide by a fraction (we have a fraction in the denominator as well) we invert it and then multiply instead:

$$\frac{100}{9.95} \times \frac{9.98}{100}$$

Now we can see that the 100s cancel out and we are simply left with:

9.98 / 9.95 = 1.003

Remember that this is not the percentage increase of one speed compared to other but rather how much faster the first place finisher was than the second. To get the percentage, you subtract 1 and multiply by 100. This way, you get the same answer of 0.3%.

SET 7, Q3. Correct Answer: E

Reasoning

We need to calculate the speed of the runner in the final, and from that calculate his speed in the previous races. Then we calculate his time in the heat (the first race) and hence the time of the unnamed runner-up in that heat. To calculate this last step, we use the information from the question text.

Calculation

First we need to calculate Carter's speed in the final. This is the distance run divided by the time taken:

100 / 10.03 = 9.97m/s

This was 1.3% faster than in the semi-final. The easiest way to calculate the semi-final speed from this is by imagining what we would have done if we had been provided the semi-final speed instead. If we knew the semi-final speed and the fact that Carter became 1.3% faster in the final, we would calculate his speed in the final as follows:

Semi-final speed × 1.013 = Final speed

Since we already have the final speed and we actually need to calculate the semi-final speed, we can work backwards:

Final speed / 1.013 = semi-final speed

With actual numbers:

9.97 / 1.013 = 9.84m/s

Similarly, this is 1.8% faster than in the heat which was:

9.84 / 1.018 = 9.67m/s

So he ran the heat at 9.67m/s. This would take:

100 / 9.67 = 10.34s

Don't forget that he beat the runner-up by 0.03 seconds:

10.34 + 0.03 = 10.37s.

SET 8, Q1. Correct Answer: D

Reasoning

The number of births is calculated by multiplying the population by the birth rate and then removing the necessary number of zeroes from the resulting figure.

Calculation

First we need to calculate the number of births in each of the two countries. For Finland this is:

5244 × 1680 = 8809920

However, we have to adjust this because of the order of magnitude of the data given. The population is given in thousands, so we would need to multiply the answer by 1000. But the birth rates are given per 100,000, and so, eventually, we would have to divide by 100,000. The net effect of these two operations is as follows:

Number of Births × 1000 / 100,000 = Number of Births / 100
8809920 / 100 = 88099.2

We then round this to the nearest whole number because you can't have 0.2 of a birth. Do the same for Ireland:

(4187 × 1844) / 100 = 77208

This gives us a difference of:

88099 – 77208 = 10891

SET 8, Q2. Correct Answer: E

Reasoning

The percentage change in the birth rate is simply the difference divided by the starting point and then multiplied by 100.

Calculation

The change in birth rate is the 2010 figure less the 2005 figure and then divided by the 2005 figure. This is then multiplied by 100 to make it a percentage. For Denmark this would be:

100 × (1612 – 1644) / 1644 = -1.9%

The negative answer indicates that the birth rate has fallen over the time period. Repeat this for the other four countries:

Finland: 100 × (1616 – 1680) / 1680 = -3.8%
Ireland: 100 × (1750 – 1844) / 1844 = -5.1%
Lithuania: 100 × (1582 – 1576) / 1576 = +0.4%
Netherlands: 100 × (1661 – 1702) / 1702 = -2.4%

If we now sort these numbers into order (it doesn't matter whether increasing or decreasing since we are looking for the *middle* number), we can quickly see that the Netherlands is in the middle.

Potential Shortcuts / Pitfalls
This question seems to involve an awful lot of work but in fact there are easy shortcuts. Because we are just comparing values and are not interested in the actual numbers, then any operation which is common to all can be omitted and so all the (100 x) can be left out. Although this will affect the actual value it will not change the order of the values.

Let's take a look at the calculations we performed one more time:

Ireland: 100 × (1750 – 1844) / 1844 = -5.1%

We already established that we can omit multiplying by 100:

Ireland: (1750 – 1844) / 1844 = -5.1%

In the above calculation, we first calculate the difference between the birth rates of the two years and then divide by the base value. Again, since we do not care about the actual figures, only their relationship to each other, we can simplify this step by simply dividing the two figures:

1750/1844 = 0.95

This figure actually tells us how many more (or fewer) births took place in 2010 than in 2005, which was not the question, but these figures will be just as good as the actual values for comparison. If we do this, our task is simplified into 5 much easier calculations:

Denmark: 1612 / 1644 = 0.981
Finland: 1616 / 1680 = 0.962
Ireland: 1750 / 1844 = 0.949
Lithuania: 1582 / 1576 = 1.004
Netherlands: 1661 / 1702 = 0.976

As you can see, the numbers are completely different but, predictably, the Netherlands is still in the middle.

Finally, Lithuania had clearly gone up and was the only one to do so. Save yourself some time and don't bother calculating the value at all as it is clearly going to be in top position.

SET 8, Q3. Correct Answer: B

Reasoning

The number of births is the population multiplied by the birth rate, which then needs to be adjusted for the correct order of magnitude. Also, the population needs adjusting because of the population growth.

Calculation

The number of births in 2010 is the population multiplied by the birth rate. The population has grown 1.6% from 2005 which is:

3416 × 1.016 = 3,470.656

The number of births is then:

3,470.656 × 1582 = 5,490,578

This needs to be adjusted for the correct order of magnitude. The population is in thousands and the birth rate is per 100,000 so, as in the previous question, the net effect is that we need to divide by 100:

5,490,578 / 100 = 54906

Similarly, for 2005 the number of births is:

(3416 × 1576) / 100 = 53836

This gives a difference of:

54906 − 53836 = 1070

SET 9, Q1. Correct Answer: D

Reasoning

The population is calculated by multiplying the density by the area. We can then calculate the 2010 population and then the 2010 density.

Calculation

First we need to calculate the population of Ireland in 2000. Since the density it defined as people / area, we need to multiply this by the area to get the number of people.

70.3 × 59.56 = 4187 (we would need to multiply this by 1000 to get the actual value, but we can skip that step)

This population grew by 6% over a decade so we multiply by 1.06:

4187 × 1.06 = 4438

Now divide this by the area to calculate the density in 2010:

4438 / 70.3 = 63.13

Potential Shortcuts / Pitfalls

The main point to make here is that in the calculation we *multiplied* by the area in the first step and then *divided* by the area in the third step. In step 2 we merely increased the intermediate result by 6%. This means that the area played no part in the result.

Because the area of Ireland remained constant, the result is dependent solely on *the change in population* which is identical to the change in density. *In short, a 6% increase in population results in a 6% increase in density.* If we realise this, the calculation becomes much simpler and faster:

59.56 × 1.06 = 63.13

SET 9, Q2. Correct Answer: A

Reasoning

The easiest way to approach this is gradually. The overall population density of Spain is 86.55 people / km².

We know that 74% live in urban areas, which means that 26% live in rural areas. For a second, let's completely disregard urban areas and people and let's assume that ALL the land in Spain is rural. If this were true, then the population density would also be 26% of the current figure:

86.55 × 0.26 = 22.5 people / km²

Now obviously this is not correct, as not all of the land in Spain is rural, only 83%. This means that we need to divide the about figure by 0.83 to get to the correct answer:

22.5 / 0.83 = 27.11 people / km²

This is the population density of the rural areas. In the section below, we also demonstrate a longer but more direct calculation method which you can use as a fallback option should the above intuition not occur in the real exam.

Calculation

If 74% of the population live in urban areas then 26% must live in rural areas. Similarly, if urban areas account for 17% of the total land then rural areas must account for the remaining 83%.

The total number of people living in Spain is, as we saw above:

Area × Population density
495 × 86.55 = 42842

This number is in thousands as the area is given in thousands of square kilometres. Now only 26% of this population live in rural areas which is:

42842 × 0.26 = 11139

We are told the area of Spain is 495 (thousand) km² but the rural areas cover just 83% of this which is:

495 × 0.83 = 410.85

Now the density of rural areas can be calculated by dividing the rural population by the rural area:

11139 / 410.85 = 27.11 people per km².

Note that we did not need to spell out all the zeroes as they cancel each other out (both the population figure and the area are in thousands).

Potential Shortcuts / Pitfalls
For a shortcut, as with the previous question, the area can be omitted from the calculation. If we had written the whole calculation in one step it would have been easier to see:

$$\frac{495 * 86.55 * 0.26}{495 * 0.83} = 27.11$$

This can then be simplified as follows:

$$\frac{\cancel{495} * 86.55 * 0.26}{\cancel{495} * 0.83} = 27.11$$

$$\frac{86.55 * 0.26}{0.83} = 27.11$$

This is exactly the same formula as the one we came up with using a different logic in the reasoning section.

SET 9, Q3. Correct Answer: C

Reasoning

We need to calculate what size of population would give Latvia a density precisely 1/3 that of France and then calculate how that differs from its current population.

Calculation

First we must calculate the target density which is:

110.49 / 3 = 36.83

The population is the area multiplied by the density and so the population that would give us this density is:

64.6 × 36.83 = 2379

However, the population is actually:

64.6 × 34.68 = 2240

And so the difference is:

2379 – 2240 = 139

Now we must adjust for the order of magnitude. The area is specified in thousands of square kilometres and so we must multiply the answer by 1000 to get 139,000.

Potential Shortcuts / Pitfalls
Once again we find that the area is being overused. It is not irrelevant as in the previous questions but it is used as a common factor. We are attempting to calculate the difference between two populations. Both of these populations are calculated using the area of the country. In effect we are doing:

A * density1 – A * density2

where density1 and density2 are the given and calculated densities. This can be shortened to:

A * (density1 – A * density2)

Density1 and density2 are 36.83 and 34.86 respectively and the calculation is then reduced to:

64.6 × (36.83 – 34.68) = 64.6 × 2.15 = 139

Alternatively, you can also think of it this way. Once we have calculated the target density (36.83), we can say that in order for Latvia to achieve that population density, we need 2.15 more people per square kilometre (36.83 – the current density = 2.15).

Since we also know how many square kilometres there are in total in Latvia (that is, Latvia's area), we can simply multiply that by 2.15:

64.6 × 2.15 = 13

SET 10, Q1. Correct Answer: B

Reasoning

The percentage increase for each country is the difference in per capita spending divided by the starting value and then multiplied by 100.

Calculation

First we calculate each percentage increase:
Belgium – 100 × (1630 – 1575) / 1575 = 3.5%
France – 100 × (1685 – 1615) / 1615 = 4.3%
Netherlands – 100 × (1715 – 1645) / 1645 = 4.26%
Spain – 100 × (1535 – 1490) / 1490 = 3.0%
UK – 100 × (1625 – 1580) / 1580 = 2.8%

And we can see that France is the highest by a small margin.

Potential Shortcuts / Pitfalls

This is a relatively easy problem but with a lot of operations to carry out. However, we only want to compare values and so the magnitude is not important. As every calculation has the same '100 x', it can be omitted.

Another shortcut which is a little more difficult to spot is that both France and the Netherlands had an increase of €70 per person. France, however, started from a lower base so this will produce a larger percentage rise. So, there is no need to calculate the Netherlands at all – it can never be the largest.

Similarly, Spain and the UK had a rise of €45 but Spain was from a lower base and must be larger than the UK so there is no need to calculate the UK either. This reduces the number of countries to calculate to three, saving us a little bit of time.

SET 10, Q2. Correct Answer: E

Reasoning

The total spending is calculated by multiplying per capita spending by the population for each year. We then take the difference between the two years' spending and divide by the starting value and multiply by 100 to make it a percentage.

Calculation

First we need to calculate the total spending in 2005:

10415 × 1575 = 16403625

For 2010 we first need to calculate the new population figure as this has increased by 454 thousand. As the population is already stated in thousands this can be omitted for the moment:

10415 + 454 = 10869

Thus the total spending in 2010 is:

10869 × 1630 = 17716470

And so the percentage increase is:

((17716470 – 16403625) / 16403625) × 100 = 8%

SET 10, Q3. Correct Answer: D

Reasoning

We need to calculate the amount spent by each country by multiplying its population by its per capita spending. We can then calculate the difference by simply subtracting one number from the other.

Calculation

First we must calculate the amount spent by the UK:

1580 × 60261 = 95.212m

Similarly for the Netherlands and Spain:

1645 × 16316 = 26.84m

$1490 \times 43060 = 64.159m$

The difference is then calculated by:

$95.212 - (26.84 + 64.159) = 4.213m$

However, the populations are stated in thousands and so this figure needs to be increased 1000x for the correct answer of €4213 million.

SET 11, Q1. Correct Answer: D

Reasoning

We need to calculate the overall average speed of the train. Speed is distance divided by time. Once we have the average speed, we can easily calculate the cruising speed by adding 15% to this value.

Calculation

The calculation of speed (distance / time) is quite straightforward, but here the time is not in an easily usable form. The hour component of the journey time is simple enough: 3 hours. The problem is with the minutes, as we do not express time in the decimal system. This means that 45 minutes is not equal to 0.45 hours, so we must first convert the minutes to a decimal value.

To do this, take the minutes, divide by 60 (minutes per hour) and then add the hours:

$45 / 60 = 0.75$
$0.75 + 3 = 3.75$

Now calculate the average speed:

$435 / 3.75 = 116$

The cruising speed is actually 15% faster than this. Remember how we convert a 15% increase to 1.15:

$116 \times 1.15 = 133.4$

Which, to the nearest whole number, is 133 km/h.

Potential Shortcuts / Pitfalls
The first part of this problem can be done more quickly without a calculator.

The time taken is 3:45, which is 3 whole hours and 3 quarters of an hour. This is a total of 15 quarter hours ($3 \times 4 = 12$, plus 3 quarters), so when we calculate the average speed we can use:

$435 / (15 / 4)$

But remember, if we are dividing by a fraction then we *invert* it and *multiply* instead:

$435 \times (4 / 15)$

This next step is difficult to spot but if you do, it can save a lot of time. 45 is 3x15 and so 450 is 30x15. So what? Well, notice that 435 is just 15 less than 450. Since 450 is 30x15, then 435 must be 29x15. Our division then looks like this:

$(29 \times 15 \times 4) / 15$

Notice how the 15 is both in the numerator and in the denominator – this means that they will cancel each other out, reducing the calculation to:

$29 \times 4 = 116$

There is one last thing we should not forget about in dealing with minutes. 45 minutes is three quarters of an hour. We are trying to convert this into the decimal system, so what is three quarters of one hundred? The answer is of course 75, with or without using a calculator.

SET 11, Q2. Correct Answer: C

Reasoning

We need to calculate the normal average speed for the train. Once we have this, we can calculate the actual average speed of the train and then the delay caused by the slowdown.

Calculation

We first need to convert the time into a usable format. To do this, take the minutes, divide by 60 and add the hours back in:

$35 / 60 = 0.583$
$0.583 + 1 = 1.583$

Now calculate the normal average speed:

$220 / 1.583 = 138.98$

Because of adverse conditions, our *actual* average was only 90% of this (which is just another way of saying that it was 10% slower):

$138.98 \times 0.9 = 125.1$

So, if we travelled all 220km at this speed it would take:

$220 / 125.1 = 1.7586$

This answer is in the decimal format, which we need to convert back to hours and minutes. Subtract the whole hours and then multiply the decimal part by 60:

$0.7586 \times 60 = 45.516$

This is what we know so far: the journey took 1 hour and 45.516 minutes. This is still not good enough, as now it is the minutes that is in the decimal format.

Now subtract the minutes and repeat the above step to get the seconds:

$0.516 \times 60 = 30.96s$

This is 1:45:31 which is 10m 31s late.

Potential Shortcuts / Pitfalls

There may be a temptation to take the time of 1 hour and 35 minutes and convert it to minutes. This would be 95 minutes. Some candidates would then take 10% of this and add it to the original 95 minutes to calculate the delay. This would give an answer of 9m30s delay, which is wrong. What this actually calculates is *how far you would be from your destination at the normal arrival time*, if you continued your journey at the normal average speed.

A shortcut we can take is *checking the level of accuracy needed* to answer the question. We initially calculated that the new journey time would be 1 hour and 45.516 minutes. We can see from the data in the table that 1 hour and 45.516 minutes is 10 minutes and × seconds longer than the normal journey time. As it turns out, this level of accuracy is more than enough, as option C is the only one which starts with 10 minutes – so we do not actually need to convert 0.516 of a minute into seconds.

SET 11, Q3. Correct Answer: B

Reasoning

We need to work out the number of trains we will pass. The easiest way to do this is to make note of when we depart and arrive and then calculate how many trains either (1) arrive after our departure time or (2) depart before our arrival time.

Calculation

To calculate our arrival time:

$08:00 + 5:20 = 13:20$

The first train leaving Berlin set off at 05:00 and so it will arrive at:

$05:00 + 5:20 = 10:20$

So, the first train of the day from Berlin to Brussels will still be en route when we set off. This means that we will pass every train leaving after 05:00 and before 13:20, when we arrive in Berlin.

Since trains leave from Berlin every two hours, this will add up to 5 trains:

05:00, 07:00, 09:00, 11:00 and 13:00, 5 in total.

Potential Shortcuts / Pitfalls

There may be a temptation to say that the journey is 5 hour and 20 minutes long and the trains set off every two hours, so we must pass only two trains (one after 2 hours, the second after 4 hours). This would only be true if we simply sat in a stationary train for 5 hours and 20 minutes! This incorrect approach disregards the fact that our train is also moving in the opposite direction.

SET 12, Q1. Correct Answer: A

Reasoning

We need to calculate the number of people in each of the two categories. Once we know this, we can use the information given in the question to figure out how many of those who do not own a car can swim 1 km. As a final step, we can calculate how many people are left, and this will be the number of people who can do neither.

Calculation

Because the numbers of men and women in the group are equal, we can use the mid-point between the percentages given, or their average, for the calculations. Also, because the group size is 100 people then the percentages correspond to the actual number of people in the category.

How do we calculate averages? We simply add up the numbers and then divide the resulting amount by the number of items we added up.

The number of people who own a car is, then:

$(83 + 79) / 2 = 81$

The number of people who can swim 1km is:

$(32 + 42) / 2 = 37$

We also know from the question that there are 25 people who both can swim and own a car. So how do we calculate how many people can swim 1 km but do *not* own a car? Quite simply, if 25 out of 37 swimmers own a car that means that 37 – 25 do not. This is:

37 – 25 = 12

Unfortunately, we are not done yet. We are looking for the number of people who, in addition to not being able to swim 1km, do not own a car either. To calculate this, we need to calculate the number of people who do not own a car. Since we have already established that 81 people do, that means that 100 – 81 do not:

100 – 81 = 19

We are now at the final step. We know that 19 people do not own a car. We also know that 12 of these people can, however, swim 1 km. This means that there must be 19 – 12 people who neither swim nor own a car:

19 – 12 = 7

Potential Shortcuts / Pitfalls

If you look at the answer options, you can see that the incorrect answers were not chosen at random. During our calculations, our interim results included:

12 as the number of people who can swim 1 km but do now own a car
19 as the number of people who do not own a car

Both of these numbers are among the answer options. This is dangerous because if you forget to take the last step and think that one of these interim values is the result you were looking for, you will find these among the answer options.

SET 12, Q2. Correct Answer: E

Reasoning

We need to calculate the numbers of both men and women who can make Hollandaise sauce. We do this by first calculating the number of men. Since we know the total number of people who can make the sauce, we can easily calculate the number of women as well. We also know the proportion of women in any representative group who can make the sauce, so we can calculate the total number of women in the group.

Calculation

The number of men or women who can make the sauce is the size of the group multiplied by the percentage of people in that group who can make the sauce. For men we are told that there are 82 in the overall group and the table tells us that 28% of them can make the sauce:

82 × 0.28 = 22.96

We can always round to nearest whole numbers (23 in this case) because you cannot have 0.96 of a man. The question tells us that there are 80 people in total in the group who can make the sauce and we now know that 23 of them are men, so the number of women who can make the sauce must be:

80 – 23 = 57

If we call the unknown number of women in the total group X, then we know that 38% of them is equal to 57. So:

0.38 × X = 57

Remember that we need to have × on one side and everything else on the other side and that we achieve this by performing the same operations on both sides of the equation. In this case, we divide both sides by 0.38:

X = 57 / 0.38
X = 150

SET 12, Q3. Correct Answer: C

Reasoning

We need to calculate the number of men in each group. If we then assume that *all* those who know the capital of Country × can also identify the Pole Star, we can simply subtract the Country × number from the Pole Star number – the resulting value will represent the minimum number of people who can identify the Pole Start but not the capital of Country X.

Calculation

First, we need to calculate the number of men who can identify the Pole Star, which is 37% of 200:

200 × 0.37 = 74

Next, we need to calculate the number of men who can name the capital of Country X, which is 18% of 200:

$200 \times 0.18 = 36$

Now, we do not know anything about the relationship between these two groups. It is possible that *none* of the people who can identify the capital of Country × can point to the Pole Star, and it is also possible that *all* of them can. Luckily, we do not have to know. We are looking for the *minimum* number who *can* identify the Pole Star but *cannot* name the capital of Country X.

Let's assume that everyone who can name the capital can also identify the Pole Star. This would mean that 36 out 74 people can do both. We now know that at least 74 – 36 people can identify the Pole Star but cannot name the capital of Country X:

$74 - 36 = 38$

Potential Shortcuts / Pitfalls
This question may seem confusing because it is asking for a minimum value from a range rather than a precise value. The key to answering the question is making the correct assumption that we get to the minimum *if we assume that everyone who can name the capital of Country × can also identify the Pole Star.* This is because whoever is left in the Pole Star group after this simple subtraction cannot possibly name the capital of Country X.

Let's also notice that the entire above calculation can only be made because fewer men can name the capital of Country × than can identify the Pole Star. If 100 of 200 men could name the capital, and 74 could identify the Pole Star, we could not make the above assumption and would be forced to say that it is impossible to answer the question. Although not likely in an EPSO test, this is also a possibility, so be prepared for an answer option like that.

SET 13, Q1. Correct Answer: D

Reasoning
The number of centenarians is calculated by multiplying the population by the proportion of octogenarians and then calculating the proportions of the other two age subgroups.

Calculation
First we need to calculate the number of octogenarians in the Netherlands in 2005. This is the population multiplied by the percentage that are over 80:

$16316 \times 5.64 / 100 = 920.22$

Alternatively, we can convert the percentage into a decimal in the way we did in earlier questions:

$16316 \times 0.0564 = 920.22$

The question tells us that only 4.3% of these people are over 90:

$920.22 \times 4.3 / 100 = 39.57$

And only 3.2% of these people are over 100:

$39.57 \times 3.2 / 100 = 1.2662$

This comes as no surprise as all the answers are similar to this value with the only difference being the position of the decimal point – in other words, *the answer options differ only in their order of magnitude.* We have already incorporated the magnitudes implied by the percentages by dividing by 100 at each step but the population was given in thousands and so this answer must be multiplied by 1000 to give:

$1.266 \times 1000 = 1266$

SET 13, Q2. Correct Answer: D

Reasoning
The number of octogenarians is the total population multiplied by the proportion who are octogenarians. The percentage rise is then the difference in numbers divided by the starting point and then multiplied by 100.

Calculation
The number of octogenarians in 2005 is simply:

$9066 * 0.0557 = 504.98$ thousand

We indicated the thousands at the end of the calculation but this is not important when calculating percentages as long as we are consistently disregarding them in all calculations.

Before we can calculate the number of octogenarians in 1985 we first have to calculate what the population was in 1985. Remember, we are told the population increase was 6% every ten years from an unknown 1985 population. Let us call this unknown population X, and we know that it increased 6% twice to reach the 2005 population of 9066 thousand.

$$X \times 1.06 \times 1.06 = 9066$$

As always, we need to achieve a situation where × is on one side and everything else on the other. We do this by dividing both sides with (1.06 × 1.06):

$$X = 9066 / (1.06 \times 1.06)$$

Let's calculate 1.06 × 1.06 to simplify things – in other words, let's calculate 1.06 squared:

$$1.06 \times 1.06 = 1.1236$$
$$X = 9066 / 1.1236$$
$$X = 8068.7 \text{ thousand}$$

We can again disregard the thousands and calculate the number of octogenarians in 1985:

$$8068.7 \times 5.44 / 100 = 438.94$$

This is a difference of:

$$504.98 - 438.94 = 66.04$$

The percentage rise is this difference divided by the starting point and multiplied by 100:

$$100 \times (66.04 / 438.94) = 15\%$$

Potential Shortcuts / Pitfalls

It might not be obvious at first glance but *the population is not needed for this calculation at all.*

Let's recall how we calculate the 2005 number of octogenarians and the 1985 number.

2005:

Population (2005) x 0.0557

1985:

$$\frac{\text{Population (2005)}}{1.06 \times 1.06} = 0.0544$$

What you might notice is that the population (2005) value is in both expressions. Always remember that if the same number is a factor (that is, we divide or multiply with it) in two values and our final goal is to calculate a percentage increase or decrease between the two values, we can simply omit the common factor. So, let's just replace the population with the number 1 to save time:

1 x 0.0557 = 0.0557

and

$$\frac{1}{1.06 \times 1.06} \times 0.0544 = 0.8899 \times 0.0544$$

If you calculate the above, you will get to the same correct answer without ever using the population figure.

Another important thing to remember has to do with the two times 6% population increase. A common error is to think that means that the population increased by a total of 12% (6% +6%) over 20 years. This is incorrect. The second 6% increase took place in relation to a population that was already 6% higher than the 1985 population, so the actual increase is calculated by *multiplying* rather than *adding up* the two increases, resulting in:

$$1.06 \times 1.06 = 1.1236$$

That is, in a total of 12.36% increase in population.

SET 13, Q3. Correct Answer: C

Reasoning

The data in the table are percentage rates i.e. the number of octogenarians per 100 of the population. If, in 1985, there are 4.11 octogenarians for every 100 Greeks, we can easily see that the per capita rate would be one hundredth of that: 0.0411 octogenarian for every Greek. This means that we do not actually need the population figure to answer the question; we will simply calculate the percentage (and NOT percentage point) increase in the octogenarian rate.

Calculation

The rise in the per capita rate is simply the difference between the rates given divided by the starting point and then multiplied by 100:

$$((4.31 - 4.11) / 4.11) \times 100 = 4.9\%$$

SET 14, Q1. Correct Answer: B

Reasoning

First, we need to calculate the passenger volume increase for both airlines between 2010 and 2015. Then we can work out the difference between the two resulting numbers.

Calculation

The passenger increase for Crown Air between 2010 and 2015 was:

9.2 – 6.5 = 2.7 million

The passenger increase for Jervis Air between 2010 and 2015 was:

5.4 – 3.5 = 1.9 million

The difference between the two numbers is:

2.7 – 1.9 = 0.8 million = 800 000 passengers

Potential Shortcuts / Pitfalls

With a stacked bar chart, it is quite easy to misread the numbers, so make sure you are working with the correct values.

Also, since the values in the chart are in millions and the correct answer isn't, it is important to perform the correct conversion.

SET 14, Q2. Correct Answer: B

Reasoning

First, we must calculate the total number of passengers carried by the 5 airlines in 2010 and 2015 and then the European totals. We can then calculate the difference between the two resulting numbers.

Calculation

The total number of passengers carried by the 5 airlines in 2010:

6.5 + 3.5 + 2.4 + 1.2 + 1 = 14.6

So the total for Europe in 2010 is:

14.6 x 2 = 29.2

The total number of passengers carried by the 5 airlines in 2015:

9.2 + 5.4 + 3.5 + 0.8 + 1.4 = 20.3

So the total for Europe in 2015 is:

20.3 x 2 = 40.6

The difference is then:

40.6 – 29.2 = 11.4 million

Potential Shortcuts / Pitfalls

Accounting for the fact that the 5 airlines represent 50% of total European air traffic could have been handled in one step instead of two. We could have calculated the difference between the number of passengers carried by the 5 airlines in 2010 and 2015, and doubled the difference rather than each of the values for the two years separately.

SET 14, Q3. Correct Answer: D

Reasoning

Since the chart provides monthly average passenger figures, we need to multiply this by the number of months in a year to get to the annual figure.

Calculation

The monthly average number of passengers carried by Crown Air is: 6.5 million.

We need to multiply this by 12 to get the annual figure:

6.5 x 12 = 78 million

Potential Pitfalls / Shortcuts

This is a very straightforward question and the only real pitfall to avoid is not noticing that the chart shows monthly figures, not annual ones. If you failed to do this, you would mark option A as correct.

SET 15, Q1. Correct Answer: E

Reasoning

The productivity of the employees is calculated by dividing the production volume by the number of employees.

Calculation

Craybourne Woodlands: 8 000 / 50 = 160 tonnes
Stirling Forest: 14 000 / 80 = 175 tonnes
Woodcombe Hills Woods: 3000 / 30 = 100 tonnes
Hampton Forest: 3000 / 30 = 100 tonnes
Frasier Green: 8000 / 40 = 200 tonnes

The correct answer is therefore Frasier Green (E).

Potential Shortcuts / Pitfalls

The above calculations are straightforward enough but we can reduce the number of calculations further. Just by looking at the ratio of production to employees, we can see straight away that Hampton Forest and Woodcombe Hills Woods employees each contribute half as much as those of Frasier Green (30:3 versus 80:4). Also, Craybourne Woodlands' employees clearly produce less than those of Frasier Green as the total production is the same but the number of employees is greater.

Be careful here to perform the calculations on production volume, not the volume actually utilised / sold.

SET 15, Q2. Correct Answer: E

Reasoning

First, we calculate the number of outdoor furniture shipments that were actually produced. Then, we calculate the total production volume for roofing, take 10% of it, and calculate how many outdoor furniture shipments that would have made up. We get the total by adding up the two numbers.

Calculation

The total volume used for outdoor furniture:

$4\,000 + 5\,900 + 1\,200 + 1\,300 + 2\,800 = 15\,200$

The total volume used for roofing:

$2000 + 3800 + 1600 + 1600 + 4000 = 13\,000$

10% of the roofing figure is:

$13\,000 / 10 = 1300$

The new total volume to be utilised for outdoor furniture:

$15200 + 1300 = 16\,500$

With 50 tonnes per shipment, this adds up to:

$16\,500 / 50 = 330$ shipments, which is Answer E.

Potential Shortcuts / Pitfalls

Notice how we saved time by only calculating the number of shipments (dividing by 50 tonnes) using the grand total, i.e. not twice, once for the original volume and once for the overall volume.

SET 15, Q3. Correct Answer: A

Reasoning

Similarly to how we calculated productivity, we need to divide the total production utilised for roofing by the total number of employees across all forestries.

Calculation

The total production utilised for roofing is:

$2\,000 + 3\,800 + 1\,600 + 1\,600 + 4\,000 = 13\,000$

The total number of employees is:

$50 + 80 + 30 + 30 + 40 = 230$

The roofing production of one employee, on average, is then:

$13\,000 / 230 = 56.52$ tonnes (rounded)

Potential Shortcuts / Pitfalls

An important thing to notice is that we calculated the average by adding up all the production volumes and we divided it by the total number of employees.

A typical mistake would be to divide each production volume by the corresponding number of employees. This is incorrect because it does not take into account the relative weight of each forestry in the average. For example, Frasier Green produces twice as much roofing wood as Craybourne Woodlands but with fewer employees.

SET 16, Q1. Correct Answer: D

Reasoning

We need to calculate the average speed of the runner, which is the distance divided by the time taken. We also need to figure out a way to convert the time given in hours, minutes and seconds into decimals.

Calculation

The distance run in the second half of the race is simply half the total distance:

$42.2 / 2 = 21.1$

The time taken to run this is the total time taken less the time taken to run the first half of the race:

2:13:31 − 1:07:50 = 1:05:41

The calculation of distance / time is simple enough but here, the time is not in an easily usable form so we must first convert it. To do this, take the seconds and divide by 60 (seconds per minute) to convert it to minutes and then add in the minutes. Now divide the minutes by 60 (minutes per hour) and add in the hours:

41 / 60 = 0.683
0.683 + 5 = 5.683
5.683 / 60 = 0.0947
0.0947 + 1 = 1.0947

Now calculate the average speed:

21.1 / 1.0947 = 19.27 km/h.

SET 16, Q2. Correct Answer: B

Reasoning

We need to calculate the average speed for each of the runners, which is distance / time. We then need to calculate the percentage difference.

Calculation

We first need to calculate the time taken by each of the runners for the last kilometre. For Dennis it was:

2:14:12 − 2:11:00 = 3:12 minutes

3:12 minutes = 3 × 60 seconds + 12 seconds = 192s

For Ekimov it was:

2:14:20 − 2:11:00 = 3:20

3:20 = 3 × 60 + 20 = 200s

Their speeds can now be calculated as distance (1000m) divided by the time taken. For Dennis:

1000 / 192 = 5.21m/s

Note that the calculated speed is in metres per second. If we had written 1 km as 1 km rather than 1000 metres, the unit would have been kilometres per second and the number would have been 0.00521 km / s. These are unusual units but we don't even have to write them out. Since we are going to calculate only the *percentage difference between them*, we can just take note of the number itself.
And for Ekimov:

1000 / 200 = 5m/s

The percentage difference is the difference divided by the slower speed and then multiplied by 100:

100 × (5.21 − 5) / 5 = 4.2%

Potential Shortcuts / Pitfalls
Because both runners are covering the same distance (1km) then their percentage difference in *speed* is actually the same as their percentage difference in *time*.

Why is this important? The reason is that *it is not necessary to calculate the two runners' speeds at all.* Once we know the time they took to cover the last kilometre (and this was the first calculation we performed), we can directly proceed to the difference in time, which is 200-192 = 8 seconds and so the percentage difference is:

100 × (8 / 192) = 4.2%

SET 16, Q3. Correct Answer: D

Reasoning

First, we need to work out Benoit's overall average speed. Then we calculate his speed in the last 150 metres. Once we have done this, we can calculate how far he was from the finishing line when Anderson finished.

Calculation

Benoit's overall average speed is distance divided by time but the time first needs converting to decimal form to make it easier to use. As above, divide the seconds by 60, add in the minutes and divide by 60 again and add in the hours:

38 / 60 = 0.633
0.633 + 12 = 12.633
12.633 / 60 = 0.211
0.211 + 2 = 2.211

Benoit's overall average speed is therefore:

42.1 / 2.211 = 19.04 km/h

He ran the final 150m of the race at a speed 5% faster than this, which is:

19.04 × 1.05 = 20 km/h

The time gap between Anderson and Benoit was:

2:12:38 – 2:12:14 = 24 seconds

The distance by which Anderson beat Benoit is then *the distance run by Benoit in 24 seconds at 20km/h*. We have a mismatch of units here, because the speed is given in kilometres / hour and the time difference in seconds, so we can *either* convert the time difference to hours by dividing by 3600 (60 minutes × 60 seconds) *or* convert Benoit's speed to metres/second by multiplying by 1000 (metres in a kilometre) and dividing by 3600 (seconds in an hour). Let's do the latter.

Why is this the way to convert km/m to m/s, you might ask? Let's see.

20 km / h = 20 000 m / hour

But we want to establish how many metres the runner can cover in *one second* (because the unit we are looking for is metres / second, not metres / hour). 1 hour is 60 × 60 seconds. 60 × 60 is 3600, so the speed is:

20 000 m / 3600 seconds

There is one last step to take, because we are interested in how many metres are covered in 1 second, so we divide by 3600:

5.56 m / second

Benoit ran for 24 seconds at this speed from the moment Anderson finished until the moment he himself crossed the finishing line.
The distance is then:

5.56 m * 24 = 133m

SET 17, Q1. Correct Answer: B

Reasoning

We need to calculate the price at which we purchased 1 share, work out the total for 2000 shares and then add the dealing charge.

Calculation

Monday's closing price is given as 2.37 and we purchase at 1.4% below this so we have to multiply by (1-0.014) or 0.986. This is so because, remember, 100% is 1, so 1.4% must be 0.014. If the price is 1.4% below another value, another way of saying that is that the price was 98.6% of that:

2.37 × 0.986 = 2.33682

The total cost is then the number of shares multiplied by the price:

2000 × 2.33682 = 4673.64

We also have to pay the dealing charge:

4673.64 + 15.95 = 4689.59

Potential Shortcuts / Pitfalls

The actual price is 1.4% below yesterday's price. This means that we needed to multiply yesterday's closing price by 1 – 0.014. If the actual price had been 1.4% *above* yesterday's closing price, we would have multiplied by 1 + 0.014 – this is an important difference not to mix up. *See also Set 20 for more on this.*

SET 17, Q2. Correct Answer: C

Reasoning

We need to calculate the price at which we sold the shares and hence the rise since yesterday's close. In order to calculate the selling price, we must add the dealing charge to our proceeds.

Calculation

We are told how much we got from the sale of the shares, but we must remember that that amount was already reduced by the dealing charge of 15.95. This means that the actual selling price was 15.95 *higher* than the figure given in the question text:

4664.05 + 15.95 = 4680

This was the amount we got for selling 2000 shares so the amount per share was:

4680 / 2000 = 2.34

Yesterday, the closing selling price was 2.25 and so the percentage rise is the difference divided by the starting value and then multiplied by 100:

2.34 – 2.25 = 0.09
100 × (0.09 / 2.25) = 4%

Potential Shortcuts / Pitfalls

First of all, there are a couple of small but important issues to notice:

The question again talks about Friday but we need to compare our selling price to that of Thursday

There is a temptation to say that in order to calculate

the price increase, we simply compare the Thursday selling price to the Friday selling price. This would be wrong because we did not sell at Friday's *closing* price but at an another price that we must calculate from our total proceeds

These were the pitfalls. There's also a shortcut. *You should be able to do this question without a calculator at all.* When dividing by 2000, be aware that this is basically division by 2 and then by 1000. Division by 2 simply means halving the number. Division by 1000 is moving the decimal point 3 places to the left.

When calculating the percentage, note that 2.25 is 2¼ which is the same as 9/4 (2 = 8/4). Remember that when we divide by a fraction it is the same as multiplying by the inverted version of that fraction, so when we divide 0.09 by 9/4 this is the same as multiplying by 4/9:

$(100 \times 0.09 \times 4) / 9$

When you multiply by 100 you can just move the decimal point 2 places to the right so 0.09 becomes 9 and now the 9s cancel out, leaving just 4:

$$\frac{9 \times 4}{9} = 4$$

SET 17, Q3. Correct Answer: E

Reasoning

We need to calculate the spread for each day as a percentage of the buy price.

Calculation

This is in essence a very easy problem because all the numbers are very similar. We can readily see the difference between the buy and sell price just by mentally subtracting the sell from the buy to get 0.05, 0.04, 0.05, 0.03 and 0.05 respectively. We can then calculate the percentage of the buy price by dividing the spread by the buy price and multiplying by 100:

Monday: $100 \times 0.05 / 2.37 = 2.11\%$
Tuesday: $100 \times 0.04 / 2.41 = 1.66\%$
Wednesday: $100 \times 0.05 / 2.39 = 2.09\%$
Thursday: $100 \times 0.03 / 2.28 = 1.32\%$
Friday: $100 \times 0.05 / 2.34 = 2.14\%$

From this we can clearly see that Friday has the largest percentage spread.

Potential Shortcuts / Pitfalls

Because we only want to know which is the largest spread we don't need to concern ourselves with the actual value, just whether it is larger or smaller than the others. Consequently, there is *no need to do all the '100 x' operations* which are common to all the calculations.

Furthermore, as all the numbers are very similar, then the largest result is going to come from the largest numerator, that is, the largest spread value. There are three which are equal at 0.05 and so only these need to be considered. Secondly, the largest result will come from the smallest denominator. Why is that?

Let's say you have some apples, you eat 5 of them and you want to work out what that 5 represents as a percentage of the total number of apples. If you had 10 apples in total, you ate half (50%) of the apples. If you had 100 apples, you ate 5% of the apples. This illustrates that the smaller the total (here 10 instead of 100), the higher the percentage a fixed number of apples represent.

On the same principle, since Friday's Buy price was the lowest, the fixed spread (0.5) will represent a higher percentage of that than of any other day's Buy price.

This can be determined without a single keystroke of the calculator!

SET 18, Q1. Correct Answer: D

Reasoning

The speed is the distance travelled divided by the time it takes. When coming to the final result, we need to take into account the order of magnitude of the distance and the unit of time given in the table.

Calculation

The Earth is 150 million km from the Sun and the question tells us that the distance round its orbit is 6.3 times this, which is:

$150 \text{ m} \times 6.3 = 945\text{m km}$

The speed is then calculated as distance divided by time:

$945\text{m} / 365.25 = 2.587 \text{ m km/day}$

This is how far the Earth travels in 1 day. For the purpose of calculating the speed per hour, then minutes, then seconds, let's add in the zeroes representing the million:

2,587,000 km/day

Divide this by 24 to calculate its speed per hour:

2,587,000 / 24 = 107,791.67 km/day

Next divide this by the number of seconds in an hour (60 minutes × 60 seconds = 3600):

107,791.67 / 3600 = 29.94 km/sec

Which is about 30 km/sec.

SET 18, Q2. Correct Answer: B

Reasoning

We need to calculate the speed of each planet, which is the distance travelled divided by the time taken. We then need to do the percentage calculation of the difference.

Calculation

The speed is distance travelled divided by time taken. The distance travelled is the distance of the planet from the Sun multiplied by 6.3.

Mercury = 365.4 million
Venus = 636.3 million

The time it takes to make these journeys is the orbital period. From this, we can calculate the speeds of both planets.

Speed of Mercury = 365.4 million / 88 days = 4.152 m km / day
Speed of Venus = 636.3 million / 224.7 days = 2.832 m km / day

Since we are going to calculate the percentage difference between these two speeds, we don't really care about what unit they are in, so we can leave them in the unusual million km / day format.

The question is how much faster Mercury is than Venus, so the percentage difference will be the difference in speeds divided by Venus's speed, multiplied by 100:

(4.152 – 2.832) / 2.832 × 100 = 46.61 %, or cca. 47%.

Potential Shortcuts / Pitfalls

The above calculation is a perfectly good way of arriving at the correct answer, but we in fact performed a couple of completely unnecessary calculations. Let's write out all the calculations we performed in one formula to see what I mean.

Mercury speed calculation: 58 × 6.3 / 88
Venus speed calculation: 101 × 6.3 / 224.7

What do we notice? The × 6.3 is present in both calculations. Since we are going to use the results of these calculations in a division, we can completely omit the × 6.3 from our process. Let's observe:

$$\frac{58 \times \cancel{6.3} \, / \, 88}{101 \times \cancel{6.3} \, / \, 224.7}$$

What does this mean? It means that *we do not need to waste our time calculating the actual speeds* when all we need for a percentage difference is their *relative* speeds in the same units.

The relative speed of Mercury is: 58 / 88 = 0.66
The relative speed of Venus is: 101 / 224.7 = 0.45

Now we can calculate the percentage difference by calculating the actual difference:

0.66 – 0.45 = 0.21

The percentage rise is this difference divided by the starting point and multiplied by 100:

100 × 0.21 / 0.45 = 47%

SET 18, Q3. Correct Answer: E

Reasoning

We need to calculate the distance between Mars and Earth and then the speed of the messages travelling between them.

Calculation

We are told that the delay in response is a minimum of 8m 40s and that this occurs when their distance is at a minimum. We are also told how to calculate this minimum distance, namely by subtracting the Earth – Sun distance from the Mars – Sun distance. This is simply:

228m – 150m = 78 million km

So, each message has to travel 78m km from Mars to Earth. But remember, the question is not about how much time it takes for the message to travel from Mars to Earth but how much time it takes to get a response. If we assume that Earth begins to reply immediately, that response still needs to travel the same distance as well, so the total distance travelled is twice as much as the Earth – Mars distance:

78m × 2 = 156m km

It takes a total of 8m 40s to do this journey. We need first to convert this into seconds which is:

8 × 60 seconds + 40 seconds = 520 seconds

So the speed is now calculated as distance divided by time:

156 million / 520 = 300,000 km/sec

Of course if you remember from school, you'll know that this is the speed of light.

Potential Shortcuts / Pitfalls
You might already know that radio signals travel at the speed of light and what the speed of light is – you should NOT, however, mark that as the correct answer without doing the calculations since the test designer is under no obligation to use realistic data (even though this is *mostly* the case).

SET 19, Q1. Correct Answer: D

Reasoning

The number of people in any group is the product of the population and their percentage. In the case of over 18-year-olds, we are given the inverse data: the percentage of under 18-year-olds, so we must subtract that from 100% to get that interim data.

Calculation

First we need to calculate the number of people who have never been outside Belgium:

10.84 million = 10,840,000
10,840,000 × 2.9 / 100 = 314,360

We know that 98.3% of these people are under 18, so the remaining percentage must be over 18:

100 – 98.3 = 1.7%

This means that 1.7% of the above number is the number of over-18's who have never been outside Belgium.

314,360 * 1.7 /100 = 5344

SET 19, Q2. Correct Answer: C

Reasoning

The number of people in any group is the population multiplied by the percentage size of the group.

Calculation

We are ultimately calculating a percentage of a group which is going to be relative to the population as a whole. As such we can ignore the population as it will cancel out. Just to be clear though, assume that the population of Belgium is B. Then the number of people who watch more than 10hrs of TV is:

59.8 × B / 100 = 0.598B

The number of people who are employed who are within this group would normally be:

0.427 × 0.598B = 0.255B

But the employed group are 25% less likely to be in this group, correct? How do we 'translate' this information into a calculation?

What this essentially tells us is that if the number of employed people who watch 10+ hours of TV was 25% higher, that is when their number would be exactly as we calculated above:

X (number of employed TV watchers) × 1.25 = 0.255B

Let's rearrange our equation again to have × only on one side:

X (number of employed TV watchers) = 0.255B / 1.25 – this is the actual proportion of employed TV-watchers: 0.255B / 1.25 = 0.204B

What's next? We need to know what the total number of TV-watchers is:

59.8% × B / 100 = 0.598B

We know that 0.204B is the number of employed TV-watchers, so the number of non-employed TV watchers must be:

0.598B – 0.204B = 0.394B

We are almost there. The total number of non-employed people is:

(100% – 42.7%) × B / 100 = 0.573B

Now we know the number of non-employed TV watchers and the total number of the non-employed, so we can calculate what percentage of the non-employed also watch 10+ hours of TV every week:

(0.394B / 0.573B) × 100 = 68.8%

SET 19, Q3. Correct Answer: D

Reasoning

First we need to calculate the number of employed people with a driver's licence. This will tell us how many drivers' licences are left as belonging to the non-employed. Once we have that, we can easily calculate what percentage this number represents of the total number of non-employed.

Calculation

The number of people who have a driver's licence is 64.7% of the population. Since we will never need to use the actual numbers, we can omit the population and just assume that the percentages are actual numbers. So the number of drivers' licences is 64.7. The number of these who are not employed but have a driver's licence will be a *minimum* when the number of employed people who have a licence is a *maximum*. Since the number of employed people is smaller than the number of licences, this means *all* employed people have a licence.

If all employed people have a licence, this leaves the following number of licences:

64.7 – 42.7 = 22

So, at least 22% of the population have a licence and are not employed. The total number of people who are not employed is the total minus the employed:

100 – 42.7 = 57.3

So, 22% of 57% of the population have a licence but are not employed:

22 / 57.3 = 0.384

This is the proportion of the non-employed people who have a licence. Multiply it by 100 to make it a percentage:

0.384 × 100 = 38.4%

SET 20, Q1. Correct Answer: D

Reasoning

We need to calculate the revenue from 2008 and then calculate the increase needed to get to the 2009 figure.

Calculation

The revenue from bread sales in 2008 was 7% below the 2010 figure of €87.2 thousand. To reduce by 7% we multiply by 1-0.07 or 0.93:

87.2 × 0.93 = 81.1

In 2009, this had risen to 86.3 thousand, which is a difference of:

86.3 – 81.1 = 5.2

We can now calculate the percentage rise, which is the difference divided by the starting value and then multiplied by 100:

100 × 5.2 / 81.1 = 6.4%

Potential Shortcuts / Pitfalls

Remember that to reduce a number by 7%, you need to multiply by (1-0.07) and not divide by (1+0.07). The latter would have been the correct calculation if the question had said that the 2010 figure was 7% *higher* than the 2008 figure rather than that the 2008 figure was 7% *lower* than the 2010 figure.

Why is this? Let's write everything out. The 2008 value was 7% lower than the 2010 value.

2008 Value = 2010 value – 7%
2008 Value = 1 × 2010 value – 0.07 × 2010 value, or:
2008 Value = 0.93 × 2010 value

If the question had said that the 2010 value was 7% higher than the 2008 value, this would look as follows:

2010 value = 2008 value + 7%
2010 value = 1 × 2008 value + 0.07 × 2008 value
2010 value = 1.07 × 2008 value

2008 value = 2010 value / 1.07

This goes to demonstrate that a small difference in wording can cause a huge difference in calculation methods and, consequently, in the result as well.

SET 20, Q2. Correct Answer: A

Reasoning

We need to calculate the value of sales of sparkling water in 2010 from the data and then adjust this back to 2009.

Calculation

First we need to calculate the value of sparkling water sales in 2010. From the table we can see that total drinks sales came to €44,900 and from the pie chart we see that sparkling water accounted for 29% of this, which is:

$44900 \times 0.29 = €13021$

The question tells us that this figure was 10% higher than in 2009. Please refer back to the Pitfalls and Shortcuts section of the previous explanation. After reading that, it will be clear that this is a case where we need to apply the *second* method. If a number rose by 10% from 2009 to 2010 and we have the 2010 value, we need to divide that value by 1.1 to get the 2009 value:

$13021 / 1.1 = €11837$

SET 20, Q3. Correct Answer: E

Reasoning

We need to calculate the value of all water sales and subtract that from the value of pastry sales. We can perform the two calculations in reverse order as well as we are only seeking the difference between the two numbers.

Calculation

First we must calculate the volume of water sales in order to calculate their value. This is the sum of their respective percentages of total drink sales:

$34\% + 29\% = 63\%$

So water was 63% of total drinks sales, which is:

$44900 \times 0.63 = 28,287$

The value of pastry sales is given as 30,100 and so the difference is:

$€30100 - €28287 = €1813$

SET 21, Q1. Correct Answer: B

Reasoning

We need to calculate the average number of responses, which is the total number of responses divided by the total number of questions.

Calculation

We need to sum the total number of responses to all questions. This is:

$99 + 93 + 90 + 102 + 88 + 110 = 582$

Then we divide the total by the number of questions, which is 6:

$582 / 6 = 97$

Potential Shortcuts / Pitfalls

This is a very easy question but there are two things to point out. First you need to read the question properly and make sure you don't divide by 110 to get 5.3, which is the average number of responses per questionnaire.

Secondly, there is a little shortcut for working out the average of a list of numbers that are reasonable similar. Choose a number that you feel is a reasonable guess. For this example you may have selected 96 as a possibility. Then add up all the differences between the actual scores and your guess. In this example, it would be:

+3 (99)
-3 (93)
-6 (90)
+6 (102)
-8 (88)
+14 (110)

The sum of the above numbers is 6.

If your guess is good and the numbers are reasonably similar this is very easy to do in your head, and much faster than you can type the numbers into a calculator. If the answer you get is 0 then your guess was spot on. In this case you have a total of 6. You need to divide this by the number of questions (6) to get 1, which you add to your guess to get the answer 97.

SET 21, Q2. Correct Answer: C

Reasoning

We need to calculate the total number of marks for each of the two questions. This is done by taking the product of the average and the number of responses. We then need to create a 'range' around this value, because the average can represent any number that can be rounded up or down to that average.

Calculation

The total number of marks received for each question *seems* to be:

Q1 99 × 8.1 = 802

Q6 110 × 7.2 = 792

We are told that both questions got the same total number of marks, which at first glance doesn't appear to be true from our calculation. However, the averages given are only accurate to 1 decimal place. What this means is that the averages can actually 'hide' a different number which was rounded up or down to that average.

Let's consider Q1 – the average is 8.1. Following the rules of rounding, this 8.1 may have been, before rounding, anywhere between 8.05 and 8.149, and it would still have been given as 8.1. So, the number of marks received by Q1 could be between:

99 × 8.05 = 797
99 × 8.149 = 807

Similarly, for Q6 it could be between:

110 × 7.15 = 787
110 × 7.249 = 797

We can now see that if both questions received the same total score, it must have been 797, as this is the only number that is present in both ranges.

SET 21, Q3. Correct Answer: E

Reasoning

We need to calculate the average score last year, taking into account the fact it is a number from which a 10% drop resulted in 7.2.

Calculation

Once again this is quite an easy question but some people get a little confused with averages going up and down. In most questions of this type, we are given a value and told that it has increased or decreased to another value by a given percentage. In that case we simply multiply our value by the percentage and then add it to, or subtract it from the original value.

It turns out that this is no different if we look at it from the point of view of 2009. If we assume that the average mark was A in 2009, then the 2010 mark would be calculated like this:

A – 10% = 7.2

Recall that we said that in percentage increases and decreases, we can always consider the original number to be 100%:

100% A – 10% A = 7.2, or in other words:
90% A = 7.2
90% is then converted to:
0.9 × A = 7.2

We can now rearrange this and solve it by dividing both sides of the equation by 0.9:

A = 7.2 / 0.9
A = 8

Potential Shortcuts / Pitfalls

You must be clear about which operation you are doing. It is very easy to multiply 7.2 by 1.1 to get 7.9 in error. That would only be the correct calculation if the question had stated that the 2009 value was 10% *higher* than the 2010 value.

SET 22, Q1. Correct Answer: E

Reasoning

We need to calculate the difference in sales between the two years and then make it a percentage.

Calculation

Let us assume that the total revenue in 2009 was T. Then the value of beer sales would be:

T × 29.1 / 100 = 0.291T

In 2010, the revenue rose by 5% to:

T × 1.05 = 1.05T

Beer now accounted for 30.4% of this new total revenue, which is:

1.05T × 30.4 / 100 = 0.3192T

This is a difference of:

0.3192T – 0.291T = 0.0282T

The percentage difference is then this difference divided by the starting value and multiplied by 100:

100 × (0.0282T / 0.291T) = 9.7%

Potential Shortcuts / Pitfalls
The total sales value doesn't actually need to be used at all, although it does make the explanation more understandable. Furthermore, none of the '/ 100' operations need be done either, as this is a percentage calculation and they all cancel out. This means that we could have calculated with 29.1 instead of 0.291, 30.4 instead of 0.304, and so on. Not only does this save time, it also eliminates a potential source of error, as you do not need to perform the 'conversion' from percentage to decimal.

SET 22, Q2. Correct Answer: B

Reasoning

We need to calculate the value of tobacco sales in 2010 and then calculate the total sales from that. We can do that because we know what percentage of the total sales that value represents.

Calculation

The question tells us that the revenue from tobacco sales in 2009 was € 122,000 and this grew by 0.3% in 2010. To increase the value by 0.3%, we need to multiply by 0.3 and divide by 100 and then add in the original value. This is the same as multiplying by 1.003:

122,000 × 1.003 = 122,336

This is the value of tobacco sales in 2010 which were 10.3% of total sales. To put it in a formula:

Total Sales × 10.3% = 122,336
Total Sales × 0.103 = 122,336

To calculate the total sales, we need to divide both sides of the equation by 0.103:

Total Sales = 122,336 / 0.103
Total Sales = 1,188,000

Now we must apply the correct order of magnitude. The answer options are in millions, so we must the decimal point six positions to the left:

1,180,000.00 = €1.188 million

SET 22, Q3. Correct Answer: D

Reasoning

We need to calculate how much the wine sales need to increase to equal those of beer.

Calculation

Assume that the total sales in 2010 are T; then the value of beer sales will be:

T × 30.4 / 100 = 0.304T

and for wine they will be:

T × 29.2 / 100 = 0.292T

This is a difference of:

0.304T – 0.292T = 0.012T

So, wine sales need to increase by 0.012T, which, as a proportion of current wine sales, is:

0.012T / 0.292T = 0.041

Note that the 'T' cancels out at this point – we in fact never needed it; it was just included for demonstration purposes. Multiply this by 100 to make it a percentage:

0.041 × 100 = 4.1%

SET 23, Q1. Correct Answer: D

Reasoning

The number of people vaccinated is the population multiplied by the percentage vaccinated.

Calculation

The number of people vaccinated in Italy is:

60098 × 94.8 / 100 = 56973

The number of people vaccinated in the UK is:

61899 × 91.6 / 100 = 56699

This is a difference of:

56973 – 56699 = 274

Now we must check the order of magnitude. The populations are given in thousands and so the answer needs to be multiplied by 1000:

274 × 1000 = 274,000

SET 23, Q2. Correct Answer: B

Reasoning

The number vaccinated is the population multiplied by the rate of vaccination.

Calculation

The population of the Netherlands in 2005 was 5% lower than in 2010, and so we must multiply by (100% – 5%), or 0.95:

16653 × 0.95 = 15820

The rate of vaccination in 2005 was 2 *percentage points* higher than in 2010. Remember that when we are talking about percentage points, we *add* and *subtract* (as opposed to *dividing* when it comes to percentage changes), which is:

54.6 + 2 = 56.6

Now we can calculate the number of people vaccinated in 2005:

15820 × 56.6 / 100 = 8954

The number of people vaccinated in 2010 is:

16653 × 54.6 / 100 = 9093

This is a difference of:

8954 – 9093 = -139

We also need to check the order of magnitude and as the population is given in thousands then so too is the answer:

-139 * 1000 = -139,000

Since the number is negative, the number vaccinated in 2005 was 139,000 *fewer* than in 2010.

SET 23, Q3. Correct Answer: D

Reasoning

The calculation for the number of people vaccinated is the population multiplied by the rate of vaccination.

Now, if we add together the number of people who have had the DPT vaccine and the number who have had the MMR vaccine, we would get more than the population of the country, because some people have had *both* vaccinations. These people have been counted twice, and so we must subtract them. Also, the people who have had *neither* vaccine have not been counted, and so we must add them in. This means that the population can be defined as:

Population = MMR + DPT – both + neither

From this point, we can fill in the known values and start figuring out how to calculate the unknown values, one of which will be the correct answer.

Calculation

Let's fill in what we know. Since most of our data is in percentages, let's stick with that for now. In order to do that, we need to express the population in percentage form, which is of course all the people who live in the country, that is, 100%:

100 = 87.3 + 83.2 – (both vaccines) + (neither vaccine)

Now remember that we are looking for the *minimum* number of people who must be vaccinated against both vaccines. Since we subtract the 'both' group and add the 'neither' group, it follows that 'both' will be lowest when 'neither' is lowest as well. What is the lowest the 'neither' group can get? The lowest possible value is of course 0, when there is nobody who doesn't have either vaccination. If 'neither' is zero, the equation looks like this:

100 = 87.3 + 83.2 – (both vaccines)

Let's solve this for (both vaccines) by re-arranging things to get it to be alone on one side, and everything else on the other side:

(both vaccines) = (87.3 + 83.2) – 100
(both vaccines) = 70.5

So, at least 70.5% of the population must have had both vaccinations. We are looking for the actual number of people, so let's multiply this by the population, which is:

1339 × 70.5 / 100 = 944

And finally we need to correct for the order of magnitude, as the population is given in thousands. This means that the final result will be 944,000.

Potential Shortcuts / Pitfalls
The most crucial points to take away from this question are the following:

1. 83.2% of the population is vaccinated against DPT. That means that 16.8% are not.
2. If ALL of those who are *not* vaccinated against DPT (all 16.8%) *are* vaccinated against MMR, that leaves 87.3 – 16.8 = 70.5%. These 70.5% are vaccinated against MMR and *must also* be vaccinated against DPT because we already subtracted everybody who was not vaccinated against DTP (16.8%).

I am sure you will agree that this realisation is the key to solving this test. Once you've done that, there really is no challenge in performing those few subtractions. In the explanations, we demonstrated two ways of coming to this realisation: one in the calculations and one in the shortcuts section.
In tests like this, it is perfectly normal to spend 80% of the time allocated for the question staring at it before coming to this realisation – and then quickly performing the actual calculations.

SET 24, Q1. Correct Answer: D

Reasoning

We need to calculate the percentage difference between the highest and lowest values from the point of view of the lowest value.

Calculation

First we need to find the highest data value in the table. This is Italy in 2005 where there are 9.6 shoe shops per 100,000 people. Similarly, the lowest value is for Spain in 2010 where there are 7.2 shops per 100,000 people. The difference is:

9.6 – 7.2 = 2.4

To calculate this as a percentage of the lower value we divide by the lower value and multiply by 100:

(2.4 / 7.2) * 100 = 33.3%

SET 24, Q2. Correct Answer: C

Reasoning

The number of shops is the population multiplied by the rate (number of shops per head of population). The population increases twice by 5% from an unknown value in 2000 to the known value in 2010.

Calculation

We need to multiply the population of France by the number of shops per person to calculate the total number of shops. First though, we need to calculate the population of France in 2000. Let's assume that it is P and it grows by 5% each five years to become 62139:

P × 1.05 × 1.05 = 62139

With this done we can now re-arrange the equation to have P (the value we are looking for) on one side, and everything else on the other side:

P = 62139 / (1.05 × 1.05)
P = 56361.9

The number of shops in 2000 is then:

56361.9 * 8.3 = 467803.77, which we can round to 467804

We could leave the order of magnitude correction to the end or do it now. The population is in thousands so we need to multiply by 1000 and the rate is per 100,000 so we need to divide by 100,000. The overall effect is to divide by 100:

467804 / 100 = 4678

Similarly, the number of shoe shops in 2010 is:

62139 × 8.6 / 100 = 5344

This gives us a difference of:

5344 – 4678 = 666

Potential Shortcuts / Pitfalls
Remember to apply the correction for order of magnitude. Multiply by 1000 for the population and divide by 100,000 for the rate.

Also, two important issues emerge when it comes to calculating the 2000 population.
1. Make sure you notice that the population figure given is for 2010, not 2000. If you fail to do this, you will end up with an incorrect population figure.

2. Also make sure you remember that if a population increases by 5% annually for two years, this is *not* the same as saying that it increased a total of 10%, because the second increase took place over an already increased population.

SET 24, Q3. Correct Answer: D

Reasoning

We need to calculate the number of shops in Spain in both years and then work out the percentage difference between them.

Calculation

The number of shops in Spain is calculated by multiplying the population by the per capita rate of shops. For now though, let's assume that the population of Spain in 2000 was P and it increased in 2005 by 7%. Why can we do this? Again, this is sufficient because *we are only interested in percentage figures*: the two values to compare are percentages, the increase of the population is a percentage, and the answer we are seeking is also a percentage. In fact, we *could* simply omit the population altogether, but let's leave the P in so we can clearly understand why it is not needed.

The population increased by 7% from 2000 to 2005:

$P \times 1.07 = 1.07P$

The number of shops in 2000 is then:

$P \times 7.3 = 7.3P$

The actual number is of course 7.3P / 100 000, but since the population is only a letter, we don't need to perform this step.

And the number of shops in 2005 is:

$1.07P \times 7.6 = 8.132P$

This is a difference of:

$8.132P - 7.3P = 0.832P$

As a percentage of the lower, 2000 value, this is:

$100 \times (0.832P / 7.3P) = 11.4\%$

This is the point, by the way, where the P cancels out (it is in both the numerator and the denominator), and this is proof that we never needed it in the first place.

Potential Shortcuts / Pitfalls

We are not given the population of Spain in 2000 or 2005 but it is not needed. In the calculation we assumed a general value for the population (P) and it cancelled out in the calculation. Furthermore, there is actually no need to bother with the order of magnitude correction as it is the same for each term and also cancels out.

SET 25, Q1. Correct Answer: D

Reasoning

The percentage rise is the difference between the two years divided by the starting value and then multiplied by 100.

Calculation

We need to calculate the difference in revenue from the electrical department between 2009 and 2010:

$1.99m - 1.87m = 0.12m$

As a percentage of the starting value this is:

$100 \times (0.12m / 1.87m) = 6.4\%$.

SET 25, Q2. Correct Answer: D

Reasoning

We need to calculate the value of sales in the garden dept. in 2010 from the data and then adjust this back to 2009.

Calculation

First we need to calculate the value of garden sales in 2010. From the table we can see that 'other' sales came to €2.23m and from the pie chart we see that the garden dept. accounted for 34% of this, which is:

$2.23m \times 0.34 = 0.758m$

The question tells us that this figure was 4% higher than in 2009. Remember the 'inverse visualisation' method we mentioned earlier? The 2009 figure increased by 4% to get to the (known) 2010 figure, that is, 2009 × 1.04 = 0.758m. To get to the 2009 figure, we must divide it by 1.04:

$0.758m / 1.04 = €0.729m$

This is the same as €729,000.

Potential Shortcuts / Pitfalls

Note that the 2009 figure rose by 4% and so we must divide by 1.04 to get back to the 2009 figure from the 2010 value. Don't confuse this with the case where we are told that the 2010 figure is 4% higher, in which case you would have had to multiply by 1-0.04 or 0.96. This is a very common mistake!

SET 25, Q3. Correct Answer: B

Reasoning

We need to calculate the value of stationery sales in 2010 and adjust back to 2009 and then calculate this as a percentage of total sales.

Calculation

First we must calculate the value of stationery sales in 2010. This is 27% of €2.23m:

€2.23m × 0.27 = €0.6021m

This was 3.2% lower than in 2009. Put another way, this means that the 2009 value minus 3.2% equals the (known) 2010 value:

2010 value – 3.2% = €0.6021m
100% 2010 value – 3.2% = 0.6021m
96.8% 2010 value = 0.6021

We need to divide both sides of the equation by 96.8% (that is, by 0.968) to get the 2010 value:

2010 value = 0.6021 / 0.968
2010 value = 0.622

The total value of all sales in 2009 was the sum of all the values in the 2009 data column:

6.62m + 1.98m + 1.87m + 2.11m = 12.58m

As a percentage of this total, the stationery sales are:

100 × (0.622m / 12.58m) = 4.94%

SET 26, Q1. Correct Answer: E

Reasoning

We need to calculate the consumption per person in each country and select the highest. The calculation required is total consumption divided by the population.

Calculation

As the figures for both population and consumption are given in thousands, they cancel each other out, which will leave the answer in tonnes per person. If we multiply this by a thousand it will give the answer in kg per person:

Belgium – (175 / 10415) × 1000 = 16.8
Estonia – (16.6 / 1346) × 1000 = 12.3
Hungary – (131 / 9973) × 1000 = 13.1
Italy – (932 / 58645) × 1000 = 15.9
Switzerland – (129 / 7441) × 1000 = 17.3

Then we can see that Switzerland is clearly the highest.

Potential Shortcuts / Pitfalls

It is easy to see that the multiplication by 1000 was not really necessary (though it does make the figures easier to see and compare.) However, there is still more we could have omitted as well.

If you had mentally increased Estonia's population and consumption by an order of magnitude (multiplied both figures by 10) then it is clear that although the population would be about 30% higher than Belgium's, its consumption would *still* be lower, so it couldn't possibly be the highest – therefore there's no need to calculate it. Hungary's population is so close to 10000 (thousand), it can easily be seen that the per capita consumption is going to be around 13. If you've already calculated Belgium's at 16.8 then clearly Hungary is not going to be a contender, so don't waste time calculating it!

The remaining 3 are reasonably close and so you would need to calculate each and compare.

This means that we managed to eliminate one step (multiplying by 1000 to get the per kilogram consumption) and two countries (Hungary and Estonia). Put together, this means that we saved about 50% of the calculations (and the time) needed to answer the question.

SET 26, Q2. Correct Answer: D

Reasoning

We need to calculate the per capita consumption (consumption divided by population) for both years and then calculate the percentage difference.

Calculation

Before we can calculate the per capita consumption in 2010, we must first calculate the population for that year, which has risen by 8.3% since 2005:

$9973 \times 1.083 = 10800.759$

Now we can calculate the per capita consumption in 2010:

$138 / 10800.759 = 0.012777$

Similarly, for 2005 it is:

$131 / 9973 = 0.013135$

We can now calculate the percentage change, which is the 2010 value less the 2005 value divided by the 2005 value. This is then multiplied by 100 to make it a percentage:

$((0.012777 - 0.013135) / 0.013135) \times 100 = -2.73\%$

Potential Shortcuts / Pitfalls

The population of Hungary is present in every term of each calculation and actually cancels out and needn't be used at all. How?

Let's write out the last calculation above using named parameters instead of numbers.

$$\frac{\text{Per capita } 2010 - \text{Per capita } 2005}{\text{Per capita } 2010} \times 100$$

Now let's recall how we calculated the per capita figures:

$$\frac{\dfrac{\text{Consumption } 2010}{\text{Population } 2010} \quad \dfrac{\text{Consumption } 2005}{\text{Population } 2005}}{\dfrac{\text{Consumption } 2005}{\text{Population } 2005}} \times 100$$

And let's also recall how we calculated the 2010 population:

$$\frac{\dfrac{\text{Consumption } 2010}{\text{Population } 2005 \times 1.083} \quad \dfrac{\text{Consumption } 2005}{\text{Population } 2005}}{\dfrac{\text{Consumption } 2005}{\text{Population } 2005}} \times 100$$

Do you notice something interesting? In all of the fractions above, the denominator contains 'Population 2005'. This means that *we can simply omit it* – since it is present in every calculation, it makes

no difference whether it is there or not. This simplifies the calculation to:

$$\frac{\dfrac{\text{Consumption } 2010}{1.083} - \text{Consumption } 2005}{\text{Consumption } 2005} \times 100$$

With numbers, it looks like this:

$$\left(\frac{\left(\dfrac{138}{1.083} - 131\right)}{131}\right) * 100 = -2.73\%$$

In addition to this being a simpler calculation, it also has an added benefit: it you try it out, you will see that the above can be entered as a continuous string of 3 operations into any calculator, even those primitive ones without memory that you will be provided (on screen or physically) at the EPSO test centre.

Using the traditional calculation method shown in the Calculation section, you would have had to jot down interim results and the whole process would have taken much longer.

SET 26, Q3. Correct Answer: C

Reasoning

We need to calculate the total volume of chocolate produced and, from that, the volume exported.

Calculation

The table tells us that the total consumption is 129 thousand tonnes and the question tells us that 78% of this is home-made:

$129 \times 0.78 = 100.62$

This represents 12% of Switzerland's total production so, to calculate the total, we must divide by 12% or 0.12:

$100.62 / 0.12 = 838.5$

(Remember the 'inverse visualisation method we discussed earlier. If total production $\times 0.12 = 100.62$, then $100.62 / 0.12 = $ total production.)

This is 838.5 thousand tonnes, which is the total amount produced. As they have eaten 12% of this, then they must have exported (100-12)% = 88% of it:

$838.5 \times 0.88 = 737.88$

which can be rounded to 738. Remember that this is in thousands of tonnes.

SET 27, Q1. Correct Answer: B

Reasoning

We need to calculate the growth in forest coverage, which is the difference divided by the starting point and then multiplied by 100.

Calculation

The growth in forest coverage is the difference between the two years divided by the 1990 value and then multiplied by 100. We need to do this for each country:

Denmark – $100 \times (67.2 - 63.9) / 63.9 = 5.2\%$
France – $100 \times (649.5 - 602.4) / 602.4 = 7.8\%$
Georgia – $100 \times (112.9 - 110.2) / 110.2 = 2.5\%$
Poland – $100 \times (706.8 - 715.9) / 715.9 = -1.3\%$
UK – $100 \times (193.2 - 189.1) / 189.1 = 2.2\%$

Clearly, France is the highest.

Potential Shortcuts / Pitfalls
Because we are just comparing relative values, we don't necessarily need the exact values nor are we concerned about any adjustments for the order of magnitude. As all calculations share the same '100 x' element, it can be omitted for all of them.

Also, taking the difference and dividing by the starting value is the same as dividing the 2010 value by the 1990 value and subtracting 1. If we are subtracting one from all of them then we don't need to bother with that either. This would result in the following calculations:

Denmark – $67.2 / 63.9 = 1.052$
France – $649.5 / 602.4 = 1.078$
Georgia – $112.9 / 110.2 = 1.025$
Poland – $706.8 / 715.9 = 0.987$
UK – $193.2 / 189.1 = 1.022$

As you can see, the numbers are slightly different and they are not percentages, but we can still clearly pick France's value as being the highest.

Another interesting thing we can notice is Poland's figure. It is a number smaller than 1 because the forest area there actually decreased from 1990 to 2010. This can be seen at a glance, so we don't even

need to calculate Poland.

What else can we see if we look closely? The growths in area for Georgia and the UK are very small, and they occur on a quite large base (i.e. the forest area existing in 1990 was already quite large). This should tell us that these growth *percentages* will be much smaller than those of France and Denmark, so we don't need to calculate those either, leaving us only two countries.

Finally, looking at Denmark and France, we can see one more interesting thing. The increase in forested hectares in Denmark in much smaller than in France, but it also occurs from a much smaller base. This is the reason we cannot simply pick France – we do need to perform the actual calculations for these two countries.

SET 27, Q2. Correct Answer: D

Reasoning

We need to calculate the proportion of Georgia that is covered by forest. We can then calculate what coverage that would mean in Denmark and work out the difference between that number and the actual coverage.

Calculation

The coverage is simply the amount of forest divided by the total area. For Georgia, this would be:

$112.9 / 69.7 = 1.62$

We need to be aware here of the units of measurement. The country area is in km^2 while the forest coverage is in hectares. The table tells us that 1 km^2 is 100 hectares.

This means that we should actually have converted 69.7 hectares into 0.697 km^2 and then performed the calculation. But remember: we are looking for a *percentage value*. In order to get a percentage, we would have multiplied the result by 100 – the exact opposite step, so these two operations cancel each other out and the above 1.62 is actually the forest coverage of Georgia as a percentage.

The proportion of coverage for Denmark is calculated the same way, by dividing the area of forest by the total area. However, we don't know what the area of forest is, as this is what we are trying to determine. We can write this as:

X / 43.1

What we *do* know is that this operation should result in 1.62 – this is when the two coverage percentages are the same:

X / 43.1 = 1.62

We can now get × on one side of the equation and everything else on the other side:

X = 43.1 * 1.62
X = 69.822

Again, we did not convert the 1.62% into 0.162 by dividing by 100 because we would have performed the exact opposite operation at the end to convert the resulting 0.69822 km^2 into hectares.

Based on the above, the amount needed to equal that of Georgia would be 69.822 (thousand) hectares. Denmark already has 67.2 (thousand) which is a difference of:

69822 – 67200 = 2622 hectares

SET 27, Q3. Correct Answer: B

Reasoning

We need to calculate the overall average which is the total forest coverage divided by the total country area, also accounting for the difference in units.

Calculation

The total forest coverage is the sum of all the forest areas listed:

67.2 + 649.5 + 112.9 + 706.8 + 193.2 = 1729.6 thousand ha

The total area of the countries is the sum of all the areas:

43.1 + 544 + 69.7 + 312.7 + 242.9 = 1212.4 thousand km^2

Since the forest coverage and the country area are both in thousands, we don't need to deal with that. We *do* need to take a moment to consider the relationship between hectares and km^2, which is 100 hectares to a square kilometre. This means that we would have to divide the forest coverage figure by 100 before proceeding with the division below, but remember, again, that the next step after that would be to multiply by 100 to get a percentage figure. The two operations *cancel each other out* and are therefore not needed.

The overall average is then:

1729.6 / 1212.4 = 1.43

Because of the above simplifications, this is already the percentage figure as well, and therefore the correct answer.

Potential Shortcuts / Pitfalls

The overall average is the total forest coverage divided by the total country area. A common mistake is to think that it is easier (and also correct) to simply calculate an average of the individual coverage areas.

This would give an answer of 1.49%, which is indeed provided as one of the answer options. The reason that this is not correct is because *each country has a different area* and the larger countries affect the overall average much more than the smaller ones.

SET 28, Q1. Correct Answer: A

Reasoning

Speed is calculated as distance divided by time. Since the answer options are in metres / second, and the distance is already given in metres, the easiest thing to do is convert the winning time into seconds.

Calculation

The total time taken for the medley was 3 minutes and 48.7 seconds, which we need to convert to seconds before we can use it. To do this, multiply the minutes by 60 and add in the seconds:

(3 × 60) + 48.7 = 228.7

The winner spent 26.2% of the total time doing the butterfly leg of the race, which is:

228.7 × 0.262 = 59.92s

So, he travelled 100m (one fourth of the total distance of 400 metres) in 59.92 seconds, which gives an average speed of:

100m / 59.92s = 1.67 m/s

SET 28, Q2. Correct Answer: C

Reasoning

The speed is calculated by dividing the distance covered by the time taken. The percentage difference is then the difference divided by the *slower* speed (since the question was how much faster the gold medallist was) and then multiplied by 100.

Calculation

Before we can calculate the speeds we must first convert the times into seconds. This is done by multiplying the minutes by 60 and then adding in the seconds:

1m 58.31s = 60 + 58.31 = 118.31
1m 59.88s = 60 + 59.88 = 119.88

The winner's speed is then:

200 / 118.31 = 1.6905 m/s

And the bronze medal winner's speed is:

200 / 119.88 = 1.6683 m/s

The percentage difference is:

100 × (1.6905 – 1.6683) / 1.6683 = 1.3%

Potential Shortcuts / Pitfalls

Because the men are racing over the same distance (200 metres), we do not actually need to calculate their speeds – the percentage difference in the *times* it took to swim the distance will be the same as the percentage difference between their *speeds* would be.

Following this logic, we can simply our calculation to:

$$\left(\frac{119.88 \ 0 \ 118.31}{119.88} \right) * 100 = 1.3\%$$

Note that we divided the difference by the higher number. Why? The higher number represents the time of the slower swimmer (the bronze medallist). Since the question asked how much faster the gold medallist was than the bronze medallist, we need to calculate the percentage increase on the basis of the slower swimmer's time.

SET 28, Q3. Correct Answer: B

Reasoning

The calculation for speed is distance divided by time and the calculation for distance is speed multiplied by time. We will use the first to calculate the silver medallist's speed in the last segment of the race, and the latter to calculate the distance he covered after the gold medallist completed the race.

Calculation

The overall average speed of the silver medal winner is calculated by dividing the distance by the time taken:

100m / 50.99s = 1.96 m/s

In the last few metres of the race he was travelling 10% faster than this:

1.96 × 1.1 = 2.16 m/s

The difference in time between the gold and silver medallists is:

50.99 – 50.91 = 0.08s

So, he was swimming at 2.16 m/s for 0.08 seconds; therefore in that time he travelled:

2.16m/s × 0.08s = 0.173m

which to the nearest centimetre is 17.

SET 29, Q1. Correct Answer: C

Reasoning

We need to calculate the total passenger-kilometres for France (which is total passengers multiplied by average journey length), and then the average kilometres per journey in the UK.

Calculation

First, we need to find the total number of kilometres travelled on all French journeys. This is the total number of passengers multiplied by the average journey length:

308.9m × 170km = 52513m km

The total number of passenger kilometres in Britain is exactly the same (this information is given in the question text), but it is travelled by 514.2m passengers, so the average journey length needs to be calculated as total distance divided by number of passengers:

52513m km / 514.2m = 102.1 km

SET 29, Q2. Correct Answer: E

Reasoning

The figure for journeys per capita is the total number of passengers divided by the total population.

Calculation

We need to calculate the journeys per capita for 2010 and 2005. But first we need to calculate the population for 2010, which is 3.7% higher than in 2005:

82409 thousand × 1.037 = 85458 thousand

The journeys per person in 2010 is then:

531.9 million / 85458 thousand = 0.00622411

As the total journeys are in millions and the population is in thousands, the result needs to be multiplied by 1000 (we divided millions by thousands):

0.00622411 × 1000 = 6.224 (we can round to three decimals here)

Similarly, for 2005 it is:

526.3 million / 82409 thousand * 1000 = 6.386

This gives us a percentage difference of:

100 × (6.224 -6.386) / 6.386 = -2.5%

The result of the division is not exactly -2.5%, but that is the closest available answer option.

Potential Shortcuts / Pitfalls
If you want to save a little time, you may realise that the order of magnitude corrections were unnecessary: you can always suspect that when the question is about *percentage changes*.

More interestingly, the population is not needed either, as that value also cancels out. (For a demonstration of how this 'cancelling' works, refer to the shortcuts section of the explanation for question 2 in Set 26.)

SET 29, Q3. Correct Answer: B

Reasoning

The journeys per capita figure is the total number of passengers divided by the total population.

Calculation

The number of journeys per capita in Italy is:

292.3 / 58645 = 0.004984

However, the passengers are in millions and the population is in thousands and so we need to apply the order of magnitude correction by multiplying by 1000 to get:

0.004984 × 1000 = 4.984

Similarly for Spain:

183.9 / 43060 × 1000 = 4.271

This is a difference of:

4.984 – 4.271 = 0.713 or 0.71

Potential Shortcuts / Pitfalls
Here, the order of magnitude IS important and does NOT cancel out. Since we are not talking about *percentages* but about the *actual number* of journeys, the multiplication by 1000 makes a big difference.

One tiny time-saver you can apply is to avoid multiplying by 1000 in both calculations and instead move the decimal three positions to the right for both results at the very end.

SET 30, Q1. Correct Answer: D

Reasoning

The percentage fall is the difference between the two years' totals divided by the starting value and then multiplied by 100.

Calculation

We need to calculate the total sales for both 2009 and 2010, which is the sum of their columns. For 2009 it is:

43.6 + 1.4 + 2.9 + 1.6 + 4.4 = 53.9

And for 2010 it is:

39.2 + 1.8 + 3.4 + 1.5 + 4.6 = 50.5

The percentage difference is then the difference divided by the starting value and multiplied by 100:

100 × (50.5 – 53.9) / 53.9 = -6.3%

SET 30, Q2. Correct Answer: E

Reasoning

We need to calculate the market share, or percentage of overall sales, for Jazz DVDs and calculate the percentage increase.

Calculation

First, we need to calculate the total sales of DVDs for both years. For 2009 it is:

43.6 + 1.4 + 2.9 + 1.6 + 4.4 = 53.9

And for 2010 it is:

39.2 + 1.8 + 3.4 + 1.5 + 4.6 = 50.5

The percentage of overall sales of Jazz in 2009 is:

(1.4 / 53.9) × 100 = 2.6%

And for 2010 it is:

(1.8 / 50.5) × 100 = 3.56%

The percentage increase is therefore the difference divided by the starting value:

100 × (3.56 – 2.6) / 2.6 = 37%

Potential Shortcuts / Pitfalls
The percentage share of the market rises from 2.6% to 3.56%. This is *not* a 0.96% rise in market share: it is a 0.96 *percentage point* rise. The percentage rise needs to be calculated as a proportion of the starting value. This is an especially dangerous pitfall you can fall into in this particular question, as 0.96 is also among the answer options.

SET 30, Q3. Correct Answer: D

Reasoning

We need to calculate the number of DVDs sold to teenagers and how many teenagers bought them.

Calculation

First we must calculate the number of Pop DVDs sold to teenagers. There are 39.2m sold in total and 94.3% of these are sold to teenagers. This is:

39.2m × 0.943 = 36.97m

There are 61.092m people in the UK and 12.1% of them are teenagers. This is:

61.092m × 0.121 = 7.392m

So, 7.392m people bought 36.97m DVDs. This is an average per person of:

36.97m / 7.392m = 5

Potential Shortcuts / Pitfalls
By keeping the millions in the calculations at all times it is easy to see how they cancel out at the end and no correction for the order of magnitude is required.

There is another, quite bold, shortcut that you could take if you are confident enough in your estimating skills. Take another look at the answer options:

2
3
4
5
6

You may notice that they are whole numbers and in terms of percentage difference, they are quite far apart from each other:

2
3 (150% of 2)
4 (133% of 3)
5 (125% of 4)
6 (120% of 5)

Now recall what percentage of pop DVD's are sold to teenagers: 94.3%. 94.3% is in fact quite close to saying that *almost all* pop DVD's are sold to teenagers. The percentage difference between 100% and 94.3% is certainly much smaller than the difference between any two neighbouring answer options.

What does this tell us? It means that we can assume that *all* of the pop DVD's were sold to teenagers, save ourselves one calculation, and then pick the answer option that is closest to whatever result we get.

If we do that, we would divide the total pop DVD discs sold by the number of teenagers, and get:

39.2m / 7.392m = 5.303

The closest answer option to this is D, that is, 5.

SET 31, Q1. Correct Answer: A

Reasoning

We need to calculate the difference in revenue between 5 glasses of wine and a whole bottle.

Calculation

Calculate the price of 5 glasses of each wine and subtract the price of the whole bottle:

Chablis – 5 × 8.95 – 31.95 = 12.80
Chardonnay – 5 × 7.50 – 28.50 = 9.00
Margaux – 5 × 7.15 – 27.00 = 8.75
Sancerre – 5 × 9.20 – 34.80 = 11.20
Tavel – 5 × 7.95 – 29.50 = 10.25

From this we can see that Chablis is clearly the highest.

Potential Shortcuts / Pitfalls
Unlike with many questions of this type, you *cannot* omit the '5 x' that appears on each line because it is not applied to the bottle price as well. If the bottle price was multiplied or divided by the glass price (for example if the question had been about the highest *percentage* of extra profit) then the '5 x' would be common to all terms and could be omitted.

SET 31, Q2. Correct Answer: C

Reasoning

We need to calculate the profit on 1 bottle of Sancerre and then work out the number of bottles sold by dividing the total profit by the profit on one bottle.

Calculation

The first thing to do is to figure out what the unknown is in the question. We can set this to be *either* the profit on one bottle *or* the price of a bottle before profit. Whichever we choose, we will end up being able to determine the profit on one bottle of Sancerre.

If the cost of a bottle of Sancerre before profit is B then:

B + Profit = 34.80

We know that the profit rate is 220%. What does this mean? It means that the profit is 2.2 times as much as the cost of a bottle before profit, so:

B + 2.2 × B = 34.80

We can now perform various operations to get 1 B (price of a bottle before profit) on one side:

3.2 × B = 34.8
B = 34.80 / 3.2 = 10.875

This is the cost of a bottle before profit, and so the profit on each bottle is the selling price minus this cost price:

34.8 – 10.875 = 23.925

If the profit on one bottle is 23.925 then the number of bottles needed to produce 287.10 profit is:

287.1 / 23.925 = 12

Potential Shortcuts / Pitfalls
This question may appear more difficult than it really is simply because the profit is more than 100%. Treat it in the same way as any other profit margin. The crucial juncture at which you could go down the wrong path is how you define the price of the bottle before profit: if you say that it is the selling price divided by 2.2, that is incorrect: it would only be correct if the profit rate was 120%.

SET 31, Q3. Correct Answer: B

Reasoning

We need to calculate the revenue from one bottle of wine when sold by the glass and then calculate the percentage difference from the point of view of the revenue when sold by the bottle.

Calculation

We first need to calculate the number of glasses in one bottle:

750 / 187.5 = 4

The revenue from 4 glasses will be:

4 × 7.95 = 31.80

The percentage increase in revenue is the difference in revenue when sold by the glass compared with when sold by the bottle, divided by the revenue when sold by the bottle and multiplied by 100:

$100 \times (31.80 - 29.50) / 29.50 = 7.8\%$

Potential Shortcuts / Pitfalls
Most of this could be done by mental arithmetic for speed. Let's see how this can be accomplished.

750 / 187.5 – this seems to be quite close to 800 / 200, which is 4 – so let's assume this is 4 as well.
4×7.95 – this is almost the same as 4×8, so let's work with that – the result is 32. We only need to subtract 4×0.05 to get the accurate result, which is 31.8.
The revenue from a bottle is 29.50. The difference in revenue would then be 2.30 and the percentage difference can then be calculated using a calculator.

With some practice and confidence, this method can be significantly faster than typing everything in.

SET 32, Q1. Correct Answer: C

Reasoning

We need to calculate the percentage growth of Dutch visitors required to return to the old level.

Calculation

The percentage growth is simply the number required divided by the starting point and then multiplied by 100. The difference between the two years is:

$170 - 164 = 6$

As a percentage this is:

$100 \times 6 / 164 = 3.66\%$

Potential Shortcuts / Pitfalls
If we had calculated the fall in visitors between 2005 and 2010 it would have been 3.53%. It is a frequently made error to assume that if this is the *fall* in percentage terms, the same percentage *increase* must be needed to recover to the previous level. This is incorrect, because that same percentage growth now takes place from a smaller base.

Not sure about this? Here is a simple example you should try to remember.

You have 10 apples and then the number of apples you have decreases by 20% (you eat two). If you then increase the number of your apples by 20%, you would not have 10 apples again, as 8×1.2 is only 9.6. You would need an increase of 25% (i.e. get two apples) to get back to the original 10.

SET 32, Q2. Correct Answer: A

Reasoning

We need to calculate the number of Dutch visitors to each country in 2015 and then take the difference between the two figures.

Calculation

We usually define percentage growth as the difference divided by the starting point, but we have noted before that we can also divide the end point by the starting point and subtract 1.
For France this would be:

$((312 / 301) - 1) \times 100 = 3.65\%$

We then need to calculate the same percentage growth for France between 2010 and 2015. When we do that, we would convert 3.65 to 0.365 and add in the original value (1), so in the end, we would multiply by 1.0365. If we realise this, we can save ourselves some time, as 1.0365 is exactly the figure we would arrive at if we do this:

$312 / 301 = 1.0365$

We can now easily calculate the 2015 projected value:

$312 \times 1.0365 = 323.4$

Similarly, for Germany:

$234 / 225 = 1.04$
$234 \times 1.04 = 243.4$

This is a difference of:

$323.4 - 243.4 = 80$

Finally, we need to apply an order of magnitude correction. Because the numbers given are in thousands the answer is also in thousands.

Potential Shortcuts / Pitfalls
All the workings are shown here to make it clear what the process is. However, it is plain to see that there is actually no need to calculate the initial growth as a percentage (i.e. subtracting 1 and multiplying it by 100) because when we want to use it in the next step we reverse this, making it unnecessary.

So, for France we could have said that the growth was simply 312/301 and then applied this to the 2010 value of 312. Above, we first calculated 312 / 301, and then multiplied 312 by this number. But what if there is an even easier way?

Let's write this down as a fraction:

$$\frac{312}{301} \times 312$$

When you see something like this (a fraction multiplied by a number), remember that you can always move the number into the numerator, giving:

$$\frac{312 \times 312}{301}$$

The numerator is now 312 to the second power, and this is divided by 301. If the calculator you have access to at the exam has the square function, this is the fastest way to calculate:

$$\frac{312^2}{301} - \frac{234^2}{225} = 80$$

SET 32, Q3. Correct Answer: D

Reasoning

We need to calculate the total number of Dutch people who visited the countries listed in the table and what that total is as a percentage of all holidays taken abroad.

Calculation

The total number of Dutch visitors to the countries shown is:

$301 + 225 + 170 + 192 + 195 = 1083$

This is in thousands and so is:

$1083 \times 1000 = 1083000$ or 1.083m

This as a percentage of all holidays taken abroad is then:

$1.083 / 1.805 \times 100 = 60\%$

SET 33, Q1. Correct Answer: E

Reasoning

We need to work out the number of cars sold by the franchise and then calculate that as a proportion of the total shown.

Calculation

The total sales by the franchise is simply the product of the number of showrooms, the number sold each month and the number of months in a year:

$44 \times 90 \times 12 = 47520$

The total sold is in thousands, so let's convert the dealer's sales into thousands as well:

$47520 / 1000 = 47.52$

As a proportion of total sales this is:

$47.52 / 1584 = 0.03$

To make it a percentage we need to multiply by 100:

$0.03 \times 100 = 3\%$

Potential Shortcuts / Pitfalls
The main problem here is applying all the order of magnitude corrections.

If you like fractions, there is also a beautiful shortcut to take advantage of. If we write out the calculation in full, it is:

$$\frac{44 * 12 * 90}{1584} = \frac{11 * 12 * 90}{396} = \frac{12 * 90}{36} = \frac{90}{3} = 30$$

You may notice that 4 is a common factor of 44 and 1584; 11 is a common factor of 11 and 396; 12 is a common factor of 12 and 36 and 90 by 3 divides simply into 30.

SET 33, Q2. Correct Answer: E

Reasoning

We need to calculate what the total sales would have been if the assumption in the question had been true, and then work out how many more Peugeot cars they would have had to sell in order for that to be one third of the new total.

Calculation

The proportion of total sales contributed by Peugeot is the Peugeot sales divided by the sum of all the 2009 sales. However, we don't yet know what the *new* total sales will be because the new Peugeot sales form a part of that total. If we assume that the new Peugeot sales total is P, then the new total sales for 2009 will be:

1710 + 1094 + P = 2804+P

The proportion of Peugeot sales from the total is then:

P / (2804+P)

And we want this to be equal to one-third of the total, so:

P / (2804+P) = 1 / 3

We now need to perform operations on both sides of the equation until we have only 1P on one side. Let's multiply both sides by 3 first:

3xP / (2804+P) = 1

Let's multiply by (2804 + P) now:

3xP = 2804 + 1P

We can now subtract 1P from both sides:

2xP = 2804

We can now calculate the value of 1P:

P = 1402

This is the volume of Peugeot sales we would have needed in 2009 for this to be exactly one third of this new, hypothetical total. They originally had sales of 1396 so this is a difference of 6.

Now we need to apply the order of magnitude correction, and as the sales are quoted in thousands, we must multiply our answer by 1000 to get 6000.

Potential Shortcuts / Pitfalls

In addition to the relatively challenging calculations shown above, there is one more pitfall we can easily fall into. If we assume that the total sales remained unchanged, and then calculate what one third of that would be and then compare that figure with the actual sales, we would get an incorrect result.

Why is that? It is because the question specifically states that the *sales volumes of the other brands mentioned remain unchanged*. So if the Peugeot sales change, *so must the total sales*.

If you make the error of simply calculating the total with the existing values (4200), take one third of that (1400) and calculate the difference from the actual Peugeot sales of 1396), you will get a result of 4000. This is especially dangerous because this is one of the incorrect answer options, so you would never realise the error in your method.

SET 33, Q3. Correct Answer: B

Reasoning

We need to calculate the total sales figure for all cars in France, using the market share and sales volume of Citroen, and then calculate what percentage of that total is accounted for by the three manufacturers in the table.

Calculation

The number of Citroen cars sold is 13.7% of all cars sold in France in 2010. Remember the 'reverse visualisation' method. The unknown is X, and 13.7% (or 0.137) of that is equal to 1107:

X × 0.137 = 1107

Rearranging the equation shows us that the total number of cars sold is:

1107 / 0.137 = 8080

The total number of cars sold by the three manufacturers listed is:

1723 + 1107 + 1422 = 4252

The percentage is the number from the table divided by the overall total and then multiplied by 100. This is:

4252 / 8080 × 100 = 52.6%

SET 34, Q1. Correct Answer: C

Reasoning

We need to calculate the number of people getting married as a percentage of the total 2010 population.

Calculation

First, we need to find the total number of people getting married. The table lists the number of marriages as 923, which is in hundreds, and of course there are *two people* involved in each marriage, so the total number is:

$923 \times 100 \times 2 = 184600$

The population is given in thousands, so let's convert the above to 184.6 thousand people.

The total population of Ireland has grown 5% since 2005 to:

$4187 \times 1.05 = 4396.4$

And so as a percentage it is:

$184.6 / 4396.4 \times 100 = 4.2\%$

SET 34, Q2. Correct Answer: D

Reasoning

The rate of marriages per 100,000 people is simply the number of marriages divided by the population and then multiplied by 100,000.

Calculation

We need to calculate the per capita rate of marriages in 2010. First we need to work out the population of Finland in 2010, which has dropped by 1.5% since 2005. To calculate a drop, we multiply by one minus the percentage:

$5244 \times (1 - (1.5 / 100)) = 5244 \times 0.985 = 5165.34$

The per capita rate in 2010 is then:

$998 / 5165.34 = 0.19321$

This is no surprise as all of the answers are this value with the decimal point moved. So, we need to correct for the order of magnitude. The marriages are stated in hundreds so we need to multiply by 100:

$0.19321 \times 100 = 19.321$

The population is given in thousands so we need to divide by 1000:

$19.321 / 1000 = 0.019321$

Finally, the question asks for the number of marriages per 100,000 of the population so we need to multiply by 100,000:

$0.019321 \times 100,000 = 1932.1$

Potential Shortcuts / Pitfalls

The whole raison d'être of this problem is to test your ability to keep track of all the hidden zeroes. Obviously, you don't need to do each step separately as shown when applying order of magnitude corrections.

The first thing to notice is that performing *the actual (initial) calculation is unnecessary*. The answer options basically only differ in their order of magnitude. In order to simplify our task, we can round the population down to 5000 (thousands) and the number of marriages up to 1000 (hundreds). By simply dividing this, we would get:

$1000 / 5000 = 0.2$

Now we need to take account of the zeroes.

The 5000 is in thousands so we will divide by 1000, the 1000 is in hundreds, so we multiply by a hundred, and finally, the questions asks about 'per 100,000', so we multiply by 100,000.

Let's see how many zeroes we have in these numbers:

1000 = 3 (to remove)
100 = 2 (to add)
100,000 = 5 (to add)

If we think of adding zeroes as a positive number and removing zeroes as a negative number, we get:

-3
+2
+5
= +4

This means that in order to get the correct answer, we need to add 4 zeroes to 0.2, or, in other words, move the decimal point 4 positions to the right:

$0.20000 - » 2000$

This is not the actual correct answer as we estimated, but it IS the correct order of magnitude, so now we can pick the correct answer.

SET 34, Q3. Correct Answer: E

Reasoning

The per capita marriage rate is the total number of marriages divided by the total population.

Calculation

The number of marriages per capita in Bosnia is:

714 / 3781 = 0.189

However, the marriages are in hundreds and the population is in thousands and so we need to apply the order of magnitude correction by dividing by 10 to get:

0.189 / 10 = 0.0189

Similarly for the others:

Finland – 1008 / 5244 / 10 = 0.0192
Ireland – 904 / 4187 / 10 = 0.0216
Slovakia – 908 / 5386 / 10 = 0.0169
Switzerland – 1120 / 7441 /10 = 0.0151
Clearly, Switzerland is the lowest.

Potential Shortcuts / Pitfalls

Once again, we have done the complete calculation for the per capita value but as we are only comparing the *relative* values of these calculations, their order of magnitude is irrelevant, provided they are all treated the same.

Also, we can *completely skip the calculation for Finland and Ireland*: their populations are smaller than that of Slovakia yet they had more marriages (or almost the same number), so their per capita figure must be greater than Slovakia's. That leaves Bosnia, Slovakia and Switzerland to calculate.

SET 35, Q1. Correct Answer: B

Reasoning

We need to calculate the proportion of total electricity generated by tidal power and then determine that as a percentage of the 2005 total.

Calculation

We need to calculate the proportion of electricity generated by tidal power. Clearly, the big unknown in this exercise is the *total* electricity generated: we aren't told this number, so let us assume that the total power generated in 2005 was E. The question states that this rose by 10% in 2010 to:

E × 1.1 = 1.1E

From the *table* we can see that 6.5% of this was generated by 'Other' means in 2010:

1.1E × 0.065 = 0.0715E

The *pie chart* tells us that 38% of this was due to tidal power:

0.0715E × 0.38 = 0.02717E

The *question* tells us that this doubled over the 5 years so in 2005 it was:

0.02717E / 2 = 0.013585E

To calculate this as a percentage of the total power generated in 2005, we need to divide by that total and then multiply by 100. We assumed that total was E at the beginning, so it is quite easy from this point on:

(0.01358E / E) × 100 = 1.3585%

which is rounded to 1.36%.

SET 35, Q2. Correct Answer: A

Reasoning

We need to calculate the total amount of electricity generated from 'other', and then calculate the solar power production.

Calculation

First, we need to calculate the total electricity generated from 'other'. The question tells us that 2.4 million kWh is the total generated from biomass, and the pie chart tells us this is 36% of 'other' generation. We can use this to calculate the total 'other' generation using the familiar 'reverse' method.

Other × 36% = 2.4
Other × 0.36 = 2.4
Other = 2.4 / 0.36 = 6.67

The table tells us that 'other' generation is, in turn, just 6.5% of the total generated which using the same method is:

6.67 / 0.065 = 102.62

5.2% of this total is generated by solar power, which is:

102.62 × 0.052 = 5.3mKwh

Potential Shortcuts / Pitfalls

It is usually good advice that you should *estimate whenever possible* to avoid the use of the clumsy calculator. This instance demonstrates that this advice has its limits. Let's say you decide to estimate the answer in this question. Quite quickly you would run into the problem that it is very hard to round up or down while also preserving at least a modest level of accuracy and therefore a chance to pick the correct answer at the end. This is made even more difficult by the fact that the answer options are quite close to each other.

Always consider these factors before deciding which method to use in calculating the answer.

SET 35, Q3. Correct Answer: A

Reasoning

We need to calculate the percentage change in fossil fuel generation.

Calculation

To calculate the total generated by fossil fuel, we need to know the overall total, which isn't given, so we can substitute the 2005 total with E. Then, the total generated by fossil fuel is:

$E \times 0.811 = 0.811E$

In 2010, the overall total rose by 10% to:

$E \times 1.1 = 1.1E$

So, in 2010, fossil fuel generation was:

$1.1E \times 0.764 = 0.8404E$

This is a difference of:

$0.8404E - 0.811E = 0.0294E$

As a percentage of the 2005 generation this is:

$100 \times 0.0294E / 0.811E = 3.6\%$

Potential Shortcuts / Pitfalls
Once again, the *actual total figure is not required* as it cancels out in the last step.

There are, however, several pitfalls you can fall into along the way:

1. At first glance, you might look at the two fossil fuel percentages and say that the change is actually 81.1 – 76.4 = 4.7 %. This would be wrong on many fronts; for example it doesn't take into account the 10% rise in total generation or the fact that this would be a *percentage point* change.

2. You could also calculate the above by dividing the difference (4.7%) by the starting value (81.1), but again, this would not take into account the rise in total production.

SET 36, Q1. Correct Answer: A

Reasoning

We need to calculate the per capita ratio of prisoners to population for each year and then calculate the percentage change.

Calculation

We need first to calculate the per capita rate of prisoners, which is the number of prisoners divided by the total population. In 2005 this is:

$702.2 / 38198 = 0.01838$

Now, this is not really correct because the prison population is given in hundreds whereas the total population is given in thousands, but since we are going to calculate percentage change, we can disregard this difference in order of magnitude.

For 2010, we calculate with the 2010 prison figure and divide that by the 2005 population figure increased by 700 (thousand):

$707.9 / (38198+700) = 0.0182$

The percentage difference is the difference divided by the 2005 value and then multiplied by 100:

$100 \times (0.0182 - 0.01838) / 0.01838 \approx -1\%$

Potential Shortcuts / Pitfalls
In previous questions rather similar to this, we have seen that we can just disregard the population and work with the other data plus the percentage increase in the population. Why not in this case? The reason is that the population increase was not given as a *percentage*, but as a *specific figure*: 700,000, and so, the population would not cancel out at the end of our calculation. Here is why:

Our final calculation was:

(2010 Per Capita – 2005 Per Capita) / 2005 Per Capita $\times$ 100

Let's break this down:
2010 Per Capita = 2010 Prison / 2005 Population + 700
2005 Per Capita = 2005 Prison / 2005 Population

Let's write this as a fraction:

$$\left(\frac{2010 \text{ Prison}}{2005 \text{ Population} + 700} - \frac{2005 \text{ Prison}}{2005 \text{ Population}} \right) / \frac{2005 \text{ Prison}}{2005 \text{ Population}}$$

This demonstrates why we cannot omit the 2005 population figure. A value in a fraction can only be omitted if it is a *common factor* in *all parts* of the calculation. A value can only be a common factor if we only divide or multiply with it – this is not the case in the first fraction, where the 700 is *added* to the 2005 population.

SET 36, Q2. Correct Answer: E

Reasoning

We need to calculate the per capita rate of prisoners in 2005 and then equate that to 2010 to calculate the population.

Calculation

The per capita rate of prisoners is simply the number of prisoners divided by the population. In 2005 this is:

22.4 / 1347 = 0.01663

We don't need to worry about the order of magnitude because we will never use this interim result on its own – we will eventually need the population figure for 2010, which *will* be in thousands if we leave everything untouched.

The per capita rate for 2010 is the number of prisoners divided by the population, which we don't know, but we are told that the result (the per capita figure) is the same as for 2005. What is our unknown? It is obviously the answer we are seeking, the 2010 population of Estonia.

Let us call the 2010 population X; then the number of prisoners divided by X (the per capita rate) is the same as in 2005, which we just calculated as 0.01663:

22.8 / X = 0.01663

Now we need to achieve a situation where 1X is on one side of the equation and everything else is on the other side. We do this by multiplying by X and then dividing by 0.01663:

X = 22.8 / 0.01663
X = 1371

As the population was stated in thousands then the answer is also in thousands which is what is required.

SET 36, Q3. Correct Answer: D

Reasoning

We need to calculate the per capita rate of prisoners in each country and then the percentage difference between them.

Calculation

We first need to calculate the per capita rate of prisoners in Austria, which is the number of prisoners divided by the population:

115.9 / 8232 = 0.01408

Here, as we have often seen before, the order of magnitude doesn't matter because we are calculating the percentage difference.

For Sweden it is:

106.8 / 9066 = 0.01178

The percentage difference is the difference divided by the base value (Sweden's rate) and then multiplied by 100:

100 × (0.01408 – 0.01178) / 0.01178 = 19.52%

SET 37, Q1. Correct Answer: B

Reasoning

We need to calculate how many pounds we have left after the transaction fee is subtracted and then exchange that into francs given the lower customer exchange rate.

Calculation

The bullion rate of exchange is 1.533 and the bank lowers this by 1.5% for its customers, so we need to multiply by (100-1.5)%:

1.533 × 0.985 = 1.51

We have £1000 to exchange but the bank is going to further line its pockets by charging £3 for the transaction, which leaves us with £997 to convert:

997 × 1.51 = 1505.47

Potential Shortcuts / Pitfalls

Remember this is a 1.5% *drop* in rate so you *multiply* by (100-1.5). If the question had said the bullion rate is 1.5% higher than the customer rate, we would have had to divide by 1.015.

Also, the surest and most frustrating way to lose a point in an EPSO test when doing a question like this would be to forget to subtract the transaction fee before making the conversion. It is also worth noting that while you could have subtracted the transaction charge *after* the conversion, it saves time to do it *before* the conversion because fewer calculations are then needed. In any case, the important thing is not to forget to do it at some point!

SET 37, Q2. Correct Answer: D

Reasoning

We need to calculate how many dollars we get for our euros at the lowered rate. Once we have that, we will see how many US dollars we are in excess of the closest multiple of 5. We can convert that amount back to euros to see how many euros we will get back as change.

Calculation

The exchange rate listed is 1.225 but the rate we get is 1% below that which is:

1.225 * 0.99 = 1.21275

We convert our money to dollars which gives:

5000 × 1.21275 = 6063.75

But we can only get multiples of $5 and so we get $6060.

From this point, we can do either of two things:

Option 1. We can calculate how much $6060 costs and see how many euros we have left of the 5000.

$6060 will cost us:

6060 / 1.21275 = 4996.91

This is a difference of:

5000 – 4996.91 = 3.09

Option 2. We can also say that $6060 is 3.75 less than what we would get for 5000 euros and see how much that 3.75 US dollars is worth in euros using the same exchange rate.

3.75 / 1.21275 = 3.09

Potential Shortcuts / Pitfalls
Be careful about rounding intermediate answers as it could make a relatively large difference because we're dealing with a large amount of money. For example, rounding the rate to 1.2128 will cause a €0.2 difference in the answer. This is because the small rounding error of 0.0005 is counted 5000 times.

Also, you need to remember that when you do the reverse calculation (using either method), you need to divide by the exchange rate, not multiply.

SET 37, Q3. Correct Answer: C

Reasoning

We need to convert into euros from francs using the lower exchange rate and also factor in the 2.5% transaction fee charged by the bank.

Calculation

The bullion rate for converting CHF to € is 0.832. This drops by 2% by the time the payment is processed. This is good news, because it means that fewer euros will be needed to 'buy' the requisite amount of CHF:

0.832 × 0.98 = 0.81536

The 49.36 then converts to:

49.36 × 0.81536 = 40.25

The credit card company adds, however, its 2.5%:

40.25 × 1.025 = 41.25

Potential Shortcuts / Pitfalls
Since the transaction fee is a percentage, it does not make any difference whether you apply it to the CHF amount or to the euro amount; so if you find the former to be more convenient, you can do that.

Of course if the transaction fee was a fixed amount (say, 4 euros), that it would have to be applied to the currency in which it is stated. In the example I gave, in euros.

SET 38, Q1. Correct Answer: E

Reasoning

We need to calculate the fuel used using distance travelled multiplied by fuel economy (litres / 100 km).

Calculation

The most important task is again to figure out what the *unknown* is in the question. The unknown in this case is, of course, the journey length – everything else is known: the fuel economies for the two types of scenarios, the proportion we travelled in each scenario and the total amount of fuel used.

It is very hard to formulate what the journey length is, but let's call it J and try to say something about it which we know to be true.

If we multiply the economy figure by the distance travelled then that will give us the amount of fuel used.

The urban part of the journey will use:

0.38 × J km * 7.8 l/ 100km / 100 = 0.02964J

Remember that you need to divide by 100 because the economy figures are per 100km. (You could apply this correction at the end if you want.) The fuel used for the rural part of the journey is (since the urban part is 0.38, the rural must be 0.62):

0.62 × J × 5.8 / 100 = 0.03596J

We now have the amount of fuel expressed as a factor of the distance travelled. This is good because we know the total amount of fuel used, so we can write up an equation in which the only unknown is the journey length – and this is exactly what we want.

The amount of fuel used during the two parts of the journey is 12.2 litres:

0.02964J + 0.03596J = 12.2
0.0656J = 12.2

We can now re-arrange to have only 1 J on one side of the equation:

J = 12.2 / 0.0656 = 186km

Potential Shortcuts / Pitfalls

If you are unsure about the calculation to perform – whether you should divide or multiply by the fuel economy, for instance – remember to *look at the units*. In the first calculation we did:

0.38 × J * 7.8 / 100

The 0.38 is a percentage so it doesn't have any units associated with it. The 'J' is the journey length which is in km. The 7.8 is 'litres per 100 km' but we are dividing by 100 to eliminate the 100 so it is

effectively l/km. Multiplying 'km' with 'l/km' will cancel out the kilometres and leave an answer in litres which is what we are seeking (the amount of fuel used). You are on the right lines. If the units do not give you what you are looking for then you probably have something wrong.

SET 38, Q2. Correct Answer: B

Reasoning

We need to calculate the amount of fuel used in each part of the journey and hence the cost.

Calculation

The amount of fuel used is the distance travelled multiplied by the economy. For the urban part of the journey this is (if 80% of the journey was rural, 20% must have been urban, which is 0.2):

120km × 0.2 × 6.3 litres / 100km = 1.512 litres

For the rural part of the journey it will be:

120km × 0.8 × 4.1 litres / 100km = 3.936 litres

This gives us a total of:

1.512 + 3.936 = 5.448 litres

At 1.48 per litre this gives a cost of:

5.448 litres × 1.48€/litre = €8.06

Potential Shortcuts / Pitfalls

There is only one conclusion to draw which is not immediately obvious, which is the fact that 20% of the journey was urban.

Always make sure you read off the consumption figures correctly – this could be an issue with certain types of graphs, so always double check. In this case, the minor gridlines are drawn every 0.2 litres.

Last but not least, it is worth mentioning that we can do part of this calculation using estimation as well.

20% of the 120 km journey was urban – this is 24 km, which is close 25 (one quarter of 100 km).

80% of the 120 km journey was rural – this is 96 km, which is almost 100.

Why is this useful?

If the rural journey was around 100 km, we can simply take the per 100 km consumption figure, which is 4.1 l – no need to calculate it for 96 km for now.

If the urban journey was around 25 km (one quarter of 100 km), then the urban consumption on this leg must also have been around one quarter of the urban per 100 km consumption figure (6.3 litres). 6.3 litres is close to 6.4, and one quarter of 6.4 is 1.6 litres.

1.6 + 4.1 litres = 5.7, and 5.7 litres of diesel cost 8.44 €. This is not one of the answer options but it *is* closest to option B, the correct answer. Since we rounded up both consumption figures, we also know that the exact result will be *slightly below* 8.44, which is another confirmation that option B is the correct answer.

Remember, however, that you can only use methods like this if you are sure that the level of accuracy needed to pick the correct answer is low enough for estimation to work. This takes practice.

SET 38, Q3. Correct Answer: C

Reasoning

We need to convert the litres per 100km to km per litre and take the difference.

Calculation

The conversion from litres/100 km to km/litre is the only challenge in the question. What exactly does litres /100 km mean? It means that X litres are used by the car in 100 kilometres. If we want to find the figure for how many kilometres the car can do on 1 litre, we simply divide the 100 kilometres by the number of litres used.

100 km / 4.1 km/l = 24.4 km
100 km / 7.8 km/l = 12.8 km

The difference is:

24.4 – 12.8 = 11.6

SET 39, Q1. Correct Answer: C

Reasoning

The total operating profit for a given year is the sum of the operating profits per satellite launch type. We calculate the total operating profit for each year and then subtract the 2005 figure from the 2015 figure to get the increase, and then convert to a percentage.

Calculation

The total operating profit for 2005 is:

0.5 + 0.8 + (-0.4) = 0.9

The total operating profit for 2015 is:

2.4 + 1.4 + 1 = 4.8

The difference:

4.8 – 0.9 = 3.9 million U.S. dollars

If we divide the difference by the 2005 starting value, we get:

3.9 / 0.9 = 4.33

Multiplied by 100 to get a percentage:

4.33 x 100 = 433%

Potential Shortcuts / Pitfalls
You must take note of the fact that the weather satellite launch profit figure for 2005 is negative, so this will decrease, not increase the total for that year.

Avoid the mistake of dividing the 2015 value (4.8) by the 2005 value (0.9) to get to the percentage. If you do this you will get (4.8 / 0.9) x 100 = 533%, which is incorrect but is given as one of the answer options.

SET 39, Q2. Correct Answer: B

Reasoning

First, we calculate the total revenue for both years. Then we divide by the number of satellite types, and finally we calculate the difference between the two years.

Calculation

The total revenue for 2005 was:

4.3 + 7.1 + 9.2 = 20.6

The average per satellite type is:

20.6 / 3 = 6.87 (rounded)

The total revenue for 2015 was:

8.2 + 14.5 + 16.5 = 39.2

The average per satellite type is:

39.2 / 3 = 13.07 (rounded)

The difference between the two years is:

13.07 – 6.87 = 6.2 million US dollars

SET 39, Q3. Correct Answer: D

Reasoning

First, we must calculate the total cost of satellite launches in 2015 by subtracting the operating profit from the revenue. Then we divide this number by the number of launches.

Calculation

The total revenue for 2015 is:

8.2 + 14.5 + 16.5 = 39.2

The total operating profit for 2015 is:

2.4 + 1.4 + 1 = 4.8

The total cost, then, is:

39.2 – 4.8 = 34.4 million US dollars

Divided by the 25 launches, this equals:

34.4 / 25 = 1.376 million US dollars

SET 40, Q1. Correct Answer: E

Reasoning

We need to calculate the total amount of fat consumed and then calculate the daily consumption.

Calculation

We need to work out the total amount of fat consumed, which is the amount per person (both saturated and unsaturated), multiplied by the number of people. This gives:

(2.44 + 2.19) × 60120 = 278356 This is now in kg/year and we want the daily rate, so we divide by 365 days/year: 278356 / 365 = 762.6 kg/day

You must be careful at this point not to think you have finished the question and mark option B as the correct answer, because you still have to correct the order of magnitude. The population is in thousands so we need to multiply by 1000, giving us 762600 kg per day. The answer options expressed in kg are much lower figures than this, but if we divide by 1000, to convert kg to tonnes, we get 762.6 tonnes, which is option E.

SET 40, Q2. Correct Answer: B

Reasoning

We need to calculate the increase and decrease in consumption of the two fat types and hence the overall net change.

Calculation

First, we need to calculate the reduction in saturated fat consumption, which is 15% of 2.02kg:

2.02 × 0.15 = 0.303

The increase in unsaturated fat consumption is 12.5% of 2.88kg which is:

2.88 × 0.125 = 0.360

This is a net difference of:

0.360 – 0.303 = 0.057 kg

This shows that there has been an *increase* rather than a reduction overall. We can therefore exclude options C, D, and E. As a percentage of the starting value this is:

100 × (0.057 / (2.02 + 2.88)) = 1.2%

This is also the increase in total consumption since the population remained unchanged.

Potential Shortcuts / Pitfalls

At first glance, it may seem intuitive that there has been a decrease in fat consumption because of the higher percentage in the reduction, but you have to notice that that higher percentage reduction took place on a much lower base.

Also, after we have excluded options C, D and E, we are left with 1.2% and 2.5%. Look at the numbers again:

0.057 kg increase over 4.9 kg consumption. This cannot be more than a 2% increase, so we can mark option B as correct without accurately calculating it.

SET 40, Q3. Correct Answer: C

Reasoning

We need to calculate the total fat consumed by both countries and then the average.

Calculation

To calculate the total fat consumed, add up the two amounts per person and multiply by the population. For the Netherlands this is:

$(1.77 + 3.02) \times 16316 = 78154$

And for Sweden it is:

$(1.82 + 3.11) \times 9066 = 44695$

This is a total of:

$78154 + 44695 = 122849$

To calculate the average we now divide this by the total number of people in the Netherlands and Sweden combined:

$122849 / (16316 + 9066) = 4.84$ kg/person/year

Potential Shortcuts / Pitfalls

There is no order of magnitude correction to do in this case because we multiply and divide by the populations and so they cancel out, provided we are consistent throughout.

Note also that the average is just another way of saying per capita or per person. The table already gives the average intake per person for both Netherlands and Sweden. However, we cannot just add these two together and divide by two to get the average between them because their populations are not the same. The population of the Netherlands is about 2/3 larger than that of Sweden and so its per capita values are going to be more heavily weighted and will influence the result more than the Swedish values.

SET 41, Q1. Correct Answer: B

Reasoning

We need to calculate the known elements of the total profit (profit on 300F camera sales and total warranty sales for both models) in order to be left with only one unknown: the number of 200D models sold.

Calculation

We calculate the profit on 300F camera sales (i.e. excluding warranties) by multiplying the units sold by the retail price and then multiplying by the profit rate.

$450 \times 5\,500 \times 23\% = 450 \times 5\,500 \times 0.23 = 569\,250$

We calculate the 300F warranty sales by multiplying the numbers sold by the unit price and then by multiplying by the surcharge percentage.

$450 \times 100 \times 8\% = 450 \times 100 \times 0.08 = 3\,600$

Remember at this point that the table tells us that *all* the sales value of warranty sales is profit.

Part of the total profit on 200D comes from sale of warranties:

Retail price $\times$ Warranties Sold $\times$ Surcharge rate

$360 \times 150 \times 10\% = 360 \times 150 \times 0.1 = 5\,400$

As the question tells us the total profit on both cameras (1 096 650), we can now calculate the profit made on 200D camera sales excluding warranties:

200 D camera sales profit = Total profit – 300F camera sales profit – 300F warranties – 200D warranties:

$1\,096\,650 - 569\,250 - 3\,600 - 5\,400 = 518\,400$

We can also calculate the profit made on one 200D camera excluding warranties:

Retail price $\times$ Profit = $360 \times 18\% = 360 \times 0.18 = 64.8$

The total profit on 200 D camera sales divided by the profit per unit will give us the number of cameras sold:

Total profit / Unit profit = Cameras sold

$518\,400 / 64.8 = 8\,000$

Potential Shortcuts / Pitfalls

You mustn't forget that according to the total profit definition shown in the footer of the table, the total profit includes the extended warranty sales as well. If you disregard this, you would get C as the correct answer.

It is also important not to forget that not all cameras were sold with extended warranty. If you erroneously add the warranty surcharge to the profit rate (e.g. 23% + 8% for the 300F), then you would get A as the correct answer.

SET 41, Q2. Correct Answer: B

Reasoning

We first need to calculate the total profit made on the 300F (profit on camera sales plus warranties). Once we have done that, we can calculate how much would be generated by selling ten times as many warranties.

We can then calculate two figures:

Current total (profit on camera sales + warranties)

Assumed Total (profit on camera sales + warranties)

To calculate the percentage difference between them, we calculate the actual difference between them and divide by the current total:

(Assumed total – Current Total) / Current Total

To express this as a percentage, we multiply by 100.

Calculation

For calculating the total profit on camera sales and warranties on the 300F, see the previous answer.

The current total is then:

569 250 + 3 600 = 572 850

The assumed total is the current profit on camera sales + the current warranty sales figure multiplied by 10:

569 250 + (3600 × 10) = 605 250

The percentage increase is:

(605 250 – 572 850) / 572 850 × 100 = 32 400 / 572 850 × 100 = 5.66%

Potential Shortcuts / Pitfalls

When you calculate the assumed total (with 10 times as many warranties sold), be sure to calculate the difference between this number and the current total *including the current warranty sales*. If you calculate instead the difference to the total profit excluding warranty sales, you would get C as the correct answer.

Also make sure that you use the correct retail price and profit rates (it is easy to misread the table), because there are distractor items that match what you would get if you picked the wrong figure from any of these columns.

SET 41, Q3. Correct Answer: D

Reasoning

We need to calculate the increase in total profit caused by a 1 percentage point increase in the profit rate on camera sales, and then compare that to the increase generated by selling 10 times as many warranties as currently, but at a reduced price (5% of the retail price).

Calculation

We calculate the increase in profit on camera sales excluding warranties by subtracting the current profit from the increased total profit made on the 300F.

Current profit (see answer 1) = 569 250.

To calculate the increased profit:

Retail price × Cameras sold × Profit rate

450 × 5 500 × 24% = 450 × 5 500 × 0.24 = 594 000

The revenue increase is then:

594 000 – 569 250 = 24 750

We calculate the increase in revenue from selling ten times as many extended warranties by comparing the current revenue to the new revenue.

Current revenue = Warranties sold × Retail price × Surcharge

Current revenue = 100 × 450 × 8% = 45 000 × 0.08 = 3600

New revenue = 1000 × 450 × 5% = 450 000 × 0.05 = 22 500

The difference is:

22 500 – 3600 = 18 900

We can now compare this to the increase in profit on camera sales:

24 750 – 18900 = 5850

which is Answer D.

Potential Shortcuts / Pitfalls

When calculating the increase in profit from selling ten times as many extended warranties, it is important to remember to subtract the *current* revenue generated from the new, increased figure, otherwise we would get C as the correct answer.

It is also important to carefully read the question text: there are distractor answer options you would get as the result if you forget that the surcharge percentage was dropped to 5%, for example.

There is in addition a quicker, more intuitive way to calculate this.

1. Express the 1 percentage point profit increase as a € 4.5 increase, multiplied by 5 500 (cameras sold). This can also be expressed as 450 × 55.

2. Express the revenue from the tenfold increase in warranties sold as 1000 (new number of warranties sold is 1000), and the revenue from this as 5% of the retail price. You can estimate that to be about €22.50.

We have two values (disregard the currency for now):

450 × 55 (extra profit on camera sales) VERSUS 900 × 22.5 (extra profit on warranty sales)

You can see that the first total must be greater because 450 is half as much as 900, but 55 is more than twice as much as 22.5. Since the first total is the additional profit from the 1-percentage point increase in camera sales, that will be the higher number, and this immediately excludes options A and B.

You can then calculate both values and you will see that the difference between them is € 4 500. This, however, doesn't take into account the revenue we already generate from the warranties (100 × 450 × 0.08), so the difference must be even greater than € 4 500.

This allows us to pick option D without having calculated the precise amount.

SET 42, Q1. Correct Answer: D

Reasoning

We first need to work out the profit the company currently makes on sofa beds by calculating the profit on one sofa bed and multiplying by the monthly output. Then we calculate the new profit with the decreased assembly costs and the increased output. We can then calculate the increase in profits.

Calculation

Let us first calculate the profit currently made from one sofa bed:

Profit = Retail price – assembly cost – material cost – packaging cost

Profit = 225.50 – 25 – 149 – 24.50 = 27 euros

We can calculate the monthly total profit by multiplying this by the output:

Total Profit = 27 × 55 = 1485 euros

Now let's calculate the new total profit with the decreased assembly costs and increased output.

The new assembly cost is 4.50 lower and, since all other costs are equal, the profit must be 4.50 higher as well:

New Profit = 27 + 4.50 = 31.50 euros

The output also increased, so the new total profit is:

Total Profit = 31.50 × 100 = 3150 euros

We can now calculate the difference in profits, expressed as a percentage increase. We do this by taking the difference between the two values and dividing by the originating value, multiplying in the end by 100 to get a percentage:

Increase % = (3150 – 1485) / 1485 × 100 = 112.12%

Potential Shortcuts / Pitfalls

Many test-takers would go about solving this question by first calculating the extra profit on the first 55 sofa beds contributed by the decreased assembly costs, and then separately calculating the profit made on the additional 45 sofa beds. This is not a time-efficient method because we need two pieces of data: the total profit made currently and after the changes.

As a shortcut, we can attempt to estimate the correct answer. Let's look at the increased output first. 100 is a little less than twice 55, so if the costs were equal, the new total profit would also have to be slightly less than double the original, which corresponds to a slightly less than 100% increase. This allows us to eliminate options A, B, and C – which are far below 100% – especially as we know that the actual increase in profits will be even higher on account of the decreased assembly costs.

Since the decrease in assembly costs is modest compared to the profit made on one sofa bed (4.50 out of 31 euros), we can conclude that this decrease in costs would only contribute modestly to the profit increase. Looking at the two remaining answer options with this in mind, option E is clearly too high, leaving only option D as a viable option.

SET 42, Q2. Correct Answer: D

Reasoning

We need to calculate what proportion the assembly cost represents of the total cost for each furniture type, by dividing the former cost by the latter, and then pick the lowest value.

Calculation

To calculate the proportions, we need to add up all the costs per furniture type, and then divide the assembly costs by these values.

Dining table:

10.50 / 10.50 + 57 + 15 = 0.127

Armchair:

8 / 8 + 30 + 10.50 = 0.165

Book shelf:

12.50 / 12.50 + 60 + 15.50 = 0.142

Sofa bed:

25 / 25 + 149 + 24.50 = 0.126

We can see that the assembly costs represent the lowest proportion in the case of the sofa bed, which is answer D.

Note that we do not need to calculate the exact figure for answer option E (dining table and sofa bed combined) because the sofa bed by itself must have a lower proportion as the dining table figure is higher.

Potential Shortcuts / Pitfalls
We must be careful to divide the assembly cost by the total cost, not the retail price. Even though we *might* get the same result using either method, this is not guaranteed as the different profit rates for each type of furniture may change this calculus.

Note also that we did not actually calculate percentages (that is, we did not multiply by 100), as this would have been completely unnecessary.

SET 42, Q3. Correct Answer: C

Reasoning

We must first calculate the total spending on materials at current output levels. We do this by multiplying the cost of materials per piece of furniture by the output for each furniture type, adding up the resulting four values. We then calculate the 12% decrease for this overall value.

Calculation

We first calculate the total spending on materials at current output levels by furniture type.

Dining table:

57 × 150 = 8550

Armchair:

30 × 200 = 6000

Book shelf:

60 × 350 = 21000

Sofa bed:

149 × 55 = 8195

To calculate the total spending, we add up these four numbers:

Total = 8550 + 6000 + 21000 + 8195 = 43 745

The new value is 12% lower, which means it is 88% of the current value:

43 745 × 0.88 = 38 495.60 euros

Potential Shortcuts / Pitfalls
Read carefully what is being asked in the question. For example, the 12% difference between the current and new spending on materials (5249.40) is also among the answer options, so it is all too easy to mistakenly mark that as the correct answer.

Also, while you should always look for any opportunity to try estimation, that would be unwise in this case. Option D is too close to the correct answer to allow for safe estimation.

SET 43, Q1. Correct Answer: B

Reasoning

First, we calculate the number of studios ABC Apartments had in 2013. From that, we can simply calculate the number of studios with air conditioning because we know that the percentage of such studios was the same as in 2014.

Calculation

The number of studio apartments in Spain in 2013 is the 2014 figure minus the number of units built in 2014:

$200 - 20 = 180$

We know that in 2013, 65% of the studio apartments had air conditioning, the same proportion as in 2014.

$180 \times 65\% = 180 \times 0.65 = 117$

Potential Shortcuts / Pitfalls

While the calculation itself is very straightforward, you can still get caught out by the design of the table, especially if in a rush. The table is very homogenous in that it shows a large number of very similar numbers: all of the percentages have two digits and the last two columns on the right contain only three-digit numbers. There are no decimals. This means that it is easy to get visually confused – so it is worth jotting down the numbers you will be working with so as to avoid any miscalculations.

SET 43, Q2. Correct Answer: C

Reasoning

We need first to work out how many additional studio apartments will be built in France in 2015, and what the new total is. We can then calculate the new total of studios with dishwasher using the percentage shown in the table.

Calculation

We know that there are a total 120 new units in 2015 and these are divided evenly across countries and categories. Since there are a total of four countries and two categories, that means that the 120 new units are split evenly across $4 \times 2 = 8$ "segments".

$120 / 8 = 15$

This means that there are 15 new studio apartments in France in 2015, so we can now calculate the new total:

$130 + 15 = 145$

We can now calculate the number of studios with a dishwasher:

$145 \times 40\% = 145 \times 0.4 = 58$

Which is answer C.

Potential Shortcuts / Pitfalls

It is essential to spot here that the 120 new units must be divided by 8 (2 types of unit × 4 countries); if you only divide by 4 (the number of countries), you would get 64 and choose option D as the correct answer. It is also incorrect to add up all of the apartment categories in all of the countries, add the 120 new units and then divide by 8 – this would give us a completely useless average.

We can also eliminate some answer options by performing a single calculation. If we first calculate 40% of 130 (the 2014 number of studio apartments in France), we get:

$130 \times 40\% = 130 \times 0.4 = 52$

Since we know that there is an increase in the number of units in 2015, we can say that the correct answer must be *more than* the above result of 52. This immediately eliminates options A and B. We can also say that the result cannot be E, as it is more than the total number of studio apartments, even with the increase taken into account, leaving for us to decide only between options C and D.

SET 43, Q3. Correct Answer: E

Reasoning

First, we need to calculate the total number of apartment units. Once we have this, we calculate the number of studio apartments without air conditioning in Germany, and then what percentage this represents of the total.

Calculation

The total number of apartment units is simply the number of units across both categories in all countries added up:

100 + 200 (Austria) + 130 + 300 (France) + 300 + 100 (Germany) + 200 + 250 (Spain) = 1580

Next, we have to calculate the number of studio apartments in Germany without air conditioning. The table tells us that the proportion of units with air conditioning is 14%, so the proportion without must be 86%:

The number of studios without air conditioning is then:

$300 \times 86\% = 300 \times 0.86 = 258$

We can now perform the final calculation to find what percentage this represents of the total:

258 / 1580 × 100 = 16.33% (rounded)

Potential Shortcuts / Pitfalls

The only real danger here is not noticing that the question talks about the number of studio apartments *without* air conditioning in Germany. If we fail to notice this, we would calculate the number of units *with* air conditioning:

300 × 14% = 300 × 0.14 = 42

If we continue with this result, we would then calculate how much this represents of the total as follows:

42 / 1580 × 100 = 2.66%

You will not be surprised by now to find that this is also among the answer options, so if you fall into this trap you will mark option A as the correct answer.

SET 44, Q1. Correct Answer: C

Reasoning

The question asks about revenue *per week* but, as the period of factory operation is the same for all models, it is far simpler to calculate the revenue *per minute* for each model. The model which generates the least revenue per minute will be the correct answer.

Calculation

We need to calculate the revenue per minute for each model. This is the retail price divided by the production time and multiplied by the proportion of units sold.

FR-7:

90 / 10 × 0.96 = 8.64 (dollars per minute)

FR-10:

110 / 11 × 0.92 = 9.2

TG-4:

115 / 24 × 0.84 = 4.03

RZ-10:

130 / 15 × 0.89 = 7.71

From this we can see that the TG-4 generates the least revenue per minute, and therefore per week, by a wide margin.

Potential Shortcuts / Pitfalls

The greatest danger here is of attempting to calculate the actual revenue per model *per week*, which would be completely unnecessary and involve a large volume of calculations that would waste valuable time.

We can, however, reduce our work even further simply by looking at the figures before reaching for the calculator.

It is readily apparent that one unit of the TG-4 takes significantly more time to produce than the other models, and the percentage sold of the TG-4 is also smaller than for the other models. The only scenario in which this model would not generate the smallest revenue is if its retail price was very much higher than that of all the other models. As you can see, its retail price *is* higher than that of two of the models, but only by a relatively small margin. Thus the fact that the TG-4 generates the smallest revenue per week can be estimated just with some approximate mental arithmetic.

SET 44, Q2. Correct Answer: D

Reasoning

We need first to work out how many FR-7 printers have to be manufactured to create $27 000 in value. We then calculate, taking account of the increased production time per unit, how long it will take to manufacture the same number of units after the technical failure. Note that we do not need to account for the percentage of units sold because the question asks simply about "$27 000 worth" of the FR-7.

Calculation

To calculate the number of units that will generate 27 000 in revenue, we divide the revenue by the unit retail price:

27 000 / 90 = 300

We know it normally takes 10 minutes to produce one unit. The question states that the production time increased by 20% due to a technical failure, so the new production time is:

10 minutes × 1.2 (20% increase) = 12 minutes

To manufacture 300 units, we need:

12 minutes × 300 = 3600 minutes

Converted to hours, this is:

3600 / 60 = 60 hours

We know that the factory operates for 12 hours per day, so we need to divide by 12 to get the number of days required:

60 / 12 = 5

Potential Shortcuts / Pitfalls

One slight pitfall to avoid is taking into account the 96% of units sold, but this is not a serious danger: none of the answer options corresponds to the result we would get that way.

Important things to watch out for are the factory operating hours (if we divide by 24 instead of 12 hours, we get 2.5 days, which *is* one of the answer options) and not to forget about the increased production time, because the total days needed at the original production rate (4) is also among the answer options.

SET 44, Q3. Correct Answer: C

Reasoning

We must first establish how much additional time would be available for manufacturing by staying open on Sunday. Once we have done that, we can divide the total time by the production time per unit of each of the four printer models and add up the resulting four numbers.

Calculation

We know that the factory operates for 12 hours per day, so opening on Sunday means that each printer model can be manufactured for 12 additional hours.

Since the production time is in minutes, we should convert this into minutes:

12 × 60 = 720 minutes

Now we can calculate how many additional printers can be manufactured in the extra time by dividing this number by each of the four production times per unit.

FR-7:

720 / 10 = 72

FR-10:

720 / 11 = 65 (this is actually 65.45, but we can round it down: 0.45 of a printer is not a fully manufactured printer)

TG-4:

720 / 24 = 30

RZ-10:

720 / 15 = 48

As a final step, we add up these four numbers to get the total number of additional units that can be manufactured on Sunday:

72 + 65 + 30 + 48 = 215

Potential Shortcuts / Pitfalls

There is one possible pitfall that you need to avoid with this question. As there are 12 additional hours of manufacture for each of the four printer models (a total of 48 hours), you might be tempted to add up the production times for the four printers as well:

10 + 11 + 24 + 15 = 60 minutes = 1 hour

If you do this, you will get 48 / 1 = 48 additional printer units, which is an incorrect result but is easy to pick by mistake because it is among the answer options. The mistake here lies in the fact that production takes place simultaneously on all four models: the above calculation would only be correct if the printer models were manufactured one after the other.

SET 45, Q1. Correct Answer: E

Reasoning

We need to use the figures for the number of boats in the South Atlantic and the share this represents of the total to work out the total fleet size in 2013. Once we have done that, we calculate the increased fleet size in 2014 and, from that, the number of boats stationed in the Atlantic Ocean in that year.

Calculation

We know from the question that in 2013 the company had 42 fishing boats in the South Atlantic, and from the chart that this was equal to 15% of its total fleet.

Let us call the total 2013 fleet size F:

$42 = 0.15 \times F$

We now need F to be alone on one side of the equation, and everything else on the other side. We achieve this by performing the same operations on both sides of the equation. In this case, if we divide both sides by 0.15, we get there in one step:

$F = 42 / 0.15 = 280$

Now we can calculate the 2014 fleet size by increasing the 2013 size by 15%:

$280 \times 1.15 = 322$

We know that 40% of the fleet is in the South Atlantic in 2014 and 10% is in the North Atlantic, so a total of 50% of the fleet is in the Atlantic Ocean:

$322 \times 0.5 = 161$

Potential Shortcuts / Pitfalls
A couple of things to look out for:
- make sure you read off the correct data from the pie chart, as it is easier to confuse things here than in a table
- do not forget about the 15% fleet increase: disregarding this results in picking Option D

SET 45, Q2. Correct Answer: C

Reasoning

The chart does not tell us the number of fishing boats the company operates in 2013, only the proportions in each ocean. However we do not need to know the *actual 2013 fleet size* to answer the question. We simply take the 2013 *proportion* of the fleet that is in the Pacific Ocean (10% North Pacific + 20% South Pacific = 30%) and compare that to the share it has in 2014 in a 15% increased overall fishing fleet.

Calculation

Even with an unknown 2013 fleet size, we can express how many boats the company had in the Pacific Ocean in that year:

$30\% \times Fleet = 0.3 \times Fleet$

Now for 2014. We know that the fleet size increased by 15%:

$Fleet\ in\ 2014 = 1.15 \times Fleet$

We also know that the Pacific Ocean share of this total is 25%:

$25\% \times 1.15\ Fleet = 0.25 \times 1.15 \times Fleet = 0.2875 \times Fleet$

We therefore have values of 0.3 Fleet in 2013 and 0.2875 Fleet in 2014. We can calculate the difference in the usual way, by taking the difference between the two values and dividing by the originating (2013) value:

$$\frac{0.2875\ Fleet - 0.3\ Fleet}{0.3\ Fleet} = \frac{-0.0125\ Fleet}{0.3\ Fleet}$$

Notice that the unknown Fleet size is present in both the numerator and the denominator. This means that they cancel out, leaving us with a simpler calculation:

$-0.0125 / 0.3 = -0.0417$ (rounded)

Multiply this by a 100 to get a percentage:

$-0.0417 \times 100 = -4.17\%$

Potential Shortcuts / Pitfalls
The major pitfall here is the possibility of getting bogged down in the issue of how to frame the calculation when you do not have any figures for the number of boats, only proportions.

One other mistake not to make is to confuse a percentage change and a percentage point change. If you calculate the difference between 30% and 28.75% by simply subtracting one from the other, it would result in 1.25%, which is wrong – but since it is one of the answer options, it is easy to think you have got it right.

SET 45, Q3. Correct Answer: C

Reasoning

Since both oceans are home to 25% of the fishing fleet in 2014 and therefore have the same number of boats, the difference in the number of boats per square kilometre is the same as the difference in ocean size.

Calculation

To calculate the difference in ocean size, we simply subtract the size of the smaller ocean (the Indian Ocean) from the size of the larger ocean (the Pacific) and divide by the size of the smaller ocean.

Since we do not know the actual size of either ocean, only that the Pacific is 2.3 times as large as the Indian Ocean, we can think of the size of the latter as being 1. The advantage of this is that the size of the Pacific will then simply be 2.3.

Based on this, the calculation is as follows:

$(2.3 - 1) / 1 = 1.3$

To convert this to a percentage, we simply multiply by 100:

$1.3 \times 100 = 130\%$

Potential Shortcuts / Pitfalls

In this case it is essential to realize that you can in fact do the calculation just with the ocean sizes, without knowing the actual number of boats. If that is not immediately obvious, you might be tempted by answer option E, "impossible to tell".

A further key thing to bear in mind is that the question text states that the Pacific Ocean is 2.3 times as large as the Indian Ocean (i.e. 2.3 times larger) – this is not the same as saying that the Pacific Ocean is 230% larger than the Indian Ocean.

This distinction is nicely illuminated by using the alternative method of calculating a percentage increase. In the calculation section of the previous chapter, we took the difference in size and divided by the smaller area. When it comes to percentage differences, we can also use the formula where we simply divide the larger value by the smaller value, in our case:

$2.3 / 1 = 2.3$

If we multiply this by 100, we get a percentage. In this case, however, we must remember that this merely gives us the *ratio* of the two values. To get the *percentage difference*, we must subtract the originating value, which is the size of the Indian Ocean in this case, which we denoted by 1 – or, in other words, by 100%:

$230 - 100 = 130\%$

Even when the values are different, using the above calculation and then subtracting 1 or 100% works, and some people will prefer this method.

SET 46, Q1. Correct Answer: E

Reasoning

First, we must determine how to work out the total cost of acquiring and operating the software and then calculate this amount for all of the software options. The total cost is calculated by adding up the licence fee for the given period, the one-off installation fee and the total working hours spent operating the software multiplied by the hourly wage of the operating staff.

Calculation

We can start by writing out the formula for calculating the total cost for each of the options.

Total cost = Installation Fee + Licence Fee (Year 1) + Licence Fee (Year 2) + (Staff Number $\times$ Working Hours $\times$ Number of Months $\times$ Hourly Wage)

Let's now calculate this for each of the options.

Accounts Pro 10:

$130 + 4\,500 + 4\,500 + (4 \times 20 \times 24 \times 20) = 47\,530$

BSheet 12:

$150 + 3\,500 + 3\,500 + (4 \times 20 \times 24 \times 20) = 45\,550$

BSheet Lite:

$200 + 8\,000 + 8\,000 + (3 \times 25 \times 24 \times 20) = 52\,200$

BookKeeper Standard (remember that this software has a one-off licence fee only to be counted once):

$550 + 9\,000 + (5 \times 15 \times 24 \times 20) = 45\,550$

We can now pick BSheet 12 and BookKeeper Standard as the two options that represent the lowest cost.

Potential Shortcuts / Pitfalls

One obvious pitfall to avoid is calculating BookKeeper Standard's one-off fee twice (once for each year). Also, there are a few opportunities where we can save time.

If you use a calculator, it is much better to start by calculating the total cost of the operating staff and only then adding the licence fees and the installation fee. Why? Because of the order of precedence between the various operations. The staff cost is the only factor which involves multiplication. Since multiplication is "higher priority" in a calculator than addition, we would either run into an error or would have to take note of an interim result – both of which make us lose time.

Let's take the BookKeeper Standard calculation to illustrate this. We started by adding up the licence fee and the installation fee:

550 + 9000

We then have to stop, memorize or write down this result, clear the calculator, calculate the staff costs and then add the above result in at the end. So what happens if we don't do that, and just continue with the calculations?

550 + 9000 + 5

A simple calculator will not wait to see which operation comes next, nor does it support the use of parentheses – it would simply add 5 to 550 + 9000, and then perform the multiplications, which would result in an obviously wrong answer.

SET 46, Q2. Correct Answer: C

Reasoning

We must first calculate the total licence fees for 5 years and then subtract the discount. We will then calculate the total cost of staff for 5 years and add up these two figures.

Calculation

Let's calculate the discounted licence fees for 5 years first. We do this by multiplying the yearly licence fee by the number of years and then calculating the discounted figure. A 15% discount can be expressed by saying that the new price is 85% of the original:

$3\,500 \times 5 \times 85\% = 3\,500 \times 5 \times 0.85 = 14\,875$

We now calculate the total staff cost, which is the number of staff needed multiplied by the monthly working hours and the number of months ($5 \times 12 = 60$), multiplied by the hourly wage:

$4 \times 20 \times 60 \times 20 = 96\,000$

The total cost is the sum of the above two figures:

$96\,000 + 14875 = 110\,875$ EUR

Potential Shortcuts / Pitfalls

Important to avoid:

- do not forget about the 15% reduction in licensing costs (if you do, you get option D)
- do not forget that the installation fee was waived (if you do, you get option E)
- do not forget about multiplying the staff costs by the number of months (if you do, you get option A or B, depending on whether you perhaps also forget about the licence fee discount)

SET 46, Q3. Correct Answer: C

Reasoning

We need to work out the total cost of introducing and operating each of the two software options for three years and then calculate the difference.

Calculation

The total cost of operating either software option for three years is as follows:

(Staff needed to operate × Working hours × Number of Months × Hourly Wage) + Licence fees + Installation fee

For BookKeeper Standard, this is:

$(5 \times 15 \times 36 \times 20) + 9\,000 + 550 = 63\,550$

For Accounts Pro 10, this is:

$(4 \times 20 \times 36 \times 20) + (4500 \times 3) + 130 = 71\,230$

Since the question was about the savings or losses if the company introduces BookKeeper Standard *instead of* Accounts Pro 10, we should subtract the costs of BookKeeper Standard from Accounts Pro 10, not the other way around:

$71\,230 – 63\,550 = 7\,680$

Since the total cost of BookKeeper Standard is lower (the result of the above subtraction is positive), this represents a net saving, so option C is the correct answer.

SET 47, Q1. Correct Answer: B

Reasoning

The lowest number of error-free files is calculated by subtracting the erroneous files from the total number of files closed for each team and picking the lowest number.

Calculation

The error rate denotes the percentage of files that were closed with errors, so in order to calculate the number of error-free files, we must subtract this percentage from 100% and calculate with those figures.

The number of error-free files for the five teams are as follows.

Team A:

$4\,500 \times (100\% - 5\%) = 4\,500 \times 95\% = 4\,500 \times 0.95 = 4275$

Team B:

$4\,500 \times (100\% - 7\%) = 4\,500 \times 93\% = 4\,500 \times 0.93 = 4\,185$

Team C:

$5\,000 \times (100\% - 11\%) = 5\,000 \times 89\% = 5\,000 \times 0.89 = 4450$

Team D:

$6000 \times (100\% - 8\%) = 6\,000 \times 92\% = 6\,000 \times 0.92 = 5\,520$

Team E:

$6\,500 \times (100\% - 9\%) = 6\,500 \times 91\% = 6\,500 \times 0.91 = 5\,915$

We can clearly see that Team B closed the smallest number of files without errors.

Potential Shortcuts / Pitfalls

If you take a moment to consider the two charts, you can easily figure out the correct answer without performing any calculations. The first thing to notice is that Teams A and B closed the smallest number of files (with or without errors). The only way one of those two didn't close the smallest number of error-free files is if their error rate was very low and the other three teams' error rates were disproportionately higher. This doesn't seem to be the case.

Teams D and E closed many more files and their error rates are only slightly higher, so we can safely disregard them. Team C closed only slightly more files and its error rate is much higher, so it is worth looking at it.

Team C closed 500 more files than either Team A or Team B, and its error rate is 11% compared to 5% for Team A and 7% for Team B. The only way Team C can be worse than A or B is if the difference in the

error rates accounts for more files than the difference in the total number of files – this, again, doesn't seem to be the case.

The maximum difference in erroneous files is between Team A (7% of 4 500) and Team C (11% of 5 000). That is 4 percentage points, and 4 percentage points of 5 000 is never going to make up for the 500-file difference between Teams A and B on the one hand, and Team C on the other.

This leaves us with Teams A and B. Since they closed the same number of files, the correct answer is the team which has the higher error rate, namely Team B.

SET 47, Q2. Correct Answer: C

Reasoning

We need first to calculate the number of error-free closed files for Team B and Team C, and then the difference between the two values.

Calculation

The number of error-free files closed by Team B:

$4\,500 \times (100\% - 2\%) = 4\,500 \times 98\% = 4\,500 \times 0.98 = 4\,410$

The number of error-free files closed by Team C:

$5\,000 \times (100\% - 17\%) = 5\,000 \times 83\% = 5\,000 \times 0.83 = 4\,150$

The difference between the two figures is:

$4\,410 - 4\,150 = 260$

Option C is the correct answer.

Potential Shortcuts / Pitfalls

Since the answer options are quite close to each other, there isn't much leeway for shortcuts and estimations in this exercise. On the other hand, you must be careful when interpreting the changes in the error rates: contrary to how a lot of EPSO numerical reasoning questions are worded, it is not the *change* in error rates that is given, but the *actual* new error rates – and this saves you a set of calculations which you don't have to perform.

SET 47, Q3. Correct Answer: D

Reasoning

We must first calculate the total number of files closed by the five teams throughout the year, and then what proportion of this total was closed by the end of September.

Calculation

The total number of files closed is simply the sum of the number of files closed by each team:

Total = 4 500 + 4 500 + 5 000 + 6 000 + 6 500 = 26 500

Since teams progress through files at a constant rate from month to month, we can calculate how many files they close in one month:

26 500 / 12 = 2 208.33

Since September is the 9th month of the year, we can multiply the above value by 9 to get the number of files closed by the end of that month:

2 208.33 × 9 = 19 875 (rounded up)

Potential Shortcuts / Pitfalls

There is an alternative way of calculating this which might be quicker and could yield an even more accurate result.

If we think of September as the 9th month in a 12-month year, we can say that the teams closed 9/12th of the files. We can then use this fraction in our calculations:

26 500 × 9 / 12 = 19875

As it turns out, this method yields exactly 19 875 and there was no need for it to be rounded to match option D.

SET 48, Q1. Correct Answer: B

Reasoning

We work out the total tax owed on 55 000 EUR of income by calculating the tax owed in each tax bracket and then adding on the total insurance tax for 12 months.

Calculation

First, let's calculate the tax owed on 55 000 EUR in each of the three systems.

System 1

First 10 000 EUR: tax free

10 001 – 30 000 EUR: The tax is the amount of income falling within this range multiplied by the percentage. Since the person's income is more than 30 000 EUR, we need to calculate the tax for the full range. This is done by subtracting the top of the previous range from the top of the current range:

30 000 – 10 000 = 20 000

The tax is then:

20 000 × 15% = 20 000 × 0.15 = 3000

30 001 – 50 000 EUR:

Using the same formula as above, the tax is:

20 000 × 0.25 = 5000

We still have 5 000 EUR left to account for. This falls into the 50 001+ range.

50 001+ EUR:

5 000 × 0.31 = 1550

We must also not forget about the insurance tax, which is a flat fee of 100 EUR / month:

100 × 12 = 1200

The total tax owed is then:

3000 + 5000 + 1550 + 1200 = 10 750 EUR

We now have to do the calculations for the other two systems as well.

System 2

System 2 has no tax free allowance.

0 – 30 000 EUR: 4500 EUR tax

30 001+ EUR: 5250 EUR tax

Insurance tax: 600 EUR

Total: 10 350 EUR

System 3

System 3 has a tax free allowance of 15 000 EUR.

15 001 – 30 000 EUR: 2 550 EUR tax

30 001+ EUR: 5 500 EUR tax

Insurance tax: 2400 EUR

Total: 10 450 EUR

From the above, we can see that the person owes the smallest amount in taxes under System 2.

Potential Shortcuts / Pitfalls

Unfortunately there aren't really any shortcuts you can use for this question. However there are some potential pitfalls to watch out for. You must make sure to check whether there is a tax free allowance in the system, and it is crucially important to read and understand the description of marginal tax rate – namely that only the amount falling within the range must be taxed at the given rate.

If, for example, you look at the table for System 3 and conclude that 62 000 EUR must be taxed at 28%, and you calculate the tax at 28% for the entire amount, you will get an incorrect result.

SET 48, Q2. Correct Answer: C

Reasoning

First we must calculate the total tax owed on 62 000 EUR, and then we will divide that amount by the income and multiply by 100 to get a percentage.

Calculation

For the general logic of how to work with tax brackets, see the previous explanation.

Let's calculate the tax owed in each bracket.

0 – 15 000 EUR: no tax

15 001 – 30 000 EUR: 2 550 EUR

30 001 – 60 000 EUR: 6 600 EUR

60 001+ EUR:

There are 2 000 EUR left to tax at this rate, so the tax is:

2 000 EUR × 28% = 2 000 × 0.28 = 560

We must also not forget about the insurance tax, which is 200 EUR / month, so:

200 × 12 = 2400 EUR / year

The total tax is then:

2 550 + 6 600 + 560 + 2400 = 12 110 EUR

Now to the effective tax rate, which is calculated by dividing the above value by the person's income and multiplied by 100:

12 110 / 62 000 × 100 = 19.53%

Potential Shortcuts / Pitfalls

One error that people sometimes make is to try to calculate the effective tax rate by adding up the rates of tax in the various tax brackets and then dividing the total by the number of tax brackets: this is obviously wrong because of the different weights of the ranges.

SET 48, Q3. Correct Answer: B

Reasoning

We must first calculate the tax owed under each of the two systems using the already familiar method. We can then calculate the difference in after-tax income under the two systems and divide that difference by the value under System 3.

Calculation

Let's first calculate the tax owed under System 1.

System 1

0 – 10 000 EUR: no tax

10 001 – 30 000 EUR: 3 000 EUR tax

30 001 – 50 000 EUR: 5 000 EUR tax

50 001+ EUR: 7 750 EUR tax

Insurance tax: 1200 EUR

Total tax:

3 000 + 5 000 + 7 750 + 1 200 = 16 950 EUR

The after-tax income is then:

75 000 – 16 950 = 58 050 EUR

And now under System 3.

System 3

0 – 15 000 EUR: no tax

15 001 – 30 000 EUR: 2 550 EUR

30 001 – 60 000 EUR: 6 600 EUR

60 001+ EUR: 4 200 EUR

Insurance tax: 2 400 EUR

Total tax:

2 550 + 6 600 + 4 200 + 2 400 = 15 750 EUR

The after tax income is:

75 000 – 15 750 = 59 250 EUR

Here we must be careful to get our figures the right way round. The question asks "by what percentage is their after-tax income greater or smaller under System 1 than under System 3". If you look at the figures for Systems 1 and 3, this will tell you that the after-tax income is smaller under System 1 so we are dealing with a negative figure:

58 050 (System 1) - 59 250 (System 3) = -1 200 EUR

We must now divide this by the after-tax income for System 3, since the question compares System 1 to System 3, and multiply that by 100 to get a percentage:

-1 200 / 59 250 = -2% (rounded)

This corresponds to answer option B.

Potential Shortcuts / Pitfalls

The risk here is that if you get the comparison the wrong way round, you will calculate:

1 200 / 59 250 = 2% (rounded)

This will "look right" because it is indeed one of the answer options, C.

SET 49, Q1. Correct Answer: E

Reasoning

We must calculate the percentage each power plant's electricity production represents of the total for that country and then see which one is in the middle.

Calculation

To calculate the proportion the production of a power plant represents in the total consumption of

that country, we simply divide its production by the country's consumption.

Since all of the operations we will perform are divisions, and there are five zeroes at the end of almost all consumption figures, we can simply disregard those. In the case of Venezuela, this means that we will divide by 858.5.

Itaipu Dam / Brazil:

98.3 / 4 557 = 0.02157121

Three Gorges Dam / China:

98.5 / 53 223 = 0.001850704

Krasnoyarsk / Russia:

20.4 / 10 165 = 0.002006886

Grand Coulee / USA:

20 / 38 864 = 0.0005146151

Guri / Venezuela

53.41 / 858.5 = 0.06221316

The numbers above are a little hard to compare because they are so small, but with a bit of care it is possible. We can see that Grand Coulee is the only one with 3 zeroes after the decimal point, so that will be the smallest proportion. Also, Guri and Itaipu Dam only have one zero after the decimal point, and the next number is greater (6 versus 2) in the case of Guri, so that will be the largest proportion, followed by Itaipu Dam.

This is what we have so far, from smallest to largest proportion:

Grand Coulee / USA
?
?
Itaipu Dam / Brazil
Guri / Venezuela

We are now left with Three Gorges Dam / China and Krasnoyarsk / Russia – one of them will be in the middle. Both of them have two zeroes after the decimal point, but the next number is greater in the case of Russia (2 versus 1), so we have our final order:

Grand Coulee / USA
Three Gorges Dam / China
Krasnoyarsk / Russia
Itaipu Dam / Brazil
Guri / Venezuela

Krasnoyarsk is clearly in the middle.

Potential Shortcuts / Pitfalls

There is a great opportunity to estimate here.

We can quite easily see that Guri tops the list for generating the highest proportion of its country's electricity. The Guri power plant generates more than half the electricity of either the Brazilian or Chinese power stations, but Venezuela's consumption is far smaller than that of Brazil or China.

The next smallest consumption figure belongs to Brazil, yet Itaipu Dam has the second largest production, so it must come second (while Itaipu Dam produces almost twice as much electricity as Venezuela's Guri, Brazil's consumption is about 5 times as large as Venezuela's).

If we compare the USA's consumption to China's, we see that they are fairly comparable (3.9 to 5.3) but the Grand Coulee generates only a fifth of the electricity generated by the Three Gorges Dam, so it must be in the last position.

We are now again left with Russia and China, but without having performed any calculations. The way to compare the Russian and Chinese power stations is to look at the relationship between their production and their national consumptions.

Krasnoyarsk to Three Gorges is 1 to slightly less than 5.

Russia to China, however, is 1 to slightly more than 5.

This means that the Three Gorges percentage will be lower, so it will be the fourth in the list, leaving Krasnoyarsk in the middle.

SET 49, Q2. Correct Answer: E

Reasoning

We must first calculate how much electricity is currently produced in Venezuela from the total consumption and the percentage which current production contributes to this. We will then add the capacity of the new power station to this total and subtract Venezuela's total consumption to see how much is left for export.

Calculation

To find the current total production, we calculate 78% of the total consumption of Venezuela. To keep things consistent, we should decide whether we are going to perform all calculations in TWh or MWh. We will use TWh on this occasion.

The electricity consumption of Venezuela is then:

85 850 000 MWh / 1 000 000 = 85.85 TWh

78% of this is produced by the existing power stations:

85.85 × 78% = 85.85 × 0.78 = 66.963 TWh

After the completion of the new power station (which has the same capacity as that of Guri), the new total production will be:

66.963 TWh + 53.41 TWh = 120.373 TWh

If we subtract the current total consumption from the above figure, we get the amount available for export:

120.23 TWh – 85.85 TWh = 34.523 TWh

Since this is not among the answer options, we must also convert this into MWh and check if that is correct:

34.523 TWh × 1 000 000 = 34 523 000 MWh

which is answer option E.

Potential Shortcuts / Pitfalls

There are two major issues to be careful with here.

First, we must notice and then not get confused by the different orders of magnitude represented by the two different units of measurement, as defined in a footnote to the table. In situations like this, it is advisable to make a decision about which one you will use and then consistently convert all values to that unit before performing the actual calculations.

Also, it is tempting to simply double the capacity of the Guri power station (since the new one has the same capacity) and compare that to the consumption of Venezuela. That, however, would disregard the information given in the question text, namely that current production represents 78% of the total consumption (which means there must be other power stations in the country).

SET 49, Q3. Correct Answer: D

Reasoning

The electricity consumption of the EU is unknown at the beginning of this exercise, but we know that the capacity of the Three Gorges Dam is equal to

3.24% of this, from which we can calculate the total (100%). Once we have that, we simply take 30% of this total to get the amount generated from nuclear power.

Calculation

Since the total electricity consumption of the EU is unknown, let's call it X. We do know that 3.24% of this is equal to the capacity of the Three Gorges Dam, and this capacity is a known value:

$3.24\% \times X = 98.5$ TWh

Let's convert 3.24% to a decimal:

$0.0324 \times X = 98.5$ TWh

Our aim is to find the total consumption of the EU, or X. Remember, in equations like this, we want 1 X to be alone on one side, and we achieve that by performing the same operations on both sides. Here, all we have to do is divide by 0.0324:

$X = 98.5 / 0.0324 = 3\,040.12346$ TWh

This is the total consumption of the EU, 30% of which is produced from nuclear power:

$3\,040.12346 \times 30\% = 3\,040.12346 \times 0.3 = 912.04$ TWh (rounded)

Potential Shortcuts / Pitfalls
There are several things to watch out for in this question.
- do not stop after having solved the equation – that is the *total* consumption of the EU, not the share of nuclear power
- do not round prematurely: if you round the total consumption to the nearest whole number and you calculate 30% of that, you would erroneously mark option C as the correct answer
- watch out for the units of measurement: all throughout the calculations, we only worked with TWh, so be careful with the answer options expressed in MWh

SET 50, Q1. Correct Answer: C

Reasoning

We need to calculate what percentage of all washing machines are energy-efficient, and then what percentage this represents of all household appliances.

Calculation

To find the percentage of washing machines that are energy-efficient, we simply add up the percentages of A+/A and B-rated washing machines:

$45\% + 35\% = 80\%$

We know that washing machines (energy-efficient and non-efficient together) represent 20% of the total of all household appliances, and 80% of these are energy-efficient:

$80\% \times 20\% = 0.8 \times 0.2 = 0.16 = 16\%$

SET 50, Q2. Correct Answer: D

Reasoning

We need to work out the current number of refrigerators and air conditioners that are energy-efficient from their percentage share of all refrigerators and air conditioners, and then increase this number by 20%.

Calculation

The current share of energy-efficient refrigerators:

$40\% + 25\% = 65\%$

And that of air conditioners:

$10\% + 45\% = 55\%$

We can now calculate the number of energy-efficient units.

Refrigerators:

$9\,000 \times 65\% = 9\,000 \times 0.65 = 5\,850$

Air conditioners:

$3\,400 \times 55\% = 3\,400 \times 0.55 = 1\,870$

The current total of energy-efficient units is:

$5\,850 + 1\,870 = 7\,720$

If this increases by 20%, we get:

$7\,720 + 20\% = 7\,720 \times 120\% = 7\,720 \times 1.2 = 9\,264$

Potential Shortcuts / Pitfalls
The key issue here is not to confuse what the question is asking and end up calculating a 20 percentage point increase rather than a 20% increase. Remember: if your share of a cake is one-half and your share

increases by 20%, you will have 60% of the cake, not 70%.

If you make this mistake you will calculate as follows:

Refrigerators:

$9\,000 \times 85\% = 9\,000 \times 0.85 = 7\,650$

Air conditioners:

$3\,400 \times 75\% = 3\,400 \times 0.75 = 2\,550$

This will give you a combined total (7650 + 2550) of 10200, and as this is one of the answer options you will think you have got the question right.

SET 50, Q3. Correct Answer: D

Reasoning

We need to calculate the number of D-rated units for each of the four appliances, and then see which number is the largest.

Calculation

The number of D-rated units is the total of appliances multiplied by the percentage share that are D-rated.

Air conditioners:

$25\% \times 3\,400 = 0.25 \times 3\,400 = 850$

Washing machines:

$10\% \times 5\,500 = 550$

Dryers:

$15\% \times 2\,000 = 300$

Refrigerators:

$10\% \times 9000 = 900$

From the above, we can see that D-rated refrigerators would be at the top of this list.

Potential Shortcuts / Pitfalls

It is easy to solve this question without using a calculator at all – let's see how.

10%

There are two values where 10% needs to be calculated – we can do this by simply taking away a 0 from the end of the figure.

15%

First we calculate 10%. Then we take half of that value and add it to the 10%. 15% of 2 000 then becomes 200 + 100 = 300.

25%

Calculating 25% of 3 400 seems to be the hardest of the four to calculate, but if you think of 25% as one quarter, it becomes much simpler. But how much is one quarter of 3 400? Again, if you think of 3 400 as 3 200 + 200, then you can take one quarter of both and add these two numbers up.

One quarter of 3 200 is the same as one quarter of 32 (plus the zeroes). Since 32 is 8×4, this is 800. One quarter of 200 is 50, so the result here is 850.

SET 51, Q1. Correct Answer: A

Reasoning

The percentage increase in production for each crop is calculated by taking the difference in production between the two given years and then dividing this by the starting (2010) value and finally multiplying the answer by 100 to make it a percentage.

Calculation

Corn: (12409 – 12211) / 12211 x 100 = 1.62%
Rapeseed: (5801 – 5472) / 5472 x 100 = 6.01%
Sugar: (2702 – 2920) / 2920 x 100 = -7.47%
Sunflowers: (21199 – 19194) / 19194 x 100 = 10.45%
Wheat: (7792 – 7719) / 7719 x 100 = 0.95%

The correct answer is therefore Corn (A)

Potential Shortcuts / Pitfalls

If you perform all the calculations above with a calculator you will use well over 100 keystrokes. This can be shortened considerably and even eliminated completely just by taking a few moments to think about the data.

The question asks for the middle crop so we don't actually need an exact figure, just a relative figure compared to the other crops. A quick look at the data shows that sugar production has actually fallen and so without any calculation we know that this will be at the bottom of the new table. Next, try rounding all the figures to the nearest hundred. Now we can see that corn goes up 2 from 122, rapeseed goes up 3 from 55, sunflowers go up 20 from 192, and wheat goes up 1 from 77. From this we can see that sunflowers have risen enormously compared to the others and will be at the top of the table, with rapeseed close behind. The remaining two are a little bit closer, and you could use your calculator if you are unsure, but given that the rounding would overestimate the wheat growth then corn is clearly going to be higher. This will make corn the third highest and hence in the middle of the table.

SET 51, Q2. Correct Answer: B

Reasoning

The percentage increase in production for wheat is calculated by taking the difference in production between the two given years and then dividing this by the starting (2005) value, finally multiplying the answer by 100 to make it a percentage. We can then reverse this process for sugar to calculate what value we should use for the 2010 production to get this same figure. Finally we need to subtract the actual amount produced to get the difference.

Calculation

Wheat: $(7719 - 7422) / 7422 \times 100 \approx 4.0016\%$

This can be called 4% to the nearest percentage point

Let the 2010 figure for sugar be X, then:

$(X - 2814) / 2814 \times 100 = 4.0\%$
$X / 2814 - 2814 / 2814 = 4.0\% / 100$
$X / 2814 - 1 = 0.04$
$X = (1 + 0.04) \times 2814 = 2926.56$

Now subtract the actual production value to obtain the difference or increase as mentioned in the question.

$2926.56 - 2920 \approx 6.56$ which is in thousands of tonnes.

Potential Shortcuts / Pitfalls
This problem can be simplified considerably by initially setting the two calculations to be equal to each other:

$(X - 2814) / 2814 = (7719 - 7422) / 7422$

We can simplify this further because when you expand the bracketed parts of the equation we get 2814/2814 and 7422/7422; these are both equal to one and since they appear on each side of the equation then they just disappear.

Now we have:

$X / 2814 = 7719 / 7422$

And so:

$X = 7719 \times 2814 / 7422 = 2926.605$

You will note that this is not the same as the answer given because this method has effectively used an exact figure for the percentage increase (7719/7422). To circumvent this, do that part of the calculation first and then only use the first two decimal places of the answer to continue with the rest of the calculation.

Don't forget to subtract the actual production figure to get the difference and remember that the figure is in thousands of tonnes.

SET 51, Q3. Correct Answer: E

Reasoning

The amount of land used for rapeseed production is the number of tonnes produced divided by the yield. We need to calculate this for 2005 and then can increase the yield by 6% and use this figure to calculate the land usage in 2015. We can then calculate the percentage increase by taking the difference and dividing by the 2005 figure.

Calculation

First, calculate the amount of land given over to rapeseed production. This is 4541 (thousand) tonnes divided by 3.1 tonnes per hectare:

$4541 / 3.1 \approx 1464.84$

Increase the yield by 6%:

$3.1 \times 6\% = 3.1 \times 1.06 = 3.286$

Now use this yield to calculate the land usage in 2015:

$5801 / 3.286 = 1765.37$

As a percentage of the 2005 rapeseed land use this is:

$(1765.37 - 1464.84) / 1464.84 \times 100 \approx 20.5\%$

Potential Shortcuts / Pitfalls
Some things leap out as obvious and some things are really quite well hidden. If we write out the whole procedure above as one equation it looks quite messy...

$((5801 / (3.1 \times 1.06)) - (4541 / 3.1)) / (4531 / 3.1)$

However, there are effectively three terms in the equation (B – A) / A, and you can see that all of them have the yield (3.1) as a common term as a divisor. As a result, this cancels out and can be eliminated from the equation entirely. *So, in a question that, at first, seems to focus on the crop yield, it turns out that it is not even required.*

SET 52, Q1. Correct Answer: B

Reasoning

The percentage increase in nuclear power generation is calculated by taking the difference in generation figures between the two given years and then dividing this by the starting (2000) value and finally multiplying the answer by 100 to make it a percentage. However we first need to increase the 2005 figure by 7.25% to take account of the increase in the total amount of energy being generated.

Calculation

First, calculate the total amount of electricity generated in 2005. This is 7.25% higher than in 2000. Let us assume that the total in 2000 was X. Then:

2005: Total = X * 1.0725

So the increase is:

(X * 1.0725 * 12.4 – X * 10.9) / X * 10.9

As there is a common term (X) in every element of the calculation both above and below the dividing line we can cancel it out, leaving:

(1.0725 * 12.4 – 10.9) / 10.9 = 0.22

Multiply this by 100 to make it a percentage:

0.22 * 100 = 22%

Potential Shortcuts / Pitfalls

This question is far more straightforward than it first looks. The main problem is what to do with the 7.25% increase given that there is no total power generation figure to use. However, provided there is a common base figure (the 2000 total power generation) that is being worked from, then it is always going to cancel out and need not even be considered.

Make sure you apply the increase to the 2005 figure before you calculate the difference for the increase rather than applying it to the increase itself.

SET 52, Q2. Correct Answer: D

Reasoning

The percentage increase in generation for each form of energy generation is calculated by taking the difference in percentage generated between the two given years and then dividing this by the starting (2010) value and finally multiplying the answer by 100 to make it a percentage.

Calculation

First, calculate the percentage change in percentage of total energy generated for each of the forms.

Fossil:	(53.0 – 66.4) / 66.4 * 100 = 20.2%
Wind:	(15.4 – 9.8) / 9.8 * 100 = 57.1%
Solar:	(12.3 – 7.8) / 7.8 * 100 = 57.7%
Tide:	(3.3 – 1.8) / 1.8 * 100 = 83.3%
Nuclear:	(9.8 – 10.4) / 10.4 * 100 = -5.8%
Other:	(6.2 – 3.8) / 3.8 * 100 = 63.2%

The correct answer is Tide/Wave (D)

Potential Shortcuts / Pitfalls

Virtually all the calculations can be made redundant just by taking a moment to examine the data and do a little bit of estimation and approximation. First and foremost, the question asks for the *largest increase* and so we can immediately eliminate Fossil and Nuclear because they have actually fallen.

The others are a little closer but other work that need not be done is the multiplication by 100 to make percentages. You only want the *relative* values of these figures and so any identical operation is going to do the same thing to all of them and make no difference to their relative values.

Take Wind: it starts at about 10% and increases to about 16% which is an increase of about 60%. Solar increases 4.5 from a starting value of about 8. This is clearly more than 50% but less than 2/3. Tide and wave power increases by 1.5 from a base of 1.8 which is 5/6 – which leaves the previous 2 way behind. Finally, 'Other' increases 2.4 from a base of 3.8 which is less than ¾, so Tide/Wave is left as the clear winner.

SET 52, Q3. Correct Answer: E

Reasoning

We need to calculate the percentage of the total power generated by biomass in 2005 and increase this by 50%. We then need to calculate the amount generated by 'Other' in 2010 and work out the proportion of this generated by biomass.

Calculation

First, calculate the percentage of total power generated by biomass in 2005. If we say the total amount generated is X, then the amount generated by 'Other' is:

$X * 2.9\% = 0.029X$

The amount generated by biomass is:

$0.029X * 20\% = 0.029X * 0.2 = 0.0058X$

This increases in 2010 to:

$0.0058 * 150\% = 0.0058 * 1.5 = 0.0087X$

In 2010 the total power is 10% higher than 2005, which is:

$X * 110\% = 1.1X$

So, in 2010 the percentage of total power generated by 'Other' is:

$1.1X * 3.8\% = 1.1X * 0.038 = 0.0418X$

The percentage of this generated by biomass is:

$(0.0087X / 0.0418X) * 100 = 20.8\%$

Potential Shortcuts / Pitfalls

As you can see from the calculation, the total power generated in 2005 (X) is unspecified and cancels out so needn't be considered at all. It is used primarily to explain the process. However, we can shorten this calculation considerably if we stop and think about the data in question and what we are trying to achieve.

In 2010 'Other' accounts for 3.8% of the total generation, which increases by 10% to about 4.2 when applied to the 2005 base (X). So 'Other' rises from 2.9 to 4.2. This is very close to 50%, which is the same rise that has applied to biomass and so they pretty much cancel each other out.

SET 53, Q1. Correct Answer: A

Reasoning

We need to work out the number of births in Croatia in 2005 and 2015 and then calculate the difference. The number of births is simply the population multiplied by the birth rate. However, before we can calculate the number of births in 2015 we must first calculate the population given the population has increased since 2005.

Calculation

First, calculate the population in 2015 given the increase from 2005 is 7.5%:

$Population = 4443 * 1.075 = 4776.225$

Now calculate the number of births in 2015:

$4776.225 * 16.8 = 80241$

Note that the population is in thousands and the birth rate is per thousand and so these cancel each other out. Also we can round to an exact number as this is a number of births and you cannot have a fractional birth.

Now calculate the number of births in 2005:

$4443 * 16.5 = 73310$

The difference is:

$80241 - 73310 = 6931$

Potential Shortcuts / Pitfalls

You must remember to take into account the scale of the units in the data tables. On this occasion they cancel each other out but this is not always the case.

Also, you can combine all the steps above by doing $(16.8 * 1.075 - 16.5) * 4443$. This is not quite as intuitive but it reduces the number of keystrokes and also saves the need to store partial results, which can lead to errors.

SET 53, Q2. Correct Answer: C

Reasoning

We need to calculate the total number of births for each country, add them together and then divide by 4, which is the number of countries.

Calculation

First, calculate the number of births for each country (rounding *each number of births to the nearest whole number*):

Croatia: 4443 * 16.5 = 73310
Denmark: 5417 * 11.9 = 64462
Portugal: 10547 * 14.4 = 151877
Sweden: 9293 * 11.2 = 104082

Now add all these together:

73310 + 64462 + 151877 + 104082 = 393731

And then divide this by the number of countries to get the average:

393731 / 4 = 98433

Potential Shortcuts / Pitfalls

It is important to understand that the average number of something is the total number of things divided by the number of data items. In this case it is births and countries. This is not the same as adding up all the populations and dividing by 4 (the average population) and multiplying this by the total of all the birth rates divided by 4 (the average birth rate). This would give the incorrect figure of 100238, and as this is given as one of the answer options you might easily think you had got the calculation right.

SET 53, Q3. Correct Answer: E

Reasoning

We need to calculate the number of births in Portugal in 2005 then add in the increase in births for 2015. From this we can calculate the population of Portugal in 2015 and hence the increase in population from 2005.

Calculation

First, calculate the total number of births in 2005:

10547 * 14.4 = 151877

Therefore the total number of births in 2015 is:

151877 + 4 = 151881

Now calculate the population in 2015 that would give rise to this number of births:

Population * 13.9 = 151881

Population = 151881 / 13.9 = 10927

Now calculate the percentage change in population:

Change = (10927 – 10547) / 10547 *100 = 3.6%

Potential Shortcuts / Pitfalls

The increase in the number of births is obviously tiny (4 extra births out of a total of some 150,000). However, this small increase comes despite the birth rate having fallen between 2005 and 2015, and this means that the population must have grown. Therefore *you can immediately dismiss 3 of the possible answers,* because they have the population falling. Furthermore, as the growth in births is virtually nothing you can deduce that the fall in birth rate is basically equal to the rise in population. So, by simply calculating the fall in birth rate (13.9 – 14.4) / 14.4 = –3.6% we know that the population increased by this much.

SET 54, Q1. Correct Answer: D

Reasoning

We need to calculate the number of bottles of red wine consumed in 2015, which is the total consumption divided by the size of a bottle. From this we can work out the total spending on red wine, which is the number of bottles multiplied by the cost. Finally we can calculate the per capita spending, which is the total spending divided by the population.

Calculation

First, let's calculate the total number of bottles consumed (and as wine consumption is in litres, we need to convert 75cl into litres, which is 0.75):

52 / 0.75 = 69.333

Remember that this figure is in millions of bottles.

Therefore the total spending on red wine in 2015 is:

69.333 * 6.63 = 459.678

This figure is millions of euros.

Now calculate the per capita spending:

459.678 / 16714 = 0.0275

Now we need to think about the order of magnitude. The total spending was in millions and the population is in thousands, so we need to multiply the answer by 1000 to get a per capita value:

0.0275 * 1000 = 27.50

Potential Shortcuts / Pitfalls

This problem can seem a bit more complicated than it really is. You just need to be methodical in following each step, converting litres to bottles, to money, etc. and you also need to be careful to keep an eye on the different magnitudes of the data items.

SET 54, Q2. Correct Answer: B

Reasoning

We need to calculate the percentage change in consumption of rosé wine between 2010 and 2015 and then apply this change to the white wine to calculate what the consumption would have been with the same percentage change.

Calculation

First, calculate the change in consumption of rosé wine between 2010 and 2015. This is the difference in consumption divided by the starting value (2010 figure) and then multiplied by 100:

(31 − 38) / 38 * 100 = −18.42%

Now we apply this change to the white wine figure:

74 * −18.42% = 74 * −0.1842 = −13.63

Now add this to the original 2010 figure for white wine:

74 + −13.63 = 60.37

Given that all the answer options are in millions then this can be rounded to 60.

Potential Shortcuts / Pitfalls

This question gives you the opportunity to make a quick estimation of the answer. If you look at the data you can see that the 2010 starting value for white wine (74) is very close to twice that of rosé wine (38). So, given that rosé wine reduced by 7 (million litres), then white wine will decline by pretty much double that, i.e. 14 (million litres), from 74 to 60.

SET 54, Q3. Correct Answer: A

Reasoning

We need to calculate the per capita consumption of red wine in 2005 and 2010. Then we can calculate the percentage change, which is the difference between the two figures divided by the starting value and multiplied by 100.

Calculation

First, calculate the per capita consumption in 2005:

63 (million) / 16316 (thousand) = 3.8612

The 2010 per capita consumption is:

61 (million) / 16492 (thousand) = 3.6988

Now calculate the percentage change in consumption:

(3.6988 − 3.8612) / 3.8612 * 100 = −4.2%

Potential Shortcuts / Pitfalls

Although it's often necessary to be aware of the difference in magnitude of the different data items, it is not actually necessary in this particular case as they cancel out.

However, we do have the little difficulty of keeping track of enough significant digits in each of the intermediate answers to ensure enough accuracy in the final answer. If you aren't accurate enough you can arrive at answers between 4.0% and 5.1% even using the correct procedure, leaving 3 of the answer options as possibly right. To get around this difficulty, you can do the calculation slightly differently. When calculating the percentage change you can use (final value / starting value) − 1 and multiply this by 100. This method is less intuitive but it has the advantage that you can do the whole calculation in one go. Remember when you divide by a fraction then you invert the divisor and multiply instead. This leads to:

61 / 16492 * 16316 / 63 * 100 = 95.8

This eliminates the need to record partial answers and gives full accuracy.

SET 55, Q1. Correct Answer: D

Reasoning

The number of unemployed is the population multiplied by the size of the workforce as a percentage of the population, multiplied by the percentage of the workforce that is unemployed. We need to calculate this for 2015, subtract 10000 from it, adjust the percentages by the given values and calculate the population of Ireland in 2010. We can then calculate the percentage change in the population.

Calculation

First, calculate the number of unemployed in 2015:

$4606 * 0.485 * 0.059 = 131.8$

This number is in thousands because the population is given in thousands. Therefore before we subtract 10000 from it we need to convert it to the same units. You can either multiply the above answer by 1000 or divide the change in unemployed figure by 1000:

$131.8 - 10000 / 1000 = 121.8$

The percentage of the workforce that is unemployed rose by 0.1 percentage points (*not* 0.1%) and so in 2010 it would have been:

$5.9 - 0.1 = 5.8$

So, the population that would have this level of unemployed people is:

$121.8 / (0.058 * 0.487) = 4312.12$

This means that the percentage rise in population is therefore:

$(4606 - 4312.12) / 4312.12 * 100 = 6.8\%$

Potential Shortcuts / Pitfalls
This is relatively straightforward but there are a lot of steps to it. Also, there are a few units that don't match up very easily. When you have calculated the number of unemployed in 2015, you cannot simply multiply in a percentage change because the change in the number of unemployed is given as an *absolute figure* rather than a percentage change. Also the change in the percentage of the workforce unemployed is given as a change in the figure rather than as a percentage change even though the data item itself is a percentage. This sort of thing is often a source of confusion.

SET 55, Q2. Correct Answer: B

Reasoning

The number of unemployed is the population multiplied by the size of the workforce as a percentage of the population, multiplied by the percentage of the workforce that is unemployed. We need to do this calculation for both Hungary and Portugal and then work out the percentage that the former is of the latter.

Calculation

First, calculate the number of unemployed in Hungary:

$11086 * 0.467 * 0.076 = 393.5$

Now do the same for Portugal:

$11602 * 0.421 * 0.087 = 425$

Now calculate the percentage Hungary is of Portugal:

$393.5 / 425 * 100 = 92.6\%$

Potential Shortcuts / Pitfalls
Just be careful to get the fraction for the final percentage the correct way round and that you don't use the wrong year for the percentage of population figure.

SET 55, Q3. Correct Answer: E

Reasoning

The number of unemployed is the population multiplied by the size of the workforce as a percentage of the population, multiplied by the percentage of the workforce that is unemployed. We need to work this out for Croatia in 2015, then modify the figures for the population and the percentage of the workforce unemployed as indicated and calculate the number of unemployed in 2010. Finally, we can calculate the difference between the two.

Calculation

First, calculate the number of unemployed in Croatia in 2015:

$4887 * 0.421 * 0.074 = 152.25$

The percentage of the workforce who are unemployed rose by 5% from 2010 to 2015, so the 2010 figure would be:

0.074 / 1.05 = 0.0705 or 7.048%

The population of Croatia rose by 3.3% and so the population in 2010 would have been:

4887 / 1.033 = 4730.88

The number of unemployed in 2010 was:

4730.88 * 0.419 * 0.07048 = 139.708

The difference in numbers of people unemployed is then:

152.25 − 139.708 = 12.542

This is in thousands and so the answer is 12542.

Potential Shortcuts / Pitfalls

Try and avoid too many intermediate results as these can rounding errors if too few significant digits are used. Also note that although the percentage of the workforce unemployed is a percentage (7.4%), when this changes by a percentage then you must treat the figure if it were any other piece of data and multiply or divide as appropriate. The fact that it is a percentage is irrelevant. Do not just add or subtract 5 percentage points.

7.   Succeeding in Abstract Reasoning Tests

In an EPSO abstract reasoning test you are presented with a series of figures in a sequence which follows some rules you are not told. You are also given a second set of figures (A, B, C, D, E) as answer options, from which you must choose the correct one to answer the question "Which of the following figures comes next in the series?" (or similar).

It can certainly be a daunting experience to face such a test for the first time. Your eyes will tend to scan the shapes of the figures in a haphazard fashion. You finally get an idea about the possible rules, and then look at the figures in the answer options to see which one fits. And then you realise that the figure you carefully selected would only fit the series pattern if just one thing was a little bit different. So now you must start all over again...

But, just as in the case of verbal and numerical reasoning tests, understanding the principles involved and a systematic approach to applying them can produce results much more reliably and quickly.

As part of such a systematic approach, let us therefore first review the various abstract reasoning test types, which are based on:

- the use or avoidance of colours
- the logical relationship between the various figures, whether they are part of a series, a grid, or if there is one figure which is the odd-one-out
- the number of dimensions in the test (two- or three-dimensional tests both exist)

Fortunately, it is now known that EPSO have chosen a type of abstract reasoning test that is very well defined:

- only black-and-white images are used (possibly with various shades of grey)

A typical abstract question: *Which figure is next in the series?*

A   B   C   D   E

- only two-dimensional tests are given

- only series-type questions are used

- five items of the series are shown, and the candidate must select the next, sixth item

- there are usually five answer options (though EPSO may vary this).

In abstract reasoning tests, the most important skill is learning to identify the components. Let us look at these one-by one:

- Building blocks: the building blocks of abstract reasoning tests are the following:

  - **Shapes and patterns** are the actual visual objects that are used to construct the figures in the test: triangles, squares, circles and other geometric shapes, as well as the physical properties of these objects: striped, dotted or solid fill patterns

  - **Operations** are various visual changes that these objects can undergo, such as colour inversion, multiplication, rotation, change of position, and countless others

  - **Rules** are text-based descriptions of the relationship between the various shapes/patterns and the operations affecting them

  In this chapter, we will:

- Introduce how abstract reasoning tests are designed: insight into the thought process that is behind the creation of abstract reasoning tests will be very valuable when you are on the other side, that is, when taking such tests

- Introduce the various building blocks, typical shapes, patterns and operations that you will encounter in abstract reasoning tests

- Discuss how to approach abstract reasoning tests

- Provide tips on how to prepare for them

By identifying the building blocks of a test item and systematically looking for the above patterns and operations, you will quickly be able to identify the rules that the question author invented to create the figures and the answer options.

Consequently, you will be able to "generate" or "anticipate" the correct figure in your mind without even looking at the answer options. This method is highly reliable since you will not select one of the answer options as the correct answer just because it seems the best or most suitable option: you will also have independent confirmation – the figure you came up with yourself based on the rule(s) you have figured out.

How Are Abstract Reasoning Tests Designed?

In this section, we will provide a look into the "workshop" of abstract reasoning test designers and, through a real test example, introduce how abstract reasoning exercises are designed.

As mentioned earlier, EPSO exclusively uses the series type tests in its competitions. In this type of abstract reasoning test, the test taker is asked to find the figure that correctly completes a series.

If we identify the rule, we will not only be able to tell which figure will be the sixth one (as in the example above), but also the ninth or the sixteenth one.

When designing an abstract reasoning test, the designer has specific steps to take:

1. The designer decides what shapes and patterns will be used in the tests. Based on the sample test above, let's say we will use basic geometric shapes (circles and squares).

2. Next, the designer has to decide on the difficulty level of the test. The importance of this lies in the fact that the number of rules (generally) correlates with the difficulty of the test.

3. Once the rules and the shapes/operations are identified and drawn, the designer needs to come up with one correct and several incorrect answer options. The trick to keep in mind here is that the incorrect answer options are not random – they all follow the rules of the test item up to a point, then deliberately err in one or more respects, thus making them *almost* correct.

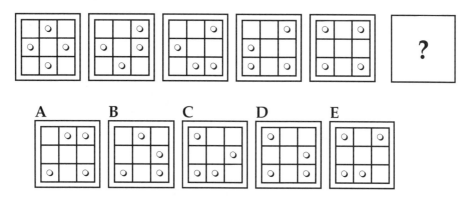

Consider the sample item above. We can identify the following building blocks:

- unshaded **circles**

- **squares** forming 3x3 areas.

    The first rule you may notice is the movement of the circles. We might describe this as follows:

Rule #1: *One by one, the circles move in a clockwise direction.*

    Based on this rule we can quickly find the correct answer – which is **option D.**

    Let's see how we could make this test item a bit harder.

    If you look at the sample item below, you will immediately realize that a new building block was introduced: **shaded squares**.

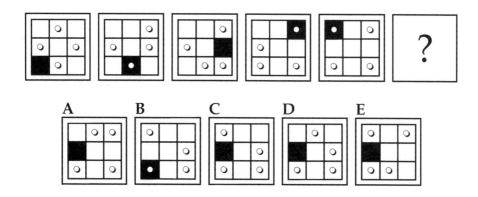

Before we try to find the rule governing the shading of certain squares, notice that the rule we came up with above still holds:

Rule #1: One by one, the circles move in a clockwise direction.

This rule, however, does not explain the appearance of shaded squares, as any number of different images could be correct from the answer options. We need to identify the second rule:

Rule #2: The shading alternatingly takes one and two steps in an anticlockwise direction.

The only answer option that matches both of these rules is **option C**.

Note how close option B is to be the correct answer, but deliberately misusing the second rule.

We can make the test item even harder by introducing another additional component:

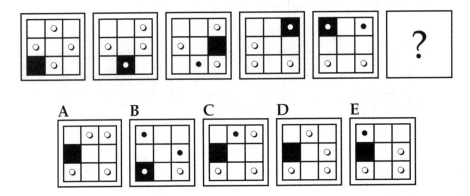

Notice that, again, a new building block and rule must have been introduced governing the appearance of the **shaded circle**. We can describe this regularity as follows:

Rule #3: Circles that stood on a shaded square will become shaded themselves for a turn.

The only answer option matching all three rules is **option E**.

As a summary, let us overview what techniques we can use to understand the thought process of the designer of the test items better:

- Determining what building blocks to use (unshaded/shaded squares and circles) and the number of rules governing their change
- Eliminating answer options based on each rule we have identified

Patterns and Operations

Now that we have seen the basic components of abstract reasoning tests and the way they are designed, it is time to turn to the various patterns and operations that you must be aware of and able to recognize in order to quickly and efficiently solve these tests.

It would be of course impossible to take stock of all the possible shapes and patterns, but we will try to give a comprehensive overview in the next section.

Rotation

Figs. 1 and 2 on the opposite page shows a simple rotation by 45° clockwise. You can gain the necessary routine in identifying rotations by taking the time to sit down with a piece of paper and a pencil, draw various shapes and then redraw them after rotating them various degrees in either direction, clockwise or counter-clockwise.

The example below shows a different kind of rotation. In strict geometrical terms, the relationship between the two figures is not rotation at all, yet for convenience's sake, we will discuss it in this section.

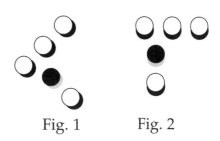

Fig. 1   Fig. 2

In the two figures, the small icons in the small squares around the larger one in the middle swap places with their neighbours in a clockwise direction. In a sense we can say that the icons "rotate" along an imaginary circle around the larger square.

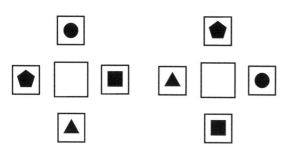

Axial Reflection

The two examples on the right show the geometrical operation called "axial reflection". The thin lines between the two figures in each of the two sets represent an imaginary mirror. In the first set, the figure on the right is the reflection of the figure on the left in the "mirror" in the middle and vice versa. This is an example of a horizontal reflection.

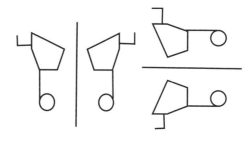

Horizontal reflection   *Vertical reflection*

The second set represents a so-called vertical reflection. While for demonstration's sake the examples show the horizontal reflection side by side and the vertical reflection with one figure below the other, in real tests this may not always be the case.

Vertical reflection

In the example on the left, the figure on the right is still the vertical "reflection" of the figure on the left, but the placement of the second figure does not correspond with where it would actually be in a strictly geometrical sense, that is, below the first image – this makes it harder to consider the relationship between the two figures as a reflection.

You can practice the recognition of this operation in the same cost-effective way as described above for rotations – all you need is paper, a pencil and loads of patience.

Patterns and Inversions

"Which of the following figures completes the series?"

In the example on the top right, a new building block component is introduced – patterns. The example features three of the next page shapes:

• Stars

- Circles
- Rhombuses

... and three distinct patterns or "fills":

- No fill (or solid white fill)
- Solid black fill
- Solid Grey fill

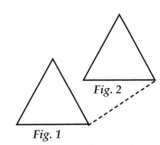

Looking at the sample test, we notice that two "operations" take place:

- The shapes in each figure change places according to some rule
- The patterns (or fill) of the rhombuses and the circle also change according to some rule
- The pattern (or fill) of the star never changes

After further observation, we can establish the following rules regarding the patterns:

Rule #1a: If a rhombus has a grey fill, change it to solid black in the next step. If it has a solid black fill, change it to a grey pattern in the next step.

Rule #1b: If a circle has a grey pattern, change it to solid white in the next step. If it has a solid white fill, change it to a grey pattern in the next step.

Rule #1c: Always leave the star's pattern unchanged.

There are of course many other combinations possible, involving more types of patterns and different relationships between them. Another typical case is so-called inversion. In such tests, the solid colour fill (usually black or white) of each shape and object turns into its exact opposite. Every shape with black fill becomes white, and vice versa.

The other component of our rule for the above example has to do with the positions of the shapes in relation to each other. We will discuss this in the next section.

Translation

In geometry, translation is an operation where each and every point of a shape is moved to a specified distance in a specified direction. In the example on the right, each point of the triangle is moved (or "translated") to the same distance and in the same direction, as indicated by the dotted line or "vector" connecting the two shapes. The vector is only shown here for demonstration purposes and would not be visible in a real exercise. We must also keep in mind that the movement sometimes occurs along an actual shape that is part of the figure:

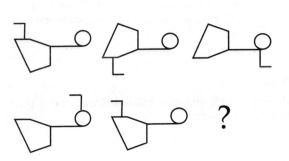

In the example on the left, the handlebar line "migrates" around the other shapes in a counter-clockwise order. The movement is not a rotation or a reflection – the points of the handlebar line are simply moved at a certain distance in a certain direction in each step of the series.

Therefore the correct answer is a shape that is the same as the middle one in the top row.

Similarly to rotation, there is also a geometrically less accurate meaning of the term "translation". Looking at the sample question with the star, the circle and the rhombus, we may notice the following rule governing the placement of the three shapes in the figures of the series:

Rule #2: Move each of the three shapes one position up. If the shape is already in the top position, it will now occupy the bottom position in the figure.

In the example, the six answer options were intentionally deleted. Based on the method described earlier in this chapter, we can mentally generate the correct figure based on the rules we have established for the series (repeated below for convenience).

Rule #1: "If a rhombus has a grey fill, change it to solid black in the next step. If it has a solid black fill, change it to a grey pattern in the next step. If a circle has a grey pattern, change it to solid white in the next step. If it has a solid white fill, change it to a grey pattern in the next step. Always leave the star's pattern unchanged."

In the fifth item in the series (the figure that will take the place of the question mark), then, the circle will become grey and the rhombus will become solid black. The star will remain white.

Rule #2: "Move each of the three shapes one position up. If the shape is already in the top position, it will now occupy the bottom position in the figure."

In the figure we are looking for, the now black rhombus will take the bottom position, the now grey circle will go to the middle, and the still white star will move to the top position.

Angles

In geometry, an angle is defined as a figure formed by two lines extending from the same point. In simple geometry, angles are usually given as being any number that is larger than zero and smaller than 360°.

When it comes to abstract reasoning tests, we need to be aware of angles for various reasons. In the case of identifying rotations, the rotation is usually done at a certain angle: 45°, 90° (also called a "right angle"), 180°, or 270°. Of course, rotation at any angle is possible, but due to the difficulty in identifying "custom" angles (say, 67°), such rotations are not likely to appear in EPSO's abstract reasoning tests.

When establishing the "rule" for a test question, we must always think about angles as well.

Consider the example below:

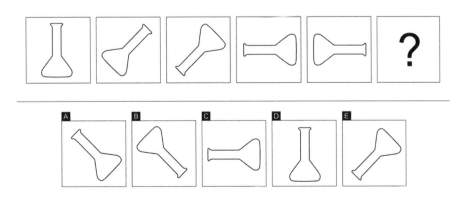

If we look at the images in the sample test above, we see a flask in various positions. After some further observation, we will notice that the flasks in the second, third and further figures are rotated at certain angles when compared to the flask in the first figure. We might describe this regularity based on angles as follows:

Rule #1: The flask is rotated around a fixed point 45 then 180 degrees, and then the cycle repeats.

Visual Arithmetic

The last typical abstract reasoning component we discuss here is sometimes referred to as visual arithmetic.

If we look at the figure extracted from a real abstract reasoning test, we see a large outer square with seven smaller squares along its sides. The top left square is black, and there are various shapes in the other squares (the fact that not all squares contain shapes is not relevant for our purposes now). What is the rule that could govern which kind of shape appears in each of the small squares? One tactic we can follow in items similar to this is to first count the number of sides the shapes have. Obviously, the triangle has three sides, the pentagon has five and the hexagon has six. How many sides should we "allocate" to the circle? Let's worry about that a bit later.

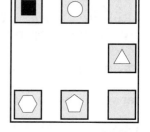

The other question is what determines why a certain shape is placed in a certain position in the figure. Counting can again help us out. If we count the distance (defined as the number of squares) between the shapes and the black square in a clockwise direction, we will notice that the position with the triangle, for example, is three steps away, the position with the pentagon is five shapes away, and so on.

We can now identify a rule:

Rule #1: The distance of a shape in any given square is governed by the number of sides the shape has.

It is important to bear in mind that EPSO's abstract reasoning tests, similarly to all such well-designed tests, attempt to measure the candidate's intuition and intelligence both visually (identification of shapes, patterns, and so on) and logically (e.g. identifying relationships and numerical regularities).

Summary and Approaches to Practice

In this chapter, we have overviewed various aspects of abstract reasoning tests:

- Test design, difficulty, rules and distractors
- Building blocks: operations, rules and patterns (rotation, reflection, angles, visual arithmetic, and so on)

Let us now add some suggestions on how to practice.

- If you feel that a geometrical operation (reflection, rotation, angles, etc.) is one of your weak points, do not shy away from sitting down with some paper and a pencil. Draw various shapes and perform the operations on them until they become routine and you are able to recognize a 90° clockwise rotation of a complex shape in a couple of seconds
- Once you are familiar with all of the typical rules and operations as detailed above, start practicing on the actual test questions in the next chapter of this book
- Since abstract reasoning tests are all about shapes, it is especially important to try to model the infrastructure of the exam while practicing – the EPSO test will be admin-

istered on a computer, which will make it harder (and stranger) to take than a paper-based test where you can scribble on the paper (even though you will be given scrap paper in the exam centre). If you have access to such services, try also to practice online

It is also important to develop a systematic approach when tackling abstract reasoning tests. One recommended approach is summarized below:

1. Quickly glance through the set of figures. Do not spend time looking at the answer options at this stage.

2. Run through all the rules, operations and patterns you familiarised yourself with during practice and try to apply them to the set of figures. Start with the one that, based on glancing at the figures, intuitively seems the most promising lead.

3. If you believe you have found the rule or rules governing the exercise, try to "generate" the correct answer figure in your mind or draw a sketch on a bit of scrap paper.

4. Look at the answer options provided and match them against the one you came up with yourself. If a test item is based on multiple rules, you may still be able to exclude one or two of the answer options based on only the first rule. If you are able to do that, you can continue looking for the second rule with a smaller set of answer options to work with – thereby speeding up the process one rule at a time.

5. If you have found a match (and only one), you can mark that as the correct answer. If there are no matches, or multiple matches to your rule(s), they probably have a flaw. Apply your rule to all the figures in the test – this will most likely reveal the flaw, which you can then correct and generate a new, hopefully correct, answer figure in your mind,

6. While practicing, you may consider writing every idea and step down for each exercise to make sure you are aware of the logic and rules at play.

In the following chapter, you will find a complete set of abstract reasoning questions that you can use to build up your your speed and accuracy.

8. Abstract Reasoning Test

160 Questions – Answers follow on from Question 160

In each question you must choose which of the figures in the bottom line - A, B, C, D or E - completes the series in the top line.

For practice purposes, you should try to complete 10 questions in 10 minutes. If you can't identify the rules for a particular question within 1 minute, move straight on to the next question rather than wasting time. For the actual number of questions, time allowed and pass mark in your exam, always check the Notice of Competition.

Comparatively harder and easier questions are mixed at random through the test, but if you want to specially concentrate on hard questions the final 40 (i.e. questions 121 to 160) are mainly of that type.

1   Which figure completes the series below?

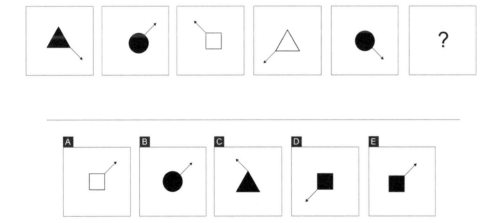

2   Which figure completes the series below?

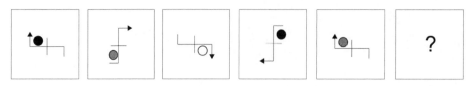

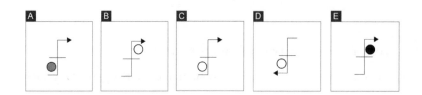

3   Which figure completes the series below?

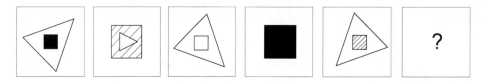

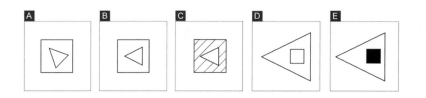

4   Which figure completes the series below?

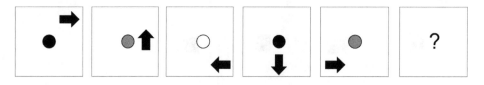

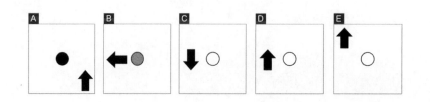

5　Which figure completes the series below?

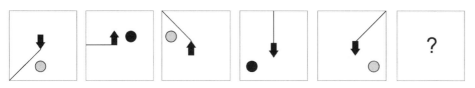

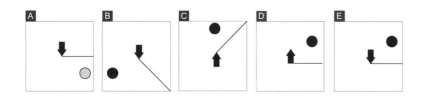

6　Which figure completes the series below?

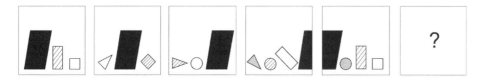

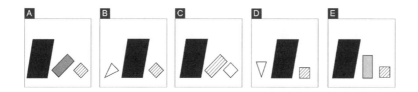

7　Which figure completes the series below?

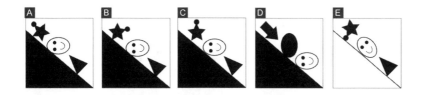

8   Which figure completes the series below?

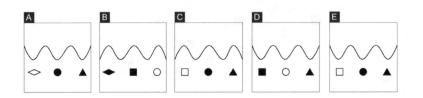

9   Which figure completes the series below?

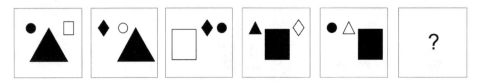

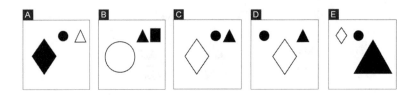

10   Which figure completes the series below?

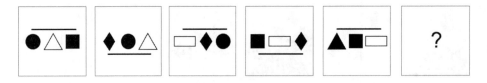

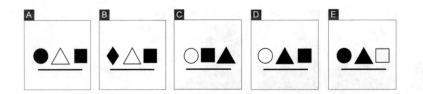

11   Which figure completes the series below?

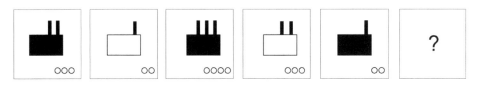

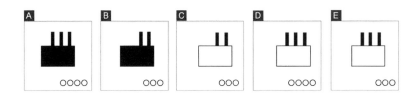

12   Which figure completes the series below?

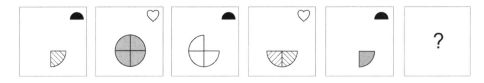

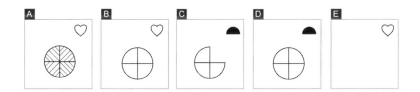

13   Which figure completes the series below?

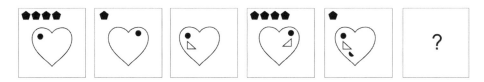

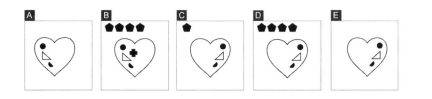

14   Which figure completes the series below?

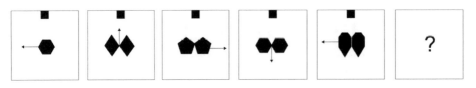

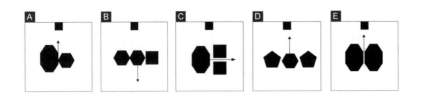

15   Which figure completes the series below?

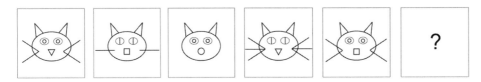

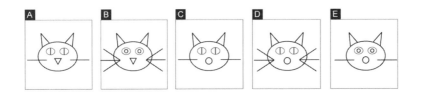

16   Which figure completes the series below?

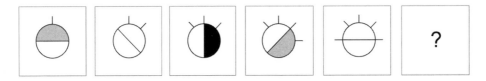

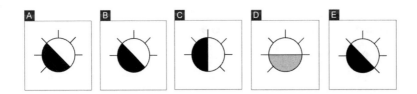

17 Which figure completes the series below?

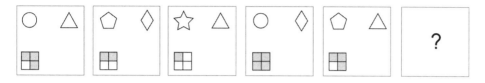

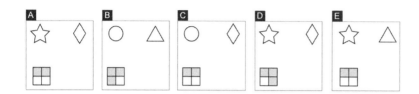

18 Which figure completes the series below?

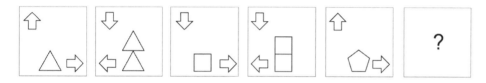

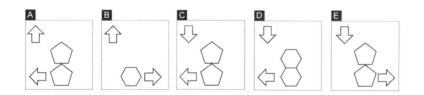

19 Which figure completes the series below?

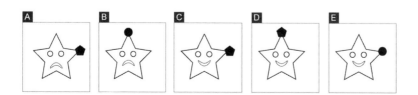

20 Which figure completes the series below?

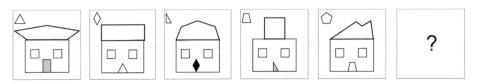

21 Which figure completes the series below?

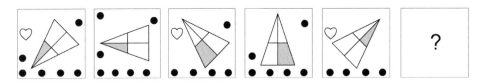

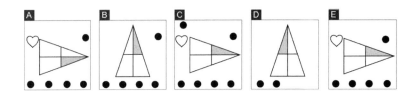

22 Which figure completes the series below?

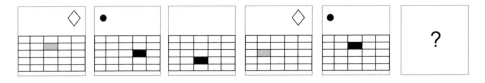

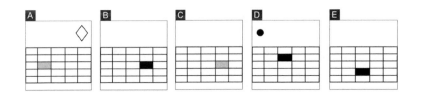

23   Which figure completes the series below?

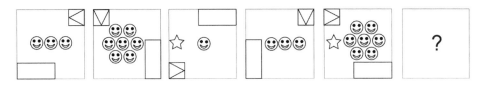

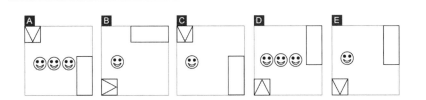

24   Which figure completes the series below?

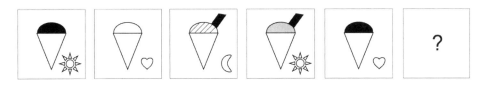

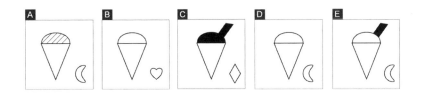

25   Which figure completes the series below?

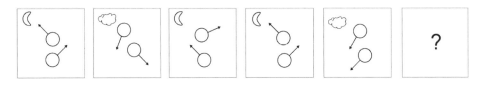

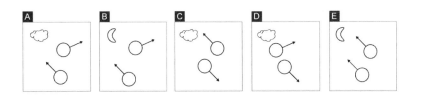

26   Which figure completes the series below?

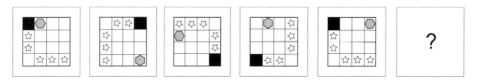

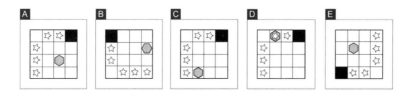

27   Which figure completes the series below?

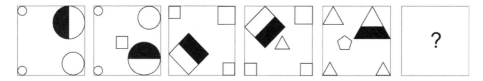

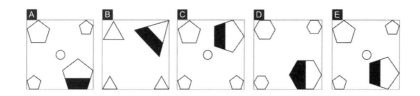

28   Which figure completes the series below?

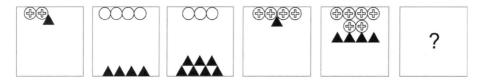

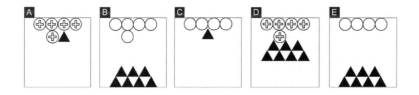

29 Which figure completes the series below?

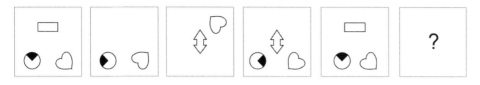

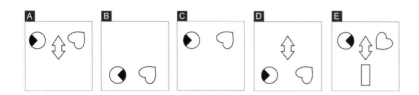

30 Which figure completes the series below?

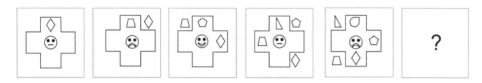

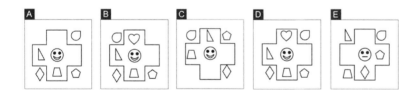

31 Which figure completes the series below?

32 Which figure completes the series below?

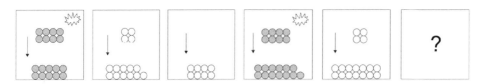

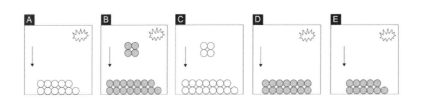

33 Which figure completes the series below?

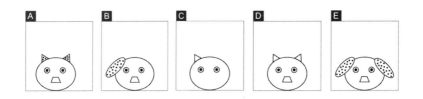

34 Which figure completes the series below?

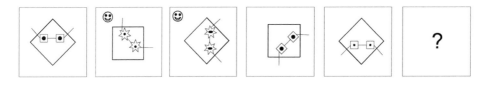

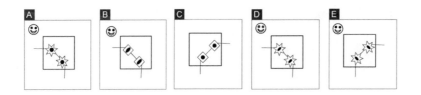

35 Which figure completes the series below?

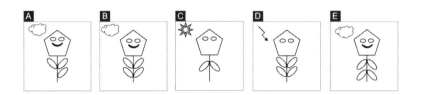

36 Which figure completes the series below?

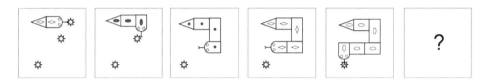

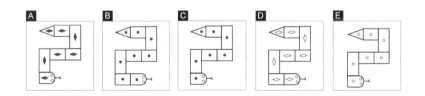

37 Which figure completes the series below?

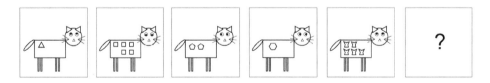

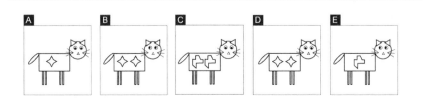

38 Which figure completes the series below?

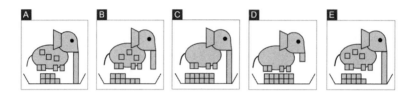

39 Which figure completes the series below?

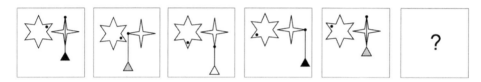

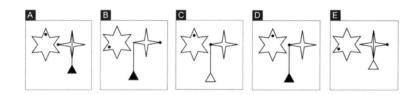

40 Which figure completes the series below?

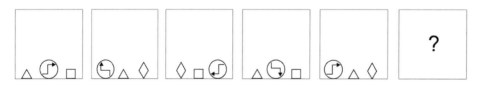

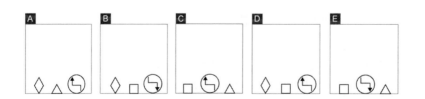

41 Which figure completes the series below?

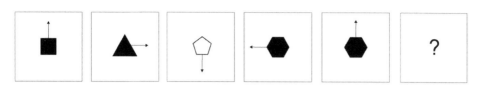

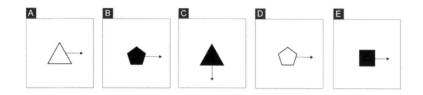

42 Which figure completes the series below?

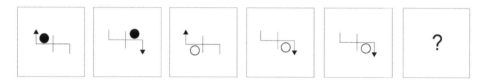

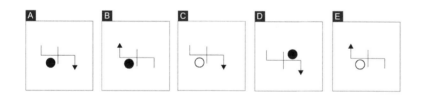

43 Which figure completes the series below?

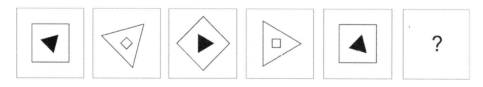

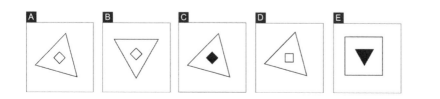

44   Which figure completes the series below?

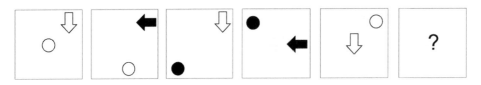

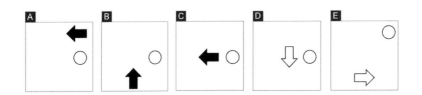

45   Which figure completes the series below?

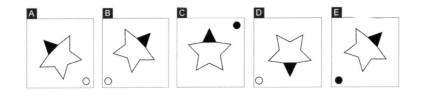

46   Which figure completes the series below?

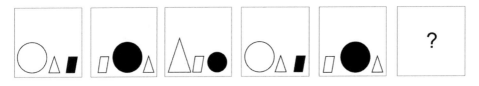

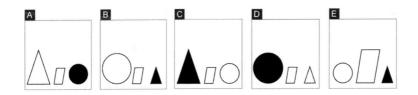

47 Which figure completes the series below?

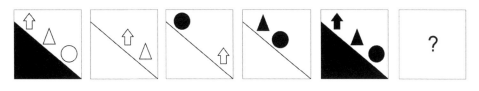

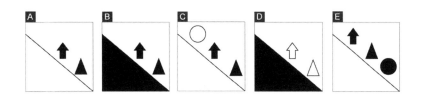

48 Which figure completes the series below?

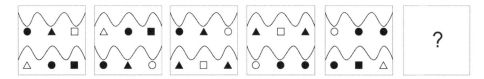

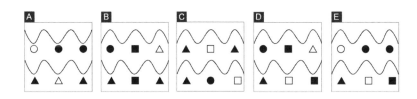

49 Which figure completes the series below?

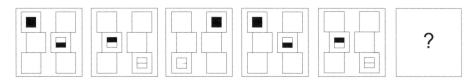

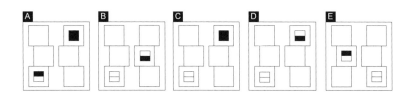

50   Which figure completes the series below?

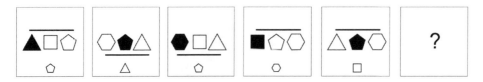

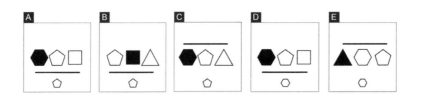

51   Which figure completes the series below?

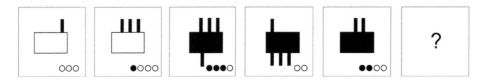

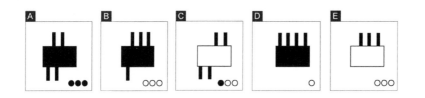

52   Which figure completes the series below?

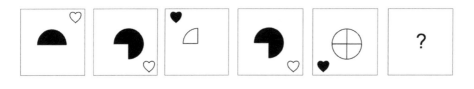

53 Which figure completes the series below?

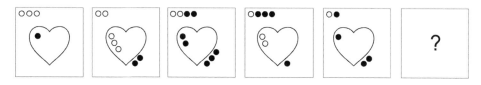

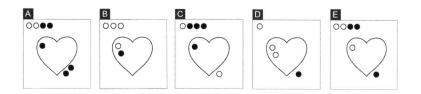

54 Which figure completes the series below?

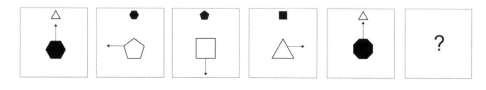

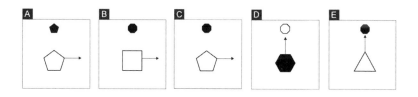

55 Which figure completes the series below?

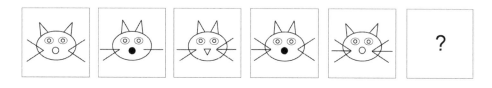

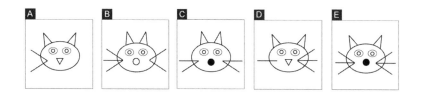

56   Which figure completes the series below?

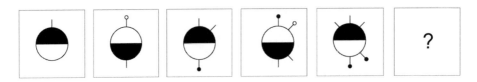

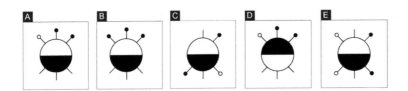

57   Which figure completes the series below?

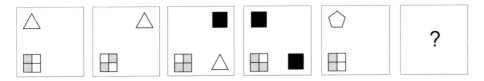

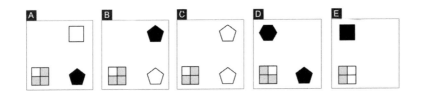

58   Which figure completes the series below?

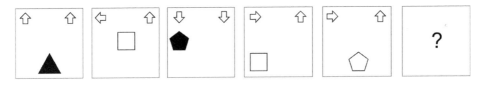

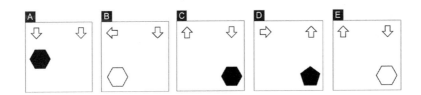

59 Which figure completes the series below?

60 Which figure completes the series below?

61 Which figure completes the series below?

62   Which figure completes the series below?

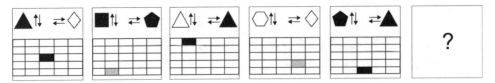

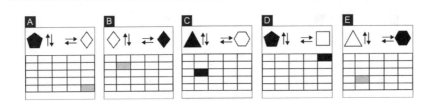

63   Which figure completes the series below?

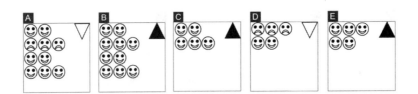

64   Which figure completes the series below?

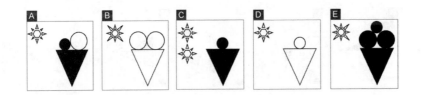

65   Which figure completes the series below?

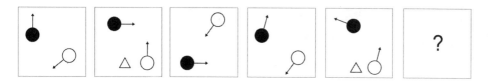

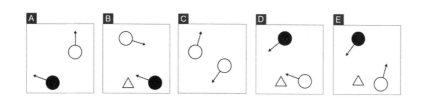

66   Which figure completes the series below?

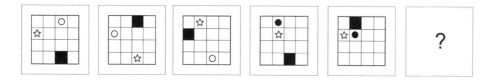

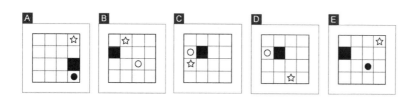

67   Which figure completes the series below?

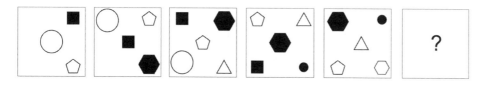

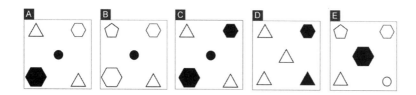

68   Which figure completes the series below?

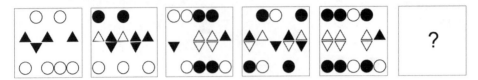

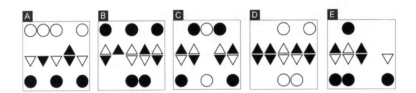

69   Which figure completes the series below?

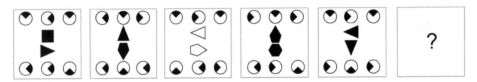

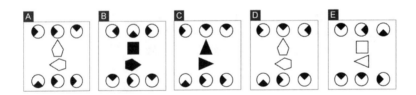

70   Which figure completes the series below?

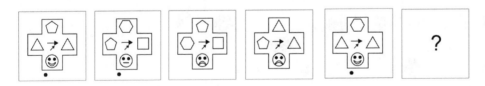

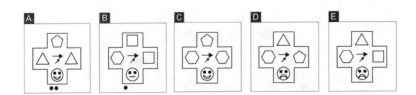

71 Which figure completes the series below?

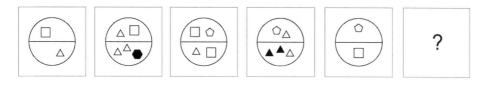

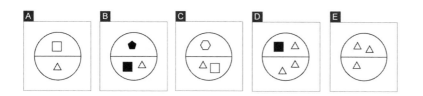

72 Which figure completes the series below?

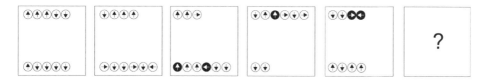

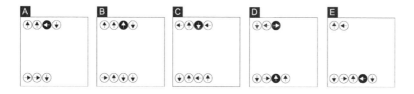

73 Which figure completes the series below?

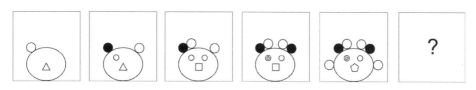

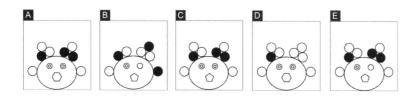

74   Which figure completes the series below?

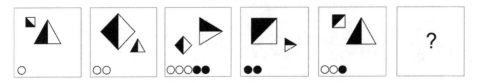

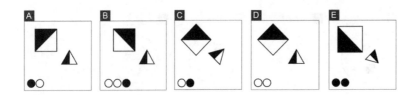

75   Which figure completes the series below?

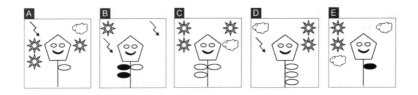

76   Which figure completes the series below?

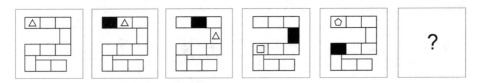

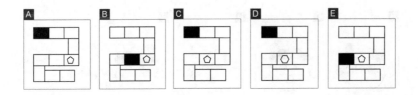

77 Which figure completes the series below?

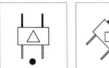

78 Which figure completes the series below?

79 Which figure completes the series below?

80   Which figure completes the series below?

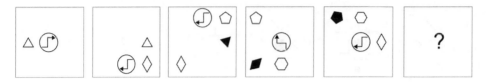

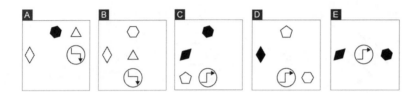

81   Which figure completes the series below?

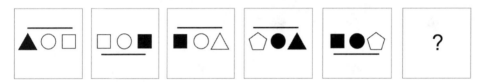

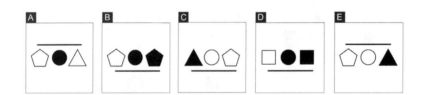

82   Which figure completes the series below?

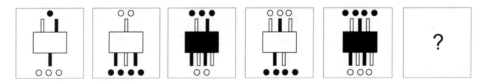

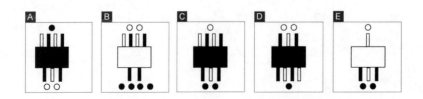

83 Which figure completes the series below?

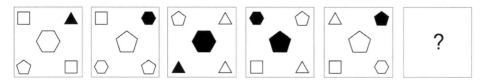

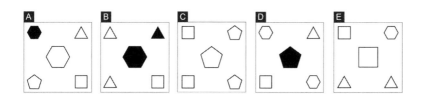

84 Which figure completes the series below?

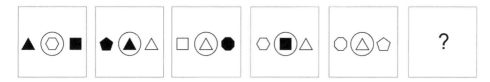

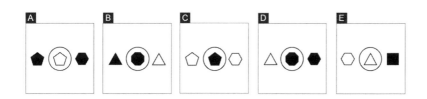

85 Which figure completes the series below?

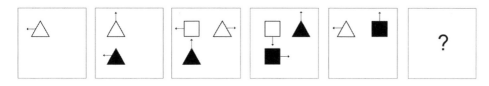

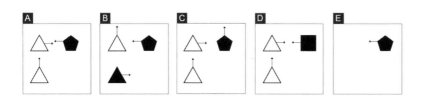

86   Which figure completes the series below?

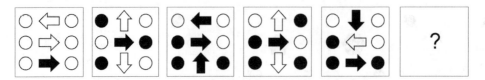

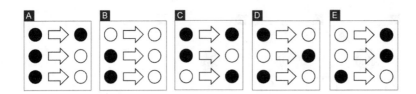

87   Which figure completes the series below?

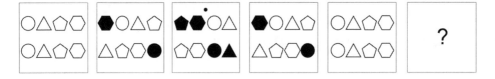

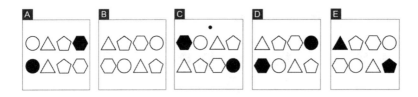

88   Which figure completes the series below?

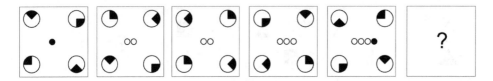

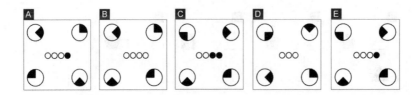

89   Which figure completes the series below?

90   Which figure completes the series below?

91   Which figure completes the series below?

92   Which figure completes the series below?

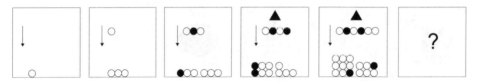

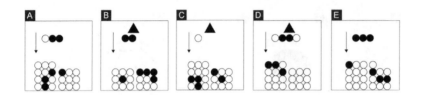

93   Which figure completes the series below?

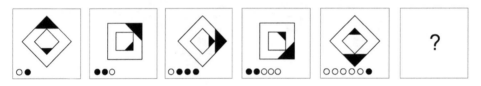

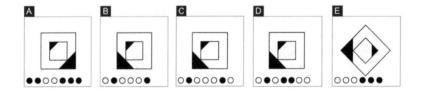

94   Which figure completes the series below?

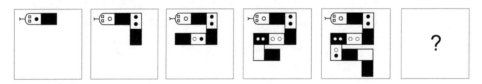

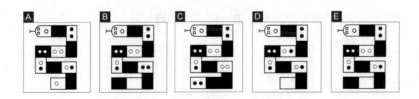

95 Which figure completes the series below?

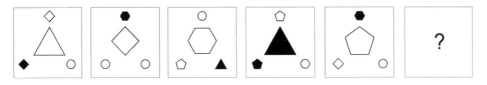

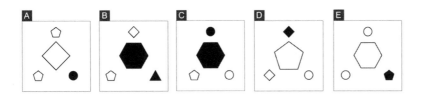

96 Which figure completes the series below?

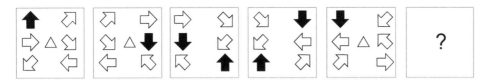

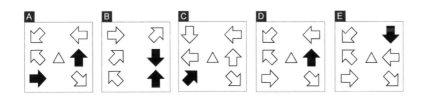

97 Which figure completes the series below?

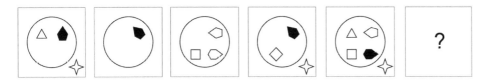

98   Which figure completes the series below?

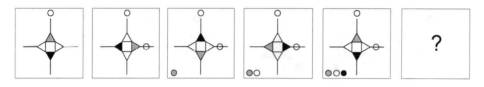

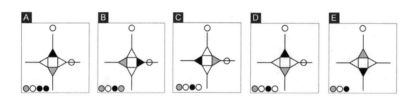

99   Which figure completes the series below?

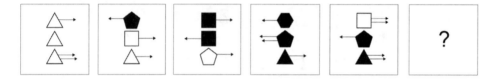

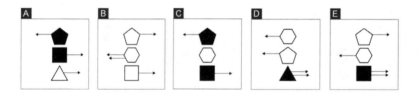

100   Which figure completes the series below?

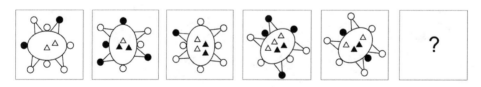

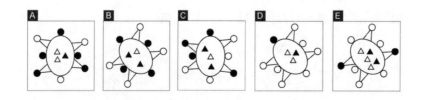

101 Which figure completes the series below?

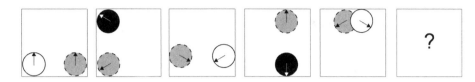

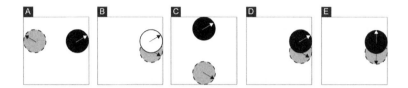

102 Which figure completes the series below?

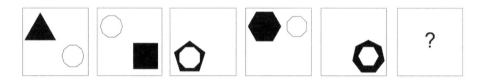

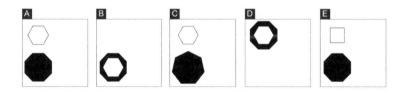

103 Which figure completes the series below?

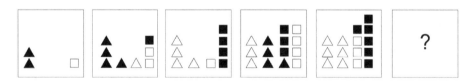

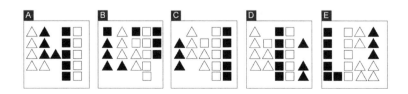

104 Which figure completes the series below?

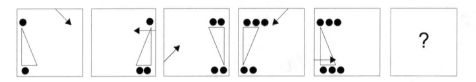

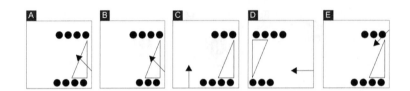

105 Which figure completes the series below?

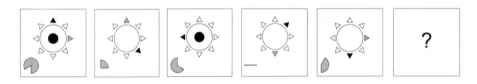

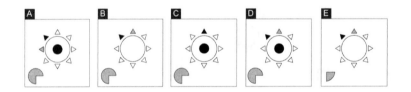

106 Which figure completes the series below?

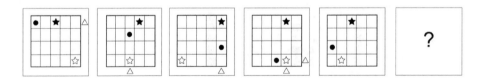

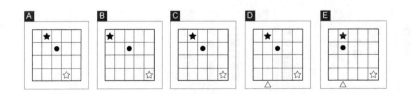

107 Which figure completes the series below?

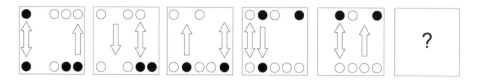

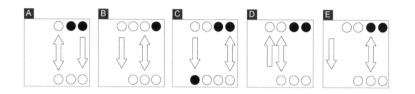

108 Which figure completes the series below?

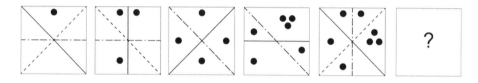

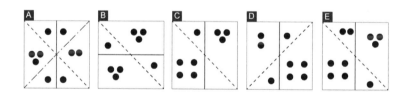

109 Which figure completes the series below?

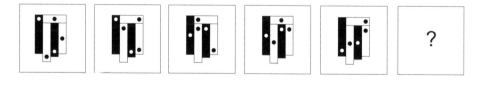

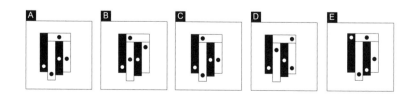

110 Which figure completes the series below?

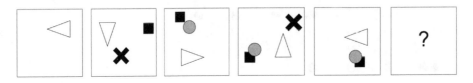

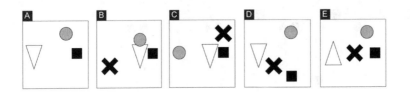

111 Which figure completes the series below?

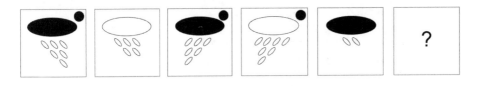

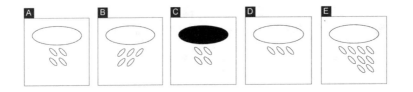

112 Which figure completes the series below?

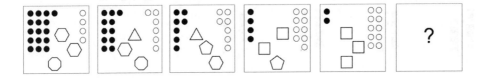

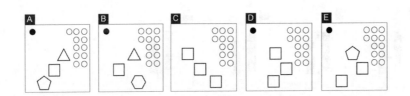

113 Which figure completes the series below?

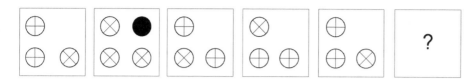

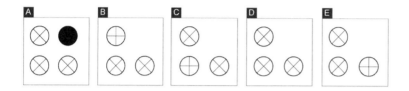

114 Which figure completes the series below?

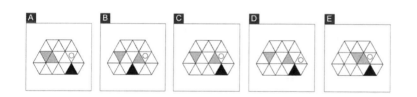

115 Which figure completes the series below?

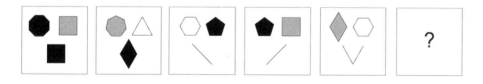

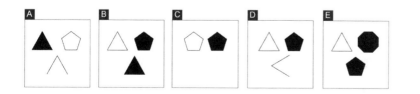

116 Which figure completes the series below?

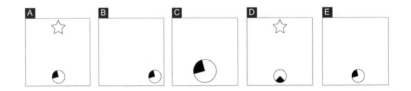

117 Which figure completes the series below?

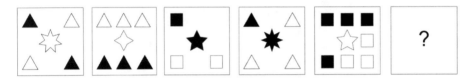

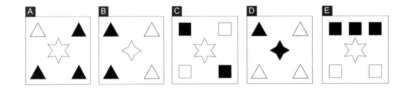

118 Which figure completes the series below?

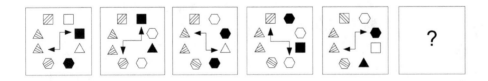

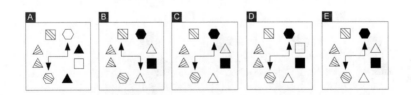

119 Which figure completes the series below?

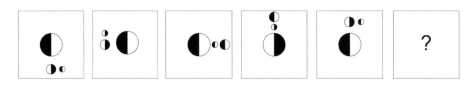

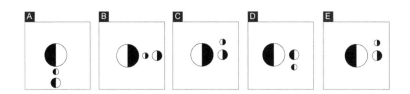

120 Which figure completes the series below?

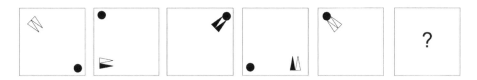

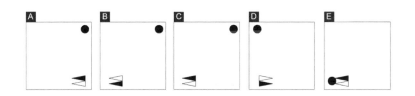

121 Which figure completes the series below?

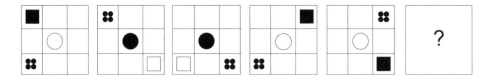

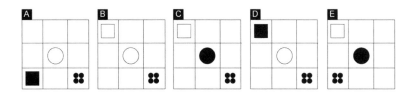

122 Which figure completes the series below?

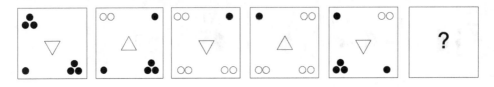

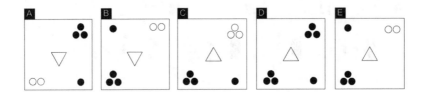

123 Which figure completes the series below?

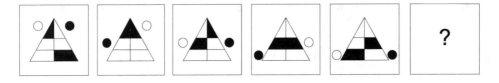

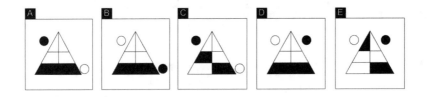

124 Which figure completes the series below?

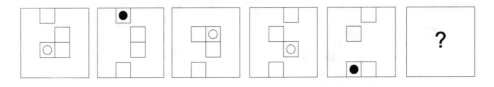

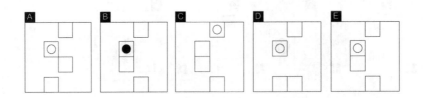

125 Which figure completes the series below?

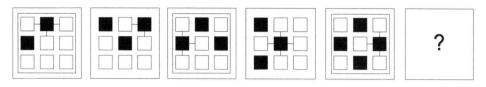

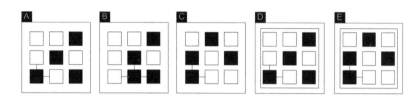

126 Which figure completes the series below?

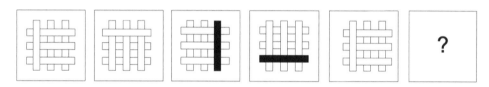

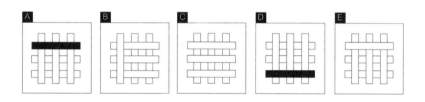

127 Which figure completes the series below?

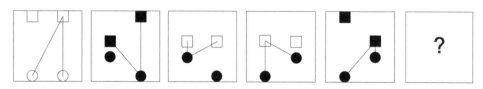

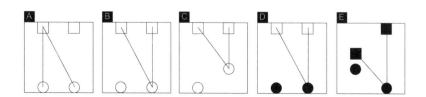

128 Which figure completes the series below?

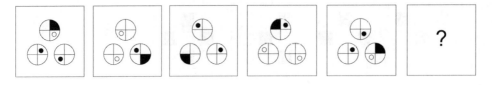

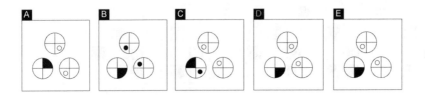

129 Which figure completes the series below?

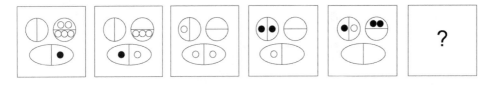

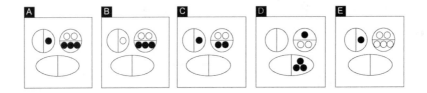

130 Which figure completes the series below?

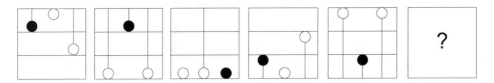

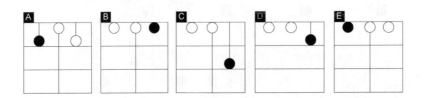

131 Which figure completes the series below?

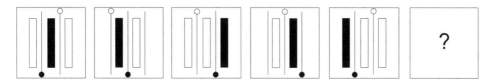

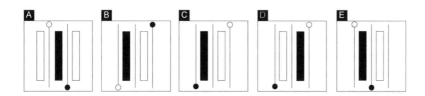

132 Which figure completes the series below?

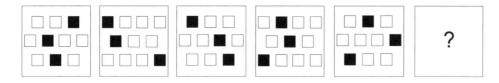

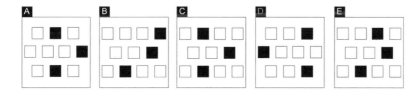

133 Which figure completes the series below?

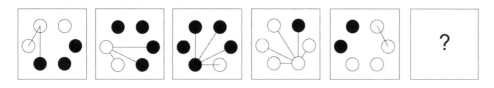

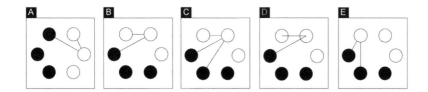

134 Which figure completes the series below?

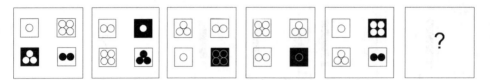

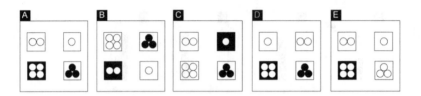

135 Which figure completes the series below?

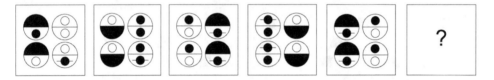

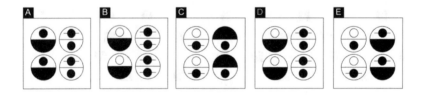

136 Which figure completes the series below?

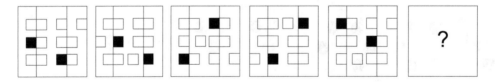

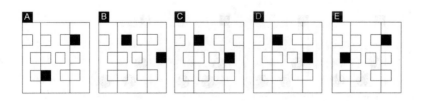

137 Which figure completes the series below?

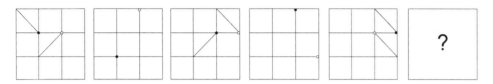

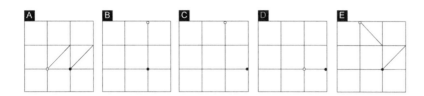

138 Which figure completes the series below?

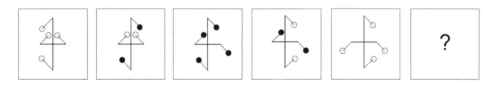

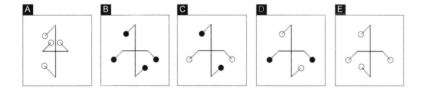

139 Which figure completes the series below?

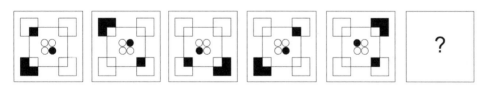

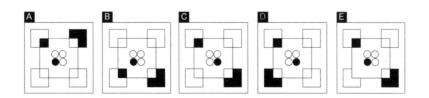

140 Which figure completes the series below?

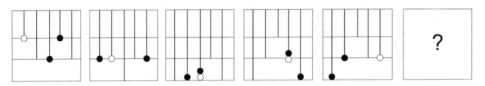

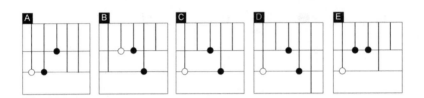

141 Which figure completes the series below?

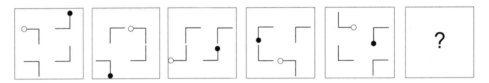

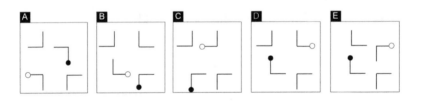

142 Which figure completes the series below?

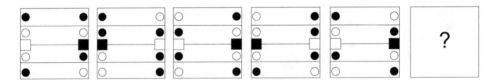

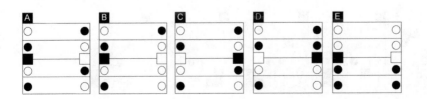

143 Which figure completes the series below?

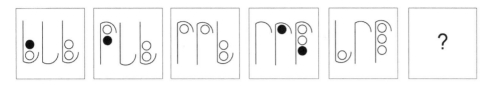

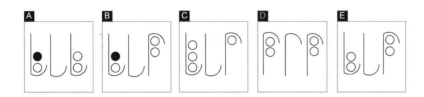

144 Which figure completes the series below?

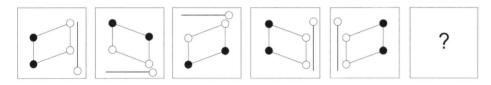

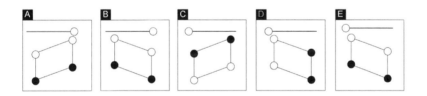

145 Which figure completes the series below?

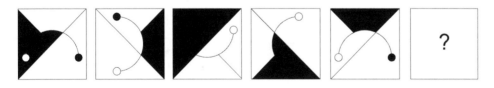

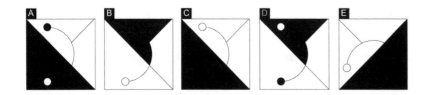

146 Which figure completes the series below?

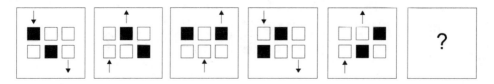

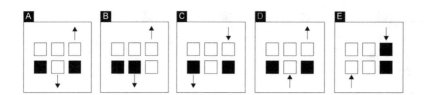

147 Which figure completes the series below?

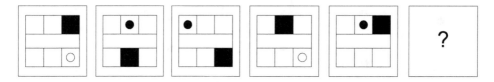

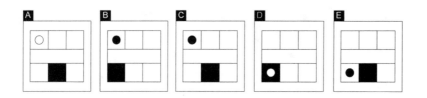

148 Which figure completes the series below?

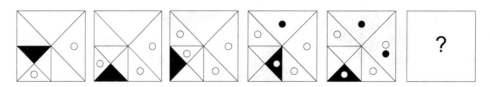

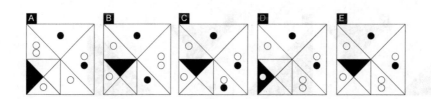

149 Which figure completes the series below?

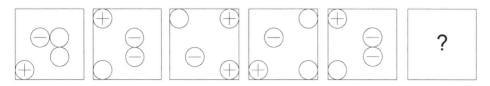

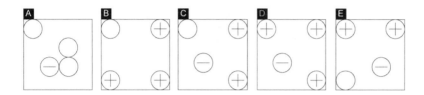

150 Which figure completes the series below?

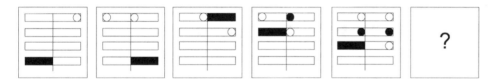

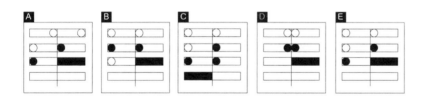

151 Which figure completes the series below?

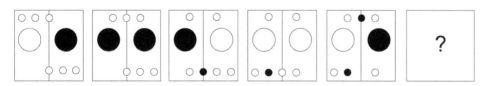

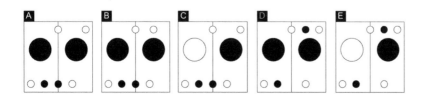

152 Which figure completes the series below?

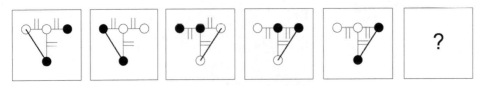

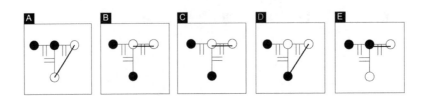

153 Which figure completes the series below?

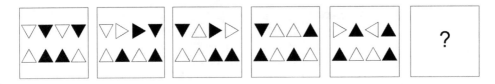

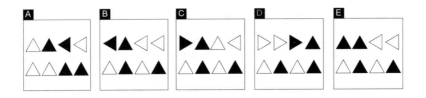

154 Which figure completes the series below?

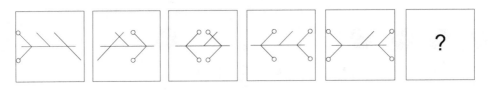

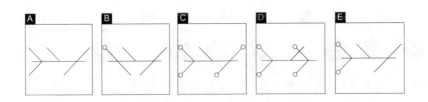

155 Which figure completes the series below?

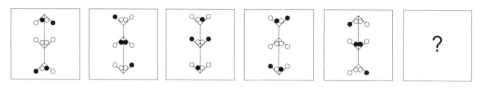

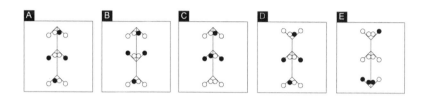

156 Which figure completes the series below?

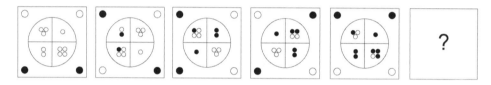

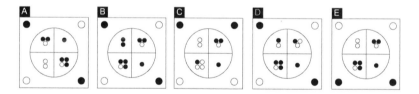

157 Which figure completes the series below?

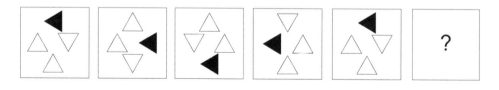

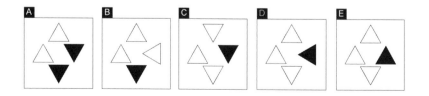

158 Which figure completes the series below?

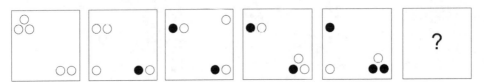

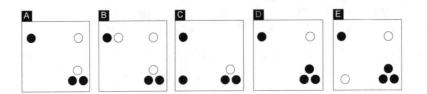

159 Which figure completes the series below?

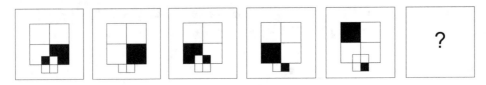

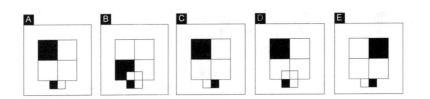

160 Which figure completes the series below?

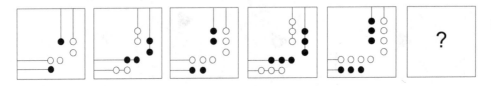

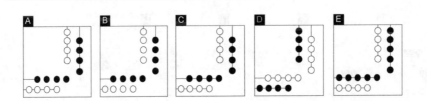

ANSWERS

1. E

Rule 1: The arrow rotates anti-clockwise 90° each time round the shape in the middle.

Rule 2: The shapes are shaded in the repeating pattern 2 black, then 2 white.

Rule 3: The shapes are in the repeating series triangle, circle, square.

2. C

Rule 1: The bent arrow rotates clockwise 90° each time round the centre.

Rule 2: The circles are shaded in the repeating pattern black, grey, white.

Rule 3: The circles move anti-clockwise around the centre, independently from the rotation of the bent arrow.

3. B

Rule 1: The triangle rotates 45° clockwise each time.

Rule 2: The fill of the square runs in the sequence black, striped, white (this leads to the square covering the triangle in the fourth of the series).

Rule 3: Which shape contains the other alternates (the square is big with triangle small, followed by triangle big with square small).

4. D

Rule 1: The arrow's position within the space moves around clockwise along the sides, progressing half the length of a side at a time (top right, middle right, bottom right, middle bottom etc.).

Rule 2: The arrow rotates anti-clockwise 90° each time.

Rule 3: The circle in the centre is shaded in the sequence black, grey, white.

5. D

Rule 1: The line connecting the arrow and the outside square rotates 45° clockwise each time.

Rule 2: The circle alternates between having a black and a grey centre.

Rule 3: The arrow points up if the circle is in the top half of the square and down if the circle is in the bottom half of the square.

6. A

Rule 1: The rhomboid moves left to right in equal steps, covering any shapes it passes over (two shapes when the rhomboid is fully visible, one shape when it is only half visible).

Rule 2: The small shapes rotate 45° each time (not visible for circle).

Rule 3: The small shapes alternate through the following shading sequence: white, striped, grey (they may have a fourth version as well but it never happens to be visible).

7. A

Rule 1: All the shapes rotate 45° each time even when not visible.

Rule 2: We move in the sequence star, smiley, triangle, arrow, ellipse one shape each time (only 3 are ever visible).

Rule 3: The slope alternates from white to black.

8. E

Rule 1: The waves move a half arc forward each time.

Rule 2: The shapes scroll horizontally two shapes at a time, through the sequence square, circle, triangle, pentagon, diamond.

Rule 3: The shapes are white in the repeating sequence second, third, first.

9. C

Rule 1: The shapes scroll one shape at a time through the sequence circle, triangle, rectangle, diamond (only 3 are ever visible).

Rule 2: The second visible shape is the largest, then the third, then the first, in a repeating pattern.

Rule 3: The shapes are white in the repeating sequence third, second, first.

10.   D

Rule 1: The shapes alternate between being below or above the line.

Rule 2: The shapes are white in the repeating sequence second, third, first.

Rule 3: The shapes scroll one shape at a time through the sequence circle, triangle, square, rectangle, diamond (only 3 are ever visible).

11.   D

Rule 1: The number of candles on the cake repeats through the sequence 2, 1, 3.

Rule 2: The number of circles is the number of candles plus 1.

Rule 3: The cake alternates between white and black.

12.   B

Rule 1: The number circle changes size in the repeating sequence whole, three quarters, half, one quarter.

Rule 2: The shape at the top right alternates between a semi-circle and a heart.

Rule 3: The circle parts progress through the repeating shading sequence striped, grey, clear.

13.   E

Rule 1: Starting with step one, every other step the number of shapes in the heart increases by one.

Rule 2: The heart is mirrored in the vertical plane after each step.

Rule 3: The number of pentagons changes in the repeating sequence 4, 1, 0.

14.   D

Rule 1: The number of sides of the shape or shapes in the centre increases by two each time (6, 8, 10, 12, 14, etc.).

Rule 2: The clock hand rotates 90° each time in a clockwise direction.

Rule 3: As the clock hand reaches the black square at the top, the number of shapes in the middle increases by one.

15.   C

Rule 1: The number of whiskers on each side of the animal's face goes through the sequence 2, 1, 0, 3.

Rule 2: The eyes alternate between slits and circles.

Rule 3: The nose changes shape in the sequence triangle, square, circle.

16.   E

Rule 1: The circle rotates 45° each time.

Rule 2: A line is added to the circle each time in equal spacing on the right side and then the left.

Rule 3: The circle is half shaded in the sequence grey, clear, black.

17.   A

Rule 1: The top left shape changes in the sequence circle, pentagon, star.

Rule 2: The top right shape alternates in the sequence between triangle and diamond.

Rule 3: The bottom left shape changes in the sequence 3 quarters shaded, 1 half shaded, 1 quarter shaded, all shaded.

18.   C

Rule 1: Each shape appears once on its own, then once stacked on top of its double.

Rule 2: When the total number of sides on the central shapes is even, the top left arrow points down. When they are odd, it points up.

Rule 3: The bottom arrows alternate between pointing right and left.

19.   C

Rule 1: The shapes on the star change in the sequence circle, square, pentagon.

Rule 2: The position of the shapes on the star moves two points anticlockwise each time.

Rule 3: The star smiles when the shape is on one of the top 3 points of the star.

20. B

Rule 1: The shape at the top left predicts the shape of the door of the house in the next figure.

Rule 2: The number of sides on the roof is the number of sides of the door plus one.

Rule 3: The doors are shaded in the sequence grey, clear, black.

21. E

Rule 1: The triangle rotates clockwise 45° each time.

Rule 2: If a heart is present, in the next figure the circles increase by one, otherwise they decrease by 2.

Rule 3: The shaded portion of the triangle shifts anti-clockwise each turn.

22. B

Rule 1. The shading of the grid piece changes in the repeating sequence grey, black, black.

Rule 2. The shapes in the upper parts of the figures are changing in the repeating sequence diamond, black circle and nothing.

Rule 3. The grid piece moves in a diamond pattern around the central rectangle.

23. E

Rule 1: The square, triangle and rectangle rotate 90° anti-clockwise and move along the following pattern around the corners. Rectangle: bottom left, bottom right, top right. Square/Triangle: top right, top left, bottom left, and then the cycle repeats.

Rule 2: If a star is present, the triangle is mirrored horizontally after the rotation from rule 1.

Rule 3: The number of smiley faces changes in the repeating pattern 3, 7, 1.

24. D

Rule 1: The ice cream colour changes in the repeating sequence black, light, stripy and grey.

Rule 2: The shapes at the bottom change in the sequence of sun, heart and moon.

Rule 3: A flake appears in the top of the ice cream in the sequence of no flake, no flake, flake, flake.

25. B

Rule 1: The top arrow rotates 120° anti clockwise each time (a third of a circle).

Rule 2: The bottom arrow alternates between rotating 90° and 180° clockwise each time.

Rule 3: If the arrows both point upwards, a moon is visible. If they both point downwards, a cloud is visible.

26. C

Rule 1: The hexagon jumps 2 spaces across the board each time, moving left to right, then down at the end of the row, before moving right to left until the end of the row. This is then repeated.

Rule 2: The board rotates 90° clockwise each turn.

Rule 3: If the hexagon would arrive on a star because of rule 1, it moves back 3 spaces, retracing where it came from.

27. E

Rule 1: The largest shape moves clockwise one each time.

Rule 2: If an extra shape appears near the middle, the shapes in the next turn change to be this shape, otherwise the shapes stay the same.

Rule 3: The largest shape alternates between rotating clockwise 45° and 90°, as seen via the shading.

28. B

Rule 1: The number of circles changes by the pattern: add two extra, take away one, add one.

Rule 2: If the number of circles is bigger than the number of triangles, crosses appear in the circles.

Rule 3: The number of triangles changes in the sequence 1, 4, 7.

29.   A

Rule 1: The shapes (even when not visible) rotate 90° anti-clockwise each turn.

Rule 2: Presence of a double headed arrow in the centre means the shapes switch whether they are in the top half or bottom half within the same turn.

Rule 3: One shape vanishes each turn until there is just one shape. Then the other 2 reappear one by one (shapes continue to rotate while 'invisible'). The process then repeats.

30.   D

Rule 1: A new random shape is added to the top of the cross each time.

Rule 2: The new shapes alternate between rotating clockwise around the cross and rotating anticlockwise.

Rule 3: The mouth on the face in the cross changes in the sequence straight, frowning, smiley.

31.   B

Rule 1: If a star isn't present the circle and its internal shapes turn clockwise 45°, otherwise the shapes rotate anticlockwise 45°.

Rule 2: The number of triangles in the circle changes in the sequence 2, 4, 6.

Rule 3: The shapes inside the circle change in the repeating sequence clear, black, grey, stripy.

32.   E

Rule 1: Balls shown at the top are added to balls at the bottom in the previous image in the repeating pattern 8, 4, 0.

Rule 2: After rule 1 is applied, balls at the bottom decrease by 3 each time.

Rule 3: If an explosion is present the balls are shaded grey.

33.   A

Rule 1: The number of ears on the creature changes in the pattern 1, 4, 2.

Rule 2: Ears change shape in the pattern round, pointy, droopy, long.

Rule 3: If a nose is present, the ears go spotty.

34.   D

Rule 1: The face rotates 45° clockwise each turn.

Rule 2: The eyes change shape in the pattern wide, point, slit.

Rule 3: If a smile appears, the glasses change to star shapes.

35.   B

Rule 1: If the flower smiles, add a leaf.

Rule 2: The weather changes in the sequence sunny, cloudy, lightning, rain.

Rule 3: The angle of the leaves goes through the pattern down, middle, up.

36.   C

Rule 1: The snake snakes down, adding a body section each time.

Rule 2: The shapes on the snake change in the repeating sequence diamond, oval, circle.

Rule 3: If the snake goes over (eats) a star, the shapes go grey.

37.   D

Rule 1: The number of spots on the cat changes in the repeating sequence 1, 5, 2.

Rule 2: The number of sides of the cat's spots increases by one each time.

Rule 3: The cat's eyes look up, down, left, then right in sequence.

38.   E

Rule 1: The elephant's trunk changes length from medium to long to medium to short in a repeating sequence.

Rule 2: The puddle in the dish grows by two squares each turn. See also Rule 3.

Rule 3: If the trunk reaches the puddle, it shrinks by 3 squares and the 3 squares appear in the elephant's stomach.

39. C

Rule 1: The 6-pointed star turns clockwise one point each turn.

Rule 2: The 4-pointed star turns anticlockwise one point each turn. The rope hangs off and moves with the 4-pointed star while holding onto the weight.

Rule 3: The weight changes colour in the pattern black, grey and clear.

40. D

Rule 1: The shapes scroll past one shape at a time through the sequence triangle, square, diamond.

Rule 2: The ball moves right to left covering one shape at a time until it reaches the far left and then reappears at the right.

Rule 3: The circle rotates 90° anticlockwise each time.

41. B

Rule 1: The arrow rotates 90 degrees in a clockwise direction in each turn.

Rule 2: If the arrow is at the top or left-hand side of the central shape, the central shape has an even number of sides. If the arrow is at the bottom or right-hand side of the central shape, the central shape has an odd number of sides.

Rule 3: If the arrow points to the bottom, the shape is unshaded.

42. E

Rule 1: The circle takes an increasing number of steps around the 'slots' of the central shape.

Rule 2: The circle is shaded if it's in one of the upper two 'slots'.

Rule 3: The arrow attached to the central shape points upwards if the circle is in one of the left-hand 'slots' – otherwise it points downwards.

43. A

Rule 1: The triangle and the square alternate between rotating 45 degrees in a clockwise direction and staying still: when the triangle rotates, the square stays still, and vice versa.

Rule 2: The shape which did not rotate from the previous turn is outside.

Rule 3: The triangle becomes shaded if it rotated compared to the previous turn.

44. C

Rule 1: The direction of the arrow shows in which direction the circle will move the following turn. If the circles reaches the edge of the image and is instructed by the arrow to move forward, it re-appears on the other side.

Rule 2: If the circle is shaded, the arrow itself will itself move in the direction in which it is pointing.

Rule 3: The arrow is shaded in every second turn.

45. E

Rule 1: The star rotates increasing multiples of 45 degrees in an anticlockwise direction.

Rule 2: The circle takes an increasing number of steps around the corners of the image in a clockwise direction.

Rule 3: The circle is shaded every time it's in one of the left corners.

46. A

Rule 1: The three shapes (triangle, circle and rhomboid) take one step to the right in each turn. When they reach the right edge of the image, they re-appear on the other side.

Rule 2: The shading starts at the rightmost shape and takes an increasing number of steps to the left in every turn.

Rule 3: The size of the leftmost shape is increased first. Then, the size increase moves an increasing number of steps to the right in every turn.

47. A

Rule 1: The four components (arrow, triangle, circle and empty space) move down the slope one step at a time.

Rule 2: The slope is shaded if all those three components that are actual, visible shapes, are visible.

Rule 3: The visible shapes become shaded the second time they appear.

48. D

Rule 1: The direction of the bottom curvy line changes from turn to turn, while the shapes underneath change randomly, without any specific pattern.

Rule 2: The only unshaded bottom shape is first the left one, then the right one and, finally, the middle one. This pattern then repeats throughout the series.

Rule 3: The top half copies the bottom half (the direction of the curvy line and the shading and arrangement of the shapes) from the previous turn.

49. C

Rule 1: The small square on the left-hand side alternates between being fully shaded, top-half shaded and unshaded.

Rule 2: The small square on the right-hand side alternates between being bottom-half shaded, unshaded and fully shaded.

Rule 3: The small squares are moving from the top to the bottom, reappearing at the top after reaching the bottom position.

50. A

Rule 1: The shapes have increasing numbers of sides from left to right when the black line is above them. They have decreasing numbers of sides from left to right when the black line is below them.

Rule 2: The shading takes an increasing number of steps to the right. When the shading reaches the rightmost shape, it reappears on the leftmost one, and so on.

Rule 3: The shape that was shaded in the previous turn is shown at the bottom of the image.

51. A

Rule 1: The circles at the bottom show how many candles will be on the cake in the following turn.

Rule 2: If a circle is shaded, the candle it represents will appear at the bottom of the cake.

Rule 3: The cake is shaded if it has an even number of candles on it (including candles at the bottom).

52. B

Rule 1: The location of the small heart determines the number of quadrants the circle at the centre will have. The top left corner means one quadrant and every other corner in a clockwise direction means an additional quadrant added.

Rule 2: The heart is shaded if it's in either of the left corners.

Rule 3: If the heart is unshaded, the quadrants it creates will be shaded and vice versa.

53. E

Rule 1: Unshaded circles outside the heart show how many circles will be inside the heart in the following turn.

Rule 2: If there are shaded circles outside the lower part of the heart, they will appear next to the unshaded circle(s) at the top in the following turn.

Rule 3: Circles inside the heart alternate between shaded and unshaded.

54. C

Rule 1: The clock hand's position shows whether the shape in the centre will have an odd or even number of sides – 12 and 6 o'clock = even number of sides, 3 and 9 o'clock = odd number of sides.

Rule 2: The shape of the previous turn is shown at the top in the current turn.

Rule 3: Shapes in the centre are shaded if they have more sides than the small shape at the top and vice versa.

55. D

Rule 1: If the cat has an even number of whiskers, its ears are farther away from each other – if it has an odd number of whiskers, the ears are closer to each other.

Rule 2: The cat's nose is shaded if it has more whiskers on the left side. It is unshaded in all other cases.

Rule 3: If the cat has more whiskers on the right side of its face, its nose turns into a triangle.

56. A

Rule 1: A new line is added to the circle in each turn, and the circle rotates in a way that the side which gets the line is always on top.

Rule 2: Every second line added gets a small circle on top of it.

Rule 3: The small circles turn shaded in their second turn of existence.

57. C

Rule 1: The shaded section of the square in the bottom left corner shows which corners of the figure have shapes in the same turn (the bottom left section of the square is always shaded as the square is always present).

Rule 2: Every shape in the corners starts as a triangle and they gain a side every consecutive turn they are present.

Rule 3: Shapes with an even number of sides are shaded.

58. E

Rule 1: The top left arrow shows which direction the shape will travel in the following turn.

Rule 2: If the top right arrow points upwards, the shape will gain a side, if it points downwards, the shape will lose a side.

Rule 3: If both arrows point in the same direction the shape is shaded in that turn.

59. B

Rule 1: Unshaded circles inside the star show how many steps (clockwise) along the points of the star the shape outside will take in the following turn.

Rule 2: Shaded circles inside the star mean an anti-clockwise movement.

Rule 3: Every time the shape crosses the top arm of the star, it gains a side.

60. D

Rule 1: The left 'window' of the house shows the shape of the 'door' in the following turn.

Rule 2: The right 'window' shows the shape of the left 'window' in the following turn.

Rule 3: 'Doors' with an even number of sides are shaded.

61. A

Rule 1: The number of circles by default shows how many 90 degree rotations the triangle will take in a clockwise direction in the following turn.

Rule 2: The number of hearts indicates how many steps the shading within the triangle will take in an anticlockwise direction in the following turn.

Rule 3: Shaded circles and hearts are 'disabled', that is, they do not exert any influence on the shape.

62. A

Rule 1: The number of sides the top left shape has indicates how many vertical steps the shaded section of the grid will take in the following turn. A shaded shape indicates moving upwards, an unshaded shape means moving downwards. When the shaded section reaches the edge of the grid, it re-appears on the other side.

Rule 2: The number of sides the top right shape has indicates how many horizontal steps the shaded section of the grid will take in the following turn. A shaded shape means moving left, an unshaded shape means moving right.

Rule 3: The shading alternates between black and grey.

63. E

Rule 1: The arrow in the top left corner shows whether a new line of smilies will be dropped on the current ones in the following turn (arrow pointing upwards) or an existing line will be removed (arrow pointing downwards) from the bottom. When new similies are added, they arrive in groups of 2-3-2-3.

Rule 2: Shaded arrows indicate that sad smilies will be dropped in the next figure.

Rule 3: Sad smilies will turn into happy smilies in the second turn of their existence.

64. C

Rule 1: The number of 'snowflakes' indicates how many balls of ice cream the cone will consist of in the following turn. Every time a snowflake appears in a figure, the cone will get an extra ball of ice cream in the following turn. Whenever a 'sun' is present, the cone will lose a random ball of ice cream in the following turn.

Rule 2: An unshaded ball of ice cream turns shaded in the second turn of its existence and then disappears in the third.

Rule 3: As long as there is a shaded ball of ice cream present, the cone becomes shaded as well.

65. B

Rule 1: The lower shape takes the posture (direction of arrow) of the upper one from the previous turn.

Rule 2: The upper circle is shaded for two turns, then the bottom one for one turn – this pattern then repeats.

Rule 3: Each time the arrow on the bottom circle is attached to the top half of the circle, a triangle appears in the image.

66. D

Rule 1: The star shows where in the grid the circle will appear next.

Rule 2: In every turn, the previous position of the circle is shaded.

Rule 3: The circle is shaded if it's next to the star.

67. A

Rule 1: The middle shape takes the form of the top right shape from the previous turn.

Rule 2: The bottom right shape shows what the middle shape will look like two turns from now.

Rule 3: The top and bottom shapes on the left do the same but with previous versions of the middle shape.

68. C

Rule 1: In each turn, both the top and the bottom row of circles start with 5 – 5 circles, but some of these circles are 'destroyed' by the shaded triangles pointing at them.

Rule 2: Circles will become shaded if they have unshaded triangles pointing at them.

Rule 3: Figures in the series alternate between having more circles than triangles and vice versa.

69. D

Rule 1: The shaded section of the circle in the top left corner shows where the shape in the middle was pointing in the previous turn. The shaded section of the circle in the middle shows where the shape is pointing in the current turn, while the shaded section of the last circle shows where the shape will be pointing in the following turn.

Rule 2: The shape in the middle is shaded for two turns then unshaded for a single turn. This pattern then repeats.

Rule 3: A second row of circles appears at the bottom, with the same rules applying to them.

70. E

Rule 1: The shape in the top arm of the cross will appear in the left arm in the following turn. This shape then will be "judged" by the smiley face. If the face is smiling, the shape will transfer to the right arm without change. If the face is frowning, the shape will transfer with one fewer side, while if the face is sad, the shape will transfer with two sides taken away.

Rule 2: Each time the face is smiling, a small dot will appear at bottom of the cross which then stays there for the rest of the series.

Rule 3: Each time the face is sad, a dot is removed.

71. E

Rule 1: The circle is divided into two halves with shapes in both. The total number of sides is always larger in the top half of the circle.

Rule 2: A shaded shape's sides are not counted towards the total number of sides.

Rule 3: In even-numbered turns (2,4, etc.), the total number of shapes (in both halves) is odd, while in odd turns, this number is even.

72. A

Rule 1: Vertical arrows within the circles indicate whether the given circle will appear/remain in the upper row or the bottom row in the following turn.

Rule 2: Circles with arrows pointing to the right will become shaded in the following turn.

Rule 3: Circles with arrows pointing to the left will be removed in the following turn.

73. E

Rule 1: The number of circles increases by two in each turn (eyes and eye segments are counted as circles).

Rule 2: In every even turn, a single circle becomes shaded.

Rule 3: The nose, starting as a triangle, gains an additional side in each odd turn.

74. D

Rule 1: The number of unshaded circles indicates how many times the smaller shape will rotate 45 degrees in a clockwise direction in the following turn, becoming the larger shape at the same time. In the next figure, the rule again applies to the smaller shape, the larger shape is always only the result of the rotation.

Rule 2: Shaded circles cause an anticlockwise 45 degree rotation similarly to the mechanism described in Rule 1.

Rule 3: The number of circles alternates between odd and even.

75. A

Rule 1: The number and location of the suns indicate how many leaves the flower will gain in the following turn. The side on which a given sun appears will determine the side on which the corresponding leaf will appear. The leaves are not cumulative, that is, leaves are removed before the new leaves are added in each turn.

Rule 2: Clouds have an effect opposite to that of suns. A sun and a cloud cancel each other out.

Rule 3: A lightning bolt will turn all the leaves black (if any) on the side on which it appears in the following turn.

76. C

Rule 1: The triangle takes an increasing number of steps down the shape. When it reaches the bottom of the shape, it re-appears at the top, continuing its movement.

Rule 2: The triangle gains a new side each time it lands on an odd section of the shape (counting from the top).

Rule 3: In each turn, the previous position of the triangle is shaded.

77. C

Rule 1: The shape within the structure gains an additional side for two turns then loses one in the third. This pattern then repeats.

Rule 2: The structure rotates 45 degrees in a clockwise direction after each turn where the shape within it was unshaded. If it was shaded, the structure rotates in an anticlockwise direction.

Rule 3: A circle appears under the structure each time the shape within has an odd number of sides.

78. A

Rule 1: In each turn, the shape above the bowl has as many sides as the number of unshaded squares in the bowl in the previous turn.

Rule 2: In each turn, the shape under the bowl has as many sides as the number of shaded squares in the bowl in the previous turn.

Rule 3: Shapes (with the exception of the squares in the bowl) change their shading from turn to turn.

79. B

Rule 1: The circle attached to the six-headed star takes an increasing number of steps around the points of the star in a clockwise direction, while the circle on the four-headed star does the same, but in an anticlockwise direction.

Rule 2: The circle on the six headed star is shaded if situated on any of the three upper arms of the star, while the circle on the other star is shaded when situated on the top or the bottom arm.

Rule 3: The triangle becomes shaded if one circle is shaded.

80. A

Rule 1: The shape shown at the base of the arrow will appear in the following turn in the position where the arrow is pointing.

Rule 2: Shapes turn shaded and rotated 45 degrees clockwise in the third turn of their existence.

Rule 3: Shapes disappear in the fourth turn of their existence.

81. E

Rule 1: A circle is surrounded by two other shapes, one of them shaded. The shaded shape will either gain a side in the following turn (when the straight line is above the shapes) or lose one (when the straight line is below the shapes).

Rule 2: If the circle is shaded, the shapes switch places in the following turn.

Rule 3: The shading goes left-right-left-right, etc.

82. C

Rule 1: Circles at the top and the bottom indicate how many 'chimneys' will be visible in the following turn. The shading of the circles changes from turn to turn.

Rule 2: Counting from the left, even numbered chimneys are shaded at the top, and odd numbered ones are shaded at the bottom.

Rule 3: If three or more chimneys are shaded, the rectangle becomes shaded as well.

83. A

Rule 1: The shape in the middle is the same as that shape from the corners from the previous turn which had the most sides (see also Rule 2).

Rule 2: Shaded shapes in the corners cannot become shapes in the middle.

Rule 3: The central shape becomes shaded every second time it appears.

84. B

Rule 1: The shape within the circle is first the shape that was to the left from the circle then to the right of the circle in the previous turn. This pattern then repeats.

Rule 2: Shapes on the left are shaded if they have on odd number of sides, while shapes on the right are shaded when they have an even number of sides.

Rule 3: The shape within the circle is shaded in every second turn.

85. A

Rule 1: An arrow pointing upwards shows that the shape will gain a side; if the arrow is pointing downwards, the shape will lose a side. An arrow pointing to the left signals that a new shape will appear, while an arrow pointing to the right shows that the shape will disappear. All transformations take place in the following turn.

Rule 2: Every second shape that appears is shaded.

Rule 3: No two arrows can point in the same direction in a given figure.

86. B

Rule 1: If a horizontal unshaded arrow points to a circle, it will be shaded in the following turn.

Rule 2: If an arrow is pointing downwards, both circles will be shaded in the given row in the following turn, while if it's pointing upwards, neither of them will be.

Rule 3: If an arrow is shaded, its effect is the opposite of the default effect described above. In the case of horizontal arrows, this means that the circle 'behind' the arrow will become shaded.

87. D

Rule 1: The top lane scrolls to the right, while the bottom one scrolls to the left. See also Rule 3.

Rule 2: Shapes change their shading if they disappear on one side and reappear on the other.

Rule 3: If a circle appears in the middle, the lanes switch scrolling direction from the next turn.

88. E

Rule 1: The top left pie chart rotates 45 degrees in a clockwise direction in each turn, while the bottom left is showing the position of the top one from the previous turn. The pie charts on the right do the same but the rotations happen in an anticlockwise direction.

Rule 2: Each time a pie chart points upwards, a circle appears which then stays there for the rest of the series.

Rule 3: The number of shaded circles equals the number of pie charts pointing downwards in the current turn.

89. A

Rule 1: The shading switches between being on the left arm – in the middle – on the right arm of the structure.

Rule 2: Each time the big central oval is shaded, the whole construction rotates 90 degrees in a clockwise direction.

Rule 3: In each turn, a small circle appears in the circle that was previously shaded.

90. C

Rule 1: The small shape in the top right corner starts as a triangle, then gains a single side for two turns, then loses one on the third. This pattern then repeats.

Rule 2: For as long as the top left shape is gaining sides, a new section is also added to the circle.

Rule 3: The circle is shaded during the turns in which the top left shape is gaining sides.

91. D

Rule 1: An increasing number of circles appear within hearts. Once a heart has three circles, a new one appears.

Rule 2: Every second added circle (circles are added as following: Left – Bottom – Right) in a given turn will be shaded.

Rule 3: A heart with more shaded than unshaded circles stand upside down.

92. A

Rule 1: An increasing number of circles are added to the bottom each turn. The circles next to the arrow show how many circles will be shaded the following turn.

Rule 2: If a circle next to the arrow is shaded, it does not have a 'shading effect' on the circles in the bottom.

Rule 3: If the total number of circles next to the arrow is even, a large triangle is added to the image.

93. C

Rule 1: The inner square is rotating 45 degrees in an anticlockwise direction while the outer one is doing the same in a clockwise direction.

Rule 2: In each turn, the number of circles increases by one.

Rule 3: In even turns, there is an even number of shaded circles, while in odd turns there is an odd number of shaded circles.

94. E

Rule 1: The snake grows by two segments in each turn and the total number of circles in it also grows by two in each turn. There will always be an odd number of total circles as the circle in the first segment is alone.

Rule 2: First, an odd number of circles are shaded, then an even number. This pattern then repeats.

Rule 3: The snake segments alternate between being shaded and unshaded.

95. B

Rule 1: The large central shape assumes the form of the shape in the left then top then right position from the previous turn.

Rule 2: The small shape that will become the large shape in the following turn is shaded.

Rule 3: The big shape is shaded every second time it appears as the same shape.

96. D

Rule 1: The arrows on the left mirror the previous turn's arrows on the right, while the arrows on the right rotate 45 degrees in a clockwise direction every turn.

Rule 2: Arrows pointing upwards or downwards are shaded.

Rule 3: A triangle appears if only one arrow is shaded.

97.　A

Rule 1: Shaded shapes will rotate 45 degrees in an anticlockwise direction in the following turn, while unshaded shapes will rotate 45 degrees in a clockwise direction. There is no rule governing the shading of the shapes or which shape is removed.

Rule 2: First, two shapes are added, then one gets taken away. This pattern then repeats.

Rule 3: A star appears every time there is an even number of shapes in the image.

98.　C

Rule 1: The structure rotates 90 degrees in a clockwise direction in each turn while circles fall on the spikes (as shown by the single circle atop the construction).

Rule 2: A given spike loses its circle when facing downwards.

Rule 3: Circles that fell off the spikes are collected at the bottom of the figure and will have the shading of the spike they fell off of.

99.　E

Rule 1: The three shapes scroll vertically downwards one at a time.

Rule 2: Shapes switch their shading each time they reappear at the top.

Rule 3: The arrows show whether a shape will gain a side (pointing to the right), lose one (pointing to the left) or stay the same (no arrows) in the following turn. The number of arrows indicates how many sides the shape will gain.

100.　B

Rule 1: Based on how many circles were shaded in a given turn, the central shape is rotating that many times 45 degrees in the following turn.

Rule 2: During even-numbered turns, there is an odd number of unshaded triangles within the shape, while during odd-numbered turns, there is an even number.

Rule 3: The total number of shaded and unshaded triangles within the shape changes in the sequence 2, 3, 4, 5, 4, 3, etc.

101.　D

Rule 1: One clock hand and clock face alternate between black on white and white on black each time.

Rule 2: The hand of the alternating colour clock moves backwards by 2 hours (60°) each time.

Rule 3: When the hand is black and the clock face is white, the clock moves as far as possible within the figure in the direction indicated by the arrow on the hand. When the hand is white and the clock face is black, the clock moves as far as possible within the figure in the opposite direction to that indicated by the arrow on the hand. It always moves in a straight line in that direction from its current position.

Rule 4: The grey clock with the dashed outline mirrors the alternating colour clock face, with the mirroring alternating between mirroring in the vertical plane and mirroring in the horizontal plane. When overlap occurs, the grey clock is positioned behind the alternating colour clock.

102.　A

Rule 1: The number of sides on the black shape increases by 1 every time.

Rule 2: The number of sides on the white shape decreases by 2 every other time, beginning with staying the same the first time.

Rule 3: The black shape moves in the following pattern within the figure, which is then repeated: top left corner, bottom right corner, bottom left corner.

Rule 4: The white shape moves in the following pattern within the figure, which is then repeated: bottom right corner, top left corner, bottom left corner, top right corner. When the white shape and the black shape occupy the same space, the white shape is visible in front of the black shape.

103.　B

Rule 1: The overall number of squares increases by 2 each time.

Rule 2: The overall number of triangles increases by 3 then decreases by 1. This pattern is then repeated.

Rule 3: The number of black squares is 1 fewer than the overall number of triangles in the previous figure.

Rule 4: The number of white triangles in a figure is the same as the number of black squares in the same figure.

104. E

Rule 1: The white triangle is reflected in a manner which alternates between the vertical plane and the horizontal plane.

Rule 2: The number of black circles increases by 1 every time.

Rule 3: The black circles are positioned at the same side as the triangle, starting from the edge of the figure. When there is an even number of circles, they are split equally above and below the triangle. When there is an odd number of circles, the extra circle is positioned near the shortest edge of the triangle rather than near the sharpest point.

Rule 4: The arrow points to the edge that the next arrow will start from.

105. D

Rule 1: The black compass point moves round clockwise by 135° each time.

Rule 2: The grey point moves round anti-clockwise by 90° each time. When it occupies the same space as the black point, the grey point is completely obscured by the black one.

Rule 3: The grey pie chart slice in the bottom left reflects the angle in the previous figure, going clockwise, from the black compass point to the grey compass point. In the first figure shown, the pie chart slice reflects where the black and grey compass points would have been in the previous figure, based on Rules 1 and 2. Please note that as the black and grey compass points shared the same point on the compass in the third figure, there is an angle of 0° between them for that figure, so consequently the pie chart slice does not appear in the fourth figure in the sequence.

Rule 4: The shaded circle appears at the centre of the compass whenever the angle of the grey pie chart slice is greater than 180°.

106. C

Rule 1: The black star moves 1 space horizontally each time. When it hits the edge of the grid it goes back in the opposite direction, following the same rule.

Rule 2: The white star moves 2 spaces to the left every time. When it reaches the edge of the grid, it continues moving left by 2 spaces from the opposite edge of the grid.

Rule 3: The black circle moves 2 spaces horizontally and 1 space vertically each time. When it hits the edge of the grid it goes back in the opposite direction, still following this same rule.

Rule 4: A white triangle appears to the right of every row and underneath every column every time there are two symbols in that row or column.

107. E

Rule 1: There are always three arrow heads, one on a single-headed arrow and two on a double-headed arrow. Whilst the left-to-right position of the arrows is arbitrary, the head of the single-headed arrow alternates between pointing up and pointing down.

Rule 2: If an arrow points to a black circle, that circle is changed into a white circle until pointed at again.

Rule 3: If an arrow points to a white circle, that circle vanishes until the space is pointed at again.

Rule 4: If an arrow points to a space, a black circle appears until that location is pointed at again.

108. C

Rule 1: The solid black line rotates through 45° clockwise each time, joining either the opposite corners or the middle of the opposite edges of the figure.

Rule 2: The line comprising alternating long and short dashes rotates through 45° clockwise every other turn. Like the solid line, it joins either opposite corners or the middle of the opposite edges of the figure. This line is not visible if it is in the same position as the solid line.

Rule 3: The dotted line of dashes of equal length rotates through 90° every time. It always joins the opposite corners of the figure. This line is not visible if it shares a position with either of the other lines.

Rule 4: When only two lines are visible in a figure, one or two additional circles are added in order to take the total number up to the first even number that is higher than the number of circles present in the last figure. When all three lines are visible, one or two additional circles are added in order to take the total number up to the first odd number that is higher than the total number of circles present in the last figure. The positioning of the circles is purely arbitrary.

109.   C

Rule 1: The circles move left to right in the top panel.

Rule 2: The circles move top to bottom in the rest of the panels.

Rule 3: The circles move in the shaded vertical panels on odd turns and in the unshaded vertical panels on even ones.

110.   B

Rule 1: The white triangle rotates through 90° anti-clockwise every time.

Rule 2: The black square always appears in the space that is just outside where the shortest edge of the white triangle was in the previous figure.

Rule 3: The grey circle always appears in the space to which the narrow point of the triangle was pointing two figures earlier. When the grey circle shares any space with the black square, the grey circle is positioned in front of the black square.

Rule 4: The black cross alternates between being absent and present.

111.   D

Rule 1: The cloud colour alternates between black and white.

Rule 2: White clouds produce an odd number of raindrops, whilst black clouds produce an even number of raindrops.

Rule 3: The rain falls on a diagonal from left to right for two figures then on a diagonal from right to left for two figures. This sequence then repeats.

Rule 4: The shaded circle next to the raindrops is present whenever there are 6 or more raindrops.

112.   B

Rule 1: The number of white circles is increased by 2 or 1 each time in an alternating sequence, starting with 2.

Rule 2: The number of black circles decreases by 1 less than the previous time every time, starting with 5, then 4, then 3, then 2, then 1.

Rule 3: The total number of sides on the three white shapes is equal to the combined number of white and black circles.

Rule 4: Reading from top to bottom, the three white shapes are always presented in order of their number of sides, with the lowest number at the top and the highest at the bottom. Shapes with an equal number of sides are presented consecutively in the downwards sequence rather than being positioned at the same height as each other.

113.   A

Rule 1: The circle with a cross in it that is located in the top left corner rotates by 45° every time.

Rule 2: The circle with a cross in it that is located in the bottom left corner of the figure rotates by 45° every other time, starting with the first time.

Rule 3: The circle with a cross in it that is located in the bottom right corner of the figure rotates by 45° every other time, starting with the second time.

Rule 4: The black circle appears in the top right corner whenever all 3 circles with a cross are oriented the same way.

114.   C

Rule 1: The black triangle moves one place at a time on a diagonal line down and to the right. When it reaches the bottom of the grid, it starts at the top of the next set of upward-pointing triangles to the right and follows the same type of diagonal movement as before.

Rule 2: The grey triangle pointing upwards moves by one place in a straight line from right to left. When it reaches the end of the grid, it starts again on the same line from the right hand side.

Rule 3: The grey triangle pointing downwards starts by moving by one place at a time in a diagonal up and to the left. When it reaches the top edge of the figure, it follows the path it would take if it was a snooker ball bouncing off the cushion of the table, and describes a diagonal down and to the left. Following the same logic, when it reaches the bottom of the figure it should next follow a diagonal that goes up and to the left.

Rule 4: The small white circle moves one triangle to the right every time, whether that triangle is pointing upwards or downwards. When it is positioned over a black or grey triangle, the circle remains visible over the top of it.

115. D

Rule 1: Although they start at different points in the sequence, the top two shapes change colour in the order black, grey, white. This sequence then repeats. The bottom shape remains black at all times.

Rule 2: The shape at the top left has one fewer side each time.

Rule 3: The shape at the top right loses one side then gains two sides. This pattern then repeats.

Rule 4: The shape at the bottom has the same number of sides as the difference between the number of sides of the other two shapes. The orientation of the shape does not matter.

116. E

Rule 1: The segmented circle alternates between being large and being small.

Rule 2: The segmented circle rotates by 120° anti-clockwise each time.

Rule 3: The segmented circle moves around the edge of the figure in an anti-clockwise direction, alternately taking up position at the corners and the mid-point of the edges. When the circle is large, it occupies the corners of the figure, when it is small it is half-way along the edge.

Rule 4: Whenever the shaded part of the segmented circle points down, a white star appears at the opposite edge or corner to the face.

117. B

Rule 1: The number of points on the star determines the number of shapes in the next figure, including the star itself. There is no fixed sequence regarding which star will be in the next figure.

Rule 2: If there are an odd number of shapes (including the star), the non-star shapes are triangles. If there is an even number of shapes, the non-star shapes are squares.

Rule 3: Half of the shapes are black and half are white. If there are an odd number of shapes, the "extra" shape is always white.

Rule 4: The star alternates between being white for two figures and black for two figures.

118. E

Rule 1: The arrow heads alternate between pointing left and right and pointing up and down. The position of the arrow heads is at the top right and bottom left for two figures, then at the top left and bottom right for two figures. After four figures, the sequence repeats.

Rule 2: The arrows on the left half of the figure have the effect of changing the fill of the shape they point to between a downward right diagonal stripe and a downward left diagonal stripe. The change itself takes place in the next figure in the sequence.

Rule 3: The arrows on the right half of the figure have the effect of changing the shape they point to. Triangles change into squares, squares change into hexagons and hexagons change into triangles. The change itself takes place in the next figure in the sequence.

Rule 4: The shapes on the right hand side of the figure all alternate between black and white each time.

119. E

Rule 1: The small and medium circles take an increasing number of steps around the large one.

Rule 2: The small circle takes a single anti-clockwise step around the medium circle in each turn.

Rule 3: The large circle changes shading each time the medium circle is in the 12 o'clock position.

Rule 4: The medium circle changes shading in every second turn.

Rule 5: The small circle changes shading in every turn.

120. C

Rule 1: The two triangles rotate by 45° anti-clockwise each time.

Rule 3: Looking at them from where their bases are joined (i.e. treating them like the left and right ears of a rabbit), the two triangles are both white, then white and black, then both black, then black and white. This sequence then repeats.

Rule 4: The black circle's position alternates between being at the corner of the figure that is closest to where the two triangles are pointing and being in the corner that is diagonally opposite to where the triangles are pointing.

121. C

Rule 1: The square alternates between jumping diagonally between opposite corners and taking two clockwise steps.

Rule 2: The circle and the square swap their shading in every other step.

Rule 3: The group of dots follows the square, indicating the square's position in the previous step.

122. D

Rule 1: The circles at the top left corner migrate from the left to the right corner one by one in every other step. The migration starts between the first and second steps.

Rule 2: The circles at the bottom right corner migrate from the right to the left corner one by one in every other step. The migration already started before the start of the series, and continues from between the second and third steps.

Rule 3: Circle clusters are shaded when there is an odd number of circles and unshaded when an even number.

Rule 4: The triangle alternates between pointing up and pointing down.

123. A

Rule 1: The shading within the triangle moves from top to bottom, alternating between the left and right side between steps. When the shading reaches the bottom level, it resets to the top level in the next step (as on the right-hand side between the first and second steps).

Rule 2: The two circles show where the shading will be the following turn.

Rule 3: The circles' shadings are the opposite of the triangle segment they are next to in a given turn.

124. E

Rule 1: The circle takes a clockwise step each turn.

Rule 2: The square the circle lands in will either move away from or towards the middle (based on its current position) the next turn.

Rule 3: The circle is unshaded when it is in squares that are in the middle.

125. A

Rule 1: The square with the connector lines to neighbouring squares moves from left to right in each step. When it reaches the right edge of the figure, it moves onto the next row down.

Rule 2: The squares which were connected to the moving square in the previous step become shaded in the next step.

Rule 3: The 9-square grid is framed in every other step.

126. E

Rule 1: The set of rectangles rotates 90 degrees clockwise in each step.

Rule 2: Every second time that either a single horizontal or vertical rectangle lies on top of the 2 lower layers of rectangles, it is shaded.

127. B

Rule 1: In each step, one or two shapes move either to the middle or to the edge. Movement starts with the two shapes on the left, and then proceeds in a clockwise direction in a 2-1-2-1 sequence (two shapes move, then one shape moves…).

Rule 2: One shape in each figure is connected with lines to the two shapes in the opposite half (top or bottom) of the figure. This connection travels clockwise from one shape to the next, starting from the shape in the top right corner.

Rule 3: Shapes that are not aligned horizontally with their pairs (i.e. if the two rectangles or circles are not in the same horizontal line) are shaded, otherwise they are not.

128. E

Rule 1: The shading of the larger circles takes a step clockwise each turn, moving from circle to circle to reach the next segment in the sequence.

Rule 2: The small circles within the circles take a clockwise step each turn.

Rule 3: The small circles are alternately either shaded or unshaded, based on whether the large circle they are in has the large shading or not.

129. B

Rule 1: Small circles move clockwise as a group (not one by one) in each step from one segment of the large shapes to another.

Rule 2: As the small circles move to and through the segments of the top right shape, they increase by 1 in each step.

Rule 3: As the small circles move to the bottom shape, their number resets to 1.

Rule 4: As the small circles move to and through the segments of the top left shape, they change their shading.

130. B

Rule 1: Circles hanging from the top move from top to bottom, stopping at the bottom for a step before starting to move upwards again.

Rule 2: The shading of the circles moves from left to right. Once it reaches the rightmost position, it reappears on the left side.

Rule 3: When a circle is shaded, it will move two positions (up or down) in the following step.

131. C

Rule 1: The setup of shapes alternates between 3 columns with 2 dividing lines and 2 columns with 3 dividing lines.

Rule 2: The shading of the columns moves one space from left to right from each 3-column shape to the next 3-column shape, and one space from left to right from each 2-column shape to the next 2-column shape.

Rule 3: The circles also move from left to right along the top and bottom points of the dividing lines.

When they reach the rightmost point, they reset to the leftmost position.

132. E

Rule 1: The setup of shapes alternates between 3/4/3 and 4/3/4 rows of squares.

Rule 2: The shading in each row moves left to right but only when the given row is visible.

133. B

Rule 1: Going anticlockwise, a circle in each step has an increasing number of connections to subsequent circles in an anticlockwise direction. This resets to 1 connection after reaching 4.

Rule 2: The number of shaded circles increases by one and the shading moves in an anticlockwise direction in each step. When the number of shaded circles reaches 5, it resets to 1.

Rule 3: The connections alternate between reaching the middle or only the edge of the circles.

134. A

Rule 1: In each square, the number of circles increases by 1 in each step, resetting to 1 after it has reached a maximum of 4.

Rule 2: Starting from 2 in the first figure, the number of shaded circles increases by 1 in each step from left to right, resetting to 1 after reaching a maximum of 4.

Rule 3: The number of shaded circles in a given step dictates how many anticlockwise steps the shading of the rectangle will take between the current and next steps.

135. D

Rule 1: Each small circle can have the following states, in the following order: unshaded, shaded, shaded with an intersecting line. When a circle reaches the third state, it remains in that state until affected another rule.

Rule 2: The shading of the large half circles moves from top left to bottom left and top right to bottom right.

Rule 3: When a large half circle becomes shaded, the small circle in that sector resets to its starting (unshaded) state.

136. D

Rule 1: The shading of the squares moves from left to right and from top to bottom in both columns. When the shading reaches the bottom, it resets to the top left positon and continues from there.

Rule 2: Shaded squares move away from the column in the following step.

Rule 3: Squares that moved away from the column in a given step move back to their original position in the next step.

137. C

Rule 1: The shaded circle takes a diagonal step towards the bottom right, then a vertical step downwards, then a diagonal step towards the top right, then a vertical one upwards, and then this pattern repeats. Diagonal steps are indicated by diagonal lines pointing to where the circle was in the previous step. When the circle reaches the right edge of the figure, the left-right direction of movement switches to right-left (although this is not visible in the series).

Rule 2: The unshaded circle takes a diagonal step towards the top right, then a vertical step upwards, then a diagonal step towards the bottom right, then a vertical one downwards, and then this pattern repeats. Diagonal steps are indicated by diagonal lines pointing to where the circle was in the previous step. When the circle reaches the right edge of the figure, the left-right direction of movement switches to right-left (although this is not visible in the series).

138. C

Rule 1: In even-numbered steps (e.g. 2,4), a circle on the vertical arm changes position, going from left to right or right to left, alternating between the top and bottom circles. In odd-numbered steps (e.g. 3,5), a circle on the horizontal arm changes position, going from top to bottom or bottom to top, alternating between the left and right circles.

Rule 2: The circles are shaded when they are in opposite positions on the same 'arm', i.e. when one is on the right, the other on the left, or when one is pointing to the bottom and the other to the top. Another way to think about it is to say that the circles follow the shading pattern of none shaded, outer two shaded, all shaded, inner two shaded, and so on.

139. E

Rule 1: The square that is three-quarters shaded moves 1-2-1 positions clockwise between steps.

Rule 2: The square that is one-quarter shaded moves 2-1-2 positions clockwise between steps.

Rule 3: The shaded circle in the middle moves 1-2-1 positions anticlockwise between steps.

140. C

Rule 1: The lines originating from the top of the figure lengthen until they reach the bottom, and then start to shorten again. The number of steps a line takes is equal to the numbers of circles on it and the line only changes length in the step after a circle has landed on it.

Rule 2: The unshaded circle jumps one step from left to right while the shaded circle jumps two steps from left to right. When circles reach the right edge of the figure, they reappear on the left side and the movement continues.

141. D

Rule 1: The unshaded circle takes left-to-right and then diagonal steps across the left/right points of the right angles.

Rule 2: The shaded circle takes diagonal and then left-to-right steps across the top/bottom points of the right angles.

Rule 3: When an unshaded circle lands on a right angle, it is mirrored vertically in the next step.

Rule 4: When a shaded circle lands on a right angle, it is mirrored horizontally in the next step.

142. A

Rule 1: Circles (both shaded and unshaded) move from top to bottom, reappearing at the top after they have reached the bottom.

Rule 2: The squares switch shading in every step.

Rule 3: When a circle 'jumps' through a square, it assumes the shading of the square in the next step. If it already had the same shading as the square, nothing changes.

143. B

Rule 1: The shapes containing the circles flip vertically one by one, going from left to right.

Rule 2: Once a shape has flipped, the circles contained in it start 'falling' out of it and into the next shape, one by one, starting with the bottom one first.

Rule 3: Falling circles change shading.

144. E

Rule 1: The line with the circle on the outside is rotated 90 degrees anticlockwise and then mirrored horizontally, then the pattern repeats.

Rule 2: The rectangular shape is mirrored vertically between each step.

Rule 3: The shaded circles at the points of the rectangle move clockwise in a 1-2-1 steps pattern.

145. A

Rule 1: The entire shape rotates 90 degrees clockwise in each step.

Rule 2: The shading takes a clockwise step across the three sections.

Rule 3: The shaded and unshaded circles swap positons in each step.

146. D

Rule 1: The arrows move from left to right between steps. Once they reach the rightmost position, they reappear on the left-hand side.

Rule 2: The arrows follow a down-up-up-pointing pattern.

Rule 3: Each shading takes one step in each row, from left to centre to right. When they reach the end of the row they move to the left position of the next row (top or bottom).

147. C

Rule 1: The shaded square moves from left to right along the row of squares in a 2-1-2 steps pattern, switching between rows when it reaches the right edge of the figure.

Rule 2: The circle is shaded while in the top row, unshaded while in the bottom row.

Rule 3: The circle moves around the rows, by two steps at a time from left to right when its starting position is in the bottom row, and by one step at a time from right to left when its starting position is in the top row.

148. E

Rule 1: The shaded triangle within the small square moves two positions and then one position clockwise between steps.

Rule 2: The circle in the small square moves clockwise around the four triangles.

Rule 3: A circle appears in a segment of the large square in each step going clockwise.

Rule 4: If the shading and the small circle appear in the same segment in a given step, the circle added to the large square will be shaded.

149. C

Rule 1: In successive steps, the blank circles become minus (–) circles, the – circles become plus (+) circles and the + circles become blank.

Rule 2: When blank circles become – circles, they move to the middle; when – circles become + circles they move to the corners, and stay in the corners when reset to blank, moving to the middle again when they become – circles.

150. E

Rule 1: In each step, a new circle is added, alternating between the left and the right columns. When a new circle is added in one of the columns, it pushes all previously added circles on that side down one row.

Rule 2: Each circle starts on the outside and then takes one step towards the centre, and then the cycle repeats.

Rule 3: The shading of the rectangle moves from left to right and top to bottom in a 1-2-1 pattern. When it reaches the bottom right corner, it continues from the top.

Rule 4: Circles become shaded when they are co-located with the shaded rectangle.

151.   D

Rule 1: The circle groups move according to the following pattern: (1) the circles at the top take a step from left to right; (2) the circle at the connecting vertical line drops to the bottom; (3) the circles at the bottom take a step from right to left; (4) the circle at the connecting vertical line ascends to the top. This cycle then repeats.

Rule 2: Circles that either dropped or ascended change their shading and stay that way.

Rule 3: The shading of the large circles changes (separately) in every other turn, i.e. the left circle changes shading in the second, fourth and sixth figure, while the right circle changes shading in the 3rd and 5th figures.

152.   C

Rule 1: The two shaded circles move one position clockwise in each step.

Rule 2: The short double lines at right angles to the main connecting lines flip direction when there are two shaded circles at either end of the main line they connect to.

Rule 3: Shaded / unshaded, shaded / shaded, unshaded / unshaded circles are connected (with a line in bold), then it repeats. An additional connecting line appears in each figure, connecting the shaded to the unshaded circle first, then shaded to shaded, and finally unshaded to unshaded, and then the cycle repeats.

153.   E

Rule 1: The shaded triangles in both the bottom and top rows alternatingly take a left to right step.

Rule 2: Those triangles in the top row that are pointed at by the shaded triangles in the bottom row rotate 90 degrees anticlockwise in the next step.

154.   E

Rule 1: The arms on the top side of the horizontal line change orientation one by one from left to right, and then right to left.

Rule 2: The arms on the bottom side of the horizontal line change orientation one by one from right to left, and then left to right.

Rule 3: Arms that are mirrored horizontally have circles on their endpoints.

155.   A

Rule 1: The inside shaded circle on the left travels from top to bottom. When it reaches the bottom, it resets to the top position.

Rule 2: The inside shaded circle on the right travels from bottom to top. When it reaches the top, it resets to the bottom position.

Rule 3: Outer circles next to shaded inner ones will become shaded themselves the following turn.

Rule 4: The direction of the arms changes whenever the two inside circles next to each other are both either shaded or unshaded.

156.   B

Rule 1: The groups of circles within the sectors of the large circle move clockwise from sector to sector.

Rule 2: The two shaded circles in the corners of the figure alternate in taking single steps clockwise.

Rule 3: One circle from each inner circle group that falls in the same position as either of the shaded outer circles becomes shaded in the next step. If a circle from the group is already shaded, an additional one becomes shaded (if there are additional circles in the group).

157.   D

Rule 1: Going clockwise, one triangle is rotated by 180 degrees in each step.

Rule 2: The shading travels along the triangles in a clockwise direction, starting from the top.

Rule 3: When the shading lands on a triangle, the triangle is rotated 90 degrees clockwise; then, in the subsequent step, it is rotated 90 degrees clockwise again.

158.   A

Rule 1: A single circle from the top left moves to the bottom left, then top right, then bottom right. Then another circle start its journey along the same path.

Rule 2: When a circle lands in the bottom left corner, a circle in the bottom right corner becomes shaded for the rest of the series.

Rule 3: When a circle lands in the top right corner, a circle in the top left corner (if available) becomes shaded for the rest of the series.

159.   A

Rule 1: The shaded quarters of both the large and small squares take alternating clockwise steps. This means that the shading in either square only moves every other step.

Rule 2: The small square alternates between being in front of or behind the large square.

160.   C

Rule 1: All circles alternate between being shaded and unshaded. Those 'hanging' from the top have a left-right alternation while those connected to the side have a bottom-top alternation.

Rule 2: In each step, two circles are added to the figure. In even steps, they are added to the bottom group on the side and to the left group on the top; in odd steps, they are added to the top group on the side and the right group on the top.

Rule 3: The lines connecting the circles alternate between being visible and invisible.

9. Succeeding in Situational Judgement Tests

> *Situational Judgement Tests have been used in some competitions in recent years but not in others. Check your Notice of Competition to see whether you will have such a test.*

Situational judgement tests (or SJTs for short) present candidates with a series of hypothetical but realistic work-based scenarios in which they are required to make a decision. It is important to understand that even though called "tests", they are very different in nature from the verbal, numerical and abstract reasoning tests you will face during the selection process as they measure how you evaluate certain situations instead of testing your harder analytical skills and behaviours.

Situational judgement tests are employed because they can be used to consistently and fairly assess at an early stage behavioural attributes such as decision-making ability and interpersonal skills that are difficult to measure by other techniques.

SJTs are a fast-growing area in the selection and development field. The basic idea of presenting a relevant hypothetical situation has been in use in recruitment since the early 1900s, but SJTs in a format comparable to today's SJTs have been more prevalent since the 1940s, used in particular for predicting supervisory and managerial potential.

More recent research has found that SJTs are strong predictors of real-life job performance. This means that in the development or review of SJTs, those people doing well in the tests were also the people who performed well in role. Not only that, but SJTs seem to measure an additional aspect of performance that is not measured by other assessment tools such as ability tests or personality questionnaires. This suggests that the SJTs are tapping into a different skill, and one that is highly relevant to job performance.

Situational judgement tests are used prior to the assessment phase, as part of the computer-based pre-selection process for Administrator profiles.

In AD competitions the following competencies are measured by means of situational judgement tests:

- Analysis and Problem Solving
- Delivering Quality and Results
- Prioritising and Organising
- Resilience
- Working with Others

Theory behind Situational Judgement Tests

At the heart of social psychology is the idea that what makes us human is our ability to make sense of social situations. When we evaluate an important or new situation most of us try to understand the intentions of others in the situation, and possible causal explanations, to guide our response (e.g. "How would you react if you discovered that your colleague had leaked some confidential information to the press?").

Social psychology theory also holds that there is a similarity in how people evaluate situations, and that most people will have a shared expectation of what is an *appropriate* response. This theory forms the basis of why situational judgement tests can be used to provide an indicator of our likely behaviour in an EU job-context or elsewhere. By presenting the candidate with relevant hypothetical scenarios and a set of responses which have been previously scored for their level of effectiveness, it is possible to assess how appropriate the candidate's response selection is, and to use this information to predict their likely behavioural response if faced with similar situations in the role.

What They Measure

The name "situational judgement test" suggests that what is being measured is indeed "situational judgement", actually tapping into an aspect of "practical intelligence" or "general intelligence". It is likely that SJTs are indeed multi-dimensional; they measure a number of different constructs including social or behavioural judgement, practical or general intelligence and aspects of personality such as conscientiousness. In the EPSO assessment process the SJT has been specifically developed for the purpose of measuring the candidate's situational judgement in relation to selected EPSO competencies.

How They Are Developed

Robust situational judgement tests are developed in the same way as other psychometric tests. The particular job profiles EPSO is seeking to select for are analysed by experts to understand what type of workplace situations occur that are critical to achieving good performance outcomes. This was done by interviewing current EU officials, heads of unit, directors and subject matter experts to gain a number of perspectives on what is important and what would be effective behaviour.

At the same time, examples of how less effective behaviour could lead to less desirable outcomes are gathered. Once these situations are identified, they are written up as possible test scenarios: a paragraph or two that summarises the situation and a range of four or more response options (from *most effective* or *desirable* to *least effective* or *least desirable*). The scenario and response options are crafted so that there is no "obvious" answer and even the "undesirable" options sound plausible. This is of course necessary to avoid the risk that candidates would be able to identify the "desired" answer too easily.

Careful consideration is given to the design of the test introduction and instructions and the scenario wording, format and content. It is well known that in the case of public opinion surveys, how the question is formulated will significantly influence the answer. As this is certainly true for SJTs as well, even subtle details of presentation must be thought through carefully.

It is important that the SJT design fits within the organisational setting and the assessment process, and that it reflects realistic elements of the job role in question. However, EPSO has said that its situational judgement tests are designed so that they require no specialist knowledge to complete: they are purely behaviourally-based assessments.

How They Work

The theory of planned behaviour states that an individual's behaviour in the past is a good predictor of their likely behaviour in the future. As with a standard competency based interview, this is the basis on which a situational judgement test is used to predict a candidate's job performance or suitability for the given job profile.

For each given situational judgement test, a *scoring key* is developed so that the candidate's response can be compared against this key. Initially, this can be developed by making rational judgements as to which are the most and least preferred responses to each scenario, based on the job analysis data collected in the design process and from additional evaluations made by subject matter experts.

The SJT can then be *validated* by demonstrating a clear relationship between good performance in the test and real-life good performance in the role. In order to validate the test design, and to select which scenarios will be in the final test, groups of existing job holders such as – for example – Administrators in the European Commission or Assistants in the Committee of the Regions will be tested on the sample scenarios and their responses will be compared to their real-life competency-based job performance (as judged by their superior's appraisal ratings).

Those scenarios for which the high performers have consistently selected the most preferred response as their *own* most preferred response will be selected as good ones for the final test. If there are scenarios for which high performers consistently select different responses, these will be brought into question as to their appropriateness and dropped from the test. When used in the organisation's assessment process, the candidate's score in the SJT will be based on their performance across all scenarios within the test and a score will be given to each competency in question.

What They Look Like

When sitting the test, you will be presented with a number of workplace scenarios, or "situations", together with options for how you should respond to the problem in the situation. You will have to choose which of the options in your view represent the most and the least appropriate responses. The scenarios will not be specifically limited to tasks and roles in the EU institutions, but instead will relate to more generic workplace situations of the sort that can arise in many jobs, involving working with colleagues and within hierarchies.

Each of the situations measures one of the key competencies for the job (although you would not be informed which is being measured when answering each question) and also cross-checks the consistency of your answers. Consequently, each competency will need to be measured more than once in order to reliably estimate your ability and therefore more than one scenario will relate to each competency. The test will have been designed especially for EPSO by expert occupational psychologists and it typically might contain 20 questions with 2 points per question.

You have been approached by your superior and asked to deliver a project within a very tight deadline. You are pleased that your head of unit has approached you to work on the project but are concerned about delivering it within the timeframe given. What do you do?

A. Review and reprioritise the projects you are currently involved in so you can start work on the new project straight away.

B. Schedule a meeting with your head of unit to discuss options for delivering the project, suggesting colleagues that you would like to involve to ensure the project is delivered within the timeframe given. (**Most Effective**)

C. Develop a plan outlining how you intend approaching the project and use this to emphasise to your head of unit your concern about the deadline and ask if it can be extended.

D. Delegate the task to another person, stressing to them the importance of meeting the deadline. Retain an overview so that you can track progress and keep the ultimate credit for the work. (**Least Effective**)

On the previous page is a sample SJT test scenario, designed to measure a generic "planning"-type competency (which is not itself a specific EPSO competency, but see the next chapter for a comprehensive sample test and explanations based on the EPSO competency framework). It also includes what can be judged to be the most and least effective courses of action (although this could vary according to exact competency definitions):

The Candidate Experience

SJTs contribute to the assessment by being a two-way process for EPSO and the candidate.

EPSO can evaluate the candidate's responses to the scenarios against the structured scoring key and evaluate the extent to which the candidate's behaviour is likely to fit in with the competencies and way of working at the EU institutions.

The candidate is also able to take a view of what it would be like to work with the EU by reflecting after the test on the types of scenarios and response options presented. These may provide a general insight into what situations or behaviours might be expected in the role. Reviewing this chapter and trying out some of the practice questions in the next chapter will prove beneficial for you: those candidates who are familiar with SJTs have been found to view the experience of completing SJTs as part of an assessment process more positively than those without that familiarity.

How to Prepare

It is a bit challenging to prepare in advance of taking an SJT: a response to a situation that may be appropriate in one role may be inappropriate in another (e.g. the way you would react to a critique from your supervisor is very different from your reaction to an issue raised by an EU citizen affected by a policy you are covering). Therefore, your answers should draw from your intuitive, *honest* responses about how you would address such situations.

However, doing some practice questions on the lines of those in the next chapter can help to alleviate stress and allow you to focus on the *content* of the questions once you start the real test, rather than spending time becoming familiar with the *format*. Also, ensure that you are familiar with the EPSO competencies, as each scenario will be based around one of these. By doing this, you will be more aware of what is likely to be looked for across all the questions. Once again, however, it should be reiterated that you must be honest in your responses and not spend time trying to second-guess what is being looked for.

If you wished to, you could look up some reference material on current best practice thinking on areas related to the competencies being assessed. Ideas for research topics on the competencies measured by EPSO through SJTs are as follows:

- **Analysis and Problem Solving** – *Identifies the critical facts in complex issues and develops creative and practical solutions*. Research areas such as troubleshooting techniques, how to approach dealing with large amounts of information, techniques to stimulate creative problem solving, how to gather appropriate information.

- **Delivering Quality and Results** – *Takes personal responsibility and initiative for delivering work to a high standard of quality within set procedures*. Research areas such as how to effectively balance quality and deadlines, how to judge when rules or procedures might be bent or broken.

- **Prioritising and Organising** – *Prioritises the most important tasks, works flexibly and organises own workload efficiently*. Research areas such as project management tools and techniques, how to prioritise effectively, how to distinguish the important from the urgent, how to respond to shifting deadlines and goalposts, when and how to delegate.

- **Resilience** – *Remains effective under a heavy workload, handles organisational frustrations positively and adapts to a changing work environment.* Research areas such as how to stay calm under pressure, how to keep an optimistic outlook, how to respond to criticism, how to balance work and home life, how to cope with ambiguity.

- **Working with Others** – *Works co-operatively with others in teams and across organisational boundaries and respects differences between people.* Research areas such as effective team working, working across organisational boundaries, how to support others.

However, it should be noted that this will be a lot of background work and it would be unrealistic to expect to become an expert in all of these areas prior to the assessment if you are not already. A better tactic might be to decide which one or two competency areas are your prime areas for development and focus upon these.

Tips for the Assessment itself

Several tips mentioned in the verbal reasoning chapter can be successfully applied for SJTs as well. Review and adapt those hints to match the specialties of SJTs.

- **Read Everything**: Read the scenario and each of the possible answers fully before responding. You may find that the answer that originally seemed to be the best does not turn out to be upon closer inspection. Remember that the options will be carefully worded and watch out for subtle differences in wording that could differentiate a truly exceptional response from an adequate one. If possible, try to judge which EPSO competency is being assessed so you have a good idea about what qualities they will be looking for you to emphasise.

- **Relative Answers**: Bear in mind that you are being asked to make *relative* judgements: you are not asked to say which courses of action are right or wrong. In other words, you may find that *all* of the possible responses are appropriate to some degree. In this case, just rank them in order of appropriateness to help you make the "most effective" and "least effective" decision.

- **Limited Context**: As with verbal reasoning exams, try not to bring in outside knowledge – base your responses solely on the information contained within the scenario itself. This is because your outside experience may colour your response in a way that means it is not relevant to the question being posed. To take a light-hearted example, you may know that in your team at work, they are all huge fans of pizza and therefore this would be a good way of motivating them. However, in the SJT test item, there may be no reference to this and the best way to motivate a team may well be to give a motivational talk. Therefore, your outside experience might negatively impact on your ability to perform well in the test.

- **Outcome Focus**: Take the time to consider what the possible *outcomes* would be, both positive and negative, of each of the courses of action you are considering. This will help you to narrow down the choices.

- **Communication is Key**: When a situation is described where you need to choose between handing responsibility for discussing an issue to your superior or discussing an issue with another party face-to-face, it is likely that the latter option will be preferred.

- **Internal Issues**: In a situation involving a conflict, try to look for options that favour keeping a certain issue in-house and involve only those affected by it; your loyalty to your unit or institution is highly valued.

- **Stay Positive**: When faced with a problem that may be resolved by making someone take the blame, avoid the temptation and try to act as fair as possible even if that means a disadvantage for you in the short term.

Though the primary focus of situational judgement tests is not your factual knowledge of EU procedures or administrative practice, it is advisable to read through the Code of Good Administrative Behaviour of EU officials. This includes fundamental principles such as lawfulness, proportionality, non-discrimination, consistency, objectivity and others which can *indirectly* help in your judgement of the questions. Another valuable source is EPSO's very own statement of the values based on which it aims to conduct its mission : integrity, ambition, professionalism, quality service, diversity and respect. If you bear these in mind when making your "situational judgement", it will surely yield the best result.

In the following chapter, you can find a sample Situational Judgement Test with detailed explanations, based on EPSO's competency framework.

10. Situational Judgement Test

The following practice situational judgement test questions have been developed to test the types of behaviours assessed by EPSO with specific exercises (rather than only by observation of behaviour in other assessment exercises). By completing this test you will gain an insight into the question types you will face and subject matter areas that will be invaluable in your preparation for the real test.

Each of the "situations" below is designed to relate in particular to one of the following EPSO competencies, and the answers at the end of the chapter tell you which one it was:

- Analysis and Problem Solving

- Delivering Quality and Results

- Prioritising and Organising

- Resilience

- Working with Others

Please complete these questions in a quiet place with few distractions. You have a series of scenarios and then four possible ways to approach that scenario. It is your task to decide which of the answers you think would be most effective and which would be the least effective.

There is no time limit in this exercise (at the EPSO exam you will likely have 40 minutes for 24 questions), although you should try not to ponder too long on any one question: your first reaction to each of the possible approaches is usually the most honest one. Try to identify which competency you think is being assessed to help focus your response, but aim to give your honest response rather than attempting to "second guess" the examiners.

If you feel that you agree or disagree with ALL of the possible options, then please choose the ones that you think are the most and least effective from those presented in a RELATIVE sense.

Remember: For each of the following situations you should pick the MOST and the LEAST effective of the options listed.

The answers come after Situation 30.

Situation 1

You have spent a lot of time putting together a long and very detailed EU report. A more experienced colleague in your Unit offered to review it for you before submission. Although they were not directly involved in the project it covers, you accepted this offer. Their review has come back to you and is highly critical of the report content and its structure. You believe that the critique is unnecessarily negative, and that many of the criticisms are unjustified. How do you respond to this criticism?

A. Submit the report as it stands. You were the person initially given the task of producing the report and were personally involved in the project.

B. Ask your colleague to explain his criticisms so you can better understand which of them to address.

C. Make all of the changes recommended by your colleague, as his experience is likely to contribute to the validity of his criticisms.

D. Dispassionately analyse the criticisms to determine which of the recommendations are sensible and which should be ignored.

Situation 2

You have been assigned a fairly lengthy project which will require you to work closely with a teammate who you have previously found to be distant and stand-offish. You have also previously overheard him saying negative things about your abilities to another team member. You are concerned about having to now work closely with him. How do you proceed?

A. Try to approach working with the teammate with an open mind.

B. Discuss your concerns with your Superior prior to starting the project.

C. Ask the teammate to explain the negative comments you overheard.

D. Adopt a high degree of caution in your interactions with the teammate.

Situation 3

You are part of a project team that provides data to DIGIT, the Commission's IT Directorate-General, which they then utilize in implementing a complex computer generated report about performance against agreed monthly targets. They are dissatisfied with the format in which your team provides the data and provide details of the alternative format they would prefer instead. This format would require additional analysis from your team and would not be viable within the timescales your team has to turn the data around. How do you proceed?

A. Continue to use the existing format in order to ensure that timescales are appropriately managed.

B. Adopt the elements of the new format that you know can be easily changed and that would not impact on timescales.

C. Adopt the new format in its entirety whilst explaining that timescales for getting the data to them will need to be longer as a result.

D. Ask the IT Unit to explain which elements of their preferred format are of greatest value to them and adopt these if timescales are not dramatically impacted.

Situation 4

You are responsible for preparing key aspects of a presentation for a more senior colleague. These will be inserted into the overall presentation, some aspects of which are already written, some of which are being prepared by other members of your Unit. The senior colleague has provided everyone with a clear overview document and she has promised to inform the relevant individuals if aspects of their part of the presentation require any changes. How do you tackle this task?

A. Frequently telephone your colleagues who are also working on the presentation to understand how the presentation is coming together.

B. Work primarily from the overview document provided by the senior colleague and from any changes that come directly from her.

C. Request that colleagues inform everyone involved in preparing the presentation of any changes affecting their area using e-mail or similar.

D. Arrange regular meetings for everyone involved in preparing aspects of the presentation where changes can be discussed collectively.

Situation 5

You have been finding your work relatively unchallenging recently and asked your Superior for more opportunities to challenge yourself. In response to your request, he put you in charge of a project, the output of which has clear visible benefits to EU policy. However, the work is taking up more time than you initially anticipated and you are finding much of the work even more tedious and mundane than your regular responsibilities. How do you act?

A. Continue to deliver the work without commenting on the fact that you are finding it tedious as the policy benefits are clearly evident.

B. Continue to deliver the work as requested, whilst informing your Superior that it is not actually challenging you as much as you had hoped.

C. Point out to your Supervisor that the work is more time consuming than anticipated and request some assistance from another team member to share the time commitment.

D. Tell your Superior that you would like someone else to take on this work as you are finding it time consuming without being challenging.

Situation 6

There are unconfirmed rumours that the roles within your Directorate are being reviewed and people's responsibilities will be changed. Your Superior has confirmed that a major restructure will take place, and although the final details are not yet clear, from the information provided it seems that your role will be affected. As a result of this uncertainty, morale is low across the Directorate. How do you approach this situation?

A. Spend some time putting together an outline of your skills so you can align them with any new responsibilities that may come your way.

B. Put most of your energy into performing your existing role as effectively as possible, thus demonstrating how much you can achieve and await further clarity.

C. Offer to contribute to tasks that are similar to those that you believe are likely to be required after the restructure has taken place.

D. Request a meeting with your Superior to understand the nature of the restructure more fully and how it will affect you.

Situation 7

One of your colleagues has become very erratic in their time-keeping, which is very out of character. In addition he is apparently trying to avoid another member of your Unit with whom he previously appeared to have a close working relationship. This behaviour is impacting on the performance of the team and the team dynamic on a project that involves all three of you. How do you act in this situation?

A. Ask your colleague in private if there are any issues underlying his time-keeping and the deterioration in both performance and dynamic in the team.

B. Ask the team member that the colleague may have difficulties with if they know of any issues that might be affecting your colleague.

C. Raise your concerns about your colleague with your Superior as you feel they ought to know and may be able to advise on how to proceed.

D. Decide that the matter is none of your business and allow the two individuals concerned to deal with the issue themselves.

Situation 8

You are in a meeting, trying to get your point of view heard, when another person interrupts you saying that you are "talking nonsense" and then puts forward his views instead. The group all agree with the other person's idea even though you did not finish describing yours and you feel it still has merit. Moreover, the other person's plan has some obvious flaws. The group is about to move onto another topic of conversation; what are you most likely to do?

A. State that you, likewise, feel that the other person's idea is "nonsense" and that if he hadn't interrupted so rudely, he might have had a chance to hear your idea as well. Then proceed to give your views.

B. As the group is about to move on, don't hold up the meeting by disagreeing now, but send round an email that outlines your alternative idea afterwards, asking for feedback and whether you could call a subsequent meeting to discuss.

C. Let them proceed with the other person's idea, as it is the group consensus decision. However, do some preparation in advance to manage the fall-out when things go wrong.

D. Despite holding up the meeting, you state clearly and firmly that whilst you appreciate the other person's idea has merit, there are some drawbacks and you would like to suggest an alternative. Then proceed to give your views.

Situation 9

You have conducted analysis on some anonymous staff satisfaction surveys relating to your Unit's output, and are writing a report on the key findings. Whilst most of the data demonstrates clear trends, responses relating to the courtesy with which the end users were treated by your Unit vary wildly, and there are no discernible trends as to who provided the poor levels of courtesy or who was on the receiving end of it, and no consistent explanations as to why that may be the case. What do you do?

A. Write your report, highlighting in it the fact that there is no discernible trend around courtesy and that no obvious explanations are apparent.

B. Inform your Superior that this part of the analysis lacks discernible trends before you produce your report and ask their advice on how to proceed.

C. Send out a short, more targeted request to those who completed the surveys to ascertain the reasons for the lack of a clear trend in this area.

D. Highlight that there are no overall trends around courtesy in your report, but choose also to include those explanations that best support your understanding of why that may be the case.

Situation 10

You are working as part of a team to discuss how to resolve a problem that has occurred with a technical system. The conversation seems to be going nowhere, with lots of people suggesting their own solutions but no-one listening. About halfway through you notice that the technical expert who was responsible for the problem has been quiet for most of the meeting, only contributing the occasional fact when asked by others. You know he is shy as you have worked with him for a while, but you definitely feel he could be contributing more. What do you do?

A. Explain that you feel the meeting is not achieving its objectives and you are running out of time. Summarise what has been discussed and then say that you want to make sure that everyone's views are heard. Then ask for the technical expert's views directly in front of the rest of the group.

B. Make a note of the fact that the technical expert not only caused the problem, but was also unhelpful in resolving the issue. Feed this back to him and his superior following the meeting.

C. Ask him for his views immediately and assertively. The meeting is already halfway through and you do not wish to waste any more time on discussions that might be irrelevant.

D. Suggest that the group pause for a moment and refocus on the purpose of the meeting. Then ask if anyone would like to comment on what we have covered so far whilst looking at the technical expert in the hope that they will take the opportunity to speak.

Situation 11

You are new to the role and one of your team members comes to you for an urgent decision. Apparently, they are in a heated debate with someone from another team about the best way to implement a new piece of software. Your team member has presented you with a large amount of information that they say backs up their case and asks you to give them your support at a project meeting tomorrow. What do you do next?

A. Demonstrate your faith in your team member's judgement and promise to give your full support at the meeting.

B. Ask if the meeting can be postponed so that you have a chance to look through the information and analyse it in more detail before arriving at a decision about what to do.

C. Go and see the individual from the other team to get their side of the story before making up your mind about what to do.

D. Start from scratch in analysing the situation for yourself and see if you can suggest something that meets both party's needs.

Situation 12

You have just been given responsibility for overseeing a special project team that has been put together to work on a large piece of translation work over the next 6 months. You have worked with everyone before and you feel you know their strengths and weaknesses. They are all hard workers and you are confident they have the motivation to do an excellent job. However, you do know that the commissioning client is likely to change the specification of the project as time progresses, so you want to keep things flexible. How would you approach the management of the team?

A. Gather the team together at the start and reiterate the faith you have in their ability to deliver. Avoid patronising them by telling them exactly what is expected of them. Ask for regular updates from them and hold ad hoc meetings to check on progress.

B. Identify the key milestones, risks and contingencies facing the project in partnership with the team and pull together a formal project plan that you can all refer to as the project progresses.

C. Instruct the team to begin by working towards the first deadline target, without looking too far into the future so that you can respond flexibly to the client's changing requests.

D. Start with a broad plan, but then arrange one-to-one meetings with every team member on a daily basis in order to check on progress and assign new tasks and responsibilities as they arrive from the client.

Situation 13

You are responsible for compiling the results of an important opinion survey that is running behind schedule and you are due to present the findings in two days' time. The work required is fairly basic data entry with some simple calculations required to get average scores. You already have a full diary and are feeling exhausted, your superior is away on holiday and you have no additional budget to spend. How do you approach the situation?

A. Decide to request an extra temporary member of staff anyway and worry about the budget later: delivering the project on time is the most important issue.

B. Scale back the scope of the project and report on what you have been able to complete in the available time and then give a follow-up presentation at a later date that covers subsequent work.

C. Work additional hours yourself in order to get the data entered, even if you already have a very busy schedule.

D. See if some extra resource is available from another team to help with the data entry.

Situation 14

You have been asked to manage the transition from an old database system to a newer replacement, a task that will require many people's contributions and cooperation. The new system has improved search facilities but data input is more complicated and time-consuming. You have a target date several weeks down the line for when the entire task must be completed, but it is up to you to determine how best to meet this deadline. How do you approach the task?

A. Break the task down into a series of smaller processes, complete with individual deadlines and targets for each task.

B. Concentrate on engaging with those required to input data into the system as these are likely to be the people most resistant to the transition.

C. Heavily publicise the target date to ensure that everyone affected is aware of when it must all be completed.

D. Focus on examining in detail the elements of the task you expect to be most challenging.

Situation 15

You submitted a report making several efficiency recommendations to your Unit and you received a lot of praise for your work. However, you recently reread your report and noticed an error in your analysis of one key process, upon which one of your main recommendations was founded. As a result of this recommendation, which has already been adopted, savings in time and money have been great. Unfortunately a previous stage for checking data has now been omitted and there is an increased risk of errors continuing into later stages. Although this has not happened so far, if it did, bad policy decisions could be made or, if the mistake was spotted, delays could be severe, as much work would need to be redone using the correct data. As your recommendations resulted in a complex process overhaul rather than tackling processes in isolation, the stage cannot easily be reinserted in its previous form. How do you act?

A. Continue with the revised processes without saying anything as they are delivering savings in both time and money.

B. Alert everyone using the process to your oversight to ensure they are especially careful in inputting the data first time round.

C. Say nothing but explore ways to address the omission which, once identified, you can include in a second set of recommendations.

D. Point out your oversight and suggest reverting to the original processes until you can formulate a new set of recommendations.

Situation 16

It is your first week back at work after two weeks of annual leave. You come back to find that a large amount of work has been set for you by different people in your Unit. All of the work is to be completed by the end of the day and you feel overwhelmed. Each of the people who set you work has asked what time you will complete it by and insists that their work is of the utmost importance. Your Superior then reminds you of another important task you have with a non-negotiable deadline of tomorrow morning. What do you do?

A. Arrange to see your Superior, explain that you are feeling overwhelmed due to the unrealistic amount of work you have been set, and discuss together how to move forward.

B. Speak straight away to each person in your Unit who set you work; explain the situation and ask them whether the deadlines can be extended, apologising for the inconvenience.

C. Take 5 minutes to reflect on the situation and take hold of your emotions before persevering with the tasks as they were set. Ask for support from your colleagues if needed.

D. Tell each person that due to a lack of communication, you have an unrealistic workload. Explain that it is not just their work which is important and if they need the work completed by today, they need to see if someone else is available.

Situation 17

You have been tasked with creating a presentation based on a project which you and some colleagues from your Unit recently undertook. Your Superior will give the presentation to the Directorate tomorrow. You want to show your Superior that you are personally capable of producing the necessary content so that your efforts and skills will be recognised. Ultimately, the most important thing is that a high quality presentation is produced. How do you proceed?

A. Create the presentation yourself based upon what you learnt during the project. Run the final version by your colleagues for feedback before sending it to your Superior.

B. Ask the other people you worked with to send you any notes they made about the project when working on it, but decide on the content yourself.

C. Invest some time reflecting on the project and deciding what is the most relevant content. Create the presentation based upon your own experiences and expertise.

D. Call together the colleagues who worked on the project with you and discuss it in order to get their views on the most suitable content for the presentation.

Situation 18

Your Superior has compiled some data for you to analyse and then include in a report. After looking at the data, you start to think that something isn't right. You believe you may have identified an error in the dataset – however you are not certain at this stage. What approach do you adopt?

A. As you are not certain, and to avoid embarrassment, include the original data in the report and send it to your Superior to review.

B. Look at the dataset in more depth before raising the issue. Carry out the appropriate analysis to confirm or deny the suspected error.

C. In order to address the potential issue, notify your Superior of the possible error straight away and explore the dataset together.

D. Ask a colleague to look over the dataset and see if they identify an error. If an error is confirmed, raise the issue with your Superior.

Situation 19

It is a very busy period for your Unit, with everyone working to tight deadlines. You've been given three tasks by three different senior staff members, all of which are to be completed before tomorrow morning. You are finding it difficult to juggle all three tasks. What are you going to do?

A. Contact the people who set the tasks. Enquire about the urgency and importance of each task and ask whether the deadlines can be extended.

B. Complete the most important task to the very best of your abilities by the deadline. Move on to the other tasks later once you have the time.

C. Persevere with all three tasks and aim to get all of them to a fairly good standard by the deadline, despite the lack of time.

D. In order to complete all three tasks, work throughout the night until all of the tasks have been completed to a high standard.

Situation 20

You are about to embark on a new project. You have had a preliminary project briefing and are due to have one final meeting with your Superior before you start, just to confirm arrangements. The project is scheduled to start by the end of the week as the timeframe is quite tight. However, due to unforeseen circumstances, your Superior has been called away and will not be contactable until the middle of next week. How do you act?

A. So as not to begin the project before having had the final meeting with your Superior, postpone the start date until after your Superior returns.

B. Before you start the project, spend however long is needed consulting your colleagues in order to get ideas for how best to approach it.

C. Attempt the parts of the project where everything is confirmed and delay the rest of the project until your Superior is back.

D. Despite no final meeting, make a start on the project based on the information gathered from the initial briefing and your own ideas.

Situation 21

Your Superior asks you to finalise a report on a major new EU initiative because the person who started it has been called into an urgent meeting. When you finish the report, you send it to the Directorate as requested by your Superior. The Directorate complains that the data in the report is inaccurate and not what they originally produced. You are sure that the data is right as you did not change it. When your Superior learns of the Directorate's reaction he is very disappointed and asks you to explain what happened. How do you handle this situation?

A. Approach the person who started the report when you next see him. Ask him to explain his approach when compiling the report and use this to see if he made any errors.

B. Contact the Directorate yourself and apologise for what happened, assuring them that you will investigate to ensure this does not happen again.

C. Inform your Superior that you used the data you were given. Suggest that he asks the person who started the report if he made a mistake or altered the data.

D. Request a meeting with everyone involved in compiling the report and try to understand what happened. Take the necessary actions and apologise where necessary.

Situation 22

You are running a Unit project and hold weekly meetings for your Unit members. One of the members repeatedly arrives late to the meetings and then wastes time and makes disrespectful comments to you whilst you are asking for input from the group on your ideas. The person is appearing increasingly agitated as the weeks go by. How do you act in this situation?

A. In order to resolve the issue, contact the person's manager and ask them to speak to the individual: he may be more likely to listen to a more senior individual.

B. Send an email to the whole project team which stresses how important the meetings are and how everyone needs to arrive on time and be fully committed.

C. Meet with the individual on a 1:2:1 basis and ask him why he is often late. Ask him for feedback on how he thinks the meetings could be improved.

D. The next time the Unit member arrives late or is disruptive, stop the meeting and challenge the person there and then to try and prevent it happening again.

Situation 23

You recently started to think that your Unit would benefit from having someone who is tasked with generating new systems and ways of working, and improving existing ones. You believe that this would benefit everyone in the Unit and the majority of people appear in favour of your suggestion. However the senior Unit managers you approach say that adding the cost of an additional role is not currently feasible. What do you do?

A. Put together a site in the intranet where all Unit members can share new ways of working. This way, all members have easy access to them and can adopt them if useful.

B. Arrange to meet with the most senior person in your Unit and put together a proposal for your ideas which is tailored to her, in order to win her support.

C. Look at other ongoing projects within your Unit that could benefit from new ways of working. Use these examples to support your case and approach the senior managers again in a few months.

D. Due to the seniority and knowledge of the managers you approached, accept their decision for now. Share ideas informally with colleagues as they arise.

Situation 24

You are managing a group of colleagues on a key project. You are eager to prove to your Superior that you are capable of leading the group to success. One way you want to show your ability is to finish the project 3 days ahead of the deadline, which means there will be ample review time for your Superior. You are aware that some of the group members have other fairly demanding tasks to complete within this timeframe, but you believe your aim to be achievable. However, you then receive a request from your Superior for the project to be completed a whole 14 days prior to the deadline. How do you respond?

A. In order to show your Superior what you are capable of, agree to the new deadline and ask the group members to invest additional hours in the project if required in order to complete it on time.

B. Agree to the new timeframe and ask other colleagues from your department not already involved in the project if they have any spare time to assist with the workload.

C. Explain that due to your group members' other commitments, you don't think that the requested deadline is feasible; however, say that you aim to complete the project 3 days ahead of schedule.

D. Inform him you are unsure whether or not you could achieve the new deadline. Work on the project as planned and let him know nearer the deadline if you think it is realistic.

Situation 25

There is a set of internal procedures that you have abided by since working for the EU. When you first started, you were told that it was important that organisational rules and procedures were followed, and any instances where they were breached should be highlighted upwards. When speaking to a Senior Manager from another Unit, he asks you if you can find a way around one of the procedures in order to help him get a report completed before an important deadline. He presents a strong rationale for his argument. How do you proceed?

A. Help the Senior Manager as he put forward a good argument and this will strengthen your working relationship.

B. Inform your Superior of the situation and ask him to respond to the Senior Manager on your behalf.

C. Explain to the Senior Manager that you cannot help him and inform your Superior of the situation that has occurred.

D. Refuse to bypass the procedure and remind the Senior Manager of the importance of following organisational procedures.

Situation 26

You have been asked to take responsibility for writing a complex policy document within the next month. One of your colleagues has offered to support you as he has experience in the subject area. There is a very large amount of available information that you could use to write the document, including a series of documents of different styles such as spreadsheets, slides and reports. A lot of the information is unfamiliar to you and you are concerned about your experience in the overall topic you are looking at. How do you respond?

A. Figure out some of the key documents and focus on understanding them first, as these may give you a good understanding of the area overall.

B. Ask your colleague to put together a plan for how to tackle the information, to ensure your approach is based on his experience.

C. Create a detailed list of all the different documents that could possibly be used so that you have a clear reference for these.

D. Meet with your colleague to propose an approach to tackle the data, stating that he is welcome to contribute insight to your plan.

Situation 27

You have been working closely with a colleague on putting together a review of recent international legislation. There are only a couple of days before the review is due. You have just found out that your colleague is unwell and will not be in the office today. While the review is almost complete, you feel that your colleague could still add value to the process. What do you do?

A. Wait until your colleague returns tomorrow to finalise the review to make sure you don't make incorrect changes to the report.

B. Focus on finishing off the review yourself and try to send it to the relevant people today, a day before the expected deadline.

C. See whether anyone else can help you finalise the review and then run the work past your ill colleague tomorrow if they return.

D. Contact the relevant people in your Unit, explaining the situation and ask for an extension to make sure the review is finalised.

Situation 28

You are responsible for managing an important project which requires input from several of your colleagues. You are reaching an important point in the project's progress and, while it is mostly running well, a few of the team have not delivered everything you expected and needed from them by this stage. While you are still on schedule overall, this may well have a knock-on impact on the rest of the team's work and change their schedules. How do you deal with this?

A. Re-work your timeline for the project and then communicate new goals for the different team members.

B. Immediately look for additional resources to ensure that you can meet your timelines comfortably.

C. Meet with the team members who were not able to meet their targets and ask how you can support them.

D. Write to the whole project team, highlighting the incomplete work and how it will negatively impact the project.

Situation 29

At a weekly meeting you are making a presentation to a large number of members of your Unit, including several senior staff. You prepared well for the presentation, but halfway through you realise you are working from an incomplete version of the slides and you do not have the final few slides that show the conclusion. There are still some slides remaining in your slideshow that you know are not missing. You have about 15 minutes left to talk, and know that it will take about 5-10 minutes to find the updated version of the slides.

A. Apologise and state that you will need to complete the talk next week as you are missing important slides.

B. Apologise and ask a colleague to find the correct slides while you continue to talk on the available slides.

C. Continue the talk but focus mainly on the slides available, discussing the conclusion briefly where possible.

D. Call a break while you find the slides, locate them, then return and talk through what you can in the remaining time.

Situation 30

You are leading a small team putting together a significant risk assessment for a piece of proposed legislation. Two of your team members are constantly getting into disputes and this is distracting other members of the team. In your current meeting you are discussing who will do what work. The two team members quickly get into an argument regarding how you have allocated the work, with one agreeing with the way you have suggested and the other stating he disagrees. They are raising their voices and this is clearly upsetting the other members of the team. How do you deal with this?

A. Assertively tell the whole team that you are leading the project so they need to follow your instructions to ensure that it is a success.

B. Ask both team members to stop raising their voices as it is having a negative impact on the meeting rather than helping with the task.

C. Try to solicit the views of each team member independently and ensure they are presenting their ideas to you rather than arguing with each other.

D. Allow the debate to continue for the meanwhile, but make a note to talk to both team members after the meeting.

Answers with Explanations

Situation 1. EPSO competency: *RESILIENCE*

The most appropriate answer in this case is **Option D**. A dispassionate approach to criticism demonstrates great resilience, whilst the analysis will ensure that effort expended in amending the report is more likely to be in areas where amendments are genuinely needed.

Option **A** is probably the least desirable as it simply dismisses the criticisms out of hand, in spite of your colleague's experience, and also means that his review of your work has been a waste of his time.

Option **C**, in contrast, whilst demonstrating a desire to take criticism on board, assumes that overall experience is everything; your colleague may not have sufficient knowledge of your particular project to be able to advise on all aspects of content.

Option **B** is arguably the second best option, but requires your colleague to invest more of his time having already done you a favour.

Situation 2. EPSO competency: *WORKING WITH OTHERS*

The most appropriate answer in this case is **Option A**. An open minded approach is the best way to give the working relationship a decent chance, and for you also to ultimately disprove their negative opinions of you.

Option **D**, in contrast, risks damaging the relationship.

Option **B** has some merits, in that your Superior will be aware of the potential issues should anything go wrong; however your teammate has not said anything negative to you directly, so it is difficult to raise this issue.

The least desirable option, however, is probably **Option C**; it means your teammate knows you may have a problem with him, which risks damaging the relationship, and also involves admitting to listening in on other people's conversation.

Situation 3. EPSO competency: *ANALYSIS AND PROBLEM SOLVING*

The most appropriate answer in this case is **Option D**. This option balances meeting the needs of the end user of the data (i.e. DIGIT) whilst recognising that timescales cannot be greatly affected if the data is used to analyse performance against monthly targets.

Option **B** also demonstrates a pragmatic approach, but without knowledge of how the data is converted into the final report, it would be difficult for you to make a call as to which elements of the proposed format should be retained and which are less critical.

Option **A** demonstrates a desire to maintain the status quo and disregard the request.

However, **Option C** is probably the least desirable option; if the reports are produced monthly, a delay in their production will make it difficult for DIGIT to react swiftly enough to the messages they contain.

Situation 4. EPSO competency: *PRIORITISING AND ORGANISING*

The most appropriate answer in this case is **Option C**. This makes the most effective use of everyone's time whilst ensuring that everyone is kept informed via a clear written record.

Option **B** is the least desirable option, as it does not keep track of any changes to other people's parts of the presentation that may impact on your own.

Option A involves time-consuming chasing of information and multiple communications of the same information.

Option D includes the benefit that changes can be discussed in a single forum, but may prove a waste of time; it can always be added into the process if changes prove to be very frequent and complex, but as a starting point is less sensible than the e-mail approach of Option C.

Situation 5. EPSO competency: *DELIVERING QUALITY AND RESULTS*

The most appropriate answer in this case is **Option B**. Your Superior will be made aware that the work is not challenging you, whilst the work continues to be done.

Option A also ensures that the important work is completed, but your Superior may believe that it is challenging you if you do not speak up, and future tasks may be at a similar level.

Option C could be seen as a rather underhand attempt to share the dull duties and could also make you look less capable in the eyes of your Supervisor.

However **Option D** is probably the least desirable option, as it is an attempt to shirk any personal responsibility for delivering output that is important to EU policy.

Situation 6. EPSO competency: *RESILIENCE*

The most appropriate answer in this case is **Option B**. It demonstrates great resilience to continue to work effectively under difficult circumstances.

Option C is probably the least desirable as everyone will wish to demonstrate their skills on tasks that will be relevant, and not everyone can do them at once. Your Superior will have assigned tasks with people's skills in mind and chasing the ones that will exist after the restructure may not be in alignment with your Superior's wishes and without further information your guesses as to what will be required may be wrong.

Option A contains some good qualities (it is always useful to be aware of your skills and consider how they could be applied), but without further knowledge of what the new responsibilities will look like, this exercise could lack focus at this stage.

Option D is also a reasonable reaction, but your Superior will likely have shared as much as they can already, and will wish to inform others according to a timetable set by the organisation.

Situation 7. EPSO competency: *WORKING WITH OTHERS*

The most appropriate answer in this case is **Option A**. A private discussion with your colleague where you seek to better understand any potential underlying issues and give the opportunity to talk about them both demonstrates concern for their well-being and potentially enables the issues to be addressed.

Option B is probably the least desirable option; if there are issues between the two teammates, it is not advisable to talk to one about the other as this could appear to be taking sides with the one you have the discussion with rather than the one who is externally exhibiting behaviours that are out of character.

Option C does allow you to get advice about how to proceed, but it also involves you highlighting someone else's potential personal issue to your Superior without their knowledge that you are doing so.

Option D is not an accurate reading of the situation; your project is being affected, and this option does not address it in any way.

Situation 8. EPSO competency: RESILIENCE

The most appropriate answer in this case is **Option D**. It demonstrates great resilience to not only come back against a challenger that everyone else has agreed with, but also to do so in a calm and measured manner. It will be far more efficient to raise the point now, even if it means extending the meeting, as it ensures all subsequent discussions are relevant.

Option A is likely to simply cause antagonism by being equally rude in return. Although your views will be heard by the group, they will also note your emotional reaction and may hesitate about engaging with you or challenging you in the future. Additionally, the person you were originally in conflict with may then feel obliged to argue back just because of the approach you adopted, in order to maintain his pride.

Option B may be acceptable, depending upon the timescales available, but it would show greater resilience to address the issue there and then, face to face. It also runs the risk of the rest of the meeting being unproductive because it will be based on the premise that the alternative idea will be adopted.

However, **Option C** is probably the least desirable as because you failed to speak out, now an entire project's success is at risk: Option C almost feels like you are getting your own back on the other person through spite. It also shows a tendency to shy away from confrontation, which shows a lack of personal confidence.

Situation 9. EPSO competency: ANALYSIS AND PROBLEM SOLVING

The most appropriate answer in this case is **Option C**. A lack of clear explanation in this case warrants trying to better understand the underlying reasons, and this targeted approach is a reasonably optimal way of achieving that.

Option D is probably the least desirable option; it would be inappropriate to present only the information that supports one explanation rather than presenting a balanced picture.

Option A is at least more honest than Option D, but raises a question that goes unanswered.

Option B has the benefit of keeping your Superior informed, but as this task has clearly been assigned to you, there is no reason why you should need your Superior's views on how to proceed and it is up to you to find an appropriate solution.

Situation 10. EPSO competency: WORKING WITH OTHERS

The most appropriate answer in this case is **Option A**. By pausing the meeting and summarising, this gives the chance to ensure everyone has the same understanding so far and also allows a pause for the technical expert to speak. Choosing Option A not only demonstrates empathy on your part, it also shows a certain drive to help the team achieve its goals.

Option B shows no real attempt to aid the team-working process and is therefore the least desirable option. It also abdicates responsibility for resolving the issue there and then yourself which would have aided the team-working process.

Option C shows a certain lack of appreciation for the technical expert's current mindset: this action may embarrass him and/or lead to him being unable to contribute by feeling too exposed. Introducing a pause in proceedings and then asking the technical expert to contribute in a non-threatening way shows far greater emotional intelligence.

Option D is unlikely to be successful as it seems from the scenario information that the technical expert is so shy or embarrassed they may not pick up on your cue to speak. More direct action is needed to encourage their contribution.

Situation 11. EPSO competency: *ANALYSIS AND PROBLEM SOLVING*

The most appropriate answer in this case is **Option B**. It is likely to be unrealistic for you to make a sound judgement before you have reviewed the evidence and it sounds like there is not only complex data to analyse, but also some internal politics to consider before reaching a conclusion. There does not seem to be an urgent deadline for a decision, other than the scheduled meeting, and therefore a delay would probably be acceptable.

The least effective is **Option A**: this shows perhaps a tendency to shy away from detailed analysis and does not take into account the possible biases of your team members in presenting their views to you. Although it may demonstrate unwavering loyalty to your team, it may result in a less than optimum outcome – especially considering you are new to the role and you presumably know little about your team members' trustworthiness to date.

Option C would be a potentially good course of action at some point, as it will help not only give you a balanced view but also build bridges with the other team and help reduce conflict. However, to go and see them before having first reviewed your team member's documentation and doing some preparation may result in you not having all the facts to hand. Therefore it would be better to do Option B first.

Option D is a possibility if you had a lot of time, but it seems an uneconomical way of problem solving if a lot of the research has already been conducted. It would be better to capitalise on the existing information, even if it is biased, and then once you have reviewed all the evidence you can then decide if a full analysis from scratch is required or not.

Situation 12. EPSO competency: *PRIORITISING AND ORGANISING*

The most appropriate answer in this case is **Option B**. Despite the fact that project scope is likely to change, in order to stand the best chance of successful delivery, an initial project plan with milestones, risks and contingencies is required. By involving the project team, not only will you formulate a better plan but you will gain their buy-in to it and show how you value their expertise. You can always build contingencies into the plan from an early stage to try and pre-empt any difficulties.

Option A reflects too much of a relaxed approach and this lack of planning is likely to lead to difficulties later on due to a lack of clarity over deliverables. Whilst you may expect this to lead to your team feeling empowered, it is actually likely to make them feel a little directionless and therefore possibly demotivated and certainly less productive.

Option C reflects a very "short-termist" approach. It may mean that some time is saved in planning, but it would be more effective to consider all the steps required in the lead up to the ultimate objective rather than dealing with each in isolation. Without a view of the bigger picture, it is impossible to plan effectively for each stage in isolation. Option C is therefore probably the least effective course of action.

Option D reflects a micro-management approach that is likely to make the team members feel a lack of empowerment, as well as taking up a lot of your time. If you are meeting that regularly with your team and issuing frequent changes of direction or new tasks, this may cause frustration: better to meet less frequently and have time to consolidate all the feedback from the commissioning client into coherent, larger pieces of information that could be fed back to all – e.g. at a team meeting.

Situation 13. EPSO competency: *DELIVERING QUALITY AND RESULTS*

The most appropriate answer in this case is **Option D**. If extra resource is available from another team, this should help to ensure the deadline is met and with no additional cost implications. If the extra resource is not available, you are still free to pursue one of the other options, meaning that this gives you the most possible flexibility.

Despite demonstrating drive and determination, **Option C** runs the risks of errors being made due to fatigue. There is the additional risk that the other work you have on the go will also suffer as a result. Therefore, this answer falls down on the quality focus aspects.

Choosing **Option B** means that you fail to deliver the project objective. There is no indication that this course of action will be acceptable in the scenario and it is likely to be unsatisfactory to the stakeholders. Therefore it is probably the least appropriate answer.

Option A shows initiative, and should get the project delivered on time and with less chance of mistakes than working extra hours yourself (although a temp will still need to be fully briefed). However the extra budget goes beyond the remit of the project and this is therefore not an ideal solution as you will not have worked within the project objectives.

Situation 14. EPSO competency: PRIORITISING AND ORGANISING

The most appropriate answer in this case is **Option A**. This converts the single overall deadline into a practical project plan that everyone involved in the transition can make use of in order to ensure that targets are being met.

Option C is probably the least desirable option, as it focuses on just one key date that will initially seem relatively distant, so will not create any urgency. As a result, the project may drift from a lack of focus in the initial stages and the final deadline may either be missed or else the latter stages may involve working under pressure with a greater risk of mistakes being made as a result of that pressure.

Option B recognises where the resistance to the project may come from, which is always useful, but concentrating too much on this aspect may result in the bigger picture being ignored.

Option D is similarly useful in so far as understanding the most complex elements will be important, but as with Option B, too much focus here could result in ignoring the bigger picture, and indeed in ignoring other elements that may be challenging but which you have not identified as such.

Situation 15. EPSO competency: DELIVERING QUALITY AND RESULTS

The most appropriate answer in this case is **Option D**. The impact of errors creeping into later stages is potentially great, so temporarily reverting to the original processes is safer than continuing with the new ones.

Option A is the least desirable option, as it does not involve any attempt to address the oversight.

Option B at least ensures everyone is aware of the issue but still relies on the data being handled accurately in the first place without a later independent check, and would probably slow down the process anyway.

Option C relies on no errors being made until you find a solution, and once you have found the solution you will need to explain why you are proposing a second set of recommendations anyway, thus demonstrating your recklessness and the fact you were not open about the issue once you had identified it.

Situation 16. EPSO competency: RESILIENCE

The most appropriate answer in this case is **Option B**. Addressing the issue yourself without showing emotion shows an ability to remain calm under pressure and to persevere with a task.

Option D is probably the least desirable as it could be seen as being defensive and shifting the blame onto the people who set the work.

Option C, in contrast, demonstrates an ability to control one's emotions and know when to take some time out. However, persevering with the workload when it is unrealistic may lead to greater pressure in the long run.

Option A is also a plausible option as a solution is being sought, but it involves passing the problem on to someone else to help resolve your issues.

Situation 17. EPSO competency: WORKING WITH OTHERS

The most appropriate answer in this case is **Option D**. Including your colleagues in the decision making process and the creation of the presentation not only allows for a greater breadth of ideas to be generated and therefore a better outcome, but the collaboration could also help to strengthen relationships.

The least desirable option is probably **Option C**: it involves no collaboration with the relevant people, thereby losing the chance of getting help in making the presentation better.

Option A is a plausible answer as feedback is sought on the presentation before it is sent off; however, collaboration during the creation of the presentation could have benefited both the presentation and team relationships further.

Likewise, in **Option B**, the colleagues are consulted but there is no direct collaboration.

Situation 18. EPSO competency: ANALYSIS AND PROBLEM SOLVING

The most appropriate answer in this case is **Option B**. This shows an ability to challenge presented data, analysing it further rather than taking it at face value. Taking responsibility is also evident in investigating whether there is an error or not before consulting others.

Option A is probably the least desirable as the issue is not being addressed but simply being avoided: further analysis/investigation should be carried out.

Option C has its merits in raising the issue, but more analysis should ideally be carried out first in an attempt to see whether or not there is an error.

Option D shows an ability to consult others in order to get a second opinion, but the data still could have been looked at in more depth first.

Situation 19. EPSO competency: PRIORITISING AND ORGANISING

The most appropriate answer in this case is **Option A**. Finding out which task is the most important/urgent, and exploring whether there is a way to reduce the workload, will lead to prioritisation and allow a high standard to be maintained on all three tasks.

Option C is the least desirable option, as although all three tasks may get completed within the timeframe, they are likely to be rushed and not completed to the same standard as if more time had been spent on them.

Option B focuses on the right priority, but without a clear plan for the remaining tasks, this could result in disappointing the other stakeholders.

Option D includes the possibility that all tasks could be completed to a high standard before the deadline. However, working throughout the night may lead to a reduction in performance levels which could lower the standard of work. Time management and task prioritisation would be better options.

Situation 20. EPSO competency: DELIVERING QUALITY AND RESULTS

The most appropriate answer in this case is **Option D**. It shows an ability to act and start the project without receiving complete instructions, using the information already gathered and one's own initiative.

Option A is probably the least desirable option, as it shows a reluctance to take the initiative and start the project despite the tight deadline.

Option B has its merits as there is an element of proactivity shown by consulting others in order to start the project before your Superior returns. However, there is a danger of over-consulting and this delaying the start date.

Option C shows proactivity in starting the project; on the other hand, not progressing past the areas confirmed with your Superior is likely to impact on completion by the deadline and again misses an opportunity to take the initiative.

Situation 21. EPSO competency: RESILIENCE

The most appropriate answer in this case is **Option D**. It demonstrates an ability to assume a degree of responsibility in trying to find out what happened but without being defensive.

Option C is probably the least desirable as it demonstrates an element of defensiveness in reaction to the Superior's disappointment and request for an explanation. Potentially, blame is also passed onto the colleague.

Option B contains some good qualities as it shows the ability to apologise and investigate an issue regardless of fault; however there is less emphasis on taking action on the current report.

Option A is also a reasonable reaction as again some responsibility is taken. But the potential blame is simply passed on to the colleague, rather than a more objective, holistic approach being taken.

Situation 22. EPSO competency: WORKING WITH OTHERS

The most appropriate answer in this case is **Option C**. By trying to find out why they are behaving in that way you are more likely to be able to find a solution. Asking the member for their feedback shows an ability to listen to others and to involve them in reaching a resolution.

Option D is probably the least desirable option – confronting the member in front of the rest of the group is unlikely to resolve the issue. It is possible that the member has some personal issues outside work, or is faced with other pressures at work: therefore trying to address the issue in front of others could be quite insensitive.

Option A does at least ensure that someone speaks to the problematic member and that his behaviour is addressed. But by not speaking to the team member yourself, you are failing to take full responsibility for your group.

Option B may be a good way of avoiding conflict, but it is not getting to the root cause of the issue or allowing the member to explain his actions.

Situation 23. EPSO competency: ANALYSIS AND PROBLEM SOLVING

The most appropriate answer in this case is **Option A**. Coming up with a different way of enabling all members to benefit, despite the rejection of the initial idea, demonstrates an ability to produce creative ideas and effective solutions.

Option B is probably the least desirable: the senior managers have already said the idea would not be feasible on cost grounds, therefore a 1:2:1 meeting is likely to be a waste of time as the resources are simply not available at the moment.

Option C is more practical than option B and budgets may have changed in a few months; however this still does not address the issue in the short term.

Option D shows respect and understanding for the views expressed by the senior managers, but there is no structure to the proposed idea-sharing, and this may well make it less likely to succeed.

Situation 24. EPSO competency: PRIORITISING AND ORGANISING

The most appropriate answer in this case is **Option C**. Being realistic about what can be achieved and by when, allows both your Superior and your colleagues to know where they stand and what the outcome is likely to be.

Option A is probably the least appropriate, as the desire to impress overrides the ability to set a realistic timeframe. You know that the other people involved in the project have other demanding tasks; therefore it is unrealistic to suppose that the project could be completed so far ahead of the original deadline.

With **Option B**, although there is recognition that the suggested deadline is not realistic without additional support, it is risky to agree to the new timeframe without arranging extra support beforehand.

Option D does not commit to the deadline; on the other hand, it fails to confirm a deadline at all, therefore creating ambiguity for both the Superior and rest of the project team.

Situation 25. EPSO competency: DELIVERING QUALITY AND RESULTS

The most appropriate answer in this case is **Option C** as it shows adherence to set procedures and a willingness to escalate situations where there is an attempt to breach procedures.

Option A is the least desirable, as it is clearly involves breaking procedures put in place by the organisation.

Whilst **Option B** demonstrates an ability to raise the issue with your Superior, asking them to deal with the situation abdicates responsibility.

Option D correctly refuses to go against organisational rules; however the issue is not raised with anyone else to prevent this happening in future.

Situation 26. EPSO competency: ANALYSIS AND PROBLEM SOLVING

The most appropriate answer in this case is **Option D**. This shows that you are thinking about how to break down the data into something manageable, but also looks to run your idea past someone who may well have insight into how effective it will be.

Option A is an acceptable response. This does not draw on your colleague's existing expertise at all but is still likely to be a logical way to tackle large amounts of data.

Option C is also an acceptable response. This detailed list could serve as a useful resource; however, it's not clear how much information there is. If there is a manageable number of documents this may well be a good starting point, but if there are a lot and some are less relevant you risk wasting valuable time.

Option B is the least effective response. You are responsible for this project and there are several ways you can tackle the information yourself rather than passing the responsibility on to your colleague. You risk losing control of the project at an early stage by handing over such a major task to your colleague entirely.

Situation 27. EPSO competency: DELIVERING QUALITY AND RESULTS

The most appropriate answer in this case is **Option C**. This ensures that you hit your original deadline and get the input of others wherever possible – while also leaving your colleague with the opportunity to contribute final comments if they are back to work in time.

Option A is the least effective response. You do not know whether your colleague will return tomorrow and you risk falling behind in finishing off the report. You should be prepared to take responsibility for getting this finished in your colleague's absence.

Option B could be seen as an acceptable response as it means you are taking full responsibility for delivering the report. However, while it is admirable that you are striving to deliver ahead of schedule, it may still be worth seeing if your colleague returns tomorrow to add additional value and, if not, seeking input from elsewhere. That way, you may add something to the quality while still delivering on time.

Option D has the merit of being open and clear about the situation. It also gives the relevant people the opportunity to insist on getting the job finished faster, if that is their priority. However, it would be better if you took the initiative yourself for meeting the deadline.

Situation 28. EPSO competency: PRIORITISING AND ORGANISING

The most appropriate answer in this case is **Option A**. This shows that you can adjust plans as needed while still setting clear timelines. By communicating clear goals, you will let your colleagues know exactly what is needed of them. It will be important to think about how to communicate the importance of meeting the new deadlines to everyone involved so as to leave no doubt about the need to stick to the plan.

Option B could help in keeping the project on track. However, you are still on schedule overall, so while this step may help the group to successfully complete the project, it may not actually be necessary. Furthermore, adding extra resources may not be possible without affecting other work, may make the project not stretching enough to get the most out of the team, and does not tackle the fact that some members of the team are not currently pulling their weight – it may even encourage the idea that if the work doesn't get done, someone else will be brought in to do it.

Option C has the merit that you are trying to get the most out of the team and this approach could well help your underperforming colleagues improve if handled well. However, it is important that you ensure that they fully understand the importance of their input to the project as a whole.

Option D is the least effective response. Sharing this information may have a deleterious effect on the team's morale. It is possible that the underperforming team members may not know what you expected of them. This is especially true as you are still on target overall, so the team are likely to feel positive about their output overall and that things are on track. A better approach is to look forward and ensure it is clear what is needed for the rest of the project.

Situation 29. EPSO competency: RESILIENCE

The most appropriate answer in this case is **Option B**. While this involves admitting that a mistake was made with the slides, it should not undermine confidence in what you have to say. By talking off script (if you have to) while the slides are located, you can demonstrate your breadth of knowledge in the topic which could actually add credibility to your talk.

Option A is the least effective response. While it is a difficult situation to find yourself in, you should seek to resolve it now. You risk losing impact and interest if you resume in a week's time. You also risk wasting the time of those who are unable to attend the meeting both weeks.

Option C is a possible response and it may actually help the presentation appear to go the most smoothly to your audience. However, it has the downside that you risk losing impact by not addressing the conclusion in as much depth as you could. You are also potentially wasting important slides that you spent time developing and could illustrate your key conclusions well.

Option D is an appropriate response. This shows a determination to fix the issue despite the difficult situation. However, by breaking off your presentation you may damage the flow of the talk, and you may also need to rush your final slides to keep to time. Thus, it would be better to ask a colleague to locate the slides.

Situation 30. EPSO competency: *WORKING WITH OTHERS*

The most appropriate answer in this case is **Option C**. It shows an interest in their input while managing the situation actively and ensuring the team know that you are leading the project. By getting them to address you rather than argue with each other, you are aiming to keep a focus on the task itself rather than their individual dispute.

Option A is the least effective response. This authoritarian approach may prevent you from getting potentially valuable input from team members – including those who are not involved in the argument. And it does not deal properly with the core ongoing issue of the two disputing team members.

Option B is an appropriate response in the sense that it is likely to help with the immediate issue and highlight the damage that they are doing to the meeting. It does not, however, take account of the possibility that they might both have valid points to make that you can listen to and try to understand.

Option D has the benefit that it may allow you to tackle the issue with the sensitivity it deserves, rather than choosing an inappropriate response in the heat of the moment when tempers are high. However, it does not deal with the immediate situation, which may have a damaging impact on morale and could undermine your credibility in leading the team.